Best Wishes Randy!

Ross Bernstein

12/4/99

Frozen Memories

Celebrating a Century of Minnesota Hockey

by
Ross Bernstein

Nodin Press

"Frozen Memories"
Celebrating a Century of Minnesota Sports
by Ross Bernstein

(www.bernsteinbooks.com)

Nodin Press, a division of Micawber's Inc.
525 North Third Street
Minneapolis, MN 55401

ISBN#: 0-931714-82-6
Library of Congress Catalog Card Number: 99-067416

Distributed by: The Bookmen
525 North Third Street
Minneapolis, MN 55401
(612) 341-3333

Printed in the USA by Printing Enterprises
Cover Painting by Minnesota Artist Terrence Fogarty
Edited by Mike Lamey

Photo Credits:
Donald Clark Collection: 11-15, 19, 20, 22, 23, 26, 27, 29, 32, 36, 37, 43, 44, 48, 50,
51, 58, 59, 68, 74, 75, 90, 92, 107, 115, 117, 128, 131, 133, 135, 137, 143, 145, 174,
U.S. Hockey Hall of Fame: 8, 14-18, 20, 21, 24, 26, 29, 30, 33-36, 38, 40, 42, 45-47,
50, 78, 91, 130, 134, 135, 140, 151, 159
TPG Sports: 28, 50, 57, 61, 62, 65, 66, 70, 114, 119, 127, 132, 152, 161, 171, 172,
Minnesota State High School League: 121-124, 136-170
Dallas Stars: 6, 63, 64, 69, 81, 175
LeRoy Nieman: 72
Charles M. Schulz: 84
Minnesota Historical Society: 121
Jamey Guy Photography: 119
Mike Thill: 118
Murray Williamson: 113
Terrence Fogarty: 4
Pioneer Press: 54, 55
Mike Lamey: 53, 70, 71, 73,
University of Minnesota: 37, 39, 42, 67, 73, 76-84, 116,
University of Minnesota Duluth: 56, 85-90
St. Cloud State University: 91-94
Minnesota State University, Mankato: 95-97
Bemidji State University: 98-101
Augsburg College: 104-105
St. John's University: 109
St. Thomas University: 103
Christian Brothers: 31
Lynn Olson: 120

Acknowledgements:
I would like to thank all of the people that were kind enough to help me in writing this book. In addition to the countless college and
university Sports Information Directors that I hounded throughout this project I would like to sincerely thank all of the men and women
that allowed me to interview them. In particular, I would also like to thank my publisher, and friend, Norton Stillman.

Donald Clark	Neal Broten	Dave Jensen	Tim Kennedy	Michelle Kultunen	Karen Zwach
Tom Clark	Brett Hull	Bob Fallen	Paul Allen	Gene McGivern	Scott Olson
Terrence Fogarty	Herb Brooks	Greg Anzelc	Ron Christian	Howard Voigt	Lynn Olson
Todd Fultz	Ann Johnson	Joe Burns	Chris Owens	Julie Arthur Sherman	Harry Sundberg
Randy Johnson	Whitey Aus	Don Stoner	Chris Blisette	John Kuderle	Bob Grant
Jim Findley	Kurt Daniels	Todd Rendahl	Anne Abicht	Charles M. Schulz	Mark "Lindy" Lindebergh
Bob Nygaard	Mike Lamey	Tim Trainor	Jim Martin	LeRoy Nieman	*H.J. Pieser*

For Sara,
my wife and best friend,
I love you.

I would especially like to thank Minnesota sports artist, Terrence Fogarty, for painting the cover of my new book. The genesis for the painting came this past spring when we got together and took a road-trip up to the Hall of Fame in Eveleth. There, after playing a round of golf at Giant's Ridge, in nearby Biwabik, and eating lunch at Lord Stanley's Restaurant (for inspirational purposes), we turned the Hall of Fame upside down looking for great Minnesota hockey treasures. We found a ton of incredible stuff, and with the Hall's blessings, Terrence took it all home with him and started to envision a picture. What he came up with, the "Legacy," is a wonderful portrayal of old-time Minnesota hockey. I couldn't be more pleased with the way it came out, and can't thank Terrence enough for letting me showcase his new masterpiece.

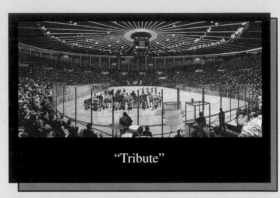

"Tribute"

One of America's premier photo realism artists, Fogarty uses oil as his preferred medium. His works have been sold throughout the world, and his clients include countless professional and collegiate sports organizations, as well as several Fortune 500 Companies. From Mickey Mantle, to Bobby Knight, to Dave Winfield's 3,000th Hit, Terrence has been commissioned to create numerous commemorative paintings over the past 17 years. In addition, his work has been featured in several major motion pictures, on baseball cards, and as cover-art for several professional sports team's programs. (In 1986 his original painting "Jays Clinch the East," sold for an astounding $38,000.)

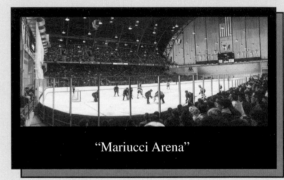

"Mariucci Arena"

Hockey has always been near and dear to Terrence's heart, so here are just a few of his many icy works for you to enjoy. If you would like to purchase a signed, limited edition print of "Legacy," or any of his other paintings, please check out his web-site or contact his new studio in Forest Lake, where you, too, can own a piece of history.

Terrence Fogarty Studio
Original Sports Art for the Serious Collector

Todd Fultz
Director
Terrence Fogarty Studio
711 Centennial Drive SW
Forest Lake, MN 55025
(651) 982-0200
www.terrencefogarty.com

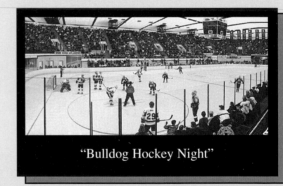

"Bulldog Hockey Night"

"Under Watchful Eyes"

"Tradition"

"Star of the North"

Table of Contents

Foreword by Neal Broten

For the kid legendary coach Herb Brooks called "the best player I ever coached at the University of Minnesota," the circle is complete. Three trips to the Minnesota State High School Tournament for the Roseau Rams, an NCAA National Championship and Hobey Baker Award with the Gophers, an Olympic Gold medal, two Stanley Cup runs with the North Stars, and finally, winning a Cup of his own with the New Jersey Devils. At 5-foot-9 and only 170 pounds, Neal Broten was not a physical giant out on the ice, but he lived out a hockey dream as only John Mariucci might have dared to imagine it. Known and loved by nearly every hockey aficionado in the state, Neal will forever be the measuring stick, the hockey player against which all others will be judged. From his laser-guided slapshots and unselfish passing ability, to his amazing sense of improvisation and remarkable peripheral vision, Neal Broten truly represents everything that is good about Minnesota hockey.

After hanging up the skates back in 1997, today, Neal, his wife Sally, and their two daughter's Brook and Lara, live in scenic River Falls Wis., where they have a 75-acre horse farm. When he's not golfing, hunting or promoting the NHL's new Wild franchise, Neal is talking about hockey, something that will remain near and dear to his heart for the rest of his life. Knowing this, when I started writing my new book about the history and heroes of Minnesota hockey, I thought who better to represent our state's wonderful hockey heritage than our most celebrated and famous native son, No. 7, Neal Broten.

"I originally met Ross back in 1992, when we got together for dinner to do an interview for his first book entitled Gopher Hockey by the Hockey Gopher," said Neal. "I was skeptical about just what this kid was up to back then, afterall his most prominent hockey credential at the time was being the mascot, 'Goldy the Gopher' for goodness sakes! But we hit it off right away and have since become good friends. I was flattered to be included in his second book, Fifty Years • Fifty Heroes as well, and when we did a book-signing together a few years ago at the High School Hockey Tournament Expo, I could see that people really, genuinely enjoyed reading his books. So, when he called me this past winter to tell me that he wanted me to write the foreword for his new book about the history of Minnesota hockey, I was not only flattered... I was honored.

"When I first saw Frozen Memories, I was immediately taken by all of the incredible pictures. There are hundreds of them, going way back to the 1800s, all the way up to today. Hockey is such a part of our culture here, and this book has somehow captured it all. It was so fun to read about all of the old teams that played here through the years as well, from the Duluth Hornets, to the Eveleth Reds, to the old St. Paul Athletic Club. And being from Roseau, I loved reading about the history of the high school tournament. Just to be able to read about so many of my childhood heroes, and to learn about all of the people that worked so hard, so that guys like myself could make a career out of hockey was incredible.

"Some of my first memories of hockey were when the Warroad Lakers would come down the road to Roseau to play in tournaments. I remember as little kids we would run down to the penalty box during the games and grab the broken sticks that the players had thrown over the boards. We would run home and have our dads glue them back together so we could pretend we were North Stars.

"Growing up, my heroes weren't the NHL guys though, they were the Roseau High School hockey players. I feel really lucky to have grown up in such a wonderful hockey town, where the tradition runs so deep into the community. I mean hockey is what that town is all about for basically eight months out of the year - it's pretty amazing, and to be a part of that is something special. In small towns like that, you start playing with the same group of guys from when you first get on skates, all the way through pee wees and finally through high school. So when its over, its like saying good-bye to family. I was lucky though. We got to play in the state tournament, and I even got a chance to go to the University of Minnesota.

"The way I feel about the Gophers can be summed up in two words, Pride and Tradition. There is just so much class there, and to be a part of that was really a humbling experience. Just the feeling of putting on that big "M" sweater with all those other Minnesota kids, and to play in front of such great fans was something I will always cherish. And getting the chance to play on that fabled 1980 Olympic team was an experience I will never forget as well. Just making that squad was an accomplishment. It's something that I always look back on proudly, because there were 12 of us Minnesotans on the team. That just showed the world what kind of kids come from Minnesota, and we were all really proud of the way we represented our state.

"From there I got to spend 13 glorious seasons with my hometown team, the North Stars. What more could a guy ask for? I mean, I could've wound up in Edmonton, or somewhere like that, and who knows what my life would be like today. In retrospect, sometimes I think I took it for granted, just how great it actually was to play for so long in my own backyard. Having the privilege of playing near friends and family, without having to move around all the time was wonderful. I feel spoiled that I got to be here for so long, and that the fans for some reason treated me like a king. I just can't thank them enough. To come home and retire, and to be treated so well by the people here is something I can't explain. I am so humbled by everyone's generosity and am just proud to have been able to have brought joy to their lives through the game of hockey.

"The state-of-the-state of Minnesota hockey is strong today, and the fact that there are five Division-I schools here now is proof that our youth programs are second to none in the nation. I know what hockey means to the people up here, and from all my traveling throughout North America and Europe, I have seen firsthand that we are well known as one of the premier hockey hotbeds in the world.

"Frozen Memories is about celebrating our past, and getting excited about our future. So many great things are happening right now at the youth level, with women's hockey, the college scene and with new Minnesota Wild hitting the ice in 2000. Ross spent the better part of a year researching, interviewing, and preserving our rich hockey heritage in this book. And for that, we all should be grateful, because the final product is awesome. If you enjoy reading about history, biographies, nostalgia and great, funny stories, then you'll love it, because it's all here."

The most sacred of Minnesota Cows — Neal Broten

Introduction

As luck would have it, millions of years ago when the glaciers melted, they left Minnesota with some 15,000 lakes. In fact, our state's name is derived from the Indian words "Minne" "Sota" meaning "land of sky-blue waters." In the summertime Minnesotans purchase more fishing and boating licenses than any other state in the country, and in the wintertime, when those lakes freeze, most of us can't wait to get out there and play hockey. It has been that way in Minnesota for more than a century, and the epiphany behind "Frozen Memories" was to celebrate that wonderful heritage of hockey that we, as Minnesotans, so dearly love and respect.

Minnesota has an amazing hockey tradition, and I am honored and humbled to be able to bring much of it to life for everyone to enjoy in my new book. When I first started writing this more than a year ago, I was immediately taken by just how much information there was about hockey in our state. This led to an interesting dilemma on just how I was going to disseminate it all. I mean there are literally hundreds, if not thousands of players, coaches, administrators, media personalities and others who are deserving of being in a book such as this, and as a result, it was extremely difficult to finalize an outline. Knowing this, I have to issue a caveat of sorts to explain my rationale for how I chose to tackle a subject that is so passionate and yet so controversial with so many Minnesotans — the game, and lifestyle of hockey.

I have chosen to focus primarily on the historical side of hockey for this book, and tried to chronicle as best as possible the true history of the game over the past 100 years. It was an arduous task, but one that was inspiring to complete. All in all, there were more than 500 sources that went into the project, not to mention nearly 100 interviews. Undoubtedly, and expectedly, whenever a book such as this is written, people usually get bent out of shape when they realize that so-and-so wasn't mentioned, or he or she got more ink than another person. I guess that is just the nature of the beast with something like this, and all I can say is that I tried to be arbitrary and objective in my research, and hopefully the vast majority of people that should be in here, are in here. For those who I have overlooked, or simply did not have the space constraints to mention, I sincerely apologize. Believe me, it was a difficult process to have to eliminate so many wonderful biographies and funny stories because I simply did not have the space. My main objective was to celebrate the positive aspects, i.e. the people, big games, history, and drama of hockey in Minnesota, and hopefully I have succeeded in my mission.

Growing up in southern Minnesota, in the hockey hot-bed of Fairmont, I would like to think that we were "old school," or as the Hanson Brothers put it "old time hockey - you know Eddie Shore, Toe Blake..." Despite playing on outdoor rinks, usually getting pummeled by our competition, and having to be sponsored by Domino's Pizza — because our high school wouldn't sanction us, I grew to love the game with a passion. I can still remember coming home from school and meeting my buddies at our rink behind our house on Hall Lake. Sometimes, oh, every couple of years or so, the lake would freeze just perfectly, without any snow on top of it, making for a hockey rink the size of New Jersey. On those rare days my friends Ryan Hall, Pat Cairns, Dave Cone, Dayn Hanson, Paul Carlson and I, would all meet at the middle of the lake, spread out, and pass the puck back and forth from what seemed like a mile away. It was special, and it got me hooked for life on the greatest sport ever invented.

After high school, back in 1987, I even had a crazy notion to try and walk-on with the University of Minnesota Gopher hockey team. There, after a few pathetic outings on the junior varsity, and a huge dose of reality, I opted instead to become the team's mascot — Goldy the Gopher. So there you have it, the extent of my hockey experience came from wearing a giant rodent costume and making a fool out of myself in front of thousands of people! One thing I learned from those experiences though, was just how much Minnesotans love hockey. It is such a part of our fabric of life here, and seems to touch nearly everyone in some way or another.

Kids here grow up in an environment where they can see the generation ahead of them making a difference. Take Cloquet for instance. There were two kids from that tiny town, Jamie Langenbrunner and Derek Plante, on the 1999 Dallas Stars Stanley Cup championship team. (Corey Millen would've made it three, but left the team only the year before.) I assure you it's not something in the water up there. Rather, it is the sense of pride that has been instilled into the community whereupon kids can see other kids making it in hockey. Success breeds success, and kids in small towns from all over our state have taken advantage of this by getting college scholarships and making careers out of hockey. Whether they turn pro or get into coaching, there are always opportunities for good hockey people, and kids at an early age seem to understand this.

As we head into the new millennium, the future of Minnesota hockey looks great. Our new NHL franchise, the Wild, is set to hit the ice next year, and our beloved high school tournament will get a new home next year as well. There are now five Division I schools in our state, women's hockey has exploded, youth hockey has been so strong that new arenas can't be built fast enough to keep up with the demand for ice-time, and in-line hockey has allowed the game to grow and expand into the inner-city. We have come a long way in the past 100 years, and thanks to the efforts of people such as John Mariucci, Herb Brooks and Don Clark, Minnesota kids today are the best coached, have the most opportunities and are leading the charge for the advancement of American hockey. Just look at the numbers. According to the College Hockey Guide, in 1998 Minnesota had 185 players on Division I college teams throughout the country, second only to the province of Ontario, which had just four more at 191, while Massachusetts was the next closest state with only 124.

In Minnesota hockey is a religion. We have provided more Olympic and professional hockey players than any other state, and show no signs of slowing down. There have been thousands of Minnesotans who have gone on to play collegiately, professionally and internationally over the past century. Just look at this past year, 1999, where there were several Minnesotans playing in the 1999 Stanley Cup playoffs: Brian Bonin (Pittsburgh), Mike Crowley (Anaheim), Matt Cullen (Anaheim), Jamie Langenbrunner (Dallas), Chris McAlpine (St. Louis), Jeff Neilson (Anaheim), Lance Pitlick (Ottawa), Shjon Podein (Colorado), Derek Plante (Dallas), Paul Ranheim (Carolina), Erik Rasmussen (Buffalo), Dan Trebil (Anaheim) and Damian Rhodes (Ottawa). Not to mention guys such as Tom Chorske (Washington), Joe Dziedzic (Phoenix), Darby Hendrickson (New York), Brett Hedican (Vancouver), Sean Hill (Carolina), Phil Housley (Calgary), Craig Johnson (Los Angeles), Trent Klatt (Vancouver), Mark Parrish (Florida) and Doug Zmolek (Chicago), who are also all playing in the NHL.

So, sit back, relax, crack open a tall beverage, and get ready to read about some good ol' fashioned Minnesota hockey. Hopefully you will have half as much fun reading about and celebrating this amazing tradition as I did getting the opportunity to bring it all to life.

To truly understand the modern game of ice hockey today, you have to go back - way back to the very beginning. There you can get to the root of the game's most fundamental origins: ice skating. Now, where and when that beginning actually is, makes for some very interesting debate. We do know, however, that what most likely first started out as a more convenient mode of winter transportation across the slippery ice and snow of frozen lakes and rivers, has evolved over time into what we now know today as ice hockey.

It seems that most every country through the ages has laid claim to the creation of one form or another of an athletic game. And, the history of advanced games, which involved using a stick to strike an object of some sort, can be traced back for thousands of years. For instance, wall-murals nearly 2,500 years old have been found in Greece which contained carvings portraying two people holding sticks in an athletic-like face-off position, very similar to what we now know as field hockey. Perhaps it was war-like in nature, possibly portraying hand-to-hand combat? Nonetheless, this is one of the ways that sports have evolved.

One such ancient game that may have led to the creation of hockey, was an old British past-time called "camp." Created in the 11th century following the Norman invasions, the game was supposedly started when the local villagers began to imitate how they booted out their intruders, by kicking rocks amongst one another for amusement. Various new games began to develop from this, and not long thereafter different sporting games that involved striking a ball or object with a stick began to emerge. Among them that may have played a part in the genesis of ice hockey over the upcoming millennium would be an amalgam of many different ice and field games including: Shinny, Hurley, Bandy, Baggataway, Ho-Gee, Oochamkunutk, Field Hockey, Lacrosse, Ice Polo, and Kolven.

Hockey's roots can be traced back for more than a thousand years

It All Started With Skating

In as early as the 1400s, Northern Europeans and Scandinavians were using not only snowshoes, but also snow skis to get around in their harsh winter's. It was not too long after that someone invented the ice skate. It is believed that the first crude form of ice skates were made of small animal bones, which were crudely fastened to one's boots. Later they evolved into wood, which was easier to carve into shape.

The Evolution of Skates

What were first hand-carved out of small animal bones, and then into wood, the evolution of ice skates have come a long way. Skates used in the early 1800s had been either hand-made out of whatever materials a person could find, or else imported from Great Britain or Holland. Called block or stock skates, because of the heavy wooden blocks that were used to hold the metal blade to the boot, the skates featured ropes or leather straps to fasten a person's foot into his skate. Those tight straps, which were necessary to hold the skates onto the boot, often times wound up cutting off the skaters circulation to his already cold feet.

A major breakthrough in the advancement of skating occurred in 1850, when E. W. Bushnell of Philadelphia invented the steel hockey skate blade. Bushnell's invention allowed skaters much more agility on the ice, and in addition, they did not have to sharpen them as frequently as they did those with the older iron blades. Bushnell manufactured and sold his new "practical" ice skates around the world. Then, another competitor began providing an even better skate in 1861. That's when the Starr Manufacturing Company of Dartmouth, Nova Scotia, began making superior quality ice skates from high quality steel. In 1863, another advancement was made when the self-fastening "Acme Club Spring Skate" was invented. Now, with just a flick of a lever, a skater could securely and quickly clamp his skates to the soles and heels of his boots. However, this trigger-type fastener often-times got hit inadvertently, which would in-turn release itself, and fly of the skaters feet in mid-stride. For an encore, the company then developed and sold what would become the most famous hockey skate in the world, the "Starr Skate." Best known for revolutionizing skating and ice hockey, the Starr Skate featured a wider, rocker-shaped blade. The blade was rounded in both the front and back, which made instant stops and starts as well as sudden turns much easier for the skater.

There are also many theories as to where the word "skate" came from. Some historians believe that it might be a derivative of the Dutch word "schaat," but there remains a controversy as to who was the first to actually use the new device. Along with the Dutch, all of the Scandinavian countries, as well as the Russians, English, Scottish and Irish, have also laid claim to skating's origins.

In the mid-1500s, the iron skate was perfected by a Scottish blacksmith. Soon after, skating became not only a popular form of transit, but also entertainment. In the mid-1600s, the Skating Club of Scotland was established, and other countries followed suit not too long after. When many of these people emigrated to North America in the 1800s, they brought their skates with them. Once ice skating became popular, ice games naturally began to emerge.

Hockey's Evolution

The word hockey seems to be as complex as the game itself. Despite all of the historical research and speculation, nobody really knows for sure who actually invented the game. The most likely scenario is that wherever there were frozen lakes, ponds, rivers, and streams; there were most likely Europeans, Scandinavians, Asians, and North American Indians alike who probably conceived and played some crude form of ice hockey.

One school of thought on how the game got its name came from Great Britain. As early as 1400, the word hockey was being used in England to describe a field game that was being played by young boys who hauled produce in "hock carts" during harvest festivals. Another theory claims that the word is an English form of the French word "hoquet," which was a shepherd's cane that resembled a modern looking hockey stick. Others claim the word had Native American origins. As far back as the mid-1700s, French explorers who voyaged up the St. Lawrence Seaway, claimed to have seen Iroquois Indians playing a primitive game which entailed using a stick to strike a ball on the ice. When a player hit the ball he would shout out "Ho-

Gee," which apparently meant, "it hurts." Yet another school of thought on how hockey got its name came from Canada in the mid-1800s. As the story goes, an English Colonel in the military whose common English family name was "Hockey," had his troops playing shinny near Windsor, Ontario, as a form of winter exercise. Supposedly, the game that they were playing became known as "Hockey's game."

Hockey's roots can be traced back to Europe, where in the 1600s the Scottish played a field hockey game called "Shinny," while the Irish played a game known as "Hurley." An additional pastime of this era was a Dutch game played on ice called "Kolven." Played with a ball, and stick that resembled a golf club, one would score a point by hitting the ball between two poles that had been stuck in the ice. Yet another game that was witnessed by French explorers in Canada in the mid-1700s, was an Indian game similar to lacrosse, called "Baggataway."

In the early 1800s, a game called "Bandy" was being played on icy rivers and lakes throughout the marshy Fen region of England. The village of Bury Fen, credited with starting the game, fielded a legendary team that supposedly went more than 100 years without ever losing a match. The game was played on skates with a short curved sticks, called "bandies." They were typically willow tree branches which were cut to the shape of a curved stick. Players used their sticks to strike a "cat," or ball, which was made of wood or cork, and eventually of rubber. Teams consisted of 11 players, and the games began when a referee threw the cat up in the air. The players would quickly fight to grab the cat and dribble it down the enormous 450' x 300' playing surface, and try to shoot it into a large 12-foot-by-7-foot goal. (Incidentally, bandy, which is considered to be the fastest team sport in the world, is currently being played in several places throughout the world including: the former Soviet Union, Scandinavia and also Minnesota. In fact, Minnesota has the only bandy program in the United States, with several leagues and teams playing at rinks in Edina, Roseville, and Bloomington.)

The Evolution of Hockey in North America

As more and more Europeans and Scandinavians emigrated to Canada, variations of these games slowly became popular on this side of the Atlantic. Hurley, an Irish game, was perhaps the first to be played competitively. One of the ways that the game was brought overseas was from Irish immigrants, who had come to

The Evolution of the Puck

The word "puck" was probably derived from the game of hurley. When a hurley ball was struck with a hurley stick, it was referred to as being "pucked." Cherry wood was the preferred material because of its dark color would show up well against the white ice.

The origins of hockey have clearly stated that the game began with the use of a round ball. One can only speculate as to why the flat puck evolved into what we know today, but a pretty good guess might entail the fact that people probably got tired of chasing after that damn ball down the river or across the lake after an errant shot. One can speculate that someone probably got smart and chopped the top and bottom off of the ball to make a puck. In the interim, between the ball and the flat disk, there were many items that were used as pucks, including: frozen manure, blocks of wood, chunks of coal, various pieces of fruit and vegetables, rocks, and even tin cans.

It is believed that the puck first surfaced as a flat disc in 1860, at Kingston Harbour, Ontario. It apparently made its big league debut during a game in Montreal, in 1875. There the game program prophetically described the puck as follows: "Some fears have been expressed on the part of the intending spectators that accidents were likely to occur through the ball flying about in a too lively manner, to the imminent danger of lookers-on... but we understand that the game will be played with a flat, circular piece of wood, thus preventing all danger of it leaving the surface of the ice."

By the late 1890s, the flat rubber puck was the standard at hockey games. But they weren't always made of rubber, rather the first pucks were made of wood. The evolution into vulcanized rubber is an interesting story in itself. Once during a game, a player shot a puck into the net. As it hit the post, it split in two. One half went in the goal, while the other half rolled out. During the mayhem which ensued as to whether or not it was in fact a goal, the referee consulted his trusty rule book. In it was stated that the puck must be one inch thick. He deduced that because the piece that was in the net was only half that width, it was ruled a no-goal. This ultimately led to the creation of a one-piece rubber puck, rather than two disk-like pieces that were glued together.

Made from carbon, sulfur, and rubber, today's NHL pucks adhere to strict guidelines. They are made of vulcanized rubber, are 1"x3" in dimension, and weigh no more than six ounces. In addition, teams freeze "les rondelles," as they are known in their native Canada, before games, in order to take some of the bounciness out of them.

work on the Shubencadie Canal near Dartmouth, Nova Scotia, in the early 1830s. Hurley was a game that was originally played on the grassy fields of Ireland with a brass ball and heavy wooden sticks called "shillelaghs." However, the fields of Eastern Canada's Nova Scotia region were much too rugged to play on, so instead they decided to play the game on ice. Soon "Ice Hurley" became the rage at Canada's first college, Windsor's King's College, located near Halifax - which was established in 1788, where students began playing the game competitively on both Long Pond and at Chester lakes.

Located on the shores of the Avon River in Nova Scotia, the region was first settled by French Acadian's. The Acadians, many of whom were farmers, lived harmoniously with the Mi'kmaq Indians, who were native to the territory. According to the Dictionary of the Language of the Mi'kmaq Indians, which was published in 1888, the Micmac's, as they were known, had invented an ice game of their own which involved using a stick and a ball, called "Oochamkunutk." The Micmac's, who were known for their superior wood-carving abilities, had mastered the art of crafting a one-piece stick. From hornbeam trees, and later from second-growth yellow birch trees, these craftsmen could carve powerful, yet durable sticks, or "hockey's" as they became known, from a single piece of the tree's root. (Later, throughout the early 1920s-30s, the "MicMac" brand evolved into a very high pedigree brand of hockey stick. It become the most popular manufactured stick of its kind in hockey, and by 1925 it was being advertised and sold around the world for a whopping 50¢ to 75¢ apiece.)

The Micmac's, who referred to ice hurley as "Alchamadijik," would gradually join with both the Acadians as well as the British soldiers in playing pick up games. Slowly their game's began to rub off on each other, and melded together. With an unlimited number of players out on the ice, some of them competed in wooden skates, while others simply wore moccasins. The games got rough, and for protection, the Micmac's used moose skin for padding on their shins and arms. Their new Canadian style of hurley featured sticks which they called "hurley's" to hit a square wooden block, through a goal. As time went by, ice hurley was referred to by many names, including: Hurley, Ricket, Cricket, and Wicket.

Long considered to be hockey's predecessor, "Shinny" was yet another informal ice game of the mid-1800s to evolve from the United Kingdom to North America. The game's rules were directly related to English field hockey, hurley, and lacrosse. The object of the game is very similar to today's hockey, in which opposing players tried to shoot a block of wood or a rubber ball into a goal, commonly made from two rocks or even tin cans, which served as markers. With no set time limits, games were played on huge rinks that were formed in rivers, lakes, ponds, and creeks.

Spectators could often-times be seen cheering for their teams by running up and down the river banks. There were no side boards of any type, so much of the games were spent chasing after the ball. One of the game's most prominent rules was taken directly from field hockey, in which during a face-off, or "bully" as it was called, players had to "shinny on their own side," which meant they had to take the draw right-handed.

Considered by some to be the greatest winter sport in North America, Shinny, or Shinty, became quite popular throughout Canada and parts of the Northern United States in the mid to late 1800s. Many kids played in their boots if they didn't own a pair of ice skates. Kids used to scour the forests to find a good "shinny stick" to play with. They would look for a solid branch from an old maple, oak, or ash tree, which might have a slight crook or growth at the end of it which would form a blade. (A good shinny stick was so durable that players would occasionally pass their sticks down generationally to their own kids.) And, getting whacked on the shins, or anywhere else for that matter, was just part of the game. The referee's typically ignored slashing, roughing, high sticking, and cross checking. Rather he would holler out the cry, "Shinny on your own side!" which was also a warning to settle down. Sometimes if a player didn't cool off, the ref would simply whack him across the shins. Most kids came home with torn trousers, and most likely, bruised shins.

While there is much debate as to whether or not the first ever hockey games played in Canada, were in fact shinny games, yet one more ice game evolved in the late 1800s after shinny and before ice hockey, called "Ice Polo." Besides shinny, it is believed that the forerunner to ice hockey in the United States was ice polo, an American conception that was probably adopted from the popular fad-sport of roller polo -- which was played on indoor roller rinks. Played much like football on ice, only with a hard rubber ball, ice polo teams featured a goaltender, a half-back, a center and two rushers. Ice polo was being played on outdoor ice by the late 1870's in parts of Minnesota, New England, and Michigan. Beginning in 1883, there was even a four-team ice polo league playing in St. Paul which sponsored annual tournaments at the infamous St. Paul Winter Carnival. But, by the early 1900's ice hockey had replaced ice polo in the U.S.

The Modern Game
As the present-day game of ice hockey started to take shape from bits and pieces of its many unique predecessors, it can safely be said that Canada is the modern game's originator. It is believed that a refined game of shinny, which included many of modern hockey's rules and characteristics, was first played in 1855 on a harbor just outside Halifax, Nova Scotia, by members of an Imperial Army unit known as "Her Majesty's Royal Canadian Rifles."

Much of the credit for the rules of the modern game have been credited to a gentleman named, J.G.H. Creighton, of Halifax, who, in the 1850s, combined the rules of British field hockey, shinny, and ice lacrosse to form the basis of ice hockey. Several rule changes were starting to be introduced to the game, including: reducing the number of players on the ice from eleven to seven players, incorporating a standard 3" x 1" puck -- instead of a ball, and also creating short side boards around the ice surfaces. In addition, ice rinks were popping up all around the country-side's. (The term rink, which referred to the designated area of play, and also meant race-course, was originally used in the game of curling in 18th-century Scotland.)

Others debate that the first real hockey game, with more defined rules and with a limited number of players, was actually played in 1875 at the indoor Victoria Skating Rink, by McGill University students in Montreal. (Incidentally, for this game, J.G.H. Creighton ordered and shipped two dozen MicMac hockey sticks to his friends in Halifax for their big game against McGill in Montreal.) Here, hockey grew and prospered. The early playing style seemed to accentuate a more rugged playing style, versus a finesse game. But, as time went by and more and more people began playing, stickhandling, passing and skating became much more refined. During this period at the University, there is also speculation that several football coaches incorporated many of the rules of rugby into the game -- which may explain for the game's rough style of play.

By the mid-1880s, hockey leagues were being played between both coasts throughout Canada. Nearly every small town had teams which played against one another, and kids began to learn how to skate as soon as they could learn how to walk. Ice hockey became a recognized sport, and in 1883, also an official event at the Montreal Winter Carnival. The carnival committee even issued a challenge for the "world championship" of ice hockey, as teams from Quebec, Ottawa, Toronto, and Montreal answered the call to play in what is believed to be the first ice hockey tournament in the world. An interesting refinement came to the game by way of the Winter Carnival a few years later in 1886. That was when one of the teams showed up for the tournament short a pair of players. The other team felt compelled to help out their opponents, and thereby agreed to drop two of their skaters to make it even. The teams found that with four less men on the ice, they could open up play and spread things out. And with that, the nine-man game finally gave way to the seven-man game.

Shortly thereafter, in 1886, representatives from several Canadian teams gathered together to finally establish a formal set of rules for consistent play. What they came up with would become known as the "Montreal Rules." A governing body was formed, and they called themselves the Canadian Amateur Hockey League (the predecessor to today's Canadian Amateur Hockey Association). They called for seven-man hockey, which featured a goal-tender, two half-backs (who played close to the goal like a modern defenseman), a rover, and three forwards. Players became quite proficient in stickhandling, because back then there was no forward passing allowed. Any forward pass was immediately ruled off-sides. Games consisted of two half-hour periods, with a ten minute breather in-between to shovel the ice.

Hockey America
America's hockey roots are not quite as complicated as those of Canada's, but nonetheless, there is some debate as to where and when the game migrated southward below the 49th parallel. The American concoction known as ice polo, muddied up the waters with regards to determining the exact origins of the game in the U.S. While some say the game started officially on the East Coast, an argument can be made that the game was also being played at the same time right here in Minnesota. One of those theories, however, takes us back to the summer of 1894, to Niagara Falls, N.Y.

There, a group of American tennis players from Yale University were competing in a tournament with some players from Canada. In between the competition, some of the players began socializing, and talking about winter ice games. Upon learning that the Americans were still playing ice polo, the Canadians, who were playing ice hockey, invited their new American friends to play a friendly exhibition of both sports. They agreed, and played a series of two-period, doubleheaders of each game throughout several major Canadian cities in front of capacity crowds. Upon the conclusion of the contests, the Canadians had swept the hockey games, while the Yanks won two and tied two of the ice polo games. When it was all said and done, the Americans agreed that ice hockey was a much better game to play. Instantly enamored with their new-found game, the American boys bought up all of the sticks and skates that they could carry and returned home. Upon their arrival, they began to play hockey full-time, which included switching over to using flat-bottom skates, a puck instead of a ball, and a longer hockey-styled stick instead of the field hockey kind. Within a couple of years, most of the universities and club teams on the East Coast had switched from ice polo to the faster and more exciting sport of ice hockey.

At about the same time that the East-Coaster's were getting indoctrinated to the game of ice hockey, the game was also being spread southward into the U.S. from other points of Canada as well. Which is why at about the same time during the late 1890s, the game was also being played in Minneapolis and St. Paul, and in Northern Minnesota, including Hallock, Eveleth, and Duluth. In addition, the University of Minnesota began playing ice hockey in 1895 against several teams from Canada, including Winnipeg.

America's first big-time league, the Amateur Hockey League, began play in New York City in 1896, and just months later the Baltimore Hockey League got started. In 1899 the Intercollegiate Hockey League was formed with teams from Yale, Columbia, Brown, Harvard, and Princeton. In addition, high school and prep school hockey was being played by the early 1900's in Minnesota, New York City, New England, and in Michigan's upper peninsula. The sport continued to grow in America to cities throughout the East Coast and Midwest. In 1903, the International Pro Hockey League became the country's first professional circuit. Michigan's Upper Peninsula mining town team of Houghton, called the Portage Lakers, became the first professional team in the U.S. Now legendary, this club often-times whipped their Canadian counterparts, and helped to put American hockey on the map.

Then, a forerunner of the National Hockey Association, which began play in 1909, the present-day (six-man style) National Hockey League was created in 1917. That same year the Seattle Metropolitans, members of Canada's Pacific Coast League, became the first U.S. team to win the Stanley Cup in its 24-year-old history, greatly embarrassing the Canadian clubs who didn't give the American teams much respect.

Ice Hockey's Early Beginnings in Minnesota

In Minnesota, where the Scandinavians and Europeans love their winters, shinny had been played on the frozen rivers and lakes since the Civil War. However, the more evolved ice game of ice polo was gaining popularity in the land of 10,000 lakes by the late 1800s. In the early 1880s, ice polo was the rage in both St. Paul and Minneapolis. The sport is believed to have evolved from the short-lived 1880s fad of roller polo, which was played on roller skates. So popular was roller polo that in 1885 Minneapolis alone had 14 indoor roller rinks, but two years later interest had died out and only two remained.

In 1883, Minnesotan, Frank Barron, an accomplished ice and roller polo player, formulated what is believed to be the first set of ice polo rules. Six (or sometimes seven) players formed a team which included the following positions: goal, coverpoint, cover goal, first rush, second rush, and center. Short curved sticks similar to a present day field hockey stick were used to hit a ball into a goal cage similar to, but smaller than a soccer goal. Barron organized the St. Paul Polo Club in 1883 and for the next four seasons they held a monopoly in the Twin City area. Members of that team were: Gus Zenzens, Con Zenzens, Frank Barron, Charles Robertson, W.J. Murnane, Paul Kleist, and Charles Trot. The club also built the first lighted outdoor rink in West St. Paul.

On January 22, 1887, the first ice polo tournament was held in conjunction with the St. Paul Winter Carnival at the Palace Grounds. The St. Paul Winter Carnival has an amazing history in itself. The annual event celebrated winter and all of its icy pleasures, which showcased several forms of ice skating, including: figure, speed, novelty, and trick skating, as well as long-jumping contests over barrels. Ice polo flourished here because of the number of people who became exposed to it.

Once again Frank Barron led the way that year. His squad, the Junior Carnival Club was awarded gold medals by beating the Royal Route Club of Omaha, and the Carnival Skating Club. The four team tournament featured two teams from St. Paul, and one from both Minneapolis, and Stillwater. The Minneapolis "Lelands" team was led by the infamous football star Walter "Pudge" Heffelfinger, who earned All-American honors as a guard at Yale in 1889, 1890 and 1891. He is still considered to be one of the greatest football players of all time.

The Barron and Murphy families, each with several members playing ice polo, played an important role in helping to promote the sport in the Twin Cities. Incidentally, there were two Edward Murphy's involved in St. Paul ice polo and ice hockey. "Big" Ed Murphy was a Canadian hockey and lacrosse player, while the other Ed Murphy was an American who did not care for the ice polo sport, but was instrumental in starting ice hockey in St. Paul. Kieffer, the goalie, the Barron's, the Murphy's, Newson, and the fast skating Harley Davidson, who was a world renown speed skater (no relation to the motorcycles), were among the best players during the heyday of ice polo in St. Paul.

Ice polo was also being played in Duluth, as the following article from the Duluth News-Tribune, on January 14, 1893, entitled "Polo on Ice," attests to: "A match game of polo has been organized between the Duluth Polo Club and the Zenith City Club. It will take place at the Central Skating Rink, foot of Fifth Avenue West, Friday night. The Zenith City team is a good club. Polo is a very popular winter sport and considerable interest has been aroused here among the fans. The attendance at this initial game of the season promises to be large. F.B. Taylor will captain Duluth and T. Moore will direct the Zeniths. Duluth: Berg, Morrison, McLennon, Thompson, Taylor (captain), Vincent, Paine, Carey, and Meining. Zeniths: Calvary, Buxton, McDonald, McIllhargie, Moran (Captain), Michaud, Maloney, Mitchell, and Grachau."

The 1892 Duluth Polo Club

The 1900 Minneapolis Athletic Club

On February 7, 1893 the St. Paul Henriette's defeated the Duluth Polo Club 2-1 for the first Minnesota ice polo title. But the next year, in 1894, Duluth defeated the Henriette's in a three game series for state ice polo championship, which was held at Duluth's enclosed Glen Avon Curling Club rink. These games are believed to be first ice polo games played on an enclosed rink in the United States.

As ice polo grew in popularity The Twin City Ice Polo League was organized, with the championships tying into the St. Paul Winter Carnival. Minneapolis and St. Paul turned up the heat on their cross town rivalry. Minneapolis teams such as The Polo Club, Acorns and Lelands would battle St. Paul teams such as the St. George's, St. Paul's, Central's, Summits, Henriette's, Fort Snelling, Mascots and Gophers. St. Paul had a more extensive program than Minneapolis. Huge crowds followed many of the games in St. Paul which were played on several popular outdoor rinks, including: Broadway, Como, Aurora, Edgerton, Central, Ramsey, Hill, Palace and Victoria. In 1894 four covered roller rinks: Jackson, Summit, Wigwam and Exposition were flooded in the winter and used for ice polo contests.

The Army Companies at Fort Snelling even formed a four-team league. In addition, several youth teams were playing the game, including: St. Paul High School, Spauldings, Summit Juniors, and Interurbans. Other cities such as: Owatonna, Stillwater and Superior (Wis.), were also playing the game at this time.

Ice polo continued to be played in the large cities of Minnesota, but by 1895, ice hockey, which had recently been introduced to the area by our neighbors from Manitoba, had quickly become the preferred sport of choice. A game much better suited to the smaller ice surface and indoor rinks, hockey was officially the rage in Minnesota by the turn of the century. The last state ice polo tournament was won by Duluth in 1899.

A Hockey State of Mind
During February, 1895, this article appeared in the St. Paul Pioneer Press: "Game of ice hockey started by Ed Murphy in 1894 as an outgrowth of the game of ice polo which flourished for years previously. Ice polo was the main winter sport in St. Paul when Ed Murphy moved in as a youngster of twenty-one years of age. Murphy an American, had watched ice hockey in Canada. He did not care for ice polo and after several attempts he finally got the game changed to ice hockey and the first St. Paul club was organized in 1893, for the season of 1893-1894."

The evolution was complete, and hockey was now gaining recognition all across our state -- especially in the Twin Cities as well as throughout Northern Minnesota (especially in Hallock), and throughout the Iron Range area. Kids and adults alike began to learn about the rules and style of this new game. All they needed now was to actually see it in action. It appears that Minnesota's first game of organized ice hockey was played between two Minneapolis teams in January of 1895. They met at an outdoor rink located at 11th Street and 4th Avenue South for a series of games against each other. These games were not only among the very first to have ever been played in Minnesota, but also in the United States.

Twin City League Dunbar Cup Winners:

1902	St. Paul Virginias
1903	St. Paul Victorias
1904	St. Paul Victorias
1905	St. Paul Victorias
1906	St. Paul Victorias
1907	St. Paul Victorias
1908	St. Paul Mic Macs
1909	St. Paul Phoenix
1910	St. Paul Phoenix
1911	St. Paul Phoenix

Later in January and early February the Minneapolis Hockey Club met the newly formed University of Minnesota team in a series of games. The first University of Minnesota team, unsanctioned by the college, was organized in January of 1895 by Dr. H. A. Parkyn, a quarterback on the Gopher football team who had played the game in Toronto. Parkyn coached the U of M team, comprised mainly of kids who were experienced ice polo players. These games would serve as a warm-up for an upcoming contest against one of Canada's best teams of that era, the Winnipeg Victoria's. A main reason why the Gophers were able to schedule a game with the Manitoba team was because at that time, there was no railroad connection between Eastern and Western Canada. So, the Victorias had to travel through the Twin Cities on their way out to play Ontario and Quebec. On February 18, 1895, the Gophers beat the Victoria's by the score of 11-3. The game was played at Minneapolis' Athletic Park, which was located at Sixth Street and First Avenue North (the present sight of the Butler Square Building, next to the Target Center). The park was also the home of the professional Minneapolis Millers Baseball Club, before they moved to Nicollet Park.

Bobby Marshall, who starred for the Minneapolis Wanderers, was also an All-American defensive end on the Gopher football team

On January 24-25, 1896, the St. Paul Winter Carnival played host to a four-team international tournament which took place at St. Paul's Aurora Rink. It was probably the first international ice hockey tournament ever held in the United States. The teams included the Minneapolis Hockey Club, two teams from St. Paul -- St. Paul I & St. Paul II, and a squad from Winnipeg. In the first round, Minneapolis beat St. Paul II 4-1, while Winnipeg whipped St. Paul I 13-2. Winnipeg then trounced Minneapolis 7-3 for the championship. On January 26 the St. Paul Globe reported: "The games were attended by large crowds. The Winnipeg team received a silver stein for winning the carnival championship while the Minneapolis team members were given sticks."

By 1896-97, there were several hockey teams, including youth teams, competing in both St. Paul and in the Mill City. In addition, informal hockey was being played throughout Northwestern Minnesota in communities such as: Argyle, Hallock, Warren, and Stephen. In 1899 the St. Paul Hockey Club was organized. The Club played several games that year, one of them against St. Cloud Normal School at the Virginia rink in St. Paul before some 400 fans. St. Paul won 6-0 with Patterson, Elliot and Newsom each scoring two goals. The team even planned a trip to the East

Coast to play teams from New York City, Washington D.C. and Philadelphia. However, the trip was canceled due to a lack of participation and quality practice time.

By the turn of the century, grade school and high school hockey programs were taking off throughout the state. By now the sport had spread to communities such as Warroad, Roseau, Thief River Falls, Crookston, Baudette, Eveleth, and Duluth. At this same time, men's and youth leagues were growing throughout the metro area. Fueling this growth were several leading industrial and utility companies who sponsored these clubs. The culmination for all of the teams came down to an annual tournament which determined the Twin Cities championship. With this organized sponsorship, hockey soon became accessible to a wide variety of men and boys alike who wished to play the game. Rinks sprouted up everywhere as the game began to take off.

As the 20th Century began to unfold, hockey continued to grow and prosper. Minneapolis even got its first indoor rink. In 1900, the old Star Roller Rink located on 4th Avenue South and 11th Street, was retrofitted for ice hockey. The Minneapolis Hockey Club, Central High School, and North High School would all use the "Star" on a regular basis for games as well as for practice.

"Senior" Hockey at the Turn of the Century

Men's senior leagues began to pop up throughout Minnesota in one form or another around the turn of the century. They have played a vital role in the development of amateur hockey in the state. By the early 1900s, there were countless men's senior hockey circuits which had sprouted up throughout the Twin Cities and Northern Minnesota. It was a social movement phenomenon, which Joseph Shipanovich -- author of the book "Minneapolis," called "industrial paternalism,"

Hall of Famer Coddy Winters starred for the 1908 Duluth Northern Hardware senior team

wherein business and corporations began the tradition of sponsoring athletic teams comprised of their employees. The first big-time league that came to fruition during this era was the Twin City Senior Hockey League.

Late in the winter of 1901, to accommodate the growing desire for organized hockey in the Gopher State, the Twin City Senior Hockey League was formed with the following four teams: Minneapolis Hockey Club, St. Paul Hockey Club, St. Paul Mechanic Arts High School, and St. Paul Central High School. During the next season of 1901-1902, the league became a six-team union when the St. Paul Virginia's and the St. Paul Mascots were added. To make it official, the world famous curler, Robert H. Dunbar, presented a silver cup which would be awarded annually to the league champion. The Virginias went on to win the inaugural Dunbar Cup.

During the 1902 season, after losing two out of three to the St. Paul Hockey Club, the Minneapolis Hockey Club withdrew from the league, leaving the alliance with only five St. Paul teams. Minneapolis HC would play a very significant game later that season though. On January 23, 1902, the world famous Portage Lake Lakers, of Houghton Mich., defeated Minneapolis HC 8-4 in a contest played at the Star Rink.

At the end of the season, the St. Paul Virginia team traveled to Houghton to face the mighty Lakers, who were for the most part Canadian imports. Considered by most to be the best team in the world, Portage Lake whipped the Virginias 11-2 before a crowd of more than 700 at the Amphidrome Arena. The Lakers enjoyed the great competition that Minnesota offered, and came back again that season to face St. Paul one more time. This time they won only 2-0. The star of the Victorias was a goaltender named Joe Jones. So impressed were the Lakers with his performance, claiming that he was the best that they had ever faced, they hired him to come tend goal for them the following season. (Later Jones would go on to play for the American Soo team of the International Hockey League, the world's first professional circuit.)

In 1903 the University of Minnesota was invited to participate in the league. Using Como Lake in St. Paul (rather than Northrop Field), as the team's home rink, the Gophers defeated both Central High School, 4-0, and the St. Paul Virginias, 4-3. A highlight of the era occurred in 1904, when a St. Paul all-star team was formed and sent to St. Louis where they competed in the World's Fair Tournament against teams from Missouri and Michigan.

Over the nine-year history of the Twin City League, which was comprised of all Minnesotans and no imports, St. Paul teams dominated the circuit with the Gotzian Victorias winning the Dunbar Cup six consecutive seasons from 1902-1907. Among the many Minneapolis teams that joined the TCL included: AAA, the Lake Shores, the Harriets, the YMCAs, the Eagles, the U of M, and the Wanderers. (The Minneapolis Wanderers were led by one of Minnesota's greatest athletes, Bobby Marshall. Marshall, one of the first African Americans to play hockey at this level in the U.S., was also a 1905 All-American end for the University of Minnesota football team.)

After the 1911 season, when as the St. Paul Chinooks and Minneapolis Wanderers withdrew from the organization, the league ceased operations. As a result of the league breakup, teams expanded their schedules in order to play a more diverse schedule. That same year, the Phoenix went on to play a series of exhibition games against several local high schools, Minneapolis Lake Shores, Duluth and Fort William. In addition, the team traveled to Cleveland and Chicago to play a series of games. Incidentally, the last two games of that season against Duluth and Fort William were played at the newly constructed St. Paul Hippodrome located in the Livestock Pavilion at the state fairgrounds. The "Hipp," as it was known, with its natural ice, had the honor of having the largest sheet of ice in North America. The ice sheet measured a whopping 270 feet long by 119 feet wide, and covered an area of more than 32,000 square feet -- more than twice as big as a normal hockey rink, which measures only 100' x 185'. Opponents who played there said it was like playing on Lake Superior! Not to be outdone, that same year the Curling Club of Duluth was built -- giving the northerners their own hockey Mecca to compete in.

The St. Paul Phoenix were an early senior team of the 1910s

During that first decade, a series of games were played against teams from Minneapolis,

Moose Goheen

White Bear Lake native Moose Goheen joined the St. Paul Athletic Club in the fall of 1915, and from there went on to become one of Minnesota's greatest hockey superstars. The crowds at his games would chant "Moose" "Moose," to which Goheen would reply by first circling his own net several times to pick up speed, and then make an end-to-end rush, usually scoring. In addition to leading the AC to several McNaughton Cups, Moose also played on the 1920 silver medal-winning U.S. Olympic Hockey team. He continued to play with the St. Paul team through 1926 when it turned professional and then on through 1932. He was offered several pro contracts from both Toronto and Boston, but opted instead to stay in Minnesota and continue working at Northern States Power Company. In 1952 Moose was selected to the Hockey Hall of Fame in Toronto, becoming one of the few Americans ever to have done so. In 1958 he was voted by the Minnesota Hall of Fame as the finest player ever produced in the state.

St. Paul, Duluth and Two Harbors to determine the State Senior champion. By no surprise the St. Paul Victorias continued their dominance in the world of Minnesota hockey, by winning the title from 1904-1907. In 1908 the Duluth Northerns won the title, and also went on to claim the U.S. Amateur championship as well. The St. Paul Phoenix won the championship in 1909 and 1910, and in 1912 the team was invited to play in Chicago, Cleveland, and Detroit.

The State's Dominion League

Another league that got underway around the turn of the century was called the State's Dominion League. This men's senior amateur league ran from 1900 into the early 1950s, with teams from all over the state competing. Included were: the Duluth Northerns, the Hallock Legionnaire's, the Thief River Falls Thieves, the Grand Forks Flickertails, Roseau, Baudette, Hibbing, Eveleth, Warroad, Two Harbors, Crookston, the St. Paul Victorias, the St. Paul Mic Macs, and the St. Paul Koppy's.

Among the leading players during the first decade of the 1900's were: Carl Struck, Cleve Benowicz, W. Lalond, Ray Hodge, Kimball Hodge, Jack Bradford, Cornell Lagerstrom, P. K. Labafle, A. Raymond, C. Fairchild, Bobby Marshall, Fred Cook, Ed Murphy, Harry and Bert Clayton, Joe Jones, Roy Sanders, Jack and Matt Taylor, Charles Kenny, Roy Moritz, Ray Armstrong, George Patterson, Bob Barron, Tom Newson, Ed Fitzgerald, Harvey McNair, Jack Ordway, Leo Leonard, Port Palmer, Fred Minser, Walter Seeger, John Foley, Charles Driscoll, Fred Bawlf, and Art Larkin (who was a quarterback for the Gopher football team in 1906 and 1907).

Minnesota Hockey from 1910 - 1920 (WWI ERA)

Following the breakup of the Twin City League after the 1911 season, the Minneapolis Senior League was formed with teams playing many of their games on the ice of Lake Harriet. Members of the league included: The ABC's, the Simokins, the North Commons, and the Lake Harriets. The Lake Harriets emerged as the team to beat during this era, considered by most to be among the best in the city. The Harriets would also play teams from not only St. Paul, but also from Duluth and even the tiny Northwestern Minnesota town of Hallock, where they would play the Lions.

The American Amateur Hockey Association

In 1914 the St. Paul Athletic Club, one of the greatest organizations in the history of Minnesota hockey, was formed and competed in an independent schedule against some tough opponents. Among them were Duluth, Grand Forks, Fort William, Port Arthur, and the Ottawa Aberdeens. The team's only two losses came from a very experienced Ottawa squad. Among the players were: Weidenborner, Goheen, Conroy, Peterson, Henderson, Kahler, Fitzgerald, McCourt and LeClaire.

Only one year earlier, in 1913, the American Amateur Hockey Association, or AAHA, was created. Many of the players in the league were imported Canadians. The inaugural teams in the league included: Portage Lake, Calumet, Sault Ste. Marie, American Soo, Cleveland Athletic Club, Boston Athletic Association, and the Boston Arenas. In 1915, the St. Paul Athletic Club joined the league. The teams competed for the coveted McNaughton Cup, which was donated by James McNaughton, president of Upper Michigan's Calumet and Hecla Copper Company, and big-time supporter of amateur hockey. The cup, which weighs some 40 pounds and towers nearly three feet tall, is hand crafted of pure silver. (Years later, in the 1940s, the cup was passed down to the newly-formed Western Intercollegiate Hockey League which later became the Western Collegiate Hockey Association, or WCHA.)

The original State Fair Hippodrome

From 1913-1915, the Cleveland Athletic Club, led by Duluth-born speed skater Frank "Coddy" Winters, won three consecutive titles. Then, in 1916, ironically in the league's last year of existence, the St. Paul Athletic Club beat the American Soo (Sault St.. Marie, Mich.) three games out of four, to win the cup. St. Paul AC was led by a high-scoring defenseman named Francis "Moose" Goheen, of White Bear Lake. Crowds at the "Hipp" in St. Paul absolutely loved the Moose. He was probably as popular back then as Kirby Puckett is today. At 200 pounds he was a bruiser, and could get the 8,000-plus fans to their feet in a hurry with one of his infamous body checks. At the time he was considered by most to be the best American developed player in western United States.

The other stars of that St. Paul squad included the high-scoring center Nick Kahler, Cy Weidenbroner, Eddie Fitzgerald, and Tony Conroy. And, all but Kahler, who had work obligations, would go on to represent the USA on the 1920 Olympic team in Antwerp, Belgium. Playing under the guidance of the International Skating Union, the Americans lost to the Winnipeg Falcons (who represented Canada), for the gold medal, in the first-ever Winter Olympic games. After winning the AAHA crown, St. Paul traveled to Montreal in March of 1916, where they beat Lachine, Quebec, 7-6, for the International Art Ross Trophy, which was emblematic of the world's amateur championship. The people of Canada were shocked that a U.S. team was that good. By the spring of 1917 World War I was underway, and the AAHA ultimately dissolved.

The St. Paul AC played an independent schedule for the season of 1916-1917. Several key players were added to the club that year. Dick Conway, a star football and baseball player at St. Thomas College from White Bear Lake, Herb Drury, a speedy winger from Midland, Ontario, who would later go on to play in the National Hockey League as a member of the Pittsburgh team, and Everett McGowan, a nationally known speed-skater. In addition to playing the American Soo, Duluth, Pittsburgh, and several Canadian teams that season, the AC also played a new team from Minneapolis - which featured a familiar face.

The Minneapolis Millers are Born

An interesting thing happened in 1917, when Nick Kahler, one of the great young hockey players of the time who had been captain of the St. Paul AC team, crossed the river to Minneapolis and formed a new team comprised mostly of Canadian imports. His new squad, the Minneapolis Millers, played the St. Paul AC and split a two game series. The first game, played at the Hipp, resulted in a 9-2 rout for the St. Paul seven, while the second, which was played at the smaller Coliseum Rink located on Lexington Avenue near University Avenue in St. Paul, ended in a 9-0 loss for the Millers. Kahler's Mill City team even sought entry in the National Hockey Association (The NHA precluded the NHL), as a replacement for the defunct Pittsburgh team, but was unsuccessful. The Millers played several of the teams in that league, which was based mostly in the East and from Canada,

The 1923 St. Paul Athletic Club

and fared well. The roster of that early Minneapolis hockey club included such stars as: Babe Elliott, goaltender; Jack Chambers Fosdale and Alex Dunlop, defense; Lyle Wright and McPherson, wings, and Nick Kahler, center. The Millers became the orphans of hockey with no league affiliation and no permanent home rink. After playing the 1919 season on a flooded roller rink at Plymouth and Washington avenues north, Minneapolis moved into the luxurious confines of the Hippodrome in St. Paul.

Tony Conroy

Tony Conroy grew up in St. Paul, where he attended Mechanic Arts High School. From 1911 to 1914, while still in high school, he even played with the old Phoenix septet. (Teams were made up of seven players in those days.) He went on to star with the St. Paul Athletic Club and later with the professional St. Paul Saints of the AHA during the 1920s. After WWI service, Conroy returned to the Athletic Club and was one of four members of that club to make the 1920 silver medal-winning U.S. Olympic team in Belgium.

The War finally came to an end on November 11, 1918. The American Amateur Hockey Association resurfaced for the season of 1919-20. The St. Paul AC again won the McNaughton Cup, this time sharing the title with Canadian Soo, because they could not agree on a neutral sight to play the championship. (It is important to note that up to this point, hockey in the United States was changing from being played with seven players to six, thus eliminated the position of rover, and there was also no forward passing. Players could skate the puck up and pass lateraly or back, but not ahead. Another key rule change of this era was the allowance of a substitute for a penalized player, so there was always a full complement of players.)

Other significant events in the world of Minnesota hockey during this decade included the growth of intramural hockey at the University of Minnesota. By 1915 some 16 fraternities were playing organized hockey on campus. Their league games were played on the flooded Northrop Field, with the playoffs taking place at the Hipp. The Bros brothers, Chet and Ben, who would later dominate for the Gophers, were the stars of that Greek league. In addition, a women's league got underway at the U of M that next year in 1916.

The late Carl F. Struck, considered the father of the ice sport in the Mill City, organized park league teams in 1916 and 1917. Two of the better known teams of that WW I period were the Vertex and the Camdens, bitter championship rivals. High school hockey was also gaining popularity. The Mechanic Arts High School was consistently one of the strongest of the Twin City high schools.

During this period, not only were college and amateur teams playing at the Hipp, but also several high school teams as well. The same was happening in both Duluth, at the Duluth Curling Club, and also in Hibbing, where the Hibbing Curling Club had recently opened. In addition, Duluth amateur teams were playing an independent schedule against Canadian and Michigan Copper-Country teams.

The United States Amateur Hockey Association

In the fall of 1920 the United States Amateur Hockey Association (U.S.A.H.A.) was formed, and the A.A.H.A. decided to become an affiliate of the new league. The U.S.A.H.A. (by virtue of an agreement with the International Skating Union, Canadian Amateur Hockey Association, and the Amateur Athletic Union) was now recognized as the sole governing body for amateur hockey in the U.S., and over the next several years its league champion was acknowledged as the national champion.

During that first season of league play in 1920-1921, there were three groups that made up the new association -- one in the East and two in the Midwest. The clubs that played in the league included: the Duluth Hornets, St. Paul AC, The Eveleth Reds, Boston AA, Boston Westminster HC, Pittsburgh Hornets, Pittsburgh Yellow Jackets, Cleveland HC, New York, Philadelphia, Cleveland, Calumet, Portage Lake, and both the American and Canadian Soo of Sault St. Marie. They were all playing a uniform version of six-man

The 1922 Eveleth Reds

Vic Des Jardins

Vic Des Jardins starred for the USAHA's Eveleth Rangers from 1921-26, before heading south, to lead the AHA's St. Paul Saints. He captured the league scoring title in 1928 before going on to play in the NHL with both the Chicago Blackhawks and New York Rangers.

hockey as well, having eliminated the "rover" position.

Eveleth got off to a great start that inaugural season. The Reds, who were playing their home games in the newly constructed Eveleth Recreation Building, finished the season by winning the Group Three Division with a record of 14-1-1. Eveleth then faced Cleveland, the Group Two champ which had beaten the Group One champ, Boston AA, in the finals. On April 2-3, in Cleveland, the Cleveland Hockey Club beat Eveleth by the back-to-back scores of 6-3, and 6-3. Then, because of the lack of ice in Northern Minnesota at the time, the series shifted to Pittsburgh -- where there was artificial ice to play on. There, the Reds beat the Clevelander's by the scores of 2-0, and 4-2 to tie it up at two games apiece. But, Cleveland was declared the winner of the four-game series 14-12 on total goals, and was awarded the league's championship trophy, the Fellowes Cup. As for the other Minnesota teams that season? St. Paul skated to a modest record of 3-5, while Duluth finished 1-7.

At the end of the 1921-22 season, Eveleth, winners of Group Three, had finished with an impressive 12-4 record. The Reds then went on to face the St. Paul AC, the winners of Group Two who posted an 8-4 record, in the semifinals on March 3rd, in Eveleth. Eveleth had a very strong team with the likes of Monette, Ching and Ade Johnson, Seaborn, Grey, Des Jardins, Galbraith, Breen and Nicklin. With the exception of Des Jardins, the entire roster was Canadian. St. Paul beat Eveleth 3-1, only to lose 4-2 the following evening. The series then shifted back to St. Paul where the teams skated to a pair of 0-0 ties, in addition to a 2-1 nail-biter victory for the AC. St. Paul wound up winning the series 7-6 on total goals. In so doing, St. Paul then went on to face Boston Westminster in the finals, only to lose in four: 3-0, 2-1, 0-0, and 2-0. Although the AC lost the championship, the playoffs proved that Minnesotans indeed loved their hockey. That's because St. Paul, with a rink that held 7,800, drew in excess of 51,000 fans for the two (seven-game) playoff series' against Eveleth and Boston.

For the 1922-23 season and thereafter, the league decided to split into two divisions -- the Eastern and Western. St. Paul along with Duluth, Eveleth, Pittsburgh, Cleveland and newcomer Milwaukee formed Group Two of the USAHA. Again St. Paul won the Western Division with an impressive 35-5 record that year, three games in front of Cleveland and four games ahead of Eveleth. Playing a big part in those wins were the addition of several new faces to the lineup that included: Taffy Abel, Dennis Breen, George Clarke and Joe McCormick. By season's end the only two teams left standing were once again St. Paul AC and Boston Westminster. Boston went on to win the Fellowes Cup for the second straight season, by winning the series in four, with St. Paul winning only Game Three by the score of 2-1. Incidentally, all four games, which were decided by one goal margins, were played in the newly constructed Boston Arena. The leading scorers in the league that year included St. Paul's Clark, who scored 15 goals, Moose Goheen, who tallied 11, and Duluth's Seaborn, who added 10.

During the 1923-24 season, the upstart Minneapolis Rockets replaced the struggling Milwaukee franchise as the sixth team in the division. The team played in the brand new Minneapolis Arena, which was located at 2800 Dupont Avenue South. Not only did the new facility have an artificial ice surface, it also had a seating capacity of some 5,400. That year Minneapolis was blessed with some of the best hockey that the Mill City would ever know. Two Winnipeg natives named Ching and Ade Johnson, who had previously played for the Eveleth Reds, joined the Rockets for their inaugural season. Ching, who at more than 200 pounds was then considered to be a giant, was an incredible crowd favorite not only back up on the Range in Eveleth, but also most everywhere around the league. His big bald head, huge grin, and rough antics on the ice made him an instant hero to hockey fans everywhere. Minneapolis, despite having the Johnson brothers as well as another star named Taffy Abel on their team, wound up in the league cellar that year tied with Duluth at 6-14-0. St. Paul, who added Wilt Peltier to their lineup that season, would up finishing the season at 14-6. Pittsburgh, who edged St. Paul for the group title by one game, went on to beat the AC in a round robin playoff with Cleveland. Pittsburgh then went on to beat Boston for the national title. At the end of the season the Duluth News Tribune selected an all-star team. Included as the best of the best that year were the Rockets' Ching Johnson, as well as St. Paul's Moose Goheen and Wilt Peltier. Leading scorers that year included St. Paul's Nobby Clarke, who finished as the league's second leading scorer with 18 points. Moose Goheen added 14 points, Duluth's Goodman netted 13, Peltier and Ching Johnson tallied 12, Eveleth's Galbraith and Rodden each scored 11, and St. Paul's Conroy added 10.

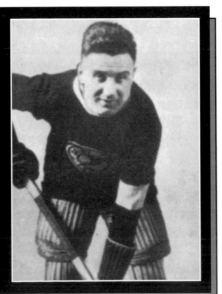

Nick Kahler

Nick Kahler was an early star on the 1913 Duluth Curling Club Team, and later for the St. Paul Athletic Club, where he served as manager, coach, and player. Later, in 1920, Kahler launched the Minneapolis Millers in the United States Amateur Hockey Association, where his 1925 team won the league title.

The 1924-25 season would prove to be an important one in for Minnesota hockey. St. Paul, coached by Ed Fitzgerald, finished its 40-game schedule with a 16-22-2 record, not good enough for the post-season. The Rockets joined the AC on the sidelines that season with an equally brutal record of 16-19-3. The last of the Minnesota contingent, Eveleth, which came on strong to finish the second-half of the season at 13-6-1, was defeated by Pittsburgh in four straight in a playoff series. Interestingly, the series was played in both Pittsburgh and Duluth, because the temperature got too warm and Eveleth did not have artificial ice. The Yellow Jackets then went on to defeat Fort Pitt, which represented the East, in the national finals. Eveleth's Vic Des Jardins was second in the league that year with 14 goals in 39 games.

Unfortunately, after running for five glorious season, 1925 was the last year of operation for the USAHA. The league was vital for jump-starting the game of hockey throughout the United States. Many of the game's best and most talented players suited up for a USAHA squad over its brief history during the early and mid 1920s, many of whom would go on to play in the NHL. Dozens of the league's elite came from the Minnesota contingent which included: Cooney Weiland (Minneapolis), Ching Johnson (Eveleth & Minneapolis), Tiny Thompson (Duluth & Minneapolis), Taffy Abel (Minneapolis & St. Paul), Herbie Lewis (Duluth), Mike Goodman (Duluth), Moose Goheen (St. Paul), Coddy Winters (from Duluth but played for Cleveland), Vic Des Jardins (Eveleth), Perk Galbraith (Eveleth & Minneapolis), Gus Olson (Duluth), Joe Bernardi (Duluth), Jim Seaborn (Eveleth & Duluth), Tony Conroy (St. Paul), Babe Elliot (St. Paul), Nobby Clark (Eveleth & Duluth), Iver Anderson (Duluth), Ade Johnson (Eveleth & Minneapolis), Ed Rodden (Eveleth), Emy Garrett (St. Paul), George Clarke (St. Paul), and Bill Hill (Eveleth).

Hockey in the Early 1920s

Hockey was going through its share of growing pains during the early 1920s, and the USAHA helped to define the game's identity. During this period, a total of seven to nine players would typically see action in a game, and often times a player might play an entire contest without taking a breather. By the mid-1920s, as many as a dozen players made up a team's roster. Goalies, were a different story. For a team to carry a spare keeper was a luxury which was unheard of. However, because they didn't wear masks, and often times got injured, this became a problem. So, in an emergency situation an extra forward or defenseman might have to strap on the pads. Or sometimes, if the team was lucky, a goalie who might be in attendance at the game would be permitted to suit up if he so desired,

Refereeing was also an enigma, especially in the early years of the association. One time, during a game in Sault St. Marie, St. Paul's coach Ed Fitzgerald protested a referee's call and proceeded to inform the official that the rule was not in the rule book. The referee took the book and said, "There ain't any rule book. Up here it is played the way I say." He then tore the rule book in half and threw it into the crowd. The term "Homers" came about from the fact that referees were usually from that particular hometown, and were easily swayed in their decision making. Timekeepers were also locals who sat on the home team's bench and often adjusted things to his team's favor.

Playing facilities also posed big problems back then. Because the East Coast teams along with Pittsburgh Milwaukee, and Cleveland had artificial ice, and the teams such as Duluth, Eveleth, and St. Paul had natural ice, they had a huge advantage. They not only got an earlier start, but they also got to play later into the Spring as well. At times some of the home playoff games of Duluth, Eveleth, and St. Paul had to be moved to their opponents home ice or to a neutral rink. But this also sped up the process of getting more arena's built in Minnesota, such as Duluth's Amphitheater and the Arena in Minneapolis, which both opened in the mid-1920s.

The rules of the early 1920s were quite a bit different, too. Gus Olson, the legendary Duluth coach and player, helped to better explain them in an article that appeared in the Duluth Herald and News Tribune in April of 1945:

"The rules of hockey have seen many changes. Originally the team was composed of seven players. A goalie, point, cover point, center, left and right wing, and a rover. The cover-point played in front of the point, who was directly in front of the goalie, and the rover played on the forward line, backing up the three forwards. Shortly after WWI, the lineup was changed to six men: a goalie, left and right defense, and three forwards. This was a big improvement, as it made for more open hockey with two less players on the ice. Often times I thought this was a great deal too many, the way I was checked.

"Under the seven-man lineup, forward passing was prohibited. Passes had to be made straight across the ice, which was later changed to permit the puck to be passed forward, but the player taking the puck had to be even or on side when the puck was passed. This sped up the game a little and later the first blueline appeared. This was 20 feet out from the goal line and permitted the defending team to pass from its end of the rink up to the blue line, but from there on it had to be played on-side. About 1927, the blue lines were moved out 60 feet from the goal mouth and forward passing was permitted in each of the three zones between the different blue lines. In 1942, the red line was added to the others, being put in the center of the rink permitting the defending team to pass from its end of the rink up to the red line. If a defending player was over his own blue line, he had to touch the puck before it crossed the red line. But if he was behind his own blue line when the puck was passed out, he was permitted to take the puck past the red line."

Travel during this era often proved to be a difficult undertaking. Because there were few hard surfaced highways and they were not maintained properly during the winter months, most of the travel was done by train. Here Gus Olson explains the problems they encountered in 1923 on a road trip to Milwaukee, Canadian Soo and Marquette:

"We had some tough road trips in the early days. The

Cooney Weiland

Ralph "Cooney" Weiland played for four seasons during the 1920s with both the Minneapolis Millers and Rockets before going on to superstardom in the NHL. Weiland would win several Stanley Cups as a member of the Boston Bruins famed "Dynamite Line."

Ching Johnson

Ching Johnson was one of Minnesota hockey's first superstars. First recruited to Eveleth from his native Winnipeg to play for the semi-pro Rangers in 1920, Ching went on to play three seasons in Eveleth before moving to Minneapolis, where he starred for the Millers and Rockets from 1923-26. From there Ching hit the big-time, signing with the New York Rangers, where he was a perennial all-star for more than a decade during the 1920s and 30s. In 1938 Ching returned home to the Millers, where he played until 1940. With his shiny bald head and hulking 200-pound frame (which was considered to be a giant back then), the hard-hitting bruiser was one of the biggest fan-favorites of all time. He was elected to the Hockey Hall of Fame in 1958.

The Duluth Hornets were led by superstars
Herbie Lewis and Mike Goodman

year Milwaukee was in the league we did not have any too many players, and on one road trip we were to go to the Copper Country for some exhibition games after playing Milwaukee. We left Milwaukee at 5:30 p.m. for the Canadian Soo, where we were to play on Monday morning between Milwaukee and the Soo, but due to a snow storm we missed connecting and as a result, we did not get anything to eat until we reached the Soo Monday at 6:00 p.m.

"Then as we had missed the regular train across the Straits, we climbed into a caboose and put our trunks on the back of the engine. We arrived at the Soo and started our game at about 10:00. We played again Tuesday night and after the game rented two toboggans and hauled our trunks across the ice as we had to catch a train out of American Soo at 5:30 am for Marquette, where we were booked for Wednesday night. We ran into more snow and did not get our game underway that night until after 10:00 p.m. Then we sat up until 4:00 a.m. to take the train back to Duluth where we were playing a team from Winnipeg on Thursday and Friday nights. That was five games in five days with all the train travel thrown in. Incidentally, we won four of the five games."

One thing has remained a constant through the years, the fact that hockey is an extremely rough sport. Many an old timer would tell of playing in games when they had injured elbows and knees and had dozens of recent stitches. The legendary hockey historian Don Clark remembered reminiscing with a couple of ice legends about what it was like back then. Emy Garrett, St. Paul forward, stated: "When we started on a road trip to the other rinks it was like going to war. Visiting teams often lost and had to be escorted off the ice by the police." Eveleth, St. Paul and Duluth dreaded visiting the small rinks in Upper Michigan. Moose Goheen thought of all the rough and rowdy games in which he had played in during his 19-year career. He said that the toughest was the 1922 playoff series between St. Paul and Eveleth when the penalty boxes were usually filled. With large crowds attending games at both home rinks, St. Paul edged Eveleth three games to two, scoring seven goals to Eveleth's six, with two of the contests ending as score-less ties.

Although the USAHA only lasted for four years, it was responsible for generating incredible growth in the popularity of the game. As a result, more leagues popped up across the country, and with them came more rinks. The level of play at this time would probably have been considered to be just below the level of Canada's top circuit -- the National Hockey League.

The Central Hockey Association and the Saints Come Marching in
With the senior leagues going gangbusters, Minnesota's appetite for hockey kept growing and growing. So, it was only natural that the hockey braintrust put their heads together to form a new league, and that's just what they did. Deciding to disband the USAHA's Eastern Division, it was decided that the USAHA's Western Division would be reorganized as the Central Hockey Association for the 1925-26 season. Pittsburgh and Cleveland withdrew from the Western Division and were replaced by two teams who were closer in proximity to the Midwest - American Soo and Winnipeg. Pittsburgh then promptly joined the National Hockey League. (To personify just how good the USAHA was, the Yellow Jackets -- using nearly the same lineup from the year before, finished third in the then seven-team NHL, which was the highest level of hockey in the world.) The new league then featured the following teams: St. Paul Saints, Minneapolis Rockets, Duluth Hornets, Eveleth-Hibbing Rangers (Eveleth joined forces with their Iron Range neighbors from Hibbing to form one team), Winnipeg, and the American Soo. The league had great parity, and each team had its share of stars. St. Paul was blessed with the talents of Moose Goheen, Tony and George Conroy, and Emy Garrett; Duluth had the amazing Herbie Lewis, Jim Seaborn, Mike Goodman, and Moose Jamieson; Eveleth featured Vic Des Jardins and Goalie Pat Byrne; Winnipeg showcased Artie Somers, Murray Murdoch, and Chuck Gardiner; and The Soo of Sault Ste. Marie, Ontario, enjoyed a smorgasbord of Canadian superstars.

Duluth Hornets goalie
Alfie Moore

That season Minneapolis, under the tutelage of Lloyd Turner of Calgary, finished on top of the regular season standings with an impressive 22-10-6 record, while Duluth was the runner-up finishing at 18-14-8. This outstanding Minneapolis team was put together by several prominent Mill City businessmen, including Paul Loudon, George Drake, and Louis and George Piper. That season also gave Minneapolis an identity of their own in the Twin Cities. They said good-bye to playing in St. Paul's Hippodrome, and said hello to their new home, the Minneapolis Arena, complete with an artificial ice surface. St. Paul placed fourth behind Winnipeg with a 15-17-6 record, while Eveleth-Hibbing wound up in fifth place at a respectable 15-16-7. In the playoffs, Duluth beat Winnipeg in a five-game series, only to meet the red-hot Minneapolis Rockets in the finals. After blanking the Hornets in the first two contests by the scores of 3-0 and 4-0, the Rockets then ventured north to Duluth, where on April 6, 1926, they won the final game of the series by the score of 2-1. The CHA crown was theirs. Some of the greatest players in the game were members of that Minneapolis team. Among them were Tiny Thompson, Cooney Weiland, Taffy Abel, Ching Johnson, Mickey McQuire, Bill Boyd, Denny Breen, Vic Ripley and Johnny McKinnon. Many would go on to star in the NHL.

That year would also mark the end of a Minnesota hockey institution, the St. Paul Athletic Club. The AC ended that year and became the St. Paul Saints. Hockey fans were blessed with the likes of countless stars that donned the AC sweater including: Abel, Goheen, Tony Conroy, George Conroy, Fitzgerald, Weidenborner, Garret, Gehrke, McCarthy, Breen, McCormick, Romnes, Shea, Wellington, Adams, Whalen, Mohan, Elliott, Clark, Drury, Nichols, Ching Johnson, Nick Kahler,

Galbraith, Weiland, Des Jardin, Somers, Gottsleig, Stewart, Worters, Jamieson, and Thompson to name a few.

The American Hockey Association

1926 was was somewhat of a tumultuous year of hockey for Minnesota, because the Central League was amateur in status, and it had become the target of raids by the upstart Eastern professional leagues. As a result, the Central League lasted just that one season. This article about the Central Association's woes appeared in the St. Paul Pioneer Press on February 13th, 1926: "The Central Hockey Association is on the verge of going professional. For the past several seasons the league has been amateur in name only. The league had to spend money liberally in order to secure good players. Now they face a new danger -- the growth of pro hockey in the East and the constant threat of raids on Central League players has made it mandatory that teams in the league protect themselves from wholesale raids. The league has acted slowly to protect the smaller cities in the circuit who could not afford to turn pro."

Ultimately the success of the league proved to be its undoing. Apparently, at the time, plans were in the works to add a new "American Division" to the professional NHL's already existing Canadian group. The talent on the U.S. side of the border was an apparent green pasture for the eastern promoters who wanted to fill their rosters. Tired of being the main suppliers of NHL talent for nothing in return, a new league was formed that next season -- the American Hockey Association. It was the first outright professional league in the Midwest at the time. They figured if they paid their players it would prevent them from packing up and heading East.

However, it was too late for a few Minneapolis stars who opted for the big bucks. The infamous Colonel John S. Hammond of the New York Rangers, who was at a Duluth Hornets -- Millers game near the end of the 1926 season, plucked Ching Johnson, Taffy Abel, Billy Boyd and Johnny McKinnon from the Millers right after the game with the allure of large offers of money as bait. Ching Johnson, after three years with Minneapolis and three years prior with the Eveleth Rangers, at the relatively old age of 29, succumbed to the intense recruiting and join the NHL's New York Rangers. He reportedly signed a three-year contract for the then unprecedented sum of $30,000. Ching went on to star in the NHL for 11 years, before returning to his Millers for a final stint from 1938-1940. He was joined by another very popular player, Taffy Abel, who played for St. Paul AC from 1922-25, and also with the Millers in 1926. (Both are members of the U.S. Hockey Hall of Fame.) In addition, the Boston Bruins later lured away Cooney Weiland and Tiny Thompson.

Due to high operating costs, the Eveleth-Hibbing franchise, along with the Soo, opted to drop out of the league to play independent schedules for the inaugural 1926-27 season. This left the Minneapolis Millers, St. Paul Saints, Winnipeg Maroons, and Duluth Hornets, along with newcomers Detroit Greyhounds and the Chicago Cardinals to form the upstart AHA. Detroit's franchise then folded after only six games, leaving it to be just a five-team league. Because the league wanted to be different from the Eastern pro leagues, that were made up of mostly Canadian players, they decided to stockpile as many American-born players as possible and ultimately challenge for Lord Stanley's Cup. This strategy was, in part, thanks to a couple of Minnesota boys named A.H. Warren of St. Paul, who served as the league's first president, and also Duluth's William Grant, who acted as secretary-treasurer.

For the 1926-27 season, the Hornets won the regular season title by finishing 20-10-8. The Millers finished second at 17-11-10, while the Saints came in fourth behind Winnipeg with a 17-15-5 record. Chicago, which finished in last place, changed their name on March 8th that year to the "Americans." The Millers went on to beat the Maroons in a three game playoff, and then met Duluth in the finals. The Hornets crushed Minneapolis by winning three straight, thus capturing the first-ever AHA championship.

The next year Chicago was replaced with a new franchise from Kansas City, called the Greyhounds. Duluth's William Grant served as the new club's president, general manager, and coach. The Hornets again finished on top of the 1927-28 regular season standings with a 18-9-13 record, followed by Kansas City, Minneapolis, St. Paul, and Winnipeg. St. Paul's Vic Des Jardins was the league's leading scorer with 28 points, followed by Minneapolis' Cooney Weiland who tallied 26, and St. Paul's Moose Goheen who added 24. In the semifinals, Minneapolis defeated the Greyhounds, and then went on to beat the Hornets for the championship. They were led by future hall of famer Tiny Thompson, who had an amazing 0.35 playoff goals-against average for the Millers that year.

Tiny Thompson was an early star for the Minneapolis Millers

Winnipeg withdrew from the league in 1928, and was replaced by both Tulsa and the St. Louis Flyers to once again make it a six team league. Tulsa went on to win the league crown that season with the Millers finishing as the runner-up. The Saints came in third, followed by Duluth and St. Louis. Turner resigned as the Millers head coach after that season to join with Seattle, of the Pacific Coast Hockey League. Lyle Wright, the manager of the Minneapolis Arena, took over the reigns for the Millers.

By 1929 the AHA was booming in popularity. Attendance was strong throughout the league and particularly in Minnesota. Duluth finished second with a 18-13-17 record that season, only to lose to Tulsa in the opening round of the playoffs. The Hornets won the opener 2-1, but then lost two heartbreakers by the scores of 1-0 and 2-1 to end their season. KC then beat Tulsa for the title that year. St. Paul's Des Jardins finished second in the league scoring race with 35 points, while Corb Denney of Minneapolis wound up third with 34, and Laurie Scott, the Hornet's speedy winger, was fourth with 32 points.

Duluth again finished strong at the end of the 1930-31 season, with a 28-19-1 record. Led by Scott, who finished third in the scoring race with 40 points in 48 games, the Hornets lost in the playoffs to KC in four games. Tulsa then beat KC for the title. In 1931-32 Duluth finished third in the regular season with a record of 21-24-3, and finally beat Kansas City in the playoffs. Although each club won two games, the Hornets advanced on the total goals by the score of 6-5. They then met the Chicago Shamrocks (they had changed their name) in the finals, where they lost three games to one. The Hornet's Forslund finished fourth in the league scoring race with 27 points. By this time

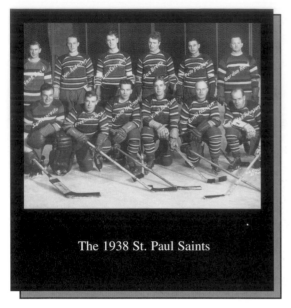

The 1938 St. Paul Saints

the AHA was developing its own players at the minor professional level. It was also a breeding ground for future NHLers, and as a result was often raided by the big-six NHL teams. So, during that season, the AHA and the NHL made an agreement of sorts which ultimately resulted in both leagues respecting one another's player contracts.

The Great Depression & Minnesota's Central Hockey League
Meanwhile, as the Great Depression started to set in, times became tough for everyone across the country. Teams were finding it hard to make ends meet, because the fans had to save their money for more important things, such as food. That year proved to be a turning point for the AHA's Minnesota contingent. Both the Saints and Millers dropped out of the league and became members of the upstart "Senior" Central Hockey League, which began as an amateur league in 1931-32, but changed to professional in its second season.

The genesis of the league is quite interesting. In 1930-31 there were two strong amateur leagues operating in Minnesota: The Twin City League, and The Arrowhead League. The Twin City League featured the Minneapolis Americans, Minneapolis Phantoms, St. Paul, and White Bear Lake. While the Arrowhead League, which had been in operation since 1927, had teams from Eveleth, Hibbing, Virginia, and Fort Frances. In 1931 Minneapolis, St. Paul, Hibbing, Eveleth, and Virginia joined forces to form the Central Hockey League. (Incidentally, the Eveleth Rangers earned a unique nickname during the league's inaugural season. Because their rink had been condemned, they had to play their entire schedule on the road. With no home ice that year, their fans dubbed them as the "Eveleth Orphans." And, even though the Millers won the championship that season, Eveleth did manage to win the regular season crown.)

Comprised almost entirely of native Minnesotans, the league consisted of the following teams: St. Paul Saints, Minneapolis Millers, Eveleth Rangers, Virginia Rockets, and the Hibbing Maroons (who changed their name to the Hibbing Miners in 1933-34). Virginia dropped out of the league after the first season, but the Duluth Hornets, who had been playing an independent schedule, were invited to join in their place in 1933. The NHL viewed the Central as a legitimate professional circuit, and its teams played a tough 48 game schedule.

The 1932-1933 AHA season was an ugly one, but did manage to feature two more Minnesota teams that "briefly" made it to the big time. That year the St. Paul Saints were replaced with another team from Pig's Eye, called the St. Paul Greyhounds. In addition, the Duluth Hornets were replaced by the Duluth Natives. During the first half of the 1932-1933 season, both St. Paul and Duluth finished behind St. Louis and Kansas City in the basement of the now fledgling four-team league. The economic turmoil was affecting the league's profitability, and as a result, the St. Paul Greyhounds franchise moved to Tulsa, and the Duluth Natives moved to Wichita.

The Rangers finished at the pinnacle of the regular season standings during the league's first year of 1931-32 with a 25-10-0 record, followed by the Millers at 22-11-3, the Saints at 17-17-2, the Maroons at 16-18-2, and the Rockets at 5-29-1. The Millers went on to tie St. Paul in the playoffs at one game apiece, but won the series 5-4 on total goals. Then went on to face Eveleth in the finals, where they beat the Rangers two games to one, winning the CHL title.

In its second season of 1932-33, the league changed from its "amateur" status to "professional." Players were now signing contracts and were being paid weekly salaries. Eveleth won the regular season crown that season with a 26-12-2 record. The Rangers then went on to beat the Millers in the playoffs in three straight to capture their first CHL championship. The league's leading scorers that year were as follows: St. Paul's Oscar Hanson (a former Augsburg College star and part of the original "Hanson-Brother" trio), led with 39 points, Minneapolis' Flood scored 36, while the Hibbing tandem of Lilly and Andrews each tallied 29 points.

Minneapolis won the regular season crown in 1934 with an impressive 28-11-5 record. The Millers then faced Hibbing, who had defeated Eveleth two games to one, for the title. Minneapolis went on to sweep the Miners in three straight to recapture the championship. The league's leading scorers that year were as follows: Hibbing's Lilly led with 35 points, Eveleth's Brink scored 34, while Hibbing's Andrews punched in 34 total points. Tragically, that spring Hibbing's rink burned down. So, they along with Duluth, which was in financial trouble, decided to withdraw from the league, leaving just three teams for the 1934-35 season.

At the end of that season, tired of beating up on each other, the Central League's "powers that be" got together to round up some more competition. They didn't have to look too far. That's because that next season of 1934-35, the AHA and the CHL, both of whom were short on member teams, decided to play an adjoining schedule against each other. It was decided that each of the seven teams in the circuit would play each team in each other's league's twice. The St. Paul Saints won the regular season crown for the 1934-35 season by going 28-10-9. Minneapolis finished second at 21-19-8, while Eveleth finished in the basement at 9-30-8. St. Paul then faced the Millers for what would prove to be the last ever CHL title. In the best-of-five series, the Saints barely beat their cross-town rivals, three games to two to win it all. Each game alternated winners, with the Saints holding on to take Game 5 by the score of 4-2. The St. Louis Flyers, champs of the AHA with

Virgil Johnson

Virgil Johnson was both a hockey star and quarterback of the football team at Minneapolis South High School. Johnson was a member of the St. Paul Saints prior to making his NHL debut with the Chicago Blackhawks in 1938, the same year they went on to win the Stanley Cup. He played with the Hawks until 1946, then spent several years with Minneapolis in the USHL, and then with the Minneapolis Jerseys and St. Paul Saints of the AAHL.

a record of 29-15-4, then met St. Paul for the Inter-League title. The Saints promptly swept the Flyers in three straight to win it all. Eveleth then defeated the AHA's Kansas City franchise to finish in third place. Crowds of more than 7,000 were commonplace for the league's games. Leading scorers in the league that year included: St. Paul's Oscar Hanson who poured in an amazing 59 points, followed by Minneapolis' Cully Dahlstrom who scored 45, and the Saints' Emil Hanson who added 40.

Yet Another Merger of Sorts

Things went so well during that interlocking schedule, that for the 1935-36 campaign the two leagues decided to merge. However, due to financial constraints, only St. Paul and Minneapolis were able to rejoin the Tulsa, Kansas City, St. Louis, and Wichita to form the "new" AHA. As a result, the Central, after four glorious years of big-time hockey in Minnesota, was no more. The Central would play an important role in the development of American hockey, with many of its players going on to compete in the AHA, AHL and

Cully Dahlstrom

Cully Dahlstrom played high school hockey at Minneapolis South and then went on to play for the Minneapolis Millers in the American Hockey Association. He won the Calder Trophy as the NHL's rookie of the year 1937-38 as a member of the Chicago Blackhawks. In addition, he led the team to the Stanley Cup title that first year as well.

NHL. One silver lining in all of this though was the fact that after the league's breakup, some three dozen former CHL players, most of them Minnesota-born and developed, were able to join one of the six AHA squads.

In 1936, another league was formed in Northern Minnesota, called The International Amateur Hockey League. The North American circuit was comprised of teams from both the Iron Range and Ontario. Its -members included: Eveleth, Duluth, Virginia, and Hibbing, as well as the Canadian teams of Port Arthur, Fort William, and Fort Frances. The Duluth Zephyrs would prove to be one of the most popular teams in Duluth hockey history, consistently playing to a full house at the Duluth Amphitheater.

Under the new "combined league" system, the Saints went on to capture the league title with a record of 32-13-3. They were followed by St. Louis. Minneapolis, which finished third in the standings, was involved in a merger of their own. On March 12th that year, the Oklahoma City Warriors franchise moved to Minneapolis, to join forces with the Millers. The Saints once again met up with St. Louis in the finals, but this time the Flyers beat St. Paul three games to two to win the cup. St. Paul's Oscar Hanson won the league's scoring title with an impressive 60 points in 49 games, and was followed by his teammate Cully Dahlstrom, who finished second with 43 points. Most impressive about the Saints victory that year was the fact that they did it with a lineup composed entirely of Minnesota players. Beef Munson and Julie Matschke were St. Paul natives, while the bulk of the Saints lineup came from both Eveleth and Minneapolis. They included: coach Emil Hanson, Oscar Hanson, Emory Hanson, Oscar Almquist, Jack Flood, Virgil Johnson, Hodge Johnson, Pete Pleban, Bill McGlone and Cully Dahlstrom.

The Saints wound up finishing third overall in 1936-37, but were swept by the Millers three games to none in the playoffs. Minneapolis was led that year by a Minnesota hockey legend, Nick Kahler, who re-emerged as the owner and promoter of the team. He hired Joe Simpson as his coach, and under the leadership of players such as Phil Hargesheimer, George Patterson and Bob Blake, the Mill City squad went on win the title by sweeping St. Louis in three straight. The Millers put the final explanation point on the season by crushing the Flyers 6-0 in the last game to seal the deal. In that series they had to face the now infamous Oscar Hanson, who was traded to St. Louis in the off-season. Hanson again won the scoring title with 62 points, followed by Minneapolis' Hargesheimer who tallied 49 points. The league was faring reasonably well at this point, but the fans weren't flocking to see the games as they had back in the 1920's when they lined up to see Ching Johnson. An example of just how good the level of play was in the minor pro AHA at that time occurred that season when Ottawa transferred its NHL franchise, the Eagles, to St. Louis. There, the Eagles were beaten soundly by the AHA's other St. Louis team, the Flyers. Incidentally, the Eagles folded after just that one season.

In 1938 the Millers finished second in the regular season standings and then defeated Wichita three games to one in the playoffs. It was then off to "old Saint-Louee" to meet their old nemesis, the St. Louis Flyers, who had beaten Tulsa to advance to the finals. The teams had developed quite a rivalry, and it was fueled by the fact that many of the players knew one another from their playing days together back in Minnesota. The Flyers decided to not get too sentimental over their old pals, and trounced the Minneapolis squad in three straight to win the championship. The Millers' G. Patterson led the league in scoring with 59 points, while his teammate Blake added 43.

Bobby Dill

Bobby Dill starred for Cretin High School in the 1930s and went on to become on of Minnesota's best ever. In 1944, after playing in the minors, Dill was called up by the NHL's New York Rangers. One of the toughest men ever to lace em' up, Dill was the nephew of former prize fighter, Mike Gibbons. During the late 1940s and early '50s Dill played for the St. Paul Saints, where he and John Mariucci used to mix it up on more than one occasion. Dill later worked as a scout for the North Stars, and was inducted into the U.S. Hockey Hall of Fame in 1979.

By 1939 St. Louis had become somewhat of a dynasty in pro hockey. That season the Millers were blessed by the return of their star centerman, Oscar Hanson, who was reacquired from their arch rivals from St. Louis. Oscar went on an unbelievable scoring barrage that season, scoring 89 points in a 48 game schedule to set a long-time standing single season record for all of professional hockey. However, despite Hanson's heroics, the Millers again finished second in the regular season standings to the Flyers with a 31-17-6 record, only to lose to Tulsa in the playoffs four games to two. It was now up to the Saints, who finished the regular season in fourth place with a

Doc Romnes

Elwyn Nelson "Doc" Romnes grew up and playing hockey in his native White Bear Lake. After starring on his high school team, Romnes went on to play with St. Thomas College, before turning professional with the St. Paul Saints of the American Hockey Association in 1928. He joined the Blackhawks during the 1930-31, and over the next 10 seasons would lead the team to a pair of Stanley Cup titles in 1934 and 1938. Romnes retired from the game in the early 1940s, and returned to Minnesota, where he took over as the head coach for the Minnesota Gophers from 1947-52. Romnes was the first American player to win the Lady Byng Trophy, for sportsmanlike conduct, when he took the honor in 1936, and remained the only American ever to win the award until Joe Mullen did it 52 years later.

24-24-6 record. After defeating Wichita, St. Paul went on to face St. Louis in the finals, only to get swept in three games.

As the new decade of the 1940s loomed in the horizon, the Saints and Millers found themselves pitted against one another for their playoff lives. The Saints, under the tutelage of Perk Galbraith, former Eveleth and Boston Bruin star, finished second in the regular season chase behind the Flyers with a 29-18-0 record, while the Millers placed third at 26-22-0. The teams faced off in the playoffs to huge crowds. Oscar Hanson couldn't work his magic this time though, as St. Paul, which was led by Jack, Saunders, Carrigan, Connelly, Virgil Johnson and LoPresti, swept their neighbors in three straight. The Saints didn't stop there, going on to whip the upstart Omaha franchise (who had upset St. Louis in the other playoff match), three games to one, to win their only playoff championship in the history of the AHA. The Saints' Jack scored 54 points, while the Millers leading scorers were N. Smith, who tallied 68 points, as well as Oscar Hanson and Farrant, who each scored 64.

The Millers and Saints finished tied for third in 1940-41, with records of 25-23. St. Paul lost three games to one to the Flyers, while Minneapolis, which was led by Tustin's 50 points that season, lost in an extremely close and controversial three games to two thriller to Kansas City. St. Louis then beat up Kansas City to win the league crown. That year a Minneapolis radio announcer and sports official named George Higgins, took over the reigns as league president. That spring the league introduced its first all-star game. Held in St. Louis, the game drew more than 9,000 to the star-studded affair -- a huge accomplishment at the time.

By 1941 the United States was mired in politics and the threat of war was fast becoming a reality. The league pressed on that year in what would ultimately be its last. Dallas and Fort Worth both joined the league for its final season of 1941-42. The league opted to divide up into two divisions that year, the Northern and the Southern. The Northern featured St. Paul, Minneapolis, St. Louis, and Omaha, while the Southern consisted Kansas City, Tulsa, Fort Worth, and Dallas. St. Paul finished second with a 28-17-5 record, while the Millers ended their season in the cellar at 22-25-3. The Saints advanced to the Northern playoffs, where they were then swept in two straight by Omaha. Kansas City advanced to the finals where they blitzed Omaha in three straight to win the last ever AHA championship. For the young men who clashed so hard on the ice, it was now off to Europe and the Pacific to fight in a real battle, World War II.

For 16 years the AHA proved to be a solid league which greatly helped advance the hockey prowess of countless Minnesotans, who were able to play big-time hockey throughout the country. At one time 14 different cities held franchises in the circuit including: St. Paul, Minneapolis, Duluth, Winnipeg, Chicago, Kansas City, Tulsa, St. Louis, Buffalo, Wichita, Oklahoma City, Omaha, Dallas, and Fort Worth. Because of this, there were as many American-born pro players in the 1920s and 1930s as there were at any time until the 1980s. Countless star players such as Doc Romnes and Cully Dahlstrom would likely never have had the opportunity to play in the NHL without first getting their chance in the AHA.

More than 50 different Minnesota players competed in the AHA during its 16 year history. Players from Eveleth included: Tom and Mike Karakas, Alex McInnes, Paul Schaeffer, Milt Brink, Andy Toth, Joe Papike, Hodge Johnson, Peter Pleban, Joe Kucler, Rudy Ahlin, Art Erickson, Mike Kasher, Oscar Almquist, John Phillips, Sam Lo Presti, John and Tony Prelesnik, Glee Jagunich and Billy De Paul. Minneapolitans included: Oscar, Emil and Emory Hanson, Manny Cotlow, Virgil Johnson, Don Olson, Phil Perkins, Burr Williams, Bill McGlone, Cully Dahlstrom, Ted Breckheimer, Bill Oddson, Jack Flood and Hub Nelson. St. Paulites included: George and Tony Conroy, Doc Romnes, George Nichols, Bob McCoy Beef Munson, Emy Garrett, Julie Matscke, Bill Galligan and Bob Graiziger. Hibbing furnished Bill Mickelich, Bob Blake and Joe Bretto while Nobby Clark, Iver Anderson and Gus Olson hailed from Duluth. Moose Goheen, Pat Shea and Doc Romnes came from White Bear Lake, while Don Anderson who played for St. Paul called Lindstrom his home. Amazingly, only five other Americans played in the league: Curley Kohlman, Muzz Murray and Vic Des Jardins came from Upper Michigan while Fido Purper was born and reared in Grand Forks, and Bob Nilan called Philadelphia home.

The United States Hockey League (1945-51)

When the war was over in the mid-1940s, countless men were anxious to get back on the ice. So, in its first season of 1945-46, the AHA resumed playing under the new name of the United States Hockey League with the following teams: Minneapolis Millers, St. Paul

Hibbing and the Hawks

During the 1930s, Hibbing became the first city on the Iron Range to install artificial ice, when it retrofitted Memorial Arena. As a result, Hibbing's Memorial Arena played host to the NHL's Chicago Blackhawks for training camp. This was quite a spectacle for the locals to watch hockey's elite right in their own backyard.

In fact, several Minnesotans got to be a part of history with the Hawks in 1938, the year the team won the Stanley Cup with a roster of mostly Americans. The Hawks, thanks to Major Fred McLaughlin, the team's eccentric owner, wanted to have an all-American roster. Now, by the mid-'30s there were only a handful of American-born players in the NHL, but that didn't deter the Major. Five Minnesotans - John Mariucci, Mike Karakas, Cully Dahlstrom, Virgil Johnson, Doc Romnes - played for the Hawks during this era, and in 1938 the team shocked the world by beating the powerful Toronto Maple Leafs to win the Stanley Cup.

Saints, Kansas City Pla-Mors, Omaha Knights, Tulsa Oilers, Fort Worth Rangers, and Dallas Texans. Kansas City finished on top of the USHL standings during that first year with a record of 35-17-4. The Saints, who finished at 28-26-2, wound up in third, while the Millers brought up the cellar with a dismal 20-33-3 record.

Over the next couple of seasons teams from Louisville, Milwaukee, Houston, and Denver would join the USHL. The league was a viable professional outlet for players both on their way up the ladder and also for those on their way down. Hockey fans in many of the cities now had the opportunity to enjoy a quality brand of hockey at an affordable price, all while receiving an education about this new sport which was foreign to them. In 1945 the International Hockey League was also organized as an outgrowth of the Windsor City Senior League near Detroit. The "I" as it is known, was, and still remains today as one of the top professional leagues in all of hockey with teams in both the U.S. and Canada.

The USHL divided into two divisions from 1946-49 with both St. Paul and Minneapolis playing in the Northern Division. The league, which was very popular, lasted in Minnesota until 1951. The Millers dropped out in 1950, and the Saints followed suit after that next season. (The USHL would reemerge in the state several years later with a group of new teams.) The Millers' best season came in 1947-48 when the squad went 34-36-6, while St. Paul's best year was in 1948-49, when they finished 36-20-10.

During those years the Saints were led by dozens and dozens of great players, among them were the legendary Bobby Dill, who from 1945-50 scored 163 points, while racking up an amazing 567 penalty minutes. John Mariucci and Gump Worsley both played on the team from 1950-51, and Gus Schwartz was the team's all-time leading scorer with 238 points. Others who made major contributions included Lloyd Ailsby, Harry Bell, Lin Bend, Harold Brown, Armand Delmonte, Joe Levandoski, Ian MacIntosh, Jack McGill, Mitch Pechet, Cliff "Fido" Purpur, Gino Rozzini, Alex Sandalack, and Joe Shack.

The Millers were blessed with the talents of several greats as well, including John Mariucci (who played from 1949-50), Virgil Johnson (1945-47), and Tom Karakas, who played in 1947-48. Others who made major contributions included: George Agar, Earl Bartholme, Tom Forgie, Ian Fraser, Wally Hergesheimer, Carl Kaiser, Harry McQueston, Walter Melnyk, Billy Richardson, Gordon Sherritt, Stanford Smith, Art Strobel and Nick Tomiuk.

Minnesota's "Short-lived" Western and Central Hockey League Participation
After a pretty lengthy absence, professional hockey finally returned to Minnesota in 1957. That year St. Paul formed a combined team with Saskatoon in the professional Western Hockey League. The St. Paul/Saskatoon Regals, as they were known, posted a 25-45-0 record during the 1957-58 season. The league lasted just one year. Some of the players who starred on this "international" team included: Ken Yackel, Doug Bentley, Bob Chrystal, Les Colwill, Gerry Couture, Lucien Dechene, Robert Kabel, Vic Lynn, Reginald Primeau, Don Raleigh, Ray Ross, and Lyle Willey.

The next year the Minneapolis Millers and Rochester Mustangs played in the "on again - off again" Central Hockey League, then a senior professional circuit. It lasted only a season before folding.

The International Hockey League (1959-63)
Big-time pro hockey came back for good that next year in 1959 when the St. Paul Saints joined the upstart International Hockey League. Later that season, the Denver Mavericks moved their struggling franchise to the Twin Cities, where they became the "new" Minneapolis Millers. Both teams played in the IHL's Western Division. The IHL featured many of the same cities from the former USHL, in addition to several more from out East. The league played a vital role in advancing the game throughout the country, and offered a quality brand of hockey to many areas that weren't yet familiar with the game.

During that first season of 1959-60, the Saints posted a league-best 41-21-6 record. St. Paul then cruised through the playoffs by beating among others, Minneapolis, which had finished the year with a very modest 39-27-2 record. The Saints kept on rolling and won the coveted Turner Cup, given annually to the league's playoff champion. That next year Minneapolis posted a whopping 50-20-2 record, only to get beat again the by the defending champion Saints, who went 46-22-4. St. Paul cruised to the finals, this time defeating Muskegon four games to one, for their second consecutive Turner Cup.

In 1961-62 the Millers went 41-26-1, while the Saints finished at 42-25-1. Both were eliminated in the playoffs. The next season Minneapolis went 36-32-2, finishing just one point behind Fort Wayne, while St. Paul slumped all the way down to sixth place. The Millers went on to beat Omaha in a tough seven-game semi-final contest, only to lose to Fort Wayne in the finals. That would prove to be the last season for the IHL in Minnesota, as both the Millers and Saints dropped out of the league that following the season.

The IHL provided a lot of excitement for Minnesota fans during this era, and many great players came through the league throughout its existence. For the Saints, many of those players included: Elliot Chorley, (the team's leading scored with 242 points in 215 games), John Mayasich, John Bailey, Dick Bouchard, Fred Brown, Rich Brown, Nelson Bullock, Jean Denis, Brian Derrett, Dick Dougherty, Ted Hodgson, Howie Hughes, Mickey Keating, Aggie Kukulowicz, Wayne Larkin, Joe Lund, Jacques Marcotte, Paul Masnick, Bud McRae, Art Miller, Reg Morelli, Danny Summers, and Gilles Thibeault.

For the Millers, those players included: Ken Yackel (the team's leading scored with 312 points in 208 games), Dick Meredith, Ed Bartoli, Bob Currie, Larry Hale, Paul Johnson, Marv Jorde,

The 1962 Minneapolis Millers

Aggie Kukulowicz, Guy LaFrance, Laurie Langrell, Bruce Lea, Bill LeCaine, Dennis Maroney, Murray Massier, Bud McRae, Jerry Melynchuk, Ray Mikulan, Harry Ottenbriet, Ed Pollesel, Joe Poole, Billy Reichart, Ken Saunders, Jack Turner, and Cy Whiteside.

The Central Professional Hockey League (1963-66)

In July of 1963, with the slogan "The Fastest Version of the World's Fastest Game!", the Central Professional Hockey League was formed. It would also be the final stop for both the Saints and Millers, as they would each be transformed into minor league affiliates of the then six-team National Hockey League. The Millers became the upstart Minneapolis Bruins, who's parent club was the Boston Bruins, and the Saints became the St. Paul Rangers, who's parent club was the New York Rangers. The CPHL featured five teams that first season, the three others included: the Omaha Knights (minor league affiliate of the Montreal Canadians), St. Louis Braves (minor league affiliate of the Chicago Blackhawks), and the Cincinnati Wings (minor league affiliate of the Detroit Red Wings). Formed as a developmental league for younger players who needed more ice-time and game experience before embarking on a career in the NHL, the CPHL was just one step removed from hockey's elite. The league rules stated that each team's roster had to be made up of 10 players under 23 years of age, five could be over 23, and the goaltender can be any age. So, with all of that youth came speed -- and that's what the fans of the CPHL got.

The Bruins played their home games in the Minneapolis Arena which had a 5,000 seat capacity. The club was owned jointly by both the Boston Bruins and three local Minneapolis businessmen: Walter Bush, Jr., attorney, Robert J. McNulty, contractor and Gordon Ritz, Time-Life executive. The general manager was Wren Blair, and Harry Sinden served as the team's first player-coach.

The St. Paul Rangers played in both the St. Paul Auditorium, which had a more than 6,000 seat capacity, as well as at Aldrich Arena. The Rangers were headed by George Cobb of Brown & Bigelow. Jake Milford was brought in to serve as the team's general manager, and Fred Shero, who formerly coached the then IHL St. Paul Saints for four years, was brought back to serve as the team's first coach.

The first season of 1963-64 saw both the Rangers and Bruins playing to packed houses as the fans immediately took to this high calibre of play. The Rangers finished second behind Omaha with a 38-30-4 record, while Minneapolis placed third at 36-29-7. Omaha then defeated Minneapolis in the semifinals, and went on to face the Rangers in the finals. There the Knights beat St. Paul in the best-of-seven series to win the inaugural J. "Jack" Adams Cup. St. Paul also featured two all-stars that season -- goaltender Marcel Pelletier, and defenseman Bob Woytowich.

In 1964-65 the league increased to six teams, with the newest member being the Tulsa Ice Oilers (minor league affiliate of the Toronto Maple Leafs). In addition, the Cincinnati franchise moved to Tennessee where they became known as the Memphis Wings. Dressed in their gold, black, and white jerseys, the Bruins finished 36-29-7 in 1964-65. Their cross-town rival Rangers, dressed in their patriotic red, white and blue sweaters, finished 41-23-6, good enough for first place in the regular season. The Bruins, who finished third during the regular season, wound up losing in the semifinals. The Rangers, on the other hand, went on to win the CPHL Championship. Both squads featured all-stars that year. Minneapolis had future North Star goalie Cesare Maniago, while St. Paul had the speedy right-winger Marc Dufour.

1965 would prove to be the last year of operation for the Minneapolis Bruins, as they packed up and moved their operation to Oklahoma City, where they became known as the Oklahoma City "Blazers." With St. Paul left as the only club in town, the team decided to changed its name to the "Minnesota Rangers" in order to unify the Twin Cities hockey faithful. It worked, because that year the team went 34-25-11, finishing first in the regular season standings. In April of 1966, more than 6,000 fans jammed into the Saint Paul Auditorium to watch the Rangers battle the Tulsa Oilers in the playoff semifinals. Unfortunately, Minnesota lost in a heartbreaking seventh game. Tulsa then went on to lose to the former Bruins team, Oklahoma City Blazers, made up primarily of the Minneapolis club from the year before, who went on to win the Adams Cup championship in their first season.

The Rangers attracted more than 130,000 fans during that season, the highest attendance in the Twin Cities since the league's inception. The team also placed three players on the CPHL all-star team that season: Paul Andrea, Al Lebrun and goaltender Wayne Rutledge. However, that would also be the last season for the CPHL in Minnesota. With the Met Center Arena under construction for the NHL's expansion Minnesota North Stars which were hitting the ice that following year, the Rangers decided not to return to the league for the 1966-67 season. The club was then relocated to Omaha, who had lost their franchise the year before to Houston. (Incidentally, after playing in 25 cities in 17 different states for some 21 seasons, the league disbanded in 1984.)

Walter Bush (right) with Gordie Howe

There were countless stars who played for both the Bruins and Rangers. Among the Bruins stars over the years were: Don Awrey, Ed Bartoli, Terry Crisp, Gary Dornhoefer, Jean Gilbert, John Gravel, Brenton Hughes, Ted Irvine, Bill Knibbs, Skip Krake, Mike Mahoney, Cesare Maniago, Wayne Maxner, Gerry Ouellette, Pete Panagabko, J.P. Parise, Wayne Schultz, Harry Sinden, Ken Stephanson, and Joe Watson.

Among the Rangers stars over the years were: Paul Andrea, Bob Ash, Terry Ball, Ron Boehm, John Brenneman, Bill Collins, Bob Cunningham, Buzz Deschamps, Marc Dufour, Trevor Fahey, Sandy Fitzpatrick, Wayne Hall, Howie Hughes, Jim Johnson, George Konik, Al LeBrun, Dave McComb, Mike McMahon, Larry Mickey, Jim Mikol, Wayne Muloin, Mel Pearson, Bob Plager, Tracy Pratt, Barrie Ross, Gary Sabourin, Bob Stoyko, Ted Taylor, Bob Woytowich, Marcel Pelletier, and Wayne Rutledge.

United States Hockey League (1961-70)

Another league that arrived on the scene about this time was the "revived" USHL, which began in 1961 and lasted in Minnesota until 1970. This league, different from the one which ended in 1951, was a senior semi-pro circuit that featured several Minnesota teams including the Rochester Mustangs (1961-70), Minneapolis Rebels (1961-62) St. Paul Steers (1962-65), and later the Minnesota Nationals (1967-68) and Duluth Port Stars (1968-69). Other teams in the league would include the Green Bay Bobcats, Des Moines Oak Leafs, Milwaukee Metros, and Waterloo Black Hawks. Teams in the league typically played a 30-35 game schedule against one-another.

One of the most influential founders of the league was Walter Bush. For some 15 years the league served as a feeder system for the U.S. National and Olympic teams. It was considered by many to be the first real attempt at a major senior hockey league which was built primarily for the advancement of Americans. The USHL quickly evolved into a very high calibre league for graduates of major U.S. college hockey programs from around the country, particularly those from Minnesota. This was important because back then there were not a lot of opportunities for American college kids to have a chance to play professional hockey. That's because in those days both the minor and major leagues still had less than 20 teams. To put that in perspective, from the period of 1951 to 1961 there were no Americans developed in the NHL. As a result, the league became a haven for young U.S. players who were leaving college and were aspiring to make it on a U.S. National or Olympic team. For players such as John Mayasich, arguably the greatest Gopher ever to wear the Maroon and Gold, this league became a wonderful opportunity for him to not only play semi-professionally, but also to represent his country at the National and Olympic level.

The league also served as a sort of collegiate minor league as well. Take Murray Williamson for example. Then a Gopher freshman in 1955, he played in the league because freshmen were ineligible for NCAA competition. His experience in the USHL helped him hone his skills, which ultimately led him to become an All-American by his senior year at Minnesota. Urged by Walter Bush, Murray later became player/coach of the USHL's St. Paul Steers in 1962, and that next year assumed ownership of the team. Under his tutelage, that Steers club became such a power in the league that by 1965 the team was converted into the U.S. National team. (Murray, the youngest man to ever coach a U.S. Olympic hockey squad, would become an icon in the world of U.S. National and Olympic coaching, leading the 1972 Olympic team to the Silver medal in Sapporo, Japan.)

The team probably the most synonymous with the old USHL would have to be the Rochester Mustangs, who won the league title during that first 1961-62 season with a 19-6-0 record. The Mustangs have played hockey in Rochester in one form or another for more than 40 years. An organization rich in tradition, they got their start in the 1950's as a senior team in the American Amateur Hockey League (AAHL), and then played in the old Central Hockey League (CHL) from 1952-60. Then, from 1961-70 the team played in the USHL. The USHL later converted over to an all-junior circuit in the late 1970s.

The Mustangs used to play at Rochester's old Mayo Civic Auditorium, infamous for being such a short sheet of ice that the players used to claim that the blue lines almost overlapped! Among the players who starred for the Mustangs over the years include: Herb Brooks, Lou Nanne, Bob Fleming, Ken Johannson, Bill Reichert, Gene Campbell, Craig Falkman, Gary Gambucci, Len Lilyholm, Oscar Mahle, Gary Schmalzbauer, Larry Stordahl, Murray Williamson, Tom Yurkovich, and of course - No. 9 Arley Carlson.

Among the players who starred for the Rebels included: former Gopher's Larry Alm, Dick Burg and Dick Meredith. Steers stars over the years included: Larry Alm, Herb Brooks, Dick Burg, Marv Jorde, Bill Masterton, Jerry Melynchuk, Wayne Meredith, and Murray Williamson. The Nationals' stars included: Doug Woog, Jerry Melynchuk, and Jack Dale.

More important than the wins and losses for this circuit was the fact that it played a vital role in the development of American as well as Minnesota hockey. (By the 1980s, the league had merged with some other junior hockey organizations and eventually became an all-junior (21-and-under) league, which today is considered to be one of the best of its kind in the country.

Senior Hockey in Minnesota

Men's senior leagues have been around in one form or another since the turn of the century, and have played a vital role in the development of amateur hockey throughout Minnesota. By the 1920s, there were countless men's senior hockey circuits which had sprouted up throughout the state. During a social movement phenomenon, which Joseph Shipanovich, author of the book "Minneapolis," called "industrial paternalism," businesses and corporations began the tradition of sponsoring athletic teams composed of their employees for competition. Desperate for state-wide braggin' rights often times meant that good hockey players could suddenly get great jobs with company's that they never dreamed of working for -- all in the name of sport.

By 1920 municipal hockey in Minneapolis fell under the jurisdiction of the Recreation Department of the Board of Park Commissioners. They established and maintained some two dozen skating rinks in the city (in addition to providing hockey rinks at Logan Park, North Commons, Lake of the Isles and Powderhorn Park), and made sure that there were warming houses at each of them for the skaters and fans alike to stay out of the cold.

According to W.W. Fox, the Director of Municipal Athletics at the time, that year was one of the most memorable ever for the sport of hockey in the Mill City. Some 20 teams representing social and community center interests from all areas of Minneapolis, were divided into both Senior and Junior Divisions I & II, with little difference in playing strength between them. The teams competed for the annual "Struck" trophy, which was given to the winners.

In the Junior I Division the Logan Parks, Stewart A.C. and Powderhorn Parks competed against the Lagoons, Camden Juniors and Maple Hills. The Logan Parks won the championship from Stewart A.C. While the Junior II Division featured four teams, including the Deephavens, Raccoons, Heatherdale A.C. and Ascensions. The Raccoons won the championship over the Ascension team in the final game. The Senior Division, on the other hand, featured several teams including the Vertex, Camden Seniors, Midway Merchants, East Side A.C., Lake Hennepin Merchants, North Commons, and ABC. At season's end the Camden Seniors and Vertex were tied, so the two paired off for a playoff game

The 1924 Virginia senior team

which was played at Logan Park. There, in sub-zero temperatures, the contest went into extra periods and ultimately, because of the cold, finished as a draw. They met again that next Sunday, and this time the Vertex won the senior championship. The stage was set for the city championship between the aggressive Logan Parks, dual champions of Divisions I and II Junior, and the savvy veteran Vertex seven, champions of the Senior Division. The championship game was played at the Logan Park rink, and the Vertex captured its fourth consecutive city title.

In the early 1920s there were eight teams which comprised the top St. Paul Senior League, they included: The Bilboas (a former junior team which won six straight league titles from 1916-1921), Tuxedos, Masters, St. Frances, Chinooks, Hook-Em-Cows, White Bear Legion and Phoenix. Among the other prominent Senior teams operating in St. Paul during the 1920's were: Armours, Sheriff Wegeners, Minnesota Mining, Fire and Marine, Van Guards, Gas Lites, Kennedy Arms, Northern Pacific, Palace, Hazel Park, Zimmerman, Sylvan and Fort Snelling.

In 1926, under the direction of both W.W. Fox of Minneapolis and Ernest Johnson of St. Paul, both city recreation department heads, the Minnesota Recreation Hockey Association was formed to create a statewide association which would promote hockey. The group elected Hibbing's George Ward to serve as president, and as their primary purpose they decided to hold the state's first ever senior (adult) hockey tournament.

The tournament quickly grew in popularity and became every senior team's goal. The following year, in 1927, the four-team tournament was held at the Hippodrome where the Minneapolis Buzzas defeated Nashwauk and the Duluth Aces for the State Recreation crown. In 1928, at Hibbing, the Minneapolis Buzzas lost to the Duluth Gateleys, the eventual champions, 4-3 in overtime in the first round of competition. The Minnesota Hockey Association continued to stage Senior state tournaments until the early 1930's. Ultimately however, outside of holding annual state tournaments, the association did little to promote the youth game or extend the growth and popularity of the game in those areas of the state where the game was not being played.

The 1932 Genoa National senior champs

The Roseau Cloverleafs

One of the more storied senior amateur teams in the state was the Roseau Cloverleafs, which, through the years participated several Senior circuits, including the States-Dominion League and also the Canadian-American Border League of the 1930s and '40s (which included: Rainy River, Fort Francis, International Falls, Grand Forks Dragons, Hallock, Winnipeg Aces, Emerson, Fosston Chevrolets, Gretna, Mahnomen, Detroit Lakes, Fargo-Moorhead, Alvarado, Red Lake Falls, and Fort Snelling Black & Tans). Years later, in 1978, the Cloverleafs won the Minnesota State Amateur Hockey Association championship under the direction of long-time skipper, Cap Nelson. The team disbanded in the early 1980s.

By the end of the decade, senior leagues were sprouting up all over the state. In the late 1920s the Southern Minnesota League was formed with teams from Winona, North Mankato, Faribault, and Owatonna. Over the next several years other teams such as: Rochester, Northfield, Albert Lea, Austin, Red Wing, Kenyon, Marshall, Cottonwood, Worthington, Wabasha, Winona, Eden Valley, Cokato, Watkins, and Paynesville also played in the circuit. The league, which briefly disbanded for to WWII, operated until the 1960s. The person that is credited with not only founding the league, but also operating it diligently through the years, was legendary hockey historian, Don Clark, of Faribault. Another new senior league during this era was the Academy League, which was formed with teams from St. Paul Academy, Blake, St. Thomas, Cretin, and Shattuck of Faribault. (In addition, one of the stronger senior teams during this era was the American Legion Post in White Bear Lake, which lost only one game from 1927-1929. They also fared well against the very tough University of Minnesota squads.)

The Great Depression Years

By the 1930s senior hockey was growing very rapidly throughout the state. Times were tough during the Great Depression, only fueling the popularity of the leagues, which proved to be an inexpensive form of entertainment for the fans. The advent of professional hockey in the area coupled with the construction of the Minneapolis Arena, all contributed to the growth of the sport in Minneapolis. Among the leading teams and programs during the period which played in the Minneapolis Arena League, included: Logan Park, Vertex, Raccoons, Deephavens, Foshays, Buzzas, Federals, Flour-City, Lake Lyndale, Wheaties, Daytons, Munsingwear, Ewalds, Jerseys, Bankers, Aces, Ascensions, Americans, Midways, North Commons, Camden, Powderhorns, Norse, Vikings, Mitby-Sather, Pershing, Red Squirrels, Nolans, East Side, Cedar-Lake, Chicago-Lake, First National Bank and St. Lawrence.

Meanwhile, in St. Paul, the Recreation Department was operating a vast array of junior and senior hockey programs for players of all ages with scores of lighted outdoor rinks being maintained for their use. And just as the Mill City had their "Minneapolis Arena League," St. Paul too had its "Auditorium League," which featured the following teams: Fire and Marine, Wards, Midland Hills, Minnesota Mining, Fort Snelling and Barnes Cafe. Among the leading players in the circuit were Howie, Al and Wylie Van, James Fletcher, Bill Toenjes, Lowell Booten, Bob McCabe, Al Trieble, Milo Gabriel, Don King, Bob Bates, Bob Meyers, Bobby Dill, Ray and Roy Schartin, Bill Galligan, Frank and Bill Haider.

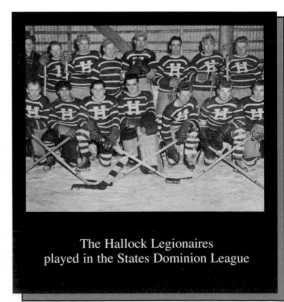

The Hallock Legionaires
played in the States Dominion League

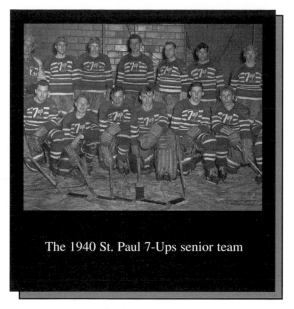

The 1940 St. Paul 7-Ups senior team

From 1930 through 1940 the Minneapolis Recreation Department sponsored the Northwest State AAU Hockey Tournament, a popular event which determined the outright champion from all the intermediate and senior winners throughout the Northwest. As many as 26 teams in two divisions participated in the annual tournament, which lasted for nearly a week. From 1936-37, the Wheaties and Jerseys, Minneapolis League teams, won the State AAU championships. While from 1938-39, the Red Squirrels and Barnes Cafe, of the St. Paul Auditorium League, won the title.

Dozens and dozens of former Twin Cities high school, as well as former University of Minnesota players, who had not turned professional, played in this popular indoor league. To put things into perspective as far as hockey growth during this era, there were some 435 teams, with nearly 6,000 players participating in Minneapolis Recreation Department hockey leagues by 1935. This was without a doubt the largest hockey program in the country and compared favorably in numbers with those in the Canada's largest cities.

Senior programs were strong in northern Minnesota during this period as well. The Senior City League, which featured teams from Taconite, Virginia, Grand Rapids, and Duluth, was dominated by the Taconite Hornets, who had won five straight City League titles throughout the mid-1930s. (Several high schools played in this league as well, including: Two Harbors and Duluth Central.) Several northern Senior teams played big time hockey

against some extremely good competition, including the University of Minnesota -- and often times won. These teams included: the Duluth Zephyrs, a very popular team that played to sellout crowds at the Duluth Amphetheatre, M. Cooke & Sons, Superior Curling, Docks, Car Shop, Bullard Mills, M.P. Goodfellowship, Hibbing Veterans and others. One of the strongest teams of this era was the Eveleth Cubs, who dominated the senior circuit, winning six straight State Senior titles from 1929-1935.

By the 1940s the Senior teams were also playing a vital role in the advancement of the sport at college and university levels. Because schools were limited in budgets, the fact that they could play these teams, who were loaded with older and more talented players, helped them to get better against their regular competitors. During this era the University of Minnesota was playing against several senior teams including: Fort Snelling, Honeywell, Bermans, and the Park League All-Stars. The University of Minnesota-Duluth was playing the West End Civic Club, Taconite Hornets, Warroad Lakers, and the Minneapolis Bungalows. Bemidji State was playing against such teams as Grand Rapids Raiders, Rainy River Legion, Bemidji Independents, Detroit Lakes Rangers, International Falls, Crookston City, and Thief River Falls VFW. And, in addition to playing against colleges and universities, St. Cloud Teachers College was also competing against several area senior teams.

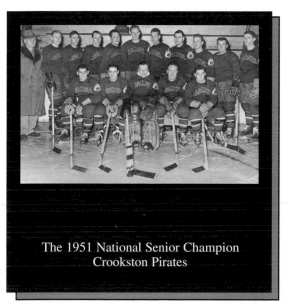

The 1938 Schmidt's Beer City Champion senior team

The American Amateur Hockey League (AAHL), another popular and successful Senior league, was formed in June of 1947 with the following charter member teams: Rochester Mustangs, Minneapolis Bermans, Minneapolis Jerseys, St. Paul Tally's, St. Paul Koppys, and White Bear 7-Ups. (Over the years the circuit expanded into neighboring states as well as into Canada before eventually becoming the semi-pro United States Hockey League in the early 1960s.)

The Advent of MAHA During the 1940s & '50s Fuels the Growth of Senior Hockey in Minnesota

During this era, the Amateur Athletic Union (AAU) was solely conducting state and district Senior tournaments. In hockey circles, it was thought that the organization was failing to adequately promote the sport throughout the state, or even the country for that matter, in the manner that the hockey community was demanding. It was felt that what hockey needed at that time was a statewide organization that, in addition to conducting tournaments, would encourage, promote and improve the standard of play at all age levels throughout the state. So, in 1947, Robert Ridder, a native New Yorker who was associated with the Duluth Herald team, of the Duluth Industrial Hockey League during the early 1940's, got the ball rolling. Ridder, then a radio and newspaper executive, was well-suited to the task of forming a statewide amateur hockey association. An organization soon materialized in affiliation with the Amateur Hockey Association of the United States (AHAUS), called the Minnesota Amateur Hockey Association, or MAHA.

The 1951 National Senior Champion Crookston Pirates

The main activity of MAHA during its first year of operation was to conduct a state Senior tournament, the winner of which would represent the state at the AHAUS National tournament. So, in March of 1948, the seven best Minnesota Senior teams, one from each league in the state qualified and met at the St. Paul Auditorium to settle the score. Those leagues included: American Amateur, States-Dominion, Southern Minnesota, Arrowhead, St. Croix Valley, Twin City Suburban and St. Cloud Municipal. (Eight other Senior circuits operating in St. Paul, Minneapolis, Duluth and Hibbing did not join MAHA in its initial season of operation, and therefore did not compete.) In the tournament, Grand Forks, of the States-Dominion League, beat both Eveleth and the St. Paul 7-Ups to win the Class A championship, while North Mankato, of the Southern Minnesota League, beat St. Cloud and Frederic to win the Class B title. St. Paul 7-Up and Grand Forks then went on to play in the 1948 AHAUS National Senior U.S. Championship at Toledo, Ohio. There, in the

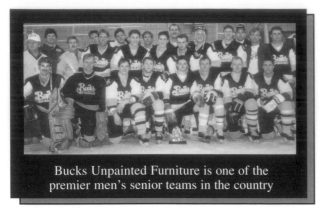

Bucks Unpainted Furniture is one of the premier men's senior teams in the country

first round of the four-team event, Grand Forks lost to Providence, R.I. 3-2, while St. Paul defeated Berlin, N.H. 7-2. In the finals Providence was able to beat St. Paul in a squeaker, 3-2.

By the 1950s MAHA was in full swing, and senior hockey was still as popular as ever. Minnesota was leading the way nationally, and bringing home the hardware to prove it. The Crookston Pirates, led by Cal Marvin, Serge Gambucci and Pat Finnegan defeated the New York Mets in 1951 to win the National Senior crown, while the Hibbing Flyers won the 1952 National Senior title that very next year.

One by one, new indoor rinks were being built throughout the state every year, making the game accessible to all who wanted to lace up a pair of skates. More and more new senior leagues were "popping up" during this era. One in particular was the "international" Thunder Bay Senior League, which consisted of five teams: Eveleth Rangers, Hibbing, Fort William, Fort Frances, Port Arthur. A Duluth promoter named Len Naymark was influential in starting the newly formed league, which was essentially a semi-pro league that featured a lot of good young junior players combined with ex-pro's and experienced veterans. Naymark would entice junior players to come play for him in return for scholarships at Eveleth Junior College. One such player who took him up was former Gopher and Olympic coach, Murray Williamson, who played for the Eveleth Rangers in 1954. With a 50-game schedule, the league offered a rough, entertaining brand of hockey for its Iron Range fans. However, in 1955, after only one season, the league folded due to financial problems.

Senior hockey went through its shares of ups and downs through the 1960s, '70s and '80s. However, the one fixture through that entire time was Cal Marvin's Warroad Lakers, who have been such an institution, that there is an entire chapter dedicated to them. The dominant Senior team of the 1980s and 1990s is without question Minneapolis-based, Buck's Furniture. The elite team has been the home of countless former Division I and even pro players for years. In 1999 the team won its eighth national senior championship since 1984, thanks to former Gopher Bobby Dustin's goal at 8:31 of overtime, to give the team a 5-4 victory over the New York St. Nicks, the oldest registered amateur team in the U.S.

U.S. Senior Champions

1932	Genoa
1949	St. Paul
1951	Crookston Pirates
1952	Hibbing
1957	Minneapolis
1958	Rochester
1964	St. Louis Park
1966	St. Louis Park
1986	Minneapolis
1988	St. Paul
1989	St. Paul
1995	Minneapolis Bucks
1997	Minneapolis Green Mill

U.S. Senior "Elite" Champions

1986	Minneapolis Bucks
1987	Bloomington
1989	Bloomington
1997	Minneapolis Bucks

The American Hockey Association

Another Senior Amateur league called the American Hockey Association (AHA), popped up in the early 90s. The circuit, which included the Minnesota Iron Rangers, Fargo-Moorhead Express, and even a reincarnation of the St. Paul Fighting Saints, played throughout the Midwest. Incidentally, the Saints, who finished with a 21-5-0 record in 1992-93, were led by several former Gopher stars, including: Grant Bischoff (who scored an amazing 69 points in 29 games), Jason Miller, Larry Olimb and Lance Werness.

Cal Marvin's Warroad Lakers

One of the biggest reasons why Warroad has been dubbed "Hockeytown, U.S.A.," is due in large part to the efforts of one man, Cal Marvin, and his passion for the game of hockey. Cal has become not only synonymous with the most successful senior amateur hockey team in the country, the Warroad Lakers, but also with Minnesota hockey in general. To fully appreciate just how amazing the Warroad hockey tradition is, you have to first understand the incredible story of one man's dedication to a town, and the sport it so dearly loves.

Warroad, a small town of some 1,700 people on the shores of the Lake of the Woods, is located just 10 miles south of the Manitoba border at the extreme tip of northwestern Minnesota. The town's biggest employer is Marvin Windows, which employs more than 3,000 locals to build and ship windows throughout the world. The owners of the company, the Marvin family, has been an intricate part of the fabric of the community for nearly a century. And luckily for Warroad hockey fans, Cal (one of five Marvin siblings), never wanted to get too involved with the day-to-day operations and management of his family's business, opting instead to pursue his love of hockey -- something that would turn out to be a huge blessing in disguise.

The youngest of six children, Cal Marvin was born on April 29th, 1924, in Warroad, where he grew up playing hockey on the area lakes and ponds. After high school Cal joined the Marine Corps, where he served in the South Pacific during World War II. After returning home from the service in 1946, Cal, along with several of his buddies, including Dan McKinnon of nearby Williams, decided to approach the University of North Dakota about the possibility of starting a new varsity program at the school. The administration thought it would be a good idea, and with that, Cal had started the Fighting Sioux hockey program. (Incidentally, the Sioux would go on to capture a national championship within just their first decade of league play.) Cal spent the next several years recruiting players from around northern Minnesota to come to Grand Forks to play hockey. All the while, Cal decided to start another "senior" team back home in Warroad, which he called the Lakers. That way, Cal and his buddies could play hockey during the week at UND, and come home to play for the Lakers on Sundays.

That first Laker's roster was loaded with talent from the Lake of the Woods area, including Williams' Clarence Schmidt (who had a brief stint with the Boston Bruins in the early 1940s), Roseau's "Masked Marvel" himself, Rube Bjorkman (who played on both the 1948 and 1952 U.S. Olympic teams), as well as Gordie "Ginny" Christian (who played on the 1956 silver-medal winning U.S. Olympic team under John Mariucci in Cortina, Italy). The team, dressed in black and gold (like the Boston Bruins), played on outdoor rinks in the now defunct States-Dominion League with other local teams such as Emerson, Dominion City, Fargo, Grand Forks, Thief River Falls, Baudette, Crookston, and Roseau. After graduating from UND, Cal returned home to play and coach full-time for the Lakers, as well as pursue business interests in the community. But, after injuring his knee during a game, Cal became the team's coach and manager.

In November of 1949, a significant event happened in the town of Warroad, the indoor Memorial Arena was opened. Affectionately called the "Gardens" by the locals, the arena was a big boost for the community's hockey programs. Cal had started the fund-raising effort to get the arena built two years earlier, and got much of the labor donated for free. Although the rink had no locker room facilities (the kids used to shower across the street from the rink at the Warroad Creamery after games), it was nonetheless a huge improvement from being outside during the frigid Warroad winters.

By the early 1950s the Lakers were competing in the Northwest Hockey League with Crookston, Roseau, Hallock, Thief River Falls and Grand Forks. Not only were they dominating their own league play, they were also whipping the best college teams in the country at that time as well. They had become regulars on many college schedules, including Murray Armstrong's tough Denver teams, as well as Michigan Tech, North Dakota and Minnesota-Duluth. The one team he didn't play was John Mariucci's Gophers. That's because Maroosh would say: "Marvin, how dumb do you think I am? It doesn't do us any good if we beat you, and we look bad if we don't!" Marvin had a deep respect and admiration for Mariucci, someone he credits personally for the USA's Olympic gold medals in 1960 and 1980.

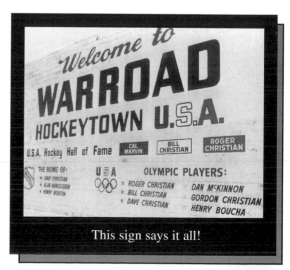

The Godfather of Warroad hockey, Cal Marvin

By 1953 Warroad had become a power on the high school scene, finishing second in the state tournament that year for the second time in five years. The stars of that team were a couple of brothers by the name of Billy and Roger Christian, two kids who's additional practice with the Lakers at night helped them to earn roster spots on the gold-medal winning 1960 Olympic team.

In 1955 the Lakers had reached the pinnacle of amateur success by beating the Grand Falls (Montana) Americans to win the U.S. National Intermediate Championship. In addition to winning the Northwest Hockey League title, something else happened that next year that really put Warroad on the map. John Mariucci, the coach of the 56' Olympic team, decided to have his squad play the Lakers before heading off to Italy. And, although Warroad lost the game (which was held in Eveleth) by the final of 6-2, nearly every U.S. Olympic team since then has kept that tradition alive by making the trek to Northern Minnesota to play the Lakers.

That same year a new teacher by the name of "Badger Bob" Johnson came to town to take over as the coach of the Warroad High School Hockey team. The U of M grad had originally signed a pro baseball contract with the Chicago White Sox, but instead had to go into the service. When he was discharged, he opted instead to try his hand at coaching and teaching. Johnson wound up coaching the Warriors for three seasons, starring for the Lakers during that same time. He had quite a schedule going in those days, too. Playing with the Lakers on Wednesdays, Saturdays and Sundays while coaching his Warriors on Tuesdays, Thursdays and Fridays, left Monday as his only day to relax. Johnson left to take over the Minneapolis Roosevelt coaching position in 1959, and of course went on to infamy as the skippers' of several college and pro teams including: Colorado College, Wisconsin, Calgary Flames, Team USA and finally with the Pittsburgh Penguins - where he won the Stanley Cup in 1991 against the North Stars.

In 1957 Marvin coached the U.S. National team to a fifth-place finish at the World Championships in Oslo, Norway. His club also became the first American sports team to play in the post-WWII Soviet Union. Marvin returned from Europe not to Warroad, but rather to a new locale that Warroad Mayor Morris Taylor had unofficially renamed "Hockeytown USA." Cal, who was now coaching the team exclusively, guided his Lakers past the U.S. National team that next year by the final score of 7-1. Perhaps feeling somewhat patriotic, Marvin abandoned the team's black and gold colored uniforms in favor of red, white and blue ones.

In 1959 the Lakers, who were led by several future NHLers including: Sugar Jim Henry (a goaltender with the Rangers & Bruins), Ed Kryzanowski (a defenseman with the Bruins and Blackhawks), won the Ontario/Minnesota Hockey League's "Cranford Cup" title. The team went on to win two more consecutive league titles as they expanded into the international scene as well to seek out new competition. In 1960 the U.S. Olympic team (led by Billy and Roger Christian) came back to town, and this time they beat the Olympians by a 6-4 margin. Just a few weeks later, in Squaw Valley, Calif., that same team won the gold medal. The Lakers had become quite the test for college and Olympic squads. Soon other countries, including Sweden and Norway, were stopping in Warroad to take a crack at these kids.

The Christian brothers played again on the 1964 U.S. Olympic team, and returned home just in time to rejoin their beloved Lakers in doing something that had never been done before. The Lakers, who, in 1962 began playing as the only U.S. team in the Canadian Amateur Hockey Association, defeated the British Columbia Kamloops to became the first American-based team ever to win a Canadian Amateur Hockey Championship. Shortly thereafter, opting to stay close to home rather than play pro hockey, the Christian brothers decided to go into business by launching a hockey stick manufacturing company under

This sign says it all!

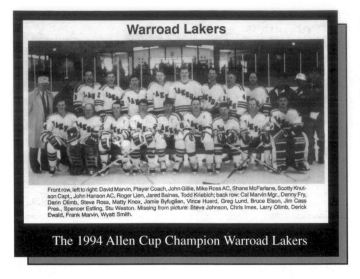

Warroad Lakers

Front row, left to right: David Marvin, Player Coach, John Gillie, Mike Ross AC, Shane McFarlane, Scotty Knutson Capt., John Hanson AC, Roger Lien, Jared Baines, Todd Kriebich; back row: Cal Marvin Mgr., Denny Fry, Darin Olimb, Steve Ross, Matty Knox, Jamie Byfuglien, Vince Huerd, Greg Lund, Bruce Elson, Jim Cass Pres., Spencer Estling, Stu Weston. Missing from picture: Steve Johnson, Chris Imes, Larry Olimb, Derick Ewald, Frank Marvin, Wyatt Smith.

The 1994 Allen Cup Champion Warroad Lakers

the slogan: "Hockey Sticks by Hockey Players." Their sticks are used today by countless pro's and kids alike from around the world.

In addition to serving as the manager of the 1965 U.S. National team, Cal guided his Lakers to Western Canada's "Allan Cup" finals, where they ultimately lost to Nelson, British Columbia. In addition, the team jumped over to the Manitoba Senior Hockey League that next year, where they won titles in 1965, 1969 and 1970. From there the team continued to play well throughout Canada, winning the Western Canadian Intermediate Championship in 1971, Central Canadian Hockey League title in 1972, and Manitoba/Thunder Bay Intermediate Championship in 1973.

In 1972 another Warroadite, Henry Boucha, who starred on the 1969 high school team that finished as the state's runner-up to Edina, won a silver medal as a member of the 1972 U.S. Olympic team that competed in Sapporo, Japan. (Boucha would go on to play with the Red Wings, North Stars and Fighting Saints before an eye injury prematurely ended his career.)

By 1974 the Lakers achieved another major milestone when they won their second Canadian Intermediate title by sweeping the Embrun (near Ottawa, Ontario) Panthers, in three straight games. With the win, the Lakers became the only U.S. team in history to ever win a "Hardy Cup," something reserved exclusively for the best Senior hockey team in all of Canada. Having to play all 17 playoff games on the road because the "Gardens" had only natural ice at the time, the Lakers long journey started in Manitoba, where they beat Thompson in five games. From there the Lakers ousted the Saskatchewan champs from Rosetown, in four, followed by a five-game win over the British Columbia champs from Coquitlam, to win the Western title. With the win, the Lakers now had the home-ice advantage. But, with no ice of their own, Warroad had to suck it up and rent ice-time from their rival neighbors from 20 miles down the road in Roseau. (For those of you who may not know, Warroad vs. Roseau is without question Minnesota's best and longest hockey rivalry. It is highlighted every year during high school's Section Eight championships, which almost always goes through one of the two towns.)

Laker Olympians:	
1952	John Noah
1956	Dan McKinnon
1956	Gordon Christian
1960, 64	Bill Christian
1960, 64	Roger Christian
1972	Henry Boucha
1976	Blaine Comstock
1980, 84	David Christian
1992	Chris Imes

The team continued its winning ways through the 1970s, winning the Manitoba Eastern Hockey League Championships in both 1975 and 1976. In 1977 the Gardens was finally retrofitted with artificial ice and the Lakers responded by beating a couple of teams from Kindersley (Saskatchewan), and Vancouver (British Columbia), to win the Western Canadian title, but ultimately losing the Hardy Cup to Cambellton (New Brunswick). The team finished as Western Canadian Intermediate finalists in 1979 as well.

The Lakers roared into the 80s getting to see yet another native son win a gold medal. This time it was Billy Christian's son, Dave, a former UND star who would go on to star in the NHL for 16 years with Winnipeg, Washington, Boston, St. Louis and Chicago, who was a member of the famed "Miracle on Ice" team of 1980. And, although the U.S. team trounced the Lakers 10-0 in Warroad that year, it was a thrill of a lifetime for Dave to get to play against his old man one last time. (Incidentally, Billy, then 42 years young, decided to finally hang em' up after that season with the Lakers.)

"It's a real tribute to our program," said Marvin," to think that the U.S. Olympic team will play in the Met Center on Tuesday, come to Warroad, and play a game on Wednesday and then play in Detroit before 20,000 a few nights later."

The U.S. National team came to Hockey-Town a few years later in 1983, where they could only muster a 6-6 draw with the mighty Lakers. The Olympic team came back in 1984, the same year the Lakers hit the road for Europe, where they went .500 against national teams from Holland, France, Austria and West Germany. Another rink, named Olympic Arena, was constructed in Warroad that year, thanks to the efforts of Bill Christian and Cal Marvin who helped raise the funds and arrange for all the volunteers to help build it.

In January of 1985 the Lakers ended their college competition when they lost to a tough Division One foe from Lowell 7-3, in Warroad. The Lakers joined the Southeastern Manitoba Hockey League that same year, where they won titles in 1985, 1987 and 1989. In addition, they won Manitoba Intermediate championships in both 1989 and 1990.

In 1990 the Lakers finished third in the Southeastern Manitoba League, and then went on to beat Altona, Morden, and Portage to win the league title. (Eagan forward John Hansen scored five goals in the final game and was named as MVP of the playoffs.) Then, in 1991, the Lakers moved to the Central Amateur Senior Hockey

Former Laker Henry Boucha with the Detroit Red Wings

Lakers in the NHL:	
Henry Boucha	Detroit, Minnesota
David Christian	Winnipeg, Washington
	Boston, St. Louis, Chicago
Chad Erickson	New Jersey
Allan Hangsleben	Hartford
Jim Henry	New York, Boston
Bob Johnson	Pittsburgh, Calgary (coach)
Bill Juzda	Toronto
Ed Kryzanowski	Chicago
Clarence Schmidt	Boston
Howard Walker	Washington, Calgary

(CASH) League, where they won the 1992 league title en route to advancing to the Allan Cup final-four. In January of that same year, the Lakers took their second trip to Europe, where they finished with a 3-1 record against French, German and Austrian teams. That year also saw Chris Imes play on the '92 U.S. Olympic team in Lillehammer, Norway, thus becoming the ninth Laker player ever to wear a red, white and blue sweater.

In 1993 Cal's family stepped up to the plate big-time, when his brothers Tot and Jack donated more than a half-million dollars of the $4.5 million price tag of the "new" Warroad Gardens arena. The state-of-the-art facility then played host to the 1994 Allen Cup finals (the Stanley Cup of senior amateur hockey), becoming only the second U.S. city ever to do so. (Spokane hosted it in 1980.) After advancing through the CASH playoffs, the Lakers, who had nearly a dozen Division I players on its roster (with several Warroad boys including: UND's Steve Johnson, Maine's Chris Imes, Gophers' Larry Olimb and UIC's Scott Knutson), made it to the finals with a 33-8 record. Then, with the new arena jammed, the Lakers, with a roster of entirely home-grown players, made history by beating Manitoba's St. Boniface Mohawks 5-2.

From there the Lakers dynasty just continued to grow. They won the Cup that next year as well, this time beating the Stoney Plain Eagles (Alberta) on their home ice thanks to Gopher Wyatt Smith's third-period goal to give the team a 3-2 victory. Playing an independent schedule, Warroad faced the Eagles that next year in the finals as well, this time in Unity, Saskatchewan. Incredibly, the Lakers prevailed 6-1 to notch their third straight Allen Cup title, something that had never before been accomplished in nearly a century of Canadian competition.

Even though the Lakers were performing so well, men's senior hockey seemed to be going by way of the dinosaur. The rise of high school and junior hockey had taken its toll on the leagues, with most folding in the 1980s and '90s. It was also taking its toll on Marvin, who was constantly battling to find a new league to play in, combined with the ever-increasing expenses of travel throughout Canada. While the Lakers decided to play in the Hanover-Tache League in 1996-97, Marvin painfully announced that after 50 years, it would be the team's final season. Wanting to take their leader out in "Knute Rockne-like" style, the Lakers somehow fought, kicked and scratched their way past a tough Flin Flon team to get back to the Allen Cup finals one last time. There, regrettably, Warroad was beaten by the final of 7-3 by the Powell River Regals from British Columbia.

A 50-year reunion was held on March 15th, 1997, the same day that Governor Arne Carlson proclaimed "Cal Marvin Day"

Christian Brothers Hockey Sticks

Bill Christian, Hal Bakke and Roger Christian

Billy and Roger Christian grew up as most kids did on Warroad's south-side, playing hockey on the river. Today the pair make up the "brothers" part of Christian Brothers, Inc., one of the world's largest manufacturers of hockey sticks and equipment. Today, the brothers only help add to the mystique of the tiny town of Warroad, otherwise known as: Hockey Town, U.S.A. The tiny town, which lies on the shores of Lake of the Woods on the Canadian border, is rich in hockey tradition, and the Christian brothers only add to that mystique.

Billy and Roger led the Warroad Warriors the 1953 State High School Hockey Tournament, where they finished runner's up to the St. Paul Johnson Governors. That team was coached by the legendary Cal Marvin, who guided the Lakers for nearly half a century. Both graduated from high school in 1956, and both played for Warroad's Lakers amateur team. They then earned spots on the U.S. National team, also coached by Marvin. That team was the first to play behind the Iron Curtain, playing both in Moscow and Prague, ultimately finishing fifth in the World Tournament, in Oslo. (Their other brother, Gordon, also played on the 56' Olympic team.) After that, the brothers returned to Warroad to work with their father as carpenters. The next year, Roger skated for the Warroad Lakers, while Bill played on the University of Minnesota freshman team.

Both brothers made the 1960 team that won a gold medal in the Winter Olympics in Squaw Valley. In that fabled event, Billy scored the tying and winning goals in the 3-2 pivotal win over the Russians. Roger and Duluth's Tommy Williams were his linemates. Roger also had a four-goal game against the Czech's, in what may have been the most memorable contest of the Games. With the U.S. down 4-3 going into the third, Roger scored a hat-trick in the final period to ice the game.

The two brothers continued to play on U.S. National teams and again made the 1964 Olympic squad in Innsbruck, Austria. The team didn't fare so well this time, but the Warroad Lakers did win the Hardy Cup, the championship of intermediate amateur hockey in Canada.

With the family's construction business prospering, Roger's brother-in-law, Hal Bakke (they're married to twin sisters), came up with a business proposition for the two brothers - manufacturing hockey sticks. The idea sounded good, so they dove right in. The three of them started their company at the old creamery in Warroad. With no money, they scraped to get by, all the time working like dogs to get the company off the ground. Then, in the 1965 World Tournament in Finland, which was coached by former Gopher Ken Yackel, and managed by Cal Marvin, the brothers got to show off their custom-made sticks to their teammates. They got a lot of great feedback, reinforcing the belief that their idea was a good one.

Back in Hockey Town, U.S.A., they continued to work nights and weekends, with little or no pay for several years, hoping to catch a break. Then, in 1969, after deciding to raise capital by selling stock in their company, they constructed a new manufacturing facility along Highway 11, that allowed them to ramp-up and become a profitable corporation. When the company started in 1964, Northland Hockey Sticks represented their main U.S. competitor. CCM in Canada, which also made sticks, got out of the stick business shortly after. "We were basically copying the Northland Stick," said Bakke. "We even toured their plant, and I think they were sorry they ever allowed us to do that. But little did we know then that we would end up owning Northland."

Today, with more than 60 loyal employees, and international and domestic sales of sticks and equipment reaching nearly $10 million annually, the company is on a roll. (They are still a distant second to the Marvin's, owners of Marvin Windows, in Warroad's economy.) Not only are they one of the nation's top hockey equipment producers, pumping out more than a half of a million sticks per year, they are also one of the most respected with regards to quality and innovation. There are more than 150 NHL players using Christian Brothers hockey sticks. The brothers still get a chuckle out of the fact that former UMD star, Brett Hull, who endorses Easton Aluminum Hockey Sticks, has refused to use it with anything other than a Christian Brothers replacement blade.

Billy and Roger, along with Cal Marvin, have all been inducted into the U.S. Hockey Hall of Fame in Eveleth. The Christian's are synonymous with hockey in Minnesota, and there are already second and third generations that have come along to carry the torch. For example, Bill's son Dave, who skated two years at UND, played on the gold medal winning 1980 U.S. Olympic Hockey team, and played for 14 years in the NHL with the Jets, Capitals, Bruins, Blues and Blackhawks, before joining the IHL's Minnesota Moose in 1995, has the most goals of any Minnesotan in the NHL.

With their trademarked Diamond Design stick blades, Christian Brothers sticks are among the best in the world. And, more importantly, they are made right here in Minnesota.

throughout the state of Minnesota. It was a fitting celebration to a man that has become the venerable Godfather of hockey in Warroad. The Lakers helped countless kids who were in transition from moving from high school to college, or from college to U.S. National or pro teams. Fully 19 U.S. Olympic and National teams have had former Lakers on their roster, and incredibly, the Lakers never had a losing season in their rich five-decade history. The man behind all of this... of course, Cal Marvin.

Yes, Marvin has done it all in the name of hockey. The financial challenges had him doing everything from running community auctions, to bingo games, to turkey shoots, to fishing contests, and even a male style show to raise money for the kids. From coaching, to selling candy at games, to pouring cement, to writing weekly newspaper columns, to selling advertising, to serving on boards, he has done it all so that each generation of children had it a little better than the one before. And most importantly, all he wants in return, is that the kids give back their time to help out the next crop of youngsters coming up after them to keep the wonderful tradition alive.

Cal Marvin has dedicated the better part of his life in the pursuit of helping others. He turned the entire community into a Laker's booster program and was fortunate to have the corporate backing from companies such as Marvin Windows and Christian Brothers to keep his dream alive. Arguably no man has done more for his community with regards to promoting the game of hockey than has Warroad's Cal Marvin. Today the town boasts one of the most complete hockey programs in the country, with kids of all ages being able to play the game for free. That's right, free. No association fees, spendy ice-time payments, travel expenses, costly equipment or uniforms. It's all donated and paid for through fund-raisers and sponsors. The coaches volunteer and the community rallies behind them to give their kids the best opportunity it can have for success. "Somebody did it for you, and you've got to pay it back," said Marvin about his town's amazing commitment to young people.

Among his many awards and honors, Cal was elected to the United States Hockey Hall of Fame as an administrator in 1982. He is also a member of the Manitoba Sports Hall of Fame, the University of North Dakota Athletic Hall of Fame and the Warroad High School Athletic Hall of Fame. He received the "Maroosh," an award presented in the name of the late John Mariucci for an individual's contributions to hockey. In addition to his Lakers, Cal operated various motels and restaurants in the community, including his Lake of the Woods Resort called "Cal's," which he ran for more than a quarter century. Presently Cal and his wife Beth

Early Youth Hockey in Minnesota

U.S. National Pee Wee Champions

1951	Duluth
1951	Duluth
1965	Duluth

U.S. National Bantam Champions

1951	Duluth
1952	Duluth
1953	Eveleth
1954	Eveleth
1958	Duluth
1970	Edina
1971	Edina
1972	Edina
1973	Mounds View
1974	Roseville

MAHA's role in the state's growth of hockey has been immeasurable. Through the efforts of gentlemen such as Don Clark and Bob Ridder, the organization has been the backbone of not only Minnesota hockey, but in many ways hockey throughout the country. By 1973, at the modest registration fee of $2, there were some 2,000 teams enrolled in the state. Their mission became more focused over time: "To encourage and improve the standard of ice hockey in the Minnesota area; to conduct ice hockey tournaments and to select representative teams to participate in tournaments; to associate with other ice hockey associations; to do any and all acts necessary or desirable in the furtherance of the foregoing purposes; to buy, sell, lease and otherwise deal in all kinds of property, real, personal and mixed, for the purpose of creating further interest in amateur hockey."

In 1951, under the direction of MAHA Secretary-Treasurer Don Clark, the state's first-ever Pee Wee tournament was held at the White Bear Lake Hippodrome. The statewide event, which included teams from Grand Forks, Wayzata, South St. Paul, East Grand Forks, Minneapolis Loans, and St. Paul Como, was the first state youth (under high school age) tournament to be held in the United States. There, Duluth Glen Avon edged host White Bear Lake 3-2 in the finals of the eight-team event before a crowd of some 700 fans. The Duluth team, led by coach Bob Fryberger and his three sons' line of Jerry, Bob and Dates, continued on to win the 1951 AHAUS National Pee Wee Championship in New York's Madison Square Garden.

In addition to the Senior and Pee Wee class tournaments, the next category to be formed was the Juvenile (today called Junior Gold), which featured players 18 years and under. The initial 1956 tournament was held in Duluth and was won by St. Paul Arlington, which defeated Mountain Iron in the finals of the four-team event. (MAHA's first state Midget tournament, held in Duluth in 1961, saw Duluth Lower Chester defeat Owatonna for the title. While the initial Junior B championship was staged at Polar Arena in North St. Paul in 1974.)

The Duluth Glen Avon Pee wees, led by coach Bob Fryberger, won the 1951 national title in New York City, and even got the Key to the City from the Duluth Mayor.

The 1973-74 Mounds View Bantams (led by future Gopher Steve Ulseth), finished with a 73-4-2 record and went on to beat Detroit for the National Championship

In 1960 Minnesota officially adopted the classes and nomenclature that the AHAUS, the national governing body, had decided to employ. The system, which had been borrowed from Canada, included Juniors, Juveniles, Midgets, Bantams, Pee Wees, Squirts and Mites. By the 1970s, girls hockey was also starting to be organized.

Walter Bush and Bob Fleming, both of whom became involved in MAHA in the 1950's, have remained active in the sport on a national level. Bush has served as president of USA Hockey (AHAUS) since 1986, while Fleming has served as director, in addition to chairing the United States Olympic Ice Hockey Committee for many years. Peter Lindberg has been a USA Hockey vice president since 1988, and Bob Ridder served as team manager of the silver-medal winning 1952 and 1956 U.S. Olympic teams. (In 1998 MAHA changed its name to Minnesota Hockey. An affiliate of USA Hockey, the organization is the governing body of amateur hockey in the state. In addition, in 1999 former NHL star and Eveleth native, Doug Palazzari was named as USA Hockey's Executive Director.)

FACT

MAHA's team registrations went from 47 teams in Minnesota in 1947, to more than 4,000 in 1999.

reside in Warroad. They have 12 children and numerous grandchildren. "We've quit, now," Cal said in an interview with writer John Gilbert several years ago. "And we're not Catholic. But I always kept the thermostat down in the winter."

"I am grateful to have worked with and to have coached so many great people over the years," said Marvin. "It was a sad day when we had to shut the team down here a few years ago, after 50 years it had become a way of life for me. But, it was just too tough. We were the only senior team between Minneapolis and Winnipeg, and all that traveling takes a toll. I have no regrets though, and would do it all over again in a second. It was a wonderful ride!"

Eveleth - The Capital of American Hockey

Synonymous with the sport of ice hockey, Eveleth has come to be known around the country as the "capital of American hockey," because of its amazing ability to produce so many elite-level players in the first half of the 20th century. Arguably, no city in the United States has meant more to hockey than the tiny town of Eveleth. Located just 60 miles north of Duluth, and a mere 100 miles south of the Canadian border, this melting-pot mining community has an incredible history. Here is its story:

In 1890 a pioneer lumberman named Erwin Eveleth emigrated from Michigan to northern Minnesota with the intent of purchasing a plot of the region's rich pine forest lands. Three years later iron ore was discovered in the area, and as a result a townsite was surveyed and later incorporated. In 1893 the tiny settlement, located a mile southwest of the city's present location, near the Adams Spruce Mine, officially became incorporated as Mr. Eveleth's namesake. At first things were very tough for the community. There was a national financial depression that year that put a great burden on the people. As a result, the townsite, which consisted of only a few buildings, almost disappeared. During that harsh winter, food became scarce, and with the exception of occasional mail service by dog sled, the town was virtually cut off from the rest of the world.

Eveleth survived though, and soon people from all over the world were packing up their lives and making the trip across the Atlantic to start over there as miners. Immigrants, mostly from southern Europe and Scandinavia, came in droves to the east end of the Missabe Iron Range in search of a better life. Before long the Slavs, Croats, Slovenians and Serbians, found themselves living among the Italians, Irish, French, Fins, Swedes, Danes, Norwegians, and English. And, because of Eveleth's cold climate, high altitude and hilly terrain, the new settlers seemed to feel right at home. In May of 1895, the Duluth, Missabe and Northern Railroad shipped its first load of iron ore from the Adams Mine, thus putting the town of Eveleth officially on the map.

By now the town was booming for these hearty people, who seemed to live by the adage "work hard - play hard." Working diligently in an open pit mine all day meant that at night and on the weekends, there was some steam that needed to be let off. Hockey would ultimately prove to be that perfect outlet. Many of the immigrants were already familiar with several ice games that were being played across the pond during the late 1800s, including shinny, bandy, ice polo and curling. So, it was just a matter of time before they started to incorporate these ice games, along with the relatively new sport of hockey (which was gradually spreading up to northern Minnesota from the Twin Cities, and at the same time down from Canada), into their new Iron Range homeland.

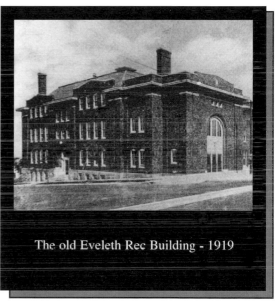
The old Eveleth Rec Building - 1919

By best guestimates, the sport of hockey was first played here in 1902 at an outdoor rink on Fayal Pond. However, the first recorded game wasn't played until a year later, on January 23, 1903, between Eveleth and Two Harbors. The contest was played on the newly constructed O'Hares' skating rink (an indoor facility with a 75' x 150' natural ice sheet), which was located at the south end of Grant Street. That following day this article appeared in the January 24, 1903, edition of the Eveleth Mining News:

"The first hockey game of the season was played last evening at the Eveleth Rink between Two Harbors and the local seven. The local team was defeated 5-2. The game was hard fought by both teams, as it was the first match game that either team had played in during the season. The visiting team did good team work and played a fast game. There was a great deal of off-side playing by both teams. Hockey is practically a new game on the Range. With proper support, Eveleth can put up a good team, as there is plenty of first class material here. A return game will be played with Two Harbors."

The old Eveleth Hippodrome

Shortly thereafter a hockey club was organized by a gentleman named John Herman, called the "City Hockey Club." The club played games against several area teams including: Two Harbors, Duluth, Biwabik and Virginia. Eveleth soon developed a great rivalry with Virginia, where they played on what was then called Rainy Lake, but is now Silver Lake. Their games against one another, more often than not, usually ended up in a brawl, proving that fighting has been a part of the game since its early beginnings. Some of the "lads" who played on those early Eveleth teams included: Alvin Skramstad, Victor Lundgren, Leonard Peterson, Tony Van Buskirk, Henry Lamier, Hart LaVigne, Ernest

Baldi, Tom Dolan, "Foxy" LaVigne, Joe Haley, Fred Viger and James Clark.

By 1910 Eveleth's population had reached 7,000. Hockey continued to flourish in the community, as did other ice sports, including curling. In 1907 the first curling club was built, on the west end of Jones Street, near the present sight of the Spruce Pit. It is readily apparent that Eveleth's ascendance as the hockey Mecca for which we know it today was clearly fueled by its mining riches. The mining company's, which were in some way responsible for nearly everyone in the town's income, figured that it was probably in their best interests to keep their employees and their families happily entertained in their new surroundings, always remembering that a happy worker was a productive worker. So, they, along with the city of Eveleth, decided to provide this entertainment in the form of constructing several new meticulously maintained public ice rinks. Recreational commissions were soon organized in conjunction with the local school board and ran by both parents and local citizens alike - all of course without pay, in order to give their kids the very best facilities.

Soon kids from every neighborhood in the city were playing hockey. From October to March, Eveleth was transformed into an annual winter-wonderland. Kids began to expect a new hockey stick under the tree every Christmas, and couldn't wait to go out and show it off to their neighborhood pals. There were countless family teams, gang teams, and even rival groups from one neighborhood street who would challenge the boys from an adjoining street. Rinks were merely a formality, as nearly half of the streets in town had become make-shift ice sheets, complete with goals made of snow and ice. From dusk till dawn, kids could be seen passing pucks

Frank Brimsek

Frank Brimsek grew up playing hockey in Eveleth. After starring on the local high school team, Frank attended St. Cloud Teachers College, where he starred as both a goalie on the hockey team, and also as a fullback on the football team. After playing for a couple of seasons with the Pittsburgh Yellow Jackets of the Eastern Hockey League and Providence of the International American League, Frank was called up to the NHL's Boston Bruins in 1938, where he replaced the legendary Cecil "Tiny" Thompson in goal. There, he became an immediate sensation, and soon earned the nickname "Mr. Zero" for his many shutouts. In fact, during his rookie season, he blanked the opposition in six of his first eight games, and 10 of 41 overall over that Stanley Cup-winning season. For his efforts, he was awarded the Calder Memorial Trophy as the league's top rookie and the Vezina Trophy as its leading goalie. A perennial all-star, Frank played for the Bruins for five years before joining the U.S. Coast Guard for a two-year term. He then returned to the Bruins for four more seasons before finally ending his active hockey career with the Chicago Blackhawks in 1950. Over 10 seasons, Brimsek's goals against average was 2.74 with 42 shutouts. He was elected to the Hockey Hall of Fame in Toronto in 1966, and the U.S. Hockey Hall of Fame in 1973. "Mr. Zero" is without question to greatest Minnesota goalie ever to play between the pipes.

back and forth across the street to one another. Some kids used branches as sticks, and instead of wearing shin pads - they put "Saturday Evening Post" magazines over their shins for protection. There even was a lot of pressure put on parents to get their kids new skates - which were a great expense for a family back then. Usually a kid would get his first pair by about kindergarten, and then hope to swap with another kid later on when he outgrew them. The result was the fact that most kids grew up on boot-hockey, perfecting their stick-handling skills way before they even learned how to lace up a pair of skates. And, that was why so many of the kids from Eveleth went on to become so polished at handling a stick and puck. Each generation of kids tried to emulate the one before them, and to no one's surprise, Eveleth soon became a spawning ground for some of the best hockey talent in the world.

In 1918 the first formal hockey organization, called the Eveleth Hockey Association, was formed in Eveleth by several business and professional gentlemen, including Edward Hatch, who later became mayor of Eveleth and then mayor of Duluth, Victor Essling, also a mayor of Eveleth, Leonard Peterson, who later managed the Eveleth team, Charles Hale and Tony Van Buskirk, both pioneer residents of Eveleth. That next year the Eveleth Recreation Building was built at a cost of $125,000. Complete with six sheets of curling ice on the ground floor, and a hockey rink on the second floor, the building was state of the art for its day. The first organized senior league, called the "Hot Stove League," was sponsored that year by Helps-Shea Hardware. That next year an all-star team of sorts, called the "Reds," was formed to play in conjunction with the Winter Carnival at the new "Rec." Building. Eveleth beat Hibbing 5-2 at the first-ever game played there. Members of that squad, many or whom were from Two Harbors and Duluth, included: Clark, Hedberg, Stein, Couture, Toppula, Sullivan, LeFleur, Bastien and Seaborn (a Canadian import who played the seventh spot better known back then as the "rover."). Playing an independent schedule against several local teams including: St. Paul, Hibbing, Duluth, Calumet, Rainy River, Virginia and Winnipeg, the team finished that 1920 season with an 18-5-1 record. It was at about that time that the Eveleth Hockey Association began importing Canadian hockey players to play for the Reds, and in return, would get them good jobs working in the mines.

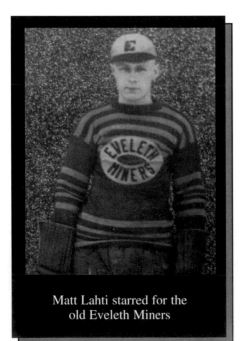

Matt Lahti starred for the old Eveleth Miners

The USAHA, Eveleth's First Taste of the Big-Time

The first high school hockey team was organized in the fall of 1920. The team was coached by hockey legend Ade Johnson, who was the brother of Hall of Famer Ching Johnson. Ade was also one of the stars of the Eveleth Reds, who had by this time a year later, graduated from playing an independent schedule, and had joined the professional ranks of an upstart big-time national hockey circuit called the United States Amateur Hockey Association (USAHA). During that first season of league play in 1920, there were three groups that made up the new association -- one in the East and two in the Midwest. The clubs that played in the league included the Duluth Hornets, St. Paul AC, Boston AA, Boston Westminster HC, Pittsburgh Hornets, Pittsburgh Yellow Jackets, Cleveland HC, New York, Philadelphia, Cleveland, Calumet, Portage Lake, and both the American and Canadian Soo of Sault St. Marie. Incredibly, the people of Eveleth now had the unique opportunity of viewing some of the greatest hockey players in the world on a regular basis. Seeing that tremendous brand of hockey no doubt inspired the youth of the Iron Range to foster a tremendous love and respect for the game.

In 1920 the Reds, who were now playing six-man rather than seven-man hockey, were designated to play in the USAHA's Group Three along with Calumet, Houghton, American Soo and Canadian Soo. The Reds were led by several Canadian imports during that first year in the league, among them were: the brothers' Ching and Ade Johnson, Perk Galbraith, later a member of the Boston Bruins and a coach at Blake School, Denny Breen, Percy Nicklin, Monette, Seaborn, Grey, and also Vic Des Jardins, a native of Sault Ste. Marie, Mich. Eveleth got off to a great start that inaugural season. The Reds, who finished the season with a 14-1-1 record, went on to win the Group Three division by beating the American Soo, 10-1, in a wild and crazy Group Three title game. This story describing that game later appeared in the Eveleth Mining News:

"Fully 600 fans came over from the Canadian Soo (Sault St. Marie) to the Eveleth - American Soo hockey game, and made themselves known by throwing coal, rotten eggs and other objects at the Eveleth players. At one time a piece of coal intended for one of the Eveleth players struck and seriously cut Stanley Skinner, a Soo player. Manager Peterson wired Eveleth that the treatment received from the American Soo management and players and local fans was fine, but the Canadians who came over to see the game were the meanest crowd of spectators he ever saw, and they abused our players so much that the two teams did not change ends, as is customary after each period, so that the Eveleth players could defend the goal farthest from the mob of Canadian soreheads during the entire game." When asked about the game, rover Jim Seaborn reportedly said: "They liked us so much that they practically presented us with the sports arena... one board at a time!"

Sam LoPresti

Hall of Famer Sam LoPresti, born in Elcor but raised in Eveleth, went on to mind the nets at Eveleth High School. From there he went on to play at both Eveleth Junior College and also at St. Cloud Teacher's College. Sam broke into the big leagues in the fall of 1939, after coach Cliff Thompson pointed him out to a scout for the St. Paul Saints of the AHA. In 1940-41, LoPresti became a Blackhawk, and although he only spent two seasons in the NHL, he might be most remembered for an amazing game in which he played on March 4, 1941, when, in a 3-2 loss against the Boston Bruins, LoPresti made a record 80 saves! (Incidentally, Boston's goaltender during that game was fellow Evelethian, Frankie Brimsek.) After the 1942 season, LoPresti entered the US. Navy. There, after having his merchant ship sunk by a torpedo, he spent 42 days alone in a lifeboat at sea before finally being rescued.

For their efforts the team was awarded the coveted McNaughton Cup. Now they would go on to face the champs of Groups One and Two for the USAHA's National Championship. They went on to play Cleveland (the Group Two champs who had beaten Boston AA of Group One), in the national finals. On April 2 and 3, in Cleveland, the Cleveland Hockey Club beat Eveleth by the back-to-back scores of 6-3, and 6-3. Then, because of the lack of ice in northern Minnesota at the time, the series shifted to the neutral sight of Pittsburgh, where there was artificial ice. There, the Reds beat the Clevelander's by the scores of 2-0, and 4-2 to tie it up at two games apiece. But, Cleveland was declared the winner of the four game series 14-12 on total goals, and was awarded the league's championship trophy, the Fellowes Cup. Even though they finished as the runner up, people from all over the country were now asking, "Just where the heck is Eveleth?" People from all over the Range just couldn't get enough of their new team. There was even a crowd of more than 1,000 Reds fans, who stood outside in the cold at the local Western Union office awaiting details of the playoff games via telegraph.

As a result of this onslaught of interest in the new team, Mayor Essling, a St. Peter native who was also a lawyer, promoter and developer, decided to get cooking on building an arena suitable for his town's Reds. Now, by 1921 World War I was over, and hockey in North America was experiencing tremendous growth, especially on the Iron Range, where there were already four indoor ice arenas: Eveleth, Hibbing, Virginia and Chisholm. The competition was becoming fierce throughout the Range, and Eveleth, in a classic case of wanting to "keep up with the Jones'," needed to keep their edge. Because the Eveleth Recreational Building had become inadequate to handle the ever increasing crowds, the city decided to build an arena like no other. The result was a 3,000-seat 230' x 150' icy masterpiece, called the Hippodrome. The giant wooden structure located on the corner of Garfield and Adams Streets, known affectionately by the locals simply as the "Hipp," soon became recognized throughout the state as the "Madison Square Garden of the Northland." It opened on January 1, 1922 before a full house, as the Reds defeated the Duluth Hornets 10-6.

This hockey shrine became so popular that before long it became the focal point of the entire community. To best capture what it might have been like to be a young boy dreaming of one day wearing an Eveleth Reds sweater, here is an excerpt from a story written by Chuck Muhich, longtime Eveleth recreation director, that appeared in the November 26, 1953 edition of the State Sports News:

"Many a boy who later wore a Ranger uniform can tell you how he got into the Hipp through the coal chute through an underground tunnel or by means of a ladder reaching to a window. A game night found everyone in the neighborhood busy stowing away their ladders out of reach of the youthful raiders. Frequently the Hipp caretaker would snap on

Mike Karakas

Hall of Famer Mike Karakas, though born in Aurora and raised in Eveleth, played goalie on the Eveleth High School team and also for Eveleth Junior College. He later led the Eveleth Rangers to the 1931 state championship. Karakas went on to star for the Chicago Blackhawks, where after posting a 1.92 goals against average and 9 shutouts in 1936, earned rookie-of-the-year honors. He dazzled the Windy City fans for more than a decade, and even won a Stanley Cup in 1938.

The Eveleth Rangers of the 1940s
were led by Andre and Elio Gambucci

the light switch only to find a group of boys perched like crows holding down an entire section."

Later many of these youngsters formed the nucleus for the strong Eveleth High School and Eveleth Junior College teams and continued on to become college, professional and Olympic performers. The "Big Time" hockey had fostered an intense interest in the game in Eveleth and soon most of the youths and many of the adults were playing some form of hockey. During the depression years many Eveleth youth and adults spent their spare time playing hockey. In 1921 the Eveleth Recreation Commission organized teams and leagues and built and maintained several outdoor rinks. Scout troops, churches, lodges, clubs and neighborhoods formed teams of various ages. Chickentown would meet Fayal, and Adams would play Hayes in intra-city games. Adults competed in Class "A" or Class "B" leagues. It seemed that almost everyone in Eveleth was playing hockey. In addition, the various mining locations adjunct to Eveleth, such as Leonidas, Genoa, Iron, Cherry, Sparta and Spruce iced hockey teams with some of them having very strong adult and Senior teams." (Incidentally, Sparta won the 1930 Minnesota Senior Recreation title with a lineup composed entirely of players of Finnish nationality.)

Those same kids couldn't get enough hockey, and as a result, the Hipp was practically open all day and all night for all levels of play. So, it wasn't uncommon for people to wake up either at the crack of dawn, or in the middle of the night, by the sounds of kids running down the streets for a game or practice at the Hipp. Sometimes, if the streets were frozen, they would simply skate to their games, with their hockey bags draped over their sticks. One of those kids, who grew up in the 1920s playing hockey as a way to stay out of trouble, was John Mariucci. Maroosh learned the game on Hayes Street, playing with his neighbor's -- the Brimsek's and Karakas'. Some people referred to it as "Incubator Street," because it was said that there were so many nationalities living there, and each house was filled to the brim with kids. (Later, in the 1940s, the next generation of kids, like John Mayasich played for Summit Street, while Willard Ikola played for Jackson Street.)

At the end of the 1921-22 season, Eveleth, winners of Group Three, had finished with an impressive 12-4 record. The Reds then went on to face the St. Paul Athletic Club, the winners of Group Two who posted an 8-4 record, in the semifinal playoffs on March 3, at the Hipp in Eveleth. Eveleth lost to St. Paul 3-1, on that night, only to lose 4-2 the following evening. The series then shifted back to St. Paul where the teams skated to a pair of 0-0 ties, in addition to a 2-1 nail-biter victory for the AC. St. Paul wound up winning the series 7-6 on total goals. In so doing, St. Paul then went on to face Boston Westminster in the finals, only to lose in four: 3-0, 2-1, 0-0, and 2-0. The Eveleth fans proved to be road warriors as well, making the trip in droves to St. Paul to support their Reds. The games played at the St. Paul Hippodrome attracted more than 8,000 onlookers per outing.

For the 1922-23 season and thereafter, the league decided to split into two divisions -- the Eastern and Western. This was largely due to the fact that Eveleth was not satisfied with the USAHA placing them in a league with the weaker Michigan teams, and consequently requesting to be placed in a group with larger cities and stronger teams. As a result, Eveleth joined St. Paul, Duluth, Pittsburgh, Cleveland and newcomer Milwaukee, to form the realigned Group Two (Western Division) of the USAHA. The Reds finished the 1922-23 season in third place, four games behind St. Paul (who won the Western Group title but lost the national championship to Boston, in a close four-game series -- six goals to four). Members of that Eveleth squad were: Bernie McTigue, Ching and Ade Johnson, Percy Nicklin, Billy Hill, Perk Galbraith, Vic Des Jardins, Bob Davis and Bob Armstrong.

During the 1923-24 season, the upstart Minneapolis Rockets replaced the struggling Milwaukee franchise as the sixth team in the division. And, unfortunately for Eveleth, Ching and Ade Johnson decided to move to the Mill City to join them. Eveleth finished fourth in the six team circuit with a 9-11 record. It was a sub-par season for the Reds, who were led by Galbraith and newcomer, Ed Rodden, who each scored 11 points.

The 1924-25 season would prove to be the last for the USAHA in Minnesota. The Reds, who came on strong to finish the second half of the season at 13-6-1, were defeated by Pittsburgh in four straight in a post-season playoff series. The games were played in both Pittsburgh and (neutral) Duluth, because the temperature got too warm for the Hippodrome's natural ice. Incidentally, the Yellow Jackets went on to defeat Fort Pitt in the national finals. Red's forward Vic Des Jardins was second in league scoring that year with 14 goals in 39 games.

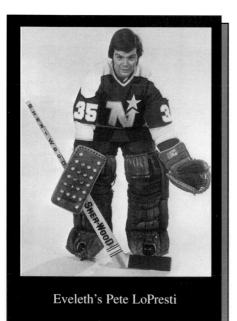

Eveleth's Pete LoPresti

Unfortunately, after running for five glorious season, 1925 was the last year of operation for the USAHA. The league was vital for jump-starting the game of hockey throughout the United States. Many of the game's best and most talented players who suited up for a USAHA squad over its brief history went on to play in the NHL. The Eveleth contingent included: Ching and Ade Johnson, Vic Des Jardins, Perk Galbraith, Jim Seaborn, Nobby Clark, Ed Rodden and Bill Hill.

The season of 1925-26 would prove to be the last in the world of big-time hockey for Eveleth. That year St. Paul, Minneapolis and Duluth along with newcomers Winnipeg and Canadian Soo, formed the re-named Central Hockey Association, while Pittsburgh and Cleveland both withdrew from the USAHA. Pittsburgh, with almost the same lineup that they had used the previous season in the USAHA's Western Division, joined the National Hockey League, where they became an instant force. As for the Reds? Eveleth and Hibbing joined forces to form one team which was known as the "Eveleth-Hibbing Rangers." The Rangers got off to a good start in the upstart CHA, but floundered in mid-season before finishing behind St. Paul for fifth place. By season's end it was the Minneapolis Rockets who would win the title over Duluth and Winnipeg. High operating costs and the problem of protecting players from raids by professional hockey clubs ultimately killed the Central Hockey Association after just that one season.

So, after six glorious years of world class "semi-pro" hockey on the Range, it was the end of the line for the Eveleth franchise. No longer would fans of the Range be able to see the best players in the world right in their backyard. Players such as: Tiny Thompson, Taffy Abel, Nels Stewart, Lionel Conacher, Herbie Lewis, Mike Goodman, Bill Cook, Bun Cook, Ching Johnson, Moose Goheen, Herb Drury, Vern Turner, Perk Galbraith, Roy Worters, Coddy Winters, Moose Jamieson, Mickey McQuire and Hib Milks.

Eveleth Says Good Bye to Semi-Pro Puck and Hello to Senior Hockey
A new outright professional circuit that had a working agreement with the NHL called the AHA was formed that next year, but Eveleth opted to sit on the sidelines. Instead they focused on producing the state's top amateur teams. And that is just what they did in 1926, when the Eveleth Cubs (using only home-town boys) won the first State Senior Championship held in Hibbing, sponsored by the Minnesota Recreation Association. Among the players on the team were: Frank DeLeo, Bill Langen, Matthew Lahti, Andrew Jagunich, Tony and John Prelesnik, Bill DePaul, and Victor Machek. The Cubs, who later became known as the Eveleth Miners, became a dynasty of their own, winning four straight AAU State Senior titles from 1929 through 1932. Incidentally, while the tiny nearby town of Genoa which no longer appears on Minnesota road maps, captured the state crown in both 1933 and 1934, the 1935 title was won by St. Cloud Teachers College, a team made up almost entirely of Eveleth natives.

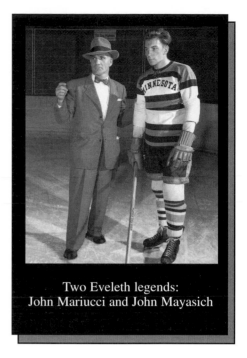

Two Eveleth legends:
John Mariucci and John Mayasich

That Eveleth team even received an invitation to be the United States representative in the 1928 Winter Olympic winter games to be held in Amsterdam. But, because the club was unable to raise the necessary funds to cover the costs of the trip, it was called off, and ultimately the U.S.had no hockey representative for that Olympiad.

From 1927-1931, another senior amateur circuit was formed in northern Minnesota, called the Arrowhead League, which featured teams from Eveleth, Hibbing, Virginia, Duluth and Fort Frances. Eveleth's team, known as the Rangers, was comprised of entirely of locals.

In 1931 a new amateur league, called the Central Hockey League, was formed with teams from Eveleth, Minneapolis, St. Paul and Virginia. Virginia withdrew from the league after the first season, and from that point on, the circuit changed over to a professional status. For the 1931-32 season, the Rangers earned themselves a new nickname -- the "Orphans." That's because the Hipp had been condemned for renovations, and they were forced to play their entire 35 game schedule on the road. This didn't even phase the team, as they went on to win the regular season crown. The league, which ultimately ran through the 1934-35 season, featured tremendous competition. An example of just how good the caliber of play was in the league was displayed in 1934, when the CHL and the American Hockey Association (a higher level professional league with teams throughout the Midwest and East Coast), played an interlocking schedule. That year the St. Paul Saints swept the AHA champion St. Louis Flyers for the title.

Amazingly, almost the entire Central Hockey League was comprised of Minnesota natives, and of them, more than 20 of the league's 65 total players were Eveleth natives. They included: Milton Brink, Glee Jagunich, Rudy Ahlin, Art Erickson, Andy Toth, Vance and Joe Papike, Hodge Johnson, Alex McInnes, Pete Pleban, Frank Ceryance, Paul Schaeffer, Bill DePaul, Tony Prelesnik, P.J. Murphy, Al Soumi, Mike Kasher, Frank DeLeo, Oscar Almquist, Sam and John Phillips, and Sandy Constantine.

By 1937 Eveleth found themselves without a league again. So, they formed a new senior circuit called the International Hockey League. They were joined by teams from Hibbing, Duluth, Port Arthur and Fort William. Later Fort William and Port Arthur dropped out and were replaced by Fort Frances. And, as in the CHL before, most of the players were from Eveleth. Unfortunately, due to the commencement of World War II in 1940, and the fact that so many of our boys were sent off to battle, the league disbanded. However, the league was soon replaced by a strong four-team industrial league which was based in Duluth during the war years.

In 1938 the Hipp was completely renovated, with brick replacing the old wooden walls. A new lobby was added along the south side of the building, additional seating was built, and locker rooms were added to the basement. The original steel beams and trusses were renovated, with everything else being replaced for the sum of $150,000. (The rink's natural ice remained though, until 1950, when artificial ice was finally installed.)

After World War II, Eveleth bounced around in several senior league's. The first was the Northern Amateur League, a senior circuit, which was formed in the early 1940s with teams from Eveleth, Duluth, Hibbing, Virginia, and Fort Frances. The league prospered through the decade, and finally disbanded in 1951. That same year Eveleth, along with Hibbing, Minneapolis, St. Paul, Rochester, and Sioux City, decided to join the American Amateur Hockey Association. The AAHA changed its name to the Central Hockey League for that next season of 1952-53. Eveleth, however, decided to withdraw from the CHL after only one year. Then, in the fall of 1954, the Eveleth Rangers joined the upstart "international" Thunder Bay Senior League, which consisted of five teams: Eveleth, Hibbing, Fort William, Fort Frances, and Port Arthur. (See Senior Hockey Chapter for more info) However, in 1955, after only one season, the league folded due to financial problems. This ultimately ended Eveleth's participation in Minnesota Senior Open competitions.

One of the greatest high school lines ever was Eveleth's 1945 trio of Neil Celley, Pat Finnegan and Wally Grant

The First High School Dynasty
There are perhaps but a few things in life which are more synonymous with Minnesota than that of high school hockey and the town of Eveleth. It can claim, arguably, the greatest all-time high school hockey program in the history of our country. It's history is a fascinating story within itself.

Eveleth Junior College

Incidentally, Eveleth Junior College was an institution in itself. So good was the team in fact, that in 1928, along with the University Club of Boston, Harvard University, University of Minnesota and Augsburg College, it was considered as a candidate by the United States Olympic Committee - under the chairmanship of General Douglas MacArthur, to represent the United States in the 1928 Winter Olympic Games in Amsterdam, Holland. However, due to a lack of financial backing, Eveleth Junior College respectfully declined the invitation to serve as the U.S. Olympic squad. (Ultimately, the USA was not represented at the 1928 Winter Games.)

In 1928-29, according to the college hockey ranking system of Princeton University's professor Theodore Tonnele, Eveleth Junior College was ranked as the number one college team in the nation, followed by Yale, the University of Minnesota, and Clarkson which was fourth. Eveleth J.C. was considered to be a power-house, and one of the reasons for its success was due, in large part, to its feeder system - the high school team, which was also coached by Thompson. Ironically, the toughest opponent that the J.C. faced that year was the Eveleth High School team, which they narrowly beat by the score of 4-3. That year was the best ever for the J.C., as they finished the season undefeated and went on to win college hockey's National Championship.

Thompson coached the Eveleth Junior College team from 1928-40, and recorded an amazing record of 171-28-7.

National Ranking of Collegiate Hockey Teams, 1928-1929

BY THEODORE MILLS TONNELE (PRINCETON).

As the result of a number of years' study of the ranking of college athletic teams, the writer has concluded that a pragmatic formula may be devised for any sport, which, upon application to any group of teams, will result in a surprisingly sound ranking of them.

A formula worked out for, and applied to, the collegiate hockey teams throughout the country, gives the following ranking for the past season:

A TEAMS.

Ranking Order.	Team.	Index No.	Ranking Order.	Team.	Index No.
1.	Eveleth Junior Coll.	(19.00)	6.	Harvard	(10.38)
2.	Yale	(16.60)	7.	Marquette	(9.55)
3.	Minnesota	(16.08)	8.	Princeton	(9.50)
4.	Clarkson	(14.00)	9.	Wisconsin	(6.33)
5.	Dartmouth	(11.44)	10.	Michigan	(4.36)

B1 TEAMS.

Ranking Order.	Team.	Index No.	Ranking Order.	Team.	Index No.
11.	Boston Coll.	(4.00)	18.	Mass. Inst. Tech.	(.87)
11.	St. Mary's (Minn.)	(4.00)	19.	Cornell	(.63)
13.	California (Berkly.)	(3.50)	20.	Brown	(.33)
14.	Michigan Tech	(2.67)	20.	Colgate	(.33)
15.	Williams	(1.50)	22.	New Hampshire	(.05)
16.	Middlebury	(1.17)			
16.	St. Lawrence	(1.17)			

High School hockey was first played informally in Eveleth around the turn of the century, but the first official Eveleth varsity high school team was organized in 1920. The townspeople had the foresight to see the potential of giving their youth as many opportunities as possible, and backed the program through extensive volunteering and support. They pressed for new rinks, and worked in harmony with the Recreation Commission, Eveleth school system and the City of Eveleth in order to provide their kids with the best facilities as possible.

The team's first coach was Ade Johnson, a Canadian import from Winnipeg who also starred for the semipro Eveleth Reds. Members of that first high school squad who played under Ade's tutelage included: Matt Lahti, Aro Ellison, Pete Brascugli, Tito Muscatelli, Bill La Vigne, Roy Damberg and Ted Juola.

Their competition during those first years included playing against other local teams which included Duluth Central, Virginia and Hibbing. Later, in the 1920s, the Rams played other teams such as: Duluth Denfeld, Fort Frances and Chisholm. On March 19, 1923, Eveleth beat St. Paul Mechanic Arts High School 9-2 on its home ice, for what was called back then as the state "mythical title." They repeated the feat two years later in a rematch at the Minneapolis Arena on March 14, 1925, this time narrowly beating Mechanic Arts 3-2. (Incidentally, there were four members of that 1925 team that later turned professional -- Billy De Paul, Glee Jagunich, Oscar Almquist and Tony Prelesnik.)

In 1926 an important event happened that forever would change the landscape of Eveleth hockey. That year Ade Johnson stepped down has the team's head coach and was replaced by Cliff Thompson. Thompson, a former Minneapolis Central and University of Minnesota player, who is considered even today as the most celebrated high school hockey coach in our state's history, also decided to take over the reigns as the coach of the Eveleth Junior College.

Under Thompson's direction, Eveleth High School quickly gained a reputation as the team to beat in the state of Minnesota, and before long teams from the Twin Cities were lining up to take a crack at the boys from the Range. Eveleth held strong though, and answered most every challenge given to them. By 1929, the Golden Bears were riding an unbelievable winning streak, not having lost a game in more than three years against all of the Iron Range and Duluth schools. That year a metro high school all-star team of sorts, called the Cardinals, was assembled by former Minneapolis Miller great Nick Kahler. The Cards, who had won the Minneapolis Recreation title that year, was composed primarily of players from Minneapolis South and West High Schools. The Cards and Bears would do battle that year in front of a packed house at the Minneapolis Arena, with the all-star team edging Eveleth in a thriller by the narrow margin of 2-1. An idea of the caliber of talent on the ice that night was personified by the fact that six of the eleven Eveleth players and five of the eleven Minneapolis players would later play professional hockey.

Eveleth's Icy Reign of Terror

Eveleth continued to dominate hockey through the 1930s, and even through the years of the Great Depression. One of the reasons for this was due to the fact that people such as coach Thompson made sure that all of his kids had a good pair of skates under their feet as well as quality protective equipment around them. By the 1940s more and more schools were playing hockey, and it was inevitable that a state-wide tournament would come to fruition. And, in 1945, mainly through the efforts hockey pioneer Gene Aldrich of St. Paul, that's just what happened when the Minnesota State High School League hosted the first-ever boys state high school hockey tournament at the St. Paul Auditorium.

Thompson led his squad to that first tournament and showed the rest of Minnesota what the people on the Range had known for years -- Eveleth was awesome! Led by what many still consider today to be the greatest ever high school hockey line of Pat Finnegan, Wally Grant and Neil Celley, the Golden Bears breezed through the tourney and captured the state's first ever crown.

The Golden Bears shut out Granite Falls 16-0 in their first quarter-final game, and in so doing set a rather unique record that still stands today: "LEAST STOPS BY A GOAL-TENDER" -- ONE, by Eveleth's Ron Drobnick," (On a shot from center ice nonetheless!)

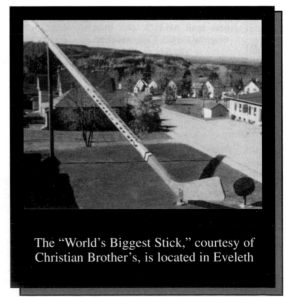

The "World's Biggest Stick," courtesy of Christian Brother's, is located in Eveleth

Eveleth rolled over St. Paul Washington 10-0 in the semifinal contest, and went on to edge a strong Thief River Falls team 4-3 for the title. Wally Grant, who would later star as a member of the infamous "G" line at the University of Michigan, tallied both the tying and go-ahead goals in that championship game.

That next season, in 1946, Eveleth narrowly missed a repeat title finishing third, only to see one of their own native son's bring home the hardware instead. That's because former Eveleth goaltender Oscar Almquist, a former Golden Ram back in the 1920s, who went on to star at St. Mary's College and later for the St. Paul Saints, coached Roseau High School to its first title. Almquist, better known as the "Giant of the North," would go on to quite a prolific coaching tenure himself. Upon retiring in 1967, after 28 years behind the bench, Almquist led Roseau to 14 state tournaments en route to winning four state titles, while compiling an amazing record of 406-150-51.

Eveleth continued its domination of the event through 1956. During that 12-year span the Golden Bears won five championships, twice finished as runners-up and claimed three third place finishes. The team earned a berth in the first 12 state tournaments and rode two amazing winning streaks of 79 and 58 games. One era in particular was the greatest possibly in the history of high school sports. That was from 1948 to 1951, when the team posted a perfect 69-0 record over four consecutive undefeated seasons en route to winning four straight titles. Incidentally, Eveleth's unbelievable winning streak ended in 1952 when Iron Range rival Hibbing bested the Golden Bears 4-3 in the title game.

Those incredible Eveleth teams were led by so many outstanding young men, including the likes of John Matchefts and Willard Ikola. But one man stands alone when it comes to "legendary status" and the high school hockey in Minnesota during that era -- John Mayasich is arguably the greatest player ever to lace up a pair of skates in Minnesota. Mayasich still holds 10 scoring records in the state tournament including most all-time points (46) and goals (36). But 1951 was the year Mayasich stole the show when he amassed 18 points in three games on 15 goals and three assists, including seven goals in a semifinal win over Minneapolis Southwest. Of course, Mayasich went on to become an All-American at the University of Minnesota, where he rewrote the Gopher record book, scoring 144 goals and 298 total points. He went on to become the only player ever to compete on eight U.S. National or Olympic teams, and has earned the title of "the greatest American ever to play the game."

Some of the outstanding players from

John Mayasich

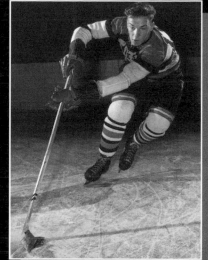

John Mayasich has long been regarded as one of the finest amateur hockey players ever produced in the United States, and is without question the greatest to ever lace em' up in Minnesota.

Mayasich grew up playing hockey in Eveleth. "We got our start learning hockey on the ponds and outdoor rinks in the city," recalled Mayasich. "The older kids would pick sides and the younger kids would learn from them. It went on from generation to generation. When the ice melted, we played street hockey and broomball. We had a lot of fun and we learned a lot playing those sports as well."

After leading the Eveleth High School team to an amazing run of four consecutive undefeated state championship seasons from 1948-51, Mayasich headed to the University of Minnesota, where he would join up with another Eveleth hockey legend, Gopher coach John Mariucci. There, John led the Gophers to a couple of NCAA Final Fours, and took college hockey by storm. Before his career was over, the perennial All-American had tallied Gopher records of 298 career points and 144 goals. His totals worked out to an incredible 1.4 goals per game average with nearly three points per game. (To put it into perspective, Pat Micheletti, the next Gopher player on the career goal-scoring list, has 24 fewer goals despite playing in 51 more games. In other words, in his 162 games, Micheletti would have had to amass 435 points just to match Mayasich's per-game average. That's an additional 166 more than his career total!) Mayasich also holds the Minnesota records for most goals and most points in a single game. In his senior year, he had an incredible six-goal game against Winnipeg and also tallied eight points against Michigan that same season. At the end of his playing career with the Gophers, Mayasich fulfilled his military obligations and then went on to star on the 1956 silver medal-winning U.S. Olympic hockey team in Cortina, Italy.

This was the dawn of modern hockey in Minnesota, and Mayasich was rewriting the record books as he went along. He was a "velvety-smooth skater," with a keen, sixth sense into the psyche of the goalie's every move. He is credited as being the first college hockey player to develop the slap shot, a new weapon that instilled fear into an already perplexed group of goaltenders who tried to stop him. John was an artist with his stick and his stick-handling skills were legendary. On opponent's power-plays, he could kill penalties by toying with opposing defenses. He used to take the puck and simply weave around the rink without ever passing to a teammate until the penalty had been killed. With amazing ability like that, it's hard to believe that he was often criticized for passing too much.

"The camaraderie was the best, those friendships go back 40 years now," recalled Mayasich on his playing days at the U of M. "Playing with the players who I had played against through my high school career was really exciting. We had great Gopher players like Dick Mere, Dick Dougherty, Gene Campbell, Ken Yackel, Wendy Anderson, and Stan Hubbard. I got to see the world through hockey, and the purity of the game is the bond that keeps these friendships together today. It was quite a time to be involved with the Gopher program as it was just taking off back then. It made me proud of the fact that I was there when all of this was happening. Now, to see what the program has grown into today, and to think that maybe, in a small way that I had something to do with it, is incredible. My time at the U of M was great."

Following college, he went on to play with eight U.S. Olympic and National teams. Declining professional hockey opportunities in the then six-team NHL, Mayasich devoted his remaining hockey career to the Green Bay Bobcats. In 1969, he was named coach of the U.S. National team. Mayasich received numerous honors during his hockey days, including being the first Minnesotan to be voted into the National High School Athletic Hall of Fame. In 1976 he had a homecoming of sorts, being inducted into the U.S. Hockey Hall of Fame in his native Eveleth.

"John Mayasich brought college hockey to a new plateau," said John Mariucci. "He was the Wayne Gretzky of his time, and if he were playing pro hockey today, he would simply be a bigger, stronger, back-checking Gretzky. The words to describe him haven't been invented. When I say he's the best, that's totally inadequate."

Cliff Thompson, Don Clark and Bob Ridder (L to R) at the Hall of Fame

that era were: Neil Celley, Wally Grant, Pat Finnegan, Clem Cossalter, John Matchefts, Willard Ikola, John Mayasich, Ron Castellano, Dan Voce, Dick Peterson, Ed Mrcronich, Andre Gambucci, Ron Martinson, Gene Klune, Bruce Shutte, Bob Kochevar, Ed Ostwald, Dave Rodda, Mike Castellano, and Dave Hendrickson.

Eveleth Hockey's Mother Lode

The answer to why Eveleth is considered as the Hockey Capital of America can be traced back like a family tree. Young boys from this community branched out across the country and laid down roots for other hockey players to grow from. Gilbert Finnegan, former Eveleth postmaster and hockey historian stated that during one particular season during the 1930s Great Depression era, there were 147 Eveleth boys playing hockey on professional, college, semi-pro and senior open teams located throughout the United States.

It seemed that wherever hockey was being played in the country Eveleth players were right in the mix of things. In many cities around the country, large companies who had their own hockey teams would stack their rosters entirely with Eveleth boys. Companies who wanted to secure a winning hockey team, made sure to take care of the Eveleth boys by giving them good jobs in an attempt to secure their services. In turn, a pipeline of sorts was created back to Eveleth. Wanting to take care of their own, players soon insisted upon "package deals," which helped them get their friends and family the opportunity of a good job as well. Even during the Depression, Eveleth boys were finding good jobs around the country, and easing the job crunch and hard economic times back home on the Range. Hockey had gone from a game, to a meal ticket into greener pastures.

One such company was Hershey's Chocolate, in Pennsylvania, which had a team of all Eveleth players. Led by the Papike brothers, a team from San Diego won a string of Pacific Coast League titles throughout the 1930s with a squad composed almost entirely of Eveleth players. In 1935 the National AAU tournament in Chicago, featured 10 different teams from across the country. Nearly two-thirds of the players on those combined rosters were from Eveleth. The winning Chicago Baby Ruth team, coached by Eveleth's Connie Pleban, had nine Eveleth natives on its 13-man roster. That same Chicago Baby Ruth team went on to beat a very strong St. Cloud Teachers College 2-0 in the National AAU Tournament. Incidentally, that St. Cloud team which posted a 45-7-0 record that year, was manned almost entirely by Eveleth players. By the late 1930s Vic Heyliger, the coach at the University of Michigan had 13 kids from Eveleth on his team. And, the University of Illinois had at one time a complete roster of Eveleth boys. In addition, during the late 1930's and early 1940's countless Eveleth players migrated to the West Coast to play college hockey, where the allure of sunshine, a good job and good education awaited. As a result, some of the best college hockey in the country was played at USC, UCLA, Loyola, and Cal.

And of course, there were four Eveleth boys on the 1956 silver-medal winning Olympic team held in Cortina, Italy: John Mayasich, John Matchefts, and Willard Ikola, who was named the most valuable player in the Olympic competition. The coach of that squad was none other than John Mariucci.

By the mid-point of the century, Eveleth had become a household name in the world of hockey. Considered as the hub of the Messabe, Vermilion, and Cuyuna Iron Ranges - which at one time produced nearly 80 percent of the world's iron ore, that in turn was used to make everything from automobiles, machines and skyscrapers, Eveleth's real "mother lode" was its exportation of top-notch players to the world of hockey. This community had embraced the sport of hockey like no other before or after, and was handsomely rewarded by the fact that it is today synonymous with the game. These Iron Rangers were passionate about sports, and not just about hockey. The sports scene in Eveleth was so intense even back in the 1920s, that they even imported a couple of refugees from the now infamous Chicago "Black Sox" team, who were banned from baseball for life for throwing the 1919 World Series, to play summer baseball on the town team. (Maybe "Shoeless" Joe Jackson himself learned to play hockey in Eveleth?)

As mentioned before, Eveleth was and still is an incredible melting pot of cultures, languages and nationalities, all brought together by the prosperity of mining. Those same mining company's used to put men of different nationality's together down in the mine's on purpose, figuring that if they couldn't speak with one another because of the language barrier, that they would, in turn, work more. But in the end, all those immigrants fooled them, by learning bits and pieces of each other's languages and culture. In the end, they celebrated their colorful diversity, while hockey gave them all a common bond in which to pull together for. Eveleth is to American hockey what Detroit is to cars and Hollywood is to film making. Its story is one of the most unique and special in all of 20th century sports.

The United States Hockey Hall of Fame: Eveleth, MN

Perhaps the most telling sign that Eveleth is indeed the hockey capital of the USA, is the fact that the U.S. Hockey Hall of Fame is located there. "Why," you might ask, "is a national shrine of this significance dedicated to United States hockey, located in a town of merely 5,000 citizens?" The answer is simple. Eveleth was chosen for its unique long-standing history and incredible contribution to American hockey. And, perhaps most importantly, is the fact that no town of its size has ever produced more elite-level players in the history of the game.

There are several reasons as to why Eveleth is so hockey crazy. Among them include the fact that when the sport of ice hockey spread to the U.S. down from Canada just before the turn of the century, Eveleth, which was situated on rail lines, was one of the many small towns where the game took hold. In the beginning, the superior Canadian players were

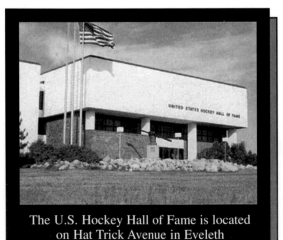

The U.S. Hockey Hall of Fame is located on Hat Trick Avenue in Eveleth

imported down to Eveleth to play for the pro teams. In return they were given good paying jobs in the mines. This ultimately served as a wonderful form of entertainment for the miners and their families. Eventually, the game rubbed off on the kids in town who grew up wanting to emulate these new stars, and before they knew it, a whole generation of superstar hockey players was born.

There is a reason that the four major hall's of fame's are located in the small town's that they are. For instance, Abner Doubleday, the founder of baseball, has roots back to Cooperstown, NY, and that is why the Baseball Hall of Fame is located there. Jim Thorpe was from Canton, Ohio, and that surely played into why the Football Hall of Fame is located there as well. And, Dr. James Naysmith first played his newly created sport of basketball in Springfield, Mass., not coincidentally where the Basketball Hall of Fame resides today. As for that "other" Hockey Hall of Fame, that one is located in Toronto, Canada. There are but a handful of Americans enshrined into the National Hockey Hall of Fame, in Toronto. Perhaps that led to the decision in 1967 to form an exploratory committee into the idea of creating a U.S. Hockey Hall of Fame. The U.S. Hall of Fame was not created to compete with the Canadian Hall, rather it was built to celebrate the accomplishments of Americans, in a game that up until recently was dominated by Canadians.

How the Hall began is an interesting story in itself. In 1967 a committee from the Eveleth Civic Association, known as the Project H Committee, began an intensive historical search program to determine candidates (other American cities) who they felt were worthy of being host cities to the Hockey Hall of Fame. Their extensive research showed that since the late 1800s, no other town had contributed as much to hockey's development; and no state had contributed more than Minnesota. So, on May 19,1968 they requested the official endorsement from the Amateur Hockey Association of the United States (AHAUS) in Boston. AHAUS gave their blessings to the project, and by 1973 the three-story U.S. Hockey Hall of Fame & Museum was completed on Hat Trick Avenue in Eveleth.

The non-profit corporation, United States Hockey Hall of Fame, Inc. was chartered in the state of Minnesota in 1968 and its first officers and directors included nine members from AHAUS: Robert Ridder, Walter Rush, Don Clark, J. Lawrence Cain, Edward Stanley, Charles Kunkle, William Thayer Tutt, Cal Marvin, and Robert Fleming. From the Project H Committee, representing Eveleth, were Larry Doyle, Tony Nemanich, and D. Kelly Campbell. (Campbell, a native of Michigan, and mining executive with the Ogleby-Norton and Eveleth Taconite companies, is the person perhaps most responsible for seeing the idea of the Hall come to fruition.)

By bringing the past to the present and to the future, the Hall serves as the focal point for preserving the history and heritage of American Hockey. Today the Hall of Fame is going through a multi-million dollar,

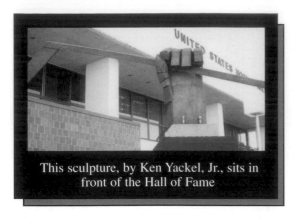

This sculpture, by Ken Yackel, Jr., sits in front of the Hall of Fame

three-phase renovation. Working in harmony with USA Hockey, the NHL, and amateur hockey associations throughout Minnesota as well as the United States, the Hall has ensured that hockey fans from around the world will have the type of museum the sport richly deserves well into the 21st century.

(Incredibly, nearly 10 percent of the Hall of Fame's inductee's are from Eveleth. Those 11 individuals (which represent more than any other U.S. city), are: Sam LoPresti, Frank Brimsek, Mike Karakas, Oscar Almquist, John Mayasich, John Mariucci, John Matchefts, Willard Ikola, Connie Pleban, Wally Grant, and Serge Gambucci.)

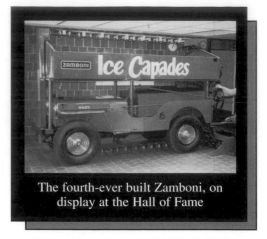

The fourth-ever built Zamboni, on display at the Hall of Fame

"The Hall is really a shrine dedicated to the contributions of those individuals who have helped put the United States on the hockey map with the rest of the world," said Jim Findley, the Hall's president. "Its goal is to celebrate the memories of its enshrinees and their contributions to the game, and in keeping with those goals, celebrating our 25th anniversary last year was a very exciting time for us. More and more people are stepping up to help us move forward, and our new renovation project is just fantastic. In judging from the feedback we have already received from our most recent improvements and additions, the Hall will be in excellent shape for many, many years to come."

The Godfather of Minnesota Hockey: Eveleth's John Mariucci

JOHN MARIUCCI DAY

The University of Minnesota's John Mariucci was the venerable godfather of American amateur hockey and the patriarch of the puck sport in our state. What John did for the sport was immeasurable. With his passion for competing, teaching, and spreading the gospel about the sport he loved, Maroosh went on to become the country's most important figure in the development of amateur hockey in America.

John Mariucci was born the son of Italian immigrants on May 8, 1916, in the birthplace of hockey in the United States, Eveleth, Minn., on the great Mesabi Iron Range. He grew up on Hay Street, also referred to by locals as "Incubator Street" because it was said that there were so many nationalities living there, and every house had eight or nine kids inside. Many of the kids would play hockey to simply stay out of trouble. Some kids didn't even have skates, so they wore overshoes, and others used tree branches for sticks. Young Johnny found his first pair of skates in a garbage can and, because he didn't have money to buy proper equipment, wrapped old magazines around his shins for pads.

Even though it was a mid-sized Minnesota Iron Range town, Eveleth was as sophisticated as New York City when it came to hockey. Eveleth was once a member of a big league pro hockey circuit that competed with cities around North America. Eveleth kids would try to emulate the many Canadians who were imported to the city to play hockey as one of the forms of entertainment provided for iron ore miners. John learned the game from legendary hall of fame coach Cliff Thompson whose tenure as the Eveleth High School hockey coach lasted nearly 40 years.

In 1936, Maroosh left Eveleth and the Range and headed 200 miles south to the University of Minnesota. There he starred as a defenseman for Larry Armstrong's hockey team and also played offensive and defensive end alongside of Butch Nash under the Gophers' legendary football coach Bernie Bierman. Although Mariucci played in between two bookend National Championship teams in 1936 and 1940, he did lead the Gophers to the Big Ten football title in 1938. "I believe I have the only lineman in America who can extract people's teeth with his fists on the line of scrimmage," said Bernie about his star end Mariucci.

In 1940, led by Bud Wilkinson, the future football coaching legend at the University of Oklahoma in the nets, Mariucci captained the National AAU Championship hockey team (at the time it was the only championship available in college hockey). After that season, Maroosh, who had been named to the All-American team, was offered the head coaching position at the U, but turned it down to play hockey professionally.

After a brief stint with Providence in the American Hockey League, Maroosh joined the Chicago Blackhawks to finish out the 1940 season. At that time the NHL employed few Americans and not many college-bred players. (To put this into perspective, by 1968, only six Americans and five collegians had played in the NHL.) Johnny played there until 1942, when he was summoned to join the United States Coast Guard. There he played for the Coast Guard team in the Eastern Amateur League during WWII. After turning down another offer to return to the U of M, he returned to the Hawks for the 1945 season. In 1947, Maroosh became the first American-developed player ever to captain an NHL team.

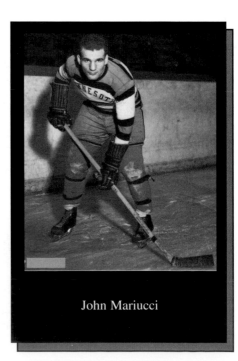

John Mariucci

The rugged Maroosh was one of the biggest celebrities in Chicago during his playing days there. He became famous among Windy City hockey fans for his brawls, one in particular with Detroit's Black Jack Stewart, which remains the NHL's longest ever, lasting more than 20 minutes. In 1948, Maroosh called it quits in Chicago. For his career in the NHL, he scored 11 goals and 34 assists for 45 points over 223 games. He also played in two Stanley Cup playoffs. More importantly, he led the team in penalty minutes, racking up more than 300 over his career. He was a role-playing hatchet man who protected and defended his teammates. That's why they loved and appreciated him.

Mariucci went on to play for St. Louis of the American League, St. Paul and Minneapolis of the United States League, and again with a Coast Guard team before hanging up his skates as an active player in 1951. After a storied career in pro hockey, he then turned to coaching, where he was named the coach of Minneapolis Millers hockey team of the A.A.L.

After a year with the Millers, Maroosh took over as the coach of his Gopher alma mater, replacing former Blackhawk Doc Romnes. It was only a part-time job for him, as he continued to also work as a salesman for the Martin Falk Paper Company.

On December 4, 1946, Chicago's John Mariucci and Detroit's Black Jack Stewart fought toe-to-toe for more than 20 minutes in one of the NHL's longest-ever brawls

"It's a good thing for me not to have to depend upon the hockey job for my livelihood," said Mariucci. "Financial independence removes me from the absolute necessity of producing a winning team, and the worry and pressure connected with it which might make me resort to some actions which -- well, you know, which are not quite above the board." In his first season he was awarded Coach of the Year honors. It was the first of many.

He got Minneapolis residents excited about college hockey, and they responded by coming out in droves to see his Gophers. The U even had to add an upper tier of seats to the Williams Arena rink to accommodate them all. Maroosh was always trying new things to keep the fans interested and was always looking for new recruits. One time while watching the giant six-foot-eleven center Bill Simonovich, from Gilbert, Minn., play with the varsity basketball team, John said: "Man, what a goalie he'd make! Give him a couple of mattresses and a pair of skis and nobody would ever score on him."

In a sport dominated by Canadians, Maroosh championed the American boys and in particular, Minnesotans. After watching an NCAA Final one time, he said: "It's asinine that the only two Americans on the ice for the NCAA championship game were the referees." Maroosh was a visionary and saw the potential growth of the sport.

"College could be a developmental program for our own country, for the Olympics and for the pros," he said. "College hockey is a state institution and should be represented by Minnesota boys," said Maroosh. "If they're not quite as good as some Canadians, we'll just have to work a little harder, that's all." It became political for Mariucci as he battled to stop the importation of the older Canadian players and give the American kids an equal playing field. In the late 1950s, the U's athletic director, Marsh Ryman, refused to play Denver's Canadian-filled teams. This ultimately led to the end of the WIHL and the creation of the WCHA in 1959.

"What I was against was the junior player who played in Canada until he was 21, then, if the pros didn't sign him, he would come to this country to play college hockey as a 22-year-old freshman against our 18-year-olds," said Mariucci. "It wasn't fair to our kids, who were finishing college at the same age Canadians were freshmen."

Mariucci left the University in 1966 with a record of 207-142-15, including conference championships in 1953 and 1954 and three NCAA playoff appearances (including Final Four appearances in 1953, '54 and '61). Although he never won the NCAA championship during his 14-year tenure at the U of M, he came pretty darn close in both 1953 and 1954 with the best line ever to play college hockey: John Mayasich, Dick Dougherty and Gene Campbell. In 1954 the Gophers lost a heart-breaking overtime game to R.P.I. in the NCAA Championship match, something that haunted Mariucci for years. Included in his tenure was an Italian homecoming of sorts, when he was led the Americans to a silver medal in the 1956 Olympics in Cortina. There were 11 Minnesota natives on the team that stunned heavily favored Canada before falling to the Soviet Union in the finals. Mariucci's successor at the U was Glen Sonmor, a former teammate and protégé with the Minneapolis Millers.

In 1966, another chapter of Mariucci's storied life unfolded as he became chief scout and special assistant to Wren Blair, GM of the NHL's expansion North Stars. There Maroosh applied his vast knowledge of recruiting, coaching, and scouting. In 1977, Mariucci coached the U.S. National team. He later rejoined the North Stars, this time as assistant GM under his former player, Lou Nanne. "One word of advice to all you coaches," said Maroosh. "Be good to your players; you never know which one might someday be your boss."

"Herbie," "Maroosh" and "Badger"

Mariucci was always a favorite of his players, and used to love telling them stories. Once, following a poor road trip, then Star's coach Wren Blair ordered an early-morning practice, as a sort of punishment for the players. That next morning, Maroosh, who was supposed to be disciplining the team, started telling some of his patented stories to the fellas. As they all sat in the bench and shot the breeze together, Maroosh would periodically stop in mid-sentence and blow his whistle. This went on for a while until one of the players asked him why the hell he was blowing his whistle. In a classic Maroosh retort, he responded simply: "In case Wren is listening, I want him to think I'm putting you guys through stops and starts!"

The Noble Roman

Described as "the noblest Roman of them all" (a line from Shakespeare's play "Julius Caesar"), John's accomplishments and honors are far too great to list here. Some of his more notable honors include being inducted as a charter member of the U.S. Hockey Hall of Fame in his hometown of Eveleth; being inducted into the NHL Hockey Hall of Fame in Toronto; and receiving the NHL's coveted Lester Patrick Award for his contributions to U.S. hockey. He also made a difference by giving to others. Maroosh devoted much of his life to something very dear to him, Camp Confidence, in Brainerd. The camp was dedicated to the belief that the mentally-retarded citizens of Minnesota have the right to experience life to the fullest. In addition, the "Mariucci Inner City Hockey Program" was honored by the NHL and given a $10,000 A.S.S.I.S.T. (Assist Skaters and Shooters in Succeeding Together) grant, to help promote the game to minorities.

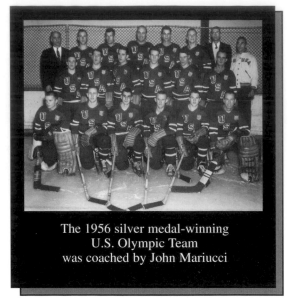

The 1956 silver medal-winning
U.S. Olympic Team
was coached by John Mariucci

On March 2, 1985, in an emotional ceremony to give thanks and immortalize the man forever, the U of M renamed the hockey half of Williams Arena as Mariucci Arena, in his honor. It was also declared John Mariucci Day in Minnesota by Governor Rudy Perpich. During the ceremony, long-time Maroosh friend Robert Ridder said: "During the 1980 Olympics, a U.S. Destroyer passed a Russian ship and signaled to it: 'USA 4, Russia 3.' Probably nobody on that boat ever heard of John Mariucci, but it wouldn't have been possible without John Mariucci." Two years later, on March 24, 1987, Maroosh died at the age of 70 after a long bout with cancer. He had seven children and several grandchildren.

Maroosh was a legend, on and off the ice. Although he was tough as nails, his wit, intelligence, and personality were one-of-a-kind. John was one of the toughest Italians who ever lived. His face has often been referred to as a "blocked punt," because it was so beat up. But what separated him from the goons was that he wouldn't just knock his opponents down, he'd pick them up and then make them laugh at his jokes.

"He was simply the bravest, guttiest man in sports," said the late Hall of Famer Bobby Dill, one of the toughest humans ever to lace 'em up. "I played against, or have seen all of the greatest enforcers and game breakers in the last 45 years. No question for sheer competitive ferocity, Mariucci and Eddie Shore were the two all time greats. Strong men backed down to them. They played every game like it was the seventh game of the Stanley Cup."

"One time Maroosh was playing in a game against a Kansas City farm team," said fellow Eveleth native and former Edina High School coach Willard Ikola. "A rookie gave Maroosh some stitches in that big honker he had with a cheap shot. Maroosh tried to run him down, but the kid, realizing who he had whacked, jumped right over the boards and ran up the stairs. Maroosh jumped up and followed him right outside. Sparks were flying from their skates as they ran up the stairs as Maroosh was yelling at him from behind. He chased him right out into the street in front of the arena, and then calmly walked back down the stairs to the ice. He was even talking to the ladies in the stands on his way back down. He went on the ice and finished his shift like nothing had happened. The next night Maroosh was still mad, but the front office wanted the kid who hit him to get some playing time, because he was going to come up to the team shortly from the farm club in Kansas City. John agreed, but only if the kid came up to him and apologized in person. That night the kid came to John's room and apologized in fear, and Maroosh laughed it off telling him to keep his damn stick down next time. Big John, the captain, took the kid under his wing after that, and helped him out. That's the kind of guy John Mariucci was."

Former player Herb Brooks, who described Maroosh as "father-like," probably said it best: "In all social causes to better an institution, there's always got to be a rallying force, a catalyst, a glue, and a magnet, and that's what John was, for American hockey. The rest of us just filled in after him." Full of wit, he was described as a newspaperman's dream-come-true. From his infamous antics, which included once breaking thumb-wrestling champion Murray Warmath's thumb, Mariucci gained a lot of mileage. Local reporters found themselves having a lot of dinners that turned into breakfasts while listening to his endless stories. The sports community was in awe of him, and he made journalists who hated the sport want to cover hockey.

He was also the pioneer in the development of hockey in Minnesota. Because of that, his legacy will live on forever. Every kid that laces up his or her skates needs to give thanks to the man that started it all. He started grass-roots youth programs, put on coaching clinics, attended new arena openings in countless cities across the state, helped former players find coaching positions, and even encouraged hockey moms to write to city councils to build rinks and develop recreation programs. Because of John Mariucci, hockey in Minnesota carries the same pedigree as basketball in Indiana or football in Texas. Described as father-like, magical, and even super-human, by nearly everyone that knew him, he was the most sacred of Minnesota cows.

The Minnesota North Stars (1967-1993 R.I.P)

Watching the Minnesota North Stars, er... sorry... Dallas Stars, win the Stanley Cup this past June was particularly painful. I think back to how close we came in 1981 and 1991 to winning it all, and just can't help but think that if it wasn't for that ?%@#!! Norm Green, maybe Lord Stanley's Cup would be here this summer, rather than in Texas. Like Dallas hasn't screwed us enough in sports! It was bad enough that the Dallas Cowboys jobbed us on that ridiculous "Hail Mary" pass in the 1975 NFC Playoffs (Yes, Pearson pushed off!!), and then they pawned off that stiff Herschell on us... OK, I'm bitter, and definitely have some issues here. First of all, let's get the facts straight. Contrary to popular belief, the Stars did not leave town because the fans didn't support them. That was a crock. They became the Texas "Lone Stars" because the owner decided to pack up and move them there for personal reasons. Period. The North Stars' attendance averaged more than 12,000 fans per

game in their last decade in Minnesota, and were outdrawing the majority of NHL clubs around the league. We supported them, and we got screwed!

Anyway, since 1967 our Stars had done us proud at the old Met Center in Bloomington. But today, regrettably, both are gone for good. Sure the Minnesota Wild will be here in 2001, complete with a brand spankin' new arena and all. But nothing was quite like tailgating with your pals at a Stars game. There were plenty of peaks and valley's with our Stars, but they were always the best show in town. So come on and take a trip down memory lane, and reminisce about one of Minnesota's greatest sports franchises, the North Stars.

By the mid-1960s, the Minneapolis Bruins and St. Paul Rangers were the only pro hockey teams in town. Both teams were minor league affiliates of the Boston Bruins and New York Rangers, respectively. Sure the Gopher Hockey team was competitive at that point, but there wasn't a professional hockey presence in town anywhere close to that of the big league's -- the NHL. Now, during this period of time, pro sports was absolutely booming in Minnesota. The Twins and Vikings had both just arrived in 1961-62, and on top of that, the Gopher Football team was in its heyday, recently winning the National Championship and Rose Bowl during that same time period. Knowing this, one could understand why there would be some skepticism about the fact that in 1965, the NHL decided to expand from its original six, to twelve teams, and a group from Minnesota was making a run at getting one of those coveted franchises. Minnesotans didn't know if the community at large could support another professional team. And on top of that, just where in the heck would they play?

The kingpin of that group leading the charge to seduce the NHL to Minnesota, was attorney, Walter Bush Jr. Bush, a former prep hockey star at Minneapolis' Breck School, played collegiately at Dartmouth, and also in the semipro ranks both as a player and coach. At the time, the former Olympic team manager was a part-owner of the Minneapolis Bruins, a minor league farm-team of the NHL's Boston Bruins. Bush's co-owners included two other Minneapolis businessmen; television executive Gordon Ritz, and ex-Yale Hockey captain and real-estate developer Robert McNulty. Now, with all of the competitive sports in town during that time, combined with the fact that the Minneapolis Bruins were forced to play in an antique arena, the group was finding it very difficult to sell their product to the public. So, they started a dialogue with Wes Adams, the Boston Bruins chairman of the board, about lobbying for one of the new NHL expansion franchises to be located in Minnesota. With 14 formal applications sent in from cities all across North America, the competition for one of the half dozens teams was fierce. The group knew that if they were going to have a shot at big-time hockey in Minnesota, they would have to come up with some big dough.

Bush immediately seized the opportunity by putting together an eight-man investment group, comprised of two groups, each from both sides of the Mississippi. He figured that it was going to take a group effort to raise the dollars necessary, and didn't want to alienate the folks from St. Paul. From the Mill City side of town, investment banker Wheelock Whitney joined Bush, Ritz, and McNulty, while from St. Paul came television executive Bob Ridder, business executive John Ordway, lumber company executive John Driscoll, and trucking mogul Harry McNeely. (Later William Rasmussen would join the group.) Their similarity's were eerie. Most all of them had played high school and college hockey, and all were graduates of Ivy League schools. They seemed well prepared for the challenge ahead of them.

Between them, the $2 million expansion fee was not going to be a problem. The group's biggest task, however, was to figure out just how they were going to convince the expansion committee that there was a suitable venue for their new team to play in. The NHL was demanding that the arena hold at least 12,500 seats, and unfortunately, the only options in the Twin Cities were the St. Paul Auditorium, with a capacity of 8,500, and the old Minneapolis Arena, which would seat only 5,000. They thought of every possible scenario on how to fit a square peg into the proverbial round hole but could not come up with a suitable solution. They even explored the possibility of remodeling and expanding the Hippodrome at the state fairgrounds. The bottom line was, they did not want to pay for a new arena, which would cost millions of dollars. (This ultimately was the reason that the NBA's Minneapolis Lakers packed up and moved to Los Angeles only a few years earlier in 1960, because they too did not have an adequate facility to play in. They were even forced to move several NBA Championship Playoff games to alternate venues around the Twin Cities, because the Minneapolis Auditorium had been committed to host ice shows and sportsmen's conventions.)

For a while it looked like this was going to be a deal-breaker, and the group was going to be stuck on the outside looking in. Just when they thought things couldn't get worse, a second group of investors from St. Paul, led by businessman Henri Foussard, emerged out of nowhere with a bid of their own. Now, as if things weren't messed up enough, there were two groups from Minnesota who wanted a hockey franchise.

Stars' goalie Cesare Maniago

Trying to keep the calm, the two groups decided to get together before their meeting with the NHL's Board of Governors in New York to see if a compromise could be worked out. It couldn't, and stubbornly both groups made the trip to the Big Apple with the intention of presenting their bids. There, the two groups got together again and had it out with each other for better than two days straight, trying to work something out for the good of Minnesota. Finally the two parties reached a compromise of sorts. Bush's group tentatively agreed that in addition to giving the St. Paul group a 10 percent ownership stake in the team, they would make a proposal to the committee for the renovation of the St. Paul Auditorium, knowing full well that a referendum would need to be passed back in Minnesota. The deal was shaky at best, and in the 13th hour the group changed their mind, deciding instead that they would either have to drop the whole thing altogether, or accept the fact that they were going to have to pony up the cash for a new arena.

In the end Bush's group decided to dig deep, and ultimately promised the Board a new arena, even though they had no idea where they were going to come up with the more than $7 million needed to build it. Not to mention the fact that they had neither architectural designs nor a chunk of property to put it on. With that, on Feb. 9, 1966, Bush's group was awarded one of the six new franchises, despite the fact that they were the smallest television market and had the smallest population of all of the applicants who were vying for a team. The NHL's expansion committee, knowing of the incredible popularity of high school and college hockey in Minnesota, was willing to gamble on the fact that a very strong fan base was already in place here. Now all the group needed to do was

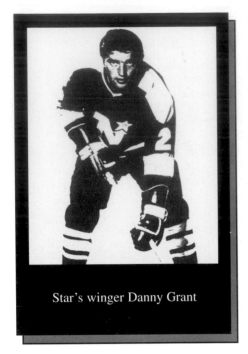
Star's winger Danny Grant

build their team a new home to play in.

(Knowing that there was no way in hell that Minnesota was ever going to get two franchises, then NHL President Clarence Campbell, upon reviewing both Twin Cities bids, reportedly stated, "In my wildest dreams I could not visualize that a franchise would come out of the chaos surrounding the Minnesota bid." Lucky for us, it did!)

Bush's syndicate rushed home and within a few months, arranged the financing for a new, state of the art hockey arena that was going to be built in the Twin Cities. But where? Now as you know, the sister cities of Minneapolis and St. Paul have not always seen eye to eye on competitive matters such as where to put a professional sports team. The bickering sisters would seemingly do anything to prevent the other from having territorial bragging rights, particularly over something as visible and full of testosterone as this. Such was the case with the Vikings and Twins only a few years before, who, in the end, wound up compromising their new homeland to a neutral "demilitarized-zone," very much like Switzerland. Yep, rather than building Metropolitan Stadium downtown, where the people and corporations were, they chose instead for a nice goat pasture, right in the middle of nowhere. The group, wanting to avoid further bickering and delays, figured that if they were going to get their arena built on time, would also build in the comfy confines of Bloomington. The local Stadium Commission agreed, and on Oct. 3, 1966, the ground was broken for the new, state-of-the-art Metropolitan Sports Center. The joke around town was that they would need to hire the construction crew that built the pyramids in order to get this impossible job done. Amazingly, in less than one year, Met Center was rushed to completion just in time for the beginning of the 1967-68 season under the direction of Bob McNulty. Upon its completion NHL President Clarence Campbell called the 15,000+ seat ice palace, "the finest facility for viewing hockey that I have ever seen."

The NHL, which had been a six team league for 25 seasons with teams in New York, Boston, Detroit, Chicago, Toronto, and Montreal, now had franchises in Minnesota, St. Louis, Los Angeles, Philadelphia, Pittsburgh and Oakland. In addition, it was decided that the original six would make the up the "Eastern Division," while the six new squads would make up the "West."

John Driscoll was named as chairman of the board, Bush became the team's president, and the other partners evolved into the team's board of directors. Now all they needed was a nickname. In 1966, some 1,200 hockey fans submitted their ideas for a new team name. Among the top creative choices included: Norsemen, Voyageurs, Blades, Mustangs, Muskies, Lumberjacks, Miners, Mallards, Pioneers, Polars, Marauders, Zips, Blades, and Puckeroos. But the overwhelming winner was, of course, "Les Etoiles du Nord" -- the North Stars.

The Bird is the Word
The team's first order of business was to hire a coach and general manager. There were numerous candidates considered, but in the end Bush decided to kill two birds with one stone by hiring Ontario native, Wren Blair, who had previously served as GM for his Minneapolis Bruins. Blair, or "the Bird" as he was affectionately called, had a long history of success while as a coach and GM of numerous professional, minor pro and junior clubs throughout Canada, as well as for the Boston Bruins, where he served as director of minor-league personnel. He also had a background in international hockey, having led the Whitby (Ontario) Dunlops, to the 1958 IHHF world championship. But Blair was especially known for his ability to scout young talent. His biggest find, none other than Bruin legend Bobby Orr. He had a very unorthodox style of coaching his players, seemingly getting every ounce of effort out of them, and ultimately everywhere he went he built winning teams. Known to have a rather large ego, the Bird simply could not stand to lose, and would tolerate nothing less from his players.

Blair's first job with the Stars would be to assemble a scouting staff in preparation of the NHL's upcoming expansion draft. Blair's first hire as his personal assistant was none other than John Mariucci, who was fresh off of coaching the U.S. National team. He then named Harold Cotton as his scouting director, followed by Ted O'Connor as chief scout. Blair's brother, Gerald, along with Leo Boivin, Bob Dill, and Murray Williamson were also named to the staff. Their job was to pound the proverbial underbelly of the hockey world for prospects. Blair even gave each scout a tape recorder, so that he could make immediate first hand observations right at rinkside.

Now the NHL's expansion draft in 1966 was nothing like today's draft lottery. This was the first time that the league had done such a thing, and to say that there were some major flaws in the system would be an understatement. The way they had set it up, was definitely in the favor of the original six clubs. The new teams were allowed to select players from the rosters of the established clubs, who were allowed to protect 11 skaters plus one goalie. Blair, a wheeler-dealer, loved the game of building from nothing, and found that he had to be very resourceful. He knew that if the Stars were going to be competitive, he would have to use every weapon at his disposal, including multi-player trades, dealing draft choices and buying unproven players from other clubs.

"Building an NHL team from the formula given us at expansion time was a real grind," said Blair in the book 'The Goldy Shuffle.' "It still is. It was like the neighborhood bully coming down the street and saying, 'Okay, let's choose up sides and play a game. I'm going to take the first 11 guys, now you can have one.' You know what the outcome of that game will be in any neighborhood in North America."

On June 6, 1967, the draft was held, and Blair went about the impossible task of selecting his team's 20 allotted nobody's and has-been's. So, with the first pick, Blair opted to draft a young goaltender from the New York Rangers by the name of Cesare Maniago, who was already known by the locals from his minor league playing stint with the Minneapolis Bruins of the CPHL. Among the other skaters he chose that day included two diamonds in the rough from the Boston Bruins: Wayne Connelly and Bill Goldsworthy. Goldsworthy, of course, would emerge as the team's first superstar, carrying the franchise on his back for its first decade of existence.

The Stars were anxious to make an immediate impact in the league, and as a result, gambled away a lot of their future draft picks in order to obtain some immediate talent. Because the established clubs had been stockpiling talent in the minor leagues, they were able to pawn off their kids, who were green, as well as their veterans, who were too old, onto the expansion teams. Add to the that the fact that the established clubs

Tragedy at the Met Center: The Bill Masterton Story

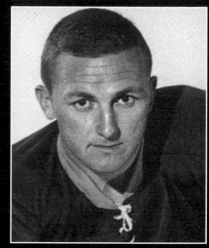

On January 13, 1968, midway through the North Star's first season, an event took place at the Met Center that forever changed the face of hockey around the world. Minnesota was playing Western Conference rival Oakland that night, when tragedy struck the sports world. Midway through the first period, Stars center Bill Masterton led a rush into the Seals offensive zone. As he got over the blue line, he back-handed a pass to his right wing, Wayne Connelly. Just then, Seals defensemen Larry Cahan and Ron Harris lined him up and nailed him with a hard, but clean body-check. Instantly, Masterton was flung over backwards, hitting his head on the ice. Now, during this era of pro hockey, he wasn't among the handful of players wearing a helmet. As a result, all of his 6-foot, 185 pound frame came crashing into the rock-hard ice surface, he was instantly knocked unconscious.

As the hushed crowd watched in horror, Masterton, who, by this time was bleeding profusely, was immediately taken from the ice on a stretcher and rushed to Edina's Fairview Hospital. For more than 30 hours doctors managed to keep him alive by use of a respirator, but regrettably, he never regained consciousness. The massive brain injury was too severe, and consequently, early on the morning of January 15th, Masterton was pronounced dead at the age of 29. Left behind was his wife Carol, and their two children.

The tragedy touched every Minnesotan, and for the upstart North Star players - it was particularly tough. "The tragic death of Bill Masterton touched us all deeply in that first year, so deeply in fact that those of us who were on that club are reluctant to discuss it even yet," said general manager Wren Blair following that 1968 season. "However, let me say this: It was real heartbreak, and leading 20 young men back from that bitter experience, convincing them that life must go on, that the North Stars had a destiny, a cause and a goal was a challenge that I certainly had not counted on that first season. These were young people, most of whom had never faced a tragedy in their lives. Most of them were young enough that they had never lost a loved one, not their mother, father, sister or brother. No one that close. Yet suddenly, someone almost as close as you can get - a fellow teammate - was gone. Still the North Stars rallied and fought back with much of the leadership supplied by Carol Masterton, Bill's courageous young wife. To this day, Bill's memory is very special to the North Stars and Carol is one of our special favorites."

Bill "Bat" Masterton was born in Winnipeg on August 13th, 1938. He grew up playing hockey like most Canadian kids, one day dreaming of playing in the NHL. He first began to show signs of greatness while playing for the St. Boniface Canadiens in the Manitoba Junior Hockey League in 1956. In 1957 Bill was offered a hockey scholarship at Denver University. While there, he steadily improved his game. During his senior year at DU, he led the Pioneers to the NCAA championship, and was named as the MVP of the tournament. The All-American recipient graduated in 1961 with a bachelor of science degree in business, and then signed with the Montreal Canadiens organization - where he was assigned to their Hull-Ottawa farm club in the Eastern Professional Hockey League.

Masterton played in Hull-Ottawa for one season, and then was promoted to the Cleveland Barons of the AHL - where he finished sixth in the league scoring race with an impressive 82 points in 72 games. By 1963 Bill was tired of the minor league rat race. None of the other five NHL teams had shown an interest in drafting him, and rather than stay the course, he opted to give up his dream of playing in the NHL and retire from pro hockey. Instead he returned to Denver to pursue his master's degree in finance. "By that time I had gotten married," he said, "and there was this offer to work in contract administration for a big, established firm like Honeywell."

So, in 1964, Masterton moved to Minnesota, where he began working as an executive with the Honeywell Corporation. He also decided to keep playing hockey as well, first with the Rochester Mustangs in 1964-65, and then with the St. Paul Steers in 1965-66 - where he tallied 67 points in just 30 games. He went on to play on the U.S. National team in 1967 - scoring 39 points in only 21 games. Then something happened. The league expanded to 12 teams, and Bill got a call from North Stars GM, Wren Blair, inviting him to training camp for a tryout.

"I went to training camp knowing it wouldn't be a picnic, especially after being out of pro hockey for four seasons," said Masterton in June of 1967. "I had the opportunity to skate quite a bit last summer when I coached in a summer league, and I think that helped me quite a bit. I was in pretty good shape when I reported. I realize it's going to be tough, but if I get the opportunity to play, I'm confident that I can make it."

He did make it. He got to fulfill a lifelong dream by playing in the "show" for 38 glorious games, even scoring the team's first-ever goal. He scored just three more after that, and added eight assists for a mere 12 points during that 1967-68 season. On paper, Bill Masterton certainly wasn't a superstar. But, unfortunately, Bill Masterton is today a hockey legend. Sometimes legends have to make the ultimate sacrifice for a cause unbenounced to them. And that is just what his legacy is all about. Bill Masterton woke up the hockey world, and forced it to take a hard look at protective headgear. As a result of Bill's untimely death, helmets are mandatory at all levels of the game today, including in the NHL. Masterton remains the only player in history to die from an injury suffered in an NHL game. And, thanks to the awareness that was brought about because of his tragedy, countless other deaths and head injuries have been averted.

Following the tragedy, the NHL governors in cooperation with the NHL Writers Association created the Bill Masterton Memorial trophy. The honor was originally given to the player who best exemplifies the qualities of sportsmanship and love of the game. In more recent years, however, the award has been given to players who have had to battle hardships due primarily to injury or illness, and have successfully returned to the game. While each team nominates one player for an overall winner, the nomination of a player in each city is a way of extending the value of the trophy and keeping Masterton's memory alive. A Bill Masterton Scholarship Fund, based in Bloomington, was also created in his memory. Montreal Canadien forward Claude Provost was the initial honoree, while other past winners include former North Star Al MacAdam, who won the award in 1980, as well as Pittsburgh's Mario Lemieux and Chicago's Tony Granato.

The North Stars, who in addition to creating an annual Bill Masterton Cup Award - which was given to the player voted most valuable by his teammates, also retired Masterton's no. 19 jersey forever into the rafters of the old Met Center in 1987.

Bill Goldsworthy

William Alfred Goldsworthy was born to Art and Manetta Goldsworthy on August 24, 1944 in the town of Kitchener, Ontario - located just northeast of Detroit. Art Goldsworthy was one of the city's best known athletes during the 1930s and early 40s, having made a name for himself as a star baseball pitcher. The Goldsworthy's had two children, Ken, and his baby brother of five years, Bill. The two brothers, who shared a small bedroom with one bed, grew up playing together. One of the things that the two brothers looked forward to most, was sitting down with their parents in front of the TV once a week to watch "Hockey Night in Canada."

At the age of six Bill laced up his first pair of skates. As a youngster, he displayed a lot of raw talent for the game. Within a year he was playing league hockey against the best kids in the city. Wanting to emulate his childhood hero, Detroit Red Wing's star right winger Gordy Howe, Goldy insisted upon playing on the right side.

Eventually Bill was selected to play on a traveling Kitchener All Star team, which kept the mischievous youngster out of trouble. Playing on the team was a big commitment, having to carry his hockey bag for more than a mile to catch a bus each time the team played. And, occasionally, if the road was icy enough, Goldy would simply put on his skates and skate to the rink.

Billy later starred as defensive safety on the high school football team. Having to practice football after school, walk home, eat, and then go to hockey practice at night, kept him in prime physical condition. Soon he was noticed by some of the local scouts. In addition to liking this skinny, temperamental blond kid's good speed and quick shot, they liked his unbridled spirit. Even back then, he was one tough S.O.B.

Goldy played his way through the Canadian amateur leagues, first with the Waterloo Siskins, and eventually for the Niagara Falls Flyers, a Junior A team in the Ontario Hockey Association that was affiliated with the Boston Bruins organization. By 1964, at the age of 20, Goldy was signed by the Bruins. However, although he was considered to be one of the organization's hottest prospects, he was only able to get called-up for three brief stints with the NHL team. It was a rough couple of up-and-down years for the 6-foot, 190-pounder, who was unable to earn a regular spot on the strong Bruins roster.

He caught a break though, when on June 6, 1967, former Bruins scout turned North Stars GM Wren Blair selected him from Boston in the NHL's expansion draft. Wanting to make the most of his opportunity, the 23-year-old worked hard to make the club's opening-day lineup. He played in 68 games with the Stars in his first season, scoring a mediocre 14 goals and 19 assists. However, at the end of the regular season, Goldy caught fire in the playoffs and led all scorers with 8 goals and 15 total points. Figuring he could parlay that success into a break-through sophomore campaign, Goldy came back that next year with another mediocre 14-goal season.

Goldy came into camp in the best shape of his life that next year, and thanks to North Stars' coach Jack Gordon putting him on the same line with center Jude Drouin and left wing Danny Grant, Goldsworthy scored 28 goals in 28 games in the second half of the season. One of the biggest reasons for his turnaround was due to the constant pushing and prodding by Blair. "I remember one day in our first year at Minnesota I told Goldy I would make a hockey player out of him if it killed us both," said Blair. "And right then I wasn't sure I was going to make it!"

Goldy continued to excel for the Stars, becoming the team's first superstar. One of the reasons why the fans seemed to love this kid so much was because of his now infamous post-scoring dance, affectionately called the "Goldy Shuffle." Yes, the "Shuffle" had taken Minnesota by storm by this point, and the fans couldn't get enough of it. You see, every time Goldy scored, he would immediately skate down the ice with one leg tucked up by his chest, and at the same time, holding his stick up in the air with his left arm, he would pump his right arm like he was trying to start a chain saw. Hard to describe, the little jig became a thing of beauty.

"I think I did the shuffle for the first time in my first year with the North Stars," he explained when asked about how it all began. "We were fighting for a playoff spot, and were playing Pittsburgh at home right near the end of the season. We needed a tie or a win. We tied 2-2, and I think I got both goals. I was so happy at the time that I did a little dance on the ice. Jeez, I got all kinds of letters from people who liked it. Then the press began to call it the "Goldy Shuffle." So now I do it whenever we're winning. When we're losing though, management doesn't like to see it too much."

Goldy was a strong veteran voice in the locker room, and the players genuinely liked him. One of his closest allies on the team was former linemate and Duluth native, Tommy Williams, who's guidance and friendship helped Goldy's career immensely. "You know, as far as I'm concerned Goldy is one of the best players in this whole league," said Tommy, who also started his career in Boston. "If he were with the Bruins now, he'd be a potential 50-goal scorer. I'm not kidding. Maybe more. Put him on Esposito's line for example. I'd say he'd score 50. He's that good."

Never one to shy away from a melee, Goldy endured himself to the fans not only because he could find the back of the net, but also because he was willing to take a few stitches every now and then for the team. Always one who could be counted upon to dress for every game, his reckless, driving, thumping style of play made him a fan favorite for more than 11 seasons in Minnesota.

Goldy finally hung em' up in 1977, but not before becoming the first player on a post-1967 expansion team to score 200 goals and the first to score 250. In 1971, Goldy became the team's leading scorer (a mark he held for more than a decade), and his 48-goal season in 1973-74 was the club's best ever - until Dino Ciccarelli broke the mark eight years later. Known as a solid team player who could play at both ends of the ice, he was the first North Star ever to reach the 500-point plateau, totaling 267 goals and 239 assists for 506 points over 670 games with the team. And, in addition to his five All-Star game appearances, he was also selected as a member of Team Canada's much celebrated "Summit Series" roster that defeated the Russians in 1972.

On February 15th, 1992, during a memorable ceremony in front of a sell out crowd, Goldy's No. 8 was retired into the Met Center's rafters. Tragically, only two years later he was diagnosed with AIDS. On May 29th, 1996, at the young age of 51, Goldy died.

Goldsworthy's untimely death from complications related to AIDS and alcoholism in 1996 is now the inspiration behind a new non-profit program called "Reality Game." With the slogan, "In the game of life, you make the call," the group is headed by Goldy's daughter, Tammy Goldsworthy Loheit. Today Loheit speaks to groups about communicating the importance of choices toward alcohol, drugs and sex.

could bargain with the expansion teams with the lure of cash, and future considerations to entice their counterparts to "pass over" their most coveted unprotected players. When it was all over though, Blair was optimistic to say the least about his new roster of players.

"Good Lord," said Blair to his scouting staff after the draft on the 20 players he had just obtained for the mere price of $100,000 each, "just look at this mess. This is supposed to be a major league hockey team. There are only four guys on this list that are major league players. Your job and mine is to unload the other 16 just as fast as we can, any way we can. I'll trade 10-for-one if I have to." Blair even wanted to stop taking players at one point in the draft, but NHL president Clarence Campbell told him that he had to take 20.

The Stars' Maiden Voyage
The stage was now set. The anticipation for big-time hockey in Minnesota was immense, and season ticket sales soared even well before the team hit the ice. The team was forced to play their first four games on the road however, because the arena's new seats weren't quite finished being installed. On Oct. 11, 1967, the Stars played their first-ever contest against St. Louis. The Stars first-ever goal was scored by Bill Masterton, but the team wound up tying the Blues 2-2. On a side note, the first fight in franchise history also took place that night, between the Stars' Bill Plager and Blues defenseman, Bob Plager - who incidentally, was his big brother. Mom and Dad must've been so proud...

On October 21st the Stars faced off against the Oakland Seals for their inaugural home opener. The packed Met Center crowd, who had seemingly waited a lifetime for the NHL to finally come to Minnesota, was delighted to see a young blonde-haired kid from Kitchener, Ontario, tally the team's first-ever goal in the new arena. His name was Bill Goldsworthy, but they would soon come to know him simply as "Goldy!" The two teams excited the crowd that night with a brand of hockey that Minnesotans had never known before, ultimately skating to a 3-3 tie.

The Cinderella Stars Go For a Ride
With the memory of teammate Bill Masterton's tragic death on their minds, the Stars played inspired hockey the rest of the way through their inaugural season. They finished the regular season with a modest record of 27 wins, 32 losses, and 15 ties - finishing fourth in the Western Division, just four points out of first. Wayne Connelly led the team in scoring that first year with 35 goals and 21 assists for 56 points.

It was off to the playoffs for the rookie North Stars, who were matched against all-world goalie Terry Sawchuk and the Los Angeles Kings. L.A. took the first two games of the best of seven series, only to see Minnesota rally back to get the series even. The Kings went up 3-2, only to see the Stars come back one more time to tie it up. Stars forward Milan Marcetta won the sixth game with an overtime goal, and with the momentum on their side, the Stars went on to rout the Kings in Los Angeles, 9-4. Minnesota, who scored a club record nine goals to win the rugged quarterfinal contest, would now face the St. Louis Blues to determine who would play in the Stanley Cup finals.

Now, even though the Stars were hot, like any expansion team, they weren't yet exactly commanding a lot of respect around town. Such was the case for the second-round playoff series against St. Louis, when it was announced that five of the seven games had to be played in St. Louis because the Ice Capades had already booked the Met Center's ice for a show. Not even phased about losing their home ice advantage, the Stars marched ahead by winning two of the first three games against the Blues.

Game Four of the series was a grinder. Through the third period the Stars were up 3-0, only to see the Blues tally twice within a two minute span. Then with only 11 seconds to go in the game, Blues forward Jim Roberts scored his second goal of the game to send it to overtime. Then, only two minutes into the OT, Gary Sabourin scored on a wrister to win it for the Blues. Excited to finally play in the Met Center, Minnesota got back on track the next night, only to lose another overtime heartbreaker. With their backs against the wall though, the guys in green came back in front of a packed house and crushed St. Louis 5-1 in Game Six.

The Seventh and final game, which shifted back to the Gateway-Arch City, would go down as a classic. It would come down to which goaltender wanted it more, Cesare Maniago or St. Louis' Glenn Hall. The game was scoreless through the first two periods until Stars winger Walt McKechnie blasted a goal past Hall with only four minutes to go in the game. But, only seconds later the Blues would tie it up, forcing the teams to play yet another extra period. Just before the end of the game, Stars winger Wayne Connelly broke lose on a breakaway, only to get mugged by a Blues defender. As Connelly went down, the fans back home thought for sure that there would be a penalty shot issued, but it never came. The score was still 1-1 after the first overtime period, which meant double-overtime. Then, only three minutes into the second OT, the Blues' Ron Shock blasted a slapshot past Maniago for the game-winner. After nearly 83 minutes of great "old-time" hockey, it was a bitter pill for the Cinderella Stars to swallow. The Blues, who were absolutely spent by the end of this emotional and physical series, went on to get swept by Montreal in the finals.

The Stars had treated their fans to some great hockey, and even made some believers of themselves along the way. The team averaged nearly 12,000 fans per game that first year, not bad for a bunch of "misfits, unknowns and castoffs." The fans wanted to show their appreciation for the team's success that season, and decided to meet the club at the airport.

"We came home on Braniff Airlines, and they had to pull the plane away from the gate area because thousands of people had come out to welcome the team," said Al Shaver, the Stars play-by-play announcer. "Everyone was quite amazed by this the reception because we didn't win the series."

"We were just thankful to have a job," said Bill Goldsworthy, who, stood atop the playoff leaderboard with eight goals and seven assists. "We were a bunch of guys who just wanted to prove something and sell the game of hockey."

"It was just a phenomenal experience," said Lou Nanne, a Gopher All-American who joined the team after the Olympics. "To be able to have NHL hockey right in your own back yard and see it every week was something that I really was excited about. Playing was just a thrill for me and that the first season we had a pretty good year, making a great playoff run. For the first time, the Stars got some credibility after that

Duluth's Tommy Williams

playoff series with the Blues."

In the end, Blair had successfully taken a bunch of no-names well beyond their natural ability, and all to way to within one goal of going to the Stanley Cup finals. All in all it was a good start for the club which Blair had pieced together on a wing and a prayer. During that first year he wheeled and dealed like no other GM in the league in order to build his team. Some deals paid immediate dividends, such as the one that sent five players off his active roster for two Toronto minor leaguers - J.P. Parise and Milan Marcetta. (In that deal, all five players dealt were out of the league in only a few years, while Parise would emerge as an early star for the team.) Another involved dealing the very popular Billy Collins to get Jude Drouin, a lightning quick young center who would later finish as the runner-up in the 1971 Rookie-of-the-Year balloting. He also irked the local scribes when he swapped the big, fast, and very popular center, Danny O'Shea, for Chicago defenseman Doug Mohns.

"In that first year we played four games against each of the six original NHL clubs," said Blair. "Amazingly, we split with Boston and Detroit and went 1-1-2 with Chicago, Toronto and Montreal. Only New York eluded us completely. Unbelievable, yet we did it. How? By driving our players unmercifully, and, in the process, driving ourselves unmercifully. The NHL was new in Minnesota, and we felt this had to be done to sell hockey here completely."

Over the next couple of years Blair would make countless more deals. He obtained Montreal goaltender Gump Worsley (a future hall of famer), and also defenseman Ted Harris, who would become the team captain and the club policeman. He followed those trades up by obtaining Barry Gibbs from the Bruins and Tom Reid from the Blackhawks. Each would go on to be big contributors for Minnesota in the years to come.

The Honeymoon Was Over Quickly...

The Stars knew it was going to be tough to top the heroics of their last season that next year. Although it was an exciting ride, it was particularly draining on Blair to serve as both GM as well as coach. It had been his intention all along to coach only until he could find the right guy to pass the reigns to. With the team sitting pretty in second place in the West, Blair named John Muckler as his new bench boss. Muckler, a minor league coach at the time, was about to receive a very rude awakening to the NHL. That's because the Stars suddenly went into a huge slump, plummeting to the divisional cellar. The fans were outraged, and as a result, Muckler became the scape-goat and got canned. (Incidentally, Muckler would go on to a long and illustrious NHL coaching career.) Blair returned to his perch behind the bench, and got the Stars fired up. They rallied late in the season, only to fall one game short of making a repeat trip to the playoffs. One of the highlights of the year was the performance of rookie Danny Grant, who's club-leading 34 goals and 31 assists earned him the Calder Trophy as the league's rookie-of-the-year. Other top performers included Ray Cullen, who tallied 63 points, and Maniago, who posted a solid 3.30 goals-against average. In the end though, the team's pathetic 18-43-15 record was just not going to cut it.

Enter: the "Gumper"

After a thorough house-cleaning by Blair in the off-season, the Stars were ready to take on the world. Early in the 1969-70 season though, Blair was ordered to take some time off by his doctor. Charlie Burns, who had started the season as the team's second-line center, was named as the team's interim bench-coach. During Burns' tenure, the team went through a horrible 20-game non-winning streak, that nearly set an NHL record. Burns, in an attempt to liven up the troops, decided to once again lace up his skates and serve as a player-coach. The team rallied behind their new skipper, had an amazing month of March, going 9-5-4, and wound up finishing third in the West. They, unfortunately were eliminated by their new nemesis, the Blues, four games to two in the playoffs. Incidentally, Goldy scored the two game-winners in the pair of home games that the Stars won.

One of the bright spots for the Stars that year was the addition of Montreal Canadien goalie, Gump Worsley. The "Gumper" was an instant fan favorite, partially because he was the last NHL goaltender to not wear a mask. The overweight, balding, often hilarious 40-something year-old Worsley, would prove to be a savior in getting the team out of their losing streak. Burns was at his wits end in the midst of the team's funk, and decided to call on the guy with the most experience to have some words of wisdom with the team.

"Charlie told me to go into the dressing room and say what I wanted to say," said Worsley in the 1972 book entitled: 'The Blazing North Stars.' "They hadn't won in so long that nobody wanted the puck. They'd come off the bench and sit there like wooden Indians. The first thing I did was talk to them. Next thing I knew they went up against Toronto and won, 8-0. I was on the bench and every time it got quiet I'd get up and start cheering and yelling. They had never had a guy like that before. When they were down a goal they'd get upset. I told them that in the NHL if you're down a goal you've got lots of time to get it back. All of a sudden we started to win. But what surprised me was that after only two practices they asked me to play." That March, Gump suited up in goal and beat Pittsburgh. Figuring the team was on a roll, Burns wanted to ride Worsley, and asked him to suit up between the pipes again that next night against the Rangers. Gump, no longer a spring chicken, hated playing back-to-back nights, but figured he'd do it for the team. The Stars played inspired hockey behind their new netminder, and thanks to a third period goal by Ray Cullen, Minnesota held on to win. "No doubt," said Worsley afterward, "it was one of the better games of my career."

Now, with the momentum on their side, the Stars faced off against the struggling Philadelphia Flyers for a shot at making the playoffs. With the Gumper in goal, North Star

Virginia's Jack Carlson

defenseman Barry Gibbs bounced a squibler past Flyer goalie Bernie Parent at 7:48 of the third period. Worsley held on to post a shut-out, and the North Stars won the game 1-0. With the win, Philly was eliminated, and Minnie was in. "Sure, we were lucky," Gump added, "but that's hockey; it's a strange game. But the main thing is that we won and got into the playoffs."

In addition to the Gumper, the driving force behind the team's second half turn-around was the amazing line of "Goldy, Tommy, and J.P." J. P. Parise led all scoring with 72 points, while Duluth's Tommy Williams put in 67, Bill Goldsworthy tallied 65, and Danny Grant added 57 of his own to help the cause.

Making History at the Forum
Wren Blair came back that following 1970-71 season, but came to the realization that he needed to hire a full-time coach - so he could focus on managing the front office. "I gotta get out of coaching," said Blair, "I love it, but it doesn't love me back."

Blair hired Jack Gordon to take over behind the bench that season. Gordon, who at the time was serving as general manager and coach of the American Hockey League's Cleveland Barons, was a former star with the New York Rangers. A four-time winner of the AHL championship in Cleveland, Gordon also served as the GM of the Rangers in the late 1960s. Gordon was a quiet man who was considered as a "player's coach." He emphasized teamwork, while his "laissez-faire" attitude allowed his players the freedom to train at their own pace. "Jackie would just tell me to be ready when the bell rings, and otherwise he doesn't care what I do," said the Gumper, who's sphelt figure was often the subject of criticism with his former Montreal coaches. "It's my own business, he figures."

The season got underway with a renewed sense of confidence that year, as the Stars came out with something to prove. They started out with seven wins, five losses and three ties over their first 15 games, and seemed to gel as a team as the season progressed. They finished out the season on a downer, however, losing four straight. But that was not going to deter this bunch, as they finished the season in fourth place with a 28-34-16 record and found themselves once again pitted against the heavily favored Blues in the playoffs. For the season, Jude Drouin led the team with 68 points, followed by Goldy, who tallied 65.

The Stars stole Game One of the quarterfinal series in St. Louis, only to lose Games Two and Three. They rallied to win Games Four and Five by the tough scores of 2-1 and 4-3 respectively. Lou Nanne got the Game Five winner in St. Louis, and ignited the team right into Game Six, where they crushed the Blues at home, 5-2, in front of more than 15,000 screaming Minnesota puckheads.

Now, it has been said that every young sports franchise requires a significant event (or series in this case) to earn the respect of its pears. For the underdog North Stars, it happened on April 22, 1971, in a classic series against the flying Frenchmen from Montreal. The Canadiens, a fabled organization which had ruled the league for years, scoffed at the thought of one of the expansion team's winning a playoff game against them. After all, up to that point in league history, an expansion team had never beaten one of the original established

Lou Nanne

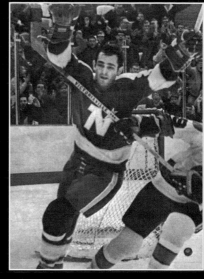

Lou Nanne has become synonymous with the game of hockey in Minnesota. A native of Sault Ste. Marie, Ontario, Louie grew up playing Junior hockey with hall of famer's Phil and Tony Esposito. Originally wanting to go to college to be a dentist, Lou came to Minnesota to as a member of John Mariucci's Golden Gopher hockey teams from 1961-1963. Nanne refers to Mariucci as his "second father," and is forever grateful to him for giving him the opportunity to play hockey at Minnesota.

Earning Gopher captain and All-American honors in his senior year, Nanne tallied a career-high 74 points, becoming the first defenseman to win a WCHA scoring title. For his efforts the newly naturalized American citizen was named as the league's MVP. "I loved playing hockey at the University of Minnesota," said Nanne, "it was a real privilege. I had tremendous fun all the way through, and it was just a great experience. I really enjoyed the atmosphere, and it was something I will always cherish."

Upon graduating from the University, Lou was drafted by Chicago into the NHL. However, Nanne got into a contract dispute with the Blackhawks, ultimately refusing to play for them, which led to a five year layoff from hockey. While he sat out, he worked for Minneapolis businessman Harvey Mackay's envelope company. He also coached the Gopher freshman hockey team for four years. During that time, he played on and off with the USHL's Rochester Mustangs, and also went on to captain the 1968 Olympic hockey team in Grenoble, coached by former Gopher All-American Murray Williamson. When the NHL expanded, Chicago couldn't "freeze" him anymore because of the new reserve list, so Nanne became a free agent. He decided to play for Minnesota's new expansion team, the North Stars.

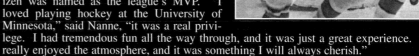

Lou quickly earned a reputation as being a good team player for the Stars. Polished at killing penalties, he also developed into a fine checking forward who was often matched against the other teams' top lines. Louie, considered as Minnesota's "Ice God," would go on to play defense and winger for the North Stars through 1978, becoming the only player to play with the Stars in all of the first 11 years of the team's existence. He also represented USA during the 1976 and 1977 World Championships, where he served as team captain. In addition, he played for the U.S. in the 1977 Canada Cup series, and later served as GM of Team USA for the Canada Cup in 1981, 1984 and 1987. For his career, including playoffs, he tallied 72 goals and 167 assists for 239 points with the North Stars.

He went from player to coach in 1978, and then was appointed general manager by Glen Sonmor from 1978-1988. "It was a lot of fun as a general manager, making very important day-to-day decisions, but there is not a better job in the world than actually playing the game on the ice. Whenever you can play something that you loved as a kid and then they pay you for it, well it doesn't get any better than that." One of the first things he did as the team's new GM, was to hire an assistant GM. Loyal to the bone, Louie hired his old coach, John Mariucci, who was scouting for the team at the time.

Of the players on the 1981 Stanley Cup team, only five were left from the team that Nanne took over in 1978. Bobby Smith was his first pick and Mike Modano would be his last. He quickly became known around the league as a wheeler and dealer of talent. He had clout with the other GM's around the league, and parlayed that into his favor. In 1979 he claimed Dave Semenko from Glen Sather's Edmonton Oilers in the expansion draft for the sole purpose of dealing him right back to Sather in a "gentleman's agreement" to leave Neal Broten available for them in that year's upcoming amateur draft. He finished his 24-year career with the Stars as the team president from 1988-1990.

Although Canadian by birth, Nanne became a well-known advocate of the Americanization of the NHL. He was one of the first to scout U.S. colleges for American talent and to take an active role in the support of player-development programs, which also included Olympic and international competition. He also wasn't just involved with the North Stars. Lou was very involved in league politics. In addition to helping lead the negotiations with the WHA that brought four new teams into the league, he also served as chairman of the General Managers Committee, as well as on the NHL's prestigious Board of Governors. In 1982, he also served as the chairman of the Central Hockey League's Board of Governors. For his many contributions to USA hockey, Nanne was honored as a recipient of the 1989 Lester Patrick award. And, in 1998 he was also inducted into the US Hockey Hall of Fame.

Possibly the most recognized hockey figure in the state, Lou is extremely well liked and respected by his peers. He had been a fixture with the North Stars from start to finish and is the authority on hockey in Minnesota today. His quick wit, colorful sense of humor and knowledge of the game have landed him several TV commentating jobs, including Stanley Cup playoffs and finals for "Hockey Night in Canada," CBS, and NBC. But his favorite color-man gig is still covering the annual State High School Hockey Tournament, something he has done now since 1964.

Lorne "Gump" Worsley

Asked once in a post-game interview why he refused to wear a facemask, he replied: "What do you mean? I'm wearing one now..." Gump Worsley, then in his 40s, only played in Minnesota for four short seasons, but he is arguably the team's most popular goaltender of all time. Here is his wonderful story.

Lorne John Worsley was born May 14, 1929, in Montreal. He grew up in a tough end of town where his neighborhood buddies proclaimed that he looked like then popular roly-poly comic-strip character "Andy Gump," and the nick-name stuck with him ever since. As a kid he loved hockey, and tried to emulate his idol, Davey Kerr, hero of the Rangers' 1940 Stanley Cup championship team.

While playing for a commercial league team in a Montreal suburb, Worsley got his first break after winning a tryout with a junior team called the Verdun Cyclones. In 1949, at the age of 20, he caught the eye of a Rangers' scout who sent him an invitation to the Rangers training camp. After a few years in the minors, he finally got the call to come to Madison Square Garden and join the Rangers in 1952. Gump would mind the nets in the Big Apple until 1963. The New York fans appreciated the pudgy goal tenders efforts, but his coach, the volatile Phil Watson, rode the Gumper hard about the size of his generous girth, and once accused him of having a "beer belly." To which the portly 5-foot-7, 200 pounder, calmly replied: "As always, Watson doesn't have the faintest idea what he's talking about... I never drink beer, only good Canadian whiskey!"

Working hard and playing hard, night after night Gump was bombarded with 40-50 shot onslaughts from the opposition. One time a reported asked the goalie which team he thought gave him the most trouble. Worsley, quick to reply, exclaimed, "The Rangers!"

Then, on June 4, 1963, after nine years of live target practice with the Rangers, he was traded to the powerful Montreal Canadiens in a multi-player deal for goalie Jacques Plante. With a modest 204-271-101 record and a 3.10 goals against average, Worsley spent a total of 10 years on a Rangers team that failed to qualify for the playoffs five times and was eliminated in the opening round the other four. For Gump, who led the NHL in losses four times during his Rangers tenure, it was great news.

Though he spent much of the next two years up and down with Quebec of the AHL, Worsley got the call of his life on May 1st, 1965, when Habs coach Toe Blake notified him that he was going to start in Game Seven of the Stanley Cup finals against the Chicago Blackhawks. For the tubby 36-year-old second-stringer, it was an opportunity of a lifetime. Worsley, who was receiving pain injections for a previously injured thigh, wanted to play his best in front of his hometown fans. Although Montreal's ace center Jean Beliveau scored 14 seconds into the game, it was the Gumper who was the game's real hero, as he went on to blank the Hawks, 4-0.

The following season, both he and Charlie Hodge shared the Vezina Trophy as the league's top keeper, en route to helping the Canadiens win a second straight Stanley Cup. Worsley earned First Team All-Star honors the following 1967-68 season as he and Rogie Vachon shared the Vezina Trophy in the team's third consecutive Stanley Cup-winning season. The Gumper helped his team win a fourth Cup in 1969, but the pressure of playing goal for the mighty Canadiens finally got to him. Disenchanted with his poor treatment from management in Montreal, not to mention the increasing problems brought on by his fear of flying, Gump decided to hang em' up. "I'd had it," he said. "I didn't want to play anymore. I didn't want to fly anymore."

Worsley was a sort of enigma. Here was a man who thought absolutely nothing of standing in front of 100 mph slap-shots without even thinking about wearing a goalie mask, but try and get him in an airplane and he would wimper like a puppy. It would be a mild understatement to say that the Gumper had an abiding distrust of air travel. His horrible fear of flying made him a complete wreck on team flights. The fear apparently dated back to his days with the New York Rovers, when, on a return flight home from Milwaukee, one of the plane's engines caught fire and forced an emergency landing. Although everyone survived unscathed, the Gumper was scarred for life. From that point on, every time he got on a flight he would sit on the aisle, clench the arm rests as tightly as possible, say a prayer, and hang on for dear life. "It's the one time I don't talk," he said, "I'm too scared to say anything!"

Another incident nearly forced him to give up the game for good. While on a Canadien's team flight, the plane hit some turbulence, causing the players to spill their meals all over themselves. Afterwards the captain calmly emerged from the cockpit and reassured his passengers that the airline was sorry about the incident and that it would pay for the dry-cleaning of their suits. At that point a freaked-out Gump stood up and screamed, "What about our shorts?"

That next year, with the Gump all but washed up, Minnesota GM Wren Blair obtained the rights to negotiate with the 41-year-old goalie and convinced him to make a comeback. For Gump, who had suffered a nervous breakdown after that season, it was another chance to play the game he loved. Playing with the enthusiasm of a rookie, Worsley, along with his new partner in crime Cesare Maniago, helped guide the Stars into the play-offs for three straight seasons. "Best move I ever made," said Gump. "We love Minnesota, and we love the team. Jack Gordon is a terrific coach. He tells Cesare and me, 'If you're having problems, don't come to me, go to each other.' So we watch each other for mistakes. We're roommates. We both know that one guy can't play for the bundle. Him and me admit it, just no way, eh?"

The Gumper gave Minnesota four solid seasons in net. And, incredibly, in his fourth and final year of 1974, after nearly a quarter-century of playing with face as a backstop, he finally decided to break down and put on a facemask. But it didn't come easily for the game's last goalie to go maskless. When asked why he would subject himself to constant cuts and stitches, he calmly replied rhetorically: "Would it have been fair not to give the fans the chance to see my beautiful face?" He took his share of licks over the years, too. Hundreds and hundreds of stitches, and dozens of concussions made the Gumper a huge fan favorite. "If Gump got hit in the face by a puck, it could only improve his looks," said Stars' scout John Mariucci. "If that's the case," Gump retorted "then you'd have to get hit in the face by a bus!"

Worsley finally played his 862nd NHL regular-season game on April 2, 1974, against Philadelphia. Conveniently, at the age of 45, the Gumper retired just about in time to start receiving his NHL pension checks. Worsley then moved into the Stars' front office, where he became a team scout - a position he retained through the mid 1980s. Playing an amazing 25 professional seasons from 1949 to 1974, Gump finished his career with a 335-353-150 overall record and a 2.90 GA average in 862 games (a number surpassed only by Terry Sawchuk and Jacques Plante). In addition to his 43 regular season shutouts, he also posted five shutouts and a 2.82 GAA in 70 playoff games. Fittingly, he was elected to the Hockey Hall of Fame in 1980.

With his trademark crew-cut , and jovial pot-belly, the happy-go-lucky soul was not only one of the game's greatest and most durable players, he was also one of the its most likable characters. A fun-loving man who claimed that his favorite post game meal was a beer and a cigarette, Gump once said of his profession: "If you want to be a good goaltender, it helps to be a little crazy. Not all goal-tenders are nuts, only about 90 percent of them..."

Forest Gump had nothing on this guy!

clubs in post-season play.

Gordon decided to start the Gumper in Game One at the Montreal Forum, hoping that he would play inspired hockey against the team that had released him the season before. Danny Grant put the Stars up 1-0 in the first, but Montreal's heavy artillery heated up after that to put the Canadiens ahead 4-1 by the end of two. The pressure was too much for Worsley as the Habs rolled over the Stars 7-2. "We had a real good 20 minutes," said defenseman Ted Harris. "The trouble is, the game was 60 minutes long."

It would be up to the long and lanky Maniago for Minnesota, who prepared to make history in Game Two. "I have nothing against the job Worsley did in the opener," Gordon said, "but my plans were to alternate the two goalies from the beginning. You can't fault Worsley because our boys weren't in the game after the first period. We stopped checking, and we didn't play our positions. They just toyed with us."

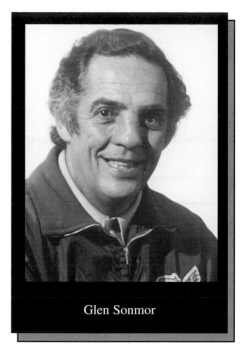

Glen Sonmor

By now, the Canadiens, who had beaten the Bruins in the opening round, had similar intentions for the kids from Minnesota. The Stars had other ideas that night however, coming out smoking. They lit up the Canadiens and embarrassed them in front of their own standing-room-only crowd. Led by Danny Grant, who dished out three pivotal assists, along with Lou Nanne's third period game-winner, the Stars prevailed in the key semifinal game. Maniago stood on his head throughout the entire game, turning away shot after shot throughout the contest. It was a milestone for all of the expansion teams, that one of their own had beaten a member of the exclusive "original six" fraternity. "Scoring the game-winning goal in that game, is still today one of the most memorable highlights of my playing career," said Lou Nanne several years later. "It really gave us a lot of confidence as a team, and got us a lot of respect and credibility around the league."

Back to Reality
Game Three switched back to Bloomington. By this time the art of tailgating had become a thing of legend at the Met Center, and rest assured, the suddenly optimistic crowd was primed and ready for our friends from north of the border. The Montreal players, still in a bit of shock over Game Two, came prepared for the team they had taken for granted. "None of us realized that the North Stars were that good," said Canadien's winger Pete Mahovlich.

The Canadiens, somewhat embarrassed over their lackadaisical performance in Game Two, came out smoking and shell-shocked the Gumper 6-3. In Game Four, both Murray Oliver and Danny Grant took advantage of power-play scoring opportunities, giving the Stars a 2-0 lead after the first bell. Montreal scored two in the second, only to see Minnesota rally behind three third period goals by J. P. Parise, Ted Hampson, and Oliver. The real hero though, was Cesare Maniago, who turned away some three dozen blasts in the 5-2 Stars win. "We wanted to show the Canadiens we didn't want to be run out of the rink," Cesare said. "We'll have a few people talking now."

With the series now tied at two games apiece, it was anybody's game. Or so they thought. Montreal, thoroughly humiliated by this point, buried the Stars in Game Five in front of their Forum fans. Maniago, starting for the injured Worsley, was thoroughly pasted 6-1.

Red Light-Green Light-Go...
With their backs up against the wall, the Stars came out swinging for Game Six, knowing that it was a "do or die" situation. On April 29, in Bloomington, the Stars dug in for one last shot at the mighty Habs. At 9:50 in the first, the crafty veteran winger Charlie Burns put the Stars up 1-0, giving the record Met Center crowd reason to believe. Montreal tied it up with less than four minutes to go, and went ahead in the second on a Claude Larose garbage goal out front. Minnesota stayed calm and played very physical against the more skilled Montreal club. Then, midway through the second, Jude Drouin beat the Canadien's All-Star keeper, Ken Dryden, with a top-shelf wrister to tie it up one more time. Maniago was solid, turning away shot after shot, until Rejean Houle beat him at 13:29 of the second to put the Canadiens up 3-2. The game went back and forth through the third period. Minnesota then pulled Maniago with just less than two minutes to go on the Met Center scoreboard. With six attackers, the Stars pressed for the equalizer. Dryden, a future hall of famer, played miraculously in the final seconds. Just when everyone thought that the game was in the bag, Stars center Ted Hampson flipped the puck over Dryden's leg pad and into the net. With no time remaining, the crowd went ballistic. As the team rushed the ice to mob Hampson, referee Bill Friday ruled that it was no goal. The green light had gone off prior to the goal being scored, and as a result the red one could not be illuminated. Time had expired on the game, and on the season for the tough-luck Stars. For the 15,422, as well as the countless other puck fans throughout the Land of 10,000 Lakes, it was a dagger through the heart. Visibly shaken, the North Stars lined up at center ice for the traditional post-series hand-shaking ceremony, and under a scoreboard that read: "NORTH STARS ARE THE GREATEST ANYWHERE!", they wished their foes good luck in the Stanley Cup finals. "The green light came on before the red one" said Jack Gordon. "I guess that's what counts. But I'm proud of these guys, they worked their guts off in this series."

"At that time, for a bunch of cast-off's like us to beat a dynasty like the Montreal Canadiens in a playoff game was quite a feat," added Goldsworthy.

Another Amazing Run
After four years of being in the league, Wren Blair had completely rewritten the team's opening day roster. Through trades over that time he had acquired several new faces, among them included: Danny Grant, Jude Drouin, J.P. Parise, Ted Harris, Tom Reid, Ted Hampson, Terry Caffery, Bob Nevin, Charlie Burns, Doug Mohns, Barry Gibbs, Gordon Labossiere, Dennis Hextall, Murray Oliver, and Gump Worsley. With all of this new talent, Coach Gordon became very good at sensing chemistry, and seemed to be able to put great lines together. In addition to the Goldy-Drouin-Grant line, he also scored big with the Lou Nanne-Dean Prentice-Murray Oliver tandem, which became one of the best in the west.

Emphasizing a strong defense, Gordon took his Stars to even greater heights in 1971-72, and made a late-season run at winning the division over rival Chicago. They would have to settle for second though, despite their impressive 37-29-12 record. Goldy led the way that year with 31 goals and 31 assists for a team-leading 62 points, while Murray Oliver and Jude Drouin each scored 56, and Lou Nanne added 49. Other key contributors in the team's success included Tom Reid, Dean Prentice, Danny Grant, Barry Gibbs, Doug Mohns, and Ted Harris. And, once again, Maniago was solid in net, posting a modest 2.65 goals against average. The fans came out in droves at Met Center that year, filling the arena to capacity for nearly every contest.

One of the highlights of the 1972 season, happened in mid-season when the Met Center played host to the NHL's annual All-Star Game. The locals were entertained by some of the game's greatest, including Minnesota's very own Bill Goldsworthy, Ted Harris, Doug Mohns, and Gump Worsley. And, although the East beat the West 3-2, the Minnesota fans thoroughly enjoyed the star-studded event.

Upon finishing second in the division, the Stars once again found themselves facing off against St. Louis in the playoffs. You know how there are just some teams that always, no matter what, just seem to have your number? Well, for the Stars, it was definitely the Blues. For whatever the reason, they owned Minnesota in the post-season. This time, however, the Blues were the underdogs - something that didn't sit real well with the Stars' coaches.

"St. Louis has been forced to fight all the way because they were battling for a playoff spot," said Jack Gordon about his team's chances against the undermanned Blues. "On the other hand, we've had our position clinched for some time and have been forced to push ourselves."

On April 5, 1972, before a record crowd of 15,482 crammed into the Met, the North Stars hit the ice on yet another quest for Lord Stanley's precious cup. Leading the charge for Minnesota was the ageless wonder, 42-year-old Lorne "Gump" Worsley. The Stars didn't disappoint either, jumping out to a 2-0 lead on goals by veterans Dean Prentice and Bob Nevin. Gump, who was hot as Georgia asphalt when it came to beating St. Louis, played huge, posting a 3-0 doughnut for the Stars. Incredibly, it was his ninth straight game against the Blues without a loss. Ever the kidder, Worsley finally admitted that a bit of "luck" may have been on his side during the streak.

Bobby Smith

One of Minnesota's favorite hockey stars of all-time, Bobby Smith grew up like most kids in Canada playing hockey. He first starred for in the major junior ranks for his hometown Ottawa 67's in the Ontario Hockey Association. In 1978 he scored 69 goals and 123 assists for an amazing 192 regular season points and then tallied another 30 points in the playoffs. He topped the OHA in both assists and points and won the Canadian Major Junior Player of the Year award. From there the North Stars selected the 20-year-old, 6-foot-4 phenom as the number one player taken in that year's draft.

Smith established a torrid scoring pace in Minnesota in his first year, scoring 30 goals and 44 assists en route to winning the Calder Trophy as the NHL's top rookie. Bobby instantly became a fan favorite in his new home. He led the North Stars in scoring four of his first five years with the club. His finest season with Minnesota came during the 1981-82 campaign when Smith achieved career highs in games played (80), goals (43), assists (71) and points (114).

In 1984, Smith was involved in one of the team's most talked-about trades ever, when be was dealt to the Montreal Canadiens for Keith Acton, Mark Napier, and a third-round pick. Smith played seven seasons north of the border, recording 70-plus points in five of those years. In 1986, he led the Canadiens to a Stanley Cup victory by scoring the game-winning goal in a 4-3 win over the Calgary Flames.

In 1991, Smith, then a 33-year-old veteran, returned to his beloved Minnesota to lead the Stars back the Stanley Cup Finals, this time against Badger Bob Johnson and the Pittsburgh Penguins. Smith's leadership and guidance on the ice and in the locker room was of great help to the younger players. He contributed eight goals and eight assists in the playoffs after a 46-point regular season, proving that he hadn't lost the edge that had always made him special in the minds of Stars fans.

For 15 seasons Bobby ruled the red line. He played in 1,077 games with the North Stars and Canadiens, scoring an amazing 1,036 points. And after 13 playoff seasons and 184 games, Smith retired with 64 goals and 96 assists for 160 points, ranking him 12th on the NHL's all-time playoff point leaders list. He also played in four NHL All-Star Games in 1981,1982, 1989, and 1990. From 1981 to 1990, Smith also served as vice president of the NHL Players' Association.

After retiring from hockey in 1993, Smith fulfilled a lifelong dream and went back to college at the U of M. He received his B.S. in Business and then went on to obtain an MBA at the Curt Carlson School of Business Management. That experience would pay quick dividends, because, in 1996, he became the Phoenix Coyotes' first executive vice president of hockey operations. Today, Bobby and his wife Elizabeth, along with their three children, reside in both Scottsdale, Ariz., and Eden Prairie. Smith presently serves as the team's GM.

Bobby was one of the greatest hockey players to ever lace up the skate. He had incredible instincts, an amazingly accurate shot, and a great passing touch. He was the ultimate competitor and team player, always putting his teammates first.

out a loss. Ever the kidder, Worsley finally admitted that a bit of "luck" may have been on his side during the streak.

In Game Two, Minnesota took a quick 1-0 lead, only to see St. Louis come out swinging, literally. Only a few minutes into the game, Blues forward Garry Unger decided to mix it up with Minnesota's Barry Gibbs at center ice. The two scrapped for a bit, with the crowd clearly declaring Gibbs as the victor. "That's the way St. Louis plays," said Blair afterward. "They try to intimidate you right away. But I think this time they made a mistake. They gave us just what we needed. That fight and rough first period turned us on."

The Blues also got fired up, coming right at Maniago in second. They went up 2-1, and then again 3-2, only to see the Stars tie it up at 3-3 going into the third. Jude Drouin, after assisting on the two previous goals, put the Stars up one more time 4-3, on a pretty shot past goalie Ernie Wakely. Blues forward Garry Unger then tallied to tie it, only to see Phil Roberto score to once again give the Blues the lead. With the seconds ticking away, 39-year-old left wing Dean Prentice pasted a shot into the top shelf of the St. Louis cage, sending the game into sudden death overtime.

Only 90 seconds into the extra session, that Stars' first line trio of Drouin, Goldsworthy, and Grant decided to get busy. With Jude skating the puck into the St. Louis zone, followed closely by Goldy and Danny, Drouin had a decision to make. Shoot or pass? He opted to shoot. His shot was tipped and flew right into Wakely's mask, where it promptly fell into the crease. Goldy, who just happened to be in the neighborhood, poked the puck through his five-hole for the game-winner. "I saw Bill," Drouin excitedly explained after the game, "and I heard him (call his name out). I was tempted to pass, but I had a good chance and he was in a perfect spot for a rebound. So I just let it go."

Despite the fact that the Stars were playing with grit, teamwork, good defense, solid forward backchecking, and solid goaltending, Gordon was nervous. They had been there before, and he knew with the series now in St. Louis that it could all change in an instant. Nearly 19,000 mental fans greeted their Blues for Game Three, as Blues wingers Mike Murphy and Phil Roberto teamed up to make it one-nothing midway through the first. Roberto tallied again in the second on a long slapper, only to see Jude Drouin score in the third to make it close. The Stars pulled the Gumper with a minute to go, but could not capitalize. The Blues took the game, 2-1.

Game Four was full of drama as Drouin and Grant scored early to put the Stars up 2-0. Then, midway through the second, a controversial no-goal entered into the equation. Parise, on a sweet two-line pass from Tommy Reid, apparently beat the Blues goaltender, Jacques Caron, on a rebound stuff-in. Caron smothered the puck, but his momentum carried his body into the net - for the conspicuous goal. But, the ref had already blown his whistle to signal a stoppage of play. Gordon went ballistic, pleading that the goal judge should've hit the lights. The play stood, and would prove to be controversial because just a few minutes later, Blues forward Kevin O'Shea scored to tie the game at 2-2. Then, with the teams mired in penalties, the Blues scored on a 4-3 power-play advantage to go up 3-2. The screened shot which ricochet off Maniago's leg pad, would prove to be the game-winner.

With the series tied 2-2, the North Stars returned to friendly confines of the old Met. There, thanks to a Jude Drouin one-timer from Goldy late in the third, the Stars won the game 4-3. The series again shifted back to St. Louis for Game Six. After the Gumper let in a couple of quick ones, Goldy scored to bring the team to within one. Then something happened that scared the hell out of the Minnesota players. With seven minutes left to go in the first period, Blues winger Bob Plager came charging into the Stars' crease and crashed head-on into Worsley. The Gumper, unable to get out of the way, smashed his head into the steel goalpost. Knocked out, the Stars could only think of one thing -- Bill Masterton. Luckily though, the Gumper would come to, and skate off on his own power. Fortunately for Minnesota fans, the Gump, who didn't wear a helmet or facemask, had taken quite a few blows to the old melon in his day. "When that happens, said Gump after that game, "there's no place to hide. I don't remember anything after he hit me." Despite Parise's late third period goal, and a respectable replacement job in goal by Maniago, the Stars lost the game 4-2.

With the series tied at three games apiece, it all came down to one last game. The Stars had earned home-ice advantage, and would need to capitalize on it right then and there if they wanted to advance to the semis. So, on April 16, 1972, a nationally televised audience of nearly 10 million puck fans from across North America crowded around to watch a little bit of playoff hockey.

It was a classic rough and tumble affair that went back and forth for both squads. Blues goalie Jacques Caron owned the Stars for the first two periods, preserving his team's 1-0 lead. "I've never seen a goalie play better," J. P. Parise would say later. "We just couldn't beat him." Then, a few minutes into the third, Stars captain Ted Harris carried the biscuit over center ice and into the St. Louis zone. Faking a shot, he zipped a pass over to Charlie Burns, who was all alone in front of the net. Burns made them pay, flipping a backhander through Caron's five-hole to even it up at one apiece. Murray Oliver brought the 15,635 Stars fans to their feet on a last-second snap-shot with less than a minute to go, only to see Caron smother it in front of the net. The score remained 1-1 through regulation, and once again, it was sudden-death overtime.

For the first 10 minutes of OT it looked like the Stars were going to put the Blues away. Time after time Caron came up huge for St. Louis, as they missed several good scoring opportunities. Then, at 10:07 of the extra session, St. Louis' O'Shea brothers, Danny and Kevin, came in on Maniago. Danny dished to Kevin, who pasted a high shot over Cesare's stick-side. The puck hit the cross bar, deflected straight back into the crease, off the back of the helpless goaltender's leg pad, and into the net. "For a moment," Maniago said, in the book 'The Blazing North Stars', "I must have been the only person in the building who knew it was in. There was a pause before the light went on, but the puck was too far back for me to reach it."

When it was all said and done, the crowd stood motionless, and in disbelief. The 1972 series, even by today's standards, is still considered to be one of the most exciting, "classic" confrontations in league history. "In a way, I'm proud," said Wren Blair. " I think we did something for expansion hockey in this series. It was a great game and a great series!"

Beaten by the "Broad Street Bully's"
The Stars finished with a 37-30-11 record in 1972-73, good enough for third in the West. For their efforts, they earned themselves a first-round playoff date with the "Broad Street Bully's" of Philadelphia. There, despite Dennis Hextall's two game-winning playoff goals, Philly beat Minnesota 4-2. Hextall, acquired from California in a May 1971 trade, emerged as the teams' leading scorer with 30 goals and 52 assists for 82 points. He was followed by Parise, who scored 75 points, and Drouin who added 73. Barry Gibbs and J.P. Parise made the All-Star team that year, while Cesare Maniago posted five bagels throughout the season as well.

The Suddenly Slumping Stars
The team took a nose-dive that next year. Wren Blair had seen enough, replacing third-year coach Jack Gordon just 17 games into the season. He was replaced with Parker MacDonald, who finished the year behind the bench. Despite another solid season from Hextall, who once again led the team in scoring, in addition to finishing third in the league with 62 assists, Minnesota finished the 1973-74 season with a disappointing 23-38-17 record -- dead last in the West and out of the playoffs. One of the main reasons for the teams' lackluster play was due in large part to their lack of defense. Where the previous year's team had scored 254 goals and allowed just 230, the 74' squad tallied only 235 and gave up a whopping 275. On a bright note, Goldy and Hextall were named to the NHL's All-Star team.

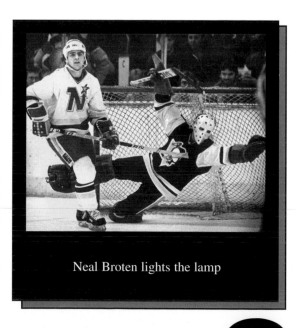

Neal Broten lights the lamp

Gordon returned as coach for the first half of the 1974-75 season, and in 38 games, recorded a lousy 11-22-5 record. Charlie Burns, who came out of coaching retirement to see if he could do any better in the remaining 41 games, posted an equally pathetic 12-28-2 mark. Scoring only 221 goals while surrendering 341 was pretty easy math for anyone to see why this club was in the dumpster. Once again Hextall and Goldy carried the team on their backs, scoring 74 and 72 points each respectively. The NHL, after expanding a few years earlier to several new cities, including: Vancouver, Calgary, Buffalo, Atlanta, New York (Islanders), Washington, Kansas City (who would move to Denver in '76), and Cleveland (who moved from Oakland/California in '76), decided to realign its divisions. The Stars managed to christen their newly created Smythe Division, by finishing in fourth place. Finding it all to be a bit too much, GM Wren Blair stepped down that year and was replaced by Jack Gordon. The Bird, one of Minnesota's most colorful characters, had been through it all, and would prove to be a vital cog in the evolution of the North Stars.

From Captain to Coach

The 1975-76 season saw former captain Ted Harris take over as the team's head coach. His first duty as the team's new skipper was to appoint Goldy to wear the "C" on the front of his green and gold sweater. The team's woes continued that year, as the Stars' finished ahead of only the upstart Kansas City Scouts in the Smythe with a dreadful 20-53-7 record. The Stars started out the year losing a whopping 16 out of their first 20 games. They had virtually no chance after that. The team scored only 195 goals while yielding 303; 16 of them of the short-handed variety. One bright spot however, was the emergence of rookie Tim Young, who's 51 points led the team in scoring. Goldsworthy's 24 goals and 22 helpers helped the cause as well, earning him a trip to the All-Star game.

Buffaloed

An old friend said good-bye at the start of the 1976-77 season. Longtime goaltender Cesare Maniago was dealt to Vancouver in exchange for fellow netminder Gary Smith. (The trade left Bill Goldsworthy as the only remaining "original" North Star from the 1967 expansion draft.) Smith split time that season in the nets with Eveleth native Pete Lopresti, who was the son of Chicago Blackhawk goaltender great, Sam Lopresti. The team had somewhat of a turnaround that year. Despite their porous defense which gave up 70 goals more than they scored, Minnesota finished second in the very weak Smythe Division with a 23-39-18 record. The team ended their four-year playoff drought by facing off against Buffalo in the first round of the playoffs. The Sabres extinguished any hopes that the Minnesota faithful had about making another run at the Cup that year, as they swept the Stars in the best-of-three series 4-2 and 7-1. Minnesota got another great year from Tim Young, who, in addition to leading the team in scoring with 95 points, was selected to his first All-Star team. Another bright spot that season included the addition of Swedish import Rolie Eriksson, who made his North Stars debut with a 25-goal, 44-assist, 69-point season.

The Merger with Cleveland

By the end of the 1977-78 campaign, things had hit rock-bottom for the Stars. They started out the nightmare season losing eight out of their first 10 games, only to follow up that streak by losing an amazing 16 out of their next 20. Ted Harris was canned as coach, and replaced with Andre Beaulieu. He would prove only to be a Band-Aid though, lasting for less than three months behind the bench before himself receiving the ax. The team finally got smart and gave the coaching position to winger Lou Nanne, who would serve as player-coach for the rest of that season. Finishing the season with a miserable 18-53-9 record, management knew something drastic had to be done quickly. Incidentally, Eriksson and Young were once more the lonely bright spots on the squad, leading the team scoring, while rookie defenseman Per-Olov Brasar also stepped up in his first season.

After six losing seasons things were looking bleak for Minnesota, which was mired in financial problems that put them in serious jeopardy of being sold-off to a new state. It was the height of professional hockey warfare throughout North America, as the World Hockey Association's battle for the best players and territory was wreaking havoc on the collective hockey world. The Stars ownership group, tired of losing their shirts, wanted to cut their losses and sell the club to new investors. Coincidentally, the struggling cash-strapped Cleveland franchise was also in the same boat, and as fate would have it, the two clubs decided to get together to further discuss the possibility a potential merger.

The owners of the Cleveland Barons, brothers George and Gordon Gund, heirs to a billion dollar fortune, had also been suffering heavy monetary losses since they purchased the former Oakland/California Golden Seals and moved the fledgling club to Ohio in 1976. Knowing that they too had to take some drastic measures to avoid financial suicide, the Gunds were determined to make something happen. After approaching both the Washington Capitals and Vancouver Canucks, two other struggling small-market teams, about their interests in a merger, they decided to pull the trigger on a unifying deal with Minnesota. Here's how it all worked out. Ultimately, the Cleveland franchise folded, and all of the players who were under contract with the Barons became the property of the "new" Minnesota North Stars. As part of the transaction, the Gunds assumed ownership of the combined team from the nine Minnesota owners.

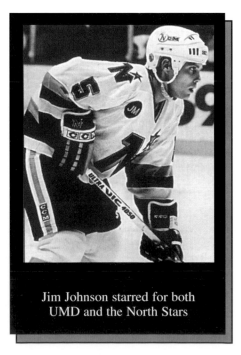

Jim Johnson starred for both
UMD and the North Stars

The league, anxious to "kill two birds with one stone," by taking its two worst franchises and putting them together, was eager to see the deal get done. Optimistic, the NHL figured that as long as the new team remained in Minnesota, where there was so much more interest in hockey than in Ohio, it would prove to be a win-win for both parties. Still, the merger was unprecedented in the history of modern sports, which gave the league reason to be concerned. At that time, only once had two pro sports teams merged within one league - and that brief union which came about during World War II between the Pittsburgh Steelers and Philadelphia Eagles, was only meant to be temporary.

While the Gunds took over as co-chairmen of the board for that upcoming 1978-79 season, John Karr was named as the team's new president, and Lou Nanne was promoted to general manager. Harry Howell was named as the team's coach, but was replaced only a couple of months into the season by former Gophers' coach Glen Sonmor.

The merger injected some new life into the team's young roster. Nanne's task now was to begin melding the best possible team from a combination of the two rosters. The new team was allowed to protect 12 players from the original North Stars including: Tim Young, Glen Sharpley, Per Olov Brasar, Bryan Maxwell and Pete LoPresti from the Stars; and from Cleveland the team acquired: Gilles Meloche, Dennis Maruk, Al MacAdam, Rick Hampton, Mike Fidler and Greg Smith. All told, their were eight former Barons that made the North Star's opening day roster. Right winger Al MacAdam, who finished second in team scoring that season, and goaltender Gilles Meloche would prove to be the best of a bunch. In addition, and perhaps most significantly, because of the team's status as the league's worst franchise, the Stars retained the rights to the no. 1 overall pick in that year's upcoming amateur draft. With that pick, Minnesota selected a young center by the name of Bobby Smith. The talented young center led the team in scoring in his first season with 74 points, and for his efforts he was awarded the Calder Trophy as the NHL's rookie of the year. Roland Eriksson was also named to that year's NHL All-Star team, as Minnesota, which had switched to the Adams Division in Cleveland's place that year, finished the season on an upswing, with an improved 28-40-12 record.

Philly Steak-Out
From April 7th, 1973 to April 7th, 1980, the North Stars won a grand total of zero playoff games, while during the same time frame made seven different coaching changes. Needless to say, it had been a bumpy ride for the past several years for the franchise. That all changed though on April 8th, 1980, when the team beat Toronto, 6-3, to end their playoff win drought. The season was a steady improvement from the one the year before, and under the tutelage of their new coach, Glen Sonmor, the Stars prepared to embark on the new decade of the 1980's with a fresh sense of purpose.

The team had started its rebuilding plans, and had been invigorated by the merger with Cleveland. Led by the young talent on the "new-look" Stars, the team went from the Adams Division's basement to third that next year, with a 36-28-16 record. The season was filled with highlights along the way, including busting up the Philadelphia Flyers unbelievable winning streak of 79'. Philly, which had broken the record for the longest undefeated streak of 29 games, previously held by Montreal, was at 35 consecutive non-loss games and counting when they were greeted by nearly 16,000 Met Center Psychos on January 7, 1980. With the eyes of the entire sports world following their every move, the Stars made a little bit of history. Behind the chants of the fans screaming "Go home Flyers, Go home Flyers," Minnesota drilled the Flyers, 7-1, thus ending their glorious ride. By winning that game the Stars set a club record of their own, by playing 12 consecutive games without a loss at home.

The post-season yielded a pair of series wins, for the suddenly surging North Stars. First the team went out and swept the Toronto Maple Leafs in the opening round of the playoffs. Next they pulled off a major upset by beating the defending Stanley Cup champion Montreal Canadiens, who were attempting to go for their fifth straight title. The series was one for the ages, with Minnesota winning Games One and Two, losing Three, Four, and Five, and then coming back to win Games Six and Seven. The finale came down to the wire, with Al MacAdam scoring on a third period wrister to put the Stars ahead 3-2. Meloche held on in goal as Minnesota won the series in front of a stunned Montreal crowd. The Stars went on to face the Flyers in the semifinals, only to see Philadelphia exact a little bit of revenge. Still upset about having their streak broken in Minnesota, Philly eliminated the North Stars in five games to earn a trip to the finals.

The season ended on a positive note, as the Stars gained a lot of confidence and a dramatic change of direction. MacAdam had a career year for the club, totaling 42 goals and 51 assists for a team-leading 93 points. The winger had earned himself quite a reputation around the league as a sharp-shooting sniper, scoring on nearly 25 percent of his shots. For his efforts he was awarded the league's Masterton Trophy, becoming the only player in team history to do so.

Gilles Meloche combined with journeyman goaltender Gary Edwards to shore up the team's defense, which for the first time since 1973, finally scored more goals (311) than it allowed (253). In addition to MacAdam's great season, Steve Payne scored 85 points, Bobby Smith added 83, and Craig Hartsburg, who made his NHL debut on defense, produced 44-points to lead the team. Hartsburg, Gilles Meloche, Payne, and former Bemidji State Beaver Gary Sargent all made the All-Star team that year as well.

The 1981 Cinderella Stars
The 1980-81 North Stars season will forever be remembered as one of the all-time greats in Minnesota sports history. It was our first taste of Stanley Cup finals' hockey, and it literally took the state by storm. A combination of youth and veteran experience played a big role in the Stars compiling a solid 35-28-17 record that season. Team leader Bobby Smith once again had a big year for the Stars, scoring 93 points on 29 goals and 64 assists. Other contributors included: Steve Payne, a 30-goal scorer, Craig Hartsburg, who escaped the sophomore jinx by scoring 43 points that year, Al MacAdam, and Brad Maxwell. They were also joined by several newcomers that season who gave the team a greatly needed boost. Dino Ciccarelli, called up in February from Oklahoma City (Central Hockey League), became a instant fan favorite when he broke teammate Steve Christoff's record for the most goals by a rookie, scoring 14. Other newcomers included Brad Palmer, who, with his blistering slapshot, was a nice addition, and so was 19-year-old goaltender, Don Beaupre, who played fabulous between the pipes. Another youngster that really stepped up that year by adding some desperately needed skill and polish to the team's backline was former University of Minnesota-Duluth Bulldog star Curt Giles. Giles, like Ciccarelli, was also called up the year before from Oklahoma City. The steady defenseman made his first major contribution that year though, in what was to be a 12-year career in Minnesota.

Brian Bellows

After leading the Kitchener Rangers to the Memorial Cup championship, Brian Bellows was selected second overall by the North Stars in the 1982 Entry Draft. Bellows would go on to score 30 goals or more in eight of his 11 seasons in Minnesota, with his best season being in 1990 - when he tallied 55 goals and 44 assists for 99 points. On August 31, 1992, Bellows was traded to the Montreal Canadiens for Russ Courtnall. During his 10-year tenure with the Stars, Bellows became the team's all-time leader with 342 goals and ranked second in both assists (380) and points (722). (Bellows would go on to star for Montreal, leading the team in his first year with 40 goals - en route to winning a Stanley Cup. He would later play for Tampa Bay, Anaheim, and in 1999 with the Washington Capitals.)

Perhaps though, the biggest "future" star of the team was someone that would get called up at the last second to join in on the post-season festivities. His name was Neal Broten, a Roseau native, and former Gopher and Olympic gold-medalist who brought more speed to an already speedy squad. The Stars had even traded away center Glen Sharpley, thus freeing up Neal's lucky No. 7 jersey.

"Glen Sonmor was a great coach, and he just let us play the game," reminisced Broten. "It all happened so fast, I had only played three games for the Stars' when we went to the Stanley Cup finals. I was so wet behind the ears, I didn't really know what was going on. Things happened so fast and the next thing I knew I was playing with guys like Bobby Smith, Steve Payne, Al MacAdam, and Freddy Barrett. It was a great experience and I will always remember that first run at the Cup."

Much to the approval of the Minnesota fans, the Stars opened the first round of playoffs on the road against rival Boston. Now, coming in to this best-of-five playoff series, the Stars were a collective 0-28-7 in Boston, having never won a game in the Boston Garden. There was clearly no love-loss between these two clubs, who, earlier in the year had beaten the hell out of each other at Met Center for a combined 406 penalty minutes (a record that still stands today!). The Stars went to Beantown expecting another blood bath. What they found however, was that Boston wanted to play some serious hockey, and with that, the fans were treated to a doozy of a series.

In Game One, with the score tied at the end of regulation, Steve Payne scored at 3:34 of the first overtime period to win the game by the score of 5-4. With the Boston "monkey" now off of their proverbial backs, Minnesota followed it up with a 9-6 victory in Game Two. The series shifted back to Bloomington for Game Three, and in what would play out to be a classic, the Stars, brimming with confidence, beat the Bruins 6-3 to sweep the series. "That had to be the biggest upset in Stars history," said legendary radio color-man Al Shaver after the game.

"Never had I seen the Met Center rocking like it was that night," added winger Steve Payne. "I remember sitting in the dressing room after the warm-ups and the building was literally rocking from the noise. People were so fired up. It was quite an experience."

Next up for Minnesota were the Adams Division champion Buffalo Sabres, who were sporting a gaudy .619 winning percentage. Steve Payne once again set the tone by scoring yet another overtime game-winner in Game One. The Stars didn't look back from that point on, winning both Games Two and Three, only to drop a Game Four double-overtime heartbreaker by the score of 5-4. They rolled on to win the series four games to one.

In the semis, the Stars found themselves pitted against another surprise team, the Calgary Flames. With Gilles Meloche and Donny Beaupre trading off in net, the Stars were proving to be a formidable force. Minnesota made a statement in the series opener by crushing the Flames 4-1. Calgary came back to win Game Two on a late third period goal to even it back up, only to see Minnesota win the next two games 6-4 and 7-4. The Flames rallied to win Game Five 3-1 back in Calgary. But the Stars hung in there and behind Brad Palmer's game-winning wrister in the third, took Game Six 5-3. Protecting their home ice throughout the series, the Stars simply outplayed the Flames and ultimately won the series four games to two. With that, after several disappointing semi-final losses over the past decade and a half, the North Stars, for the first time in franchise history, had finally made it to the Stanley Cup finals.

"Getting the opportunity to play in the Stanley Cup finals was incredible," reminisced Bobby Smith years later. "I can still remember standing on the bench as the conference finals game against Calgary was winding down, and Brad Palmer had just scored an insurance goal for us. Just realizing that you had spent your whole life watching the Stanley Cup finals and now you were going to be playing in them, was tremendously exciting."

Dino Ciccarelli

If Wayne Gretzky's "office" was the area just behind the net, then the "doorstep" area just to the side of the crease would have to be reserved for Dino Ciccarelli, who made his living redirecting and stuffing pucks past unsuspecting goalies from his favorite spot on the ice.

Dino Ciccarelli grew up in Sarnia, Ontario, and first emerged as a star on his London Knights junior team (OHA), where, at the age of 17, he won second team all-star honors in 1977-78 after a 142-point season. That next season though, Dino suffered a near career-ending knee injury that caused his draft stock to plummet. Consequently, he went unpicked in the NHL's amateur draft that year, and instead was signed as a free-agent by the North Stars. After spending a season with Oklahoma City, Dino battled back to make the Stars' roster in 1980-81, becoming an instant hit with the Met Center faithful. Ciccarelli set a rookie record by scoring 14 goals in the playoffs that year, helping to lead the team to the Stanley Cup finals. It wasn't long before the fans were bringing "Dino the Dinosaur" dolls to games, to cheer on their new hero. (Conversely, many of those dinosaurs were also maliciously destroyed and burned at rinkside in places such as Chicago, and St. Louis when Ciccarelli came to town!)

Scoring 55 goals and cracking the Top 10 in league scoring with 106 points, Ciccarelli emerged as a superstar that next season. He scored 40 or more goals four times in the next eight years in Minnesota, twice going over the 100-point plateau. A five-time team goal-scoring leader, Dino's 332 goals rank second in franchise history behind only Brian Bellows' 342. In addition, he ranks third in total points with 651, and owns two of the team's three 50-goal seasons. On March 7, 1989, in what Minnesotans considered to be a very controversial trade, Dino was sent packing in a blockbuster deal, to the Washington Capitals in exchange for Mike Gartner and Larry Murphy.

Dino went on to star for the Cap's, and also for the Detroit Red Wings, who he was later dealt to in 1992. Early in 1994, Dino banged home his 500th career goal, putting him a very elite fraternity. In 1996 Dino wound up in Tampa Bay, only to be dealt once again to the Florida Panthers two years later. There, on February 3, 1998, against his old mates from Detroit, he became just the ninth player in league history to score 600 career goals. (To put that into perspective, Mario Lemieux has 613 career goals.)

At 5-foot-10, 175 pounds, Dino Ciccarelli is not big, quick or flashy. An appropriate comparison might be that of the NBA's Dennis Rodman, in the sense that they both earned their bread and butter doing dirty work. While Rodman prides himself on being a relentless rebounder - constantly getting hammered in the paint - Dino thrived at absorbing severe beatings at the hands of bigger, tougher, defensemen in order to hold his ground and pounce on rebounds and deflections in front of the net. A relentless "goalmouth garbage sniper," Ciccarelli has gone on to become one of the most prolific goal scorers in NHL history, making him a sure-bet for Hall of Fame. After 19 seasons in the NHL, in 1999 Dino retired with 608 goals and 592 assists in 1,232 games with five teams.

The finals would prove to be a classic case of Cinderella vs. Goliath. Goliath, in this scenario, was the defending Stanley Cup champion New York Islanders, who's path to the finals went through Edmonton, and then Madison Square Garden, where they swept their cross-town rivals, the Rangers, in the semis. The Stars were now in uncharted territory as they geared up for the Isles, who were no strangers to the hoopla surrounding Lord Stanley's Cup. Afterall, the Islanders, who were used to the media circus, were the toast of the Big Apple. While Minnesota, however, was a bit "star-struck" by it all - and it would show. The Isles were an intimidating bunch. Their roster was a regular who's who of hockey during that era, featuring legends such as Brian Trottier, Mike Bossy, Dennis Potvin, and Butch Goring. Their leader, Billy Smith, a feisty goaltender who seemed to make a habit out of lodging his stick into his opponents flesh whenever they came too close to his crease, was playing outstanding in the net for the Isles.

"So close you could taste it..."

Minnesota, primed on speed and enthusiasm, opened the best-of-seven series in New York City. There, in front of some 15,000 Long Island freaks, the Stars prepared to make history. It wouldn't be easy. The Stars, visibly nervous and scruffy-looking (from not having shaved [superstitiously] in weeks) took the ice with aspirations of winning professional hockey's most coveted prize. Things got off to a bumpy start for Minnesota as New York jumped out to a quick 1-0 lead on a goal by Anders Kallur. The Stars then caught a break when Bob Bourne was assessed a major penalty for spearing. Unfortunately, the Islanders jumped right back as Kallur and Brian Trottier scored two unanswered shorthanded goals during the five-minute disadvantage, and the Stars were never able to regain their composure. A pair of third-period New York goals on only three shots secured an easy 6-3 Isles victory.

Game Two got off to a better start for Minnesota as Dino Ciccarelli scored a power-play goal to go ahead early. (Dino emerged as a star in the playoffs, scoring 14 goals and 21 points in 19 games, both NHL playoff records for a rookie.) Then, precisely one minute later, Bossy tied things up for New York, only to see both Potvin and Nystrom each score a goal. But the Stars rallied and came back to tie it at three apiece in the second, on goals from Palmer and Payne. The defending champs got nervous, but their experience prevailed as Potvin, Ken Morrow, and Bossy each scored in an eight-minute stretch to mirror the result of the 6-3 series opening victory.

Game Three brought puck mania to the then so-called hockey capital of the world, Bloomington, Minn. The Met Center was the site of many tailgate bashes as the adoring North Star fans welcomed home their heroes from the Big Apple. The Stars jumped out to a 3-1 lead after the first, and the crowd went crazy. But Goring tallied twice in the second as the Islanders took a 4-3 lead into the final period. Again, the Stars rebounded, tying the game at the 1:11 mark of the third, only to see the Islanders regain the lead less than a minute later. With New York up by one, Goring put the final dagger in the collective hearts of Minnesota, scoring again at the six-minute mark for the hat-trick to all but seal it up. The Isles added an empty-netter and came away with the 7-5 victory.

"We knew what to expect from their dominant guys, Potvin, Bossy, and Trottier," said Star's coach Glen Sonmor after Game 3. "but I don't think we were prepared for so much offense out of Goring."

Refusing to lie down and be swept by Islanders, Minnesota played brilliantly in Game Four. Utility man, Gord Lane opened the scoring for the Isles to silence the crowd early in the first period. Then, midway through the period, with Minnesota on a power play, Brad Maxwell tallied on a blistering slapshot from the blue line. Or so he thought! Referee Andy Van Hellemond apparently never saw the shot, which was later seen on reply to rip right through the net. The crowd went nuts over the no-goal call, only to see Craig Harstburg's shot from the point seconds later beat Billy Smith. This time the red light was turned on and as a result, the crowd went berserk. With the score tied up at two apiece through two, Minnesota took the lead on Steve Payne's top-shelf slapper midway through the third. Bobby Smith added an insurance goal late in the game to seal the deal, and insure a 4-2 victory for the Stars. The 19-year-old phenom goaltender Donny Beaupre played huge in Game Four, turning away shot after shot against the mighty Islanders, who were held to fewer than five goals only three times in 18 post-season games, significantly, losing all three. The Stars kept their cool during the game and it paid off. Of the four North Star goals scored in the game, two came on power plays and a third was scored three seconds after an Islander penalty had elapsed.

With the win, the Stars had lived to skate yet another day. The series once again shifted back to Uniondale, Long Island for Game Five. Unfortunately for the Stars, New York came out flying out of the gate. And, once again it was Butch Goring who would do most of the damage. At 5:12 of the first period a North Star clearing pass deflected off referee Bryan Lewis and right onto the stick of Bob Bourne, who promptly fed the rushing Goring for the goal. Then, less than a half of a minute later, John Tonelli and Bob Nystrom dug the puck out from behind the Minnesota net and fed it to a wide open Wayne Merrick, who beat Beaupre to make it 2-0. That line was amazing. It was their 18th goal of the playoffs, all scored while at even strength against their adversaries' top lines. A few minutes later, Goring, who would capture the Conn Smythe Trophy as the playoff's MVP, scored again on a wrister, putting the game out of reach. Behind legendary coach Al Arbour, the Isles went on to win the game 5-1 and the series. For New York, who had established themselves as one of the game's greatest hockey dynasties, the win would be the second in what would be a string of four-straight Stanley Cups.

North Stars' winger Dave Gagner

The Stars had lost to one of the greatest teams of all time, and could still hang their hats high. New York went into the series with a game-plan. They were a stronger, more physical team which clutched, grabbed, hooked, and interfered with the younger, speedier Stars, thus neutralizing their superior skating attack. They also converted on five of 16 power play opportunities - allowing no shorthanded goals, compared to Minnesota, which could muster just six goals out of 33 power play chances.

The Stars' Cinderella fairy-tale escapade would prove to be a huge shot in the arm for Minnesota hockey though. The fans had fallen in love with their guys in green, and the future of the organization looked to be very bright indeed.

On the Rebound

Expectations were running high for the young Stars, who had gotten a whiff of Lord Stanley's coveted prize the year before. Because of league expansion and realignment, Minnesota started out the 1981-82 season by switching from the Adams Division to the Norris Division. Feeling that they had something to prove, the club went out and won the first divisional championship in the team's history, finishing atop the Norris Division with a 37-23-20 record. Their 94-point campaign matched the then-club record for wins in a season.

In the first round of the playoffs, the Stars found themselves pitted against their old foe's from the Windy City, the Chicago Blackhawks. The series opened on April 7th in front of 15,597 Met Center mentals. The crowd was eagerly anticipating a return trip to the finals, and saw the lowly Hawks as merely a bump in the road. Boy were they wrong! Chicago stunned the Stars in Game One, when Hawk winger Greg Fox beat Gilles Meloche at 3:32 of the first overtime period to win the game 3-2. Chicago's Denny Savard beat Don Beaupre for the game-winner in Game Two, as the Blackhawks beat Minnesota for the second straight night - this time by the score of 5-3. The series shifted back to the Chicago Stadium for Game Three, and there, in front of more than 20,000 fans, the Stars finally busted loose. Led by Dino Ciccarelli's game-winner, the Stars pulverized Chicago 7-1. But, the next night Hawks defenseman Al Secord put the final nail in the coffin for Minnesota, as Chicago went on to beat the Stars 5-2. With the win, Chicago had eliminated the Stars from playoff competition. It was a disappointing loss, not to mention a major upset, for the young Stars.

There were some bright spots however. Bobby Smith had a break-out year, scoring 43 goals, and 71 assists for an amazing 114 points. Ciccarelli also stepped up by scoring 106 points on 55 goals and 51 assists, while Neal Broten added 98 points on 38 goals and 60 helpers. Ciccarelli, Hartsburg, Meloche, and Bobby Smith were all named to the 1982 All-Star squad.

The Curse of the Blackhawks

Minnesota helped itself during the offseason, when they struck gold in the 1982 entry draft. Now, the amateur draft had long been considered as a crap-shoot by most of the NHL general managers, who hated to leverage the future of their respective organizations of the shoulders of some unpolished 18-year-old kid from Moose Jaw, Saskatchewan. With the second overall pick in the first-round of the draft, the Stars selected a young left winger from St. Catherine's, Ontario by the name of Brian Bellows. Luckily for Minnesota fans, the Boston Bruins decided to go with defenseman Gord Kluzak with the first overall pick of the draft. Kluzak, plagued by injuries throughout his career, never panned out for the Bruins. But Bellows on the other hand, proved to be worth his weight in gold.

The Stars came out smoking for the 1982-83 season, losing only nine of their first 40 games. Then, on January 13th, 1983, longtime Stars coach Glen Sonmor stepped down as coach, and was replaced by his assistant, Murray Oliver. Oliver led the Stars to a second-place finish in the Norris Division with 40 wins and 96 overall points, both franchise records.

While Broten and Smith tied for the scoring lead with 77 points apiece, Stars rookie Brian Bellows finished with 65 points in 68 games. Beaupre and Meloche formed a solid tandem in goal, with Meloche posting a 20-13-11 record (3.57 goals against average) and Beaupre compiling a 19-10-5 record (3.58 goals against average) during the regular season. The entire line of Broten-McCarthy-Ciccarelli was invited to play at the 1983 All-Star game, and they were also joined by Craig Hartsburg. (Another important event happened that year as well. Craig Hartsburg took over the captain's position from Tim Young, it was a title he would keep for more than seven years.)

Oliver led the Stars back to the playoffs, where they met the Toronto Maple Leafs in the first round. There the Stars disposed of the Leafs three games to one. Bobby Smith scored both the game-winners for Games One and Two, with the latter being an overtime winner. They lost Game Three in Toronto, but came back to take Game Four, and the series, thanks to Dino Ciccarelli's overtime game-winner at 8:05 of the first extra session. Next up were their new arch-rivals from Chicago, the Norris Division champion Blackhawks. In a very physical and emotional series, the Hawks came out and took Games One and Two by the scores of 5-2 and 7-4. Minnesota came back to win Game Three at the Met Center, where Ciccarelli scored the eventual game-winner of a 5-1 blowout. Thinking that the tide was turning, the Stars battled Chicago again that next night, only to see right winger Rich Preston beat Meloche at 10:34 of overtime to win the game, and take a commanding three games to one lead in the series. Now back at the Stadium, the Hawks took Game Five, 5-2, to win the series. For the Stars, it was yet again another disappointing early exit from the playoffs.

So-Long Bobby and Hello Gretzky

The Stars thought that they could once again help themselves during that offseason, when they had the first overall pick in the NHL's entry draft. With the likes of Pat LaFontaine, Steve Yzerman, and Tom Barrasso on the board, the Stars surprised everyone by drafting a New Jersey high schooler by the name of Brian Lawton. Touting their new rookie, the Stars prepared to bid for the Cup yet another time.

At the beginning of the season, knowing they had to make some changes at the top, Minnesota hired long-time Canadian college coach Bill Mahoney to take over behind the bench. Then, in a shocker, just 10 games into the 1983-84 season, the Stars pulled off a blockbuster deal, trading Bobby Smith to the Montreal Canadiens in return for Keith Acton and Mark Napier.

"I was really very excited about going to the Canadiens," said Smith years later. "I realized that it would be an excellent opportunity and would lead to a very exciting time for me. I won a Stanley Cup in 1986 with them and without question, that is the biggest highlight of my career. On the other hand, it was very difficult to leave Minnesota. It was the place where I wanted to live. Although it was a very good move for my career, it was sad to leave Minnesota."

Rather than laying down and pouting over the loss of Smith, the Stars rallied and actually played some inspired hockey. Under Mahoney the Stars once again regained the Norris Division crown, by posting a 39-31-10 regular season record, their finest performance of the decade. Helping to fill the void created by Smith's absence, Neal Broten led the attack with 89 points while Brian Bellows added 42 goals and 41 assists for a phenomenal sophomore campaign. Defenseman Brad Maxwell contributed not only 19 goals and 54 assists, but also 225 hard earned penalty minutes. Dino scored 38 goals and 33 assists, and newcomers Keith Acton and Mark Napier also were major contributors by scoring 55 and 41 points respectively. The downside to it all was the fact that both Beaupre and Meloche were both over the 4.00 goals-against mark, a tell-tale sign that the defense was soft.

The Stars were given a very tough test in the first round, facing off against their nemesis from Chicago. But the Stars hung tough, and ultimately prevailed. It wasn't easy though, as the Blackhawks stole Game One at the Met Center, 3-1 on Al Secord's slapper to put it away. Neal Broten scored the game-winner for the Stars in Game Two though, in a heroic come-from-behind 6-5 thriller in front of a packed house in Bloomington. The Stars split the next two games in Chicago, winning Game Three 4-1, only to lose Game Four 4-3. But the series shifted back to Minnie for Game Five, and there the Stars prevailed, winning the contest by the score of 4-1 to win the series.

Full of confidence from beating the Hawks, the Stars now prepared to take on the St. Louis Blues in round two. Dino Ciccarelli brought out the inflatable "Dino the Dinosaur" dolls by the thousands at the Met Center on April 12th, when he scored the game-winner of a 2-1 nail-biter for the Stars. Doug Gilmour rained on their parade that next night though, beating Donny Beaupre at 16:16 of overtime to beat the Stars in Game Two. The Stars lost Game Three in St. Louis by the score of 3-1, only to come back and take Game Four by the score of 3-2, on Tommy McCarthy's game-winner in the third. With the series tied at two games apiece, the series returned to Minnesota for Game Five. There, Donny Beaupre blanked the Blues 6-0. In Game Six though, St. Louis returned the favor, this time shutting out Minnesota 4-0 in front of their home crowd to once again even it back up at three each. Game Seven would prove to be a classic, with both teams beating each other up at both ends of the ice. But, with the score tied at 3-3 at the end of regulation, it all came down to one shot. And luckily for Minnesota, it was Steve Payne who made the difference. At 6:00 of the extra session, Payner knocked in a dribbler past Blues netminder Mike Liut to give the Stars the series victory.

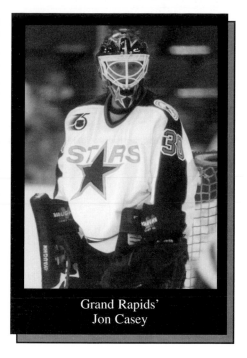

Grand Rapids'
Jon Casey

The Minnesota fans were starting to sense another run at Lord Stanley's hardware, and now only Edmonton stood in the way. This is where the story gets really ugly, as the Stars were suddenly and maliciously beaten over their heads with a very stiff dose of reality. The Oilers, led by the "Great One" Wayne Gretzky, pummeled the Stars in the Campbell Conference finals. Gretzky, Coffey, Messier, Linesman, Fuhr, and Kurri, led the assault as the powerhouse Oilers, which would go on to win the first of four Stanley Cups in five years that season, swept Minnesota in four straight games to win the series. For the Stars, it was a bitter pill to swallow.

The Blackhawk Blues
Thoroughly distraught by their disappointing early final-four exit the year before, the Stars tried to do right by their fans in 1984-85. They opened the season with a miserable 3-8-2 record, and as a result, Glen Sonmor came down from the front office and returned to the bench to resume his coaching duties from Bill Mahoney. Glen didn't do much to help his cause, as the Stars finished 18 games under .500, with a 25-43-12 record. The 62-point campaign was the team's worst finish in eight seasons.

Despite their dismal season, the team managed to squeak into the playoffs. There they faced the first-place Blues. While most were expecting a quick series, as in a quick exit for the Stars, it just so happened that it was the other way around. That's right, the Stars shocked everyone by coming out and sweeping the Blues in three straight. Keith Acton was the hero of the first round playoff match, scoring the game-winners for both of the first two games in St. Louis. A pair of nail-biters, the Stars won Game One 3-2, and Game Two 4-3. Tony McKegney got the third game-winner in Game Three, as Gilles Meloche posted a 2-0 shutout to seal the fate of the Blues.

Thinking that they could make a run much like in 1981, Minnesota was quickly brought back down to earth in Round Two by their old nemesis' from the second city - the Blackhawks. With the series opening in Chicago, Minnesota came out and steamrollered the Hawks in Game One by the score of 8-5. Chicago, none too pleased about being beat in their own house, came back the next night and manhandled the Stars 6-2. They then proceeded to take Games Three and Four as well, on game-winners by Al Secord, and Daryl Sutter. Game Five was back in Chicago, and Minnesota refused to roll over and play dead. In a bloody match, the Stars prevailed on Dennis "Pee Wee" Maruk's overtime goal just over a minute into the extra session.

To the melodic chants of "Secord Sucks!" "Secord Sucks!", the Stars played strong, but came up short in Game Six. They lost yet another overtime thriller, this time by the score of 6-5, when Chicago winger Daryl Sutter scored his second game-winner of the series, at 15:41 of the first overtime. With the win, Chicago took the Conference finals, 4-2.

Brian Bellows, the sturdy, hard-working winger, led all scorers that year with 26 goals and 36 assists for 62 points, while Maruk finished second with 60. A trio of Minnesota goalies shared the netminding duties that year, as Donny Beaupre and Gilles Meloche were joined by Rollie Melanson, who appeared in some 20 times contests for the Stars. Beaupre had the best goals against average of the bunch with a 3.69, while Meloche finished with a 3.80, and "Rollie the Goalie" compiled a respectable 4.10 GAA.

Enter the Mighty Casey
At the beginning of the 1985-86 season, North Stars GM Lou Nanne named ex-New York Islander player and coach Lorne Henning as the teams' 13th head coach. Henning would quickly find out that the fans were starved for a winner here, and wanted one sooner than later. Knowing he was in the hot-seat, Lorne led his Stars to a respectable 38-33-9 record that year, good for second place in the Norris. In the first round of the playoffs, they met St. Louis, which was anxious to avenge its previous year's shocking upset at the hands of the Stars.

Despite Donny Beaupre's nearly 40 saves, the Stars lost Game One at the Met 2-1. They rebounded in Game Two, though, behind Dirk Graham's game-winner. Back in St. Louis, Bernie Federko scored the 4-3 winner for the Blues in Game Three. It was Graham playing hero yet one more time for the Stars in Game Four, as he once again got the game-winner in a 7-4 Star's equalizer. With the series tied at two games apiece, the series came back to Minnesota. There, in front of 15,953 screaming fans, the North Stars got waxed, 6-3, to lose the series. "That was one of the toughest losses I've ever been a part of," said Donny Beaupre after the game.

Neal Broten had a career year, scoring 29 goals and 76 assists for a 105-point season - a first for an American-born player. Ciccarelli scored 44 goals and 45 assists for 89 points, while Bellows added 31 goals and 48 assists for 79 points to lead the Stars. The Stars also had a great season out of former Gopher, Scott Bjugstad, who scored 43 goals. While Beaupre played 52 games in goal that season, a newcomer, Jon Casey, a Grand Rapids native, made 26 appearances, en route to posting a respectable 3.89 goals-against average. Incidentally, Casey replaced long-time North Stars keeper Gilles Meloche, who was traded to Edmonton (later Pittsburgh) for winger Paul Houck.

Some Lean Years

1986-87 and 1987-88 were not particularly good years if you were a Stars fan. Despite the fact that the team came within one point of the Norris Division crown in 1985-86, the North Stars missed the playoffs for the first time in eight seasons in 1986-87. Glen Sonmor once again returned to the bench to serve as the interim coach, this time replacing Lorne Henning with only a month to go in the season. The team finished with a dismal 30-40-10 record, good enough for only a fifth place finish in the Norris. Neal Broten, who lit it up the year before, was plagued by injuries that year, and despite the continued efforts of Ciccarelli and Bellows, the other players simply did not get the job done. An example of the scoring disparity was the fact that Ciccarelli, who scored 52 goals and added 51 assists for 103 points, finished the season more than 40 points ahead of that of his nearest teammate, Brian MacLellan. Kari Takko joined Donny Beaupre in goal that year, while Casey got some minutes under his belt in the minors.

On April 23, 1987, St. Paul's Herb Brooks became the 14th coach of the North Stars. Brooks, then 50 years old, had won 100 NHL games faster than any coach in the history of the league when he coached the New York Rangers during a 1981-85 stint on Broadway. "Herbie" was a Minnesota icon. A former Gopher coach who won three NCAA titles in the 1970s, he gained most of his notoriety as the coach of the infamous 1980 Miracle on Ice team that won the Olympic gold medal in Lake Placid. A brilliant tactician, and student of the European game, he simply did not have the players to get the job done in only a year's time. Despite Brooks' taking over behind the bench, the team finished with a 19-48-13 record, and once again missed the playoffs. After only one season, Brooks was replaced by Pierre Page. Incidentally, Ciccarelli and Bellows led the way for the Stars that year, scoring 86 and 81 points respectively. Bellows was named to the All-Star team as well.

The Stars were indecisive and without direction at this point. Later that year, with the team clearly in a funk, Lou Nanne resigned as the team's GM, opting instead to move upstairs to the front office. There he replaced John Karr as the team's new president.

It's Ciccarelli for Gartner in a Blockbuster

Jack Ferreira, who took over as the North Stars new GM, decided to shake some things up from the top down. A major trade surprised the North Stars in 1988-89, and got them back on track. The blockbuster deal, which took place in March of 1989, sent fan-favorite Dino Ciccarelli packing to the Washington Capitals in exchange for star winger Mike Gartner. The trigger was pulled on the controversial deal after much deliberation from the Stars' front office. Nonetheless, the Stars responded by playing much better that season. Newcomer Dave Gagner, who was traded to Minnesota from the New York Rangers for Jari Gronstrand and Paul Boutilier back in October of 1987, was called up in 1988 and made a big impact in his first full season. He came out of nowhere to lead the club in scoring with 35 goals and 43 assists for 78 points. That year, the line of Neal Broten, Mike Gartner and Brian Bellows was also one of the hottest trio's in the league.

Gagner, Gartner, Broten and Bellows, along with goaltender Jon Casey, who took over as the team's full time starter that year, led the way for the Stars. Pierre Page's squad played much better than it had in year's past and wound up finishing in third place in the Norris Division with an improved 27-37-16 record. Making a return trip to the playoffs, after a two-year drought, the Stars took on the Blues in round one. The Stars lost both Games One and Two in St. Louis by the identical overtime scores of 4-3. Down but not out, the Stars tried in vain to win Game Three back in Bloomington. But, Blues winger, and former UMD Bulldog, Brett Hull got his second third-period game-winner of the series, beating Jon Casey on the top shelf, to lead St. Louis past the Stars 5-3. Minnesota, refusing to be swept, came back behind Don Barber's third period game-winning slapshot to win Game Four, 5-4. The series shifted back to St. Louis, where the Blues proceeded to crush the Stars 6-1, thus ending their season. To add insult to injury, Gartner was held scoreless in the series. Afraid of losing him to free agency, the Stars traded Gartner to the Rangers for Ulf Dahlen the next season. (In retrospect, although Dahlen would develop into a solid two-way player, it was a horrible trade - considering Dino tallied more than 600 career goals and assists for an amazing 1,200-plus points, and played through the 1998-99 season before finally retiring.)

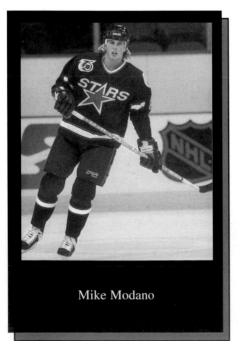

Mike Modano

Enter Rookie Sensation Mike Modano

The North Stars finished fourth in the Norris with an improved 36-40-4 record in 1989-90. However, they were blessed by a talented young rookie phenom by the name of Mike Modano, who tallied 75 points on 29 goals and 46 assists en route to finishing second in the NHL's Calder Trophy voting that season. (He was awarded the rookie-of-the-year award by The Hockey News as well.) Team captain and resident goon Basil McRae kept pretty busy that year protecting his flock of young stars. Among them included: Brian Bellows, who racked up 55 goals and 44 assists for 99 points, Neal Broten, who's playmaking earned him 85 points, and Dave Gagner, who added 78 points.

The Stars back-doored it into the playoffs that season, where they once again found themselves facing Chicago. The Stars stole Game One in the Windy City thanks to a Brian Bellows goal late in the third which gave Minnesota a 2-1 victory. The Hawks rallied in Game Two, evening up the series on a Jeremy Roenick wrister that beat Jon Casey on the short side. Chicago returned the favor back in Bloomington, stealing Game Three 2-1. Minnesota tattoo'd the Blackhawks in Game Four, as Casey garnered a coveted 4-0 shut-out. With the series once again even, Game Five took place back at the old Chicago Stadium. There, in front of more than 18,000 fans, the Hawks beat up the Stars 5-1. Back at the Met the Stars rallied, and thanks to Larry Murphy's goal midway through the third, Minnesota won the game by the score of 5-3. Tied again at three games apiece, Chicago, behind a pair from Jeremy Roenick, ended the Stars' season with a 5-2 pasting at the Stadium. (I can still hear the deafening blast of that damn diesel locomotive horn ringing in my ears from whenever the Hawks would score a goal!)

"Do You Know the Way to San Jose?"

The 1990-91 season was without a doubt the craziest in the history of the franchise. An unbelievable turn of events took place that season, starting when the brothers Gund, faced with continuing financial losses in the Twin Cities, began exploring the possibility of moving the team to another city. Basically holding the state hostage, and demanding $50 million dollars to sell the team, or else they would pack up and leave, the league stepped in as a sort of symbolic "hostage negotiator" to try and make sense of it all.

Their main suitors were a group of financiers from Northern California. (It is kind of ironic when you think about it. After all, that was the precise location of the former home of the California Golden Seals - the team which the Gunds purchased back in 1976 to move to Cleveland, because they couldn't survive financially in the area. Go figure?) The group, located in San Jose, had a new arena and an interest in luring an NHL franchise to relocate there.

The NHL, which wasn't particularly interested in the concept of franchise relocation, saw a unique opportunity. What happened next was an unprecedented compromise that saved one franchise, and gave birth to another. Here's what went down. The league, sympathetic to the Gunds, decided to award them a new expansion franchise in San Jose. At the same time, the North Stars were to be spared from relocating, or worse, folding. As part of the arrangement, a new management/ownership group was to be set up in Minnesota. The Gunds, knowing that a new management team was going to come in and clean house, relocated many of the front-office personnel to San Jose to run the new "Sharks" franchise. Among them were GM Jack Ferreira, who would be eager to draft many of the North Stars' players, of whom he was very familiar with, when the expansion draft took place.

As part of the "deal," the San Jose Sharks were allowed to select several key players from Minnesota at a dispersal draft which was held on May 30, 1991. There, as per prior agreement, San Jose claimed four players from the Stars' NHL roster and yet another 10 from their farm system. Among the big names claimed by the Sharks were enforcer Shane Churla and goaltender Brian Hayward. Now, because the Stars were taking such a hit from all of this, and basically getting raided by the Gunds new team, the NHL decided to allow Minnesota to select several players from other NHL clubs during the 1991 Expansion Draft. There, they used the opportunity to claim several veteran players including Edmonton defenseman Charlie Huddy - who was later traded to L.A. for Todd Elik, and also Rangers centerman, Kelly Kisio - who was later dealt back to San Jose in return for fan favorite, Shane Churla. Among the then lesser known minor leaguers who were also claimed included Stars' former No. 1 pick, and Rochester native, Doug Zmolek.

Meanwhile, back in Minnie, a new ownership group had finally come together. It consisted of Howard Baldwin, a former managing partner with the Hartford Whalers and California yogurt and movie guru, and financier partner Morris Belzberg. Now, here's where it gets confusing. Shortly after the transaction was completed with the Gunds, former Calgary Flames co-owner and mall developer extraordinaire, Norman Green, in a very shady deal, assumes control of the North Stars by buying out the Baldwin's ownership group, which then immediately became involved with the Pittsburgh Penguins ownership group, to emerge as the team's sole owner. Green came in and immediately started firing the front office staff at Met Center. Among the casualties were Jack Ferreira and Pierre Page, who were replaced by former Philadelphia Flyers star Bobby Clarke, who was named as the team's new GM, and former Montreal hero Bob Gainey, who was named as the team's new coach.

One Last Shot at Lord Stanley's Cup

The 1990-91 season began ominously enough for Minnesota. To say that the fans were expecting big things from this team at the onset of the season, would be quite an understatement. Afterall, only 5,730 fans showed up for the season opener. Things snowballed from there, as the team managed only one win in their first nine games, en route to a pathetic opening three months of the season. The fans weren't coming to see the team, the media was apathetic, and even free money giveaways from Norm himself couldn't get people off their butts and into the arena.

But, thanks to Stars new GM Bob Clarke, things were about to change. He bolstered the defense by trading offensive-minded defensemen, Larry Murphy, to Pittsburgh for defensive minded Jim Johnson and Chris Dahlquist - both Minnesota natives. In addition, he went out and got Calgary center Marc Bureau, who was a solid backchecking forward that could play tough defense. Other players began to step up as well, including Ulf Dahlen, who caught fire in the second half of the season by scoring 19 of his 21 goals in the last 42 games, including a hat trick against the Red Wings late in the year. Clarke's strategy of a strong defense was starting to take shape, and goaltender Jon Casey, who posted a 2.98 goals-against-average that season, was starting to play some good hockey.

Under the tutelage of first year coach, Bob Gainey, the Stars went 14-6-6 from late January until mid-March. With the team finally started to heat up, the fans started to trickle in. The Stars finished the regular season with a very marginal record of 27-39-14, good only for fourth place in the Norris Division. Miraculously, a late-season slump almost dropped the Stars out of the playoff picture, but with a little luck and a few friendly bounces, they managed to squeak into the playoffs. They were led once again by the usual suspects. Dave Gagner, the team's lone All-Star that year, had 82 points, while Bellows posted 75, Broten added 69, Modano contributed 65, and Brian Propp, who had starred throughout the 1970s with Philadelphia, bequeathed 73 points. And, Bobby Smith, who was reacquired from Montreal prior to the season, added a much needed veteran leadership presence to the young squad.

Hardly anyone gave the squad much of a chance at doing much in the postseason that year, and virtually no one thought that they would have a chance of being around playing hockey in May. It was a marginal season at best for a fourth-place team

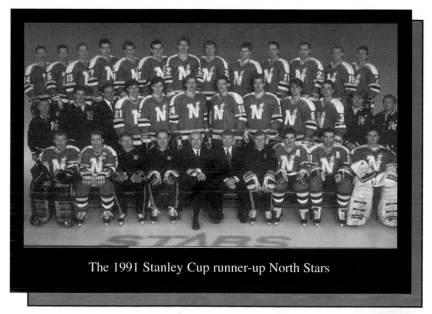

The 1991 Stanley Cup runner-up North Stars

that had finished 12 games under .500, and there were clearly much better teams in their division that they would have to get through to go anywhere in the playoffs. To put it into perspective, the Las Vegas odds going into the playoffs on the Stars winning the Stanley Cup were a staggering 25-1. But, the two Bobs, Bob Gainey, who played on five Stanley Cup winners during his brilliant 16-year career with the Canadians, and Bob Clarke, who had a couple of his own from his playing days in Philadelphia, knew what it was going take for their team to garner any postseason success. By stressing a team approach to defense, and controlling their own end, the Stars were primed and ready to go in the playoffs. Tired of being written off by the media as a fluke, sub-.500 team, coach Gainey put things into perspective before the opening face off in Chicago. "The regular season is there to prepare teams for the playoffs. The teams you respect are the ones that are still playing in late May." And so began one of the most extraordinary playoff sagas in NHL annals.

First up for the Stars were the Norris Division champion Chicago Blackhawks, who, by virtue of their top regular-season record in the NHL that year, were the odds-on favorites to win it all. The series opened in Chicago, where the Stars began their miraculous journey that will forever be remembered as one of Minnesota's greatest hockey seasons ever. In Game One, the Stars had suc-cumb to the Hawks bullying tactics, and found themselves not playing very disciplined hockey. They settled down however, and stuck to their game plan. The Stars took Game One 4-3 when Minnesota winger Brian Propp scored just minutes into the first overtime session. They knew to go upstairs on Chicago goalie Ed Belfour, who liked to go down when under pressure, and that's just where Propper put it to get the game-winner.

Cloquet's Corey Millen played for the Dallas Stars from 1995-1997

In Game Two, Chicago retaliated by beating up on the Stars 5-2. Casey, who was replaced late in the game by backup goaltender Brian Hayward, was shell-shocked by Chicago's massive artillery. Minnesota wasn't focused and played stu-pidly, setting a team record for most penalty minutes in a playoff game. Game Three brought the series back to the Met Center, where the Minnesota fans could hardly contain themselves from going completely nuts. In the history of professional hockey in Minnesota, there is with-out question no bigger hated rival than Chicago. Dave Gagner carried the Stars on his back in the first period when he set an NHL record for the most points scored in a single period, scoring two goals and two assists. The Hawks played tough though, and in the end it was Jeremy Roenick's wrister late in the third over Casey's shoulder that gave Chicago a 6-5 victory.

Game Four was a different story, as Minnesota forced Chicago to play a slower, more defensive game. It worked as Mike Craig scored the sec-ond of two goals for the Stars, which was all Casey would need for the "W," as Minnesota prevailed 3-1. With the series even, they headed back to the Second City for Game Five.

Gainey stressed playing physical without playing foolishly, and that turned out to be the difference in Game Five. The Hawks displayed their frustrations by taking a series of bad penalties. Minnesota, executing Gainey's strategy to perfection, was able to cash in on its opportunities, scoring five goals on power plays en route to a 6-0 shellacking. Casey stood on his head, and earned every bit of the coveted playoff shutout. Game Six once again returned to Bloomington, where the humiliated Hawks found themselves fighting to stay alive. On April 14th, 1991, the Stars, behind Brian Bellow's fourth goal, and 12th overall point of the series, beat the Hawks 3-1. Thanks to the spectacular goaltending of Jon Casey, who simply outplayed his rookie-of-the-year counter part Eddie Belfour, the Stars KO'd Chicago in six games. With the win, Minnesota had become the first team in 20 years to upset the top ranked team in the regular season in the first round of the playoffs.

Even though there were an amazing 487 total penalty minutes in the series, the Stars played with a high degree of discipline and were deadly on the powerplay. For the heavily favored Hawks, it was devastating. "They deserved to win," said Chicago head coach Mike Keenan.

"They [Chicago] were predicting a Stanley Cup and it was kind of like we were just in the way," said Stars left wing Basil McRae after the game. "That's what fired us up."

Feeling Blue

If the Stars thought that they could relax and coast through the playoffs, they were sorely mistaken. That's because the next opponent they faced was another old rival, the St. Louis Blues, who had finished the season with the second best record in the league. They were led by the dynam-ic duo of "Hull & Oates," better known as Brett Hull and Adam Oates, who had combined for over 240 points that season en route to finishing second and third respectively in league scoring.

St. Louis had 20 more victories and 37 more points than the Stars did that season, and they had no intention of suffering the same fate as their friends from Chicago. Shane Churla was the unlikely hero of Game One, as the Stars beat St. Louis on their home ice to take a 1-0 series lead. The Blues came back in Game Two, as Adam Oates beat Casey twice in a 5-2 St. Louis win. With the series back at the Met, Stew Gavin got the game-winner as Minnesota beat the Blues 5-1 in Game Three. Minnesota continued to roll in Game Four, pounding the Blues by the score of 8-4. Modano, Broten, Propp, Smith, Bellows and Gagner all got into the action for the Stars, who were playing inspired hockey. Game Five went back to St. Louis, where the Blues won a tight 4-2 end-to-end battle.

FACT: The Stars' thrill ride would play a significant role in what was considered by many as the greatest-ever sin-gle year of sporting events. In addition to the Stars' Stanley Cup run, the Twins won the 1991 World Series, both the NCAA's Final Four as well as Super Bowl XXVI were held at the Dome, and Golf's U.S. Open was held at Hazeltine.

Then, back at the Met for Game Six, with the Stars were leading 1-0 at 3:50 of the third period, Brian Bellows took a long pass and pushed it into the slot. There, the long armed Bobby Smith reached around a Blues defenseman and poked the puck through the crease. Old No. 18 then sturdied himself, gained con-trol of the puck, and backhanded what would be the game-winner into the top right side of the net past St. Louis goalie Vincent Riendeau. The Blues threatened with a few minutes left, but Casey played big once again, as the Stars won the game 3-2, as well as the series.

The Stars had played with the same discipline and style that had gotten them past Chicago. Perhaps the key to the Minnesota victory was its ability to shut down the Blues' deadly one-two punch of 86-goal scorer Brett Hull and super-playmaker Adam Oates. Gatean Duchesne and Stewart Gavin kept Hull and Oates in check by serving as their constant shadows, ultimately holding the tandem to only a combined 13 shots on goal during the series. Another factor was the play of defenseman and resident tough-guy Mark Tinordi, who's aggressive style of play was effective at both ends of the ice. And, of course let's not forget about goalie Jon Casey, who was once again nothing short of phenomenal in the second-round matchup.

The Stars were suddenly red-hot, and the hockey world was starting to take notice. Said Blue's coach Brian Sutter after the game: "If anybody out there takes them for granted, they don't know what's going on."

The "Gretzky-less" Oilers
So, after beating the league's two best teams, the Stars were only four wins away from a Campbell Conference championship. It would not be easy though, because their next opponents were the defending Stanley Cup champion Edmonton Oilers. "The cliche's are all used up," said Stars owner Norm Green before the series. And that was exactly how the Stars players felt, knowing that they now had to go out and prove to everyone that they weren't just a fluke and really were for real.

Despite the fact that Gretzky had been dealt to the L.A. Kings, Edmonton was still a great team. Ignoring the five giant Stanley Cup banners that were hanging from the rafters of Edmonton's arena, combined with the fact that they hadn't won in Edmonton in more than 11 years, the Stars went out and kicked some butt in Game One. "Speed Kills," said Edmonton coach John Muckler after the game. He was referring, of course, to Minnesota's young horses, who out-hustled his bigger and stronger Oilers to a 3-1 victory. Led by Dave Gagner's second period game-winner, the Stars hung on behind an outstanding night in goal by Mr. Casey.

The Oilers rallied to crush the Stars in Game Two, winning the match by the score of 7-2. With the series now in Minnesota, the Stars used speed and skill to their advantage in Game Three. Bellows and Modano each scored breakaway goals, while Bobby Smith got the game-winner, en route to a 7-3 Stars' victory. "They play like we used to play," said a disgusted Oilers owner Peter Pocklington after the game.

Edmonton lost their composure and played ugly in Game Four, racking up 49 penalty minutes. The Stars capitalized on several of those five-on-four advantages, scoring two power play goals. Mikey Modano got the game-winner, with Broten dishing out a couple of helpers as well. Stars' keeper Jon Casey stopped 20 of 21 shots for a 5-1 Minnesota win. "There is another hero every night," said Stars winger Dave Gagner.

Game Five back in Edmonton was a much closer contest. With the game tied at two apiece early in the third period, Stars forward Stew Gavin dished a sweet pass to a breaking Bobby Smith, whose long reach was just enough to extend around Edmonton goalie Grant Fuhr's outstretched stick for what would prove to be the game-winner. The Stars went on to win the game 3-2. In so doing, Minnesota had earned themselves a trip to the Stanley Cup finals for the second time in franchise history.

Once again it was hot goaltending that led the way. Casey, who really made a name for himself during the series, recorded an outstanding .991 save percentage. And, much like in the previous two series, Minnesota made the most of their opportunities by turning powerplay advantages into goals. Amazingly, the team converted on four first-period power plays goals in the five-game series.

Next up for the "new Cinderella Stars" was a trip to the finals against the Pittsburgh Penguins and their feisty coach, former Gopher and Minneapolis native "Badger" Bob Johnson.

"Super Mario" and the Mighty Pittsburgh Penguins
The North Stars, upon returning home from their trip to Edmonton, received a hero's welcome from the fans. Suddenly, they were front page news. "We're used to two reporters writing 'Stars Win' or 'Stars Lose', -- See Page 10C," said Brian Bellows sarcastically about the media horde covering the team during the finals.

Now the only thing standing in the way of Lord Stanley's Cup for the North Stars, was the Wales Conference champion Pittsburgh Penguins, who had just beaten the Boston Bruins in a seventh-game overtime thriller. In addition to two-time MVP winner Mario Lemieux, the league's most explosive and dominant player, the Pen's featured a solid blend of young speedsters as well as several experienced veterans. While Kevin Stevens, Mark Recchi, and Jaromir Jagr provided a balanced scoring punch, Stanley Cup veterans Paul Coffey, Bryan Trottier, and Joe Mullen added skill and character. Tom Barrasso, the team's goalie, was also playing excellent hockey at the time.

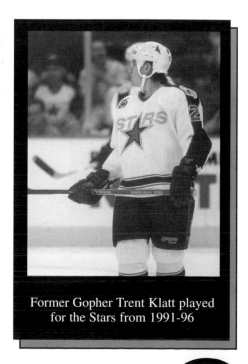

Former Gopher Trent Klatt played for the Stars from 1991-96

On paper this was a boring series. Minnesota, who finished the regular season with the sixth-worst record in the 21-team league, and Pittsburgh, a team which had made the playoffs only once in the previous eight years. The series had many subplots. Among them was the fact that it was the first time that two teams who had missed the playoffs the previous year had come back to make the finals. The Stars-Penguins series also marked the first time since the Red Wings and Blackhawks met back in 1934, that both finalists had never won a Stanley Cup. It was also the first finals meeting between two of the league's 1967 expansion teams.

Minnesota knew that if they wanted to win this thing, they would have to do two things. First, they would have to stay cool, force the Pen's to take stupid penalties, and capitalize on their power-play, which had registered 31 goals in the first three rounds of the playoffs. Secondly, and perhaps most importantly, they would have to try to contain both Mario Lemieux and Jaromir Jagr.

The Stars opened the series in Pittsburgh, and thanks to a pair of Neal Broten goals, the Stars, much like they had done in their past three openers, took Game One 5-4. Bobby Smith got the game-win-

ner late in the third, as the Stars, who were visibly excited, tried to remain calm and focused on the task at hand.

The Penguins got revenge in Game Two, spanking the Stars 4-1. Bob Errey and Kevin Stevens put Pittsburgh ahead 2-0, only to see Mario Lemieux score one of the most incredible goals that will surely live-on forever in NHL highlight films. In one of the most dazzling solo efforts in recent memory, "Super Mario" waltzed around two Minnesota defensmen, deked left, then right, and then flipped the puck up and over a "used and abused" Jon Casey. As the Stars' defenders harmlessly watched Lemieux fly through the air and eventually land head-first onto the ice behind the net, the crowd went absolutely nuts. What makes his graceful antics even more incredible is the fact that Lemieux, a six-foot-five, 230 pound centerman, is considered a giant by hockey standards.

The North Stars returned home from Pennsylvania to find that the state had gone hockey-mad. "I have been in seven Stanley Cup finals as a player and manager," said Stars' GM Bob Clarke on the hype surrounding the series. "There has never been anything like this. Never anything close."

The team was welcomed back to the Met by a standing-room-only crowd for Game Three. They also got a bit of good news during the pregame warm-up when they found out that while lacing up his skates in the locker room, Mario Lemieux had strained his back and would not be able to skate that night. With Lemieux out of the game, the Stars rolled. Dave Gagner beat Barasso late in the second on a nice wrister, only to see Bobby Smith get his second straight game-winner for Minnesota less than 30 seconds later. Jon Casey held the Pen's in check throughout the entire match as the Stars cruised 3-1 and took the series lead two games to one. Was destiny in control of this "Cinderella" team? At this point it looked like Lord Stanley's cup was going to be hanging out at Lake Minnetonka for the summer, but there were still two games to be won.

Mario came back for Game Four, and just like that the Penguins were an entirely different team. Badger Bob had his boys play all-out from the opening face-off, and they responded by scoring three quick goals in the first three minutes of the game. Pittsburgh got the Stars to take dumb penalties, and took them right out of their game plan. Gagner kept it close for the Stars, but when former Islander Brian Trottier scored midway through the second to give the Penguins a commanding 4-1 lead, it didn't look good. Minnesota miraculously fought back on a Mike Modano powerplay goal to get the team to within one goal by the end of the second, but couldn't capitalize on several good scoring chances to tie it up. Their best chance came on a missed doorstep one-timer by Neal Broten late in the period. An empty-netter by Phil Bourque late in the third iced the 5-3 series-tying win by the Pen's. Much to the chagrin of Minnesota checkers - who had so brilliantly shut down the likes of Jeremy Roenick, Brett Hull, and Mark Messier in rounds one, two and three, they could simply not contain the game's premier player -- Mario Lemieux.

The series moved back to the Steel City for Game Five, and unfortunately for the Stars, the Pen's went straight for Minnesota's jugular. For the second straight game, Pittsburgh came out of the blocks quickly and Minnesota was once again left to play catch up. By the time Penguin winger Mark Recchi scored his second goal of the game at the 13:41 mark of the first period, Pittsburgh had already jumped out to a 4-0 lead. While Ron Francis added a goal in the third, Troy Loney scored what would be the game-winner on a wild goal-mouth scramble late in the contest for the Penguins. Former North Star, Larry Murphy, also finished with four assists. The Stars made it close late in the game on some nice plays by Broten, Gagner, Bellows and Smith, but ended up on the short side of the 6-4 final.

With their backs against the wall, the Stars returned to the Met Center to try and even the series at three games apiece. What happened next, however, was one of the ugliest chapters in Minnesota hockey history. Anyone who was at the Game Six massacre, would probably attest that it was one of the most difficult things they have ever witnessed. It would be safe to say that after this fiasco, Jon Casey would need a large can of Solarcaine to help soothe all of the proverbial "goalie sunburn" on the back of his neck that was caused by all the red lights going off behind him.

Ulf Samuelsson started the barrage by scoring what would be the first of eight unanswered goals for the Penguins. Pittsburgh, who found the back of the net early and often, wrapped up the series in a 8-0 laugher. Team captain, Mario Lemieux , who scored four of his playoff-high 44 post-season points in the game, was named as the winner of the Conn Smythe MVP Trophy. And in the end, in front of the thousands of disappointed Minnesota fans, it was he who was presented Lord Stanley's Cup by NHL president John Zeigler. While the fans respectfully applauded the league's newest champions, many of the Stars' players could be seen consoling one another and even fighting back a few tears. It would prove to be the most lopsided Cup winning game in NHL history for the Pen's, who would go on to repeat as champions the next season as well.

The clock had struck midnight for the Cinderella Stars. But in the end, the underdog North Stars had won the respect of the league and the loyalty of their fans, making believers out of countless hockey enthusiasts from around the country in the process. The Stars could hang their heads high.

One of the main factors for the Stars' success that year was due to the play of the team's goon squad: Basil McRae, Shane Churla and Mark Tinordi. During the playoffs, instead of beating the hell out of people, they played effective rough hockey while suckering their opponents into

Herb Brooks

Born in St. Paul, Herb Brooks came from a hockey-crazy family. His father was a well known amateur player in the 1920s, and his brother, David, played for the Gophers in the early 1960s and also on the 1964 U.S. Olympic team. As a boy growing up on St. Paul's tough East Side, a training ground for many future Minnesota hockey stars, he was a typical hockey playing rink-rat. He went on to star as both a hockey and baseball player at St. Paul Johnson High School from 1952-1955. As a senior, the forward led Johnson to a 26-1-2 record en route to winning the state championship. In the title game, Brooks scored two goals in the 3-1 victory over their Mill City rivals, Minneapolis Southwest.

From there Herb went to the University of Minnesota, where he became known for his blinding speed. "He was one of the fastest, if not the fastest, player in college hockey in that era," said his coach, John Mariucci. Brooks would learn a lot from "Maroosh," saying that he had more to do with shaping his ideas in hockey than any other individual. Brooks wore a Golden Gopher sweater from 1957-59, scoring 45 points over his three-year career. He graduated from the U in 1961 with a B.A. in Psychology.

The next phase of Brooks' life involved his lifelong dream - the Olympics. After graduation, he began to build a successful career in the insurance business, but never fully got away from the game that continued to dominate his life - hockey. Herb tried out for the 1960 Olympic team which was played in Squaw Valley. He eluded every cut except the last one, when he was the last player to be released. "My father said that they must have cut the right guy, because they won the gold medal," Herb said jokingly.

Brooks then spent nearly a decade playing for either Olympic or National teams. From 1961 to 1970, there were two Olympic teams and five national teams in all, more than any player in the history of United States hockey. In addition, he captained the 1965, 1967, 1968, and 1970 teams. Herb went into coaching at this point. After a brief stint as the skipper of the Minnesota Junior Stars in the Minnesota/Ontario Junior-A League, he became an assistant under Gopher coach Glen Sonmor at the U of M. That next year Brooks took over as the team's new coach, becoming the youngest college hockey coach in the country. He inherited a program at it's lowest point, though, coming off a last place finish just the season before. Herb was up for the challenge, and went on to make history.

The chant "Herbee, Herbee" was an all too familiar sound throughout the tenure of the man who would become Minnesota's greatest hockey coach. Brooks instilled a new brand of pride and tradition that next season, starting with his newly designed jerseys which proudly featured the classic block-style Minnesota "M" on the front. Brooks promised he would bring, "exciting, dynamic people into the Gopher program," and he kept his word. In only seven years, Brooks had built a hockey dynasty in Minnesota. More importantly, he did it all with Minnesota kids.

With his extensive knowledge and experience in European hockey, Herb became an advocate of the Russian style of play and in particular, the coaching style of Anatoli Tarasov. He would instill this philosophy in motivating his own players. From 1972-1979, Brooks won the only national championships in University of Minnesota hockey history. There were three in all: 1973, 1976, and 1979. His record may never be equaled. While at Minnesota, Brooks won 175 games, lost only 100, and tied 20 for a .636 winning percentage. Twenty-three of his protégés went on to play in the NHL.

The next chapter of Brooks' life is the one that made him a household name, the "Miracle on Ice." After coaching the U.S. National team in the World Games in Moscow, in 1979, Herb took over as coach of the fabled 1980 U.S. Olympic Hockey team. Brooks guided the squad to their incredible upset of the heavily-favored Soviet Union team, setting the stage for the U.S. win against Finland in the gold medal game. That victory was one of the most memorable moments in U.S. sports history.

After a brief coaching stint in Davos, Switzerland, Herb's coaching success continued with the NHL's New York Rangers, where he collected 100 victories quicker than any other coach before him and, as a result, was named NHL Coach of the Year in 1982. His Broadway stint with the Rangers lasted until 1985. Then, in an amazing move, Brooks came home and accepted the head coaching position at St. Cloud State University in 1987. He was the school's savior, leading them to a third place finish in the national small-college tournament, and more importantly, moving them to NCAA Division I status. He stayed for only a year, but with his clout, got the school a beautiful new arena and really got the Huskies' program turned around.

Next stop in the Brooks' hockey adventure was another homecoming of sorts - Bloomington, where he over took over the reigns from Lorne Henning as the new coach of the North Stars. The season, however, didn't go well for Brooks. Unable to overcome an enormous number of injuries, the Stars finished in the Norris Division cellar. Citing philosophical differences with management, Brooks resigned and was replaced by Pierre Page that next season.

Brooks took some well deserved time away from coaching for a few years to get into private business and serve as a hockey color commentator on television. Then, in 1991, he first took over the New Jersey Devils minor league team in Utica, and was later promoted to be the head coach of the NHL team in 1992. Herb became a scout with the Pittsburgh Penguins in 1995, and in 1998, even took over as the coach of the French Olympic team at the Nagano Games in Japan.

One of the greatest college hockey coaches ever, Brooks was enshrined in the U.S. Hockey, U of M, and East Side Hockey halls of fame. Among his numerous awards and achievements, he was named AP and ABC "Sports Athlete of the Year." Herbie is a legend in the world of sports and is very much a hockey icon in the United States. Whether he's competing in the business world, on the ice, or even on the diamond of a world championship fast-pitch softball team, he takes the same attitude and intensity to whatever he does, and that's why he's so successful. He is a true Minnesota treasure.

"The name on the front of the sweater is more important than the name on the back," said Brooks. "They always forget about individuals, but they'll always remember the teams. That has always been the cornerstone of my philosophy."

stupid penalties. Once it was five-on-four, Minnesota's power-play proved to be deadly. Although the trio combined for almost 200 penalty minutes (and countless stitches) throughout the playoffs, they chose their battles and were there for every step of the way to protect their team's goal-scorers.

Brian Bellows and Dave Gagner led the way for the Stars in the playoffs, scoring 29 and 27 points respectively. (The two also led the team in the regular season, with Gagner scoring 82 points and Bellows adding 75 for the team.) And, while Neal Broten and Mike Modano each added 22 & 20 points of their own, it was Bobby Smith's eight goals and eight assists in the playoffs (on top of a 46-point regular season), that made the biggest difference for the team. While everyone had written off the 13-year veteran, who was supposed to be looking at his best hockey through his the rear-view mirror, he proved that he had not lost his edge. His leadership and presence were immeasurable for the young Stars.

Player after player stepped it up during that series, making it truly a team effort. Mark the "Tin Man" Tinordi, once written off as a bruising goon, found himself skating on the team's coveted power-play line, where his defense was rock solid. And how about Jon Casey, who's 3.04 GAA over the playoffs established him as one of the league's big-time "money" keepers. He carried the team, often-times gambling and coming way out of the net to single-handedly bust up break-aways. Incidentally, following the series, he became the team's winningest goaltender in the postseason with 14 victories.

Credit should also be given to Stewart Gavin & Gaetan Duchesne, who fought in the trenches gallantly for the Stars. The two wingers were assigned the toughest jobs in the world during the playoff run -- stopping each team's superstar. The two blue-collar wingers became the shadow of their targets, implementing a grinding brand of defensive offense that was crippling to a speedy center who wanted to get free in center ice. Finishing the playoffs with an impressive +9 plus-minus ranking, Gavin and the Duke even held Brett Hull to a single shot on goal in Game One of the St. Louis series.

"I thought it was great for me to finish my career in Minnesota," said Bobby Smith. "I had played 12 years in the league at that point and was pretty excited about the opportunity to play for a team coached by Bob Gainey and managed by Bob Clarke. There was a huge interest in hockey in the Twin Cities at that point, and it was very exciting for the players. We had a lot of success that year and going back to the Stanley Cup finals was a real thrill for me."

Back to Reality

The euphoria of the team's amazing cup run soon wore off as the team finished in fourth place in the Norris Division in 1991-92, posting a very mediocre 32-42-6 record. They backed into the playoffs, where they would face the Detroit Red Wings. Just when everyone was about to write them off, a little bit of the magic came back as the Stars beat the Wings 4-3 and 4-2 at the "Joe" (Joe Louis Arena) in Detroit. Back at the newly remodeled Met Center, they lost a close Game Three, only to come back and take Game Four. With Minnesota firmly in the driver's seat up three games to one, the fans started to get a little nostalgic. Playing inspired hockey, the Wings threw the Stars a pair of 3-0 and 1-0 shutouts in Games Five and Six. The series then shifted back to the Motor City for Game Seven, where Detroit prevailed over the worn-out Stars, 5-2.

After blowing a three games to one lead, things got pretty testy back at home. Owner Norman Green started to complain publicly that the team was losing money, and started talking about the possibility of moving the team. The off-ice distractions drifted onto the ice and into the lockerroom as the team struggled to stay focused. Green had shaken up the front office as well. With GM Bobby Clarke departing to take over the expansion Florida Panthers, coach Bob Gainey was left to wear both hats. Under Gainey, and with relocation rumors running rampant, the Stars tried to save face.

One Final Ugly Chapter

Here is a rough chronology of what supposedly transpired during that very ugly and painful 1992-93 season: Let me first preface this nightmare by explaining that shortly after signing Mike Modano to a four-year $6.75 million contract (then the fifth highest salary in the NHL), Norm Green made it pretty clear to the world that the team was losing money, and could not make it here without some major concessions.

Green, a real-estate developer, apparently had high hopes for turning a remodeled Met Center into an extension of the Mall of America. Complete with an enclosed skyway connection to the Mall, there were talks of developing the land around the Met Center for a Phase II expansion of the Mega Mall. When it became clear that this was not going to happen, all hell broke loose between the North Stars, the City of Bloomington, State of Minnesota, and the Metropolitan Sports Facilities Commission. Ultimately, Green, who had his eyes set on much greener real-estate development pastures, knew that he wasn't going to make as much money by operating just the hockey team.

So, early in 1992, the team implied that unless the Metropolitan Sports Facilities Commission gives them an improved lease deal, the team may be forced to move. Among the places that the team threatened included: Anaheim, where a group of interested investors was apparently in place; St. Paul, to play in the old Civic Center; and Minneapolis, where a deal was in the works to play alongside of the Timberwolves at the Target Center.

By November of that year, on top of everything else, rumors circulated that Green's assistant was considering filing a sexual harassment lawsuit against him after his behavior forced her to quit back in August.

On January 30th, 1993, Green received bids from both the Target Center and Civic Center. On weighing the feasibility of moving the team from Bloomington, Green was quoted in the Star Tribune as saying: "I want to find out whether we can sell 10,000-12,000 tickets if we move downtown. I lost about $5 million last year and I'll lose more money this year. I am not going to lose any more money operating a hockey team."

Pittsburgh Penguins coach Badger Bob Johnson holds the Stanley Cup after his Pen's beat the Stars

As the suspense drags on as to just what the hell Green is going to do with our Stars, Twin Cities celebrity author and envelope tycoon, Harvey Mackay, steps up and offers to personally guarantee the sale of 1,000 season tickets if the team will stay in Minnesota and play at the Target Center. Green declines the offer, instead choosing to keep his options open. Ironically, later in February Green has the audacity to say that if indeed the North Stars have to move out of the state, that it is because the fans did not buy enough season tickets.

On March 8th, upon returning from his Palm Springs mansion, Green called for a team meeting in which he criticized his skaters for their recent poor play. Two days later, after ruling out selling the team to local owners, an agreement was finalized to move the team due south down Interstate-35 to Texas, where they would become the "Dallas Stars." (Interestingly, the Stars' new home would be the dumpy, luxury suite-less Reunion Arena, home of the NBA's Dallas Mavericks.)

"I signed a 10-year lease" proclaimed Green. "It is a demonstration of our commitment to Dallas. We intend to stay here for a long time."

Hearing the bad news, the team finished its last month of the season as lame ducks. On April 15, tax day of all days, the North Stars played their final game against the Detroit Red Wings. Just before that last game, the Metropolitan Sports Facilities Commission, fearing that the fans were going to trash the joint in protest, placed an ad in the Star Tribune, entitled: "The Puck Stops Here; Please be Gentle" Underneath the headline it read in part, "We know that many people are disappointed that the team is leaving Minnesota. We agree it's unfortunate. But we want to remind everyone that the public, and not the hockey club, owns Met Center. And that we need to keep the building intact and in good repair for future uses." (Amazingly, only 19 months later, the rocket scientists from the Metropolitan Sports Facilities Commission decided to blow-up the Met Center, which, with its newly retrofitted burgundy seats and impeccable site-lines, was considered by many to be one of the NHL best arena's, to make way for it's new owner -- the Twin Cities International Airport, which wanted the land for a new runway construction project.)

Incidentally, the Star's final game was played. People did wreck and steal stuff. And the Stars, like anybody gave a rip, lost 5-3, finishing out their final season in Minnesota with a record of 36-38-10, and out of the playoffs. As the players took one last lap around the ice and saluted the fans who had stuck with them through thick and thin, the chants of "Norm Sucks!" "Norm Sucks!" "Norm Sucks!" echoed throughout the Met Center rafters. For those black, green and gold faithful, it was a sad and very cruel day.

"It was the worst day of my life," said Mike Rendahl, arguably the North Stars' greatest all-time fan, "and I still get upset thinking about how it all ended. I really miss my Stars, and their logo... oh I loved that logo!"

With the Stars leaving town, many of the players chimed in on how they really felt about the country's biggest hockey state not having an NHL franchise.

"Minnesota is one of the top two or three best hockey areas in the U.S. with unbelievable support for high school, college and junior associations," said former Star Dino Ciccarelli upon learning that the Stars were leaving Minnesota. "To not have an NHL team there doesn't make sense. With all that cold and snow, it was a great hockey atmosphere and I've got to believe they'll get a team, but it will be a team in trouble and you'll be starting from the bottom."

"It was like losing a relative," said Lou Nanne. "It was just a really disheartening experience for me."

"It was a very sad day for the NHL and certainly for hockey in the Twin Cities and the state of Minnesota," said Bobby Smith.

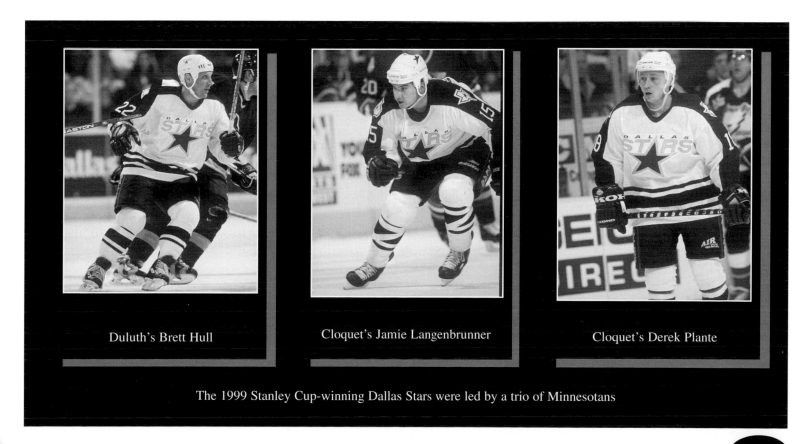

Duluth's Brett Hull   Cloquet's Jamie Langenbrunner   Cloquet's Derek Plante

The 1999 Stanley Cup-winning Dallas Stars were led by a trio of Minnesotans

"It was tough for me to take," said Neal Broten. "A lot of people took it pretty rough, and it was a real big deal. I remember this strange feeling and thinking that this can't be happening to me. You didn't really think it was going to happen until it happened, and then you're moving and driving down to Texas."

It was tough for me, being from Minneapolis, and seeing that franchise leave even though it was really supported well by the public," said Jim Johnson. "And I mean that, because we averaged about 16,000 fans that year before the team moved. So, I had mixed emotions about moving to Dallas."

Fittingly, only a couple of years later, Green wound up selling the Dallas Stars, and in 1999, following Brett Hull's Game Six "toe in the crease" game-winner over Buffalo, the "Greenless" Lone Stars went on to win the Stanley Cup Championship.

Blowing up the Met Center... Gee, that was a brilliant idea!

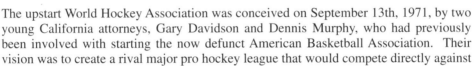
The Fighting Saints

Maybe it was because they played during the North Stars' bleakest era? Or maybe it was because Glen Sonmor was somehow able to magically bring together a mix of pint-sized speedy, goal scorers, with a bunch of outcast prospects and goons who played with a reckless abandon. For whatever the reason, the Saints were one of the most colorful teams in Minnesota hockey history. And, although they only lasted for five years in downtown St. Paul, they managed to build a loyal grass-roots fan base that was second to none throughout the Twin Cities. Whether it was playing hard on the ice, or partying hard off of it, the fans fell in love with these guys and simply couldn't get enough of them. Here is there story:

The upstart World Hockey Association was conceived on September 13th, 1971, by two young California attorneys, Gary Davidson and Dennis Murphy, who had previously been involved with starting the now defunct American Basketball Association. Their vision was to create a rival major pro hockey league that would compete directly against the powerful NHL, something that hadn't happened in more than 50 years.

The league then recruited potential investors throughout the U.S. and Canada who were interested in purchasing franchises. A year later the WHA set up shop with 12 teams in two divisions. Among them included: the New England Whalers, Cleveland Crusaders, New York Raiders, Quebec Nordiques, Ottawa Nationals and Philadelphia Blazers (all of the Eastern Division), in addition to the Minnesota Fighting Saints, Winnipeg Jets, Chicago Cougars, Houston Aeros, Edmonton Oilers and Los Angeles Sharks (all of the Western Division).

On February 12, 1972 the WHA held its first draft. The owners of the new league, wanting quick returns on their $7 million franchise fee investments, went right after the NHL by attacking their deep rosters and farm teams. They knew that if they lured away a few big-name stars, to give themselves some instant credibility, and combined them with a bunch of other lesser-known younger players, they would have a decent product to sell to the fans. They began by paying existing NHL players more money to jump ship, and also did their best to sign away junior prospects, minor leaguers, and Europeans who wanted an opportunity to play for more money and recognition.

At first, the NHL laughed at the new league, thinking it would dissolve much like the others that had come and gone through the years. But when the WHA's Winnipeg Jets signed Chicago Blackhawks superstar Bobby Hull to a multi-million dollar contract, the NHL quickly took notice. The NHL soon realized that these guys were for real, and knew that they had to do something to protect their interests. As a result, the NHL dug deep into its financial reserves and tried to tie-up a lot of its players' contracts, to prevent them from straying to the renegade league.

The WHA responded with a variety of political ploys to attract players to their side of the fence. Among them included drafting 18-year-olds, instead of the NHL's then-usual draft age of 20. This infuriated NHL scouts and GM's alike who didn't want to gamble on the abilities of inexperienced kids. The NHL answered back by raising their own salaries, lowering their draft age eligibility, and even went as far as adding new franchises in strategic cities around the U.S. and Canada (Atlanta and the N.Y. Islanders for instance) as a sort of "preemptive strike" to add even further competition

The Saint's Mike "Shaky" Walton

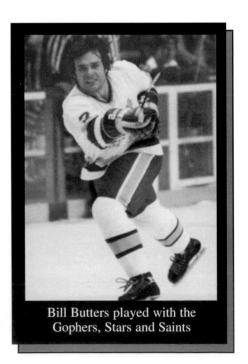
Bill Butters played with the Gophers, Stars and Saints

and expense to the renegade WHA teams who were going to be residing there.

The WHA also knew that they had to differentiate themselves from the other guys to win over the fans. One of the things that they did was to allow its players to use big banana curves on their hockey stick blades. While the NHL allowed just a 1/2 inch curve, the WHA allowed for a whopping 1 1/4 inches for its players to lift the puck into the arena's rafters. Another thing that they did was to use a different colored puck. Much like the old ABA used red, white and blue basketballs to separate itself from the NBA, the WHA also wanted its own identity from the NHL. So, instead of using traditional black pucks, they decided to try a flaming red puck. But, because the paint quickly peeled off of it, they went to a color called "Superpuck-Blue." And, even though these proved to be soft and often bounced erratically on the ice, they became the instant trademark signature of a very different league.

Now, the genesis of the Minnesota Fighting Saints is an interesting one. When the new league was formed, they immediately considered Minnesota as one of its prime candidates to house a franchise. By the early 1970s the North Stars were struggling, and had been playing to half empty crowds at the Met Center. Several Twin Cities businessmen with ties to local hockey, including Lou Kaplan, Frank Marzitelli, John Massaff and Len Vannelli, realized that there was an opportunity for another team to come to town and give the Stars a run for their money. They got together and successfully lobbied the city of St. Paul to transform the newly constructed Civic Center into the Saints' new home arena. The group was awarded a franchise in August of 1971, and immediately started to put together the pieces of their new organization.

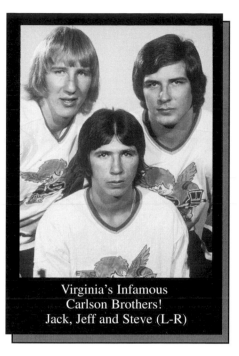

Virginia's Infamous
Carlson Brothers!
Jack, Jeff and Steve (L-R)

Their first appointment was then Gopher hockey coach, Glen Sonmor, who was hired to serve as the team's first coach and GM. Next, they prepared for their team's inaugural draft. Now, the way it all worked back then, was that each team picked four "preferred players" to put on their wish-list so that the owners could determine which teams wanted which players. One of those players that the Saints picked was former Warroad High School star, Henry Boucha. But, Boucha, fresh off of playing on the 1972 silver-medal winning Olympic team in Japan, opted instead to sign with the NHL's Detroit Red Wings. The Saints first player they did manage to sign was U.S.Olympic goalie and International Falls native, Mike Curran, while their first NHLer was former North Star Wayne Connelly - then of the Vancouver Canucks. Other players from that inaugural draft included North Stars' legend Bill Goldsworthy, Montreal Canadiens forward Peter Mahovlich, and Vancouver winger Dale Tallon. In addition, they brought in a bunch of local Minnesota boys — a tactic that would lure lots of fans to the Civic Center. Among them were Mike Antonovich, Keith "Huffer" Christiansen, Craig Falkman, Jack McCartan, Len Lilyholm, Dick Paradise and Bill Klatt.

Gary Gambucci starred for the Gophers, Saints and North Stars

It was a veritable gold mine for players, who, for the first time's in their careers, now had a choice. But some thought that It was too much too soon, and that ultimately these inexperienced players would dilute the game's talent pool to a lower level.

"From my Olympic team alone there were eight players, some of average ability, who were offered lucrative contracts," said 1972 Olympic coach and former Gopher All-American Murray Williamson. "They were jumping quickly. Our goaltender, Mike Curran, left a $12,000 teaching job in Green Bay for a $35,000 contract with the Minnesota Fighting Saints. Frank Sanders, Wally Olds, Jim McElmury, Dick McGlynn, Kevin Ahearn, Tim Sheehy, Craig Sarner, Bruce McIntosh, Tom Mellor and Henry Boucha, all fresh from the Olympic team, were looking at offers from both leagues. Perhaps one or two were ready for major pro hockey at that time."

Sonmor drafted a roster chock full of potential stars, unproven wannabe's, has-been's, maybe's, and in keeping with traditional Sonmor values - a bunch of tough guys who could really mix it up. All of whom were delighted to be playing pro hockey in the Twin Cities. They opened their training camp in Duluth that first year, and prepared themselves to battle in the WHA's Western Division.

Wayne Connelly scored the first-ever Saints goal at the 13:04 mark of the first period against the Winnipeg Jets on October, 13, 1972, and although they lost that game 4-3, they did go on to get their first-ever win against the Chicago Cougars on October 13th, when Mike Antonovich got the 3-2 game-winner late in the third. The Saints had their ups and downs that first year, but all-in-all played well as the team went on to finish the season with a 38-37-3 record, good for just fifth place ahead of Chicago in the six-team Western Division. The Saints provided some dramatics at the end of the year though, when they managed to squeeze into the playoffs by beating a tough Edmonton Oilers team in a sudden death overtime thriller. And, although they lost in the first round of the playoffs to Winnipeg, four games to one, they had laid the foundation for a solid team. The fans came out to see them, and they proved that the Twin Cities could indeed support two pro hockey franchises.

Paul Holmgren

Former Gopher and St. Paul Harding High School star Paul Holmgren, played hockey professionally with the WHA's Fighting Saints, North Stars and Philadelphia Flyers. He is also one of the few Americans to have ever coached in the NHL, having led both the Philadelphia Flyers and the Hartford Whalers during the late 1980s and early '90s. One of the toughest men ever to lace em' up, Holmgren played more than 10 years in the NHL.

LeRoy Neiman

Minnesota's very own LeRoy Neiman is one of America's premier artists. He is without question the most famous sports artist of the 21st century, and has painted nearly every famous American athlete over his career. His vivid colors and unique brush-strokes are brilliant and have made his works instantly recognizable. LeRoy Neiman was born on June 8, 1921, in St. Paul, and grew up in the Frog Town neighborhood of the city. He loved sports and painting as a kid, and used to go ice fishing and sledding on White Bear Lake, as well as attend the St. Paul Winter Carnival. He got into hockey at an early age, and used to admire fellow St. Paulite, and Hall of Famer, Bobby Dill.

"I was always a goalie," said Neiman in a recent phone interview. "I wasn't a good player that's why I was a goalie. I played in Uniondale Playground in Frogtown, that was our domain and we used to play out there all day long. I also loved going to the Auditorium and watching the Saints play against the Millers, that was a great rivalry."

Neiman attended Washington High School in the late 1930s, until going into the Army. After his discharge from the service, in 1946, Neiman enrolled in courses in basic drawing techniques at the St. Paul Gallery and School of Art. There, he learned the principles of composition espoused by the French Impressionist Paul Cezanne, one of his early influences. Neiman later moved to Chicago and entered the School of the Art Institute of Chicago, where he would go on to become a teacher as well. He gained wide recognition early in his career as contributing artist for Playboy, in the 1950s. Neiman went on to become one of the world's most recognized figures. He was the official artist at five Olympiads, and has become good friends with everyone from Mohammed Ali to Wayne Gretzky. It has been estimated that the more than 150,000 Neiman prints that have been purchased to date around the world "have an estimated market value exceeding $400 million."

St. Paul native and world famous artist LeRoy Neiman with his good friend, Wayne Gretzky

"Blue Hockey"
Depicting the 1980 U.S. Olympic Team

Today Neiman lives in New York City and continues to do what he loves most - paint. He has written nearly a dozen books, given millions to charity and to museums, and shows no signs of slowing down. In 1995 he gave the School of the Arts at Columbia University a gift of $6 million to create the LeRoy Neiman Center for Print Studies. After speaking with him this past summer, he told me that he had just finished painting Mark McGuire, Sammy Sosa and Joe DiMaggio. In addition, he has painted several hockey stars including Gretzky, Bobby Hull, Mario Lemieux, Stan Mikita, Glen Hall, and even his childhood idol, Bobby Dill. He also said that he is planning to immortalize our new Governor, Jesse "The Mind" Ventura.

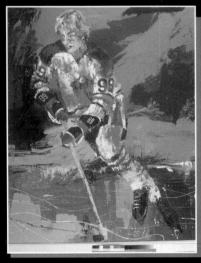

"Great Gretzky"

One of the bright spots on the team that first season was Wayne Connelly, who led the Saints in scoring with 40 goals and 30 assists for 70 points. But, the Saints scored only 250 points in 78 games that year, which ranked 11th among the 12 WHA teams. That was reason enough for Sonmor to make some changes. He needed to bring in some heavy artillery, and that's just what he did for the 1973-74 season.

After combing the countryside with new coaches Harry Neale and Jack McCartan looking for new talent, Sonmor added seven new faces to the team that next year, including the likes of Mike "Shaky" Walton, Murray Heatley and Steve Cardwell. Those seven men paid big dividends for Sonmor's Saints, scoring a combined 132 goals and 195 assists. (That's not even counting goalie John Garrett!) That new blood, plus a solid nucleus of veterans helped to propel the Saints to a 44-32-2 record in year two, good for second best record in the WHA and a trip to the playoffs. The team went on to beat Edmonton four games to one in the first round of the playoffs, and then go on to face the Houston Aeros in the second round. The Aeros were led by none other than Gordie Howe, who had come out of his two-year retirement that year to join his two teen-aged sons, Mark and Marty, to form the famed "Howe-Line." Gordy, who scored 100 points that year even in his 40s, proved to be too much for the young Saints, as Houston went on to just barely beat them four games to two in the best-of-seven series.

Although they lost that disappointing series that Spring, it was still a much improved year overall for the Saints. Walton, a former 50-goal scorer with the Boston Bruins, proved to be the biggest acquisition for the young Saints. By season's end the speedy winger had tallied 57 goals and 117 points, both tops in the league. At one point during the season, he went on a tear, scoring in a league record 16 straight games - including a stretch where he tallied 11 goals in three consecutive nights against Los

Native Minnesotan Saints:

Mike Antonovich	Calumet
Bill Butters	St. Paul
Henry Boucha	Warroad
Jack, Jeff & Steve Carlson	Virginia
Mike Curran	International Falls
Craig Falkman	St. Paul
Gary Gambucci	Eveleth
Paul Holmgren	St. Paul
Billy Klatt	Minneapolis
Len Lillyholm	Minneapolis
Jack McCartan	St. Paul
Dick Paradise	St. Paul
Frank Sanders	St. Paul
Craig Sarner	St. Paul
Pat Westrum	Minneapolis

Angeles, New England and Winnipeg.

Gord Gallant proved to be another major contributor. After coming to Minnesota from Cleveland, the tough defender, who played on a line with Mike Walton and Jim Johnson, wound up leading the league in penalty minutes with 223. Wayne Connelly also played big for the Saints, scoring 42 goals and 53 assists for 95 points. One of the biggest highlights from that season included George Morrison's amazing 43-second pure hat trick in a game against Vancouver. The offense was so good that it even set a league mark with 332 goals.

Another trademark of Sonmor's teams was tough defense, and that year's Saints squad was no exception, as John Arbour, Rick Smith, Mike McMahon, Terry Ball, Dick Paradise, Bob Boyd and Ron Busniuk patrolled the blue line with authority. In addition, the goaltending was solid. While Mike Curran and Jack McCartan shared the netminding duties during the first season, John Garrett was added to the mix in 1974. Both Curran and Garret played great all year. At one point midway through the season, Curran reeled off a fabulous record of 13-1-1, while Garrett posted eight consecutive wins at the end of the season and into the playoffs.

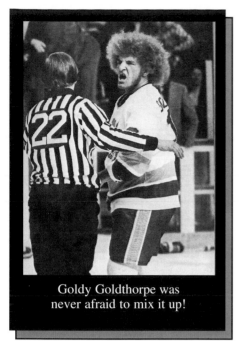
Goldy Goldthorpe was never afraid to mix it up!

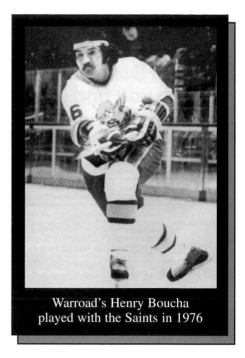
Warroad's Henry Boucha played with the Saints in 1976

Most importantly though for the Saints that year, was the fact that the fans came out in droves to support them. Averaging better than 6,500 for the season, the Saints averaged more than 9,000 during the playoffs against Houston. So popular were they, that during one playoff game some 17,211 Saints fans piled into the Civic Center. Not only was it a WHA attendance record, at the time it was also the largest crowd ever to watch a hockey game in Minnesota. Another highlight from that 1974 season occurred that winter at the Civic Center, when the WHA's All-Star Game was played before a sell-out crowd. There, in front of his home fans, Saints winger Mike Walton earned the game's MVP award.

Ever the perfectionist, that next year Sonmor was at it again, tinkering with his lineup card to the extent of bringing in yet another dozen players to enhance his club's roster. Among them included: forwards Fran Huck, Gary Gambucci, Don Tannahill and Danny O'Shea, two-way defenseman Ron Busniuk, and tough guy's Bill "Goldy" Goldthorpe, and Curt Brackenbury. Perhaps his most interesting signings that year were the brother's trio of Jack, Jeff and Steve Carlson, as well as Dave Hanson - who were then playing for the Johnstown Jets of the NAHL. Now for those of you who don't quite remember, Jeff, Steve and Dave made up the original "Hanson Brothers" from the classic movie "Slapshot." Jack was supposed to be the third Hanson, but got called up from Johnstown to St. Paul and had to have Dave take his place on the set at the last minute.

The Carlson brothers, as well as Dave Hanson all got called up that next year. So did former Gopher Bill Butters, who added a solid defensive presence to the team. The Saints finished the 1974-75 season with a very respectable 42-33-3 record, and went on to first beat New England in the first round of the playoffs, only to lose a seventh game heart breaker to the Quebec Nordiques in the second round of the playoffs. It would be the closest the club would ever get to sipping from the Avco Cup.

Several star players joined the Saints in 1975-76, including former Gopher Paul Holmgren, Hall of Famer Dave Keon, John McKenzie and even Warroad's Henry Boucha. The team's future appeared to be as bright as ever that year, but unfortunately, and unexpectedly, the economics of the game finally caught up to the club. Poor attendance and rising salaries all contributed to the fact that in February of 1976, after playing only 59 of 81 scheduled games, the ownership group was forced to file bankruptcy and terminate the team. A stunned Saints faithful was left in a state of shock. The team had a 30-25-4 record going up to that point that season, and was really caught off guard when the news was announced.

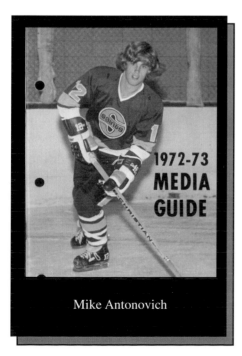
1972-73 MEDIA GUIDE

Mike Antonovich

The pity-party was short lived though. That's because just a few months later, Cleveland Crusaders owner, Nick Mileti, who also owned Cleveland's Indians and Cavaliers pro baseball and basketball franchises, decided to move his struggling WHA franchise to downtown St. Paul, where it would be transformed into the "New" Fighting Saints. The new team would replace the team's old blue and gold sweaters with scarlet, white, and gold uni's - giving the franchise a new makeover. Mileti then installed Robert D. Brown as the team's new president and also rehired Glen Sonmor as his GM. To get the fans back, Sonmor immediately brought back some of the old Saints favorites such as Dave Keon and Mike Antonovich. With that, the second incarnation of the Saints had officially begun.

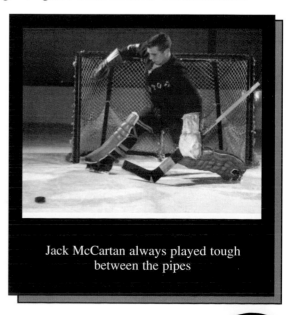
Jack McCartan always played tough between the pipes

Having moved over to the Eastern Division, the Saints start out the first half of the year on a good note by posting a respectable 19-18-5 record. But, in January of 1977, after just 42 games into the season, the team announced that it was folding, leaving all of its players as homeless free agents. Yes, the Saints had been killed yet again, this time due to slumping ticket sales - or so they said. For whatever reason, it was a sad final chapter to an otherwise wonderful story. (Ironically, the Crusaders were the first of two Cleveland hockey teams that would ultimately move to Minnesota, as the Cleveland Barons made the trek north just a year later to merge with the fledgling North Stars.)

Saints Reunion

In the Fall of 1991, as a good faith gesture, the North Stars staged an exhibition game against the Winnipeg Jets at the Civic Center and tied it in with a reunion for many of the old Fighting Saints' players. While the exhibition game proved to be a great homecoming of sorts for South St. Paul's Phil Housley, and Roseau's Butsy Erickson, the real reason the fans came to the event was to see the incredible reunion of some 21 former Saints who were introduced during the game. Among them were: Mike Antonovich, Bill Butters, Jack Carlson, Huffer Christiansen, Craig Falkman, Gary Gambucci, Ted Hampson, Dave Keon, George Konik, Len Lillyholm, Mike McMahon, Dick Paradise, Frank Sanders, Mike Walton, and Pat Westrum.

The WHA lasted just two more seasons after that, ultimately following the Saints into early retirement in 1979. While that WHA had won many of the battles along the way, in the end it had appeared that the NHL had won the war. But the WHA had some "conditions" that had to be met before they signed a final settlement treaty. Now, much like the American Football League and the American Basketball Association before them, the WHA also wanted to become a successful "second" league that was every bit as good as its big brother predecessor. And, ultimately, much like the AFL merged with the National Football League, and several ABA franchises merged with the National Basketball Association; in the end a victory of sorts was declared for the WHA, as four of its better teams were merged into the National Hockey League. Those four franchises were the Hartford Whalers (now the Carolina Hurricanes), Quebec Nordiques (now the Colorado Avalanche), Winnipeg Jets (now the Phoenix Coyotes), and the Edmonton Oilers. And maybe, just maybe, a teen-aged hockey phenome from Brantford, Ontario by the name of Wayne Gretzky, who was emerging as a superstar for the Oilers at the time had something to do with the NHL's sudden can't beat em' - join em' policy? We'll never know!

All-in-all there were 32 teams that played in 24 cities, during the WHA's tumultuous seven-year tenure, with New England, Winnipeg, Houston and Quebec each taking turns holding the championship Avco Cup. The WHA proved itself in the end, by showing that a rival league could produce top-level players and break the "anti-trust" mentality of its bully big brother. It became a safe-haven for many Hall of Famers who wanted to extend their careers, as well as a showcase for countless European players who wanted to play in North America. In the end, many of the kids who were given a chance to prove themselves as teen-agers in the WHA, went on to become the stars of the NHL in the 1980s. Perhaps, and most importantly though, was the fact that the WHA became a portal of sorts for American hockey players everywhere who wanted to advance in the professional game. As a result, the WHA proved to be a sanctuary for American talent in the Canadian-dominated NHL, which also translated into countless more opportunities for Minnesota kids to play pro hockey. The WHA changed the rules of the game forever, and in the process, brought a lot of joy to countless hockey fans everywhere.

The Minnesota Gophers

It appears that Johns Hopkins University of Baltimore may have been the first college in the United States to "officially" play the sport of ice hockey, when they tied the Baltimore Athletic Club on December 26, 1894, but that honor can certainly be disputed with the University of Minnesota. While the Gophers had "officially" began playing the sport just a month later, in January of 1895, the game had been played on campus "unofficially" for several years prior.

The first University of Minnesota team, unsanctioned by the college, was organized by Dr. H. A. Parkyn, a quarterback on the Gopher football team who had learned the game in Toronto. Parkyn coached the U of M team, comprised mainly of kids who were experienced ice polo players. These games would serve as a warm-up for an upcoming contest against one of Canada's best teams of that era, the Winnipeg Victorias. A big reason why the Gophers were able to schedule a game with the Manitoba team was because at that time, there was no railroad connection between Eastern and Western Canada. So, the Victorias, who had to travel through the Twin Cities on their way out to play Ontario and Quebec, decided to schedule a tune-up match along the way. On February 18, 1895, the Gophers beat the Victoria's by the score of 11-3. The game was played at Minneapolis' Athletic Park, which was located at Sixth Street and First Avenue North (the present sight of the Butler Square Building, next to the Target Center). The park was also the home of the professional Minneapolis Millers Baseball Club, before they moved to Nicollet Park.

This article describing the gala event appeared in the Minnesota Ariel on February 16, 1895: "The University of Minnesota hockey team will play a game for the championship of Minneapolis against the Minneapolis Hockey Club at their rink, at the corner of Fourth Avenue and Eleventh Street South. The game is preparatory to the game to be played Monday afternoon by Winnipeg and the University of Minnesota. Winnipeg is

The old barn

The 1922 Gophers vs. Wisconsin

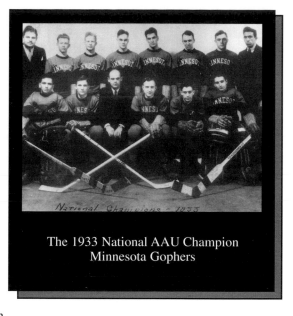

The 1933 National AAU Champion
Minnesota Gophers

champion of the world. *(Incidentally, this statement was incorrect: Winnipeg did not win the Stanley Cup until the following year, in 1896.) Winnipeg has returned from a rough trip through eastern Canada and has defeated without too much trouble Montreal, Toronto, Victoria, Ottawa, Quebec, and the Limestone's. The University started practice two or three weeks ago and played against a Minneapolis team, being defeated 4-1. A week and one half ago they defeated the same team 6-4. Tonight they play the tie off for the championship. Dr. H.A. Parkyn has been coaching the boys every afternoon. He has a couple of stars in Willis Walker and Russel. Walker plays point and Russel coverpoint, with Van Campen in goal. Parkyn and Albert are center forwards. Dr. Parkyn's long experience with the Victoria team of Toronto, one of the best, makes him a fine player. Thompsen and Head, the other two forwards, are old ice polo players and skate fast and pass well. Van Campen, quarterback on last year's football team, plays goal well. Many tickets have been sold for tonight's and also Monday's game. Tickets are 25¢, ladies come free. The excitement of these games is intense, and surpasses that at a football game."

Three days later, on February 19, 1895, this article ran in the St. Paul Pioneer Press: "The first international hockey game between Winnipeg and the University of Minnesota was played yesterday, and won by the visitors 11-3. The day was perfect and 300 spectators occupied the grandstand, coeds of the University being well represented. Features of the game was the team play of the Canadians, and individual play of Parkyn, Walker, and Head for the University. Hockey promises to become as popular a sport at the University as football, baseball, and rowing."

From those humble beginnings, the U of M got its start. The game continued to grow in the coming years, with more and more kids wanting to get involved. The first attempt to organize varsity ice hockey on the U of M campus took place in November of 1900 when a committee composed of George Northrop, Paul Joslyn, and A.R. Gibbons was appointed to draw up a constitution for the club and look into other problems concerning playing the game at the school. A committee conferred with the Athletic Board and decided not to flood Northrop Field, and instead to play at Como Lake in St. Paul several miles distant. No scheduled games were played during the season of 1900-1901, and it was not until late in the season of 1903 that the University of Minnesota played any games on a formal basis. Only two contests were played that season, both resulting in wins for the Gophers. Minneapolis Central High School was defeated 4-0 and the St. Paul Virginias 4-3. Team members were: John S. Abbott, Frank Teasdale, Gordon Wood, Fred Elston, Frank Cutter, R.S. Blitz, W.A. Ross, Arthur Toplin, and captain Thayer Bros.

The season of 1903 proved to be the last for ice hockey on a formal varsity-sport basis at the U of M until 1920, nearly two decades later. In 1910 unsuccessful efforts were made to revive the sport and even to persuade several other midwestern universities to form a Big Ten Conference for hockey.

In January of 1914, the school's Board of Control finally voted to outfit a hockey team. The next year a series of unofficial "pick-up" games were played against Minneapolis and St. Paul high schools, St. Thomas College and even some of the school's fraternity teams. Many of the games were played outdoors at Northrop Field with the finals and playoffs often being played at the indoor "Hippodrome" on the state fairgrounds in St. Paul. This continued for the next several years with more and more intramural teams becoming involved, including women's hockey teams as well -- many of whom were coached by the frat boys.

The 1940 Gopher
National AAU Championship Team
(Mariucci is front row, third from the right)

Under the direction of St. Paul's Beaupre Eldridge, a student at the time, the Gophers finally became an official varsity sport just after WWI, in 1920. One of the team's biggest games that year came against St. Thomas (then considered as the state's collegiate champions), who they beat by the final of 3-1 in a game played at St. Paul's Coliseum Rink (which was located on Lexington Avenue near University Avenue). While the team beat Hamline that year as well, most of its games were canceled due to warm weather. Many of the other large university's around the midwest were also organizing teams by this point, making it possible for the Gophers to travel to other schools for competition.

The 1921-22 team, under new coach I.D.

Bud Wilkinson

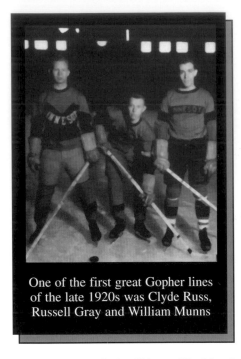

One of the first great Gopher lines of the late 1920s was Clyde Russ, Russell Gray and William Munns

MacDonald and captain Chet Bros, defeated Wisconsin, Luther Seminary, Hamline and Michigan Mines, while losing only to Hamline and Michigan Mines (twice), en route to an overall record of 7-3. The next year, Emil Iverson, an exhibition skater and skating instructor from Denmark, took over as the Gophers' new skipper and led the team to a 10-1-1 record. That next year, behind captain Frank Pond and goalie Fred Schade, Iverson led the team to an impressive 13-1-0 record, and in so doing the Gophers were declared as the National Champions. One of their biggest rivals that year was Marquette University, which was incidentally coached by Iverson's brother Kay.

In 1925 the Gophers moved into the newly constructed Minneapolis Arena, complete with artificial ice, where they brought the "U" no less than a share of top national honors for six consecutive seasons. From 1923-1929, Iverson's teams compiled a tremendous record of 75-10-11, with Chuck McCabe, Joe Brown and John H. Peterson each earning All-American honors to boot. Iverson left the program in 1930 (he would later coach the Chicago Blackhawks), the same year his 11-2-1 club shared the national title with Yale. Among the Gophers' competition during the 1920s included Michigan Mines, Michigan, Marquette, Notre Dame, Hibbing, Eveleth Junior College, North Dakota, North Dakota Aggies, St. Thomas, Hamline, Luther Seminary, Ramsey Technical School, Manitoba, Dallas A.C. and Tulsa A.C.

Gopher Teams in the NCAA Finals

1953 - Colorado Springs, Colo.
Michigan 7, Minnesota 3.

1954 - Colorado Springs, Colo.
RPI 5, Minnesota 4 (OT).

1971 - Syracuse, NY
Boston University 4, Minnesota 2.

1974 - Boston, Mass.
Minnesota 4, Michigan Tech 2.

1975 - St. Louis, Mo.
Michigan Tech 6, Minnesota 1.

1976 - Denver, Colo.
Minnesota 6, North Dakota 3.

1979 - Detroit, Mich.
Minnesota 4, North Dakota 3.

1981 - Duluth, Minnesota
Wisconsin 6, Minnesota 3.

1989 - St. Paul, Minn.
Harvard 4, Minnesota 3 (OT)

A large number of Gopher players during the '20s came from Minneapolis, with a few from St. Paul, Duluth and the Iron Range mixed in. Among the stars of this era included: Chuck McCabe, Joe Brown, Osborne Billings, Frank Pond, John H. Peterson, Cliff Thompson, Ed Owen, W.B. Eldredge, Chet, Ken and Ben Bros, Don Bagley, Reuben Gustafson, Fred Schade, Walt Youngbauer, Vic Mann, Ed Olson, Phil Scott, Jack and Bill Conway, Lloyd Russ, Herb Bartholdi, Leland Watson and H.J. Kuhlman.

Former team captain Frank Pond took over the program in 1930. The Two Harbors native iced very strong nationally ranked teams during his five-year tenure, ultimately finishing in 1935 with an impressive 46-21-4 record for a .676 winning percentage. The 1932 team, led by future Gopher athletic director Marsh Ryman, became the first Minnesota team to play a team from the East Coast, when they lost to a formidable Harvard team, 7-6 in Boston. As a result, the Gophers would finished ranked No. 2 in the country (according to the Tonelle system of rating), to those same Crimson. The maroon and gold were led that year by a group of kids from Eveleth (Alex MacInnes, Andy Toth, Ben Constantine and John Suomi), a pair from Duluth (Gordon Schaeffer and George Todd), and the rest from Minneapolis (Howie Gibbs, Laurie Parker, Bucky Johnson, Phil La Batte, George Clausen, Harold Carlsen, Fred Gould and John Scanlon). The next year, the "Pony Line" of Russ-Gray-Munns, combined with Wagnild and La Batte at defense, and Clausen and Scanlon tending goal, the Gophers pummeled Wisconsin 14-1 at the Hipp. La Batte was later selected as a member of the 1936 U.S. Olympic team.

Former St. Paul Saints coach Larry Armstrong became the team's third coach when he took over the program in 1935. One of his first highlights came in 1937, when the Gophers, behind All-American goalie Bud Wilkinson, defeated the University of Manitoba for the first time in 11 seasons. The 1938-39 sextet finished second in the National AAU finals with a modest 15-6 record. They won their first two games, swamp-

Herb Brooks starred for the Gophers from 1957-59

ing the Philadelphia Arrows 10-1, edging the St. Nicholas Club 3-2 and then losing in the finals to Cleveland Legion 4-3. Had there been a 1940 U.S. Olympic team several members of the Gopher team would undoubtedly have been selected. That next year would be a special one for Gopher boosters, as the team posted an undefeated 18-0 record en route to winning the National Amateur Athletic Union of the U.S. (AAU) title. (At the time, that was considered the country's national championship since there was no NCAA tournament back then.) Before rolling over the New England All Stars (Amesbury) 9-4 and Connecticut's Brock Hall 9-1, in playoffs, the Gophers took care of Michigan, Michigan Tech, Illinois, London (Ontario) and Yale. Led by such performers as John Mariucci, Babe Paulson, Frank St. Vincent, Hayden Pickering, Jim Magnus, Ken Cramp, Fred Junger, Dave Lampton, Al Eggleton, Norb Robertson and goalie Marty Falk, the team outscored their opponents 138 goals to just 25.

During the war years the Gophers schedule was curtailed as many colleges did not ice teams and the government discouraged travel. Minnesota scheduled a

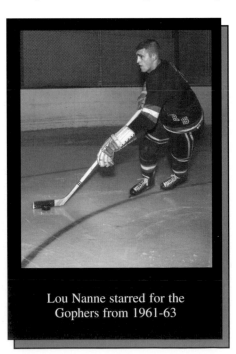

Lou Nanne starred for the Gophers from 1961-63

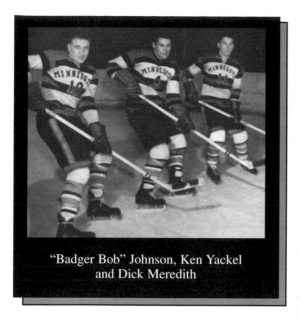

"Badger Bob" Johnson, Ken Yackel
and Dick Meredith

few college contests against Dartmouth, Michigan and Illinois, but the bulk of their schedule was against local amateur clubs such as Honeywell, Fort Snelling, Berman's and Wold Chamberlain and Canadian Junior teams from Winnipeg, Fort William and Port Arthur. Among the leading players during the war period were Bob Graiziger, Paul Wild, Bill Klatt, Bill Galligan, Bob Carley, Allan Van, Al Opsahl, Dick Kelley, Mac Thayer, Jack Behrendt, Pat Ryan, Don Nolander, Bob Arnold and Burton Joseph.

By the season of 1946-47, Armstrong's last, the Gophers had a nucleus of a strong team. Minnesota-bred players such as Bill

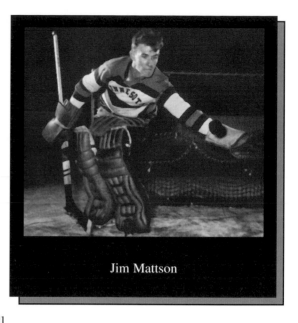

Jim Mattson

Hodgins, Roland DePaul, Bob Harris, Jim Alley, Ken Austin, Al Opsahl, Dennis Rolle, Jerry Lindegard, Cal Englestad, Bill Klatt, Jerry Remole, Dick Roberts and Tom Karakas were welcome additions to the club. Harris, Roberts, Austin, Alley, Lindegard and Englestad were among the first players form northwestern Minnesota to play for the Gophers. They were natives of such small communities as Warroad, Roseau and Hallock. Injuries and ineligibility dogged the team, but they managed to finish the 1946-47 season with a respectable 12-5-3 record. Armstrong held the Gopher coaching spot for 12 seasons, finishing with a 125-55-11 overall record.

White Bear Lake's Elwyn "Doc" Romnes, a St. Thomas grad and former Chicago Blackhawk star, took over for the 1947-48 season. One of the highlights of Romnes' tenure happened on February 17, 1950, when the Gophers defeated the Michigan State Spartans, 12-1, before a crowd of 3,734 in the inaugural game in the "new" Williams Arena. The facility, which had been constructed in 1928, was retrofitted with a wall that divided the arena into two ends, one end for basketball and the other for ice hockey. Finally, after playing like nomads for their first 31 years at places such as the St. Paul Auditorium, the Minneapolis Arena, and the Fairgrounds Hippodrome, the Gophers finally had a home of their own.

Romnes' best season came in 1951, when the Gophers started out slow but came back to win their last nine to finish with a 14-12 record. The team's senior line of Rube Bjorkman, Gordon Watters and Cal Englestad led the offense, while Jim Sedin, Frank Larson and Tom Wegleitner were the team's leading defensemen. The next year was the beginning of one of Minnesota's most glorious, the John Mayasich era. The kid from Eveleth, who would go on to become the greatest ever to wear the maroon and gold, was joined by a cast of all-stars that year including Dick Dougherty, Gene Campbell, Dick Meredith, Ken Yackel, Gordy Watters, Larry Ross and Jim Mattson, as well as the Duluth line of Bodin-Strom-Nyhus. Together they would finish the season with a 13-13 record, good enough for fifth in the newly formed Midwest Collegiate Hockey League. (The league, which was the first forerunner of the WCHA, included Colorado College, Denver, Michigan, Michigan State, Michigan Tech, Minnesota and North Dakota.) In addition, Rube Bjorkman, Ken Yackel and Jim Sedin were members of the Silver Medal winning 1952 U.S. Olympic team. Doc, who finished with a modest 52-59 overall record, turned the coaching reigns over to John Mariucci in 1953.

Larry Ross

Larry Ross graduated from Duluth, Morgan Park High School in 1940 and later attended the University of Minnesota, where he was an all-American goaltender in both 1951 and 1952. From there Ross went on to become one of the state's greatest high school hockey coaches at International Falls. Over the next couple of decades Ross' Broncos made the state tournament on 13 different occasions and won it six times. From 1963-1966 the team went undefeated in 58 straight games. In all, his teams compiled a record of 566-169-21. Fully 12 of his players would go on to play in the NHL. In addition, Ross also started ed the Rainy River Community College hockey program, and for a stretch, ran both teams at the same time.

Former Minnesota Governor
Wendy Anderson

Maroosh, a former Gopher football and hockey star in the 1930s, led his 1953 squad to a 22-5-0 record and an WIHL conference title in his first season behind the bench. From there, the Gophers just kept on going, all the way to the NCAA college hockey final four in Colorado Springs. In the first game the Gophers beat a tough Rennselaer Polytechnic Institute (RPI) team by the final score of 3-2, only to lose in the finals to rival Michigan 7-3 for the title. Soon record crowds were pouring into Williams Arena to see these kids. (In 1954 Minnesota led the nation in college attendance by attracting some 103,000 fans for 18 home games, compared to North Dakota, who was second with 54,000 and Michigan who had only 39,000.)

The Gophers finished the 1953-54 season with a 24-6-1 record, the best in the nation, and won their second straight

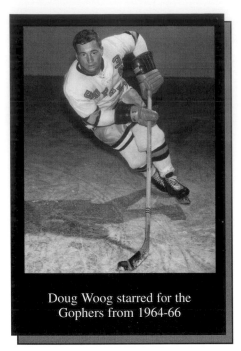

Doug Woog starred for the
Gophers from 1964-66

WIHL title. Minnesota pummeled Boston College in the semifinals 14-1, behind an amazing effort from the best line in college hockey. John Mayasich scored three goals and added four assists. Dick Dougherty scored four goals and added two assists, and Gene Campbell added three goals and two assists. Next up was RPI, which had upset the defending champs from Michigan. The Gophers rallied from a 3-0 deficit to tie it back up in the third on goals from Kenny Yackel, Dick Dougherty and John Mayasich. Mayasich then set up Dougherty on a pretty "five-hole" goal to finally take the lead late in the third, only to see the Engineers tie it up with just minutes to go to send it into overtime. There, at 1:54 of the extra session, after a mix-up out in front of the net, RPI's Gordie Peterson, found a loose puck in front of Mattson and promptly drilled it home to win the game 5-4. It was a devastating defeat and a big blow to coach Maroosh, who wanted so badly to win the big one for Minnesota. After the game, the players huddled around their coach to shield him from the press and their cameras. It was the first and only time Minnesota hockey players would ever see this giant of a man cry openly. Despite the loss, Yackel, Mattson, Dougherty, and Mayasich were all named to the All-American team.

"It's a loss that sticks with me still today," said Mayasich on the loss to R.P.I.. "To lose in overtime was bitter. It's not the ones you won that you remember, it's the ones you lost. To me, that was probably my biggest individual disappointment in all my years of hockey."

In 1956 Maroosh coached the U.S. Olympic team to a silver medal in Cortina, Italy, with several members of his team including John Mayasich, Dick Meredith, Gene Campbell, Dick Dougherty, Wendell Anderson, and Jack Petrosky.

In 1958 Maroosh flexed his muscles about an issue that was very important to him, Americans playing college hockey. Back then there were no restrictions on the eligibility and recruiting of older, more experienced Canadian junior players. While Maroosh's rosters were made up predominantly of Minnesota kids, other schools in the league had recruited lineups full of the top Canadian juniors who couldn't foresee making it in the six-team NHL, and thought it would be better to go to college rather than bounce around in the minors until they got called up. (Michigan even had a kid on its roster that had played briefly for the Toronto Maple Leafs!) This all came to an impasse during a series at Colorado College, when Minnesota got waxed by several teams who were comprised mostly of these players. Maroosh took his frustrations out on who he felt was the main perpetrator, Denver coach Murray Armstrong, in what evolved into one of the most bitter feuds in college hockey history. One by one, each team withdrew from the WIHL, ultimately forcing the league to fold in protest. The teams all cooled down and came back together a year later, this time as the WCHA, but with an understanding that things were going to be different. As a result, the NCAA tournament, which had always been held at the Broadmoor World Arena in Colorado Springs, was relocated to Minneapolis that next year — where Denver beat North Dakota 6-2. It would be quite a few years before Maroosh would be comfortable playing Denver. When he was forced to do so years later at the NCAA tournament in 1961, he had Lou Nanne, a naturalized American from Canada, carry a sign in front of the press that read, "We fry Canadian bacon."

Maroosh coached at his alma mater until 1966, when he decided to take a position with the newly formed Minnesota North Stars. He was replaced by longtime friend Glen Sonmor, a former teammate with the Saints. Mariucci amassed a 215-148-18 record during his tenure, capturing league titles in 1953 and 1954, while placing second in 1961 and 1966, and third in 1955, 64 and 65. There best showing following their upset loss in 1954 came in 1961, when they finished in third place in the NCAA Tournament. After losing to the hosts from Denver, 6-1, they battled back to beat RPI 4-3 to finish third.

John Mayasich was the star of this era, not only leading the Gophers in scoring for four consecutive seasons (1952, 53, 54 and 55), but also the entire league as well. Mayasich would also be joined by Dick Meredith and goalie Jack McCartan as members of the 1960 gold medal winning U.S. Olympic team, while Herb Brooks, Dave Brooks, Gary Schmalzbauer and Jim Westby all played on the 1964 U.S. Olympic team. During Mariucci's tenure, the following players were selected to the All-American team: John Mayasich (1953, 54, 55), Jim Mattson (1954), Ken Yackel (1954), Dick Dougherty (1954), Jack McCartan (1957, 58), Dick Burg (1958), Mike Pearson (1958), Murray Williamson (1959), Lou Nanne (1963), Craig Falkman (1964) and Doug Woog (1965).

Other highlights from this era included the success of former Gophers Herb Brooks, Larry Johnson, Ken Yackel, Murray Williamson, Bob Johnson, Lou Nanne and Doug Woog, all of whom continued on to brilliant coaching and management careers after their playing days. In addition, Eveleth and St. Paul Johnson High Schools made quite an impression on the Gopher landscape during this era. Along with Herb Brooks, Johnson produced nearly all of two famous lines: the "Buzzsaw Line" of David Brooks-Len Lilyholm-Gary Schmalzbauer (Lilyholm was from Robbinsdale), and the Mike Crupi-Greg Hughes-Rob Shattuck trio. It is also interesting to note that in the four-year period of 1961-64, three of the scoring leaders, namely Norman, Constantine and Nystrom, were Eveleth products.

Glen Sonmor, who at one time had been Mariucci's freshman coach, became the Gophers seventh mentor in 1966. With a record of 21-12, and an 18-8 finish in the WCHA, the Gophers captured the 1969-70 season title edging out Denver and Michigan Tech. Goalie Murray McLachlan and the pint-sized Mike Antonovich from Greenway of Coleraine led the maroon and gold to the league championship. In the finals of the WCHA playoffs, Michigan Tech edged the Gophers 6-5 to dash any hopes that they had of going to the NCAA Tournament. In 1971 the upstart Gophers saddled with a losing regular season of 11-16-2, advanced to the NCAA finals at Syracuse before losing to Boston University 4-2. In the semifinal game Minnesota edged Harvard 6-5 in one of the most exciting overtime games in team history.

Former Gopher and Warroad
Coach Dean Blais hoists the
McNaughton Cup as the Coach of
the UND Fighting Sioux

Neal Broten

Born on November 19, 1959, Neal Broten is one of Minnesota's most sacred of cows. To understand Neal, you have to go back to his hometown just south of the Canadian border, Roseau - a tiny town of some 3,000 people, yet it has three hockey arenas. Roseau has sent a team to the State High School Hockey Tournament an unprecedented 29 times, en route to winning six championships in 10 title games. The tiny community has one of the richest hockey traditions of anywhere in the country, thanks to the three Broten brothers — Neal, Aaron, and Paul. They all played for the Roseau Rams, the Gophers, the Stars (in both Minnesota and in Dallas), and for National Teams.

For the Broten brothers, it started at sun-up, when their parents would awaken before 6:00 a.m. on frigid winter mornings and drive their kids to hockey practice. "When he was a pee wee, he was scoring five, six, seven goals a game," said Gary Hokanson, Broten's coach at Roseau. "You could see then that he was going to be something special. He was a little guy who could handle the stick and put it in the net like nothing I'd ever seen."

Neal starred for the Roseau High School Rams alongside his brother Aaron, and best pal Butsy Erickson. They took the Rams to State several times, but could never bag the big one. In 1978, shortly after leading his Rams to a tough semifinal loss to Edina in the state tournament, Neal Broten, considered to be the best prep hockey player in the nation, made it official. He would become a University of Minnesota Golden Gopher. Some were skeptical as to how the small-town kid would do in big-time college hockey under the demanding U of M coach Herb Brooks. But it only took Neal less than one season to establish himself as one of the Gophers greatest hockey players of all time. In 1979, as a freshman, Broten easily exceeded everyone's expectations when he broke John Mayasich's 25-year-old school assist record when he dished out 50 helpers to his teammates. In the process, the WCHA's Rookie of the Year winner led the Gophers to an NCAA title.

The next chapter of Neal's life story proved to be the one that may well have linked his name to the sport of hockey forever. That off-season, Neal was selected to be a member of the much-celebrated 1980 U.S. Olympic team that shocked the world in Lake Placid. Neal would play center on the storied squad, finishing as the teams' fourth-leading scorer. Named as one of Sports Illustrated's "Athlete's of the Year," Neal gained instant celebrity status.

After the Olympics, Neal could've easily turned pro, having been drafted in the second round by the North Stars. Instead he returned to the U of M to be reunited with his two former linemates from Roseau, his brother Aaron, and Butsy Erickson, who had recently transferred to the "U" from Cornell. There, new Gopher coach Brad Buetow quickly assembled the three to make up one of the most feared scoring lines in all of college hockey. The trio led the Gophers to the NCAA Championship game for the second time in three years, ultimately losing to Wisconsin 6-3 in the 1981 finals, which was held in Duluth. Neal went on to earn All-American honors as well as being selected as the first-ever recipient of the Hobey Baker Memorial Award, which recognized the nation's top collegiate player. Over his incredible career at Minnesota, Broten scored 72 goals 106 assists for 178 points in only 76 games.

That season marked the end of Broten's collegiate career. But for Minnesota hockey fans it would only be the beginning. Neal left the "U" just in time to join the Cinderella North Stars as they were heading into the Stanley Cup playoffs. The Stars had even traded center Glen Sharpley, freeing up Neal's lucky No. 7 jersey for him. The Stars made it all they way to the finals that year, before losing to the New York Islanders in five games. He finished as the runner up Winnipeg's Dale Hawerchuk in the NHL's Rookie of the Year balloting in 1981-82.

One of the biggest highlights of his career happened in March of 1990, on a weekend when Roseau High School won the state high school hockey tournament. The North Stars hosted "Broten Brothers Day," during a game against the New York Rangers at the Met. Neal and Aaron were both playing for the Stars at that time, and baby brother Paul was in town playing for the Rangers. "It was great supporting the Rams, the town, and to see them win the championship like that was incredible."

He led the Stars back to their only other Stanley Cup finals appearance in 1991, where, after scoring nine goals and adding 13 assists in 23 playoff games, as Minnesota lost to the Pittsburgh Penguins. Later that summer, a contract dispute forced Broten to hold-out, and ultimately start the season with Team Preussen in the German League. The Minnesota fans freaked-out at the possibility that Neal would not return to Minnesota and demanded that he get signed. Their cries were heard, as his return to the lineup was met with a standing ovation from his loyal fans.

For 13 seasons Broten dazzled the Minnesota faithful as a member of the North Stars. His stats are remarkable. A four-time All-Star, Broten led the Stars in scoring from 1982-1986 with 405 points, and was an 80-plus point producer four times in the decade. He became the first U.S.-born player to score 100 points in a season when he tallied 105 in 1986.

When the North Stars moved to Dallas, Broten played two seasons in Texas before Bob Gainey traded him to the New Jersey Devils during the 1994-95 season. Ironically, he was dealt for fellow Northern Minnesotan Corey Millen, of Cloquet. There, Broten became the final piece in the Devils' Stanley Cup puzzle. He ignited New Jersey's offense by scoring seven goals, including four game-winners, while dishing out 12 assists during their playoff run to become the first Gopher player ever to have his name inscribed on Lord Stanley's Cup. "I can remember sitting there in the locker room with him after they won it," said Neal's father Newell. "He looked at me and said, 'Dad, can you believe it after all these years?'"

Neal competed in his 17th and final NHL season in 1996-97, back with the Dallas Stars. He still holds many franchise records, among them — most assists (634), most games (1,099), most points (923 — 289 goals + 634 assists), most NHL seasons (16), most assists in a season (76), and most points by a rookie (98). He is second all-time in points by an American with 923, (surpassed only recently by Joe Mullen) and has played in the most games as an American with 1,099.

In addition, Broten was awarded the Lester Patrick award in 1998 for outstanding service to hockey in the United States. That same year, Broten, along with fellow Gopher John Mayasich were selected to the All-Time USA Hockey Team by the members of USA Hockey as a component of the organization's 60th anniversary celebration. Then, on February 7th, 1998, Broten's No. 7 jersey was retired by the Dallas Stars in a special ceremony before a game against the Chicago Blackhawks at Reunion Arena, recognizing his outstanding 16 years with the franchise — 13 of them in Minnesota. The next stop for "Brots," is most certainly the U.S. Hockey Hall of Fame in Eveleth, and perhaps, the Hockey Hall of Fame in Toronto as well.

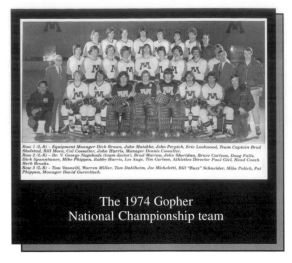

Row 1 (L-R) – Equipment Manager Dick Brown, John Matshke, John Perpich, Eric Lockwood, Team Captain Brad Shelstad, Bill Moen, Cal Comsaler, John Harris, Manager Dennis Comsaler.
Row 2 (L-R) – Dr. V. George Nagobads (team doctor), Brad Morrow, John Sheridan, Bruce Carlson, Doug Falls, Dick Spannbauer, Mike Phippen, Robby Harris, Les Auge, Tim Carlson, Athletics Director Paul Giel, Head Coach Herb Brooks.
Row 3 (L-R) – Tom Vannelli, Warren Miller, Tom Dahlheim, Joe Micheletti, Bill "Buzz" Schneider, Mike Polich, Pat Phippen, Manager David Gurovitsch.

The 1974 Gopher
National Championship team

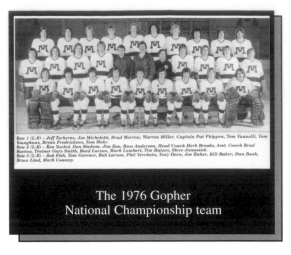

Row 1 (L-R) – Jeff Tscherne, Joe Micheletti, Brad Morrow, Warren Miller, Captain Pat Phippen, Tom Vannelli, Tom Younghans, Bryan Fredrickson, Tom Mohr.
Row 2 (L-R) – Ken Yackel, Don Madson, Jim Boo, Russ Anderson, Head Coach Herb Brooks, Asst. Coach Brad Buetow, Trainer Gary Smith, Reed Larson, Mark Lambert, Tim Raines, Steve Janaszak.
Row 3 (L-R) – Bob Fish, Tom Gorence, Rob Larson, Phil Verchota, Tony Dorn, Joe Baker, Bill Baker, Dan Bonk, Bruce Lind, Mark Conway.

The 1976 Gopher
National Championship team

Frank Sanders, Mike Antonovich, Dennis Erickson, John Matschke, Wally Olds, Craig Sarner, Doug Peltier and Dean Blais were among the players who took a leading role in the surprising finish of the 1971 team. From the Sonmor era, Wally Olds (1970), Gary Gambucci (1968) and Murray McLachlan (1970) were chosen to the All-American team. In addition, Bill Klatt led the WCHA in scoring in 1968 with 23 goals and 20 assists in 31 games. Players from this era who played or coached for the U.S. during the Olympics included: Herb Brooks, Jack Dale, Craig Falkman, Len Lilyholm, Gary Gambucci, Tom McCoy, Lou Nanne, Larry Stordahl and Murray Williamson all in 1968; and Wally Olds, Bruce McIntosh, Frank Sanders, Craig Sarner, and Murray Williamson in 1972.

Glen left the program early in the 1971-72 season to join the newly formed Minnesota Fighting Saints of the WHA. He was replaced by interim coach Ken Yackel, himself a former Gopher three-sport star in the 50's. Sonmor posted a 79-82-6 record in his five-plus seasons, and became a big-time fan favorite on campus.

Yackel was replaced at the beginning of that next season by another former Gopher, Herb Brooks. Brooks became the eighth Minnesota coach when he replaced Yackel for the 1972-73 season. Brooks, who grew up in the hockey-happy East Side of St. Paul came from a hockey conscious family. His father had been a well known amateur player in the 1920's and his brother, David, had been a member of the Gophers in the early 1960s and the 1964 U.S. Olympic team. In addition to his playing for Minnesota in the late 1950s, he had been a member of five U.S. National sextets and the 1964 and 1968 U.S. Olympic Teams. Prior to his appointment as Gopher mentor, Brooks had coached at the junior level, and had also been an assistant to Glen Sonmor. Having extensive playing experience in European hockey it was only natural that he became interested in the game as played by the Russians and Czechs. He became an advocate of the Russian style of play and the coaching of Anatoli Tarasov. Brooks, who had a degree in psychology from the University of Minnesota, employed some of his learning in this field to motivate his players with the will to win.

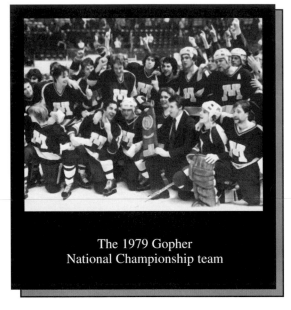

The 1979 Gopher
National Championship team

In 1974, the Gophers made history. Led by their second-year coach, Herb Brooks, they went on to win the first ever NCAA hockey championship. After finishing sixth in the WCHA the season before, the Gophers came full circle that season, proving to the world that Minnesota was indeed, the hockey hot-bed of America.

After starting 0-4-1, the Gophers put together a nine-game winning streak that included series sweeps of North Dakota, Michigan State, and St. Louis. Minnesota went on to lose only two of it's final 16 home games at Williams Arena. They finished with a 14-9-5 record, good enough for second place in the WCHA, behind Michigan Tech.

The Gophers went on to beat two tough Michigan and Denver teams in the WCHA playoffs, and suddenly they had found themselves on their way to Boston, where they faced the top-ranked, hometown Terriers of Boston University in the NCAA final-four. The Cinderella Gophers felt right at home in the Boston Garden, as they proceeded to knock off BU in a nail-biter, 5-4, thanks to Mike Polich's shorthanded goal at 19:47 of the third period to make it into the finals. There they faced their old WCHA nemesis, Michigan Tech, for the title.

Aaron Broten

Aaron Broten is the middle of Roseau's three Broten brothers. Aaron played 12 years in the NHL and was the first player in New Jersey Devils franchise history to top 200 assists and 300 points in a career. Aaron, who also played with the North Stars for a few seasons, represented the USA at the World Championships in 1981, 1982, 1985, 1986 and 1987. In addition, he played in two Canada Cups, both in 1984, where he played on the same line with his big bro Neal, and also in 1987.

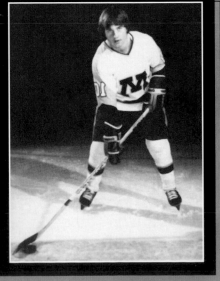

The Gophers went back and forth with the Huskies throughout the first period, until John Sheridan scored late to give the maroon and gold a one-goal lead. John Perpich then beat the Tech goaltender to make the score two-zip in the second. The Huskies came back though, scoring at 3:24 of the same period, to get within one. It remained that way until the third, when John Harris and then Pat Phippen both scored 12 minutes apart to put the Gophers up for good. The Huskies added another one with less than a minute to go, but it was too little, too late. With an impressive 39 shots-on-goal, the Gophers held on to win the title 4-2. Brooks had hit the jackpot, and Minnesota had its first NCAA hockey crown.

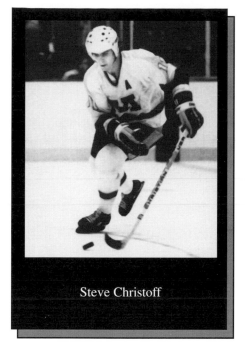

Steve Christoff

Gopher All-American Bill Baker

Brooks had led the Gophers to a 22-12-6 overall record, becoming the first team in 25 years to win the title with a team comprised exclusively of American players. And, he did it with only two years' worth of talent that he had recruited. For his efforts, Brooks was named WCHA Coach of the Year. Team captain Brad Shelstad, a product of Minneapolis Southwest, was chosen as the tournament's MVP and was also selected as an All-WCHA selection. Les Auge and Hibbing's Mike Polich were named to the All- Tournament team. That season, centers Polich and Harris led the team in scoring. Polich went on to a successful career in the NHL, while Harris has emerged as a star in another sport, golf, where he won the 1993 U.S. Amateur Golf Championship and is a perennial member of golf's Walker Cup team.

Moving from last place in the WCHA to first could not have been accomplished without unique leaders. "My first year, our two captains, Billy Butters and Jimmy Gambucci, were tremendous leaders who just did a great job of getting the program returned to a good, solid footing," said Brooks. "It was tremendously gratifying getting the school's first championship coming from where we did. The players weren't in awe of anything, and they were extremely strong mentally, plus they could really compete. They played well on the road, they played against the odds and overcame a lot that season. That first title was very special to me."

After beating Harvard 6-4 behind Warren Miller's hat trick, Michigan Tech got their revenge against Minnesota that next year, beating the Gophers 6-1 in the finals which were held in St. Louis. Miller and defenseman Reed Larson were picked for the All-Tournament team. Herbie's boys rallied back in 1976 though, winning the WCHA with a 24 8 0 mark. The Gophers opened the postseason by playing a classic against Michigan State in East Lansing. In that game the Gophers downed the Spartans 7-6 in triple overtime behind goalie Jeff Tscherne's NCAA record 72 saves. From there they advanced to the to the NCAA Tournament in Denver, where they downed Boston University 4-2 in the semifinals. Next up were the Huskies from Michigan Tech. Down 3-0, the Gophers rallied behind goals from Tom Vannelli, Micheletti, Baker, Gorence, Phippen and Miller to beat Michigan Tech 6-4.

Minnesota's Tom Vannelli, who led the Gophers in scoring that year with 69 points, was also named as the tournament's MVP. After the win Gopher forward Pat Phippen said, "They called us shabby, they called us inconsistent, now they call us NCAA champions."

Three years later, in 1979, Brooks led his team back to the promised land yet again. The final series of that season featured a tough North Dakota team coming to town in what would prove to be a WCHA championship showdown. The Gophers took the opener 5-2, but the Sioux rallied to take the title, in one of the best series ever witnessed at Williams Arena. In the playoffs, the Gophers went on to sweep both Michigan Tech and then the University of Minnesota at Duluth at home. They then knocked off Bowling Green, winners of the CCHA, earning a trip to Detroit and the NCAA tournament.

Dave Snuggerud

Paul Broten

Paul Broten, the youngest of the three Broten brothers, went on to play in the NHL after his stint with the Gophers. After graduating from the U of M in 1988, where he scored 116 career points, Paul went on to play for eight seasons with the New York Rangers, Dallas Stars and St. Louis Blues. From 1988-1996 Paul scored 101 points in 322 career NHL games.

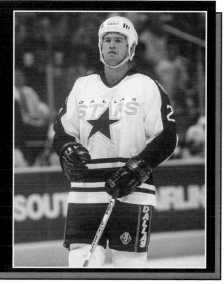

In the first game of the Final Four tournament, led by Eric Strobel's hat trick, Minnesota held on to beat New Hampshire 4-3. It was on to the finals, where they would meet their neighbors from North Dakota. Minnesota got out to an early lead on goals by Steve Christoff, John Meredith, and captain Bill Baker, to make it 3-1 after the first. The Sioux rallied in the second, narrowing the gap to 3-2. Then early in the final period, Broten the freshman sensation from Roseau, scored on a fabulous, sliding chip shot in what would prove to be the game winner. UND added another goal late, but the incredible goaltending of Gopher senior netminder Steve Janaszak proved to be the difference as the Gophers held on to win, 4-3, and the right to be again called national champs.

With 35 saves, Janaszak, fittingly, was voted the tournament's MVP. Three other Gophers also made the all-tournament team including freshman defenseman Mike Ramsey and forwards Steve Christoff and Eric Strobel. Additional honors would cascade down to a couple of other future Gopher legends as well. Billy Baker, who scored a then single season

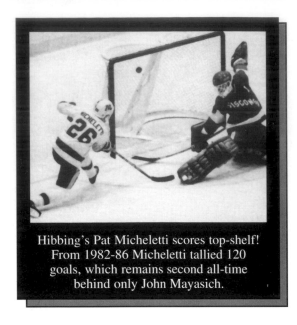

Hibbing's Pat Micheletti scores top-shelf! From 1982-86 Micheletti tallied 120 goals, which remains second all-time behind only John Mayasich.

record of 54 points by a defenseman, was selected as an All-American, and Broten was named WCHA Rookie-of-the-Year. As a team, the Gophers rewrote the record books that season, as they scored an amazing 239 goals in 44 games, led by Steve Christoff and Don Micheletti who both tallied 36 goals each. They also set a record for most wins in a season with 32.

"We were playing against a tremendous North Dakota team," said head coach Herb Brooks. "I think they had 13 guys that turned pro that next year. Broten scored a dramatic goal, sliding on his stomach and hitting a chip-shot over the goalie. It was incredible. I remember speaking at a Blue Line Club meeting the year before and saying that we were going to win it all that next season. It leaked out in the press and went across the country, putting a lot of pressure on our team. I kind of wish I wouldn't have said it now. But I just felt real strong about that team. I put a lot of pressure on those kids and I really raised the bar. But, because of their mental toughness and talent, we won the championship."

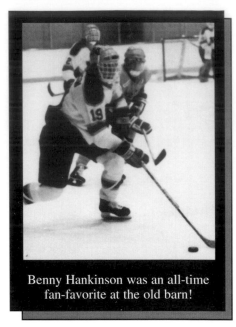

Benny Hankinson was an all-time fan-favorite at the old barn!

"I remember playing at the old Olympia Arena in Detroit," added Broten. "Just being in there and thinking about Gordy Howe and all those old Red Wings teams that had played there was really neat. North Dakota was our biggest rival back then, and beating them in the finals was a great win for us. That year was great, and I have a lot of great memories of my teammates from that season, it was pretty special."

Brad Buetow, who had played under Brooks and was his assistant coach, took over the head coaching duties at Minnesota on an interim basis for the 1979-80 season as Brooks was at the helm of the U.S. Olympic team. Nine Gophers (Neal Broten, Bill Baker, Steve Janaszak, Eric Strobel, Phil Verchota, Mike Ramsey, Buzz Schneider, Rob McClanahan and Steve Christoff), were selected by Herbie as members of that famous 1980 gold medal U.S. Olympic team. In addition, Les Auge, Mike Polich, Tim Harrer, Neal Broten and Steve Ulseth were all named as All-American selections during the Brooks era.

Buetow, a former three-sport Gopher athlete from Mounds View, took over as the team's new head coach in 1980 when Brooks opted to pursue a coaching career in the NHL. Despite losing a truck-load of players to the NHL that year, Gophers finished with an overall record of 26-15-0 and surprisingly second in the league. The team was led by Tim Harrer, who won the WCHA scoring crown and set a school record of 45 goals for the season. Aaron Broten, one of the three brothers from Roseau who have played for the Gophers, Steve Ulseth, Peter Hayek, Bob Bergloff, David H. Jensen, Mike Knoke and goalies Jim Jetland and Paul Butters were among those who helped fill the spots left by those who departed to play for the U.S. Olympic team.

With an overall finish of 31-12 Buetow led the 1980-81 team to the WCHA title, finishing ahead of Michigan Tech and Wisconsin by six points. Neal Broten returned from the Olympics to join his brother Aaron and Butsy Erickson, to form the best line in college hockey. With a roster composed of Minnesota natives, the Gophers defeated Colorado College and UMD in the 1981 WCHA playoffs. After beating Colgate by 9-4 and 5-4 scores in the NCAA Playoffs, Minnesota entered the NCAA final four in Duluth. There the Gophers outlasted Michigan Tech 7-2 in the opener, but were upset 6-3 in the finals by former Gopher "Badger" Bob Johnson's Wisconsin team. In the end, despite Steve Ulseth capturing the WCHA scoring title, and Aaron Broten leading the nation in scoring with 106 total points for the season, Neal Broten was awarded the innaugural Hobey Baker award as hockey's top collegiate player.

In 1982-83 Minnesota won its second league crown in three years as they posted a 18-7-1 WCHA finish and a 33-12-1 overall season. In the league playoffs the Maroon and Gold defeated UMD but lost to Wisconsin in the WCHA finals. Minnesota, behind Scott Bjugstad and Corey

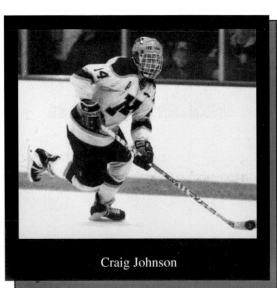

Millen, beat New Hampshire 9-7 and 6-2 in the playoffs to advance to the NCAA final four in Grand Forks. There, the Gophers lost to Harvard 5-3 in the opener and then to Providence 4-3 in the consolation contest.

While UMD dominated league play for the next several years the Gophers continued to play well, advancing to two more NCAA tournaments. Brad Buetow left the Gopher program following the 1985 season, with a 171-75-8 record. During his reign, Tim Harrer (1980), Neal Broten (1981), Steve Ulseth (1981) and Pat Micheletti (1985) were accorded All-American hon-

The 1989 Gophers following that heart-breaking overtime loss to Harvard at the Civic Center

Craig Johnson

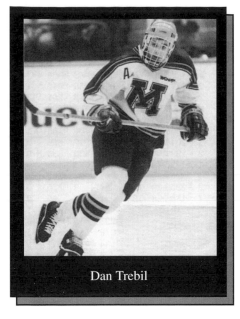
Dan Trebil

ors. Another significant event happened in 1985, when, in an emotional ceremony, the structure was renamed Mariucci Arena in honor of the "Godfather of Minnesota Hockey," John Mariucci. (Maroosh would pass away just two years later.)

Former Gopher All-American and South St. Paul prep star Doug Woog took over in 1985-86. Woog, who had previously coached the St. Paul Vulcans and the Minnesota Junior Stars of the USHL to league and national titles, led the Gophers that first year to a new school record of 35 wins and to a spot in the NCAA final four in Providence, where they ultimately lost to Michigan State 4-3. Behind Corey Millen and Pat Micheletti, who led the Gophers in scoring that year, and John Blue, who led all WCHA goalies with a 3.08 GAA, the Gophers rallied back to beat Denver 6-4 to take third place.

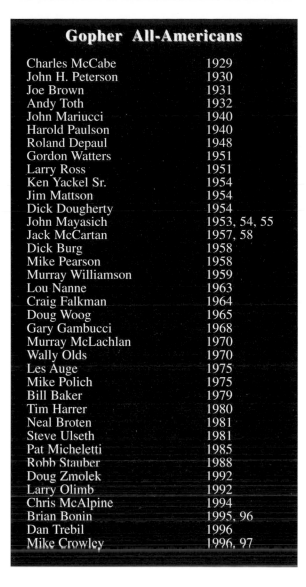

In his second season Woog posted a 34-14-1 record and led the team back to the NCAA's final four, this time Detroit. There the Gophers took third place by beating Harvard 6-3, after losing in the first round to Michigan State 5-3.

After losing Corey Millen, Dave Snuggerud, Tom Chorske, Todd Okerlund and John Blue to the 1988 U.S. Olympic team, Duluth Denfeld goalie Robb Stauber led the Gophers to the 1988 WCHA crown, and yet another trip back to the final four, that year in Lake Placid, NY. After beating Michigan State 4-2 and 4-3 in the playoffs, the Gophers wound up losing to St. Lawrence and then Maine in the semifinals to finish fourth.

In 1989 Woog led his squad back to the promised land, which was coincidentally held at the St. Paul Civic Center that year as well. After winning their second consecutive WCHA crown Minnesota went on to beat the cheese heads from Wisconsin in the opening round of the playoffs. From there the Gophers downed Maine 7-4 in the NCAA finals opener, only to lose one of most heartbreaking games in team history the next night to Harvard. In a back and forth game, the Gophers wound up heading into overtime with the Crimson. Midway through the sudden death session, Gopher defenseman Randy Skarda nailed the pipe on a blistering slapshot. Moments later, Harvard scored on a fluke goal to win the national championship.

"It was probably the most crushing defeat of my life," said Skarda. "Kenny Gernander set me up, and I hit the inside of the pipe. After the game I couldn't leave my house for two weeks, I was devastated."

As for the other shot at the other end: "I don't like to think about it," said goalie Robb Stauber. "I remember the shot, and I reached for the rebound but missed it. There were so many things in that game I would've done differently. Sometimes in big pressure games you tend to be more reserved, and play more conservatively than you'd like to. But, that was a great year, and we had nothing to be ashamed of that season at all."

Brian Bonin

Minnesota finished with a 33-11-0 record in 1992, Woog's seventh season as Gopher coach. They went on from there to beat UND for the WCHA crown, followed by a 5-1 win over Colorado College in the opening round of the NCAA playoffs. With the win the Gophers found themselves once again in the final four, this time in Detroit. There, they lost a tough opening round heart-breaker to Northern Michigan by the final score of 4-2 to end their season. They got a new arena that next season when the "new" state-of-the-art Mariucci Arena was built right across the street from "old" Mariucci - which was turned into the Gopher women's sports pavilion.

They went back in both 1994 and 1995, for a pair of third place finishes at the NCAA final four. After beating St. Cloud State, 3-2, in a WCHA playoff overtime thriller, the Gophers went on to beat UMass-Lowell 2-1 in another overtime fiasco to reach the final four. There, in St. Paul at the Civic Center one more time,

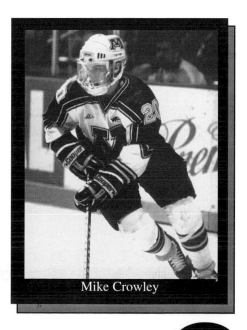
Mike Crowley

they lost a tough one to Boston University 4-1. In 1995 they beat Denver, RPI and Colorado College all in the playoffs to get to the finals, this time in Providence. But, they met up with Boston University again, who won 7-3 to knock them out of contention for the second straight year.

The Gophers made a return trip to the NCAA tournament in 1997. After beating Alaska Anchorage for the conference title, Minnesota advanced to beat Michigan State 6-3 in the opening round of the playoffs. But, after losing to Michigan 7-4 that next night, the season was over for the boys in maroon and gold. The Gophers went through a slump of sorts for the next couple of years, despite the outstanding play of Brian Bonin, who led the WCHA in scoring in both 1995 and 1996, Mike Crowley who led the league in 1997, followed by Reggie Berg, who snagged the league scoring crown in 1998. Coach Woog, who resigned in 1999 to take a fund-raising position with the Athletic Department, finished with an amazing record of 389-187-40, and four WCHA crowns over his 14-year tenure. He posted seven 30-win seasons and coached seven All-Americans (Robb Stauber, Doug Zmolek, Larry Olimb, Chris McAlpine, Brian Bonin, Dan Trebil and Mike Crowley).

Woog's replacement in 1999 was Grand Rapids native Don Lucia, who had previously been the skipper at Colorado College. Lucia, who posted an impressive 166-68-18 record over his six year tenure at CC, signed a six-year contract with the Gophers. "I'm excited and honored to be chosen as the new head men's hockey coach at the University of Minnesota," said Lucia. "I'm looking forward to coming home where hockey is king. I'm looking forward to building a program that the University and state of Minnesota can be proud of."

The Gopher Hockey program, which has taken great pride in its teams' reliance on home-grown talent, has one of the greatest traditions in the world of college athletics. Although the expectations area high, Lucia is a proven winner and will surely bring the maroon and gold back to that promised land that only Herb Brooks was able to get to.

The "new" Mariucci Arena

Charles Schulz

World famous cartoonist Charles Schulz was born in Minneapolis on November 26, 1922, and grew up in St. Paul loving hockey. As a kid he loved going to St. Paul Saints and Minneapolis Millers games, and even had a rink in his family's backyard. After graduating from St. Paul Central High School, Schulz went on to art school in Minneapolis. There, he created a comic strip about the adventures of a group of preschoolers (including a kid named Charlie Brown) called "Li'l Folks," which appeared in the St. Paul Pioneer Press in 1947.

United Features Syndicate bought the strip in 1950 and renamed it "Peanuts" because 'Li'l Folks" sounded too much like "Li'l Abner." Seven newspapers carried the original "Peanuts" cartoon strip on October 2, 1950, and the numbers have grown ever since.

He later moved on to California, where he became one of the world's most famous cartoonists. The multiple Emmy winner's cartoons are now read by several hundred million people in 68 countries, who speak 26 different languages. (Charlie Brown is Carolius Niger and Snoopy is Snupius in the Latin version.) He has been one of the Top 10 highest-paid entertainers in the U.S., and has built an empire surrounding that lovable pooch, Snoopy.

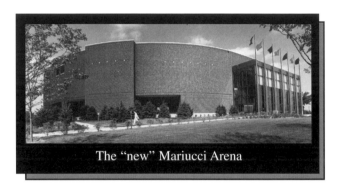

Through it all his love of hockey has only grown. Schulz even started a senior hockey tournament at his arena (which he purchased) in the early 1970s. From a dozen first-year teams, it has grown into the world's largest senior hockey tournament. Charles now plays a mean left wing in the "over-70" bracket. In 1981 Schulz was honored by winning the Lester Patrick Award for outstanding service to hockey. He was also inducted into the U.S. Hockey Hall of Fame as well. Today, the Minnesota Cartoonists League meets at O'Gara's piano bar in St. Paul under an original portrait of Snoopy drawn and signed by Charles himself. The reason they meet there is because that building was, from 1942 to 1952, Charles Schulz's father's barbershop. "Good Grief!"

The Minnesota-Duluth Bulldogs

The University of Minnesota Duluth Bulldogs have established a hockey tradition that is second to none in Minnesota. For many, hockey is a religion in northeastern Minnesota, and the Dogs have gained a tremendously loyal following. The history of this school, which dates back to 1895, when it was founded as the Duluth Normal School, takes us back to when ice polo was just evolving into ice hockey along the shores of Lake Superior.

Hockey first began in Duluth as an outgrowth of the game of ice polo in the 1890's. By 1893, the Glen Avon Curling Club Rink was in full swing, with ice polo teams from Duluth battling squads from the Twin Cities on the 126' x 80' ice surface. By 1900 adult hockey teams in Duluth and Superior were playing teams from Two Harbors, Eveleth and from Upper Michigan's Copper Country. The first strong Duluth hockey team was probably the Northern Hardware team, a men's senior team that after earning the 1908 Minnesota title, defeated Cleveland and Detroit for the national championship. By 1913 interest in the game peaked in the port city when the new Duluth Curling Club Arena was built on the corner of 13th Avenue East and London Road, complete with a large ice surface and seating for 2,000 fans.

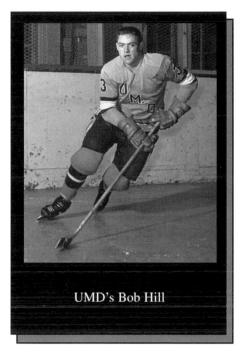

UMD's Bob Hill

The Duluth Hornets emerged in 1920 to play in the United States Amateur Hockey Association with such teams as Eveleth, St. Paul, Minneapolis, Cleveland, Chicago, Winnipeg and Pittsburgh. To accommodate the large crowds, the Duluth Amphitheater, with seating for more than 4,000 fans, was built, becoming one of the first buildings in the state to feature artificial ice. With so much hockey going on, it only seemed natural that the high school and college games would emerge. Cliff Thompson's Eveleth Junior College team already had their own little dynasty going 60 miles up the road by this time. Duluth's college hockey team would soon join in the fun.

On December 10th, 1930, Duluth State Teacher's College, which had been converted a few years earlier from a two-year normal school to a four-year teachers college, announced that intercollegiate ice hockey would be added to the institution's varsity sports program. The Bulldogs first hit the ice on Tuesday, January 13th, 1931, at the Amphitheater against Duluth Central High School. The team's first coach was Frank Kovach, who also helped start both the football and basketball programs that same year as well. That first roster included the likes of Gary Bartness, Cliff Heidman, Woody Wanvick, Cliff Johnson, Lawrence Rudberg, Benny Knutila, Merrill Boreen, Walt Thygeson, Herman Jappe, Gordy Pomroy, Henry Antoskiewicz, and A. Caldwell.

Connie Pleban

Eveleth's Connie Pleban, in addition to his international successes as both a player and manger of several U.S. National teams, coached at UMD during the 1950s. There, he led UMD's transition from small to major-college status, and in four years there his teams never lost a game in the MIAC.

The Dogs were blanked by the young Trojans that opening night by the final score of 3-0. The goalic on that first Bulldog team was Duluth native Gary Bartness. "Actually, losing to the high school team was not that great a disgrace, although we might have taken it harder if we had known to what heights the college's hockey teams would one day rise," said Bartness. "Central had had teams for a number of years and playing college teams was not exactly new to them. The only other high school team in the Duluth area was Duluth Cathedral, so the Trojans had to schedule high school and junior college teams from the Iron Range."

The Bulldogs wound up losing their only other two games of the season in their inaugural campaign, the other two coming at the hands of mighty Eveleth Junior College, 8-2 in Eveleth, but only 4-2 later at the "Amp." "I like to think the latter score reflects our progress during our abbreviated season, added Bartness. "Losing by only two to a team as strong as Eveleth was an achievement."

Bartness had a lot of fond memories about that first season, including the late arrival of the team's equipment. "By the time we put on our brand new green-and-gold uniforms, the season was almost over," he joked. He also remembered scrimmaging against many other teams that year, including a tough bunch called the "Amphitheater Rink Rats." The Rats were the maintenance guys who swept

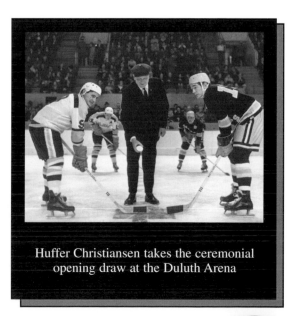

Huffer Christiansen takes the ceremonial opening draw at the Duluth Arena

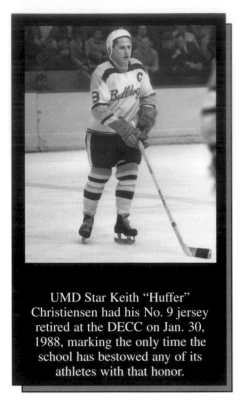

UMD Star Keith "Huffer" Christiensen had his No. 9 jersey retired at the DECC on Jan. 30, 1988, marking the only time the school has bestowed any of its athletes with that honor.

the ice between periods of the games played by the Duluth Hornets at the Amp, and in return got all the free ice time they wanted. Among those players included Rip Williams, the Godfather of Duluth hockey.

The next season the Dogs sported a 2-5-0 season, winning their first game in a 3-2 decision over Two Harbors High School. But, following that 1931 season, the college dropped the sport for what would amount to 14 years, until finally reinstating it for the 1946-47 season. (One of the players who played at the school during this "unofficial" period was Hall of Fame goalie Sam Lopresti from Eveleth, who played on a club team from 1936-38, after spending a season between the pipes at St. Cloud Teachers College in 1935.)

The Depression and War were consuming most people's spare time in the 1930s, but hockey managed to survive. While the semi-pro Hornets packed up and moved to Wichita in 1933, several senior leagues popped up throughout the area. Under long-time Duluth hockey booster Rip Williams, Duluth joined the International Amateur League (along with Eveleth, Virginia, Port Arthur and Fort William), which later evolved into the Duluth Industrial League, which was composed of the Coolerators, Butlers, Coast Guard and Clyde Club. During that stretch of the mid-1930s, the thing to do in Duluth was to go and watch the Duluth Zephyrs at the old "Amp." The "Zeph's" won the IAHL title in 1936, and proved to be the big show in town during the Great Depression era.

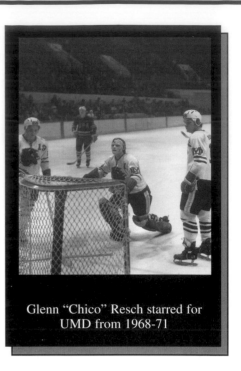

Glenn "Chico" Resch starred for UMD from 1968-71

In 1939, an event took place which set back hockey's development in Duluth. One night, during a Fireman-Policeman benefit game in front of some 4,000 fans, the roof of the Amphitheater caved in. Although no one was injured, the growth of hockey suffered until 1953, when artificial ice was installed in the Curling Club Arena.

On June 10, 1946, hockey made its triumphant return to the school, where the Bulldogs, playing an independent schedule, posted a respectable 11-6-1 record under coach Joe Oven. In 1949 two major things happened to the school. First, Duluth State Teacher's College was evolved into a coordinate campus of the University of Minnesota, and secondly, the new University of Minnesota Duluth Bulldogs joined the Minnesota Intercollegiate Athletic Conference (MIAC), where they could now compete regularly against other colleges from around the state including Augsburg, St. Mary's, Macalester, St. Thomas, St. John's, Hamline, Carleton, Gustavus and Concordia. On February 24th, of that year, Bulldog goalie Norm Thompson shut out Carleton College 3-0 to close out the year with a 7-0-0 overall record for what would prove to be the school's only unbeaten, untied season in history.

In 1955 Connie Pleban, a veteran of international coaching, took over as the team's skipper. He would prove to be instrumental in leading the school's transition from small-college to major-college in status. (Among other things, Pleban successfully solicited NCAA rule-makers to expand body checking from half to full ice - a major change for the game.)

The team continued to dominate the MIAC, and at the same time play competitively against many of the country's largest university teams. In 1957 UMD beat Michigan Tech by the score of 5-3 for its first triumph over an NCAA Division I institution. Another highlight from this era happened on February 18th, 1959, when junior center Orest Wojcichowsky tallied 10 points (four goals and six assists) en route to beating Concordia College 16-0, in what would stand as a Minnesota-Duluth (pre-NCAA Division I) single-game record. A lowlight happened that next season when UMD's star center John McCormick, from Fort William, lost his eye after being hit in he face by a puck during a game at the Curling Club.

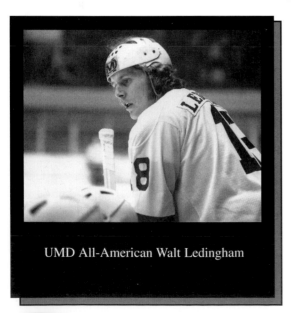

UMD All-American Walt Ledingham

In four years, Pleban's UMD teams never lost a game in the MIAC. Pleban left in 1959 and was replaced by Ralph Romano, a former goaltender at Duluth Central. Romano kept up the winning tradition, adding on to Pleban's winning streak until finally getting to 56 straight wins over MIAC opponents. Duluth was so good, it really wasn't fair, often times winning games by margins of 10 to 20-plus goals. Teams would try anything to slow

Bill Halbrehder

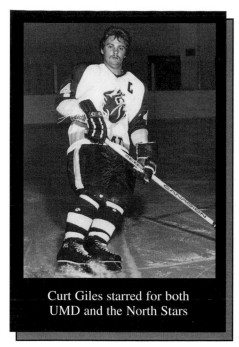

Curt Giles starred for both
UMD and the North Stars

these guys down, even letting the grass grow up through the ice in an attempt to gain equal ground. Finally, in 1961, after winning nine consecutive MIAC titles, the Dogs left the conference to play an independent schedule against big-time Division I Schools. (Some of the teams that the Dogs played in addition to the MIAC schools

Mike Sertich

One of only two individuals to be named the WCHA's Coach of the Year on four different occasions, Mike Sertich has stood behind the University of Minnesota-Duluth's bench for 18 seasons. With nearly 350 career wins, he has become the Bulldogs' all-time winningest coach.

throughout the 1940s and 1950s included: Eveleth Junior College, Duluth Junior College, Virginia Junior College, Hibbing Junior College, West End Civic Club, Eveleth Rangers, St. Cloud State, Bemidji State, Taconite, Warroad Lakers, Fort Francis, UND, Michigan Tech, Regina Pats, Minneapolis Bungalows and Minneapolis Millers.)

In hopes of landing in the prestigious Western Collegiate Hockey Association (which included: Minnesota, North Dakota, Colorado College, Denver, Michigan, Michigan State and Michigan Tech), the Dogs began playing a rigorous schedule against much stiffer competition. One of those games came on December 19th, 1964, when UMD senior goaltender Bill Halbrehder made an amazing NCAA record 77 saves in his team's 6-5 overtime loss to the University of Michigan in Ann Arbor. After paying their dues for a few years, the Dogs were finally admitted into the WCHA in 1965 - where they have remained a formidable force ever since.

With the move came word that the city of Duluth was going to finalize the plans for a new state-of-the-art facility which was to be built along the city's Canal Park waterfront, called the Duluth Arena. After starting out 0-14, the Dogs finally got a win that first year when they beat North Dakota in Grand Forks, 3-2 in overtime. Although the Dogs finished last in the WCHA their first year, they did manage to get a huge win that next season. On November 19th, 1966, the hated Gophers came to town to baptize UMD's new icy palace, which would later become known as the Duluth Entertainment and Convention Center, or DECC for short. The star of the UMD team was a kid from International Falls by the name of Keith "Huffer" Christiansen, who played the Gophers that night like a fiddle, scoring six points in an 8-1 drubbing before a sellout crowd of 5,700. Huffer went on to earn All-American as well as conference MVP honors that year, in addition to leading the WCHA

The DECC is one of the most picturesque hockey arena's in the country

in scoring with 46 points in just 23 games. And, on top of that, his two wingmates, Pat Francisco and Bruce McLeod, finished second and third in WCHA scoring as well. (McLeod, would eventually go on to become UMD's athletic director.)

Terry Shercliffe took over as the Dog's new coach in 1970, replacing Bill Selman, who had been behind the bench since 1968. One of the highlights of his coaching tenure came that next season on December 17th, 1971, when UMD tattooed the Gophers 15-3 in Minneapolis. More than a dozen new single-game records were shattered that night as All-American centers Walt Ledingham and Pat Boutette each tallied hat tricks to lead the scoring onslaught for the Dogs - who struck for nine goals in the second period alone. Another highlight came on January 13th, 1973, when the Dogs rallied from a 6-2 deficit with just over five minutes remaining in regulation to edge Michigan Tech 7-6 in overtime at the Duluth Arena for one of the school's greatest all-time comebacks. Led by Pat Boutette's natural hat trick in a span of 2:37 in the third, the Dogs won the game on rookie right winger Tom Milani's overtime game-winner at 3:02 of the extra session.

Gus Hendrickson took over behind the bench for UMD in 1975. One of his first highlights came on October 24th of that year, when, in his first collegiate game, freshman right winger John "Bah" Harrington took an Ernie Powell centering pass and flipped it past goaltender Blane Comstock at 4:04 into overtime to give the Dogs a 4-3 win over the U.S. Olympic Team.

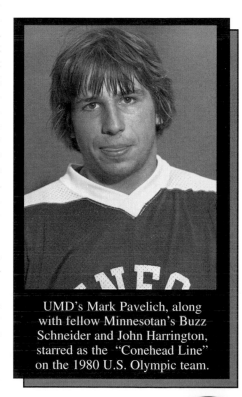

UMD's Mark Pavelich, along with fellow Minnesotan's Buzz Schneider and John Harrington, starred as the "Conehead Line" on the 1980 U.S. Olympic team.

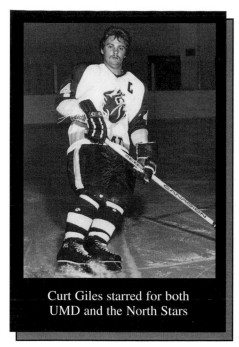

Dave Langevin starred at UMD during the '80s

The Bulldogs continued to grow as a team and com-

Brett Bull

mand the respect of its WCHA rivals. In 1979, for the first time, the team won a two-game, total-goal WCHA quarterfinal playoff series with the Denver Pioneers 7-6 at the Duluth Arena to advance to the second round of the league's post-season tournament. All-Americans Curt Giles and Mark Pavelich helped guide the Dogs that year to their third place finish in the final WCHA standings.

In 1980 UMD was blessed to have a couple of Olympians on its roster: Mark Pavelich and John Harrington, who starred on the "Miracle on Ice" team in Lake Placid, and also Curt Giles, who would go on to play for his native Canada in 1992. Another significant event happened that year when Dan Lempe graduated as the team's all-time career points leader (a record he still holds) finishing with 79 goals and 149 assists for 222 points.

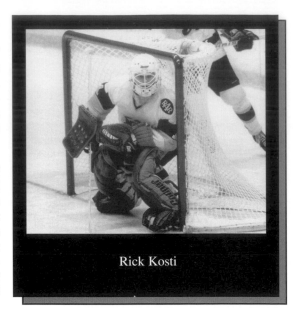

Rick Kosti

In 1982 a new coach took over for the Dogs, by the name of Mike Sertich. The Virginia native, who has been the team's skipper ever since, was himself a former defenseman for the Dogs in the late 1960's. "Sertie" didn't take long to make his mark with the team, leading them to their first-ever NCAA playoff appearance that next year. And, although they lost to Providence College, the Dogs had become a force in college hockey. They came back that next season with something to prove.

UMD's Hobey Baker Finalists

UMD has had Six Hobey Baker Finalists, with three winners: Tom Kurvers, Bill Watson and Chris Marinucci.

Tom Kurvers	1984
Bill Watson	1985
Brett Hull	1986
Norm MacIver	1986
Derek Plante	1993
Chris Marinucci	1994

In 1984, the Dogs finished with an impressive 29-12-2 overall record, the best in school history, while going 19-5-2 in the WCHA, good enough to win their first-ever conference title in their 20 years in the league. Led by All-Americans Tom Kurvers and Bill Watson, UMD came as close as a team can possibly come to winning a national championship, in what many say was the greatest game ever played in college hockey.

UMD coach Mike Sertich's team, fresh of their first-ever showing in the NCAA playoffs against Providence the year

The 1984 WCHA Championship team

before, started out their magical season by receiving a lesson in humility by getting spanked by the U.S. Olympic team, 12-0. Winger John Harrington of Virginia, and goaltender Bob Mason of International Falls were both former Bulldogs who played on that 1984 squad. Another highlight that season came in December, when the Dogs split a two-game exhibition series with the Junior Red Army in Leningrad and in Moscow to become the first American collegiate ice hockey team to tour the Soviet Union.

Tom Kurvers

UMD settled down after that and kicked off the WCHA season by sweeping Colorado College. From there, the Bulldogs won eight of nine and finished the regular season losing only four of their final 16 games. They swept Wisconsin at the season's end to win their first McNaughton Cup, signifying the conference title.

Forced to host a "home" series at Williams Arena in Minneapolis due to a scheduling conflict with the Duluth Arena, the Dogs slaughtered North Dakota, 8-1 and 12-6, before near-capacity crowds in the WCHA championship series to advance to the NCAA quarterfinals at home against Clarkson College. They split with Clarkson, and earned themselves a trip to Lake Placid for the right to take on North Dakota again, this time in the Final Four. In an overtime thriller, the Dogs beat the rejuvenated Fighting Sioux, 2-1.

Their opponents in the championship game were the champions of the CCHA, Bowling Green, who had knocked off Michigan State in the semifinals. It was a tale of two teams and two different playing styles.

Bill Watson

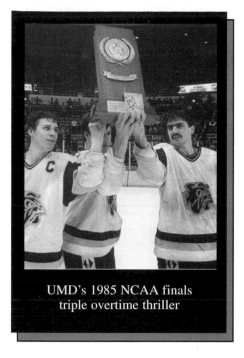

UMD's 1985 NCAA finals triple overtime thriller

Bowling Green, whose lineup was dominated by Canadians, had only four Americans on the squad. Duluth on the other hand, comprised mostly of home-grown Minnesotans, had only four Canadians. The sellout crowd of nearly 8,000 people had no idea that they were about to be a part of intercollegiate hockey history when the opening puck dropped.

For the first time in two games, UMD fell behind as Bowling Green defenseman Garry Galley crashed into Bulldog goalie Rick Kosti, and went "top-shelf" on a backhander at 5:58 of the first. The Dogs came back, as they had done so often that season, when Aurora's Bob Lakso stole the puck in the Bowling Green zone, and slipped a pass to Chisholm's Mark Baron, who flipped the biscuit under the crossbar to tie it at one apiece.

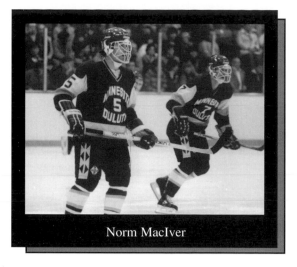

Norm MacIver

Then, after being stymied on their first three powerplay attempts, Hoyt Lakes' Matt Christensen directed a face-off to the left point and Watson proceeded to tip in a Kurvers blast to go up by one. In the third, Lakso, who would be named to the all-tournament team, spurted between two Falcon defensemen and fired a low wrister to beat Falcon goaltender Gary Kruzich on the short side. Things were looking pretty good for UMD as they went up 3-1. It didn't last long, as Falcon forward Jamie Wansbrough, pressured by Bulldog defenseman Jim Johnson, went five-hole on Kosti. UMD answered back at 11:55 on a hard wrister by International Falls' Tom Herzig.

As it went back and forth throughout the third, Bowling Green scored once again at 12:42. Kosti stopped a blue line blast by Falcon, Mike Pikul, but got caught up in traffic in front of the net as he tried to recover. Forward Peter Wilson put in the garbage goal to make it 4-3, Duluth. Then with 1:37 to go, Bowling Green tied it up on a fluke goal. With their goalie pulled, the Falcons dumped a long, off-target shot into the zone from beyond the red line that many people felt was off side. Oddly, the puck bounced off the end boards and past Kosti, who had stepped behind the net to control a puck which would never arrive. The puck hit a crack in the dasher board, deflected to the net, hit the left post and stopped in the crease. With Kosti way out of position, John Samanski, who had sprinted down the slot, tapped in a "freebie" to tie it up.

"I've never seen it happen, but I've heard of it happening. However, it never happened to me" said the goaltender on the tough-luck bounce. "It happened so fast that I didn't know what to do. I felt helpless."

The teams went to OT. In fact, it would be four overtimes! Save after save, both goalies battled to stay alive. In the blur of the overtimes, Kruzich and Kosti, both freshmen goalies, played out of their heads. Kruzich stopped three UMD breakaways while Kosti stopped 19 shots in the final 37 minutes. Time stood still. It was unbelievable. Both teams were visibly fatigued and seemed to be skating only on adrenaline.

UMD Goalie Chad Erickson

Derek Plante and the McNaughton Cup

Finally, at 7:11 of the fourth overtime, it ended. And with it broke the collective hearts of UMD hockey fans forever. Falcon forward Dan Kane sped into the Bulldog end from the neutral zone and, from the high slot, threaded a pass to Gino Cavallini, who broke in all alone on Kosti. Cavallini took the puck from left to right, and put a back-hander in to make college hockey history.

Kosti, who tied a tournament record with 55 saves, really had no chance on the game-winning goal. Kane made the perfect pass, and Cavallini made the perfect shot. That was it. As soon as the puck hit the back of the net, Kosti skated straight to his bench, where he was met by his teary-eyed teammates, who sat motionless in disbelief.

The Bulldogs and Falcons had skated for 97 minutes and 11 seconds at Olympic Arena, in a game that took nearly four hours, while taking part in the (then) longest and most memorable game in college hockey history. The historic arena in Lake Placid that housed the famed "Miracle on Ice" Olympic team four years earlier, had now played host to the "Marathon on Ice."

UMD All-Americans	
Bob Hill	1966
Keith Christiansen	1967
Murray Keogan	1970
Walt Ledingham	1971, 72
Pat Boutette	1973
Ron Busniuk	1970
Curt Giles	1978, 79
Mark Pavelich	1979
Tom Kurvers	1984
Bill Watson	1984, 85
Rick Kosti	1985
Norm MacIver	1985, 86
Brett Hull	1986
Chad Erickson	1990
Brett Hauer	1993
Derek Plante	1993
Chris Marinucci	1994

UMD Star Chris Marinucci

"The thing I remember most about the over-times was being really tired and gasping for air during the whistles," said team captain Tom Kurvers. "I think we only played four defensemen for most of the game. After a while, you didn't take any chances. You just played your position and tried not to make a mistake. The whole overtime was confusing. I hardly remember any of it. I was hugely disappointed at the loss, but it was an incredible game."

"Just to be going into overtime was a huge letdown, and we didn't feel that we had to be there," said Bill Watson. "It's one thing to score late to get into overtime, and it's another thing to squander the lead to get into overtime. The excitement level was incredible. The overtimes went on and on and on, and it just became a situation of survival and mind over matter as to just how much you wanted to win. It was tough playing on the much bigger Olympic ice surface too. It was probably my toughest loss ever as a hockey player."

Duluth hockey hero Gus Olson with some of his old Duluth hockey memorabelia

UMD turned the corner that night in the world of college hockey. No longer were they just the second-best team in Minnesota. Bulldog hockey had arrived big time. In an ironic twist, UMD returned to the Final Four again the following year. This time, led by a young freshman named Brett Hull, they lost a three-overtime heart-breaker 6-5, to RPI in Detroit. They rebounded to finish third in the nation by winning the consolation game 7-6 over Boston College, in, you guessed it, overtime. For his team's efforts, third-year head coach Mike Sertich was selected the WCHA's Coach of the Year for an unprecedented third season in a row.

Another major milestone came for Hull that following season, when, on March 1st, in the Bulldogs' WCHA quarterfinal series with Northern Michigan at the Duluth Arena, he beat goalie Chris Jiannaris at the 15:38 mark of the third period for his 50th goal of the year (and fourth of the night) to eclipse the previous Bulldog single-season mark of 49 goals set only the year before by Bill Watson.

The Dogs roared into the 90's though some up and down seasons. In 1993 the team rebounded to win their third WCHA title by blanking visiting St. Cloud State University 4-0, on junior winger Chris Marinucci's two goals. The team went on to sweep Alaska Anchorage in the first round of the WCHA playoffs at the DECC, thus finishing the year with a 17-1-0 home record and a .944 winning percentage, the best single-season mark in school history. After beating Brown, the team ultimately lost to Lake Superior State 4-3 in the NCAA's Western Region finals. But, as a small consolation, the Dogs did manage to clean up at the annual WCHA Awards Banquet. Senior center Derek Plante was named as the league's MVP, and fellow All-WCHA first team defenseman Brett Hauer was named the Student-Athlete of the Year (a Bulldog first). Sertie rounded out the evening by bringing home his fourth Coach of the Year trophy, becoming only the second coach ever to do so.

One of the biggest moments in Bulldog history happened on March 15th, 1998, when the team, left for dead and down 4-0 with less than 14 minutes remaining in regulation, rallied back to beat the Gophers 5-4 in the third and deciding game of their best-of-three WCHA playoff series at the DECC. Five different Dogs scored in the historic victory, including senior Mike Peluso who got the game-winner at 10:49 of sudden death. After the game, in a classic display of emotion, Sertie flew down the ice and slid into his team's net on his back.

Since their first game back in 1931, the University of Minnesota Duluth has established a rich hockey tradition that is second to none throughout the ranks of college hockey. The program, which started from humble beginnings, has grown into a consistent NCAA power. Since 1983 the Dogs have compiled a very respectable 6-6-0 lifetime record in NCAA post-season play, all of which have come under the coaching reign of Mike Sertich. The program is first rate and with the luxury of being the "only show in town," enjoys the support of the entire community. Much like the Nebraska football program has the total support of its community, the Dogs too have the run of the joint and show no signs of slowing down.

Rip Williams

Rip Williams is a legend in Duluth hockey. He did more to help develop the game in the Port City than probably anyone. The father of two NHLers, Tommy and Butch, Rip was involved with promoting and legislating for youth hockey throughout his life. In addition to being involved in youth hockey, he was also instrumental in promoting junior and senior hockey as well. In the early 1960s he got to play alongside of his son, Tommy, on the Duluth Chun King senior team. Rip, himself an avid player, also starred on the Duluth Coolerator team. Among his many accomplishments include founding the Lower Chester Youth Hockey Association, where the kids today play on the Rip Williams Hockey Rink. There was also a junior tournament, named the Rip Williams Challenge Cup, in his honor.

Minnesota's Lester Patrick Award Winners:	
1972	Ralph "Cooney" Weiland
1973	Walter Bush
1975	Donald Clark
1977	John Mariucci
1980	U.S. Olympic Team
1981	Charles Schulz
1988	Bob Johnson
1989	Lou Nanne
1994	Robert Ridder
1998	John Mayasich
1998	Neal Broten

Founded in 1896 as the state's third "Normal" school, St. Cloud State University was once known primarily as a teacher's college. By 1899 the school had a hockey team that was competing against several teams in the state including the mighty St. Paul Hockey Club. While the St. Paul AC shut-out St. Cloud in their first-ever game 6-0 at the Virginia Rink in St. Paul before a crowd of some 400 fans, it put the city on the map as one of the state's hot-spots for hockey growth.

The game continued to grow in the area, and by the 1930s, St. Cloud Teacher's College was one of the state's biggest hockey powers. The school's first official team hit the ice in 1931, and under the tutelage of head coach Ralph Theisen, the squad posted an impressive 8-1-7 record. Ludwig Andolsek took over that next year and found the key to his team's success to be a couple hundred miles to the northeast, in hockey-crazy Eveleth. From 1933 through 1935, St. Cloud Teacher's College, manned almost entirely by Eveleth players, posted an astonishing 42-4-1 record. In 1935 the 25-2-0 Huskies finished second in the National AAU Tournament (which was the national championship back then), in the Windy City, losing 2-0 to the Chicago Baby Ruth's, who coincidentally was composed entirely of Eveleth players. The stars of that era also included a pair of Hall of Fame goaltenders: Frankie "Mr. Zero" Brimsek, and Sam LoPresti, both from Eveleth. (Both would go on to play between the pipes first for the Eveleth Rangers [USAHA], followed by the then six-team NHL -- Brimsek with Boston, and LoPresti with Chicago.) Others included Roland Vandell at right defense, Walter DePaul at left defense, Ray Gasperlin at right wing, Bernard Bjork at center and Cletus Winter at left wing.

St. Cloud continued to dominate against the local small colleges and produce top players throughout the 1930s and '40s, rising to a prominence which provided college hockey with a tremendous boost. "No institution did more for collegiate hockey in the '30's and '40's than St. Cloud," said John Mariucci, who would also have come to play for St. Cloud had it not been for the $100 scholarship that the Gophers offered him to come their instead. "The Vandell brothers, Bjork, Gasperlin, Gambucci, Strand and DePaul all ended up at St. Cloud State and were instrumental in helping the hockey program. Gambucci (later) started the high school hockey program in Grand Forks and Robert DePaul was the coach at International Falls."

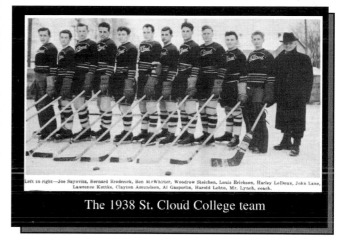

The 1938 St. Cloud College team

George Lynch led the Huskies from 1938 to 1942, posting a modest 20-15-2 record. The school then shut down its hockey program from 1942-46, due to WWII. In 1946 former star player Roland Vandell took over behind the bench, and over the next five years led the Huskies to an impressive 39-19-2 record against such schools as the University of Manitoba, Minnesota Duluth, North Dakota, Michigan Tech, Bemidji State, St. Thomas, St. Olaf, St. John's, Concordia, Macalester, Hamline, Carlton, Gustavus and St. Mary's. The star of that era was Eveleth's Sergio Gambucci, a two-time team captain who twice led the team in scoring. The Huskies, after posting a 12-4 record, won the 1948 St. Paul Winter Carnival Championship after beating St. Thomas, St. John's and St. Olaf. The title was symbolic of the college hockey championship of Minnesota at time. One of the school's other big wins of that era happened on February 20, 1949, when St. Cloud State beat Bemidji State by the final of 13-0.

After five different coaches in five years, Jack Wink finally took over as the team's new skipper in 1956. Wink would lead the Huskies to a 68-69-2 record over a 12-year span until 1968, when he was replaced by Charles Basch. During that time St. Cloud played tough against several newcomers, including the University of Colorado, Lake Superior State and Augsburg. Basch came in and got the program focused on playing bigger and better schools, eventually joining the NAIA with several other local colleges, while later gaining Division II status. Ultimately, Basch would guide the Huskies to a 181-193-7 record from 1968-1984. During that period, the team played several new teams including: the Air Force Academy, Alaska Anchorage, Illinois-Chicago, Chicago State, Iowa State, St. Scholastica and several Wisconsin State schools. Basch posted a winning season every year he served as the team's coach, while his best stretch was from 1979-84, when he posted an outstanding 127-75-60 record against a lot of bigger Division I and II schools.

The 1970's produced five all-American's in Ronald Gordon (1970), Paul Oberstar (1971), John Fitzsimmons (1973), Pat Sullivan (1974, '75), and

KMSP-TV Ch. 9 News anchor Jeff Passolt was a star winger (and bruiser) for the Huskies from 1977-81.

Hall of Famer Frank Brimsek was St. Cloud's first star

Tim Hanus is St. Cloud State's #2 all-time leading scorer

Dave Reichel (1978, '79). Reichel (a current member of the United States Bandy Team), led the Huskies in scoring from 1977-79, and currently ranks fifth on the SCSU all-time scoring list with 138 points. Meanwhile, Fitzsimmons, who led his teams in scoring in 1971 and 1973, ranks 17th all-time with 103 points.

In 1980, long-time coach Charlie Basch led the Huskies into the Northern Collegiate Hockey Association, the inaugural season of the league. It was the school's first step in getting to what they felt was a realistic level, NCAA Division I. Some of the stars of that era included TV news anchor Jeff Passolt, who remains sixth all-time in team scoring with 67 goals and 69 assists for 136 career points from 1977-81, as well as goalie Rory Eidsness and defenseman Dan Pratt, who were both named as All-Americans in 1981-82.

Upon his retirement from coaching in 1984, Basch was replaced by former Gopher John Perpich, who also played the game professionally for the St. Paul Fighting Saints in the late 1970s. Although Perpich would only stay for two seasons in St. Cloud, he led the Huskies to

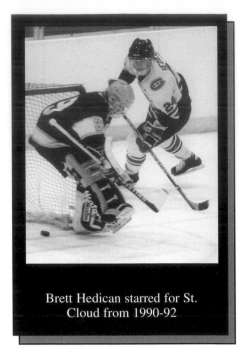

Brett Hedican starred for St. Cloud from 1990-92

back-to-back winning seasons and renewed interest in Husky hockey. During his tenure, Perpich posted a 30-24-4 record, highlighted by his 1985 second-place finish in the NCHA. The following season, after leading the NCHA on six different occasions before darkhorse Mankato State and perennial power Bemidji State took over, the Huskies recorded a 16-11-2 overall record and finished fifth in the league. The Hibbing native left the Huskies in 1986 to become the head coach at Ferris State, a Division I school in Michigan.

After Perpich left, the school really got serious about getting to the next level. What they needed was someone to come in that had a lot of credibility and clout. Someone with enough star power to get legislation passed to finally move the program to the Division I level. Their prayers were answered in 1986, when former Gopher, Olympic and NHL coach Herb Brooks agreed to come to St. Cloud and take over as the team's 15th ever coach. "It was a wonderful opportunity for a Division I school and would provide more opportunities for kids," said Brooks. "There are more kids in Minnesota than there are places to play."

With the big news, a whole new wave of excitement erupted onto the St. Cloud community. The first step in implementing their long range plan for turning the program into a Division I Hockey power from its current Division II status, required lobbying for a new arena. Design plans soon got underway for an heir apparent to Municipal Ice Arena, the "National Hockey Center," complete with two Olympic-sized sheets of ice and seating for more than 6,000 fans.

In Brooks' first and only season as head coach at SCSU, the Husky hockey team broke or tied 45 school records on the way to posting a 25-10-1 record and placing third at the NCAA Division II Ice Hockey Championships. Playing to capacity crowds Herbie worked his magic, gaining grass-roots level support and starting a massive recruiting initiative to get the state's best blue-chip players to come there. The Huskies went 17-4-1 on their home ice, finished first in the NCHA with a 13-6-1 record, and won the conference's post-season tournament. The Huskies were seeded first in the Western Division and went on to defeat Salem State in the first round of the NCHA Division II Championships. The series win over Salem State sent the Huskies to the Final Four held in Plattsburgh, N.Y. While the Huskies dropped their opening game to Oswego State 5-2, they did rally to defeat conference rival Bemidji State 6-4 to finish third in the nation. One of the stars of that team was two-time All-American selection Mike Brodzinski, who remains third all-time in team scoring with 146 points. Brodzinski, from Blaine, had 18 goals and 29 assists for 47 points to lead the team in scoring. "Herb breathes winning," added walk-on Burnsville senior forward Herm Finnegan, "I think we were afraid to lose."

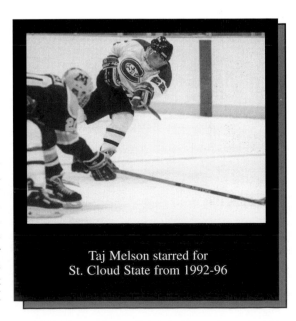

Taj Melson starred for St. Cloud State from 1992-96

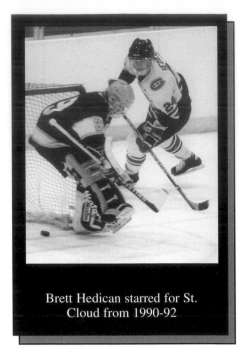

Herb Brooks came in and brought the program to the next level

"We had a commitment from the president," said Brooks, who was inspired to take the position on some advice from John Mariucci. "He encouraged me to go up there for at least a year and put something back into the game. It was more for philosophical reasons that I went there, and that year went fast for me. Basically, that was one of the most enjoyable years I ever spent in hockey; it was fun."

In late May of 1987, after an arduous battle with the state legislature, the school's arena proposal was approved under Governor Rudy Perpich's Olympic and Amateur Sports Initiative, which included building various sports facilities around the state. While the construction of the National Hockey Center was underway, the Huskies decided to join the ranks of Division I hockey as an Independent among the nation's best NCAA Division I teams. Brooks, who left the school to take over as the North Stars new head coach after a year in St. Cloud, passed the torch to his top assistant, former University of Wisconsin-River Falls and Bethel College hockey coach Craig Dahl. Dahl now began the long journey of getting his team prepared for the rigors of Division I hockey.

The Huskies got a little "baptism by fire" in their first game that year, when they got waxed by the Gophers 6-0 in Eveleth for the annual Hall of Fame game. It wasn't easy at first, but Dahl led the Huskies to a modest 11-25-1 overall record in his first season. His Huskies showed a big improvement at the end though, when they won five of their last eight games, including an impressive 4-3 upset win over third-ranked Lake Superior State on the final night of the season.

The Huskies opened the 1988-89 season by beating Division I mainstay Notre Dame by the final of 4-3, giving St. Cloud a much needed shot of confidence. Dahl's club went on to win three of their first five games, and began to peak the interests of recruits from all around the state. Another big event happened early that season as well, when, on December 16, 1989, the Huskies christened

Jeff Saterdalen, who played at St. Cloud State from 1988-92, remains as the school's all-time leading scorer with 179 points

the National Hockey Center by beating Northern Michigan by the final score of 5-4 in front of some 4,000 fans. The team beat several established Division I teams that year including Notre Dame, Alaska-Fairbanks, Clarkson, Air Force, Dartmouth, Brown and Alaska-Anchorage, to finish with an impressive 19-16-2 record. For their efforts the team received an invitation to the first round of the NCAA Division I playoffs in Sault Ste. Marie, Mich., for a best-of-three series against Lake Superior State. There, the Huskies ended their season with a pair of toughly contested 6-3 and 4-2 losses. Winger Lenny Eseau led the team in scoring with 39 points.

The Huskies kicked off the 1989-90 season with a 5-4 and 4-2 sweep of former NCAA Champion Northern Michigan. Dahl's boys went on to garner a 17-19-2 record that year, which included big wins over Denver, Wisconsin, Michigan Tech, Air Force, Bowling Green, and a tie with UMD. Not only were new recruits taking notice, but so were other college coaches. At the end of the season, the Huskies were ranked second in the NCAA Division I Independent Coaches Poll behind only Alaska-Anchorage. Bloomington's Jeff Saterdalen led the team in scoring that season with 24 goals and 33 assists for 57 points.

In the fall of 1990, the Huskies' wish finally came true — they were accepted into the prestigious Western Collegiate Hockey Association. In their first-ever WCHA game, the Huskies tied the Gophers in a 3-3 overtime thriller in front of a record home crowd of 7,051 screaming fans. The Huskies played a great rookie season in the conference that year, ultimately finishing fifth in the league with a 12-16-4 record. The season came to a climax when they took North Dakota to three games in the first round of the conference playoffs. After opening the series with a 4-2 win, the Sioux tied it up by beating St. Cloud 10-2. Then, in the third and final game, the Huskies blew a 4-0 lead by giving up seven unanswered goals to lose the game. While winger Brian Cook had 50 points for the team to lead all scorers, junior defenseman Bret Hedican of North St. Paul was St. Cloud's first All-WCHA First Team pick.

Hedican opted to leave the Huskies the following season to play for the 1992 U.S. Olympic Hockey team in

St. Cloud Head Coach Craig Dahl

The man who has been through it all over the past decade at St. Cloud is head coach Craig Dahl. Dahl, who is entering 13th season as the Huskies' head coach, has been the constant factor behind a program that continues to improve throughout the ranks of Division I hockey.

A native of Albert Lea, Dahl turned down a chance to play hockey at Dartmouth and instead accepted a scholarship as a football quarterback under Murray Warmath at the University of Minnesota in 1971. But, when Cal Stoll took over for Warmath in 1972, Dahl's Gopher gridiron career came to a screeching halt. Dahl then decided to transfer to Pacific Lutheran University in Tacoma, Wash., where he played both football and also defense for the Burien Flyers Junior hockey team in Seattle. Upon graduating with a degree in physical education and social sciences in 1976, Dahl found a job teaching and coaching football and track at Winona State and later in Billings, Montana. One of his buddies there, who went on to coach football at Bethel College in St. Paul later recommended him for his school's open hockey coaching position. Eager to learn the art of college hockey coaching, Dahl sought the advice of several Minnesota hockey coaching legends, including: Ed Saugestad, Brad Buetow, Gino Gasparini, Don Roberts and Chuck Grillo. Grillo signed him for a summer hockey camp, where Dahl did as much listening and learning as he did instructing. In 1980 Dahl began his collegiate coaching career at Bethel. There, he produced a modest 61-75 overall record, led the Royals to a MIAC championship in 1982, a NAIA consolation title in 1984, and was named as the MIAC Coach of the Year in 1985. That same year he left Bethel to take over for the University of Wisconsin-River Falls, where his Falcons knocked off St. Cloud for the final spot in the Northern Collegiate Hockey Association playoffs.

It was at Bethel though, where Dahl caught another break. Herb Brooks, who was leaving the country to coach in Switzerland, was looking for someone to house-sit his home near Bethel. He had heard that Bethel had a new hockey coach, so he called Dahl to see if he was interested. The result was a beautiful friendship that would later pay big dividends for the young Dahl. In 1986, Brooks accepted the SCSU coaching position, and as fate would have it, his top assistant (and predecessor in waiting) would be Craig Dahl. Dahl of course took over the head coaching position in 1987, and after a season of playing Division I hockey as an independent, led his team into the WCHA in 1988.

One of the hardest things for Dahl to overcome, was the fact that because state dollars were ultimately used to fund the program's new arena, many critics expected Dahl to "do the right thing" by recruiting only Minnesota kids - like the Gophers did. So, when Dahl recruited some top-notch Canadian kids, some people got bent out of shape. "Unfairly, I think, we took some heat," Dahl said. "It was said that this program was supposed to be a program for Minnesota kids. In my mind, it will be," he added. And he has done that through the years, by giving countless Minnesota kids scholarships and opportunities to advance their hockey careers at St. Cloud State.

This season will mark his 18th overall as a head collegiate coach, having posted a 266-290-31 career record. In addition, his 200-plus wins at St. Cloud State have made him the winningest coach in school history. His Huskies have advanced to the WCHA Final Five four times in the last six seasons and have become a force on the national college hockey scene. Exciting hockey is not the only product of Dahl's program though. Academics are as important as winning as evidenced by the fact that some 50 SCSU players have been named to the WCHA All-Academic Team since the Huskies joined the league. Dahl is a proven winner, and sometime soon in the next millennium, he will bring a national championship back to the people of St. Cloud.

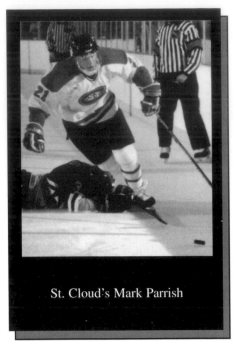

St. Cloud's Mark Parrish

Albertville, France. Then, upon returning from the Olympics, Hedican decided to join the St. Louis Blues. (He was later traded to the Vancouver Canucks, where he has since played in a Stanley Cup Final, as well as an All-Star game.) The Huskies posted a 14-21-2 record in their second season as a member of the WCHA. While freshman winger Sandy Gasseau was named to the WCHA All-Rookie team, seniors Jeff Saterdalen and Tim Hanus completed their careers with 179 and 172 career points, respectively, to become the number one and two scorers of all-time in Husky Hockey history.

While St. Cloud State's program continued to grow and gain respect throughout the annals of college hockey, they quickly learned that there was going to be no free lunch in the tough WCHA. In 1992-93 the team posted a 15-8-3 record, good only for seventh place in the conference. Centerman Fred Knipscheer, who led the team with 34 goals and 26 assists for 60 points, was named to the 1993 All American squad - the team's first as a Division I school.

On March 5,1994, the main ice rink inside of the National Hockey Center was officially named as the Brendan J. McDonald Ice Rink. McDonald, who served as the school's president from 1982-1992, was a strong advocate for the school's move to Division I. Defenseman Kelly Hultrgren's 37 points led the way for the Dogs in 1994, as the team once again cracked the 20-win plateau. The biggest highlight of the year came during the postseason, where after defeating UMD in the first round of the WCHA playoffs at home, St. Cloud went on to beat the University of Wisconsin 3-2 in overtime in the semifinals at the Bradley Center in Milwaukee. After goals from Dave Paradise and Tony Gruba in the second, Dave Holum got the game winner at 1:04 of the extra session to give the Huskies their first-ever birth in the WCHA Championship Game. There, it would be another overtime contest that would determine the winner, and unfortunately for SCSU, it was the Gopher's Nick Checco who beat Husky goalie Grant Sjerven at 1:47 of the sudden death session to give the U of M the win. Dave Paradise and Gino Santerre each scored for St. Cloud in the loss. While SCSU ended their season with a 21-13-4 overall record, they proved to be lethal at home, losing just once at the National Hockey Center.

In the 1994-95 season, the Huskies posted a 17-20-1 overall record en route to finishing fifth in the WCHA with a 15-16-1 mark. After winning seven of their last eleven games, SCSU earned home ice for the WCHA playoffs but ultimately lost to the University of North Dakota in two games. Center Brett Lievers' 48 points were tops for the Dogs in 1994, while freshman goaltender Brian Leitza was named to the WCHA All-Rookie team.

After finishing in the WCHA basement in 1995-96 with a 10-18-4 record, Craig Dahl's Huskies rallied to make their second appearance in the WCHA Final Five by upsetting the No. 3 ranked Denver Pioneers in the first round of the playoffs. The Huskies won Game One 3-1, lost the second match 6-4, and then came back behind Brian Leitza's 4-0 shutout to win the final game. From there SCSU went on to face Michigan Tech in the WCHA Final Five, ultimately losing to Tech 4-3 in overtime. Sacha Molin opened the scoring for the Huskies at 4:45 of the first, followed by a sweet power-play goal set up by two great passes from Mark Parrish and Taj Melson to Matt Cullen with just under four minutes to go in the second. Geisbauer added the third at 7:21 of the third, but it was too little - too late as Michigan Tech went on to beat SCSU 4-3. Freshman sensation Matt Cullen, who would go on to play for the NHL's Anaheim Mighty Ducks, was named to the WCHA All-Rookie Team.

The 1996-97 season was the best ever for the Huskies, who finished not only with an impressive 23-13-4 overall record, but also finished third in the conference with an 18-10-4 mark. The team advanced to the WCHA Final Five for the second consecutive year, where, on March 14th, they lost to the Gophers 5-4 in an overtime thriller at the Civic Center in St. Paul. Matt Noga, Sacha Molin, Jason Goulet and Matt Cullen all scored for the Dogs in what was arguably one of the most crushing defeats in school history. Gopher All-American Mike Crowley got the game-winner at 9:37 of sudden death to end the game. After the season, two of Huskie hockey's greatest players, Matt Cullen and Mark Parrish, left school early to join the NHL -- Cullen for the Anaheim Mighty Ducks and Parrish for the Florida Panthers.

In 1998 the Huskies posted their second consecutive 20-win season, finishing third in the WCHA with a 22-16-2 record. For their efforts the squad earned a trip to their third straight WCHA Final Five, where they decided to make some noise. On March 19th, in Milwaukee, the Dogs played a wild one against UMD. While Jason Goulet opened the scoring for St. Cloud at 12:05 in the first, Matt Noga and Mark Parrish tied it up at 3-3 in the third. Then, at 3:40 of overtime, Huskie winger Matt Bailey beat Duluth goalie Gino Gasparini up high to give his team a thrilling 4-3 victory. Up next for SCSU that next night were the mighty Sioux from North Dakota. After falling behind 3-0 through the second, the Huskies rallied behind goals from George Awada, Jason Stewart and Ryan Frisch, but came up on the losing end of a 4-3 heart-breaker. That next night the Dogs got pounded by Colorado College 6-1 to end their season. While SCSU head coach Craig Dahl was named as the WCHA Coach of the Year, sophomore phenome Josh DeWolf decided to leave school early at the end of the year and signed with the NHL's New Jersey Devils.

In 1999 the Huskies finished the season with a respectable 16-18-5 record. Some of the highlights of the season included series sweeps of UMD, Mankato, Nebraska-Omaha and Wisconsin. Perhaps the biggest win of the year came on October 24th, when they beat the Gophers 6-5 in front of a jam-packed "dog pound." The Huskies' Ritchie Larson opened the scoring in that game at 9:24, when he beat Gopher netminder Willie Marvin. Just four minutes later winger Brian Gaffaney made it 2-0, only to see the Gophers tie it up just five minutes after that on goals from Wyatt Smith and Dave Spehar. At 7:21 of the second Mike Pudlick scored a power-play goal on assists from Jason Goulet and George Awada to regain the lead. Then, just five minutes later, Brandon Sampair found the back of the net to give

St. Cloud State All-Americans

Name	Pos	Year	Hometown
Ronald Gordon	G	1970	Minneapolis
Paul Oberstar	F	1971	Hibbing
John Fitzsimmons	F	1973	Roseville
Mike Brodzinski	F	1986, 87	Blaine
Pat Sullivan	F	1974, 75	Crookston
Dave Reichel	F	1978, 79	Hopkins
Rory Eidsness	G	1982	Fargo, ND
Dan Pratt	D	1982	Minneapolis
Fred Knipscheer*	F	1993	Fort Wayne, IN
Mark Parrish*	F	1997	Bloomington

* Division I

the dogs a two-goal advantage. The Gophers rallied on scores from Nate Miller to get to within one again, but Pudlick's second of the night made it 5-3. The Gophers continued to press, as both Reggie Berg and Nate Miller beat Huskie keeper Dean Weasler to tie it up at five-apiece with only 46 seconds to go. Craig Dahl's boys then came through huge when George Awada and Tyler Arnason set up Jason Goulet with just 16 seconds to go in the game to give the Huskies a thrilling 6-5 victory over their rivals from the Minnie.

After a pair of huge 5-2 and 3-2 wins over Wisconsin, in Madison on March 13th and 14th, the Dogs found themselves pitted against the Gophers in the WCHA playoffs. There, despite a pair of goals from George Awada and another from Matt Bailey, SCSU wound up on the losing side of a 5-3 game to end their season. Matt Noga led the team with 33 points that year, followed by Tyler Arnason's 31 and George Awada's 30. In addition, senior captain Kyle McLaughlin was named as the 1999 WCHA Student Athlete of the Year, and Winnipeg's Tyler Arneson was named to the WCHA's All-Rookie team.

St. Cloud has always had a rich hockey tradition, and who knows just where SCSU's program would be today had they gotten an artificial sheet of ice decades sooner. Craig Dahl has done a marvelous job of creating a winning program in St. Cloud, and the future definitely looks bright with him steering the ship.

The Minnesota State, Mankato Mavericks

On January 16th, 1970, Maverick winger Jim Lang scored a goal that would signal the beginning of a pilgrimage of sorts. The goal, just one of two in an otherwise meaningless 8-2 drubbing from the hands of St. Cloud State, would prove to be much more significant than just the first ever in MSU men's varsity ice hockey history. It was the first step of a 30-year long journey that eventually led this Division III school into a Division I contender that will begin the new millennium as members of the prestigious Western Collegiate Hockey Association.

In 1868 Mankato Normal School first opened its doors in the picturesque river valley town of Mankato, with its primary role being to train teachers for work in rural schools throughout southern Minnesota. In 1921 the school became Mankato State Teachers College and was authorized by the State to offer a four-year curriculum. With enrollment at the school averaging some 700 students through the 1930s and 40's, a surge in the late 1950s strained the capacity of the tiny Valley Campus. So, a new campus on the hilltop overlooking the city began, and with it came a growing reputation for academic and athletic excellence.

By 1969 Mankato State's first varsity ice hockey program began playing an independent small college schedule. Leading the program was the St. Louis Park native Don Brose, who joined the Mankato State coaching staff in 1965 as a baseball assistant. On January 24th, 1970, Dave Kramer's hat trick (the first in school history) led the Mav's to their first-ever win, a 5-2 upset over UW-Stout. The Mav's went 5-8-1 during their inaugural season, which also included wins over St. Olaf, St. Cloud State and Rochester Junior College. While freshman winger Bill Techar was named as the team's captain and MVP, defenseman John McNamara earned small college All-American honors.

Mankato exploded out of the gates in their second season, winning their first six games en route to an impressive 15-2-1 record. On February 5th, 1971, Greg Jagaros scored the 100th goal in school history at 15:47 of the third period, the final goal in an 8-0 pummeling of Iowa State. The Mav's went on to crush the Cyclones 13-4 the next night as well.

The Mav's continued to flourish over the next couple of seasons. In 1975 the program got a much needed boost when it gained university status, and with it came an opportunity for the school to compete in post-season play. On March 3, 1975, making their first-ever Western Intercollegiate Hockey Association (WIHA) post-season appearance, the Mav's beat Illinois-Chicago, 7-3, behind two third-period goals by Steve Forliti. They went on to beat Hamline 5-2 that next year for their second WIHA championship, and then finished second in 1977 after first losing to St. Cloud State 5-4 in the finals.

In 1978, after first losing to Lake Forest, 5-2, in the WIHA finals, MSU then went on to earn a third-place finish at the NCAA Division II National Championships. The Mav's lost to Merrimack in the opener, 6-1, but then rallied to beat Elmira (NY) 5-3 in their first-ever NCAA appearance. Maverick goalie Dave Pilot made 33 saves while Marc Peckham scored an empty-netter with only seconds to go to secure their third place finish. Mankato went on to earn a second-place finish the following year after first beating Salem State 5-3, but then falling to Lowell 6-4 in the finals. One of the highlights of that season came on November 16th, when forward John Passolt's five points led MSU to an 8-3 victory over Hamline for the team's 150th win.

The 1979-80 season was filled with highlights for the Mavs. On December 7th, during a 13-2 rout of UW-Eau Claire, Mankato center Paul Mattson scored a school-record six goals, while his linemate, Steve Forliti, set records for assists, with seven, and points, with nine. MSU rolled that season, first over St. Scholastica 14-6 in the Western Regional finals, and then through Lowell by the final of 8-1 to reach the NCAA Division II championship game. There, behind All-American goalie Steve Carroll's 42 saves, the Mavs beat Elmira (NY) 5-2 to win their first national title. It was a spectacular end to a spectacular 30-9-1 season for Mankato.

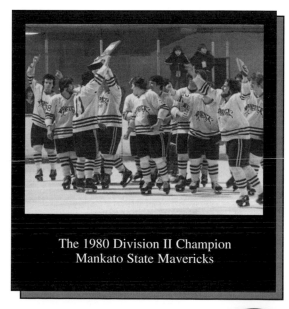

The 1980 Division II Champion
Mankato State Mavericks

That year the team decided to join the newly formed Northern Collegiate Hockey Association (NCHA), which was created by the dissolving of the WIHA. The D-II-III conference included Mankato State, Bemidji State, St. Cloud State, UW-Eau Claire, UW River Falls and UW Superior. MSU would gain another third-place finish at the NCAA's the following year by beating Concordia 9-7, after first falling to Lowell in a heart-breaking 8-7 overtime thriller the night before. They lost to Merrimac in the 1982 NCAA D-II quarterfinals, only to do the same in 1983 against Rochester Institute Tech. After that season, one of the greatest players ever to wear the purple and gold hung em' up. Tom Kern, the 1983 NCHA Player of the Year, graduated as the Mavericks all-time leading scorer with 129 goals and 110 assists for 239 points from 1979-1983. (He remains number one on the list even today.)

The NCAA decided to dissolve the Division II post-season tournament following the 1983-84 season, and as a result, MSU decided to switch to Division III competition for the next seven years. And, although they missed the post-season in 1984, the Mavs rebounded in 1985 to win the NCHA title and get back to into the tourney. After beating Gustavus in the Western finals, they lost a tough-fought series against Bemidji State in the NCAA quarterfinals.

In 1986 Mankato won their second NCHA title and went on to finish fourth at the 1986 NCAA Division II-III Tournament, after losing a pair of games to Plattsburgh State and Rochester Institute Tech. But, something exciting happened along the way. Thanks to a couple of Dan Horn goals, the Mavs got coach Don Brose his 300th career victory, a 6-5 win over St. Thomas in the first game of their NCAA quarterfinal series.

After a couple of dismal seasons in the late 1980s, the Mavs made a return trip to the NCAA Division III Tournament in 1991. The season opened on a mixed note. While Dan Brettschneider scored the 3,500th goal in team history, the Mavs opened their season with a 5-2 loss at Alaska-Anchorage. They went on to post a very modest 23-7-6 record that year though, en route to winning their third NCHA title. MSU rallied in the post-season to first beat Gustavus in the D-III quarterfinals, 4-4 and 7-2, to advance to the NCAA D-III Final Four held in Elmira, NY. There, after beating the hosts from Elmira, 7-2, MSU lost a tough 6-2 contest to UW-Stevens Point, to finish in second place in the nation.

After that season, the school announced its intentions to elevate their program to NCAA Division I, a move that would prove to be full of conflict and political debate. What started the ball rolling was the fact that in 1992, NCAA legislation deemed that the Mavericks, along with several other of the better, larger, Division II affiliated schools, could not compete at the Division III level. Forced to make an affiliation decision, the Mavs chose to go D-I. They knew though, that in

Minnesota State, Mankato All-Americans		
Name	**Position**	**Year**
John McNamara	Defense	1969-70*
Dave Gross	Goal	1972-73*
Bill Techar	Center	1972-73*
Jim Stangl	Left Wing	1973-74*
Greg Olson	Defense	1974-75*
Tom Anderson	Defense	1975-76*
Tom Anderson	Defense	1976-77*
Dave Saatzer	Defense	1977-78*
Bill Essel	Center	1977-78*
Dave Saatzer	Defense	1978-79*
Larry Ward	Right Wing	1978-79*
Mike Weinkauf	Defense	1979-80*
Steve Carroll	Goal	1979-80*
Mike Weinkauf	Defense	1980-81*
Steve Carroll	Goal	1980-81*
Tom Kern	Right Wing	1982-83*
Scott Jenewein	Defense	1986-87*
Ken Hilgert	Goal	1986-87*
Dan Horn	Defense	1987-88*
Terry Hughes	Defense	1989-90*
Glen Prodahl	Goal	1990-91*
Bill Rooney	Center	1990-91*
Derek Cooper	Defense	1990-91*
Tim Potter	Defense	1991-92*
Brian Lyke	Defense	1994-95*%
Jason Krug	Defense	1994-95%
Ryan Rintoul	Center	1994-95%
Ron Bookler	Goalie	1994-95%
Tyler Deis	Right Wing	1995-96%
Jason Krug	Defense	1995-96%^
Ryan Rintoul	Center	1995-96%
Jason Krug	Defense	1996-97+
Jason Krug	Defense	1997-98+

* ACHA All-American
% NCAA II SID All-American
^ CoSIDA College Division Academic All-American
+ CoSIDA University Division Academic All-American

order to play at that level, they would need to get out of Four Seasons Arena and into a new, bigger facility. In October, a $25 million bond referendum was presented to the people of Mankato to build a new arena, complete with an Olympic sized sheet of ice, which was to be called the Mankato Civic Center. Many of the locals opposed the measure because it included the addition of .5percent sales tax to cover bonding costs. But, thanks to high turnout in student precincts, the referendum was passed. With the approval by the community of a bond referendum,

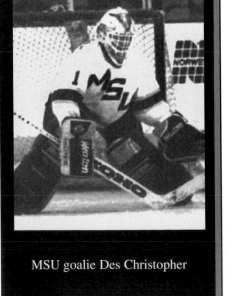

MSU goalie Des Christopher

former MSU president Margaret Preska announced that the program would join the NCAA Division I ranks for the 1992-93 season. That announcement would later be rescinded in the fall, however, when the school's board denied the program's attempt to make the switch. Mired in controversy, the Mavs began playing as a Division II "Independent" squad for the 1992-93 season, while construction began on the new Mankato Civic Center.

Despite losing in the 1993 NCAA Quarterfinals, Dan Brettschneider's two-goal effort in a 4-2 win over UW-Superior enabled Don Brose to become just the 14th coach in NCAA history to record 400 career wins. The Mavs finished the '93 season with a 12-17-5 record, followed by a 11-15-1 record in 1994.

On February 3rd, 1995, Chris Hvinden christened the newly completed Mankato Civic Center with a goal at 1:58 of the first period. In addition, forward Ryan Rintoul's goal at 6:55 of the third, which began a late four-goal rally in MSU's 6-3 win over Alabama-Huntsville, was also the 4,000th goal in school history. The 1995-96 year ended with the Mavericks holding an overall record of 16-12-4 in their final season as a NCAA Division II Independent.

In December of that same year, after years of lobbying from the private sector, including a group of business leaders which later formed the team's Blue Line Club, the Board of Minnesota State Colleges and Universities finally approved MSU's bid to become an NCAA Division I member. In January of 1996 the NCAA made if official when they too approved their status as Division I.

"I think it's great," said former 1980 All-American goaltender Steve Carroll. "I feel happy for coach

Brose and the program, especially with what they've gone through the past few years. He's really persevered to bring a first class hockey program to MSU."

On October 11th, 1996, the Mavs, now an independent member of NCAA Division I, hit the ice against Ferris State, in Michigan. Despite Todd George's power-play goal at 6:28 of the second for the team's first-ever D-I goal, MSU wound up on the losing end of a tough 4-3 overtime contest. They rallied back that next night though, this time beating the Bulldogs, 5-4, behind Andy Fermoyle's goal 55 seconds into overtime for their first D-I win. And, thanks to a pair of Aaron Fox goals in front of a packed Civic Center crowd, the Mavs got their first home win on November 2nd in a 5-3 victory over Ferris State.

That was just the beginning, as the Mavericks played several big-time teams that "transition" year including: Michigan Tech, Notre Dame, Air Force, Ferris State, and Army to finish with an impressive 17-14-3 record. After 27 years of D-II and D-III hockey, the boys from Mankato had officially arrived. But they wanted to get to the next level, and that meant only one thing - the WCHA. So, that summer the team petitioned the Western Collegiate Hockey Association for admission, and received notice that they would be allowed to participate in the league's 1998 post-season tournament as the 10th ranked team.

"When we were having success in the late 1970's and early 1980's, when we were one of the top Division II-III teams in the country, I felt we could be competitive with the Division I teams," said head coach Don Brose. "Then when St. Cloud State made the move to Division I and starting having success, both in the win column and at the gate, I felt maybe it was something we should be looking at."

With its first completely Division I schedule in place, MSU, behind goalie Des Christopher's 36 saves, opened the 1997-98 season by handing the Bulldogs a 2-1 loss in Duluth. The Mavs went on to record wins that year against Denver, Air Force, Alaska Anchorage, Nebraska-Omaha and Ferris State, as well as ties from St. Cloud, Michigan Tech and Union. In addition, they played the Gophers to a tough 4-3 loss, letting the hockey world take notice that they were indeed for real. On March 14th, 1998, the Mavericks concluded their 15-17-6 season after a heartbreaking 5-4 loss to the top-ranked Fighting Sioux from North Dakota in WCHA first-round playoff action. So impressive was their showing, that after that season, Brose was named as one of 10 finalists for the Spencer Penrose Award as the NCAA Division I Coach of the Year.

Minnesota State University, Mankato Coach Don Brose

Don Brose celebrates with
Steve Forliti (L) and Steve Loomis (R)
after winning the 1980
D-II National Championship

Mankato State hockey and Don Brose are synonymous. With 500 wins in four different decades, he is a Minnesota hockey institution. Starting with nothing, Brose built the MSU program into prominence through a lot of hard work and dedication. His teams have earned a "lunch bucket" reputation for their spirit and desire, both direct reflections of their tireless leader.

Born and raised in St. Louis Park, Brose received his bachelor's degree in 1962 from Concordia College in Moorhead, where he was a three-sport athlete, earning 12 varsity letters in hockey, baseball and football. He then went on to earn his master's degree in physical education from the University of Maryland in 1964 while coaching freshman baseball. Brose returned to Minnesota and assumed the football and baseball coaching duties at Heron Lake High School before joining the Mankato State coaching staff in 1965. Brose, who was serving at the time as a baseball assistant to Jean McCarthy, was asked to start Mankato's hockey program in 1969.

From 1969-1999, Brose's Mavericks have accumulated a 512-322-70 record for an impressive .630 winning percentage. Having posted winning records in 25 of his 29 years at the helm, some 34 of his best players have gone on to earn All-American honors. In addition, his Mavs have been to the NCAA national tourney on 11 different occasions. The pinnacle came in 1980, when he won an NCAA Division II national title. In addition, the 1979 and 1991 squads finished as the national runners up, the 1978 and 1981 teams took third, while the 1986 club placed fourth.

Brose was named as the American Hockey Coaches Association "Coach of the Year" in 1980 and the Northern Collegiate Hockey Association "Coach of the Year" in 1987 as well. He has also been very active in the promotion of hockey by serving on committees and through association memberships. He has been a member and chairman of the NCAA Ice Hockey Committee, was selected to the coaching staff of the national Midget Camp (1981, 1982 and 1985) in Colorado Springs, and was a member of the coaching staff of the 1992 US Olympic Trials. Brose was selected to a four-year term on the Board of Governors of the AHCA and was the AHCA president from 1992-94. He has also served in the past as president and vice-president of the Western Intercollegiate Hockey Association as well as being the chairman and a member of the NCAA rules committee for seven years. Brose also spent the 1983-84 season studying and learning European hockey techniques in Sweden and also studied in Russia for three weeks in 1976.

With a rock-solid work ethic and a firm commitment to his kids, Brose, a tenacious taskmaster, has been the driving force behind getting the program to where it is today. "This is a dream come true," said the legendary coach. "The progress has been long, but amazing. It is hard to believe we started as a club team with no indoor or outdoor hockey rink in Mankato. Thanks to the tremendous support of the Mankato community and leadership from several individuals, MSU and Mankato can be very proud of the new heights reached by MSU Hockey."

On May 1st, 1998, MSU's prayers were answered when the WCHA announced that their application for membership had been accepted and that the team would begin playing a full conference schedule in 1999-2000. The event marked the Association's first expansion since the addition of the University of Alaska Anchorage as a league member back in 1993-94.

In issuing a joint statement on behalf of the WCHA, league commissioner Bruce McLeod and chair of the association Norm Chervany (Faculty Representative from the University of Minnesota) said, "We are delighted to welcome Mankato State University into the Western Collegiate Hockey Association family. Mankato State is a quality academic institution with an outstanding athletic and Division I ice hockey program and an impressive commitment to the student-athlete."

To celebrate the team's accomplishment, University officials decided to give the Mavs a new identity. On September 18th, 1998, Mankato State

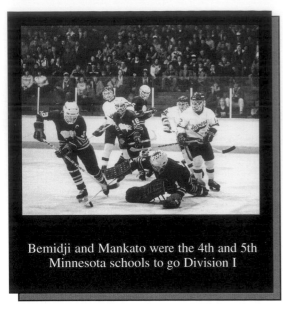

Bemidji and Mankato were the 4th and 5th Minnesota schools to go Division I

University officially changed its name to "Minnesota State University." (The last time the program did something drastic was back in 1977, when Mankato State changed its nickname from the "Indians" to the "Mavericks," due to sensitivity issues regarding Native Americans.)

"This is a significant step forward for our University," said MSU president Richard R. Rush. "The new name will help us better accomplish our mission as one of the premier higher education institutions in this state and region. Our goal is to make this University the other great public University in Minnesota. This name change coupled with our outstanding programs is the next step toward accomplishing that goal."

The Mavs opened the 1998-99 season by winning their first five games. Ultimately finishing with a tremendous 18-16-5 overall record, the Mavs ended their last ever season as a D-I Independent by knocking off the No. 1 nationally ranked Fighting Sioux in the WCHA playoff series opener, only to lose the three-game series. An overtime goal from junior defenseman Andy Fermoyle gave the Mavericks a 3-2 win over UND, while freshman goaltender Eric Pateman stopped 44 of 46 Sioux shots for the win. Meanwhile, winger Aaron Fox led the Mavs in scoring in 1998 with 22 goals and 25 assists for 47 points.

The highlight of the year by far though, happened on October 26th, in an 11-3 victory over Canisius. With the win, head coach Don Brose entered college hockey's pantheon by earning his 500th career win. In so doing, he became only the 13th coach in U.S. college hockey history to reach the coveted 500-win plateau. Brose now stands in 11th place on the all-time list and ranks seventh amongst active coaches in career wins. With some 15,000 students on the MSU campus, and Brose behind the bench, this program is destined for greatness in the WCHA. More importantly, being the fifth school in the state to go D-I in hockey, it is great for the kids of Minnesota.

The Bemidji State Beavers

Bemidji State began as a state Normal School in 1919 and soon became one of the leading teachers colleges in the region. By the 1930s and '40s the school was bustling with students from across Minnesota, the Dakota's and even Canada.

In 1947 John S. Glas, the school's then vice president of finance, approved a $100 budget to ice the school's first 15-man Beaver hockey squad. The money went for hockey sticks, some old football jerseys and a set of goalie pads. Under coach Jack Aldrich, the team's first "intercollegiate contest" took place on January 26th, 1947 against Itasca Junior College. Official records indicate that Ken Johnson scored the first goal in Bemidji State history, while Ledge Burhans got the assist in the loss. The first ever game played at the Bemidji Sports Arena was against the Grand Rapids Raiders. The senior team squashed the Beavers 12-1, as goalie Ed Johnson got a rude welcome to the world of college hockey.

Eric Hughes took over as the team's coach in 1948. The Beavers finished with 9-6-0 record in their second season, finally getting their first win on February 1st, 1948, when they beat International Falls 6-2. John Whiting also recorded the school's first hat-trick in the win. After playing to an 8-7-0 record in 1949, something tragic happened in the Bemidji Sports Arena. The facility, which was not originally intended to house a hockey rink, was plagued by problems from the beginning, ranging from poor sight lines to poor seating, not to mention its undersized ice surface. On January 4th, 1949 at 2:20 PM, during an open skating session, the roof collapsed due to structural failure. Several children, who were skating directly under the caved in section, miraculously escaped the falling beams and timbers. As a result though, the team ultimately had to abandon the structure a year later, and for nine years the team's lack of a rink forced the school to cease its hockey program.

Some of the school's opponents during the late 1940s included North Dakota State, UMD, St. Cloud State, Augsburg, Rainy River Legion, Fort Frances Aces, Bemidji Independents, Detroit Lakes Rangers, Grand Forks Legion, Crookston City, Thief River Falls VFW, Itasca JC, Concordia and Ontario.

The team persevered through the slushy confines of a semi-frozen Lake Bemidji on an informal basis until Dr. Vic Weber revitalized the Beaver men's ice hockey program in 1959, after a nine-year absence. That year hockey was reintroduced on campus, first at the 17th Street Rink near the high school for a couple of games, and then at the College Rink located on 19th Street. Some 200 fans came out to celebrate the return of Beaver hockey on February 13th, 1960, as BSU lost to St. Cloud State 4-2 on their new outdoor campus rink.

The program grew and prospered through the early 1960s, as the Beavers finished the 1960-61 sea-

Gary Sargent
was a Bemidji State legend

son with a 6-4 record. They went on to win eight games in 1962 and 1964, followed by 10 in 1965 and an impressive 12 in 1966. Some of the stars of this era included Ron "Red" Aase, Paul Lafond, Vic Chaput, Jim Thomson, Marv Sanderson, Jerry O'Neil, John Hopkins and Rich Budge.

In 1966 the program got great news. Then University of North Dakota head coach Bob Peters decided to leave the NCAA Division I hockey program he was currently coaching in lieu of a small college program in its early stages of existence, Bemidji State. "I knew a new arena was going up," said Peters. "All we needed was a foundation to build on. Every time a new arena goes up, there is another hockey base to build on."

While Peters led the Beavers to a 13-5-1 record in his first season, it was his second that helped put Bemidji on the map. After closing out their last game ever at the College Rink February 4th, 1967 with an 8-1 thrashing of UW-Superior, the Beavers opened the 1967-68 campaign by christening their newly constructed arena, the BSU Fieldhouse -- a state-of-the-art facility that rivaled most Division I arenas. The Beavers also joined a new four-team league that year as well, called the International Collegiate Hockey Association (ICHA), that included St. Cloud State, UW-Superior, and Lakehead of Thunder Bay, Ontario.

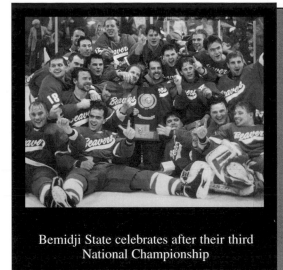

Bemidji State celebrates after their third National Championship

<table>
<tr><td colspan="2">Bemidji State's 13 National Titles:</td></tr>
<tr><td>NAIA</td><td>1968, 1969, 1970, 1971, 1973, 1979, 1980</td></tr>
<tr><td>NCAA II</td><td>1984, 1993, 1994, 1995, 1997</td></tr>
<tr><td>NCAA III</td><td>1986</td></tr>
</table>

The first win at the Fieldhouse came on November 28th, when the Beavers beat Fort Frances 4-3. They kept rolling from there, ultimately going on to post a 16-8-0 record en route to their first ever NAIA national tournament crown (small college hockey's championship), defeating Boston State 11-0 in the semifinal and Lake Superior State 5-4, in overtime, in the finals to win the title. Terry Bergstrom got the game-winner at 3:57 of the extra session for the Beavers, while Len Kleisinger made 18 saves in goal. Terry Burns and Ric Anderson captained the team while Bryan Grand, the tournament's MVP, along with Burns, Barry Dillon, Jim McElmury and Terry Bergstrom garnered NAIA All-Tournament honors. For the Beavers, the title was the school's first national championship in any sport.

BSU finished the 1968-69 season with a sensational 23-2-0 record. After beating Lakehead 8-0 to win the ICHA Championship, the Beavers once again joined three of the other 23 NAIA intercollegiate hockey teams in Sault Ste. Marie, Mich., for the second annual NAIA hockey championships. In the semifinal games, Bemidji State wiped out Salem State 14-2 and Lake Superior State moved past Gustavus 6-2 to set up a rematch between two programs which were slowly emerging as college hockey powers. There, the Beavers rolled over Lake Superior State 6-2 to win the title. Blane Comstock, Austin Wallestad, Terry Burns, and NHL draft picks Charlie Brown and Jim McElmury earned All-Tournament honors, while Bryan Grand was named as its MVP.

The good times just kept on rolling for Peters and his boys from Bemidji. After finishing with a 24-3-0 record, and their second ICHA Championship, the Beavers went on to skate past Gustavus Adolphus 5-2, to meet their new rivals from Lake Superior State for the third straight year in the NAIA title game. The Lakers, who crushed Alaska Methodist 22-3 in their semifinal game, were anxious to exact a little revenge. But, like both times before, the Beavers hung on to beat Lake Superior State on their home ice in Sault Ste. Marie, Michigan, 7-4. Blane Comstock earned MVP honors, while Bryan Grand, Jim McElmury, Charlie Brown and Dennis Lemieux were named to the All-Tournament Team.

By 1971, the word dynasty was being associated with Bemidji State. The Northern Minnesota juggernaut made it four in a row in 1970-71, as they once again finished with a 20-7-1 record, and yet another ICHA title. After cruising to a 12-1 semifinal win over Augsburg, the Beavers found themselves pitted against Lakehead University, who had slipped past Gustavus 6-5 to reach the finals. The finals, which were being held that year at the recently dedicated John S. Glas Fieldhouse in Bemidji, gave the locals a

Joel Otto

Born on October 29, 1961, in St. Cloud, Joel Otto grew up playing hockey just outside the Twin Cities in Elk River. A 1984 graduate of Bemidji State University, the three-time All-American led the Beavers to their first NCAA D-II National Championship in 1984, en route to becoming only the second team in NCAA history to record a perfect season at 31-0. For his efforts, Otto was awarded college hockey's most prestigious honor, the Hobey Baker Memorial Award (NCAA II). Otto remains today as the third all-time leading scorer at Bemidji State with 204 points.

Drafted by the Calgary Flames in 1984, Otto recently completed his 14th season in the NHL as one of the games premier two-way centers. One of the highlights of his career came in 1989, when he got his name engraved on Lord Stanley's Cup as a member of the Calgary Flames. His game-winning goal in Game Seven of the Smythe Division finals that year proved to be a defining moment in his storied career. "You think of all the things that went your way during the season and in the playoffs to win it, and it's really incredible," said Otto. "This is one of the hardest won trophies in sports."

A veteran of several U.S. Olympic and National teams, Otto played for Team USA at the Canada Cup in 1987 and was co-captain of the team that reached the finals of the 1991 event. In addition to serving as captain of the 1996 U.S. team that beat Canada in the World Cup, Otto also played for Team USA at the 1998 Olympics in Nagano, Japan.

Blessed with size and great hands, Otto has become one of the best all-around centermen in the game. His tough and physical playmaking skills have earned him a host of NHL accolades, including nominations for the Bill Masterton Memorial Award, given for dedication and sportsmanship, and the Frank J. Selke Trophy, awarded to the game's best defensive forward.

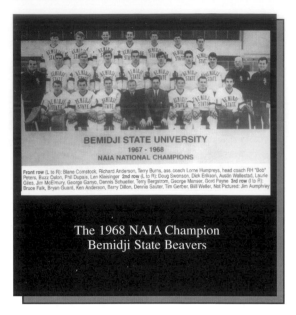

BEMIDJI STATE UNIVERSITY
1967 - 1968
NAIA NATIONAL CHAMPIONS

Front row (L to R): Blane Comstock, Richard Anderson, Terry Burns, ass. coach Lorne Humphreys, head coach RH "Bob" Peters, Buzz Oslon, Phil Dupais, Len Kleisinger 2nd row (L to R): Doug Swonson, Dick Erikson, Austin Wallestad, Laurie Giles, Jim McElmury, George Ganye, Dennis Schueller, Terry Bergstrom, George Manser, Gord Payne 3rd row (l to R): Bruce Falk, Bryan Guard, Ken Anderson, Barry Dillon, Dennis Sauter, Tim Gerber, Bill Weller, Not Pictured: Jim Aumphrey

The 1968 NAIA Champion
Bemidji State Beavers

chance to watch small college hockey's best two teams duke it out. The Beavers made quick work of Lakehead, winning the game easily 6-2 to win their fourth straight NAIA national title. Bruce Falk, Dennis Lemieux, Blane Comstock, Charlie Brown and Jim McElmury earned All-Tournament honors for the Beavers.

The 1971-72 season was a reality check for Bemidji State, who finished the season with a very modest 13-12-1 record. After losing the final two games of the year to Lake Superior State, the season was over for the Beavers. But, on the bright side, defensemen Jim McElmury and Charlie Brown starred on the 1972 silver medal winning hockey team at the Olympics in Sapporo, Japan.

The Beavers rallied back in 1973 to finish with a 23-6-1 record and another ICHA Championship. Then, in the playoffs, the Beavers upended Boston State 8-1 and Gustavus 6-3 to reach the NAIA finals against Lakehead, who had beaten Augsburg 8-7 and Lake Superior State 8-4 to get there as well. Playing in Lakehead's backyard, Thunder Bay, Ontario, Bemidji forward Mark Eagles got both the game-tying and game-winning goals in a 3-2 overtime thriller, as BSU took its fifth NAIA national title.

The Beavers won the ICHA title in 1974 with a 20-10-1 record, but wound up finishing as the NAIA runner-up's after being ousted by Lake Superior State in the finals 4-1. In 1975 the school achieved university status - which was about the only good news for the slumping 13-15-0 Beavers, who failed to make the playoffs. They came back to win their sixth ICHA Championship in 1976. After first beating Stout, the Beavers lost in the play-offs to UW-Superior to wind up in the consolation round. There, BSU got beat 4-3 by Gustavus to finish fourth in the NAIA national championships in Superior, Wis. They won their seventh ICHA crown in 1977. After first losing first to St. Scholastica, the Beavers then beat Augsburg 5-2 to finish third in the 1977 NAIA national championships, which were once again held in Superior, Wis.

In 1978 Bemidji State finished strong with a 25-5-1 record and their unprecedented eighth ICHA title. After pounding St. Francis (Maine) 16-2 and St. Thomas 7-1, the Beavers lost a 4-3 heartbreaker to Augsburg in the NAIA finals. The 1979 squad was finally able to bring the hardware back to Bemidji, in what would prove to be an exciting round of playoffs. After pummeling St. Francis 17-1 and then UW-River Falls 7-5, the 27-2-0 Beavers went on to capture the school's sixth NAIA crown with a 5-1 victory over Concordia-Moorhead. Rod Heisler was named MVP and Mike Gibbons, Pat Kinney and John Murphy earned All-Tournament Team honors.

It was more of the same in 1980 as the Beavers won their seventh and final NAIA national title with a 4-3 victory over the University of Michigan-Dearborn. Brian Carlton got the game-winner at 18:29 for BSU, on assists from Irwin Frizzel and Gary Krawchuck. After finishing with a 24-8-0 record, the Beavers beat St. Olaf 5-2 and then UW-Superior 8-3 to reach the title game. Jim Scanlan, Irwin Frizzel, Gary Krawchuck and Dale Baldwin were named to the All-Tournament Team.

In the summer of 1980 the NCAA Division II-III Northern Collegiate Hockey Association (NCHA) was created from a combination of college teams belonging to the now-defunct International College Hockey Association and the Western Intercollegiate Hockey Association. It's six charter members included Bemidji State, Mankato State, St. Cloud State, UW-Eau Claire, UW-River Falls and UW-Superior.

On Bemidji Going Division I...

"The first stage of our move to Division I requires a tremendous amount of work," said Bob Peters, "and I am unequivocally committed to the development of a solid Division I hockey program at Bemidji State."

"The transition to Division I will not be an easy one," added former Beaver and current NHL star Joel Otto. "It's not something you just turn on. It will take some time and a lot of work."

"The timing is perfect for this to happen because I believe Bemidji can become competitive relatively quick," said former Beaver and current US Air Force hockey coach Frank Serratore.

"Division I hockey is the best advertising a community can get," said former U.S. Olympic coach Murray Williamson. "It will put Bemidji on the map."

The Beavers finished third in 1981 when, after losing to UW-Superior 6-4, they rallied to hammer Michigan-Dearborn 11-2 in the consolation game. Although the Beavers won back-to-back NCHA titles in 1982 and 1983, they finished as NAIA runner-ups in both years as well. After beating Hamline 6-2 and UW-River Falls 7-0, the Beavers lost to Augsburg 8-3 in the 1982 finals. Then, after beating Gustavus 6-3 and then Babson 3-1, the Beavers once again lost to Augsburg, this time 6-3. (Incidentally, coach Peters took a leave for the 1983 season, and was replaced by former player - turned interim coach, Mike Gibbons, who led the team to an impressive 30-6-1 record.)

Bemidji State All-Americans

Terry Bergstrom	1968
Terry Burns	1968
Barry Dillon	1968
Austin Wallestad	1969
Bryan Grand	1970
Glen Beckett	1970
Jim McElmury	1968-71
Charlie Brown	1970, 71
Blane Comstock	1970, 71
Bruce Falk	1971
Denny Lemieux	1971
Gary Sargent	1973
Chuck Scanlon	1973, 74
Mark Eagles	1973-76
Jack Horner	1977, 78
John Murphy	1977, 79
Rod Heisler	1978, 79
Mike Gibbons	1978, 79
Dale Baldwin	1980
Tony Montebello	1981
John Hansen	1981
Jim Scanlan	1981, 82
Brian Hartman	1982
Joe Knudson	1982
Joel Otto	1982-84
Drey Bradley	1983, 84
Mark Liska	1983-85
Dennis Gibbons	1985
Eric Gager	1985
Mike Alexander	1985, 86
Greg Biskup	1986, 87
Ian Resch	1987, 88
Todd Lescarbeau	1987
Steve O'Shea	1988, 89
Dan Richards	1989
Tom Shinabarger	1989
Scott Johnson	1991
Pat Cullen	1991
Paul Ferry	1992
O.J. Kennett	1992
Gary Gustafson	1993
Jamie Erb	1993
Jim Karner	1994
Chris Morque	1994
Omer Belisle	1995
Robin Cook	1995
Jude Boulianne	1995
Bernie Adlys	1996
Shawn Pomplun	1997
Jeff Sobb	1997
Troy Edwards	1996, 97
Aaron Novak	1998
Mike Donaghue	1997, 98

Coach Peters returned in 1984 to lead his team to its first NCAA Division II national title in style by posting college hockey's finest unbeaten record of 31-0. Led by future NHL star Joel Otto, the Beavers defeated Alaska Fairbanks 9-6 and 4-2 in a two-game total-goal series format, and then went on to defeat Merrimack 6-3 and 8-1 for the title. That game featured the largest crowd ever to see a game in the Fieldhouse as 2,773 Beaver fanatics jammed in to see the festivities. Joel Otto, Drey Bradley, Eric Gager, Galen Nagle and Dave Jerome earned All-Tournament honors. Otto, a three-time All-American, also went on to be named as the 1984 NCAA D-II Hobey Baker winner as the nation's top player.

Beaver Olympians:	
Charlie Brown	1972
Jim McElmury	1972
Blane Comstock	1976
Gary Ross	1976
Joel Otto	1984, 98

On January 1st, 1985, the Beavers finally lost to Augsburg, 9-2, bringing an end to an incredible NCAA record unbeaten streak of 43 straight games. After losing to the Rochester Institute of Technology (RIT) in the 1985 finals, 5-1, the Beavers came back in 1985-86 to finish the season with a 25-9-1 record. On February 1st, 1985, something happened at the Fieldhouse that hadn't happened in nearly four seasons. The Beavers finally lost a home game, 5-4 to St. Cloud in overtime. That's right, since December 16th, 1981, BSU had won 55 consecutive games at home. Bemidji State captured its only NCAA Division III national title with a championship game victory over Plattsburgh State 8-5 at the John S. Glas Fieldhouse. After beating Elmira in a best-of-three format 4-2, 3-5, 3-0, BSU earned a dramatic 5-4 overtime victory in the semi-finals over the Rochester Institute of Technology, scoring a last second goal to force the extra period. Mike Alexander, Bucky Lescarbeau, Todd Lescarbeau and Jim Martin each earned All-Tournament honors. (Apple Valley's Mike Alexander, a two-time All-American in 1985 and 1986, remains as Bemidji State's all-time leading scorer with 252 points.)

In 1987, after winning seven straight NCHA titles, the 22-12-1 Beavers wound up finishing fourth in the NAIA finals after losing to St. Cloud 6-4 in the consolation game. The 1988 squad fared no better, this time losing to UW-River Falls 6-4 and 5-3 to once again place fourth in the nation. And, believe it or not, the 1989 team did the same thing by finishing fourth after getting stomped by Stevens Point 11-0 and 6-3. It

Bemidji Head Coach R.H. "Bob" Peters

Bob Peters is not only the winningest coach in the history of Minnesota college hockey, he is also the second winningest in the history of all of college hockey. That's right, only one coach (Ron Mason of Michigan State) has won more games than Peters. Synonymous with hockey in Minnesota, Peters has become a coaching legend at Bemidji State.

A native of Fort Frances, Ontario, Peters went on to star as a goalie at Fort Frances Collegiate High School. A 1960 graduate of the University of North Dakota, Peters spent his college days playing goaltender for the Fighting Sioux. (His son Steve followed his old man to play between the pipes at UND as well in the late 1980s.) Upon graduating, he coached on the high school level for one season before rejoining the UND staff as an assistant coach. In 1964, Peters was named as UND's head coach and during his initial campaign his team won the WCHA championship and finished third at the NCAA Championships. For his efforts he also earned WCHA Coach of the Year honors. Peters finished his reign at UND with a 42-20-1 coaching mark.

In 1966, Peters opted to move to Bemidji and take over the school's fledgling hockey program. Within three years his team captured its first NAIA National title, and as the people of Bemidji would soon find out, it was just one of many, many more championships to come. There would be 26 post season playoff appearances, 15 conference championships, and 13 National Championships in all over the next 34 years under Peters... and he's still going strong! In addition, Peters owns the distinction of being the only collegiate head coach to have teams reach the final four in each division of national collegiate hockey championships; NCAA-I, NCAA-II, NCAA-III and the NAIA. He also holds college hockey records for most wins in an undefeated season (31-0, 1984), and the longest unbeaten streak at 43 straight games (Nov. 8, 1983 to Jan. 1, 1985). But by far the most impressive statistic in Bob Peters' coaching arsenal, is his amazing number of wins, 728 and counting through 1998-1999. A recipient of more than a dozen Coach of the Year awards, he was also honored by having the NCHA Playoff Championship trophy, called the "Peters Cup" named after him.

Coach Peters is reunited with Beaver Hockey Alumni Frank Serratore (left) and Buzz Christianson (right). Serratore, now head coach at Air Force, played for Peters from 1980-81, and Christianson, a college hockey official and former BSU hockey player, served as asst. coach under Peters in 1980-81.

Peters' Coaching Milestones:

Win	Date	Result	(opponent)
1	11/20/64	13-1	(Brandon Wheat Kings)
100	12/14/69	10-2	(Winnipeg)
200	1/4/75	8-1	(St. Mary's, MN)
300	2/11/79	9-1	(Lakehead)
400	2/3/84	5-3	(St. Cloud State)
500	1/30/88	4-3OT	(UW-Superior)
600	2/27/93	7-0	(UW-River Falls)
700	1/17/98	8-4	(UW-Stout)

During his tenure, Bemidji State has produced more than 80 All-Americans, eight US National Team Players, five Olympians, four NHL players and a host of minor professional players in the US and Europe. Most importantly to Peters, however, is the growing list of Beaver alumni who have gone on to work in the hockey ranks as high school and college coaches, officials and administrators.

Ever the task-master, Peters still remains a student of the game. His routine behind the bench often includes writing notes on his opponents' shooting tendencies, studying the mannerism's of his opposing goalies, and constantly making sure that his boys are skating hard. "When you play a Bob Peters team, you better be ready to skate," said legendary Augsburg Hockey Coach Ed Saugestad. "You won't see many teams that go harder for 60 minutes than the Beavers."

Today Peters serves as not only the Head Men's Ice Hockey Coach, but also the Athletic Director for Hockey. In addition he runs one of the best hockey camps in the country during the summers at Bemidji with long-time friend and former Olympic coach, Murray Williamson, called appropriately enough "Bemidji International Hockey Camp." His 728-257-46 record will certainly be put to the test in the new millennium as his Beavers enter the world of Division I hockey on a full-time basis. But one thing is for certain, Bob Peters is a winner, and given time, he will bring another national championship to the people of Bemidji, a feat he has done some 13 times before.

would be safe to say that New York was not Bemidji's "kind of town," seeing as all three of their disappointing fourth place finishes took place there, in Plattsburgh, Elmira and Rochester, respectively.

The 1990 team finished out of the playoffs altogether, while the 1991 squad rebounded to win the school's eighth NCHA championship with a 21-6-3 record. After a disappointing 1991-92 season, the 1992-93 BSU team looked to be the beginning of the next Beaver hockey dynasty. Finishing with a 24-7-1 record, the Beavers first beat UW-River Falls and then UW-Stevens Point en route to welcoming the NCAA Division II championship back with a title series victory over Mercyhurst 10-6 and 5-0 at the Fieldhouse. (The NCAA had discontinued the Division II event from 1985 to 1992.)

In 1994 BSU won its 11th national title after shocking Alabama-Huntsville on its home ice with a comeback victory in the first meeting between the schools. The Chargers, who entered the series ranked No. 1 in the NCAA's poll, took the first game 5-3, but the Beavers battled back to take Game Two by a 2-1 count, followed by a 3-2 sudden death victory in the mini-game to secure the title. In that exciting overtime match, Bemidji winger Jason Mack took a Kris Bjornson pass at 15:48 and beat Charger goalie Derrek Puppa on a nice wrister to seal the deal.

The Beavers took to the road for their 12th national championship in 1995, edging Mercyhurst 5-4 in Game Two of the title series after a 6-2 win the previous night in Erie, Pa. The Lakers entered the championship with a perfect home record of 13-0-0 and a 23-1-2 record overall, but BSU rallied to take the title on the Lakers' home ice. Bemidji center Eric Fulton's hat trick late in the third period gave the Beavers the dramatic win.

After losing to Alabama-Huntsville to finish second in 1996, the Beavers came back for revenge in 1997 by winning their 13th and final Division II championship over those same Chargers from Alabama. Meeting for the fourth time in the titles series, the Beavers edged the rival Chargers 3-2 in the first game, and then came out to win the second 4-2, thanks to a pair of goals from winger Josh Klingfus in the second and third periods. The packed Fieldhouse in Bemidji saw some great hockey, as the Beavers went on to win their fourth D-II title of the 1990's.

Bemidji State and Alabama-Huntsville met yet again that next year in the 1998 finals, this time on the Chargers' home ice in Huntsville. The boys from 'Bama got even this time, winning both games 6-2 and 5-2 to bring the D-II title back down to Dixie. In an effort to get ready for their big jump to Division I hockey, the Beavers played an independent schedule against NCAA I, II and III teams for the 1998-99 season, ultimately finishing with a 17-13-0 record in their 18th and final year in the NCHA.

On May 26th, 1998, Bemidji State University announced, that its men's ice hockey program would be joining the National Collegiate Athletic Association (NCAA) Division I ranks. The decision was made following a 60-day campaign to raise funds needed to support the move. "This is a landmark day in Bemidji State hockey history," said BSU athletic director for hockey and men's head ice hockey coach Bob Peters. "This is a natural evolution for our program. Our tradition has endured and prospered since 1947, and this is the dawn of a new era."

"By recommendation of the Division I Exploratory Committee, we have decided to go forward with our commitment to moving the Bemidji State University men's ice hockey program to Division I," said Dr. Jim Bensen, Bemidji State University president. "Based on the results of our fundraising efforts and the response from the community and our alumni, we have every confidence that Bemidji State will have the necessary support to fund a quality Division I men's ice hockey program."

BSU, who will start its first full Division I schedule in the fall of 1999, joins the University of Minnesota, the University of Minnesota-Duluth, St. Cloud State University and Minnesota State University, Mankato, as the fifth Minnesota school with an NCAA Division I ice hockey program. The Beavers will not play in the WCHA with the aforementioned teams however. They will instead be playing in the newly formed College Hockey America Conference, a seven-team Division I league that will begin play in 1999-2000. The seven founding institutions and charter members include: Bemidji State, Alabama-Huntsville, Air Force, Army, Findlay (Ohio), Niagara (NY) and Wayne State (Mich.).

Minnesota's Small College Programs

The Minnesota Intercollegiate Athletic Conference (MIAC)

M.I.A.C.
Minnesota Intercollegiate Athletic Conference

In the early 1900's the organization and control of hockey was for the most part student-centered. Issues such as eligibility restrictions, scheduling procedures, awarding championships, and the establishment of consistent rules and regulations were sporadic at best. As a result, conferences and associations began to appear in an attempt to formalize athletic competition.

One such organization was the Tri-State Conference, which was made up of colleges from both Minnesota and the Dakotas. In 1919, after a heated debate between the two state factions regarding rule changes and eligibility, the Minnesota contingent broke away and formed their own conference called the Minnesota Intercollegiate Athletic Conference. The MIAC's first charter members included: Carleton College, Gustavus Adolphus College, Hamline University, Macalester College, St. John's University, St. Olaf College and the University of St. Thomas. (Concordia College-Moorhead joined the conference in 1921, Augsburg College in 1924 and St. Mary's University in 1926. Bethel College later joined in 1977.) In addition, Macalester College ended its MIAC hockey run in 1973, and the University of Minnesota Duluth, which had joined in the 1950s, made the jump to Division I in 1962.

Recognized as one of the toughest and most prestigious NCAA Division III intercollegiate athletic conferences in the country, today, the MIAC sponsors championships in 23 sports; 12 for men and 11 for women. And, because its members are all private undergraduate colleges, none of them can offer athletic scholarships to its student athletes. So it really is about the kids, and hockey.

The University of St. Thomas' Hockey History

Founded in 1885, in what was once a farmers field, the University of St. Thomas originally began as St. Thomas Aquinas Seminary. From those original 62 students, the school has evolved into Minnesota's largest independent university with more than 11,000 students. With a rich hockey tradition that goes back to the turn of the century, St. Thomas has been a small college hockey power in Minnesota for nearly a hundred years.

The St. Thomas College hockey program began in 1899, when the students from the school began playing against some of the local high school, college and senior teams. Among the school's first opponents throughout the early 1900s included the Mic Macs, Virginias, Victorias and Chinooks as well as Mechanic Arts and St. Paul Central High School's, and Luther College.

In 1915, St. Thomas College played a series of games against a team representing the University of Minnesota. However, the team was not recognized by the U of M Athletic Board at that time and the games played were classed as only "pick-up" contests. The Tommies also played several games during this era against some of the better U of M fraternity teams. The matches were often played on outdoor ice at Northrop Field with the finals and playoffs often being played at the indoor "Hippodrome" ice arena at the State Fairgrounds in St. Paul.

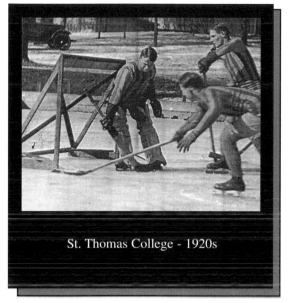

St. Thomas College - 1920s

By 1921, the Tommies, who were considered in hockey circles as the Minnesota State Champions, played the "now-varsity" Gophers to a tough 2-1 loss at the Coliseum Rink on Lexington Avenue near University Avenue in St. Paul. Head coach Harold Dudley led the Tommies to a 6-1 record that year, as the team went on to defeat Hamline and St. Mary's that season as well. The next year St. Thomas helped to create the newly formed Minnesota Intercollegiate Athletic Conference (MIAC), which would include several teams during that era, including Augsburg, Hamline, St. Mary's, Gustavus, Macalester, St. Olaf, St. John's, Bethel and Concordia.

The team won its first MIAC title in 1923, under then head coach Joe Brandy. It would be the first of many for the Tommies. A couple of the team's toughest losses that year came at the hands of the Gophers and also Eveleth Junior College - both of whom were top-10 nationally ranked powers. By the mid-1920s St. Thomas was by far the strongest of Minnesota's small colleges, winning several more conference championship throughout the late 1920s.

Some of the stars during this era included White Bear Lake's Dick Conway, and Hall of Fame winger Elwin Doc Romnes, also of White Bear Lake. In 1926 Romnes, and his teammates Falk, Emond and Starrett, led the Tommies past nationally ranked Michigan Tech 8-1, at Calumet, and 8-0 in a return contest in St. Paul. Upon graduating from St. Thomas, Romnes would go on to star for the NHL's Chicago Blackhawks, where he led the team to the 1938 Stanley Cup Championship. In 1936, as one of only a handful of Americans playing in the NHL, Romnes was awarded the NHL's coveted Lady Bing Trophy for outstanding sportsmanship - an award Wayne Gretzky would later win.

St. Thomas went on to win MIAC titles in 1934 and again in 1939, 40, 41 and 42. They played many of their games during this era at the State Fair Coliseum, which was originally known as the Hippodrome. Its 260-foot ice surface was like skating on a lake! One of the biggest games for the Tommies came in the late 1930s against a St. John's team that was led by future U.S. Senator Eugene McCarthy. The War years put a damper on hockey, but by the late 1940s, under head coach Bill Funk, the Tommies were back in action, winning MIAC titles in 1947, 49, 51, 52, and 53. During the early 1950s the team was playing many of its games on the corner of Selby Avenue and Finn Avenue, on some flooded tennis courts. One of the biggest games of this era came against future WCHA power Colorado College, who beat the Tommies in a pair of 1954 contests.

In 1953 Duluth came into the league and dominated it until the early 1960s, when they finally left to go Division-I. The Tommies, who were now playing their home games at St. Paul Academy, played competitively throughout this period under head coach Gus Schwartz, but didn't win a title until 1974, when Jeff Boeser, who tallied 201 points from 1971-75, led the way. That year the Tommies made it all the way to the NAIA Championships (small college hockey's championship), which were held in Bemidji. There, the Tommies lost to Gustavus in the Final Four to finish fourth in the nation.

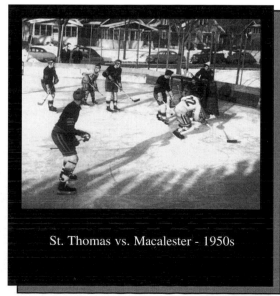

St. Thomas vs. Macalester - 1950s

In 1976 the Tommies played Hamline at the Fairgrounds Coliseum, beating the Pipers 7-4. The Coliseum has been the home of St. Thomas hockey ever since. In 1977 the school went co-ed, giving young men from around the state all the more reason to come to St. Thomas. In 1978 St. Thomas made it back to the NAIA Championships, this time held in St. Paul. There, the Tommies beat Gustavus 6-5 in overtime to advance to the championship round, where, after losing to Bemidji State in the semis, they beat UW-River Falls 7-6 to finish third in the nation. A couple of the stars from this era include: and Jeff Keys, who scored 186 points from 1973-77, and Mark Hentges, who scored an amazing 226 points from 1977-81. (Hentges' 83-points in just 28 games in 1979 remains No. 1 all-time for points in a season.)

In 1980 and 1981 the Tommies advanced to the NAIA Tournament, but were knocked off by UW-Superior both times. In 1981, after losing to UW-Superior 7-6, the Toms then rallied to defeat St. Mary's (6-4) and St. Olaf (12-3) to take the consolation title. They picked up where they left off in 1983, winning three MIAC titles (and a runner-up in '84) through 1986, when former Hill Murray High School coach Terry Skrypek took over from then head coach Terry Abram - who led the team from 1982-87. In 1985 the Toms made it to the NCAA Division III Tournament but lost to Rochester Institute of Technology (NY) 5-3 and 5-2 in the quarters. One of the stars of this era was Hopkins native Bo Snuggerud, who scored 121 points from 1983-85.

In 1986 the Tommies made it to back to the D-III Tournament, but lost this time to Mankato State in a best-of-three games series 6-5, 1-6 and 2-0 at Augsburg Arena. They made it back in 1988, only to lose this time to Bemidji State 5-1 and 3-1. In 1989, in his second season at the St. Thomas helm, Skrypek led the Toms to yet another MIAC title, and for his efforts was named as the conference's Coach of the Year. In 1990 the College of St. Thomas became the University of St. Thomas, but it was still business as usual for the hockey team. UST won the MIAC crown again in 1990, and achieved a No. 5 national ranking and a berth in the NCAA Final Eight.

By 1992 Skrypek had made it four MIAC titles in a row and again took his team into the NCAA quarterfinals. Again selected as the MIAC Coach of the Year, the St. Paul native's squad had to pull of a couple of 3-2 and 3-1 victories over his alma-mater, St. Mary's, during the final weekend of the 1993 regular season for his fifth consecutive MIAC title. The Toms made it six straight MIAC titles under Skrypek in 1993-94, and made it back to the NCAA quarterfinals as well, where they lost to eventual NCAA runner-up UW-Superior. The 1994-95 Toms extended the MIAC title streak to seven but lost in the MIAC tourney finals. The Tommies took third in 1996 and second in 1997 before getting back the MIAC title in 1998. They won it again in 1999, only to lose to UW-Superior in the NCAA playoffs.

Now in his 13th season as head coach, Terry Skrypek has established himself as one of the top collegiate coaches in the country. Skrypek, who won a State High School title in 1983 as the skipper of Hill Murray High School, earned his 200th career victory in 1998, and has put together a 12-year mark of 233-107-21, including a stellar 149-32-11 record in the MIAC. From 1986 to 1999, Skrypek has led the Tommies to an astonishing nine MIAC titles, a pair of second-place finishes, and one third. The team has also advanced to the MIAC postseason playoffs in all 13 years the format has been in existence, and reached the finals 13 of the 14 years.

Overall, St. Thomas has made eight trips to the NCAA Division-III Hockey Tournament, more than the rest of the schools in the MIAC combined. And, its all-time total of 813 wins ranks it first nationally among Division III institutions and 16th among all college hockey programs.

Augsburg's Hockey History

Augsburg Auggies

Founded in 1872, Augsburg University is one of Minnesota hockey's pioneer institutions. The program first got going "officially" in the early 1920s, but had "unofficially" been playing for several years prior.

By the late 1920s the school was pounding schools from around the area, and in 1927, the undefeated Auggies won their first MIAC title. The leaders of that team were none other than the "original" Hanson brothers: Oscar, Emil, Julius, Joe and Lewis. That's right, not to be confused with the three Virginia, Minn. Hanson Brothers, from the 1977 hit movie "Slapshot," the Augsburg Hanson's were some of the first hockey superstars Minnesota would know. Other members of the team included Gordon Schaeffer, George "Red" Malsed, Wallace Swanson, Willard Falk and Chuck Warren.

The next year, former Minneapolis Millers star - turned team owner, Nick Kahler, a future hall of famer, was selected to coach the Augsburg College team, which had recently been picked by the Amateur Athletic Union (AAU) Ice Hockey Committee to represent the United States in the 1928 Olympics, in St. Moritz, Switzerland. The fame of that Augsburg team and its five Hanson brothers made them a top candidate for selection by the AAU, who also approached Harvard, University Club of Boston, and Eveleth Junior College regarding participation in the games. (Either due to lack of funds or absence from school for such a long period of time, all of the clubs but Augsburg passed on the chance.) Kahler helped to formulate the necessary plans, and even led a fund-raising effort to help with the team's expenses as they prepared for the big event. But, after much internal wrangling with the United States Olympic Committee, General Douglas MacArthur, who served as the committee's chairman, came out and termed the Auggies "not representative of American hockey," and vetoed them as their choice. As a result, no U.S. team was sent to the Olympics that year and a dark cloud loomed over amateur hockey in America.

For the boys from Augsburg, the news was devastating. They had been deprived of their greatest opportunity for international fame, and the community was very upset as well. Undeterred, the Hanson's and the Auggies went on to dominate small-college hockey throughout the late 1920s and early 30's, both in the MIAC as well as against other local senior teams. Upon graduation, Oscar went on to enjoy an amazing professional career with the St. Paul Saints, Minneapolis Millers and Chicago Blackhawks. In addition, Oscar won three AHA scoring titles in the 1930s, highlighted by his 1939 season with the Millers, when he scored 89 points in just 48 games to set a long standing season scoring record for all of professional hockey. Emil, like his brother, would also go on to play for the Millers, Saints and Detroit Red Wings.

The 1928 Augsburg team was led by the five infamous Hanson Brothers: Oscar, Emil, Julius, Joe and Lewis

After a brief layoff during the War years, the program resumed in the late 1940s. One of the team's stars during the 1950s era was a kid by the name of Ed Saugestad, who also served as a hard-nosed tackle on the Augsburg football team. In 1958 the biology major was asked to take over as a playing coach. He agreed, and the rest, as they say, is history. Later taking a teaching position as well, Saugestad led the Auggies through some dark years in the MIAC, but slowly but surely got better and better over time. By 1971 the

Auggies were one of the strongest small college teams in the country, and went on to beat Gustavus 8-6 to finish third in the NAIA finals (small college's national championship).

In 1973 Augsburg lost to Boston State 4-3 to finish sixth in the NAIA championships. That next year the program got a huge boost when Augsburg Arena, complete with two rinks, was built on campus. "People get excited about a rink on campus," said Saugestad. "But it can be an educational tool as well. It gave us visibility at the very least. You go to Southdale and find a kid with a hockey jacket and he knows where Augsburg Arena is."

Although they came close on countless occasions (including posting undefeated regular seasons in the MIAC in both 1973 and 1975), the Auggies finally won a MIAC championship in 1977, nearly 20 years after Saugestad first took over behind the bench. "I think we were second 10 of 12 years," said Saugestad.

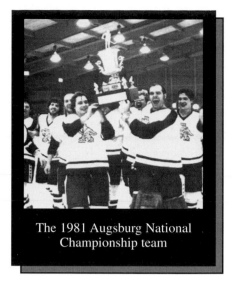

The 1981 Augsburg National Championship team

With their new rink, coupled with the addition of a huge new centerman by the name of Stan Blom, the Auggies repeated as MIAC champs in 1978. But they didn't stop there. After beating Ferris State 6-4 in the quarters, and UW-River Falls 10-2 in the semis, Augsburg went on to beat Bemidji State 4-3 to win the NAIA championship.

In 1979 Augsburg won its third straight MIAC title, and went on to lose to Concordia 5-3 in the NAIA championship quarterfinals. The same thing happened in 1980, only this time they lost in the quarters to Michigan-Deerborn 6-3. The next year, 1981, would prove to be a break-out year for the Auggies.

Led by star winger John Evans, who had spent a season in Austin playing in the USHL, the Auggies, after winning yet another MIAC title, advanced on to the NAIA playoffs. There, after beating UW-River Falls 9-2, and then Michigan Deerborn 7-4 in the semifinals, Augsburg beat UW-Superior 8-3 to win their second NAIA championship. Once again the Auggies were the best small college team in the land.

After posting an all-time MIAC best 16-0 record (which included averaging nearly eight goals per game), the Auggies made it six MIAC's in a row in 1982. Then, after beating UW-Eau Claire 7-6, and Michigan Deerborn 5-4 in the playoffs, Augsburg found themselves back in the NAIA championship game. There, the Auggies went on to beat Bemidji State 6-3 to finish as back-to-back national champs. The Augsburg program was now a dynasty, and the pride of Minnesota.

Although the Auggies continued to play well in the conference as well as throughout the ranks of Division III, that would be the last MIAC title for the team through the millennium. Aside from advancing to the NCAA D-III Final Four in 1984, the Auggies had a relatively quiet stretch until the mid-1990s.

But, for coach Saugestad, who's achievements included garnering three national championships, seven MIAC titles and 15 runner-up finishes over his storied career, the best was yet to come. That's because in 1996 Ed Saugestad won his 500th career game, joining an elite fraternity of just 12 other college hockey coaches to have done so. After 37 years

Ed Saugestad

behind the Augsburg bench, and fostering 24 All-Americans later, the coach retired from the game after that season with a final record of 503-354-21. His 503 wins rank him fifth all-time in NCAA Hockey history. His honors include three NAIA Coach of the Year awards, six MIAC Coach of the Year awards, and the governor even created an Ed Saugestad Day (February 17, 1996).

A brilliant tactician and teacher, Ed Saugestad has become synonymous with Augsburg hockey, and will forever be a Minnesota hockey coaching legend. He was later honored by the league when it named its playoff championship trophy as the Ed Saugestad Cup.

"At Division III, you are always a teacher first and a coach second," said Saugestad. "What I have always tried to do is teach my players that sports, like life, is made of decisions. Decisions come from reactions. Now my system of playing hockey may not have changed much in thirty-some years, but the options have. That's what you teach a player. Use your options."

Mike Schwartz, a 1983 Augsburg grad, took over as the team's new coach. A former scout with the NHL's San Jose Sharks who also coached in Italy, Schwartz had spent the past four years as a high-school head coach and physical education teacher. Schwartz had some huge shoes to fill, but in only his second season he led the Auggies to a fourth place in the NCAA Division III championships and was named as the MIAC Coach of the year. In addition to claiming their first MIAC regular-season championship since 1982, the Auggies also won their first-ever MIAC playoff title. After sweeping UW-River Falls in the NCAA quarterfinals, 3-2 and 4-3, the Auggies qualified for their second-ever trip to the NCAA Final Four (the last trip came in 1984). The Auggies lost their national semifinal game 5-2 to eventual national champion Middlebury (VT), and then lost 9-5 to host Plattsburgh State (NY) in the third-place game. Finally, despite finishing 11-12-4 in 1999, the future looks bright for the Auggies.

St. Mary's Hockey History

Founded in 1912, St. Mary's College of Winona, located 45 miles west of Rochester, has had a glorious hockey history. Then known as the Redmen (now nicknamed the Cardinals), St. Mary's hit the ice "officially" in 1928. Led by several natives of Eveleth, including goalie Oscar Almquist, (who would go on to become a legend as the coach of Roseau high school), Tony, Ed and Louis Prelesnik, and Matt Lahti, as well as Chick and Chester Eldridge of St. Paul, the Redmen won their first MIAC title in 1929. (Almquist, Prelesnik and Lahti would all go on to earn All-American honors.)

Quickly becoming a force to be reckoned with in college hockey, the team competed against a broad array of local and national schools, including St. Thomas, Macalester, Eveleth Junior College, Fort Snelling, Michigan Tech, North

Rainy River Community College

Rainy River Community College has been a power in Junior College hockey for more than 30 years. As members of the National Junior College Athletic Association (NJCAA) and the Minnesota Community College Conference (MCCC), Rainy River has sent numerous young men into the ranks of Division I, II and III, MIAC and NCHA schools.

In 1967 legendary International Falls High hockey coach Larry Ross started the Rainy River Community College hockey program from the ground level while also coaching the Broncos high school team. Two years later, George Schlieff took over behind the bench and led his team to the 1971 State Title, and was instrumental in hosting the first ever National Junior College Athletic Association National Tournament in 1972. That same year, the Voyageurs finished second in state (to Itasca CC), Regional, and National play.

In the early years of Voyageur hockey, the team played several big-time schools, including: the Gophers, Badgers, UMD, St. Cloud State, UND, Michigan Tech, and the Air Force Academy. By the early-1970s, the conference was made up of Rainy River, Itasca, Hibbing, Crookston, Northland, Mesabi, and Lakewood. In 1976, Anoka-Ramsey entered into the picture, and in early 80's, Rochester, Brainerd, Fergus Falls, and Vermilion joined the circuit.

In 1976, coach John Sirotiak led the Voyageurs to the state finals, only to lose to the Hibbing Cardinals, which won their third title in a row. Former Voyageur Terry Thompson took over in the fall of that year and led the Voyageurs to the National Title in his first season. The Voyageurs were 21-3-1 and won the Triple Crown: State, Region XIII, and National Championships. Rainy River beat Mesabi 7-3 to win the State Championship, then went on to beat Canton ATC, 5-2, for the National Championship.

The 1977-78 season brought together the most prolific forward line combination in school history. Thompson put sophomore All-American Dave Olson with freshmen Kevin Gordon and Chuck Green. This combination provided the Voyageur fans with 197 points in their 20 games. Kevin Gordon finished his Rainy River career with 105 goals and 87 assists for 192 points in 45 games (a 4.26 points per game average), while receiving All-American honors after his second season as well. The Voyageurs finished second in the 1978 MCCC State Tournament as Mesabi revenged the loss in the 1977 State final.

In 1979-80 Thompson earned his second Triple Crown in four years. Rainy River was led by the All-American duo of Barry Woods and Steve Readmen, as well as Mike Auran, Bill Mason and goaltenders, Tim Port and Mark Pelowski, who were all instrumental in the State and National run. A fourth place conference finish put the Voyageurs against Hibbing in the first round of the Minnesota Community College Conference (MCCC) State Tournament. The upset minded Voyageurs beat Hibbing and then beat Mesabi 5-4 for the State Title. Rainy River traveled to Eveleth for the 1980 NJCAA National Tournament and beat powerhouse Canton, 6-5 in OT, then lost a three-goal lead in the second period and lost 8-7 to the College of DuPage in the championship game.

Thompson finished his coaching career at Rainy River in 1985 as the schools all-time winningest coach with a final record of 158-60-1. Former UMD Bulldog Bill Mason was called upon to fulfill the coaching opening, but the league had dwindled. By the late 1980's, the conference included only Rainy River CC, Itasca CC, Hibbing CC, and UM-Crookston. Mason would coach the Voyageurs for five seasons before turning over the duties to another former Voyageur, Scoff Riley, in 1990. In 1994, the Voyageurs were upset in the first round of the State Tournament by Hibbing and missed their chance at earning a birth in the 1994 National Tournament. Chad Shikowsky led the team in scoring and was named to the All-American team. That same year Dan Huntley took over as the team's new skipper.

Crookston dropped out of the conference following the 1994 hockey season as the school evolved into a four-year institution, and NDSU-Bottineau (now MSU-Bottineau) joined what would be a new conference, called the Western Junior College Hockey League.

In 1995 the Voyageurs, seeded third, needed two overtimes to beat Itasca 4-3. The Voyageurs then faced conference champion Bottineau for the right to advance to the National Tournament in Lake Placid, N.Y. The Voyageurs lost a nail biter 6-4, but responded the next day beat Hibbing 4-3 to finish as Region XIII runner-up. Goaltender Pat Fermoyle made 73 spectacular saves to earn the victory over Hibbing, while Chad Mitchell was named to the All-American team.

On the 20th anniversary of Rainy River's first National Championship the Voyageurs would return to the National Tournament. Once again the Voyageurs were the third seed in the Region XIII tournament and would have to dig deep to outlast Bottineau. The Voyageurs pulled off the 4-3 upset on Derek Bilben's goal with 1:08 left in the third period. The next night, Rainy River would face conference champion Itasca for a shot at the National Tournament. For the second year in a row, there would be a double overtime game against Itasca. Goaltender Todd Sether played spectacularly and Ross Gruye scored the game-winner to send the Voyageurs packing to Lake Placid. Rainy River lost all three games in the National Tournament but raised expectations for the program. Todd Sether, Barrett Olson, and Jon Cooper were named to the All-American team.

In the 1997 Region tournament, Rainy River lost a heart breaker to Bottineau 2-1, and in 1998 the Voyageurs lost to the Lumberjacks, 6-0, for the second year in a row in the Region title game. In 1999 Rainy River ripped off 13 victories in a row to win the conference championship for the first time since 1980, and would sweep through the Region XIII playoffs. In round one of the 1999 NJCAA National Tournament (which was hosted by the Voyageurs), RRCC beat Erie CC 4-3 on a Lee Jenke breakaway goal with 5 minutes left in regulation. In round two, RRCC beat MSU-Bottineau for the fifth time with a 6-4 victory. Round three would bring national power SUNY-Canton, and the Voyageurs would fight from behind to win 6-3 and gain their second National Title in school history.

Rainy River National Junior College Athletic Association All-Americans:

Paul Brown	1977
Ken Sirois	1977
Dave Olson	1978
Kevin Gordon	1979
Barry Woods	1980
Steve Readmen	1980
Steve Readmen	1980
Gerald Boistad	1983
Patrick Ganshore	1986
Steve Crosby	1991
Chad Shikowsky	1994
Chad Mitchell	1995
Barrett Olson	1996
Todd Sether	1996
Jon Cooper	1996
Barrett Olson	1997
Todd Sether	1997
Joe Jenke	1998
Matt Rissanen	1998
Tom Larson	1999
Dale Sager	1999
Shawn Sirotiak	1999
Scott Aikenhead	1999

Dakota and Waterloo (Iowa). In addition, the Redmen traveled throughout the Midwest and to the East Coast on several occasions to play teams such as Harvard, Yale, Princeton, Providence Athletic Club, Crescent Athletic Club of New York City and Chicago. (They even beat Crescent AC in Madison Square Garden back in 1932, 3-2, on Tony Prelesnik's game-winning goal.) Big Ten schools such as Minnesota, Michigan and Wisconsin would not play St. Mary's though, because the school allowed freshmen to play - something that was frowned upon by most institutions, who red-shirted their frosh. On Sundays, many of the St. Mary's players would suit up with the local senior team - the Winona Owls, to battle other teams from neighboring Faribault, Owatonna, Rochester, North Mankato and even South St. Paul, to name a few.

The 1931 St. Mary's College team was a national power which often-times beat large East Coast teams

Because of the fact that the team didn't have indoor facilities, and they were always facing the disadvantages of outdoor ice in southern Minnesota. During mild winters, they sometimes had a month less of ice-time than did the kids of northern Minnesota. In 1933 St. Mary's decided to drop the sport, after just five seasons.

Hockey was eventually revived on the St. Mary's campus during the late 1950s. The conditions were suspect to say the least, as the kids played on an old outdoor rink called affectionately the "Rink on the Hill." One time the snow knocked out the power transformers and the players had to finish their game by having both team buses shine their brights on the ice from both ends of the rink. There wasn't even a warming house to get dressed in, just an outdoor barracks of sorts that was near the rink. The team struggled through a few sub-par seasons, until the early 1960s, when something happened that turned the program around for good. That's when a big, strong a barrel-chested forward defenseman from Shawinigan, Quebec, by the name of Andre Beaulieu came to town.

Beaulieu was a legend back in Quebec. At just 15, he won the scoring title in the Quebec Junior A League, and just a few years later he was already playing for Muskegon of the International Hockey League. He didn't want to play pro hockey (Montreal had his draft rights), but instead wanted to pursue a life as a teacher and coach, Beaulieu worked with his high school counselor to find a college in the States that would be a good fit for him. One of those schools was St. Mary's. "I was looking for a place to go to college," said Beaulieu. "I wanted to learn English badly. I knew I didn't want to end up working in a foundry in town the rest of my life."

Because he had played in the IHL, he was ineligible to play NCAA D-I hockey. But, St. Mary's, a member of the NAIA at the time, had no such restrictions. Head coach Max Molock worked out the details and got Andre a student work study job, appropriately enough, building a new rink on campus. Starting from scratch, Beaulieu and his buddies took that summer and built St. Mary's their new outdoor rink -- goals and all.

St. Mary's hit the ice in their new rink in 1961 with Beaulieu leading the way. As both player and assistant coach, he scored an amazing 41 points in just 16 games that season. That next season Bob Paradise, a star defenseman from Cretin High School who would later star in the NHL, joined the team. This combo proved to be lethal for St. Mary's, which went on to win back to back MIAC title in 1964 and 1965. (In those days, with Duluth out of the league to play D-I, Macalester and St. Thomas were the teams to beat.) Thousands of St. Mary's fans would brave the freezing temperatures at the outdoor rink to see the team and its new stars tear up the ice.

Beaulieu went on to score 62, 63, and 68 points respectively over his next three years, finishing with an unbelievable 134 goals and 99 assists for 233 points in just 63 games. (That's an average of 3.7 points per game on an outdoor rink!) Beaulieu once even scored nine goals in a 9-0 win over Augsburg. He finally got some national attention by being featured in Sports Illustrated's "Faces in the Crowd," after scoring 13 goals in a pair of weekend games against St. Olaf and Carleton. (Beaulieu, who later became a pro scout and even briefly coached the North Stars in 1978, went on to become a math teacher and head hockey and tennis coach at Stillwater High School, but his legend lives on in Winona.)

In 1972 another star came to town by the name of Tom Younghans. He only stayed for two seasons though, before going on to star for the University of Minnesota and then in the NHL with the North Stars. A few years later Don Olson took over as the team's new coach, got them a new facility, and has been steering the ship of a very successful program ever since.

Olson led the Cardinals to the 1981 NAIA Championships, but were knocked off in the quarterfinals by Bemidji State 5-1. The Cards then made it to the NCAA Division III National Tournament in 1989, but lost to Bemidji State 5-4 and 7-2 in the best-of-three games. Their last trip came in 1994, when the St. Mary's team advanced to the NCAA Division II National Tournament in Huntsville, Ala., only to lose to UW-River Falls in the quarters.

Today the Cardinals play in SMU Ice Arena, a new structure that was built where the old rink (which had a bubble roof installed in 1983) stood for years. The team has been consistent through the late 1990s, and posted a modest 11-10-4 overall record in 1998-99, good for fourth in the MIAC.

Gustavus Adolphus' Hockey History

Founded in 1862 by Swedish immigrants, Gustavus Adolphus College bears the name of the famous 15th century Swedish monarch, Gustav II Adolph, better known as the "Warrior King." Fittingly, today's Gustavus Adolphus College boasts one of the premier Division III hockey program's in the nation.

The Gusties hockey program was originally founded back in 1928 by a group of seven students, including Gustavus Hall of Famer Charles Frawley, who starred as a defenseman. In addition to playing the other MIAC schools, the

Gusties took on local senior teams from towns throughout the Minnesota Valley area. Bill Young and John Holcomb, both Hall of Famer's, were members of the first "recognized" team, which played in 1937. Holcomb, already an accomplished goalie from the Shattuck School, had an offer to play for the Gophers but came to St. Peter instead to play both football and hockey for coach George Myrum. In addition to providing all of the protective pads for the team, he is likely to be remembered as the person who first legitimized hockey at Gustavus. While Thief River Falls native Robert Hansen served as captain of the '41 team, the 1949 team, which played indoors on Myrum Memorial Fieldbouse's natural ice surface, was the first Gustavus squad to produce a winning record with six wins and five losses. In addition, Dwight Holcomb, who starred during this era, went on to serve as the team's coach in 1951.

The program got a big boost in 1964, when the school decided to formally recognize the sport on a varsity basis. They needed someone to take over as the team's new coach, and decided to ask former Gustavus football star, Don Roberts. Roberts, despite knowing very little about hockey at the time, jumped in head first and started recruiting. After playing a solid first season, Roberts led the team to its first MIAC title in 1965-66.

One of Roberts' first players, Chuck Linnerooth (who would go on to become the first hockey player inducted into the NAIA Hall of Fame), reminisced about those first few years, "Don didn't know a thing about hockey," joked Linnerooth. "Sometimes, during a game the ref would blow the whistle for icing or offside and Don would turn to us and ask, 'What was that whistle for?'" Don picked up the game quickly, though, and wound up leading his Gusties to an amazing 10 MIAC championships from 1966 through 1977 (including a record eight straight titles from 1966-73).

In 1971 the team welcomed one of the most intense and aggressive players in Gustavus hockey history, Jim Miller, who brought his massive shot and bone-crushing checking skills to St. Peter from Rainy River Junior College. Miller tallied 39 goals in 39 games in his two-year playing career and ranks third in school history in career points per game at 1.82 (39 goals and 33 assists for 72 points). A two-time all-conference and All-America selection, Miller, who would later turn pro, led the Gusties to two MIAC titles and two NAIA National Tournament appearances, finishing fourth in 1971 and second in 1972.

After losing to (now D-I power) Lake Superior State 11-3 to finish fourth in the NAIA tournament in 1973, followed by a 6-5 victory of St. Thomas to finish third in 1974, Roberts led his Gusties back to a second place finish at the NAIA National Championships in 1975. In 1976 the Gusties annihilated Portland-Gorham (Maine) 22-1 in the quarterfinals, only to lose to St. Scholastica 6-5 in an overtime thriller in 1976. In 1977 the team finished third in the nation after beating Augsburg 5-2 in the quarterfinals.

In 1982 the Gusties placed third at the NCAA Division III Championships, and went on that next season to make the quarterfinals of the 1983 Division II championships in Lowell, Mass., as well. All in all, the Gusties played in virtually every NAIA tournament from 1968-1982, in addition to several D-II & D-III tourney's throughout the late 1980s. Gustavus regained the MIAC title in 1984, and then again in 1993. Since then the Gusties have been a formidable force in the world of Division III hockey.

In 1997, after 33 years behind the Gustavus bench, Don Roberts retired as the winningest D-III coach in the history of hockey with a record of 532-278-25. In fact, when he retired he was also the third winningest coach all-time, for all divisions of hockey, behind only Bemidji's Bob Peters and Michigan State's Ron Mason. Not bad for a guy who never even played hockey before! In fact, he had to learn the rules from his players and from reading instructional books.

After serving as an assistant coach for 16 years, Larry Moore, who played for Roberts from 1973 through 1976 and earned All-America honors as a goalie in 1976, became the Gusties' new head coach in 1997. The Gusties compiled a mark of 13-12-2 in Moore's first season, while posting a modest 13-11-1 record in 1999 as well. The future looks bright for Gustavus, which has been a leader in Minnesota hockey for more than 70 years.

Don Roberts

Donald E. Roberts, a native of Appleton, Wis., was a high school football, track, and basketball star who was recruited to play football for the Gusties in 1952. There, he went on to earn All-Conference honors as a fullback under coach Lloyd Hollingsworth, in addition to also lettering in basketball and baseball as well.

After graduating from Gustavus in 1956, Don went on to coach baseball and football for the Marines at Camp Pendleton before returning to Gustavus in 1959 to coach baseball, football and wrestling. In 1964 he took a hockey program in its infancy and turned it into a dynasty.

From 1964-1997 Don's career record in St. Peter was 532-278-25. The first coach to ever win 500 games, his teams won 13 Minnesota Intercollegiate Athletic Conference titles, played in three national championship finals, and missed postseason play only three times. The eight-time MIAC Coach of the Year was named as both the NAIA and American Hockey Coaches Association Coach of the Year in 1975. In 1993, he received the AHCA's John MacInnes Award for his lifetime commitment to the sport of hockey. Recently he was honored with the creation of the Don Roberts Trophy, which is awarded annually to the MIAC Conference Champion. In addition to developing 28 All-Americans and 66 All-Conference players, Roberts led the Gusties to a fifth place ranking on the all-time Division III win list.

Upon his retirement from the game in 1997, Don reflected: "The winning and the losing, that's something we all do as coaches. Starting the youth hockey program in St. Peter and building the indoor rink (Lund Arena) at Gustavus are among the most rewarding things I've done. I'll always remember the great friendships I've made and all the traveling I've done because of hockey."

St. John's Hockey History

Founded in 1857, St. John's University has a long tradition of hockey success. Hockey at the school first began informally on Lake Sagatagan around 1910. Then, in 1925, Friar Damian Baker organized the school's first intramural program. In preparation of the new game, the administration had the carpentry shop construct some ice scrapers, to clear away the snow, and also some ankle high goals were built out of two-by-fours as well.

In 1929 one of the better intramural squads began playing regularly against the St. Cloud Lions, a senior team. Then, in 1932, Simon Ryan, a football player who had played on the Minneapolis West High School hockey team, proposed that St. John's should sponsor a team. Friar Damian agreed to be the team's new coach, and soon the Johnnies were playing against several of the MIAC schools. Led by future Minnesota Senator (and presidential candidate) Eugene McCarthy, St. John's beat St. Cloud Normal School 4-1, in their first official game.

After going 0-6 in 1933, the school rebounded behind the Maus brothers from St. Cloud, Eddie and Dick. Eddie went on to become one of the most prolific scorers in St. John's history. By 1935 the school had won its first MIAC hockey championship. Led by Maus, McCarthy and goalie Bill Dreher (who allowed only three goals that entire season against conference teams), the Jays went 4-0 in conference play that year. In addition, the roster included five natives from St. Cloud: Leonard Werner, Willard Nierengarten, Robert Kyle and the Maus brothers.

In 1942, because coach Vernon McGee had enlisted in the army, Eugene McCarthy, now a teacher in the college, became the team's new coach. He lasted just a season, as all intercollegiate competition was suspended in the MIAC during the war years of 1943-46. The 1947 team put together a seven-game winning streak, then won the St. Paul Winter Carnival championship by defeating Eveleth and St. Cloud. Later the team defeated a couple of local semi-pro outfits out of the States Dominican League from Crookston and Grand Forks.

Former 1980 US Olympic
star John Harrington
will lead St. John's University
into the new millenium

The 1950 Johnnies finished their best season in years with an 8-2-1 record to win their second MIAC title. In addition, the team won its second St. Paul Winter Carnival title in four years. A few of the leaders of that team included goalie Ted Joyce, Lou Cotroneo, Fred Schultz and Frank Macioch. In 1952 Bob Boeser took over as the team's new coach. A graduate of De La Salle High School in Minneapolis, Boeser was selected by the Olympic Committee to represent the U.S. as a member of the 1948 Olympic team. After the Games, he traveled with amateur teams in England, France and Eastern European countries before settling down at the University of Minnesota, from which he transferred to St. John's in 1951.

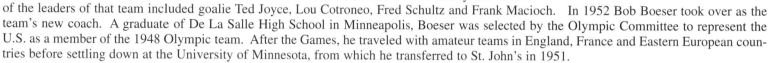

In 1955 legendary football coach John Gagliardi was appointed as the new coach of the hockey team. By his own admission "Gags" was clearly underqualified for the post. When asked why he had been selected as the new skipper, he replied, "I had an uncle in Chicago who once went to a Blackhawks' game!" Gags led St. John's to a fourth place conference finish that year, highlighted by a 5-4 victory over the powerful Duluth Bulldogs. Gagliardi (who would go on to become the second all-time winningest coach in the history of all divisions of college football), led the hockey Johnnies until 1960, finishing with a modest 69-46-1 record.

In 1966, led by all-conference winger Jim Trachsel and Wally Blaylock, the Jays stunned the mighty University of Wisconsin Badgers, whose coach had scheduled St. John's to pad his schedule in anticipation of an easy win. That next year the Johnnies, who were now playing indoors at the new St. Cloud Municipal Ice Arena, finished 12-5-1, good for second in the conference. A highlight of the season came in the first Minnesota Small College Hockey Tournament, when St. John's got by Gustavus and St. Mary's, only to lose to a Canadian-loaded Bemidji team in the finals.

In 1976, Stacy Christensen, a product of Minneapolis West High, finished as the school's (then) all-time scoring leader with 66 goals and 76 assists for 142 points, thereby supplanting Mike Musty's 111 points registered in 1968. For his efforts, he was awarded All-American honors. Two years later, SJU goalie Bob Hanson was awarded back-to-back NAIA All-American honors as well. The Johnnies featured two more All-Americans a few years later: Dick Gunderson, who finished with 102 career points from 1976-79, and Pat Conlin, who tallied 112 points from 1979-82. In addition, centerman Rick Larson scored 113 points of his own during this same era.

Finally getting a facility worthy of its program, the Johnnies began playing in the newly constructed state-of-the-art National Hockey Center in nearby St. Cloud in 1989. The team went through its share of ups and downs through the 1980s under coaches Jerry Haugen, Denny Hartman and Todd Delveaux, who led the Jays until 1993. One of the highlights of this era was the play of two individuals -- Craig Herr and Steve Persian. Herr scored 80 goals and 77 assists for 157 career points from 1988-92, the most in school history, while Persian tallied 65 goals and 79 assists for 144 career points from 1984-88, the second most in school history.

In 1993 the Johnnie hockey program caught a huge break when former Olympic star John Harrington agreed to take over as the team's new head coach. Harrington, a former prep star at Virginia High School, went on to star for the UMD Bulldogs from 1975-1979. After gaining fame as a member of the famous gold medal winning 1980 U.S. Olympic hockey team, Harrington played hockey in Lugano, Switzerland for one season (1980-81) before returning home as a member of the U.S. National Team in the 1981, 1982, and 1983 World Hockey Championships. He then completed his international playing career as a member of the 1984 U.S. Olympic Hockey team that competed in Sarajevo. From there Harrington became an assistant coach at the University of Denver from 1984 to 1990. Prior to his jump to Collegeville, Harrington worked as an assistant coach at St. Cloud State University from 1990 to 1993. (A member of the U.S. Hockey Hall of Fame, Harrington received the Lester Patrick Award in 1980 for outstanding service to USA Hockey. In addition, he is a charter member of the U.S. Olympic Hall of Fame and was a 1990 inductee into the Minnesota Olympic Hall of Fame.) Harrington came out of the gates and won a pair of MIAC Coach-of-the-Year awards in both 1993-94 and 1995-96, by posting 14 and 17-win seasons respectively. In 1995-96, Harrington directed St. John's to its first MIAC regular season title since 1950, its second trip to the MIAC playoff finals and its first-ever bid to the NCAA Division III tournament. In 1996-97, the Johnnies repeated as MIAC regular season and playoff champions and entered the NCAA D-III tournament as the No. 1 seed in the West Region. The Johnnies proceeded to advance to the NCAA D-III hockey final four and brought home the third-place trophy, which was the highest finish ever for a MIAC hockey team in the NCAA tournament. The building process continues for Harrington's Johnnies, who posted a modest 13-12-2 record in 1998-99.

Harrington has guided the Johnnies to a 110-73-13 record during his first six years with the program. The winningest hockey coach in school history, Harrington has led the Johnnies to the MIAC playoffs five times and the NCAA tournament twice during his tenure in Collegeville. In addition, he is also the president of the American College Hockey Coaches Association for the 1999-2000 season. Harrington is a proven winner, and fits perfectly into the unbelievable winning tradition that St. John's has carved out for itself over the past century. He has demonstrated that it just a matter of time before he brings home a national championship to the people of St. John's -- the same way coach Gag's has done time and again on the gridiron.

Concordia's Hockey History

Concordia College was founded in 1891 as a mostly Norwegian Lutheran school. The first hockey team in the history of Concordia College took the ice in 1928 under the direction of player/coach Rene Wambach. The Cobbers' first win came against Moorhead State Teachers College, by the final of 9-1. The team went on to post two more wins that first year, over North Dakota State, 6-5, and Moorhead High School, 20-5. The team played for several years, until finally quitting the program on a formal basis until 1946. Hockey returned to campus that year under the tutelage of Bob Bain, who led the Cobbers to a 2-3 record that season.

By the 1950s the Cobbers were playing against both MIAC schools as well as in the Fargo Senior League. In 1974 the Cobbers made it all the way to the NAIA playoffs, ultimately losing to (now D-I power) Lake Superior State by the final of 7-1. Led by NAIA All-American Dan Travica, of Greenway, who set a Cobber single-season record that year for scoring by a defenseman with 32 points, the Cobbers posted a 16-6-1 record in 1975, and earned another invitation to the NAIA National Tournament.

Defenseman Gary Samson, a Hibbing native, earned his second NAIA All-American nomination in 1977, the same year he received the MIAC award as the league's MVP. Samson led the Cobbers to a 13-10-1 overall record that season, as the Cobbers gave up their bid in the NAIA by losing 8-5 and 5-2 to Gustavus in final season action.

Under the guidance of coach Al Rice and his star wingers' Jeff Frider of Hibbing, and John Villalta of International Falls, the Cobbers had an outstanding season in 1979. Concordia made it back to the postseason this time by beating Augsburg 5-3 in the quarterfinals, followed by St. Scholastica 6-3 in the semifinals to reach the NAIA championship game. There, they lost to the tough Bemidji State Beavers 5-1 to finish as the nation's runner up.

They made it back in 1980, this time losing to UW-River Falls 5-4 in the quarterfinals in St. Paul. In 1981 the Cobbers skated to their first ever MIAC title. Later that next year Steve Baumgartner, a senior center from Regina, Saskatchewan, became the first Cobber ever to be invited to play in the senior all-star game, held at the Met Sports Center in Minneapolis. Baumgartner even tallied in the final minute to put the West ahead of the East 5-4. In addition, Coach Al Rice was selected by the American Hockey Coaches Association to coach the West all-star team.

In 1987 Steve Baumgartner took over as the team's new coach. Right out of the gates he led the Cobber hockey team to its second ever MIAC championship with 12 wins in 16 conference games. Highlighted by a huge overtime win over rival St. Thomas, the Cobbers went on challenge longtime foe Bemidji State in the first round of the NCAA Division III playoffs, but lost 8-6 in a two-game sweep. Moorhead's Mark Rice was named to the All-American team as well as finishing as the league MVP that year, while Thief River Falls native Brian Johnston earned All-Conference honors.

"The team's success did not come in individual flash, but in the 28 players' team effort," said Baumgartner. "We had the most balanced scoring of any team in the league. That's why we got as far as we did."

Through the 90's the Cobbers have been competitive in the MIAC. In 1994 All-American Marc Terris helped a talented Cobber team finish tied with Augsburg for fourth in the league, and in 1999 the Cobbers finished with a respectable 14-12-3 record, good for second in the MIAC regular season standings. The future looks bright for the Concordia-Moorhead Cobbers.

Bethel's Hockey History

Bethel College, in Arden Hills, began its four-year Christian liberal arts instruction in 1947, but can trace its roots all the way back to Bethel Seminary, with was founded in 1871.

Bethel's formal program began in 1979-80, when Craig Dahl, who is presently the head coach of St. Cloud State University, took over as the team's first coach. From 1980-1985, Dahl led the Royals to a modest 61-75 overall record. The highlight came in 1982, when he guided the Royals to their first MIAC regular season title. The star of that team was NAIA All-American winger Dave Johnson, who led the team with 48 points.

In 1984 Dahl led Bethel to the NAIA National Tournament consolation title, and was named as the MIAC Coach of the Year in 1985. That same year he left Bethel to take over for the University of Wisconsin-River Falls, before eventually going to St. Cloud State. The stars of that era were Division III All-Americans John Abrahamson and Doug Voss. Abrahamson scored 148 points from 1983-86 to become Bethel's all-time leading scorer, while Voss finished his Royal career with more than 1,017 saves in the nets.

Steve Larson took over for Dahl in 1985-86 and led the team to a second place finish in the MIAC in his first year with a 11-5-0 conference record. Over the next seven years Larson guided the Royals to a 36-80-7 record. Peter Aus took over as the next Royals skipper in 1992-93. Aus, who has dedicated much of his life to traveling throughout the United States and Canada working with Christian Athlete Hockey Camps as a power skating specialist, has led the team on and off ever since. Aus, a former Murray High School and then St. Olaf hockey standout, has more than 30 years of high school coaching experience at both Litchfield and Willmar. (In addition, his brother, Whitey, was the longtime coach at St. Olaf until retiring at the end of the 1997 season.)

In the mid 1990s, Bethel began playing its home games at Mariucci Arena on the U of M campus. In 1996 former Gopher Coach Bill Butters, a former Gopher, North Stars and Fighting Saints star in the 1970s, joined the coaching staff as well. The school showed immediate improvement under Butters, and in 1997, his son, Ben, earned All-American honors. The Royals skated to a 11-13-1 record in 1998-99, while finishing with a modest 8-7-1 record in the MIAC. The school's hockey program, which is relatively new compared to many of its conference counterparts, has done an outstanding job of creating a winning environment on campus. It's winning tradition will only continue to grow through the upcoming millennium and beyond.

Macalester's Hockey History

Founded in 1874, Macalester College has long been one of Minnesota's premier higher learning institutions. The school began its hockey program in during the early 1920s, when it was formally recognized on an official basis. The Scots proved to be one of the best teams through the 1930s, winning outright MIAC titles in 1930, 31, 33, 36 and 37 and then shared the honors in 1932 with Hamline, and again in 1939 with St. Olaf. Macalester continued to field several outstanding teams throughout the early 1950s and early 60s as well, winning additional MIAC crowns in 1950, 1951, 1962 and 1963. Then, in 1973, after finishing in the MIAC cellar with a 1-13-0 record, Macalester decided to end its hockey program due to lack of interest and suitable facilities.

Hamline's Hockey History

In 1854 a pioneering group of Methodists founded Minnesota's first university. The school began playing hockey as a varsity sport in 1920, when the Pipers played several games against both the University of Minnesota and also St. Thomas. In 1922 Hamline split a two game series with the Gophers, winning 2-1 and losing 3-2.

The Pipers went on to be one of the better teams in the MIAC through the 1920s, 30s' and 40s, as their three only MIAC titles came in 1923, 1932 and 1948. That 1948 title team, which was led by Arnie Bauer and George Karn (now a famous artist and painter), was the last to bring home the conference hardware.

John Neihart coached the team from the 1950s and into the 1970s, producing many solid players and competitive teams. In 1982 the Pipers had a resurgence, making it all the way to the NAIA National playoffs, which were held in Superior, Wis., that year. Although they lost to the Bemidji State Beavers in the quarterfinals 6-2, it was a significant achievement for the program to advance that far into the postseason.

Tim Cornwell was the coach for nearly a decade from the 1980s and 1990s, and was replaced in the early 1990s by Kurt Stahura, who won a National Championship as a member of the Wisconsin Badgers in 1990. Pat Cullen took over late in 1999 and will lead the Pipers into the new millennium.

The program's top assistant coach through the late 1980s and 1990s is St. Paul native and 1950s Hamline hockey star, Gordy Genz, who's leadership and coaching experience has proved invaluable for the young Pipers. Genz, who retired from high school coaching and teaching after a 35-year Minnesota head hockey coaching career at both Warroad High School (1959-62) and Roseville's Alexander Ramsey High School and Roseville Area High School (1962-1994), is a member of the Minnesota Hockey Coaches Hall of Fame. Genz, a former star on the 1952 and 1953 Humboldt High School tourney teams, went on to lead the Pipers in the late 1950s. One of the highlights of that era was the 1959 team, that just barely lost to UMD in the MIAC finals.

In addition to winning more than 500 high school games, Genz has coached six conference championships and seven Minnesota State Tournament teams. His Alexander Ramsey teams were Region Champions in 1963 and 1965, and the 1973 team was runner-up to Hibbing in the Minnesota State High School Hockey Championship. In 1995, he was the recipient of the Minnesota High School Coaches Association "George Haun Award" for outstanding service and leadership. Furthermore, Genz was selected by USA Hockey and U.S. Olympic Committee to be assistant coach to Brad Buetow and the West hockey team at the 1983 National Sports Festival. The West team won the gold medal and many of its members were selected to the 1984 Olympic team including Roseville's Steve Griffith.

"It's always nice to come back to your alma mater," said Genz. "Hamline has always had such a long tradition of hockey excellence, and I am just proud to be a small part of it."

St. Olaf's Hockey History

Founded in 1874 as a co-ed, residential, four-year private liberal arts college, St. Olaf's hockey program first began in 1926, when the team started playing against local college and senior teams in the area. The school began MIAC competition shortly thereafter and soon developed several good rivalries with Shattuck, Augsburg, Macalester and St. Thomas. The team was one of the best in the state through the 1930s, and went on to win what would prove to be the school's only two MIAC titles in 1938 and 1939.

After the War years, the program went through its share of highs and lows, ultimately leaving the MIAC in 1950 to play in the Midwest Conference. The team, under the tutelage of coach Tom Porter, himself a 1951 St. Olaf star, twice tied for the Midwest Conference championship in 1961 and 1966 and then won it outright in both 1969 and 1970. One of the best era's of Ole Hockey came in the late 1950s and early '60s, when standouts such as Jerry Roce, Duane Swenson, Whitey Aus and Harrold Vinnes were all starring for the squad.

By 1971, after 12 years behind the Ole bench, Porter had posted an impressive 70-27-1 record. The Oles played at various rinks on campus until the late 1970s, something that hurt the team's productivity. During one stretch in 1974, coach Porter's Oles had to delay the start of their season due to a fire at the school's home rink at the Shattuck School in Faribault.

St. Olaf returned to the MIAC in 1975. That next year, 1976, Whitey Aus took over as the team's new skipper. It would be a position he would hold for 20 seasons in Northfield. Aus had been coaching for the past 15 seasons prior at Roseville High School. Over his two-decade tenure on The Hill, Aus would win MIAC and NAIA Coach of the Year honors, as well as become the school's all-time winningest coach.

One of the highlights of the program came in the early 1980s, when the Oles made a couple of runs at the NAIA National playoffs. In 1980 the team got beat by Bemidji State 5-2 in the opening round, and then lost to Michigan-Deerborn in the 1981 quarters. They rallied back to beat UW-River Falls after that, only to lose to St. Thomas in the consolation finals. They made it again in 1983 and 84, losing to UW-River Falls and Bemidji respectively. Some of the stars of the '80s included: Chuck Abrahamson, a goalie from Roosevelt, Steve Nelson, an All-American from White Bear Lake, Guy Considine, who remains as the Oles' all-time leading scorer with 161 total points, and Edina's Craig Ranheim, who tallied a record 70 goals in 1983.

MIAC Titles Won or Shared (1919-1999)		
School	No.	Last Title
University of St. Thomas	23	1998-99
Gustavus Adolphus College	13	1992-93
Macalester College	12	1962-63
*UM-Duluth	9	1960-61
Augsburg College	7	1981-82
St. John's University	4	1996-97
St. Mary's University	4	1987-88
Hamline University	3	1947-48
Concordia (Moorhead) College	2	1986-87
St. Olaf College	2	1938-39

No Longer a Member of the MIAC

Up and down throughout the 1980s and 90s, the Oles played solid, fundamental hockey under Aus. Some of the team's stars during the '90s include: All-American Brent Eilefson, who remains second all-time in scoring with 150 career points, John Klaers, who is third with 137, and Adam Rice, an All-American from Cottage Grove.

In 1997, 500 games later, Aus retired both from coaching, as well as from teaching at St. Olaf. He remains a school coaching legend to this day. One of his top assistants that last year was former Ole winger Tod Dungan, himself a former prep legend at the Marshall School in Duluth. (In addition, Aus' brother, Peter, has coached for more than 30 years at both the high school level, with Litchfield and Willmar, and has been the skipper at Bethel College since 1993.)

Throughout the program's checkered history, the Ole's have competed both as independents as well as in the NAIA. Today, however, the team competes entirely in the MIAC, which is an NCAA Division III affiliate. Late in 1999 the Ole's played in their 1,000th game, beating Gustavus 2-1. Today, Sean Goldsworthy, the son of former North Stars legend Bill Goldsworthy, is the coach of the Ole program. He guided the team to a 8-16-1 overall record in 1998-99, and continues to work on building the rich St. Olaf Hockey tradition.

All-Time MIAC Champions

Year	Champion	Year	Champion	Year	Champion
1919-20	Hamline/Mac/St.Thomas	1944-45	No Champion	1971-72	Gustavus
1920-21	No Champion	1945-46	No Champion	1972-73	Gustavus
1921-22	No Champion	1946-47	St. Thomas	1973-74	St. Thomas
1922-23	Hamline	1947-48	Hamline	1974-75	Gustavus
	Macalester	1948-49	St. Thomas	1975-76	Gustavus
	St. Thomas	1949-50	Macalester	1976-77	Augsburg
1923-24	No Champion		St. John's		Gustavus
1924-25	No Champion	1950-51	Macalester	1977-78	Augsburg
1925-26	No Champion		St. Thomas	1978-79	Augsburg
1926-27	No Champion	1951-52	St. Thomas	1979-80	Augsburg
1927-28	Augsburg	1952-53	St. Thomas	1980-81	Augsburg
1928-29	St. Mary's		UM-Duluth		Concordia
1929-30	Macalester	1953-54	UM-Duluth	1981-82	Augsburg
1930-31	Macalester	1954-55	UM-Duluth	1982-83	St. Thomas
1931-32	Hamline	1955-56	UM-Duluth	1983-84	Gustavus
	Macalester	1956-57	UM-Duluth	1984-85	St. Thomas
1932-33	Macalester	1957-58	UM-Duluth	1985-86	St. Thomas
1933-34	St. Thomas	1958-59	UM-Duluth	1986-87	Concordia
1934-35	St. John's	1959-60	UM-Duluth	1987-88	St. Mary's
1935-36	Macalester	1960-61	UM-Duluth	1988-89	St. Thomas
1936-37	Macalester	1961-62	Macalester	1989-90	St. Thomas
1937-38	St. Olaf	1962-63	Macalester	1990-91	St. Thomas
	St. Thomas	1963-64	St. Mary's	1991-92	St. Thomas
1938-39	Macalester	1964-65	St. Mary's	1992-93	St. Thomas/Gustavus
1939-40	St. Thomas	1966-67	Gustavus	1994-95	St. Thomas
1940-41	St. Thomas	1967-68	Gustavus	1995-96	St. John's
1941-42	St. Thomas	1968-69	Gustavus	1996-97	St. John's
1942-43	No Champion	1969-70	Gustavus	1997-98	St. Thomas/Augsburg
1943-44	No Champion	1970-71	Gustavus	1998-99	St. Thomas

Junior hockey has played a vital role in the development of hockey in America, and the genesis of how this division of 17-20-year-olds came to be makes for an interesting story. Although junior hockey had been highly successful in Canada since the turn of the century, it was a relatively new thing for Minnesotans back in the mid to late-1960s.

In the early 1960s it was becoming readily apparent that kids who weren't quite good enough to get college scholarships out of high school were dropping out of hockey altogether because they had no organized place to play competitively. With that, a group of Minnesota hockey boosters started a summer-league program for post-high schoolers and college freshman, to give some of these kids an opportunity to improve their skills and get noticed by some of the local colleges. In 1965, a group led by Ron Woodey, Larry Hendrickson, Jim Steichens, Harry Sundberg and others, took a team of Minnesota junior all-star players from the Junior Olympic Hockey Association summer-league to Colorado Springs to play in the National Junior Championships. The team, called "Duff's Bar" (the only sponsor they could get), went on to surprise a few people by winning the national title over a highly touted team from Detroit.

Suddenly enlightened, that next year Walter Bush, Jr., Win Stephens, Jr., Bob Somers, Ron Woodey, Harry Brown, Red Kairies, Harvey McNair, Harry Sundberg, Ken Austin and several other local hockey boosters, organized the first junior hockey league in Minnesota, called the Minnesota-Ontario Hockey League. The circuit, which initially played throughout the Twin Cities and Ontario consisted of just four initial teams: The Win Stephens Buick Juniors, who were first coached by Larry Hendrickson (as in the dad of NHL star Darby), the Minneapolis Bruins (who were later led by the Carlson brothers -- as in the "Hanson Brothers" of "Slapshot" infamy), and two teams from Thunder Bay -- the Vulcans and Flyers. (A team from Fort Frances also played briefly.)

The league, which evolved into the Canadian-American or Can/Am League, progressed over the next couple of years, with solid results. It was giving post-high schoolers more experience and also getting more scouts to check out the Minnesota hockey scene as well. (It would be safe to say that Rodney Dangerfield's famous line of "I went to a boxing match and a hockey game broke out..." was very applicable during the first couple of years of the league.) One of the early fan-favorites was one of the toughest hombres ever to hit the ice, Goldy Goldthorpe (like Ogie Ogelthorpe in the movie "Slapshot), who starred for the Thunder Bay Vulcans. He led the team to a couple of early titles, and took no prisoners along the way. (Goldy later played for the Fighting Saints as well.)

Now, after a couple of seasons, the Win Stephens team evolved into the Minnesota (Bloomington) Junior Stars. Herb Brooks coached the team for part of the 1971-72 season, and when he took over the Gopher coaching position from Glen Sonmor later that year, he handed the coaching reigns over to future Gopher coach, Doug Woog. Woog then led the Junior Stars to the national championship that year. The Junior Stars went on to win the Can/Am title in 1973, and then proceeded to gain a berth in the Centennial Cup, the tournament held to determine the best Canadian Tier II juvenile team. There, after advancing to the semifinals, the Stars wound up losing a tough seven-game series to the Pembroke Lumber Kings.

Going back to the Fall of 1972, Bush and Murray Williamson (the coach of the 1972 U.S. silver medal-winning Olympic team in Sapporo, Japan, who was with the North Stars at the time), decided to explore the idea of starting a new circuit that would rival Canada's most prestigious Tier II leagues, complete with 60-game schedules and eventual international competition. It was an ambitious goal, but they felt that the timing was right.

Now, there were a number of factors in their decision to start this new league. First of all, this was a very tumultuous time in not only American hockey, but also in politics, as the Vietnam War was winding down. With the termination of the draft, an influx of 18-year-old men soon became readily available to play hockey after high school. Among the other factors fueling their decision included the fact that by 1972, professional hockey was exploding across North America. While the upstart World Hockey Association (WHA) was rapidly expanding into new markets, the NHL, in an effort to protect their interests, was counteracting by aggressively expanding themselves. Both rival leagues began bidding wars for players, and anyone with a heartbeat and a slapshot was seemingly getting a tryout to play somewhere. The WHA rolled out 14 new pro teams, and the NHL had recently expanded from six to 16. So, in less than five years, from 1967-72, pro hockey went from six franchises to 30, creating the biggest demand for hockey talent in history. It was a boom era for fringe players, probably unparalleled in any other pro sport's history. Suddenly there were some 400 professional job openings available, and teams needed personnel fast. Not only did they need players at the top levels, but they also needed to fill in their suddenly depleted minor-league systems as well.

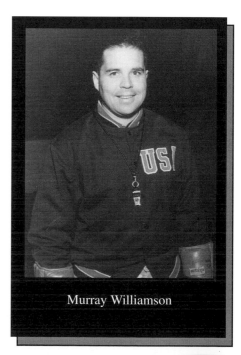

Murray Williamson

The Canadian dominated NHL, feeling the pressure big-time, began looking to the U.S. for hockey talent, something they never would have dreamed of doing before. The NHL Board of Governors, led by then commissioner Clarence Campbell, who had been contributing financially to the Canadian junior systems for years, figured it would be a good opportunity to start developing a junior hockey feeder system in the U.S. similar to the one they had created north of the border. So, after some lengthy negotiations, they agreed to help subsidize the new league financially.

Couple in the fact that American colleges, who were overflowing with Canadian players, were begging for experienced American talent, and that our state's high school hockey program was producing top-level players who wanted to take their game to the next level, but had few opportunities, and

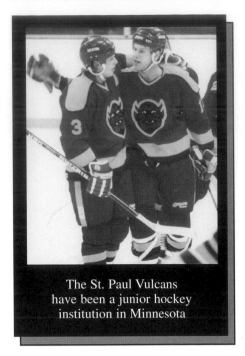

The St. Paul Vulcans have been a junior hockey institution in Minnesota

it all started to make some sense. With that, Walter and Murray smelled a giant opportunity. The timing was right, and they knew that they would be doing a tremendous service for not only American hockey, but for Minnesota hockey as well.

In February of 1973, the new Midwest Junior Hockey League (MJHL), via merging with several of the now-defunct Can/Am teams, opened for business with six franchises. They included Bloomington, St. Cloud, St. Paul, Fargo-Moorhead, Chicago, and Thunder Bay. (Here's where it gets confusing. The Thunder Bay Vulcans and Flyers both merged into one team, now called the Hurricanes. The Minnesota Junior Stars franchise was sold to a new group in St. Paul that included Somers, Woodey and Sundberg, where they renamed their new team as the St. Paul Vulcans. And finally, a new group, led by Walter Bush, then president of the North Stars, and his executive assistant Murray Williamson, took the "old" Minnesota Junior Stars name and created a new team called the "Bloomington Junior Stars," and set up shop at the Met Center.)

As the league started to come together, next came the issue of recruiting top-level players and coaches who could ultimately give the league the appearance of being Tier II in status by Canadian standards. As it turned out, that would be the easy part. While Ken Austin of Owatonna agreed to become the league's first president, St. Mary's star Andre Beaulieu went from Hill-Murray to the Bloomington Junior Stars, Bob Gernander left Coleraine High School to take over the Fargo Sugar Kings, former Blackhawks star Ken Wharram took over the Chicago Nordiques, and finally, Rich Blanche (and later Frank Zywiec) left his assistant coaching job at Denver University to head up the St. Cloud Saints franchise. With that kind of coaching talent, it wasn't long before some of the state's top players joined on. Numerous future NHL stars, including: Reed Larson, Gary Sargent, Paul Holmgren, Steve Short and Dave Geving all jumped on board.

The league got off to a good start that year, the competition was fierce, and the fans began to come see what it was all about. Pretty soon scouts from most WHA and NHL teams were frequenting the action, and in no time, college recruiters were bypassing the long trek to Canada to check out the new league.

It wasn't without its share of controversy though. Opposition to junior hockey immediately surfaced from existing high school, senior and small colleges teams. High school coaches suddenly found themselves fighting for their collective lives. They knew that they were stuck with the fact that they could only schedule 20-game seasons, while the MJHL could offer their top players three-times as much game experience - against much tougher competition. They were forecasting that eventually the state's top high school players would simply skip their junior and senior year's to play juniors. On the other hand, college coaches such as Herb Brooks at the U of M, were basking in their own private minor-league feeder system. No longer did they have to gamble on a scholarship with a young, unproven player, when they could now send him to the juniors for a year to get a little "seasoning," and then reevaluate his progress a year later. (Incidentally, Brooks would have some 15 former Vulcans alone on his three NCAA titles teams in the 1970s.)

Williamson, a veteran of U.S. international play, desperately wanted to get AHAUS involved at that point, to create a world junior team. After a little politicing, the league sent an all-star team of sorts (which became the U.S. National Junior Team), to Russia, to take part in an international junior tournament. The league figured that it would not only be great experience for its top players, but it would also serve as a good recruiting and publicity tool for themselves. Once there, after being stranded for five days without their equipment in Leningrad, the U.S. team hit the ice against the national junior teams from Sweden, Russia, Finland and Canada. And, although they lost all four games, they did rally back to beat the Czechs to finish fifth in the six-team tournament.

Later that season, a two-game series was arranged with one of Canada's premier junior teams, the Peterborough Pete's, from the prestigious Ontario Hockey Association. Virtually every scout in North America flew to Minneapolis to watch the super-hyped match, as the U.S. National Junior team beat the Pete's by the final score of 2-1. The win only solidified what Minnesotans had known all along, this league and these kids were for real.

Phil Housley

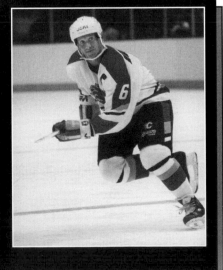

Drafted straight out of South St. Paul High School in 1981 by Buffalo, Phil Housley went to the pros after first playing in the USHL. There, after 18 NHL seasons, he became the highest scoring U.S. born player in league history, when, on March 11, 1999, when he tallied three assists for the Calgary Flames to bring his career total to 1,066 points. Housley has played for the Buffalo Sabres, Winnipeg Jets, St. Louis Blues, New Jersey Devils, Washington Capitals, and Calgary Flames, and ranks as the fourth highest scoring defenseman in league history and the fourth defenseman to ever score 300 goals.

The Thunder Bay Hurricanes tied the Junior Stars for the lead league that inaugural 1973-74 season, only to see the Vulcans defeat the Junior Stars 5-4 in the post-season championships to win the coveted Don Clark Cup. By all accounts that first season was a success. One barometer for just how good the league fared that year came during the 1974 amateur draft, when fully 21 players from the league were selected by either the NHL or WHA. In addition, some 26 MJHL players were offered D-I college scholarships that first year - 22 in the WCHA alone.

Another significant event happened in February of 1974, when the Vulcans became the first American Junior team to beat a Canadian Tier I team, the Westminster Bruins, who, as winners of the Memorial Cup, were Canada's top Tier I Junior A team. The game, which was played in Bismarck, ND, saw the Vulcans beat the Bruins 4-2, despite the fact that the Bruins had seven players get drafted and go into the NHL following that season, including N.Y. Ranger's future all-star Ron Greschner.

Then, a major road-block hit the league. After that first year, a competing junior league operator in Chicago blew the whistle to the NCAA on the "suddenly successful" amateur league, for accepting money from the NHL. Now, at the time, the NCAA had strict standards regarding subsidies and sponsorship from professional organizations. As a result, on August 28th, 1974, the NCAA ruled that the MJHL was professional in status. The news was potentially deadly for the league, and its players who suddenly got very nervous about the possibility of losing their college eligibility. After a short legal battle, however, the ruling was reversed and the league resumed as business as usual. But, unfortunately, some collateral damage had been done. The league's image had been tarnished, and the NHL, which was mired in financial problems of its own, decided that it could no longer help out financially.

Chicago dropped out after that season, while a new franchise, the Austin Mavericks, which was headed by Leon Abbott, was added. Following that next season, after suffering heavy financial losses, Fargo and St. Cloud both dropped out as well. But the league pressed on, and continued to get kids into the next level. The Vulcans repeated in 1975, as Doug Woog's team dominated. (Some of the top players in the mid to late 1970s included: Paul Holmgren, Butsy Erickson, Pat Phippen, Steve Ulseth, Jim Boo, John Sheridan, Craig Hanmer, Paul Klasinski, Mitch Horsch, Tommy Gorence, Mark Wenda, Russ Welch, Jim Cunningham, Bob Graiziger, David Hanson, Kevin Hartzell and Frank Serratore.)

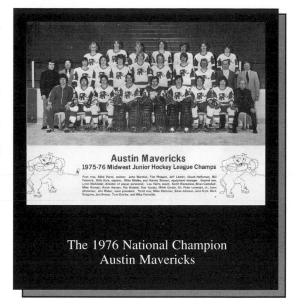

Austin Mavericks
1975-76 Midwest Junior Hockey League Champs

The 1976 National Champion
Austin Mavericks

After a last place finish in their inaugural season, Austin, led by Ray Kurpis, won it all in 1976, beating the Vulcans 5-3 to win the U.S. Junior A title. The Mavs' coaching reigns were handed from Leon Abbott (who became St. Lawrence University's head coach) to Lou Vairo, a native New Yorker who would later coach the 1984 Olympic team.

In 1977 the Vulcans won the MJHL title, and were awarded the Anderson Cup. That year, five Vulcans went on to play for Michigan State, while several others earned D-I scholarships. Coach Doug Woog left after that season to take over the South St. Paul High School team, and was replaced by former Vulcan Kevin Hartzell. "Those were the days," recalled the Wooger. "It was a great time for hockey in Minnesota and really a wild ride! I can remember all the ups and downs we went through to get that whole thing going, it was exciting to be a part of it all."

By now, the league was struggling financially. The teams, which made money not only from the NHL (which was drying up), but also by getting kick backs from pro teams that signed the MJHL players, were hurting. This, in itself was a driving factor in the type of players that the league was producing. Because the pro leagues at that time wanted big, tough kids who could not only play physical, but also fight, those types of players began to be the ones who got drafted. As a result, the toughest guys on the team were actually the most valuable, because they were generating income for the clubs. In a sense, the goons were dictating the style of play in those days, and that too remained controversial.

Desperate, the league had to do something drastic to stay alive. That's when the United States Hockey League (USHL) came calling. The USHL had been a men's senior league up until that point, with several teams having played in Minnesota during the 1960s and '70s, including the Minneapolis Rebels, Minnesota Nationals, St. Paul Steers, Duluth Port Stars and Rochester Mustangs. Once the backbone for U.S. National team development, they too were having financial troubles, and proposed a merger. They agreed, and a year later the MJHL became the "junior" USHL.

The 1977 USHL featured six teams -- The Bloomington Junior Stars (who finished first with a 51-20-29 record), Austin Mavericks, St. Paul Vulcans, Sioux-City Musketeers, Waterloo Blackhawks and Green-Bay Bobcats. In 1978 the Austin Mavericks won another Junior title, and that same year the Anoka Nordiques were added to the league. By 1979 the league had officially gone 100 percent juniors, as there had been some cross-over for the past two seasons between the junior and semi-senior teams. The league started out well and proved to be a very exciting brand of hockey in the state. In 1985 the Rochester Mustangs, a perennial senior league power since the 1950s, with one of the richest hockey traditions in Minnesota hockey history, merged with the Austin Mavericks to join the league. The team played its first season in Austin, winning the title that year, thanks in part due to the efforts of star defenseman Ken Martell.

In 1982, Vulcans star Phil Housley was drafted by the Buffalo Sabres as the No. 6 overall pick of the first round. That same year the St. Paul Vulcans were sold to Stanley Hubbard, owner of Hubbard Broadcasting (KSTP-TV). Hubbard's sons had played on the team, and he knew the importance of having a strong junior program in the state was. He even bought the team a new airplane, so that

Minnesota Junior College & Community College History

While there was once a flourishing Junior College or Community College circuit during the 1930s in Minnesota, which played in the Little Ten Conference, today there remains only a four-team league, called the Western Junior College Hockey League. Started in 1994, the league includes: Rainy River CC, Itasca CC, Hibbing CC and MSU-Bottineau (North Dakota).

Some of the other Junior College and Community College programs through the years in Minnesota have included:

1. Itasca Community College, Grand Rapids
2. Hibbing Junior College
3. Rainy River Community College, International Falls
4. Eveleth Junior College
5. Anoka Ramsey Community College
6. Fergus Falls Community College
7. Century Community College, White Bear Lake (NE Metro Tech & Lakewood Combined)
8. Northland Community College, Thief River Falls
9. Central Lakes Community College, Brainerd
10. Mesabi Community College, Virginia
11. Vermillion Community College, Ely
12. Rochester Community College
13. Duluth Junior College
14. U of M Crookston

they would have a competitive advantage. (To this day the Hubbard family has done more for junior hockey in Minnesota than probably anyone.)

Under Hubbard, the team now had the resources to travel abroad. In December of 1984 the Vulcans became the first team (other than a U.S. National team) to play in Czechoslovakia. There, on live Czech TV, the Vulcans won the Liberation Cup, the championship trophy awarded to the winner of a 16-team holiday tournament in Brno, Czechoslovakia. That next year the team became the first American team, amateur or pro, to play in Hungary, where in front of some 10,000 fans, they lost to the Hungarian National team. (Some of the Vulcan's top players of this era included NHL stars Shaun Sabol and Jim Johnson.)

The Mustangs then moved to Rochester in 1986, where, under former Bemidji State All-American goalie Frank Serratore, they soon became a power in the league. In their first six years in Rochester, the "new" Mustangs won three National Junior 'A' championships. In 1987 the Mustangs swept the USHL's Anderson (season champion) and Clark (playoff champion) Cups, and the AHAUS National Junior A Championships. Incredibly, 14 players moved into Division I college hockey from that team. Among them was Rochester native, Shjon Podein, who attended UMD before going on to star with the Philadelphia Flyers.

Serratore left after that season to take over as an assistant at UND. "The team has now come to reflect Rochester, a pretty glamorous place to play junior hockey," said Serratore when the franchise shifted to Rochester in 1986. "The franchise, in my opinion one of the five best Tier II programs in North America, has become a great thing for hockey and southern Minnesota."

Minnesota's Junior B's

Junior B hockey has also played a vital role in the development of the game in Minnesota. When the Minnesota Junior Hockey League became the USHL back in the late 1970s, the league went from a Junior A to Junior B, one step down. That era was tough for junior hockey everywhere. The costs of running a team became exorbitant, the 18-year-old drinking age diverted many young men from participating in sports, and the growing amount of youth players took much of the available ice time at local arenas. Despite these hurdles though, teams such as the St. Croix Stallions, North Suburban Junior Hawks and Tri-Metro Junior Whalers were able to remain intact. Coaches Dave Sanden of the Whalers and Dick Jenkins of the Junior Hawks were two of the key people who worked hard to keep the league operating for the countless young men who weren't yet seasoned enough to get a good look from a college or Junior A scout.

One of the ways that the MJHL gets its kids noticed is by scrimmaging many of the local Division III and Junior College teams in the area. This gives the college coaches ample time to scout upcoming talent to fill their future rosters with. There have been numerous high school graduates who have continued to develop into outstanding hockey players using this league as a medium for acquiring a college education.

By the late 80s, two more teams were added to the MJHL, the West Suburban Junior Kodiaks and the Northland Voyagers from Duluth. (The Northland's team is named so because they played their home games in Cloquet, Coleraine, Silver Bay, Eveleth, Two Harbors, Duluth and Superior. The team was coached by Butch Williams, the son of Rip Williams, who was very influential in promoting junior hockey throughout Minnesota. In addition, there was even a Rip Williams Challenge Cup, a junior tournament in Duluth, which was created in his honor.) In 1989 the Tri-Metro Whalers won the 1988-89 International Junior Championships, a first for a Minnesota Junior B squad. That next year the Northlands Voyagers won the National Junior B championship by beating the Amherst (NY) Knights, 6-3, in Royal Oak, Mich. The Whalers added another title in 1992 as well.

By the mid 1990s the South Suburban Steers, East Metro Lakers, North Metro Owls, Junior Kodiaks, Minnesota Ice Hawks and the Shattuck St. Mary's Sabres comprised the MJHL. During that era, the Kodiaks brought home the hardware on three different occasions: 1993, '95 and '97. That same year, 1997, the Lakers made it to the Junior B National Tournament in Toledo, OH., and in 1998, the Lakers won the league championship and then went on to finish second at the Junior B National Tournament in Simi Valley, CA. In 1999 the Iron Range Yellow Jackets (out of Coleraine), were added to the circuit. That same year the East Metro Lakers under team owner and GM Ralph Hayne, and head coach Mike LaValle, beat the St. Paul Steers 8-1 to win the MJHL title. The Lakers then went on to win the Minnesota Junior B Hockey League's double-elimination KSTP Cup Tournament, which was held at the newly constructed Blaine Super Rink.

In 1988, led by Hutchinson's Mark Bahr, who would go on to play for the Gophers, the Mustangs won their second National Junior A title, by beating Detroit Compuware under the tutelage of Kevin Constantine (a former all-state goalie from International Falls during the late 1970s, who would go on to become the head coach of the San Jose Sharks and Pittsburgh Penguins), on their home Rochester ice.

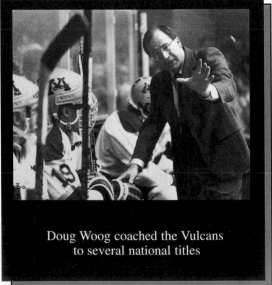

Doug Woog coached the Vulcans to several national titles

Serratore returned to the USHL in 1989, this time as the new head coach of the fledgling Omaha Lancers. The Lancers, who had gone 0-48 in 1987, did a complete 180 under Serratore, who led them to the USHL regular season and playoff championship in 1990. The worst-to-first Cinderella season earned Serratore the league's GM and Sportsman of the Year awards. (Serratore, who finished with a 247-103-6 record in the USHL, went on to become the coach at Denver University, followed by the IHL's Minnesota Moose, and finally at the Air Force Academy, where he remains today.)

In 1990, led by two-time USHL All-Star Jay Ness, the Mustangs won their third National Junior Championship in four years, by once again beating Detroit Compuware 4-2 in Madison, Wis. Not to be outdone, the St. Paul Vulcans then proceeded to win yet another National Junior Championship in 1991 as well. The USHL went through its share of ups and downs in the '90s, but overall the league has been very successful. Expansion teams were added as well, including the Des Moines Buccaneers, Dubuque Fighting Saints, Green Bay Gamblers, Lincoln Stars, North Iowa Huskies, Omaha Lancers, Rochester Mustangs, Thunder Bay Flyers, and the Fargo-Moorhead Ice Sharks in 1996. In addition, the Sioux Falls Stampede and Cedar Rapids Rough Riders have joined the league as well. (Sadly, in the summer of 1999, the "Twin Cities" Vulcans announced that they will be moving to Kearney, Neb., thus ending their storied history in St. Paul.)

Today the state of junior hockey in Minnesota is a mixed bag. From what started with very humble beginnings in the '60s, has grown into an essential and vital cog of that which is the machine of American hockey today. While some of the USHL franchises are extremely popular and lucrative in places such as Omaha, where they are the only show in town, Minnesota is faced with much more competitive hockey environment. The fans are more knowledgeable about the game here, and have a wide variety of hockey choices with which they can spend their time and money following. The successful clubs have found new and innovative ways to provide their fans with a fresh and exciting means of sports entertainment. Nonetheless, the junior level is growing and constantly giving more 17-20-year-old Minnesota kids new opportunities to play college and pro hockey every year.

The USHL, which is now governed by USA Hockey, has positioned itself to be the No. 1 Junior A hockey league in the country. It is one of the prime feeder programs for the country's top Division I colleges, not to mention the international, Olympic, professional and small college ranks. The junior programs have also helped to level the playing field, by proving that more and better playing opportunities for American kids was better than legislating and restricting against the Canadian game.

For the coaches who work with these kids on a daily basis, the job is tough. With annual team turnovers sometimes approaching 60-70 percent, for team's to be competitive year after year is an arduous task. But there are some coaching advantages. "It's usually when a kid is humbled by the fact that he's not going to the U of M, or anywhere on scholarship, that they start looking at other programs," said former Mustang's skipper Kevin Constantine, on the art of coaching in the juniors. "That's why coaching juniors is so easy. The players have already been humbled, they didn't get a scholarship. They know they have shortcomings and are eager to work at them."

The numbers are staggering though, as to just how many opportunities the junior levels have provided for our Minnesota kids. Thousands of players who have come through their ranks, kids who possibly would've given up on the game had their not been somewhere in between the high school and college levels to go, have gone on to get an education. The Rochester Mustangs alone, have sent more than 120 players on to Division I college hockey schools, and even more than that on to play in Division II and III programs throughout the nation. Highlighting speed, skill, discipline and basic fundamentals, the USHL and MJHL are two of the top developmental leagues in the nation. Kids from all over the world transition from high school to college in these leagues, and are both huge assets to Minnesota hockey's past, and to its future.

In-Line Hockey in Minnesota

Roller skating has had a long and storied history in America with roots that can be traced back for centuries. The four-wheeled version (quads - two in front and two in back) had been the mainstay since the creation of in-line skates in the late 1970s. The design for four straight wheels (in a line) actually goes back much further though. In fact, the first record of inline skates actually dates back to the early 1700s, when a Dutchman attempted to simulate ice skating on a road by fastening wooden spools to strips of wood which he attached to the bottom of his boots.

By the mid-1800s, an American developed the first "conventional" roller skates, with wheels arranged side by side. Soon the sport of ice polo had evolved into roller polo, a short-lived fad that hung around until the early 1900s. So popular was roller polo, that in 1885, Minneapolis alone possessed 14 indoor roller rinks. Leagues soon sprung up throughout the East Coast as well as in the Midwest, with teams traveling by train to compete. As ice polo transformed in to ice hockey, so too did roller polo emerge into roller hockey - just after the turn of the century. Ice hockey's modern ancestor was nothing like roller hockey as we know it today, but nonetheless, it gave hockey players something to do in the when there was no ice. Roller skating however, soon became a slice of American pop culture that had it all -- exercise, entertainment and even romance. That's right, when the roller polo craze died off in the early 1900s, roller rinks became the ultimate cheap date.

In 1937 the Roller Skating Rink Operators Association created the United States Amateur Confederation of Roller Skating in Detroit. By the late 1960s the organization began facilitating some of the country's first roller hockey tournaments. The game was still clumsy, due to the fact that the skates wouldn't permit the skater to maneuver very well. Unlike ice skates, roller skates were heavy, and awkward to try and play hockey in - not to mention the adventure of trying to stop in them without eating some pavement.

Still, kids in places such as Minnesota, New England and Canada, played many a game on the old tennis court with "quad" roller skates. (One of the hot-spots for organized "quad" roller hockey in the late '70s was in New York City, where the Fort Hamilton (Broooklyn) Roller Hockey League was producing such future NHL stars as Joey and Brian Mullen.) It was painful, but hey, it was hockey in the summertime. Then, somebody got smart and invented a training tool for hockey players and Nordic skiers alike in what we now know as in-line skates. I can still remember seeing that first pair in the late 1970s. Some guy had taken an old pair of skates, removed the blades, and riveted on a steel chassis with three bright orange wheels. My buddies and I all rushed out and got a pair of our own. They weighed about a hundred pounds, but they finally allowed a hockey player to actually simulate a true skating motion.

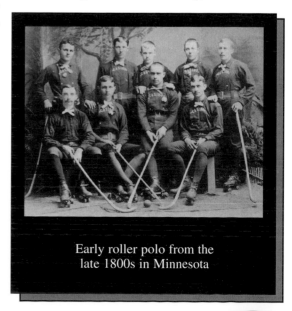

Early roller polo from the late 1800s in Minnesota

The genius behind those first contraptions was Scott Olson, who can be considered as the pioneer of in-line skates. The genesis of in-line skates began in 1979, when Olson, a former St. Louis Park High School hockey star in the late 1970s, saw a pair of those first in-line skates while rummaging through a sporting goods store. Immediately seeing the

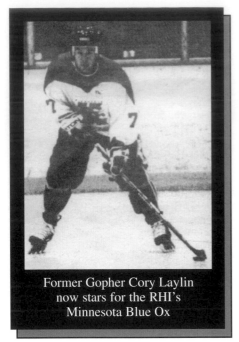

Former Gopher Cory Laylin
now stars for the RHI's
Minnesota Blue Ox

potential as a valuable tool for hockey players who couldn't get ice time during the summer, he contacted the manufacturer of those skates (which were really just a set of wheels on a chassis - the buyer had to then rivet them onto a pair of old hockey boots), a California-based start-up company called Super Sport Skate Co., which marketed the product under the name of Ultimate Street Skates. Olson then became the company's Midwest franchisee of sorts, distributing the devises under his own company name called, Super Street Skates. He then began selling the products on a grass-roots level out of his house and car.

Two years later, after deciding to manufacture his own skates designed specifically for hockey players, Olson launched his own in-line skate business out of his parents basement called "Ole's Innovative Sport Systems." Inspired by a 1966 Chicago Roller Skate Company in-line skate design patent intended to simulate ice skates, Olson set out to create a product that was maneuverable, light-weight and affordable for kids and adults everywhere. He started out by going around to sport shops such as Penn Cycle, in Bloomington, and buying pairs of molded boot skates (like the old Lang's). He would then remove the steel blades, sell them as scrap iron, and use the boots to attach his blades to. He decided to call his new, improved in-line creation, Rollerblades.

Rollerblades became an instant hit with hockey players around the state, and soon Olson hired his brother, Brennan, to begin mass-producing "blades" in their new Edina office. Now, at the time, they were buying roller skate wheels from a small company called Kryptonic (today an in-line wheel manufacturing giant), and taking them to the machine shop, where they were then shaved in half, to make an in-line sized wheel. Capitalizing on the fact that most every hockey player had an old pair of skates laying around in the basement (which could be easily converted into Rollerblades), the $35 cost was nothing when compared to buying a new pair of skates, which were hundreds of dollars. Soon kids everywhere where bringing in their old skate boots to have the new blades attached, and for $15, they could keep rotating back and forth between in-line and ice hockey blades every other season.

Soon Olson wanted to construct the complete skate, boot and blade, together as one. So, he packed up and went to Italy, home of the world's premier plastic ski boot manufacturers, to design custom molded boots for his Rollerblades. By the early 1980s, the bike path's at Lake Calhoun were bustling with in-line skaters, and parking lots around the state were being transformed into pick-up hockey rinks during the summer. (Amazingly, 3M couldn't figure out why it was suddenly selling a ton of electrical tape in the area, until they realized that the kids were using the rolls of tape as pucks.)

Before long the Olson's were assembling and selling Rollerblades across the country. As part of Olson's vision to market the products, he ventured to New York City, to play some pick-up games against those kids from Brooklyn who were using the old quad skates. There, the kids compared in-line skates vs. the old-fashioned quad skates, and before long kids everywhere could be seen playing roller hockey and blading around the East Coast on Olson's Rollerblades. Business grew in the early '80s, but the market was underdeveloped and limited geographically. With some 25 employees and limited resources, the company needed capital to expand and go big-time. It was at that time that Olson made the decision to sell his company to outdoor advertising magnate Bob Naegele Jr. (Naegele later led the ownership group to buy the Minnesota Wild NHL franchise.)

"Looking back, it was a dream come true to be able to start the craze that got it all going," said Olson. "Being a hockey nut, I was just happy to have brought a new hockey training tool to the people of Minnesota. Besides being able to cruise around as a means of transportation, to be able to play hockey during the off-season was awesome. It all happened so quickly from there, and I had no idea that it would lead to where it has gone today. It's been great to see so many kids having fun and being able to play and learn the game, and I am really honored to have played a part in that. In retrospect, I think Rollerblade really helped to advance the sport of hockey in America." (After selling his company, Olson then started a new in-line skate company which manufactured interchangeable in-line-hockey skates called "Switchits." The skates, which could be converted from in-line skates to ice hockey skates with the flip of a switch, proved to be a huge hit. After selling the company in 1992, Olson later invented a new work-out phenomenon called the "RowBike" -- which is an amalgam between a rowing machine and a bicycle on wheels. Today the Waconia-based company manufac-

Riedell In-line Skates

Riedell Skate Company was founded in 1945 by Paul F. Riedell, and has been a mainstay in Red Wing ever since. During Riedell's life he received many awards for his outstanding achievements within the skating industry. His innovative designs, his commitment to his company and the skating industry resulted in his receiving numerous awards, such as the "Great Skate Award" from the Ice Skating Institute of America, his induction into The Roller Skating Hall of Fame, the "American Designers Award" from the leather industry and his induction in 1979 to The Ice Skating Institute of America Hall of Fame. From the beginning, Riedell has had an unparalleled commitment to comfort and fit - both of which are essential for skating enjoyment and top performance. Today, the third generation of Riedell's, Paul's grandsons Scott, Paul, Bob, and Dan Riegelman - along with 160 skilled employees, handcraft the best fitting figure, hockey, speed, roller and inline skates in the world, and are currently the largest manufacturer of white figure skates in the U.S.

Riedell, of Red Wing,
has been in the hockey business
for more than a half century

tures and ships RowBikes all around the world.)

In 1985 Bob Naegele Jr. purchased Ole's Innovative Sport Systems, renamed it as Rollerblade, Inc., and supplied the leadership and resources necessary to take the company to the next level. Rollerblade soon not only became a noun, but also a verb. "Blading" quickly became all the rage throughout the country, making Rollerblade the undisputed leader of in-line skates and protective equipment. From the company's Minnetonka headquarters, he implemented a strategic marketing effort to position in-line skating as a new sport. His tactics, such as giving skates to rental shops along trendy Venice Beach in California, became a huge success.

The company's first big hit was the Lightning, the skate that really got it all started. Soon Rollerblade was innovating such things as polyurethane boots and wheels, metal frames, dual bearings and heel brakes. (Today the company holds approximately 200 issued and pending patents for in-line skating products.) For the next decade Naegele served as the chairman of Rollerblade Inc., repositioning the brand and fueling the explosive growth of in-line skating.

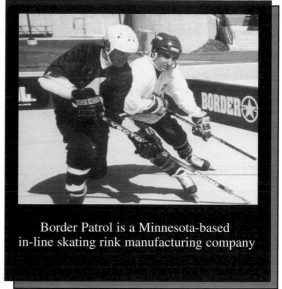

Border Patrol is a Minnesota-based in-line skating rink manufacturing company

In the late '80s, inline skating was dubbed as the sport of the '90s by the New York Times and Forbes magazine. One of the biggest boosts to the sport came in 1988, when Wayne Gretzky was traded from Edmonton to the Los Angeles Kings. Southern California instantly went hockey crazy, and Rollerblade was there to lead the charge. From there, in-line skating spread like wildfire to warm-weather climates throughout the world. Soon Rollerblade owned an estimated 75 percent of the marketshare, as the business continued to grow like no other fad in history. In addition to roller-hockey, in-line racing, stunt competitions, marathons and good old fashioned exercise, the sport had evolved into a simple and efficient means of transportation. People everywhere could now be seen "blading" to work in suits and ties.

Rollerblade also really got involved at a grass-roots level in promoting the sports of in-line skating, roller hockey and extreme skating (a la the X Games). They even sponsored one of the first in-line tournaments with teams from across the US, Canada and Europe, called the World Roller Hockey Championships, which were held at St. Paul's Aldrich Arena in the late '80s.

Minnesota soon became the Mecca for in-line skates. In addition to Rollerblade, First Team Sports (Ultra Wheels) and Riedell - both Minnesota based company's, got into the action. In the mid 1990s, according to the National Sporting Goods Association, in-line skating was the fastest growing sport in the U.S. and the world, rising at nearly a 50 percent annual growth rate. It was now a billion dollar industry as nearly 500 million pairs of in-line skates had been sold throughout the world by 1995. In-line hockey was booming and people couldn't get enough of it.

By 1993 two professional leagues had emerged: Roller Hockey International (RHI) and the World Roller Hockey league (WRHL). While the WRHL was a TV-only league, the RHI hit the pavement with a dozen teams located mostly in warm-weather markets around the country. After a year, the two leagues merged under the name RHI. (This was nothing new to RHI owner Dennis Murphy, who also founded the WHA and ABA.) The new and improved league featured 24 teams, among them was the Minnesota Arctic Blast. The Blast entered the league in 1994, and played at the Target Center. Although they won the conference title that first year, the franchise folded after that first season. (The Arctic Blast came back in 1996, won their conference title, and promptly folded yet again after that season.) So did most of the others as well. By 1997 there were just 12 teams remaining, with no television deal to boot. Another pro team entered the mix in 1995, the Minnesota Blue Ox, who played their games at Aldrich Arena in St. Paul. They, too, folded after a season, but were reincarnated in 1998.

In 1999 the Ox were led by several Minnesotans, including former Gopher hockey star Cory Laylin, Roseau's Billy Lund, Richfield's Dave Shute, Bloomington's Joe Bianchi, Edina's Charlie Wasley, Cottage Grove's Jay Moser, Wayzata's Brady Alstead, Inver Grove Height's Eric Rud, Birchdale's Chris Imes, and Eagan's John Hanson, among others. The team, which plays their games in the new Mariucci Arena, is coached by Minnetonka native Steve Martinson. In addition, the RHI team is co-owned by former NBA Minneapolis Laker's legend George Mikan.

The game continued to grow, with new leagues of all ages, genders and abilities popping up around the world. The game needed some direction, and in 1994 it got it when Bob Naegele III, son of Rollerblade owner Bob Naegele Jr. and himself a college goalie at Brown University, formed the National Inline Hockey Association (NIHA). In addition to promoting and providing organization for the sport, NIHA also sponsored several major tournaments around the country, including the NIHA National Championship in Las Vegas. At about the same time, USA Hockey had created a program called USA Hockey Inline, which also aimed to provide structure, stability and administration to the game at the grass-roots level. (With 36 teams entered, USA Hockey held its first national championships in 1996, in the Twin Cities.) In 1997 USA Hockey acquired NIHA to become the solo governing body of in-line hockey in America. (The unification saw USA Hockey register more than 100,000 players in nearly 1,000 leagues in 1999, a number that is still growing exponentially.)

Minnesota hockey's first-family, the Naegele's: Robert Jr. and Robert III

In addition to founding NIHA, Naegele also started another hockey business called In-line Sport Systems, which designed an innovative new rink product -- Border Patrol. Border Patrol defined a new category, portable hockey rinks. Today the St. Louis Park-based company designs, manufactures and ships rinks all over the world so that people can play roller hockey comfortably and safely outdoors. In 1995 the Naegele family sold Rollerblade to Benneton, the famous Italian clothing manufacturer. That next year they purchased a small start-up roller hockey company based in

Ultra Wheels In-line Skates

Inspired by the Rollerblade phenomenon, First Team Sports, makers of Ultra Wheels in-line skates was founded in 1986 by three men: John Egart, Dave Soderquist and Ron Berg, who started the company out of a garage in Anoka. In October of 1987, the company went public (ironically on Wall Street's Black Monday), to raise additional funding to launch their products nationally. Ultra Wheels could be seen everywhere, as the in-line skate craze began to boom. Their strategy of making quality skates at affordable price points proved to be the recipe for success in the new in-line skate market. In 1990 the company signed an endorsement contract with superstar Wayne Gretzky, who had recently moved to Los Angeles. Soon the company was shipping in-line skates around the world from its Alexandria plastics molding plant. By 1995 First Team Sports was recognized by Fortune Magazine as one of the top 100 "Fastest Growing Companies in America." Two years later the company partnered with Wayne Gretzky to acquire the Canadian-based Hespeler Hockey Company, which manufactures an elite line of skates and protective equipment. In 1999 Ultra Wheels Biofit Skates were launched and received rave reviews. The new athletic shoe-like skates are the next generation of in-line skates, and have positioned the company as an industry leader for years to come.

Orange County, Calif., called Mission. Today Mission produces some of the best hockey and in-line skates, as well as protective equipment, in the world.

At the moment, the International Ice Hockey Federation estimates that nearly 40 countries compete at roller hockey. (Many are non-traditional hockey countries such as China, Spain, Italy and Brazil, where roller hockey is second in popularity only to soccer.) The much quicker, four-on-four style of play has opened the door to a whole new generation of hockey fans everywhere. The game is evolving like never before. There is even a Pro Beach Hockey League, which is played on the beaches of Southern California. Complete with ramped tracks behind the nets to allow the skaters to literally fly around the net, music is played during the games and scantily clothed bikinis can be seen prominently in the crowd. (That's got to be quite a bit better than watching an outdoor pee wee game in Warroad in January!)

Overall, in-line hockey is good for the sport of ice hockey. With more than an estimated 50 million in-line skaters in the USA today, kids everywhere are getting the opportunity to play and learn the game. (According to the NSGA, more than 60 percent of all 11-year-olds in the country have a pair of in-line skates. And, in-line skating is now the fastest growing sport in the country, surpassing baseball, football and soccer in total number of participants.) Let's face it, hockey is an expensive, regional, elitist sport. It may have started out in the North and East because of the cold weather, but today the sport is regionalized because of its great expense for ice-time and equipment. Basketball and soccer can be played anywhere for virtually no money, while to play hockey planets must align. Roller hockey is bridging that gap though. Kids in inner cities and in warm-weather climates can strap on a pair of blades and play some pick-up hockey in the cul-de-sac for very little money. This is revolutionary, and will definitely change the game of hockey as we know it. As more and more of these kids who learn the game on the street move inside to the frozen pond, the game will evolve and become more culturally diverse, something long overdue, and great for the game.

Women's Hockey in Minnesota

The history of women's hockey goes back for more than a century in North America, with the first recorded women's hockey games taking place in 1891, in Barrie, Ontario, and also in Ottawa. Soon Lord Stanley of Preston (Canada's sixth Governor General and namesake of the NHL's Stanley Cup), was regularly hosting mixed skating parties which often featured pick-up games on Ottawa's Rideau Hall rink. Stanley's daughter, Isobel, took to the game and began playing it with her friends. She would later play for a Government House team that competed against the Rideau ladies' hockey team, among others. One of the first organized teams was called the "Love-Me-Littles" from Queens University in Kingston, Ontario. Before long, organized women's circuits throughout Canada called "Bakers Leagues," had popped up.

The ladies' game soon spread to the State's after the turn of the century to both the East Coast and also into Minnesota and Upper Michigan's Copper Country. In 1916, according to U of M yearbooks, some 30 women tried out for the first-ever Gopher Women's team. This article appeared in the "Gopher" that same year describing the team:

The 1925 Lady Gophers hockey team

" 'But girls can't play hockey,' protested everyone when they heard that the girls at Minnesota intended to indulge in this strenuous sport. Just to prove that they could, and could do it well, the girls organized four strong class teams, with subs for each one. They didn't need to learn how to skate, for they were already experts, so they devoted arduous hours of practice under skilled coaches to developing teamwork. This resulted in a tournament of fast games which called forth an unusual amount of interest, and convinced people that girls really could play hockey. The first game was between the Freshmen and the Juniors, and the newly entered girls succeeded in winning from the upper classmen 5-0. The Sophomores lived up to their reputation as a fast team by defeating the Seniors 2-0. On February 27, the Sophomores and Freshmen fought for the class championship. Both teams displayed remarkable teamwork and the Sophomores only succeeded in carrying off the title by the narrow margin of 1-0."

The Gopher women's program sported at least two squads per year, with 15 ladies on each roster. Although most of their competition came against other U of M teams, there was an annual cup awarded for the school's championship team. In addition, each woman that tried out had to have at least a C average in their studies to be considered. The teams often practiced their stick handling skills in the gymnasium, until after the Christmas break when they would venture outdoors to practice on the skating rink at Northrop Field. While Gopher men's hockey coach Emil Iverson helped to coach them on occasion, the majority of the women's teams' coaches were fraternity boys who were also playing intramurally. The women played through the 1920s, often times drawing big crowds to come see their games.

The women wore long dresses and overcoats, always remaining "lady-like" on the ice. But, while they wanted to play like the boys, they surely didn't want to take a beating like the boys. In fact, in 1927, to protect her face from flying pucks, Queen's (Canada) goaltender Elizabeth Graham became the first recorded hockey player ever to wear a face mask - more than three decades before Montreal Canadiens' keeper Jacques Plante, then considered the originator of sporting a cage over the old melon.

This came at an empowering time for women, who were now in the midst of the women's suffrage movement which challenged society for equality in education, work and play. In addition to fighting for equal rights (Incredibly, women were finally allowed the right to vote in only 1926!), women were having to prove to the world that they could do anything men could do. Male doctors were even claiming that the women's unique anatomy, coupled with their moral obligation to bear children, was not suitable for vigorous physical activity, especially with something as rough as hockey. But large numbers of women pressed on and continued to compete for the love of the game.

Women's hockey at the Goodrich Rink in St. Paul during the 1920s

In 1929 the University of Minnesota women finally got a home of their own, when a hockey rink was constructed behind the old library on campus. These were the heydays for women's hockey, as the Gophers now were playing teams from Duluth and the Iron Range, as well as from nearby Carleton College. In addition, the Gopher women played against other women's club teams, co-ed fraternity and sorority teams, and even some men's teams. While other women's sports were emerging on campus, it was thought that many of the school's most talented female athletes were hockey players.

But, when the Great Depression hit in the early 1930s, the women's program at the U of M came to a halt. The game continued to flourish in Canada though, as the Rivulettes, a women's squad from Preston, Ontario, posted an unbelievable win-loss record of 348-2 throughout the 1930s, often-times beating local men's teams.

During the war years women's hockey continued to blossom. With most of the men overseas, women began working, supporting their families, and enjoying a new independence they had not known before. While women's baseball flourished during this time (a pro league called the AAGPBL was started in the midwest, which included the Minneapolis Millerette's, and was featured in the movie "A League of Their Own"), other women's team sports, including hockey, were often-times the only game in town. But, after the war ended, men's hockey began to boom, which ultimately meant less ice-time for the ladies, and as a result, the growth of the women's game slowed down.

In 1956, a nine-year-old girl by the name of Abby Hoffman forever changed the game of hockey for women. The young defenseman from Brantford, Ontario, made headlines across Canada that year when she brought the issue of gender equity to the front-burner in a rather unique way. You see, Abby had been playing on the boy's team that entire season, while disguised as a boy. Because the kids dressed at home, and she wore her hair short, nobody seemed to notice. At the end of the season Abby was selected to play in the Timmy Tyke minor hockey tournament, which also included a post-season swimming party at the local pool. Busted! Still determined to play in the league (because there were no girl's youth teams back then), Abby and her family took their case all the way to the Ontario Supreme Court. There, the court ultimately ruled against her, and as a result she was banished from the league. Life went on for Abby though, as she later went on to become a Canadian Olympic track and field star. In 1982, in remembrance of her struggle to "just play hockey," the Ontario Women's Hockey Association created a national women's tournament in her honor called the Abby Hoffman Cup.

By the late 1960s women's-only programs began forming throughout the U.S. and Canada, and by the early '70s, teams had popped up in Sweden, Finland, Japan, China, Korea, Norway, Germany and Switzerland. By now, several U.S. college varsity and club teams had formed throughout the East Coast, and also in the Midwest. The U of M re-established a club team during the early '70s as well. The girl's game was developing quickly, but still had a long way to go at this point. Soon special protective chest and pelvic gear was designed especially for women, as their game began to evolve into its own style.

In the mid 1970s, in addition to community-based grass-roots programs, girls ice hockey was starting to be included in the athletic programs of several Minnesota school districts. Inspired by Billie Jean King, who defeated professional male tennis champion Bobbie Riggs in a "Battle of the Sexes" tennis match broadcast around the country, little girls everywhere saw that they were capable of achieving anything. In 1974, the first state pee wee and bantam tournaments were held with White Bear Lake winning the pee wee title and Mounds View taking the bantam crown. (The pee wee tournament lasted from 1974 to 1976, until being resuscitated in 1989, while the bantams lasted from 1974 to 78. Midgets, which was for 16-19 year-olds was later added as well.) While most of the programs folded within only a few years, a few stayed together and continued to play into the early 1980s. Many of those same girls who got their start at the youth level went on to star on women's midget, senior and club teams around the state.

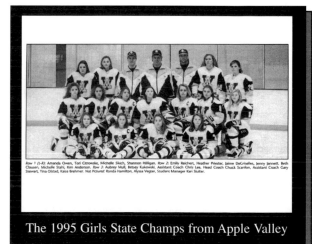

Row 1 (L-R): Amanda Owen, Tori Citrowske, Michelle Skich, Shannon Hilligan, Row 2: Emily Reichert, Heather Priester, Jaime DeGroelles, Jenny Jannett, Beth Clausen, Michelle Stahl, Kim Anderson, Row 3: Aubrey Mull, Betsey Kukowski, Assistant Coach Chris Lee, Head Coach Chuck Scanlon, Assistant Coach Gary Stewart, Tina Obtad, Kaisa Brehmer. Not Pictured: Rondia Hamilton, Alyssa Vegter, Student Manager Kari Sutter.

The 1995 Girls State Champs from Apple Valley

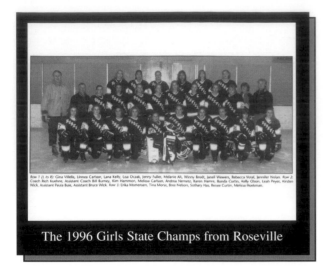

The 1996 Girls State Champs from Roseville

In 1980, USA Hockey, the governing association of amateur ice hockey in the United States, organized the first-ever girls pee wee and midget National Championships at which Wayzata took home the National midget title. Women's senior A and B divisions were added to the championship the following year, while several colleges and universities on the East Coast were now offering women's hockey as part of their sports curriculum's.

In the late 1970s a woman by the name of Lynn Olson, the venerable "Godmother" of women's hockey in Minnesota, started the Minnesota Women's Hockey League. With no age limit per se, high school aged girls as well as middle aged women in their 40s all came together in the new league to have a little fun and play some competitive hockey. Several teams, including the Blue Jays, Rink Rats, Shooting Stars and Gold Diggers, emerged as the team's to beat in the league. Into the early 80s, as the sport continued to grow, a new elite midget team from Wayzata, called the Checkers, burst onto the Minnesota hockey scene. (One of the people that helped a lot in the development of the girls game was Dr. Bob May, who, in addition to helping start the Checkers, also coached at North Dakota.) In 1980 the Checkers came home with the national Open B Division women's title. Then, led by Laura Haldorson (today the Gopher women's hockey coach), and Jill Pohtilla (the Augsburg women's hockey coach), the Checkers went on to win a couple of USA Hockey National Midget Championships in the early-1980's in both the 15-and-under, and later in the 19-and-under categories. In 1987 a new powerhouse team called the Thoroughbreds took the women's game to a new level. The elite team from Minneapolis dominated league play and often-times played against the best amateur club teams from around the nation.

By 1982 there were 116 teams registered in the women's division of USA Hockey, covering the spectrum from squirts through seniors. In 1984 Providence College won the inaugural Eastern College Athletic Conference Women's Championship, which would later come to serve as the equivalent of the women's college hockey national title. In 1986 Lynn Olson formed the Minnesota Women's' Hockey Association, which then became a part of the Minnesota Amateur Hockey Association (MAHA) and USA Hockey. This really opened the door for women everywhere to get involved in hockey. International women's hockey was growing too, as the U.S. defeated Sweden, 5-0, to win the bronze medal in the first-ever Women's World Invitational Tournament held in North York and Mississauga, Ontario, in 1987.

In 1988, Minnesota hosted the USA Hockey Girls National Tournament (they would host it again in 1992). That next year the girl's and women's section of USA Hockey was established for the purpose of overseeing the development of girls' hockey throughout the country. In addition to legislating rules and regulations, the division would also help run national tournaments and developmental training camps as well. The director of the new program was Lynn Olson, a position she would hold for six years. One of the first big hurdles Olson faced was the issue of recognition: "When I first started, the girls' program was not really recognized," said Olson. "That's the way I felt and so did a lot of the rest of the country and we were very happy to see that USA Hockey was appointing a director to help establish a better program. We grew from 150 teams to over 700 teams; just the visibility that was created and the credibility of being a part of USA Hockey helped establish that."

There would be other issues as well, including the fact that at that time, there were a lot of men who simply were not comfortable with the idea of girls playing hockey: "I believe USA Hockey is firmly behind the program but not everybody at the amateur level is necessarily interested in promoting it because it takes time away from their sons," added Olson. "It has been a problem over the years, but it's getting better."

Although the sport went through somewhat of a lull in popularity during the late '80s, it really picked up speed in the early '90s. In 1990 Minnesota had 29 amateur youth teams in the state. That same year, Minnesota led the nation in the total number of registered women's hockey players, with just less than 6,000. By this time the age classification for girl's hockey was broken down into 10-and-under, 12-and-under, 15-and-under and 19-and-under, or midget.

In 1990 the first-ever IIHF Women's World Championships were held in Ottawa. There, after blowing a 2-0 lead, the U.S. lost to Team Canada by the final score of 5-2 in the championship game. While bodychecking was allowed in the contest, it was later ruled illegal in the sport.

Something else interesting happened in the development of the game in 1990, when, as part of a gender equity requirement set forth by state and federal laws, schools were required to give equal athletics opportunities to both boys and girls. That next year, according to a Minnesota Department of Education survey, only 35 percent of Minnesota's high schools were in compliance with these new gender equity regulations. In an attempt to become compliant, many state schools introduced the game of ringette (a game similar to hockey that uses a straight, bladeless stick to slide a rubber ring across the floor and into a goal). While the game was pretty well received, most girls wanted to play the game of ice hockey.

By 1992 there were 39 girls and women's teams registered with MAHA and USA Hockey in Minnesota, and a record 25 teams took part in the five divisions of the MAHA State Hockey Tournament that year as well. After that season, the Minnesota State High School League took a survey called "Girls Really Expect A Team!" or (GREAT!) to gain a more accurate assessment of which sports high school girls were most interested in playing. Nearly 8,000 girls signed a petition saying that they would love to play high school hockey if it were only offered.

On November 19, 1994, South St. Paul and Holy Angels played the first high school girl's hockey game in state history. Later that year, in response to the overwhelming outcry for more organization in the sport, eight teams representing 11 state schools

The 1997 Girls State Champs from Hibbing

hit the ice for the inaugural girls state tournament, which, incidentally was not yet sanctioned by the MSHSL. Blaine/Coon Rapids beat Anoka/Champlin Park 3-0 for the "unofficial" 1994 state title. That same year, there were 78 amateur youth teams registered in the state, up from 29 only four years earlier.

Something else dramatic happened that year for women's hockey as well, when Farmington's Amber Hegland played third-line center for the Tigers' boys state tournament team, thus becoming the first girl ever to play in the boys' state tournament. Amber, who had skated since she was two, and played on boys' teams since she was five, also played cornerback on the Tigers' varsity football team, which competed in the 1991 state tournament.

In 1995, after seeing how the experiment would fare, the Minnesota State High School League's Representative Assembly took a giant leap of faith by voting to become the first such organization in the country to sanction girls' ice hockey as a varsity sport. The news was viewed as a major advancement for women's sports everywhere. "Now the younger girls will have role model's and know that they can get better," said Lynn Olson. "It will give them more encouragement to start playing."

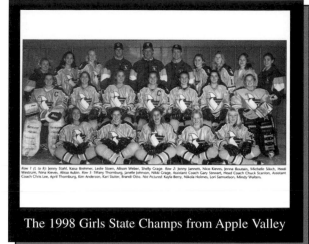
The 1998 Girls State Champs from Apple Valley

Twenty-four varsity teams took to the ice that season, while an additional 12 schools featured junior varsity teams, giving more than 1,000 girls in Minnesota the chance to play hockey at various high school levels. Then, on February 24, 1995, with the eyes of the nation upon them, the MSHSL sponsored the first-ever girls' state high school hockey tournament.

Held at the 3,500-seat Aldrich Arena in Maplewood, the inaugural tournament field included teams from Stillwater Area, Apple Valley, South St. Paul and Henry Sibley. The 22-0-1 undefeated Apple Valley Eagles, who came into the tournament as the favorite, faced Stillwater in the opener. Stillwater's Jenny Ginkel then made history by scoring the first goal of the tourney, just 92 seconds into the first period. But the Eagles screamed back behind the play of senior defender and Star Tribune Girls' Hockey Player of the Year Jamie DeGriselles (who went on to star and coach at the University of New Hampshire). Despite being a defenseman, she led the Eagles with 43 goals and 35 assists for 78 points that season. In addition to DeGriselles great play, freshman Michelle Sikich, who tallied 70 points that season, netted a hat trick in the third period to rally Apple Valley to a 6-4 win. South St. Paul, behind goalie Jenny Retka, defeated Henry Sibley in the other semifinal game, 4-0 to advance to the championship game. Then, in front of a standing-room-only crowd in the title game, freshman goaltender Jenny Jannet posted an 18-save shutout to lead Apple Valley to a 2-0 victory over the Packers for the first girl's high school hockey championship.

As high school hockey grew, so too did the college game. In 1995 Augsburg College made history by becoming the first fully funded women's varsity hockey program not only in the state, but in the nation. At the same time, the Minnesota Legislature was making strides to help the girl's game grow as well. Believe it or not, a lot of the women at the state capital like to skate themselves, and many even play in a league of their own on Sunday nights. They wanted to do their best to see to it that girls everywhere had the same opportunities that the boys did. So, in 1995 the legislature passed a bill requiring that 15 percent of all ice time in both public and private rinks, be reserved for girls, increasing to 30 percent in 1996 and 50 percent in 1997. Arena owners throughout the state could no longer get away with giving the girls undesirable time slots either at the crack of dawn or in the middle of the night, and report that they had filled their quota. In addition, the Minnesota Amateur Sports Commission, the body runs all amateur sports in the state, received funds through the legislature called the Mighty Ducks Bill, which was earmarked for either the construction of dozens of new arenas or for the renovation of existing ones. In 1995, 23 grants totaling nearly $3 million were awarded to 23 communities throughout the state, and to date more than $20 million has been awarded for the sole purpose of giving more kids the chance to play hockey in Minnesota.

The University of Minnesota women's team also turned varsity in 1996, due in part to rising gender equity issues at the collegiate level. Both the Big 10 Conference, as well as the NCAA were enforcing strict rules about equity and making sure that member school's were providing an equal number of sports for both male and female athletes. This was one way the school saw fit to satisfy them both. Former Colby College coach Laura Haldorson took over as the team's first head coach that year, as the team hit the ice at the new Mariucci Arena. One of their biggest problems out of the gates was a lack of competition. Other than Augsburg, there weren't any other varsity programs in the area, so many of the team's games that year were played on the East Coast, against the more established programs.

In addition to the U.S. National Women's Championships being held in Bloomington in 1996, it is interesting to note that the number of girls programs had nearly doubled that year to 47 teams now playing throughout the state. Roseville, Blaine/Coon Rapids, Burnsville and the Blake School rounded out the 1996 tournament field, as Roseville (led by the fabulous Curtin sisters - Ronda and Renee, who scored some 20 points between them in the tourney), went on to beat Burnsville for the second annual girl's high school hockey championship.

By now women's ice hockey had become one of the fastest growing sports in the world, growing from 5,573 women registered with USA Hockey in 1991, to more than 23,000 by 1997. (While there were just 35 teams in Minnesota in 1986, in 1997 there were 332 teams -- broken down like this: 235 youth + 68 high school + 17 Junior Varsity + 12 college. Those 332 teams in Minnesota represented more than one-third of all the teams in the country at the time.) That same year, in addition to the Gophers and Augsburg, who had varsity teams, there were numerous club teams which were playing in the Midwestern Collegiate Women's Hockey Alliance, including: Carleton, Gustavus Adolphus, Mankota State, UM-Duluth, St. Catherine's and St. Thomas, St. Cloud State, St. Mary's and St. Olaf.

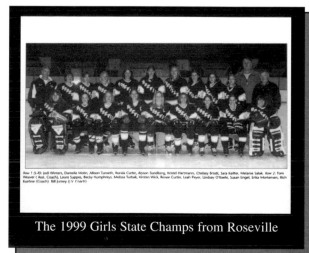
The 1999 Girls State Champs from Roseville

Krissy Wendell

In 1999, junior defenseman Krissy Wendell became the first high school player (boy or girl) in the nation to score 100 goals (not to mention her 38 assists) in a high school season, when she tallied 100 goals in just 22 games (she even missed three games while she was playing in a World Tournament in Finland). She eventually finished with 109 goals and 40 assists for 149 points (including the playoffs) that year, to lead the Pirates to an undefeated 25-0 regular season, a sectional title and the 1999 Girls' State Consolation Championship. The Park Center High School phenom had played on the boy's junior varsity team up until that year, where she was one of the leading scorers on a team that finished third at the state tournament. A dominating two-way player, she twice scored eight goals in a game this past season.

She had played on boy's hockey teams all of her life, and was even the catcher on the boy's little league team that went to the Little League World Series in 1994 - becoming just the fifth girl ever to do so. While nearly every team refused to try and steal second base on her cannon-arm, as a switch-hitter she belted out several home runs from both sides of the plate throughout the year. So amazing was her story, that Sports Illustrated for Kids Magazine did a full-color page feature story about her. (In addition, as an 8th grader she led the girl's varsity softball team to the state tournament.)

Making the jump to the girls team in 1998-99 however, was a tough decision. She probably would've played on the boy's varsity team had she not gotten injured before the season, but has no regrets about her new team. "I improved a lot each year because the (boys) game is played at a much faster pace," said Wendell. "You have to go on instinct and not just natural skills. But, the boys kept growing and I didn't. This was a good year to switch. The girls program definitely is stronger than it used to be."

Last summer, after leading a Minnesota All-Star team in scoring in a win over a Massachusetts team, she was invited to try-out for, and made, the prestigious U.S. Women's National Team - along with several other Olympians. Look for Krissy to be the next superstar on the 2002 Olympic team in Salt Lake City.

With some 68 schools now offering girl's high school programs in the state in 1997, the tournament moved to the bigger State Fair Coliseum. In addition, the field also expanded from a four to an eight-team format, as Hibbing, Roseville, Blaine, Eagan, Owatonna, Stillwater, Mounds View and Hopkins battled it out for the right to be called champion. Hibbing went on to win it all that year by doing something that had never been done, they beat the 51-0 (all-time) Roseville Raiders (who had the state's two leading scorers - Ronda and Renee Curtin), in the first quarterfinal game. Led by Beth Wolff's goal with just 18 seconds left in the game, the Bluejackets scored three unanswered third period goals to win 4-3. After knocking off Blaine in the semis 4-2, thanks to Amber Fryklund's hat-trick, the Hibbing Blue Jackets then met Eagan in the finals. Eagan, which was led by the state's most exciting player, seventh-grader Natalie Darwitz, advanced to the title game by first beating Owatonna, and then Mounds View. In the quarterfinal win over Owatonna, Darwitz scored four goals and had three assists in the 9-3 rout, while against Mounds View, which was led by All-Stater Laura Tryba, she scored all of her team's three goals in a 3-2 win. In the championship game, however, Darwitz could only muster a pair of goals, as Hibbing, behind Amber Fryklund's four scores and Haley Walters one goal and two assists, went on to beat the Wildcats 6-3 for their first title. The tournament drew record crowds at the State Fair Coliseum, as some 13,000 fans came to cheer on the ladies.

The 1998 hockey season was a huge one for women's hockey everywhere. Not only did the U.S. bring home the first-ever Olympic gold at the Winter Games in Nagano, Japan, but the Lady Gophers (after finishing with a 21-7-3 overall record), shocked the hockey world by finishing fourth at the American Women's College Hockey Alliance National Championships. (They lost to New Hampshire 4-1, and then Northeastern 4-0.)

The number of Minnesota high schools with varsity girls hockey teams jumped to 85 that year, as the defending champs from Hibbing were joined in the tournament field by Anoka, Apple Valley, Bloomington Jefferson, Burnsville, Mounds View, Roseville and South St. Paul. After beating Burnsville 2-1 in the Section Two finals to advance to the tournament, Apple Valley, led by Bethany Petersen, defeated Anoka 3-1 in the quarters, and then Mounds View 8-2 in their semifinal game to get to the title game. Meanwhile, Hibbing, who beat Bloomington Jefferson 3-1 in the quarters, narrowly squeaked by Roseville 4-3, in the semis to make it to the finals.

Apple Valley, which was eager to avenge an earlier 3-2 regular season loss to Hibbing, played the Blue Jackets tough throughout regulation. In a defensive gem, both goalies, Apple Valley's Jenny Jannett and Hibbing's Natalie Lamme, played tremendously as the teams headed into sudden death overtime with the score tied at 0-0. Then, at 1:25 of the extra session, Apple Valley's sophomore winger Leslie Stoen flipped a rebound past Lamme for the game-winner. For Jannett, who's 14 saves were enough to garner a coveted shutout, stopping Beth Wolff's breakaway shot late in the third period, as well as numerous Amber Fryklund blasts (one of which hit the pipe), proved to be the difference in the game. One of the highlights of the tournament was the fact that for the first time ever, it was broadcast live throughout the state on television by KMSP-TV, ch. nine.

The final significant event which really put women's hockey on the map in 1998, was the amazing gold-medal run of the women's Olympic team in Nagano, Japan. Led by Minnesotan's Jenny Schmidgall of Edina, and Alana Blahoski of St. Paul (both of whom scored five points in the Games), as well as Karyn Bye, from River Falls, Wis. (who finished as the third-leading scorer in the tournament with five goals and three assists in six games), Team USA defeated Team Canada 3-1 to win the first-ever Olympic gold medal in women's hockey history. The upset victory was sweet for the Americans, who had finished as runner-ups to their north-of-the-border neighbors in all five of their previous Women's World Championship meetings.

The game, which was televised throughout the world, was back and forth through the first period. Then, behind second and third period goals from both Gretchen Ulion and Shelley Looney that beat world famous Canadian goalie Manon Rheaume (who had played on several men's pro teams), the U.S. went up 2-1. Finally, with just eight seconds remaining in the game, Sandra Whyte intercepted a loose puck and tallied an empty-netter to clinch the 3-1 victory. It was an accomplishment that would thrust women's hockey into the national spotlight. Following the telecast, USA Hockey was inundated with thousands of phone calls from curious girls around the country who wanted to start playing hockey, as well as women who wanted to start their own leagues. In addition, a huge media blitz followed the historic win, including appearances on numerous national morning variety shows as well as a cover shot on the front of the Wheaties box.

While the game did not have the same global implications of the 1980 Lake Placid "Miracle on Ice" men's game, it did represent just how far women's sports has come. Fully each of the women on that team had been told at least once in her life that she couldn't play ice hockey, and most had to scrape by for years on unappreciative boy's teams because there was simply no other alternative.

For Karyn Bye, who grew up playing hockey on boy's teams (she kept a short haircut and had just her initials on the back of her uniform, instead of her name, so she could play undetected as a girl), it was a dream come true. As a young girl, Bye even wrote to the Olympic Committee to find out more about the women's Olympic team, to which they replied by simply sending her information about field hockey. "I just wanted to show everyone how thankful I am to be an American and to be on the first women's ice hockey team to win the gold medal," said the 1995 USA Hockey Women's Player of the Year from the University of New Hampshire, after the game. "Just holding this medal in my hand, I can picture all the sprints we ran, all the hard work we did, and it was all worth it. It's just unbelievable."

The Gopher women's team made it back to the Final Four in '99 for their second time in a row. There, the 28-4-3 Lady Gophers took

Natalie Darwitz

Simply put... Natalie Darwitz is a phenom. As a 6th grader Natalie was voted as the captain of the boys pee wee A team, where she led the team in scoring. Then, in 7th grade, she was asked to try out for the new varsity girls team. How would she handle the transition from playing with 12 & 13-year-olds to high school seniors? By most accounts she did pretty well, scoring a mere 90 goals and 32 assists for 122 points, and leadint the team to the state title game.

In 1997 Natalie led the state in scoring with 85 goals and 60 assists en route to leading the Eagan Wildcats to a perfect 25-0 regular season record and the state's top ranking. (That's 145 points in 25 games - or better than five points per game while averaging a hat-trick per outing!) Eagan was expected to go all the way that year, but was upset by Roseville and the amazing Curtin sisters in the quarterfinals of the state tournament. For her efforts, she received all-state honors as well as the Star Tribune's Metro Player of the Year award.

Burnsville High School hockey coach Tom Osiecki felt certain that she could've played on the 1998 women's gold medal winning Olympic team. Jack Blatherwick, a U of M and Olympic skating and conditioning coach, said "she can skate with college men," and added that her skating times were very close to men's Olympic times. "I've got to think she's the best in the nation, if not in the world," said Eagan coach Merlin Ravndalen.

It is amazing to see someone so young, have so much talent and poise. "It's a great honor to have kids look up to you," said Darwitz. "Most importantly though it's great to see that girls have an interest in hockey, and that our sport continues to grow."

In 1999, Natalie was invited to try out for, and made, the U.S. Women's National Team. The team's youngest player began touring Europe in the summer of '99. Her goals are simple. In addition to hoping to lead her Wildcats to the State title, in both hockey and softball, she is tentatively planning on graduating a year early so she can play in the 2002 Winter Olympics in Salt Lake City. "My biggest goal and dream in life right now is to work hard and make that team."

on a top ranked University of New Hampshire team in the semis on their home ice at Mariucci Arena. The Gophers, led by several Minnesota stars including: Jenny Schmidgall of Edina, Winny Brodt of Roseville, and Laura Slominski of Burnsville, jumped out to an early 2-0 lead on a pair of goals by Nadine Muzerall. But, UNH rallied to tie it and then send it into overtime. After a back-and-forth exchange by both teams, Melisa Heitzman finally beat Gopher goalie Erica Killewald at the 12:37 mark of the extra session. It was a heart-breaking loss for the Gophers, who, in only their third season are already one of the game's elite teams. They did rally that next night to beat Eastern power Brown University 3-2 on third period goals from both Tracy Engstrom and Nadine Muzerall, to win third place honors.

"This was a huge win for us," said Gopher coach Laura Halldorson. "Last year, we were just happy to be in this tournament and to come in fourth. This year, we knew we had to finish better. This continues our growth and gives us momentum going into next year. This is a team that is learning as we go, and the experience we're gaining means a lot to us."

The future of the Gopher program looks strong as well, due to the fact that their local recruiting pool is overflowing and that they are about to break ground on a new arena of their own on campus.

The 1999 High School Tournament once again featured sell-out crowds and plenty of excitement. The '99 tournament field included: Bloomington Jefferson, Burnsville, Duluth, Mankato, Mounds View, Park Center, Roseville and South St. Paul. Led by the 1999 Ms. Hockey Award winner Ronda Curtin, who scored 91 points that year, the undefeated 21-0-1 Roseville Raiders roared into the finals to win their second state title. (Maybe there's something in the water in Roseville? Her next door neighbor growing up was Gopher star Winny Brodt, also a Ms. Hockey Award winner!) Curtin scored a pair of hat-tricks in the quarterfinal and semifinal wins over both Burnsville and Duluth to lead her squad to the finals.

In the other bracket, Krissy Wendell, the first-ever prep player in the nation to score 100 goals in the regular season, led her undefeated Park Center Pirates into the first round of the tournament to face South St. Paul. There, the Packers, who were led by freshman sensation Ashley Albrecht and Erika Hockinson, recorded one of the biggest upsets in tourney history. Despite a pair of Wendell goals late that beat Packer goalie Sarah Ahlquist, South St. Paul hung on to a tough 3-2 win. The Packers then faced Bloomington Jefferson, which had beaten Mounds View 4-3, in the semis. In a back-and-forth thriller, Packer winger Erika Hockinson missed an empty netter that would have won the game, only to see the Jag's Jessica Brandanger come right back and score the equalizer with just seconds left to send the game into overtime. Two overtimes later, Jaguar senior winger Lindsey Christensen slid the game winner past Ahlquist to give Jefferson a ticket to the finals.

In the title game, Curtin exploded for four goals, as the Raiders went on to crush the Jaguars 8-2. Curtin's 10-point performance over the three games, solidified her as the best female hockey player in state history. As Minnesota's all-time leading-scoring hockey player, boys or girls, with more than 400 total points, she will attend the U of M in 1999-2000. Her sister, Renee (the second leading scorer in the state that year),

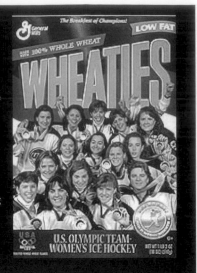

who scored four goals and two assists in the tournament as well, may surpass her big sister's scoring record in 2000 - stay tuned! With the win, Raiders coach Rich Kuehne's four-year record now stood at the incomprehensible 100-4-3.

During the summer of 1999, the Thoroughbreds (19 & under midget all-stars) made their sixth straight appearance to the USA Hockey National Championships, this time in Washington DC, where they earned the silver medal after losing to the Connecticut Polar Bears in the title game. In addition, the Blue J's, the state's top women's senior team, won the USA Hockey National Championships, also in Washington D.C., by beating the Massachusetts-based Nighthawks 7-0 in the finals. The J's, who were led by Olympic star Alana Blahoski, St. Cloud State coach Kerry Brodt, and former Thoroughbred Joy Woog, outscored their opponents that year by the amazing margin of 32-3. Additionally, many of the women from both of these teams came together during the summer of '99 to play in the first "Minnesota Dream Team" Tournament. The event, which featured 23 of the state's top high schoolers, 23 of the top college players, and 23 of the top senior women's players, mixed up the teams with all age groups for a weekend of competition. The event, arguably, brought together one of the greatest single women's talent pools in the history of the sport.

Another exciting advancement for women's hockey happened in 1999 as well. The Minnesota Intercollegiate Athletic Conference (MIAC) was awarded a supplemental grant of $440,000 from the U.S. Olympic Committee and the NCAA to help develop women's hockey as a sport on the varsity level. While the current conference members include Augsburg, Gustavus Adolphus, St. Benedict's, St. Catherine's, St. Mary's and St. Thomas, with the news Bethel, Concordia (Moorhead), Hamline, St. Olaf and Carleton all announced their intentions to move forward with advancing their program's from club status to varsity as well. The MIAC is the second conference in the nation, and the first in the Midwest, to offer a championship in women's hockey, and will also be the first to offer women's hockey completely at the NCAA Division III (non-athletic scholarship) varsity level. While most of these schools have competed in recent years in the Midwestern Collegiate Women's Hockey Alliance (MCWHA), the MIAC will finally be their own conference with similar Division III schools. Other Minnesota schools, including the U of M, UM-Duluth, Bemidji State and Minnesota State (Mankato), have all made, or are in the process of making the varsity jump to Division I, and will compete in the Women's Western Collegiate Hockey Association (WWCHA) along with Ohio State and the University of Wisconsin. The WWCHA is now the second D-I women's conference in the nation, along with the East Coast Athletic Conference (ECAC). With more than 40 colleges across the nation now offering women's hockey at the varsity level, the "emerging sport" has come a long way to catch up to the boys, who presently have just more than 50 D-I programs nationwide.

While Title IX legislation proved to be a major influence on the development of women's sports in the US, another factor in favor of female athletes was that medical studies were also beginning to reveal the benefits of sports and exercise to women's health. One such study indicated a decreased risk of breast cancer among women who were more physically active, while others found that women who were active in sports often-times had more self-esteem and confidence, and were even less likely to become pregnant or drop out of school. For whatever the reason, Minnesota has proven to be the model for the rest of the country, showing what girl's and women's hockey can become if given a chance.

The game has come a long way. Equipment manufacturers are now designing protective equipment, skates and even sticks, especially for girls and women. The sky is the limit for women's hockey. Who knows where it will all lead? Will they be able to parlay their '98 Olympic victory into a professional "league of their own" like women's basketball (WNBA), gymnastics and figure-skating have done? Perhaps Mia Hamm and the U.S. Women's Soccer team is wondering the same thing after their amazing World Cup win over China in the summer of 1999. There are still rumors about the Women's Professional Hockey League, which plans on awarding five pro women's hockey franchises to several cities on the East Coast and Canada. Time will tell if it will fly or flop. Is America ready for women's pro hockey? Stay tuned!

The Minnesota Connection

Alana Blahoski, who tallied five points during the Games, graduated from Johnson High School in St. Paul, in 1992, where she starred as member of the hockey, softball and soccer teams. She went on to be named as the 1996 Eastern College Athletic Conference Player of the Year at Providence College, and then played on two U.S. Women's National Teams in both 1996 and 1997. Following the Olympics she became a coach at Minnesota State University, Mankato. She is presently training for the 2002 Games in Salt Lake City, Utah.

Jennifer Schmidgall, who also tallied five points during the Games, graduated from Edina High School in 1997, but played on the elite Minnesota Thoroughbreds women's team. Schmidgall appeared on two U.S. Women's National Junior Teams in 1995 and 1996, before making the Olympic team. At just 19, she was one of the youngest women on the squad. After the Olympics, she attended the Gophers for a season, and after the 1999 season, decided to transfer to UM-Duluth. She is presently training for the 2002 Games in Salt Lake City, Utah.

The Hobey Baker Memorial Award
A Minnesota Tradition

Each April the nation's best player receives the Hobey Baker award, college hockey's equivalent to the Heisman Trophy. The recipient is the player who best exemplifies the qualities that Hobey Baker himself demonstrated as an athlete at Princeton University in the early 1900s. Baker was considered to be the ultimate sportsman who despised foul play, picking up only two penalties in his entire college hockey career. With his speed and superior stick handling, Baker opened up the game of hockey and set new standards for the way the game was played. A true gentleman, his habit of insisting upon visiting each opponent's locker room after every game to shake their hands became a model for today's players. A hero, Baker gave his life as an American pilot in World War I.

In 1981 Bloomington's Decathlon Club founded the Hobey Baker Memorial Award and each year presents the coveted honor to the nation's top player. Fittingly, the nation's top hockey state hosts the top hockey player finalists from around the country for the gala event. The club also commissioned a Twin Cities sculptor, Bill Mack, to create its beautiful signature trophy, simply known as the "Hobey." The balloting for the award is voted on by the nearly 50 NCAA D-I coaches who are asked to pick the top three players in their league as well as the top three in the nation. Since the awards' inception in 1981, three Gophers and three Bulldogs have won it. All were first team All-Americans, and all have gone on to successful professional careers.

Gopher Hobey Baker Winners:
Neal Broten, Brian Bonin and Rob Stauber

Minnesota's Hobey Baker Award Finalists:

Year	Player	Hometown
1981	*Neal Broten, Minnesota	Roseau
	Steve Ulseth, Minnesota	Roseville
	Steve Carroll, Mankato State	Edina
	Mark Hentges, St. Thomas	New Hope
1982	Bryan Erickson, Minnesota	Roseau
1983	Bryan Erickson, Minnesota	Roseau
	Scott Bjugstad, Minnesota	New Brighton
	Kurt Kleinendorst, Providence	Grand Rapids
	Tom Kern, Mankato State	
1984	*Tom Kurvers, UMD	Bloomington
	Jon Casey, UND	Grand Rapids
	Joel Otto, Bemidji State	Elk River
1985	*Bill Watson, UMD	Powerview, Manitoba
	Pat Micheletti, Minnesota	Hibbing
1986	Scott Sandelin, UND	Hibbing
	Brett Hull, UMD	West Vancouver, B.C.
	Norm MacIver, UMD	Thunder Bay, Ontario
1987	None	
1988	Robb Stauber, Minnesota	Duluth
	Paul Ranheim, Wisconsin	Edina
	Ken Hilgert, Mankato State	
1989	*Robb Stauber, Minnesota	Duluth
1990	None	
1991	None	
1992	Larry Olimb, Minnesota	Warroad
1993	Derek Plante, UMD	Cloquet
1993	Fred Knipscheer, St. Cloud	Fort Wayne, IN
1994	*Chris Marinucci, UMD	Grand Rapids
1994	Kelly Hultgren, St. Cloud	Bloomington
1995	*Brian Bonin, Minnesota	White Bear Lake
	Chris Imes, Maine	Birchdale
1996	Brian Bonin, Minnesota	White Bear Lake
	Mike Crowley, Minnesota	Bloomington
1997	Mike Crowley, Minnesota	Bloomington
	Jason Blake, UND	Moorhead
1998	None	
1999	Jason Blake, UND	Moorhead

*Denotes the Hobey Baker Winner

Neal Broten
Roseau native Neal Broten won the inaugural Hobey in 1981. The Gopher center, and Olympic gold-medalist became the first American player ever to score 100 points in a single NHL season, when he notched 105 in 1986 with the Stars.

Tom Kurvers
Bloomington native Tom Kurvers won the Hobey in 1984. During his tenure at UMD, Kurvers scored 43 goals and 149 assists for 192 total points - all three of which remain all-time records for a defenseman.

Bill Watson
Powerview Manitoba native Bill Watson won the Hobey in 1985. The right winger scored 89 goals and added 121 assists for 210 total points during his tenure at UMD, and still holds the record for most assists in one season with 60.

Robb Stauber
Duluth native Robb Stauber won the Hobey in 1988. The first goaltender ever to receive the award, Stauber set career records for games played (98), minutes played (5,717), wins (73) and save percentage (.906) for the Gophers from 1986-1988.

Chris Marinucci
Grand Rapids native Chris Marinucci won the Hobey in 1994. The right winger played in a team-record 149 consecutive games during his four seasons at UMD, scoring more points than any other collegian from 1992-1994.

Brian Bonin
White Bear Lake native Brian Bonin won the Hobey in 1996. The speedy center who finished his Gopher career with 216 career points, was named as the league's Player of the Year in both 1995 and 1996, after leading the nation in scoring.

By the year 2000 there will be upwards of 50,000 women playing some form of organized ice hockey in the United States. Presently, Minnesota has some 300 amateur girls hockey teams, plus an additional 115 girls high school hockey teams, along with another 50 or so with JV squads. The majority of the growth today is coming from the small towns outside the metro, in non-traditional hockey hot-beds, such as Fairmont, in southern Minnesota. Our youth feeder-programs have paid big dividends as well, with girls graduating into higher levels each year. High school teams are getting stronger, and those girls are in turn graduating and leading our state college and university teams into the future. Not even John Mariucci could have imagined that it would have come this far!

FACT: In 1991 Edina's Jan Hanley became the first female goalie in the state to play regularly for a boy's varsity team. Her big break came on March 2nd, 1991, when Willard Ikola, after 33 years of coaching, started her in the nets against rival Richfield in a game at the sold-out Met Center. Hanley, who had gone undefeated during the season, led the Hornets to a 4-2 victory, earning herself a lot of national attention. She later attended both Hamline and St. Thomas Universities, and went on to play on the U.S. Women's National Team. Today she is the head coach for the Burnsville girls high school team, where she led the Braves to the 1999 State Tournament.

The 1960 U.S. Olympic Team

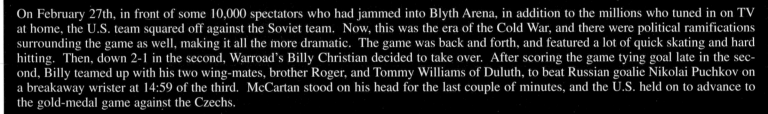

Twenty years before the now famous "Miracle on Ice" team of 1980, which brought home the gold in Lake Placid, N.Y., there was another team making history on the other coast of the country, in Squaw Valley, Cal. They were the underdog 1960 U.S. men's hockey team, and with the help of some eight Minnesotans, they upset some of the biggest hockey powers in the world that February, to give America it's first taste of Olympic hockey glory.

The U.S. held its' preliminary tryout camps at Williams Arena, at the U of M campus, under the guidance of the 1956 silver-medal winning Olympic Coach, John Mariucci. After finalizing the roster, the team spent several months playing exhibition games against teams from all over the world.

The Olympic tournament got underway with the Russians and the Canadians being the overwhelming favorites to bring home the gold. The Americans, on the other hand, were not even expected to get past the first couple of rounds. The U.S. came out swinging though, and thanks to five John Mayasich goals, they defeated Australia 12-1 and Czechoslovakia 7-5 to advance into the medal rounds. Then, after beating the favored Swedes 6-3, thanks to Roger Christian's hat trick and his brother Billy's three assists, they went on to beat Germany 9-1, setting the stage for a showdown with the mighty Canadians. There, behind former Gopher Jack McCartan's 39 saves, the U.S. beat Team Canada by the final of 2-1.

On February 27th, in front of some 10,000 spectators who had jammed into Blyth Arena, in addition to the millions who tuned in on TV at home, the U.S. team squared off against the Soviet team. Now, this was the era of the Cold War, and there were political ramifications surrounding the game as well, making it all the more dramatic. The game was back and forth, and featured a lot of quick skating and hard hitting. Then, down 2-1 in the second, Warroad's Billy Christian decided to take over. After scoring the game tying goal late in the second, Billy teamed up with his two wing-mates, brother Roger, and Tommy Williams of Duluth, to beat Russian goalie Nikolai Puchkov on a breakaway wrister at 14:59 of the third. McCartan stood on his head for the last couple of minutes, and the U.S. held on to advance to the gold-medal game against the Czechs.

The U.S., which had earlier beaten the Czechs, weren't going to take anything for granted. Despite the U.S. team being noticeably fatigued, they came out strong, and found itself tied at three apiece after the first period. The American squad fell behind 4-3 after two, but then, behind Roger Christian, they roared back for what would prove to be one of the greatest third periods of Olympic history. Roger struck first at 5:50, followed by Harvard's Bill Cleary, who took a Mayasich pass to put the Americans ahead 5-4. From there, it was all red, white and blue. Roger added two more goals that final period, to give the U.S. a stunning 9-4 win, and their first Olympic gold medal. Roger Christian led Team USA in scoring with eight goals, while Mayasich added seven of his own, and McCartan, who was named to the "All World" team, signed with the N.Y. Rangers immediately following the game.

Warroad's Roger Christian scoring against the Soviets during the 1960 Olympics

Name	Hometown	College/Club
Roger Christian	Warroad, Mn.	Warroad Lakers
William Christian	Warroad, Mn.	Warroad Lakers
Paul Johnson	W. St. Paul, Mn.	Rochester Mustangs
John Mayasich	Eveleth, Mn.	Minnesota
Jack McCartan	St. Paul, Mn.	Minnesota
Richard Meredith	Minneapolis, Mn.	Minnesota
Robert Owen	St. Louis Park, Mn.	Harvard
Thomas Williams	Duluth, Mn.	Duluth Swans
James Claypool	Duluth, Mn.	(Manager)
Dr. William Atmore	Duluth, Mn.	(Team Physician)

The 1980 Miracle on Ice

The 1980 United States Olympic Hockey run will forever remain etched in our memories as one of the greatest sporting events of American history. There have been numerous books written about the historic event, and it will forever remain as the team every other Olympic hockey team will have to measure up to. It put the sport, which at the time was perceived by some as a "hobby," and by others as merely a regional game found primarily in the North and East, into the national spotlight. It is, in some way I'm sure, partially responsible for the fact that the National Hockey League now has franchises in Florida, Texas, California, Arizona, Tennessee, Georgia and North Carolina. And, be honest, whenever you see that replay of the players throwing their sticks up into the crowd, piling on the goalie, and crying to the sounds of Al Michaels saying, "Do you believe in miracles?", as they upset the heavily favored Soviets in the medal round, do you get goose-bumps? Yeah, me too!

A Dozen Home-Boys

The Americans, who, since the inception of the Winter Games, had won one gold medal (1960), four silver medals (1924, 1952, 1956 & 1972), and one bronze (1936), were eager to bring home some hardware on their native soil. Having finished fourth during the previous Olympics, in 1976, at Innsbruck, Austria, under Minnesota native and coach "Badger" Bob Johnson, the U.S. knew it would never have a better opportunity than the one they had in front of them right then in Lake Placid, N.Y.

The coach of that now fabled squad was Herb Brooks, who was no stranger to the USA Olympic hockey program. After being the last man cut from the gold medal team's roster in 1960, Brooks went on to play on the 1964 and 1968 Olympic teams, as well as on five other U.S. National Teams. Herbie, who had just finished leading the Golden Gophers to the National Championship in 1979, now had the responsibility of selecting the 20 players to represent the United States. Brooks went with what he knew, local boys. While 12 of the 20 were native Minnesotans, nine of them were players whom Brooks had coached as Gophers, including: Roseau's Neal Broten, Grand Rapids' Bill Baker, White Bear Lake's Steve Janaszak, Rochester's Eric Strobel, Duluth's Phil Verchota, Minneapolis' Mike Ramsey, Babbitt's Buzz Schneider, St. Paul's Rob McClanahan and Richfield's Steve Christoff. The three other Minnesotans on the fantasy team were: Warroad's Dave Christian, who played at North Dakota, and Virginia's John Harrington and Eveleth's Mark Pavelich, both of whom played together at Minnesota-Duluth.

"Having played international hockey for so many years, it gives me an awfully warm feeling to be selected as head coach for the 1980 Olympics," Brooks said. "I'm extremely honored and humbled. To be picked when there are so many outstanding amateur hockey coaches in the nation, well, let's just say it's something I never really expected to happen."

In early September, the team began as challenging an exhibition schedule as had ever been organized for an American Olympic squad. Beginning with an initial European tour in early September, the team played a 61-game pre-Olympic schedule against foreign, college and professional teams, ultimately finishing with a 42-16-3 record. It was during this time together that the players were introduced to Brooks' new offensive game-plan called, the "weave." Brooks felt that if his club was going to compete against Europeans, they had better learn how to play like Europeans.

Entering the XIIIth Winter Olympic Games, the team was a decided underdog, an evaluation that seemed to be confirmed by a 10-3 defeat at the hands of the Soviets in the final exhibition game in New York City. Though seeded seventh in the 12-nation pool, the Americans felt that they had something to prove. The Yanks took on Sweden in the opening game, as Bill Baker scored with 27 seconds remaining in the third period to give the U.S. a 2-2 tie. The goal acted as a catalyst for the young Americans, who then upset Czechoslovakia, and their amazing Stastny brothers, 7-3, thanks to goals from Pavelich, Schneider, Verchota and McClanahan. After beating both Norway and Rumania, now only West Germany (the team that knocked them out of the bronze medal in 1976), stood in the way of getting into the medal round.

Down 2-0 in the first, the Minnesota boys came through big as McClanahan and Broten each tallied to tie it up. McClanahan then scored again on another breakaway in the third, and Phil Verchota lit the lamp late to give the U.S. a 4-2 win over the Germans. This gave the Americans a round robin record of 4-0-1, and a date with the mighty Soviets - who were led by Vladislav Tretiak, the world's premier goaltender. The Soviets, who had outscored their opponents 51-11 through their first five games, were just another of a long line of dynasty teams which had won the last four Olympic gold's, and five of the last six. In fact, the only team to beat them since 1956 was the U.S. squad 20 years earlier in 1960.

Do You Believe in Miracles?...Yes!

The game had all the hype in the world, with political and social implications written all over it. The "Iron Range" line of Pavelich, Harrington and Schneider got the Americans on the board, when, down 1-0, Pavelich fed Schneider for a nice slap shot which found the top corner. The Russians answered back three minutes later, only to see Mark Johnson tie it up with just seconds to go in the period. When they returned to the ice following the intermission, the U.S. team was shocked to see that Soviet coach Victor Tikhanov had replaced Tretiak in goal with backup keeper Vladimir Myshkin. While it would appear that the great bear was wounded, the Soviets came back to take the lead, having now out-shot the Yanks 30-10 through two. Johnson got his second of the game at 8:39 of the third to tie it at 3-3, setting up the heroics for the Iron Rangers.

Midway through the third, Schneider dumped the puck into the Russian zone and Harrington dug it out to his old UMD wingmate Mark Pavelich. Pavelich then floated a perfect pass to the top of the circle where team captain Mike Eruzione fired home "the shot heard 'round the world." The final 10 minutes of the game were probably the longest in U.S. hockey history, but the Americans held on as goalie Jim Craig played brilliantly down the stretch. Then, as the crowd counted down the final seconds, Al Michaels shouted "Do you believe in miracles,...Yes!" And with that, the Americans had made it into the gold medal game.

As the players went nuts on the ice, Herbie, ever the psychologist, quickly put his team back in its place. He screamed at them not to get too cocky, and that they were just lucky, and hadn't won a damn thing yet. The next day at practice, Brooks put the team through a grueling workout, constantly reinforcing to his men that he was not their friend, and they had proved nothing yet. This was part of his ingenious master plan, to get the players to despise him, and force them to rally amongst themselves to become a stronger team.

In the final game the U.S. faced Finland, who had beaten the Czechs in the other semifinal. Down 1-0 in the second, Steve Christoff got the Americans on the board at 4:39 with a nice wrister down low. The Finns regained the lead, however, and went into the third up 2-1. After an emotional speech between the intermission from Brooks, reminding his players ever so eloquently that they would regret this moment for the rest of their collective lives if they let it slip away, the U.S. came out inspired and tried to make history. The hero this time would prove to be Phil Verchota, who took a Dave Christian pass in the left circle and found the back of the net at 2:25. With that, the Americans started to smell blood and immediately went for the jugular. Just three minutes later, Robbie McClanahan went five-hole with a Mark Johnson pass to give the U.S. a 3-2 lead. Johnson then saved the day by adding a shorthanded backhand goal of his own just minutes later to give the U.S. a two-goal safety net. Jim Craig then hung on for the final few minutes of the game as Al Michaels this time screamed: "This impossible dream, comes true!" It was suddenly pandemonium in Lake Placid, as the team threw their sticks into the crowd and formed a human pile at center ice to the chants of "USA! USA!"

Many of the players were visibly moved by what they had done, as evidenced during the singing of the National Anthem, where the entire team gathered on the top podium. Still wringing wet with their jersey's on, goaltender Jim Craig, with an American Flag draped around him, sang the Star-Spangled Banner. The country went crazy with a newly found sense of national pride. Sports Illustrated named the team, collectively as "Sportsmen of the Year," Life Magazine declared it as the "Sports Achievement of the Decade," and ABC Sports announcer, Jim McCay, went on to call the amazing achievement, "The greatest upset in the history of sports."

Instant Super-Stardom
A grateful nation, depressed by the Iranian hostage crisis and mired in an economic recession, hailed the team as heroes. A visit to the White House followed, as well as appearances in cities across the land. The Wheaties box, magazine covers, awards, honors, speaking engagements and a whole lot of hoopla would follow for all the players.

The icy miracle was achieved by enormous ambition coupled with great passing, checking, speed, and sound puck-control. Shrewdly, Brooks refused to play the typical dump-and-chase style of hockey that was so prevalent in American hockey. "I didn't want the team throwing the puck away with no reason," said Brooks, who went on to coach the N.Y. Rangers that next season. "That's stupid. It's the same as punting on first down. The style I wanted combined the determined checking of the North American game and the best features of the European game."

"They were really mentally tough and goal-oriented," said Brooks of his team. "They came from all different walks of life, many having competed against one another, but they came together and grew to be a real close team. I pushed this team really hard, I mean I really pushed them! But they had the ability to answer the bell. Our style of play was probably different than anything in North America. We adopted more of a hybrid style of play - a bit of the Canadian school and a little bit of the European school. The players took to it like ducks to water, and they really had a lot of fun playing it. We were a fast, creative team that played extremely disciplined without the puck. Throughout the Olympics, they had a great resiliency about them. I mean they came from behind six or seven times to win. They just kept on moving and working and digging. I think we were as good a conditioned team as there was in the world, outside maybe the Soviet Union. We got hot and lucky at the right times, and it was just an incredible experience for all of us."

In 1998 the Olympics went to an NHL All-Star format, something Brooks has strong feelings about. "To me the Olympics are not about 'Dream Teams,' it's more about dreamers. And, it's not about medals, but the pursuit of medals. The Olympics are not about being number one, it's about sacrificing and trying to be number one. That's why I am real disappointed with the Olympic movement today. The 'Dream Teams' for me are 'ho-hum', business as usual for pro-sports. I think it's killed the hopes and dreams and inspirations of many young people that have hopes of playing in the NBA or NHL. I know that times change and I understand all those things. But I've always felt that our country didn't have to prove that we were better than the vehicle of the Olympic team. That's why the Olympics were always really special to me."

The Fall-Out
Most importantly perhaps, was the fact that the historic win brought hockey to the front-page of newspapers everywhere, and forever opened the door to the NHL for American-born players from below the 49th parallel. While all of the Minnesota boys went on to play hockey after the Games in the professional ranks, seven went on to become regulars in the NHL, including: Bill Baker, Dave Christian, Mike Ramsey, Neal Broten, Mark Pavelich, Rob McClanahan and Steve Christoff.

The Minnesota Connection in Lake Placid

Name	Hometown	College
Bill Baker	Grand Rapids, Mn.	Minnesota
Neal Broten	Roseau, Mn.	Minnesota
Dave Christian	Warroad, Mn.	North Dakota
Steve Christoff	Richfield, Mn.	Minnesota
John Harrington	Virginia, Mn.	Minnesota-Duluth
Steve Janaszak	White Bear Lake, Mn.	Minnesota
Rob McClanahan	St. Paul, Mn.	Minnesota
Mark Pavelich	Eveleth, Mn.	Minnesota-Duluth
Mike Ramsey	Minneapolis, Mn.	Minnesota
Buzz Schneider	Babbitt, Mn.	Minnesota
Eric Strobel	Rochester, Mn.	Minnesota
Phil Verchota	Duluth, Mn.	Minnesota
Herb Brooks	St. Paul, Mn.	Head Coach
Ralph Jasinski	Mounds View, Mn.	Manager
Warren Strelow	Mahtomedi, Mn.	Goalie Coach
Dr. V.G. Nagobads	Edina, Mn.	Physician
Gary Smith	Minneapolis, Mn.	Trainer
Bud Kessel	St. Paul, Mn.	Equipment Mgr.

**1980
UNITED STATES OLYMPIC HOCKEY TEAM
XIII WINTER OLYMPICS
GOLD MEDALIST**

Front Row (L-R) Steve Janaszak, Bill Baker, Mark Johnson, Craig Patrick (Ass't Coach/Ass't GM), Mike Eruzione (Captain), Herb Brooks (Head Coach), Buzz Schneider, Jack O'Callahan, Jim Craig

Middle Row (L-R) Bob Suter, Rob McClanahan, Mark Wells, Bud Kessel (Equipment Manager), V. George Nagobads (Physician), Gary Smith (Trainer), Robert Fleming (Chairman), Ralph Jasinski (General Manager), Warren Strelow (Goalkeeping Coach), Bruce Horsch, Neal Broten, Mark Pavelich

Back Row (L-R) Phil Verchota, Steve Christoff, Les Auge, Dave Delich, Jack Hughes, Ken Morrow, Mike Ramsey, Dave Christian, Ralph Cox, Dave Silk, John Harrington, Eric Strobel

The Minnesota Moose

Early in 1994, Minnesota rejoined the long-running International Hockey League (the Millers and Saints played in the IHL back in the early 1960s), when the expansion Minnesota Moose, led by businessmen Kevin MacLean and Roger Sturgeon, hit the ice at the Civic Center. The group named Frank Serratore as their head coach and director of hockey operations while Glen Sonmor was named director of player development. The team, which competed in the Midwest Division of the Western Conference (along with Atlanta, Houston, Kansas City and Milwaukee), featured Dave Snuggerud and John Young as its first two stars.

The team got off to a shaky start, losing its first regular season game on the road at Denver by the final of 4-1. Blair Atcheynum notched the team's first-ever goal in the loss. The Moose rebounded a few nights later, when, on October 16, 1994, thanks to Stephane Morin's game-winning goal, they notched their first win in a 6-1 victory at Chicago. After losing their home-opener to Milwaukee, they finally got their first home-win on November 15th, when they beat the Chicago Wolves 4-3. The team was an instant hit with the fans, who immediately started to buy up all of the Minnesota Moose paraphernalia they could get their hands on. Within a short period of time, the team's logo became so hot that it led all of minor league hockey in merchandise sales.

With the North Stars gone to Dallas, the community was eager to rally behind a new club. Soon their games were being carried on MSC-TV, and near-capacity crowds were showing up at the arena to support their new team. The club was up and down throughout that first year, but one of its first highlights came on January 18th, 1995, when winger Stephane Morin garnered three assists for the Western squad at Las Vegas in the IHL's annual All Star Game. After winning their final home game against Las Vegas, the Moose, led by the league's leading scorer, Stephane Morin, finished their inaugural 1994-95 season with a 34-35-12 record. With their fourth-place record in the division, the team also clinched a spot in the Turner Cup playoffs. There, the Moose were swept by the eventual champion Denver Grizzlies, despite losing a heart-breaking Game Three at the Target Center by the final of 4-2.

That next season the team signed a working agreement with the Winnipeg Jets to become an affiliate "minor league" team. And, after finishing the 1995-96 season in the divisional cellar, with a 30-45-7 record, and out of the playoffs, Winnipeg soon became the team's permanent address. That's because following that season the team decided to move to Winnipeg, where they became the Winnipeg Moose. It was widely speculated at the time that there was going to be a "swap" of sorts, with the NHL's Winnipeg Jets coming to Minnesota, and the Moose going there. But, in the final hour the whole thing was botched, and the Jets wound up going to Phoenix instead. Meanwhile, Minnesota was left with no pro team.

In addition to Snuggerud, some of the other players with a Minnesota connection over the team's two-year stint here included: Scott Bell, John Brill, Dave Christian, Parris Duffus, Tod Hartje, Chris Imes, Reed Larson, Kris Miller, Larry Olimb, Mark Osiecki, Frank Pietrangelo, Gordie Roberts and Brett Strot to name a few.

Warroad's David Christian played for the Saints after starring in the NHL for more than a decade

Number of Indoor Rinks in Minnesota 1904-1998

Year	SM	TC	CWC	NE	NW	Total Number
1904	0	1	0	1	0	2
1913	0	1	0	1	1	3
1920	0	1	0	2	0	3
1930	0	3	0	7	1	11
1940	2	4	1	6	6	19
1950	1	3	1	3	5	13
1960	2	5	1	4	5	17
1970	4	25	3	15	13	60
1982	17	60	10	22	21	130
1998	26	106	26	28	30	216

SM - Southern Minnesota
TC - Twin Cities Metropolitan Area
CWC - Central/West Central Minnesota
NE - Northeastern Minnesota
NW - Northwestern Minnesota

Sled Hockey allows physically challenged players of all ages to continue to play the game

The Minnesota Wild

On June 25, 1997, the NHL Board of Governors unanimously voted to award an expansion franchise to Minnesota, to begin play in a new St. Paul arena, for the year 2000-2001. Just hours later a celebration erupted in downtown St. Paul, where a parade of 22 Zamboni's took to the streets. That next day, more than 100 starved hockey fanatics lined up to put down their deposits on season tickets, three years before the first puck would ever be dropped. It would be safe to say that Minnesota was ready for the return of pro hockey!

"We accomplished something that gives us a niche in history," said majority owner Bob Naegele Jr., who's investment group ponied up the $80 million expansion fee. "We were part of a group that returned the NHL to Minnesota, at a time when there was seemingly no chance of doing so. And there were so many nay-sayer's and doomsday prophets along the way."

Minnesota has been without NHL hockey since the North Stars were hijacked to Dallas back in 1993, and the anticipation of the new team has been great. In the fall of 1998 the team sponsored an exhibition game between the Dallas Stars and Phoenix Coyotes at the Target Center, and to their amazement, some 18,294 fans, the largest crowd to ever watch a hockey game in Minnesota, came to support the return of the pro hockey in our state. It wasn't without it's hurdles though, and one individual who should be given a lot of credit for making this whole deal happen is St. Paul Mayor, Norm Coleman, who lobbied hard to get the new $130 million, 18,600-seat arena built in downtown St. Paul.

On January 22, 1998 the team held a bash at Aldrich Arena in St. Paul to formally announce that it was going to be named as the "Wild," with its official colors being "Iron Range Red," "Forest Green," "Harvest Gold" and "Minnesota Wheat." Sales of team merchandise have been phenomenal, and the team's web-site has been inundated by fans from throughout the world.

Leading the way for the new team is CEO Jac Sperling, who is no stranger to Minnesota hockey. Sperling, a Colorado attorney specializing in pro sports transactions, was part of the group that originally tried to work a deal that would have brought the Winnipeg Jets to town back in 1995. While the Jets opted instead to move to Phoenix, where they became the Coyotes, he tried again in 1997 to lure the Hartford Whalers to Minnesota, only to see that franchise wind up instead in Carolina, as the Hurricanes. Three times was the charm for Jac, however, as he now sits firmly in control of a new franchise in the best hockey market in the country. And, to make sure that the proverbial honeymoon won't end too quickly, in September of 1999, Jac hired former Montreal Canadien's and Calgary Flames' star, Doug Risebrough, as the team's first general manager.

The Wild will become the NHL's 30th franchise and will join the league's newly realigned Northwest Division of the Western Conference, along with the Calgary Flames, Colorado Avalanche, Edmonton Oilers and Vancouver Canucks. And for those keeping score at home, the league has changed quite a bit since the last time the NHL expanded here, back in 1967, when the North Stars were one of six new teams that made the league's total skyrocket to 12. In fact, it has changed a great deal even since the Stars' Norris Division heyday's of the early 90's.

By the year 2000 the average NHL season ticket price will be nearly $45, and while the average NHL salary back in 1992 was $467,000, by 2000 it will have tripled to an estimated $1.4 million. The numbers are insane. While the North Stars reached the 1991 Stanley Cup Finals with a payroll of around $9 million, the 1999 Dallas Stars payroll was nearly $50 million. But, one thing the Wild has today that our North Stars didn't have back then, is a $600 million national TV deal. The North Stars, who only received about $1 million from local cable and radio contracts back in the early '90s, will receive some $4 million annually from that revenue right out of the gates. And, based on the fact that the team has already sold more than 12,000 season ticket deposits, and pre-sold nearly all of the new arena's 74 luxury suites, the outlook looks great.

"McGyver," otherwise known as Richard Dean Anderson, is from Roseville. He loves hockey and plays in Hollywood.

Mr. Hockey Minnesota Winners

Year	Player	High School	College
1985	Tom Chorske	Southwest	Gophers
1986	George Pelawa	Bemidji (Killed in auto accident)	
1987	Kris Miller	Greenway	UMD
1988	Larry Olimb	Warroad	Gophers
1989	Trent Klatt	Osseo	Gophers
1990	Joe Dziedzic	Edison	Gophers
1991	Darby Hendrickson	Richfield	Gophers
1992	Brian Bonin	White Bear Lake	Gophers
1993	Nick Checko	Bloomington Jefferson	Gophers
1994	Mike Crowley	Bloomington Jefferson	Gophers
1995	Erik Rasmussen	St. Louis Park	Gophers
1996	Dave Spehar	Duluth East	Gophers
1997	Aaron Miskovich	Grand Rapids	Gophers
1998	Johnny Pohl	Red Wing	Gophers
1999	Jeff Taffe	Hastings	Gophers

Simply known as the "Tourney," the Minnesota State High School Hockey Tournament is, in a word, amazing. In what has evolved into the largest high school sporting event in the country, it can also be compared on many levels to that of the Indiana Boys' Basketball Tournament and the Texas State Football Championship, in terms of popularity, attendance, revenues, community support, pride, and world-wide mystique. To play in the spectacle known simply as "March Madness," is probably the single greatest highlight of any young boy or girl's athletic life. And, with college and professional hockey futures hanging in the balance, it has evolved into a proving ground of sorts which can make-or-break young careers.

Although the State High School Tournament officially began in 1945, a lot of people don't realize that high school hockey in Minnesota goes back much, much further than that. The tradition and history that have made those three wonderful days in March so special today, has actually been a work in progress for more than a century. Its genesis from rovers - to red lines - to Cooperalls, is a journey that starts from its humble beginnings at the old St. Paul Auditorium. From there it went to the Met Center, then back to the Civic Center, followed by a two-year hiatus at the Target Center, and lastly to its final resting place at the new RiverCentre for the year 2000. The pinnacle of amateur hockey achievement in our state, the Tournament, in all of its glory, has become synonymous with Minnesota.

High school hockey's roots in Minnesota can be traced all the way back to the late 1890s, around the same time that the sport of hockey evolved from the game of ice polo. By then hockey had spread both up from from the Twin Cities, and also down by rail from Manitoba, to communities such as: Warroad, Roseau, Warren, Hallock, Argyle, Stephen, Thief River Falls, Crookston, Baudette, Eveleth, and Duluth. As the sport grew in popularity throughout the state, industrial sponsored men's leagues began to emerge. With that, more and more rinks started to be constructed, spreading the game's popularity even further throughout the youth levels.

The first high schools to form varsity teams in Minnesota were St. Paul Mechanic Arts, St. Paul Central, St. Paul Academy, Minneapolis North, Minneapolis Central, Minneapolis East and Minneapolis West. By as early as 1899, in addition to playing one another, the high school squads played against several local men's senior league teams including the St. Paul Hockey Club, St. Paul Athletic Club, Minneapolis Hockey Club, Mic Macs, Victorias, Laurels, and Chinooks, as well as the University of Minnesota, St. Thomas and Luther Colleges. By 1900 two of the schools, St. Paul Central and St. Paul Mechanic Arts, were playing in a newly formed four-team men's senior amateur circuit along with the St. Paul and Minneapolis Hockey Club's, called the "Twin City Senior Hockey League." Many of the games were played in Minneapolis' first indoor arena, the old "Star Roller Rink" (located on 4th Avenue South and 11th Street), which had been retrofitted with natural ice for hockey that year. That next season of 1901-1902, the league expanded to six teams by adding the St. Paul Virginia's and St. Paul Mascots. To make it official, then world famous curler, Robert H. Dunbar, presented a silver cup to the league which was be awarded annually to its champion. The Virginias went on to win the inaugural Dunbar Cup during that first season, while in 1903, the University of Minnesota, which had since joined the league, defeated both Minneapolis Central High School 4-0, and the St. Paul Virginias 4-3, on a frozen Como Lake in St. Paul to take the Cup. (The star of that Central team was a kid by the name of Bobby Marshall. Marshall, one of the first African Americans ever to play the game, went on to star as an All-American End on the Gopher football team.)

That same year, several of the high school teams competed in the first-ever "Mythical" State Amateur Championship, which featured teams from St. Paul, Minneapolis, Duluth and Two Harbors. Soon, to meet all of the demand, another roller rink (located at Washington and Broadway Avenue North), was outfitted with natural ice. Electric lights were even installed on the 150' x 50' ice surface, so that the high school and senior teams could play all night long. In 1905 the Minneapolis Amateur Hockey Association constructed an outdoor ice hockey rink (located at the corners of Lake Street and Girard Avenue South), which featured not only a large warming house but also long bleachers for the large crowds. Before long high schoolers from around the Twin Cities were rooting against one-another at this new fan-friendly venue.

Hockey continued to flourish throughout the prep ranks of the state through the first decade of the new century. In 1908 Warroad and Roseau began their high school hockey rivalry, and in 1909 the St. Paul Public High School Championships were held for the first time. Mechanic Arts won the first three years, only to see Central win it from 1912-1914. (The two schools would share the crown exclusively on and off until 1933.) By 1914 the Minneapolis High School Hockey Conference (which included East, West, Central and North), as well as the St. Paul City Conference (which included Mechanic Arts, Central, Humboldt and Johnson), were up and running smoothly with teams maintaining their own outdoor rinks. Minneapolis West, coached by W.W. Bradley, dominated the Minneapolis High School Conference early on, winning 14 championships from 1908-1932. (During the late 1920's and early 1930s, the dominant West High School was led by Phil Perkins, Jack Flood, Laurie Parker, Burr Williams, Earl Barthelome and Manny Cotlow, who all amazingly went on to play professional hockey.) West's close proximity to the "lakes," combined with their nearness to the Minneapolis Arena proved to be factors in their early success. When the St. Paul champion met their Minneapolis counterparts for the Twin Cities Championship, the contests usually took place in front of large crowds at both the Hippodrome (on the State Fairgrounds in St. Paul), and also at the Coliseum (located on Lexington Avenue near University Avenue). Some of the really big games were held at the Minneapolis Arena, which had the advantage of having artificial ice - a real rarity back then.

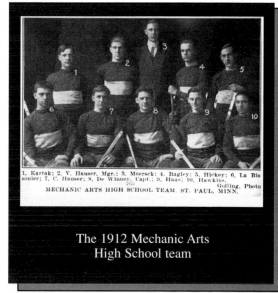

1. Kartak; 2. V. Hauser, Mgr.; 3. Moersck; 4. Bagley; 5. Hickey; 6. La Bissonier; 7. C. Hauser; 8. De Winney, Capt.; 9. Haas; 10. Hawkins.

Golling. Photo

MECHANIC ARTS HIGH SCHOOL TEAM, ST. PAUL, MINN.

The 1912 Mechanic Arts
High School team

The feeder programs for the high school kids were also growing. Countless youngsters who wanted to someday play for their hometown teams were taking up the game. Juvenile

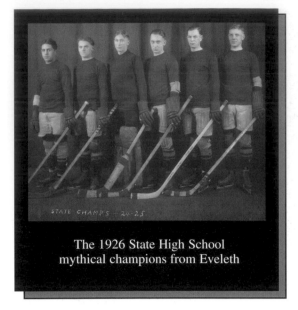

The 1926 State High School mythical champions from Eveleth

teams sprouted up, as well as organized youth leagues. In 1919 the first national youth hockey tournament for boys under high school age was sponsored by the Amateur Hockey Association of the United States (AHAUS).

As the decade of the 1920s began to unfold, the metro teams, tired of beating up on each other, began playing the northern teams more frequently. One of the first big games between the "North & South" took place in 1922, when St. Paul Central defeated Duluth Central 5-3 in Duluth. On March 19, 1923, Eveleth beat Mechanic Arts 9-2 in Eveleth, for what was billed as the second-coming of the State "Mythical" Championship - an event that hadn't taken place in some 20 years. The two teams then met again at the Minneapolis Arena on March 14, 1925, where Eveleth won again 3-2. Although the games were unofficial state championship games, they nonetheless proved that there had been a shift of power in the game of hockey in Minnesota. The North had made a statement that they wanted some respect, and in time, they would be heard loudly.

No actual statewide amateur tournament was held until 1926, when the Minnesota Recreation Association conducted the first of several yearly tournaments in Hibbing. Later, the Minneapolis Park Board and the Minneapolis Arena held yearly tournaments at the Minneapolis Arena. That same year the Northeastern Minnesota High School League was formed with teams from Duluth (Central and Cathedral) and the Iron Range cities. Duluth, Eveleth, Virginia, Hibbing and Chisholm all had enclosed rinks during this era, which put them on an equal playing field with the metro schools. (Two Harbors, Cloquet and Buhl were also fielding competitive high school teams at the time as well.) But, when you factor in the fact that it was much colder that far up north from the Twin Cities, the northern schools probably got an extra month or so of valuable ice-time over the metro schools. In addition, many of the teams played in the Senior City League, which included high school and college players from local senior teams in Northeastern Minnesota.

And it wasn't just the northern kids who were taking up this booming sport. Shattuck Military Academy in Faribault is thought to have organized the first ice hockey team in Southern Minnesota when they started a hockey program in 1922 -- due in large part to the fact that many of the school's faculty and students were from out East and were already familiar with the game. Throughout the 1920s Shattuck regularly played against many of the state's private schools and colleges who had started programs of their own, including Blake, De La Salle, Cretin, St. Paul Academy, St. Thomas Academy, Pillsbury Academy (in Owatonna), St. Paul Luther, St. Olaf College, and Carlton College. (Incidentally, Marty Falk, Wally Taft and Bud Wilkinson, all Shattuck products, went on to star for the U of M. So good was Wilkinson as a goalie, that in 1932, he led Shattuck to an undefeated season and Northwestern Academic Championship, and in the process, he went unscored upon over the entire season. Wilkinson then went on to even bigger stardom. The former Gopher football and hockey All-American defensive end, and goaltender, later became a nationally acclaimed football coach at the University of Oklahoma - where he led his Sooners to five straight undefeated seasons.)

As the sport branched out across the state, it also started to hit in the suburbs. In 1925 natural ice was installed in the Hippodrome (on the Ramsey County Fairgrounds) at White Bear Lake. (Incredibly, this was the only Twin Cities suburb to possess an indoor facility for the next 25 years.) White Bear Lake High School formed a varsity hockey team at that same time, thus becoming the first Twin Cities suburb to have a high school team. The Bears, who were led by future Gopher coach and NHL star Doc Romnes, played against the public schools of both Minneapolis and St. Paul, as well as the private schools of Cretin, St. Paul Academy and St. Thomas Academy.

In 1929 former St. Paul Athletic Club star, Nick Kahler, assembled a High School All-Star team called the Cardinals. The team, which played older, Senior teams, went on to win the Minneapolis Recreation League title that year. Members of the teams, most of whom were from South and West High Schools, included: Phil Perkins, Bill Oddson, Bubs Hutchinson, Red Malsed, Harry Melberg, John Scanlon, Evy Scotvold, Kelly Ness, Bill Cooley, Mack Xerxa and Bill Munns. One of the team's biggest games that year came against Eveleth High School. In a contest played at the Minneapolis Arena, the Cardinals edged Eveleth, who had not been defeated in the past three seasons of competition against Iron Range and Duluth schools, by the score of 2-1. An idea of the caliber of players that these teams possessed can be gathered from the fact that 5 of the 11 Minneapolis players and six of the 11 Eveleth skaters later played hockey professionally.

By the end of the decade hockey was sponsored by approximately 25 high schools in Minnesota. While most of the schools were both in the northeastern part of the state and in the Twin Cities area, high school hockey was slowly expanding. The 1930s however, were a difficult time in America and Minnesota was no exception. While many public schools in the state were forced to drop their hockey programs during the Great Depression due to financial hardship, other communities embraced the high school game as an inexpensive form of live entertainment. In addition, in many of the small towns during this era, where economies were more isolated and insulated from the rest of the world, the game flourished. Among the areas where high school hockey began to take off was northwestern Minnesota, where communities such as Roseau, Warroad, Thief River Falls, Hallock, Williams, Baudette, Crosby, Crookston, and even Detroit Lakes had begun building enclosed rinks. (Some of the schools, including Roseau and Hallock, used to also play the University of North Dakota, as well as in Senior leagues on a regular basis.)

High school hockey was finally taken off life support in the late 1930s, but went back on hiatus during the time surrounding WWII in the early 1940s. Here is how some of the local teams fared during this era: Cretin, led by John Quesnell, Doc Reardon, Bobby Dill, Bill Galligan, Bob Pates and Jim Mooney, posted a 45-10-2 record from 1936-39. In 1939

The 1928 Virginia High School squad played a tough schedule against many of the area's local senior teams

Humboldt, led by Bob Meyers, Joe Guertin, Elmer Monge and goalie Ray Gipple, winners of the St. Paul Public School title, defeated Minneapolis Marshall, winners of the Minneapolis City League title, before 2,600 fans at the St. Paul Auditorium by the score of 3-2 to win the Twin Cities Championship. Washington, under coach Frank Bergup, and led by Hal Younghans, Bob Graiziger, George Path and Joe Borsch won back-to-back St. Paul City titles in 1939 and 1940 with a combined 25-1-5 record. Coached by former Princeton goalie John Savage, Blake, led by Jock and Tel Thompson, Bert Martin, Lindley Burton, Monty Wells and captain John Brooks, went undefeated during the 1937-38 season. Washburn won their second and third championships in 1937 and 1939, while Roosevelt captured their first title in 1940. And, Max Sporer's St. Paul Academy team, led by future Gophers Bob Carley and Harry Bratnober, sported a 33-2-0 record from 1941-43.

Gene Aldrich

Gene Aldrich (the namesake for whom Aldrich Arena on White Bear Avenue in St. Paul is named for), was truly a pioneer, and someone who should be given sincere thanks to. His dedication to young people and his belief that playing sports was something for all to enjoy, led him to try and innovate new ways of making athletics a great experience for everyone. In addition to working to keep ticket prices low so students could always attend sporting events, it was Aldrich who also suggested that cheerleaders and ice pageant shows perform skating routines between periods, and that high school bands should be in the stands rooting on their teams.

During this era, countless Minnesota high schoolers went on to play professionally at various levels, among those who cracked the NHL included Bobby Dill (Cretin), Virgil Johnson (Minneapolis South), Cully Dahlstrom (Minneapolis South), Bill Moe (Minneapolis), Emil and Oscar Hanson (Minneapolis), Doc Romnes (White Bear Lake), Sam LoPresti (Eveleth), Frank Brimsek (Eveleth), Mike Karakas (Eveleth), Vic DesJardins (Eveleth), John Mariucci (Eveleth), LeRoy Goldsworthy (Two Harbors), and Fido Purpur (from Grand Forks, N.D.).

"Tourney-Time!"

1945: Eveleth vs. Thief River Falls

As our boys returned home victoriously from battle following WWII, hockey was thrust to the front burner in Minnesota. People just couldn't seem to get enough of this rough and tumble high school game, which was in desperate need of some new leadership and direction. Enter the savior, Gene Aldrich.

In February of 1944, Gene Aldrich, the longtime Director of Athletics for St. Paul's public schools, thought that a statewide high school hockey tournament would be a good idea. (There was an unofficial state tournament held in Roseau in 1942, when, then school superintendant C.D. Hollister organized a "northern school" high school hockey tournament, which was won by Thief River Falls.) Seeing how well the St. Paul schools were already drawing for their games, combined with the popularity of the game in northern Minnesota, Aldrich figured the interest and support would be there for a big-time tournament. With the complete approval of the State High School League and financial backing from St. Paul Book and Stationery owner Elmer Englebert, Aldrich began putting the pieces together for what would be the first of its kind in the United States. (Although the first "official" state tournament was claimed to have taken place in Massachusetts back in 1938, but with only 500 people in attendance, Minnesota's was the first "real" state high school hockey tournament, sponsored by the schools and done to this magnitude.)

At the time, in 1945, there were only 26 high schools playing varsity hockey in Minnesota. Nonetheless, Aldrich had devised a system of regional groupings in which the top eight teams from around the state would have equal opportunity to come together and compete for the right to be called champion. Those first eight teams competing in that inaugural tournament included: the powerhouses from Eveleth (Region 7), and Thief River Falls (Region 8), the darkhorse contenders from St. Paul Washington (Region 4), White Bear Lake (Region 2) and Rochester (Region 1), and the unknowns from St. Cloud Tech (Region 5), Granite Falls (Region 3) and Staples (Region 6).

The old St. Paul Auditorium

Now, for the most part, the majority of those aforementioned teams were moderately schooled in the modern rules of the game. But, a few of the schools, who had become accustomed over the years to playing the game under their own "house" rules, came down to the St. Paul Auditorium that winter, without even so much as a clue. For instance, Granite Falls and Staples had never played with blue lines before, and as a result didn't know what offsides were. In addition, the boys weren't familiar with how to line up for the opening face-off either. So, before (and during) the game, referee John Gustafson gave the boys a few quick lessons on how the game was played down in the big city. There were other issues that first go-around as well, such as the formality of uniforms. The Granite Falls and Staples teams came to play in hodge-podge variety of non-matching long pants and sweatshirts, with perhaps the most storied feature of their outfits being the newspapers and magazines that the players had stuffed into their pant legs for shin-guards. (Now that is truly old-time hockey!) It was a rough initiation for the teams, who also got their first taste of just how big a regulation sized rink was too.

With all the formalities out of the way, just after 2:00 PM on Thursday, February 15th, 1945, the Thief River Falls Prowlers and the White Bear

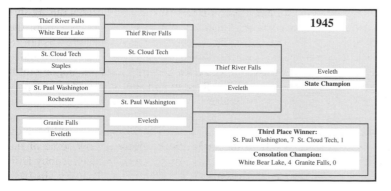

Thief River Falls				
White Bear Lake	Thief River Falls		**1945**	
St. Cloud Tech	St. Cloud Tech			
Staples		Thief River Falls		Eveleth
St. Paul Washington		Eveleth		**State Champion**
Rochester	St. Paul Washington			
Granite Falls	Eveleth			
Eveleth				

Third Place Winner:
St. Paul Washington, 7 St. Cloud Tech, 1

Consolation Champion:
White Bear Lake, 4 Granite Falls, 0

The 1945 Innaugural State Champs
from Eveleth

Lake Bears hit the ice before a crowd of 856 onlookers. When that first puck was dropped, so began history. The Bears opened the scoring of that first match, when at 9:29 of the first period, defenseman George Kieffer made an end-to-end rush and flipped a shot past Prowler goalie Ralph Engelstad for the tournament's very first score. Falls' winger Wes Hovie tied it up only to see Bears winger Bob Shearen score just 27 seconds later regain the lead. But the Falls rallied behind Bob Baker's game-tying goal at the end of two, followed by his eventual game-winner at 3:56 of the third. Thief River Falls hung on to win that first game by the score of 3-2.

While the second game of the afternoon saw St. Cloud Tech beat Staples 2-0 on goals by Chet Jaskowiak and Bill Clark, the first evening game saw Washington's Julius Struntz tally the first hat trick of the tourney, en route to a 5-0 drubbing over Rochester. (Rochester made quite a showing, considering the fact that they didn't have a high school program until the early 1940s. Even more amazing is the fact that Rochester sits in the only county in the state of Minnesota that does not have a natural lake within its boundaries. However, they were able to play in the Mayo Auditorium, which featured artificial ice as early as the late 1930s.)

In the last game of the day, as fate would have it, the underdog Granite Falls Granites were matched up against the mighty Eveleth Golden Bears. The Granites, who wound up borrowing uniforms and some equipment from nearby St. Paul Monroe High School (although goalie Gorman Velde decided to stick with his trusty football helmet), had no idea what they were in for. Eveleth, on the other hand, showed up like they owned the joint. They came in sporting jerseys from the Eveleth Junior College team, with breezers, skates and sticks that were given to them by the NHL's Chicago Blackhawks team, which then had its team training camp in nearby Virginia.

In what still stands today as the most lopsided win in Tournaments history, Eveleth waxed Granite Falls 16-0. Falls didn't stand a chance against the Golden Bears, who usually played against amateur junior and senior teams from the Iron Range in 20-minute period games, rather than the typical 12-minute periods of high school games. Led by legendary coach Cliff Thompson, Eveleth was merciless. For the Granite Falls players, who had to have the off-sides rules explained to them throughout the game, it was a rude welcoming. Neil Celley, Wally Grant Pat Finnegan and Milan Begich all had hat tricks for the Golden Bears, while Eveleth goalie John Drobnick had only one stop in the entire game. The half-ice shot still stands today in the record book: "LEAST STOPS BY A GOALTENDER" — ONE, by Eveleth's Ron Drobnick."

The championship semifinals were both runaways. While Thief River Falls smoked St. Cloud 12-0, on four Wes Hovie goals and three by Les Vigness, Eveleth beat up on Washington 10-0. In that game, Pat Finnegan, Wally Grant and Neil Celley showed why they are still to this day regarded as the greatest ever high school hockey line in state history. While Celley and Finnegan each scored hat tricks, Wally Grant (who would later skate as a member of the famous "G" line at the University of Michigan), tallied four goals of his own.

In the championship game Eveleth battled Thief River Falls in a game of northern giants. When Eveleth's Pat Finnegan scored the game's first two goals within the first three minutes of the game, most thought it was over. But the Falls hung in there, behind goals from Gene Brossalt at 4:12 of the first, followed by Watt Vigness' two goals in the second to put his team ahead 3-2. This maneuver apparently upset Grant, who decided to take the game into his own hands from that point on. He was unstoppable after that, scoring yet another two goals in the third. That would prove to be enough for the Golden Bears. With Drobnick standing firm in goal, the Eveleth juggernaut rolled on to win the state's first-ever title by the score of 4-3. For the undefeated Bears, it was simply business as usual - and a warm-up of things to come in the future.

The inaugural tournament proved to be a reasonably successful venture for Aldrich. In the end, some 8,434 spectators flocked to the St. Paul Auditorium, paying more than $4,000. in admissions fees -- good for a $135.06 profit. From this meager beginning, the High School Tournament was born. Seeing how successful the event was, the Minnesota State High School League (MSHSL) decided to take full control of the tournament that next year and assumed complete responsibility for its financing as well.

1946: Roseau vs. Rochester

The 1946 Tournament saw the return of several teams, as well as the addition of a few new ones. Heavily favored Eveleth was back, along with Rochester, White Bear Lake, Granite Falls and St. Cloud. While Minneapolis West, St. Paul Johnson and Roseau, led by its bespectacled superstar forward Rube Bjorkman, came in as tournament rookies.

In the opening round, Eveleth got a late goal by Tom Pavelich to barely etch out a tough St. Cloud team, while Rochester's Allen Gilkenson scored at 3:25 of the first overtime period to beat West. While Roseau's Lowell Ulvin and White Bear's Bob Shearen each scored in the first period of the initial evening game, it was Bob Harris scoring the overtime winner just three minutes into the extra session to give Roseau a 2-1 victory. Then in the last game of the day, Johnson's three big guns of Jim Rentstrom, Jim Sedin and Orv Anderson each scored two goals apiece to lead the Governors past Granite Falls 6-2.

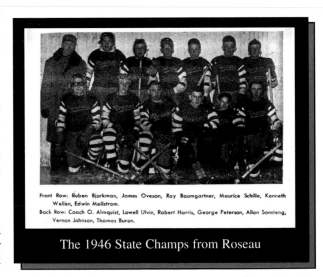

Front Row: Ruben Bjorkman, James Oveson, Ray Baumgartner, Maurice Schille, Kenneth Wellen, Edwin Mellstrom.
Back Row: Coach O. Almquist, Lowell Ulvin, Robert Harris, George Peterson, Allan Sonsteng, Vernon Johnson, Thomas Buran.

The 1946 State Champs from Roseau

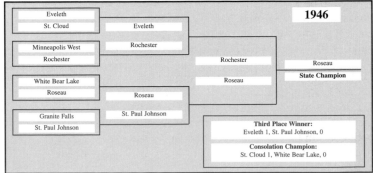

					1946
Eveleth					
St. Cloud	Eveleth				
Minneapolis West	Rochester				
Rochester			Rochester	Roseau	
White Bear Lake			Roseau	**State Champion**	
Roseau	Roseau				
Granite Falls	St. Paul Johnson				
St. Paul Johnson					

Third Place Winner:
Eveleth 1, St. Paul Johnson, 0

Consolation Champion:
St. Cloud 1, White Bear Lake, 0

Oscar Almquist

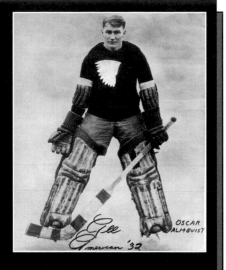

Eveleth's Oscar Almquist played goalie for the high school team from 1923 through 1927. After a two-year stint with Virginia of the Arrowhead Amateur League, he went on to star at St. Mary's College in Winona, where he earned All-American honors in 1932 & '33. Almquist then began his professional career, first with the Eveleth Rangers, followed by three seasons with the St. Paul Saints. He then went into high school coaching, the career for which he would become legendary. After coaching for a year at tiny Williams in 1937, Almquist moved to Roseau, where he began coaching, and also playing for the amateur Cloverleaf's. In 1941 the "Big O" became the team's head coach, a position he would hold until 1967. During this period Roseau High School became a perennial power winning state titles in 1946, 1958, 1959, and 1961. The Rams appeared in the state event 14 times, and in addition to the state championships they were runner-ups on four occasions. Before retiring to become the school's athletic director and principal, the "Giant of the North" had posted a record of 404-148-21, including a 49-game winning streak from 1957 through 1959.

In the semis, Rochester's Ray Purvis and Allen Gilkenson both hooked up for a pair of goals, as Rochester came up with the tourney's first big upset, knocking off the defending champions from Eveleth 2-1. In the other semifinal contest Roseau's Rube Bjorkman, who wore goggles much like a WWII aviator, scored the 2-1 game-winner at 8:21 of the third period to beat Johnson. In the finals, Rochester hoped to make history, but was denied. The masked marvel, Rube Bjorkman, took the game into his own hands, scoring a hat trick, en route to leading his Golden Rams to a 6-0 victory and their first championship.

1947: Johnson vs. Roseau
The 1947 Tournament started out with a bang, as all of the opening round matchups were won by shut outs. The masked marvel, Rube Bjorkman, pulled another hat trick out of his bag in the first game, leading Roseau to a 5-0 win over St. Cloud. Eveleth also rolled into the semi's, blanking Willmar 6-0 on Dick Peterson's hat trick. And, while Dave Riepke's three goals led Johnson to a 4-0 win over Rochester, West out-muscled South St. Paul 6-0, with Bill MacFadden and Lloyd Lundeen tallying two goals each.

The amazing Bjorkman continued his antics, scoring yet another hat trick in the 4-1 drubbing of Eveleth in the first semifinal game. Johnson also advanced on goals by Jim Rentstrom, Howie Eckstrom and Dave Riepke, to give the Governors a 3-1 victory over West.

Then, on Saturday, February 15, 1947, in front of a packed Auditorium of some 7,404 fans - many of whom arrived via street-cars to downtown St. Paul, Roseau took on Johnson in what would turn out to be one of the classics. Interestingly, it had become a North vs. South affair at the tournament, with the battle lines clearly drawn in the dingy-gray Auditorium ice sheet. Defending champion Roseau, who finished the season at 13-2-3 (having lost twice to Crookston Cathedral), had nine of their players back from the year before. Bjorkman, who centered Dan Baumgartner and Tom Buran, was the star, while defensemen Vernon Johnson and Lowell Ulvin, both 200-pounders, seemed to be an impenetrable force. Roseau coach Oscar Almquist, himself a legend in Minnesota hockey, had his boys ready to go. Johnson, on the other hand, came into the finals with an amazing 31-1 record with its only blemish coming on a loss to Blake. Coach Rube Gustafson's Governors, chock full of Swedes and Italians, were led by the formidable first line of Dave Reipke, Jim Renstrom, and Jim Sedin, with Orville Anderson and Howard Eckstrom on defense.

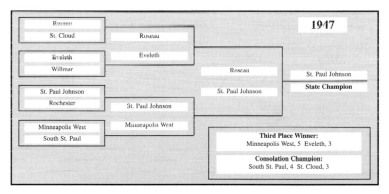

The game got underway with Johnson scoring at 2:58 of the second on a goal by center Orvin Halweg. Bjorkman then answered early in the third to tie it at one apiece. The game was tight from there on in, with Johnson goalie Jack McGahn playing large. The Johnson players seemed focused on stopping Bjorkman, a strategy that seemed to be working. Then, with just 1:18 to play, Johnson defenseman Howard Eckstrom dished to Dave Reipke at mid-ice. Reipke, rushing in, deked around the Roseau defenders, and flipped the game-winner over Roseau goalie Maurice Schille's left shoulder for the game-winner. Johnson had slain the giant.

1948: Eveleth vs. Warroad
In 1948, for the first time ever, the defending champion did not make a return trip to the Tournament. That's because Johnson was knocked-off in the regional championships by newcomer Harding, from St. Paul. The favorite of the tourney however, seemed to be Eveleth, who was led by All-Stater John Matchefts and a freshman phenom by the name of John Mayasich. Other contenders that year included Rochester and St. Cloud, (both making their fourth consecutive appearances), South St. Paul, and first-timer's Warroad, Minneapolis Washburn and St. Louis Park.

The 1947 State Champs from St. Paul Johnson

On February 19th, in the opening game of the tourney, St. Cloud, led by a pair of Jim Broker goals, beat Washburn 4-2. In the second game of the day, despite Rochester goalie Jack Nichols' 41 saves, Eveleth trounced Rochester 7-2, thanks to multiple goals from John Matchefts, John Mayasich and Dick Peterson. Harding's honeymoon was then abruptly ended by South St. Paul in the first evening game, despite peppering Packer goalie Rudy Lindbeck with 41 shots. South St. Paul's Henry Bruggeman scored both goals in the 2-1 victory. Then, in the last game of the day, Warroad, led by George Guibault's four goals and Max Oshie's three, bulldozed over a shell-shocked St. Louis Park team, 10-0. Despite giving up 10 goals, Park keeper Jim Mattson (who would later star at the U of M), registered an amazing 49 stops -- 20 of which came in the second period, a record which stood for several years.

John Matchefts' four goals easily led Eveleth past St. Cloud 8-1, in the semi's, while in the other semifinal, five different Warroad boys tallied for a 5-3 win over South St. Paul. On February 21st, before a sell-out Auditorium crowd, Eveleth hit the ice to battle fellow northerners Warroad. Eveleth jumped out early, only to see Warroad's Oshie brothers, Max and Buster, keep it close. But John Matchefts and Tony Tassoni each scored hat tricks, as the powerhouse Eveleth went on to beat Warroad 8-2, for their second title in four years.

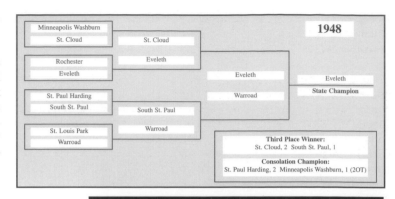

1949: Eveleth vs. Williams

In 1949, because it was determined that the southern part of Minnesota was exhibiting less interest in hockey than that of the Twin Cities and northern Minnesota, the format was changed for determining the regional champions. The result was a change in three regions that ultimately made it possible for more suburban metro schools to enter the Tournament. The champions of those three new regions who entered the field that year included Minneapolis Central (Region One), Williams (Region Three), and St. Louis Park (Region Six). The other five finalists included the returning champs from Eveleth, Warroad, Minneapolis Washburn, White Bear Lake, and St. Paul Murray - first time winners of the St. Paul title.

Eveleth, led by John Mayasich's hat trick, came out right where they left off the year before, crushing White Bear 6-0, despite Bear's goalie Dick Doyle's 42 saves. Buster Oshie led Warroad with three goals, while George Guibault and Sammy Gibbons each scored twice as Warroad advanced to the semis by beating Central 7-1. The evening games were much

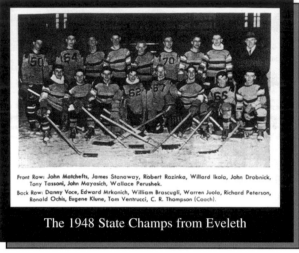

Front Row: John Matchefts, James Stanaway, Robert Rozinka, Willard Ikola, John Drobnick, Tony Tassoni, John Mayasich, Wallace Perushek.
Back Row: Danny Voce, Edward Mrkonich, William Brascugli, Warren Juola, Richard Peterson, Ronald Ochis, Eugene Klune, Tom Ventrucci, C. R. Thompson (Coach).

The 1948 State Champs from Eveleth

tighter affairs, as Williams beat Washburn 2-0 on goals by Chet Lundsten and Sid Bryduck. Then, in the final game, Murray edged out St. Louis Park in a 2-1 overtime thriller, as winger Tom Wegleitner scored on a power play to give Murray the victory.

In the first semifinal game, Eveleth found themselves in a rematch of the last year's title game against Warroad. Eveleth didn't even make it close, rolling over Warroad 8-0 on yet another hat trick by John Mayasich. His wingmate John Matchefts added a goal and three assists to lead the Golden Bears in a laugher. The other semi would prove to be a barn-burner, as Williams and Murray battled for three overtimes. Down 3-2, Murray pulled their goalie with 55 seconds to go in regulation. Shortly thereafter, center Tom Wegleitner responded by scoring and sending the game into overtime. It was back and forth for two overtime periods, until forward Chet Lundsten tallied early in the third extra session to give Williams a 4-3 victory.

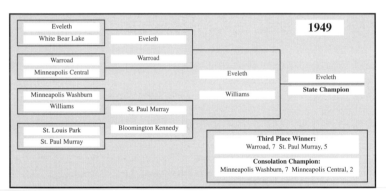

Once again, the title would be given to a northern Minnesota team that year, as Eveleth found themselves pitted against tiny Williams High School for all the beans. More than 7,000 fans jammed into the Auditorium's wooden seats to watch the Williams Wolves (a town of only 375 souls which was coached by Eveleth native Al Braga), try and make history. Coach Cliff Thompson's Eveleth team came out smoking in the championship game, as Ron Castellano opened the scoring late in the first. Williams kept it close through two though, as John McKinnon beat Eveleth goalie Willard Ikola on a penalty shot late in the second to make it 2-1. But then John Matchefts and Ron Castellano each scored to bust it open in third. John Mayasich added his seventh goal of the tournament at the 8:10 mark to give Eveleth a 4-1 victory, and their second consecutive championship.

Front Row: John Matchefts, John Drobnick, Dan Voce, Ronald Castellano, Willard Ikola, John Mayasich, John Nelson, Tom Ventrucci, Robert McCarty.
Back Row: C. R. Thompson, Coach—Thomas Roberts, David Hendrickson, LaVerne Hammer, Edward Mrkonich, William Brascugli, Robert Halstrom, James Mudge, Jack Gornik, Mgr.

The 1949 State Champs from Eveleth

1950: Eveleth vs. Williams

Riding their remarkable 47-game winning streak, Eveleth once again entered the 1950 Tournament as the heavy favorite. The juggernaut from the Iron Range flew through Region Seven by absolutely annihilating both Duluth Central, 23-0, and then Grand Rapids 18-0, before finally beating International Falls 5-1. The Falls also got into the tourney field via the "back door." (In those years, Regions Seven and Eight alternated in sending their second place teams to the tournament to represent the "geographically-nonexistent" Region Three.) Also joining the Bears and Broncos in the big dance were Williams, St. Paul Murray, St. Cloud, Minneapolis Central, Minneapolis South, and South St. Paul.

Johnny Mayasich got a pair of goals while Dan Voce added three of his own as Eveleth continued its domination by spanking Central 6-0 in the opener. St. Cloud took care of South St. Paul in the afternoon game 4-1, while Williams, led by Ray Beauchamp's four goals, beat South 8-2. The best was saved until last though, as International Falls battled Murray into double-overtime. The two squads went into the extra session tied at one apiece, when, in the first overtime, Bill Wegleitner scored at 2:30 to give Murray a 2-1 lead. But, not to be outdone, the Dougherty brothers, Bill and Dick, combined to tie it up less than a minute later. Then, just after the opening face-off of the second overtime, the

Dougherty's struck again, this time with Dick scoring on a pass from Bill to give Williams a 3-2 win. (At this point of the tourney's history, overtimes weren't sudden death.)

In the first semifinal contest, John Mayasich proved why he is still to this day the best player ever to hail from Minnesota, when he put on a clinic, scoring an amazing six goals in Eveleth's 7-0 shellacking of St. Cloud. The other semi saw Cinderella Williams beat International Falls by the score of 4-2, thanks to a couple of first period goals by Dick Lundgren and Sid Bryduck as well as a pair in the second by senior forward Chet Lundsten.

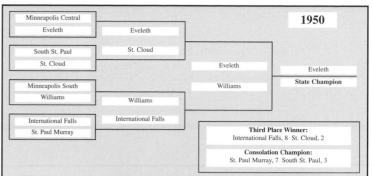

Another capacity crowd gathered at the Auditorium to witness the championship game rematch between Eveleth and tiny Williams. Eveleth captain Willard Ikola, who was coming off of two consecutive shut outs, knew he would have to play big in order to beat the Wolves from Williams. Mayasich opened the scoring by notching two quick goals for the Bears. Dan Voce then put Eveleth up 3-0, only to see Chet Lundsten score two of his own, followed by a Ray Beauchamp wrister over Ikola's sprawled out blocker to tie it up late in the third. Then, with only 20 seconds left in the game, Castellano hit Mayasich on a quick centering pass at the top of the circle. Mayasich deked, and fired a low snapper into the back of the net to give Eveleth its third consecutive title, and its 50th consecutive victory.

1951: Eveleth, er... Mayasich vs. Johnson

In 1951 Eveleth arrived in St. Paul with the title of "three-time defending champion" in front of its name. The boys from the Range were somewhat of an enigma with the Twin Citians, who by now had heard of them much like they had heard about Paul Bunyan and Superman, with a sort of mythical God-like connotation. Led by All-Staters John Mayasich, Ron Castellano and Dan Voce, the Golden Bears came in with an amazing 66-game winning streak, fresh off of yet another undefeated 16-0 season in which they scored 179 goals, while yielding only 30.

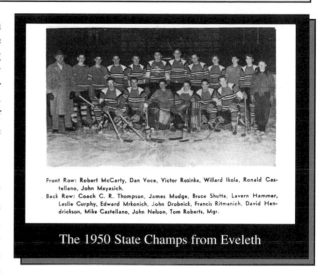

The 1950 State Champs from Eveleth

In the opening game of the first round, Thief River Falls, which was riding a 16-game winning streak of its own, edged out St. Cloud 3-2 on three first period goals by Alan Steenerson, Jack Erickson, and Darryl Lund. St. Cloud's sibling trio of Ron, Don and Dick Saatzer rallied their team back late to get to within one, but in the end they just couldn't beat Falls' keeper goalie Bill Maruska for the equalizer. In Game Two, Johnson handed White Bear a big doughnut, beating them 7-0 thanks to a couple of two-goal performances by both Bob Youngquist and Hugo Anderson. In the first evening game, Minneapolis Southwest, led by the Meredith brothers, Bob and Dick, edged St. Paul Murray 2-1. Then, in a replay of the last years' finals, Eveleth took on Williams in the nightcap. When Mayasich scored just 57 seconds into the game, people knew it was going to be ugly. He didn't stop there though, going on to score three more in that first period alone, as the Golden Bears hammered the Wolves 12-0.

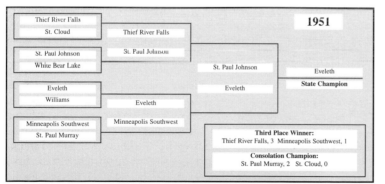

In the semis, John Mayasich showed why is the greatest, scoring an unbelievable tournament record seven goals against Southwest. After a quick goal by Eveleth winger Dan Voce, Mayasich pumped in three quick ones of his own in the first period. Southwest came back to make it interesting behind three goals by the Meredith brothers. That was apparently all the wake up call Mayasich would need though, as he scored again in the second, and added another hat trick in the third. The Castellano's added one each as well for the Bears, as Eveleth cruised to an 11-5 victory. That put the Bears into the title match against Johnson, who had beaten Thief River Falls in the other semifinal contest by the score of 6-2, thanks to a pair of goals each from Bob Youngquist and Ray Youngberg.

On Saturday, February 24th, 1951, in front of 7,163 Auditorium fans, Eveleth hit the ice to try and make it four-straight crowns. Johnson Coach Rube Gustafson knew that he would have to get a near perfect performance from his boys if they were going to have a chance. There was speculation before the game as to what kind of defense the Governors were going to throw at the Bears. Some teams had achieved a marginal level of success against them that season by running a "1-5" defense, in which one skater stayed at the blue line and the other four hung around the goalie. Or, perhaps he would just have the other four hang around Mayasich? Deciding to play it straight and take their chances, Johnson came out strong and held the Bears scoreless through the first on tough goaltending by Johnson keeper Warren Strelow. But, just a minute into the second, who else but John Mayasich beat Strelow to go up 1-0. Ten minutes later he scored again, and decided to add two more in the third just for good measure. His fourth and final goal of the game was a beauty, beating Strelow on a 20-foot blast from the point. Johnson's Bob Schmidt added a meaningless goal late, but to no avail, as Eveleth and John Mayasich prevailed 4-1. For Mayasich, who finished with 15 goals and three assists for 18 points, which is still a tournament record, it was sweet.

The 1951 State Champs from Eveleth

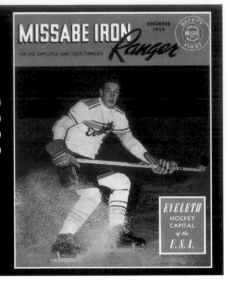

John Mayasich's Unbelievable High School Hockey Tournament Records:

Most All Time Total Points:	46 (1948-1951)
Most All Time Total Goals:	36 (1948-1951)
Most Consec. Games Scoring a Goal:	12 (1948-1951)
Most All Time Hat Tricks:	7 (1948-1951)
Most Points One Tournament:	18 (1951)
Most Goals One Tournament:	15 (1951)
Most Points One Game:	8 (1951)
Most Goals One Game:	7 (1951)
Most Points One Period:	5 (1951)
Most Goals One Period:	4 (1951)

"I remember that St. Paul Johnson game was a tough one," recalled Mayasich, "and there was a lot of pressure on us to keep the winning streak going through that fourth year. When it was all over we couldn't believe what we had done, it was very special."

"When we were growing up, we didn't think about college hockey or the Olympics or the pros," he added. "We thought about making the high school team and getting to the state tournament. Eveleth had won the first state tournament in 1945, when I was in sixth grade, and that gave us something to strive for. In Eveleth you were expected to win and it was just assumed you would. As a result, we didn't take any time for sightseeing in St. Paul. All we did was watch and play hockey."

1952: Eveleth vs. Hibbing

Defending champion Eveleth made its return to the tournament via the "back-door," fresh off of having their unprecedented 85-game winning streak snapped by Hibbing in the regional finals. In the opening game, Humboldt beat Winona 2-1. Winona forward Roger Neitze opened the scoring in the first, only to see Humboldt's Carl Weber tie it up in the second. Winona ran out of gas in the end though, as Humboldt's Bernie Weber got the game-winner with 3:45 left to go. Despite Dick Larson's 33 saves, Winona lost the game 2-1. The afternoon match featured the Mayasich-less Golden Bears from Eveleth against Thief River Falls. Eveleth winger Mike Castellano's first period goal was matched by Falls' winger Jack Erickson's at 2:08 of the third to make it 1-1. Eveleth rallied though, behind goals from Jack Curphy, and Dave Rodda, to give the Bears a 3-1 win - their 13th straight tournament victory. In the evening sessions, Southwest beat Johnson 2-1 on goals by Ray Karnuth and Don Berg, while Hibbing smashed St. Cloud 10-0, on hat tricks from both George Jetty and Jim Lipovetz.

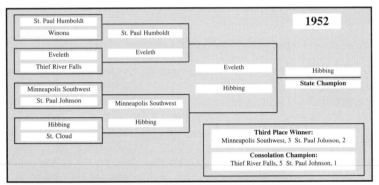

In the semis, Dave Hendrickson and Bruce Shutte each got two goals for Eveleth as they beat up on Humboldt 6-1. The second semifinal featured Hibbing against Southwest, in what would prove to be a battle of solid goaltending. Both keepers, Don Vaia from Hibbing and Howie Cammack from Southwest, played big through two, as the score remained 0-0 going into the third. Finally, at 4:43 of the third period, Hibbing's George Jetty put the Bluejackets up 1-0 on a low wrister. Then, less than two minutes later Hibbing's Jim Lipovetz made it 2-0 on a nice pass from Jack Petroske. Jim Blanchard scored for Southwest late, but Vaia held strong in net as Hibbing went on to win by the final of 2-1.

The stage was set for an all-northern Minnesota championship match, with the perfect storyline. Because Hibbing had beaten Eveleth just a week earlier in the regions, everyone figured that the Bears would be eager to exact revenge on their Iron Range pals. Mike Castellano opened the scoring for Eveleth at 9:15 of the first on a nice slapper from Palkovich. Then in the second, Hibbing fired back to take a commanding 3-1 lead on goals by Jack Petroske, George Jetty, and Howard Wallene. At 1:21 of the third, Jetty tallied again for Hibbing, only to see Eveleth's Dave Hendrickson and Bruce Shutte each score to make it 4-3 late. But Don Vaia stood on his head, turning back 13 shots in the third period alone to get the win. For Hibbing it was their first championship. For Eveleth, who had won five of the first seven Tournaments, it was the end of a dynasty. (Incidentally, as of the year 2000, Eveleth's 85-game winning streak still remains the second longest ever in the history of high school hockey in the US.)

Left to right: George Jetty, Herbert Sellars, Jack Petroske, William Webb, Frank Fields, Donald Holcomb, Donald Vaia, William Fena, Howard Wallene, James Lipovetz, Jerry Callengar, Martin Sundvall, Joe Ban, Stu. Mgr., Mauritz Uhrbom, Coach.

The 1952 State Champs from Hibbing

1953: Johnson vs. Warroad

Behind by Jack Stoskopf's two goals and one assist, and Billy Christian's one goal and two assists, Warroad kicked off the opening round by blanking Humboldt 5-0. South St. Paul and Roseau got together for the second game of the day, with each team scoring two in the first. Both goaltenders, Henry Metcalf of South St. Paul, who posted 19 saves, and Roger Norberg of Roseau, who saved 12 of his own, played marvelously and forced the game into overtime. Then, at 3:25 of the extra session, Bob Sharrow fed Dick Lick on a beautiful one-timer to give South St. Paul a 3-2 victory.

In the first evening game, Southwest played Eveleth as tough as they had been played in several years at the Tournament. With the score tied at 0-0, Southwest's Jack Thomas beat Eveleth goalie Tom Yurkovich only nine seconds after the puck dropped in the second period. Eveleth winger Bob Kochevar tied it up at 8:20 in the third period, and then Gerald Palkovich got the game-winner with less than a minute to go in the game to give Eveleth a 2-1 win. Finally, Johnson, who was led by coach Rube Gustafson, and St. Louis Park got together for what would prove to be second longest game in the history of the tournament -- four overtimes! Johnson opened the scoring in the game on Jack Hoistrom's rebound goal at 7:34 of the second period, only to see Park's Dennis Stedman tie it up at 7:32 of the third to send it into overtime. From there both goalies, Gene Picha and Gerald Norberg played fabulously. But, at 2:28 of the fourth overtime, with the players barely able to move from exhaustion, Johnson's Roger Bertelson slapped a 47-foot prayer that somehow got past Norberg's stick and found the back of the net. The Governors won the thriller 2-1.

The opening semifinal contest featured something that hadn't been seen in the history of the Tournament -- Eveleth got pummeled. Roy and Rod Anderson put the Governors up 2-0 in the first, and then Bob Wabman added three goals of his own, as Johnson beat the heck out of the Bears by the score of 7-1. In the other semi, Warroad and South St. Paul battled back and forth for the better part of two periods before Roger Christian finally beat Henry Metcalf at the 6:16 mark to give Warroad a 1-0 advantage. Jack Stoskopf made it 2-0 just two minutes after that, only to see Dick Lick bring it back to 2-1 a few minutes later. But Bob Lewis played great between the pipes as Warroad held on to beat the Packers 2-1.

In the finals, Johnson, which won the title in 1947, found themselves pitted against the Christian brothers from Warroad. Johnson came out strong, taking the early lead on two first-period goals by Roger Bertelson, followed by two more in the second by Rod Anderson and Ray Karnuth. Warroad finally got on the board at 6:33 of the third when Roger Christian's pass found Jack Stoskopf's stick in front of the net. Johnson went on to win the contest 4-1, behind some great goaltending from Gene Picha. The real hero of the game though, was probably Warroad's goalie Bob Lewis, who came up with an astonishing 39 saves in the losing effort. With the win, Johnson broke the five-year stranglehold of championships that the northern schools had enjoyed at the Tournament.

Front Row: Roger Johnson, Gary Shea, Jack Holstrom, Gene Picha, Duane Quatman, Glenn Peterson, William Johnson.
Back Row: Larry Paul, Jerry Gehrig, Robert Wahman, Rod Anderson, Roy Anderson, Roger Bertelson, Ray Karnuth, Rube Gustafson (Coach).

The 1953 State Champs from St. Paul Johnson

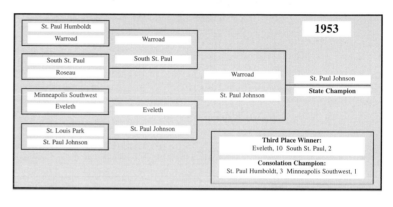

1953

St. Paul Humboldt				
Warroad	Warroad			
South St. Paul	South St. Paul			
Roseau		Warroad		St. Paul Johnson
Minneapolis Southwest		St. Paul Johnson	**State Champion**	
Eveleth	Eveleth			
St. Louis Park	St. Paul Johnson			
St. Paul Johnson				

Third Place Winner:
Eveleth, 10 South St. Paul, 2

Consolation Champion:
St. Paul Humboldt, 3 Minneapolis Southwest, 1

1954: Thief River Falls vs. Eveleth
Bob Helgeland's hat trick in the opener kicked off the tourney, as Thief River Falls continued their undefeated season with a 6-1 win over South. South St. Paul beat up Duluth Central 6-0 in the afternoon game, as Dick Lick led the way with a pair of goals for the Packers. The first evening game featured Wayzata and Johnson, which came out and scored on their first shot and didn't look back from there. In addition to Rod Anderson, Stu Anderson, and Jim Pasuik, who each had a pair of goals, a kid by the name of Herb Brooks also added three assists in Johnson's 7-0 shellacking. Then, in the last game, Eveleth beat Harding 5-2 on a pair of Jerry Judnick goals. Dick Jinks scored two for Harding, but the Bears pounced on Harding goaltender Ed Kohn, with 36 shots on goal to seal the deal.

Thief River Falls' forward Darryl Durgin netted a hat trick while Lyle Guttu added a pair in the first semifinal contest, as the Prowlers tallied five in the third to beat South St. Paul by the final of 8-1. Then, in the other semifinal game, Eveleth earned its sixth trip in seven years to the finals by beating Johnson 3-2. In what proved to be a very tight game, Eveleth jumped ahead in the first on goals by Gene Klun and Dave Rodda.

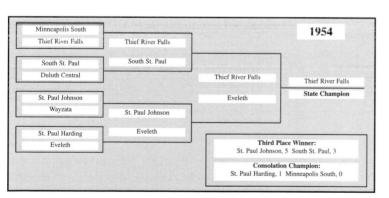

1954

Minneapolis South				
Thief River Falls	Thief River Falls			
South St. Paul	South St. Paul			
Duluth Central		Thief River Falls		Thief River Falls
St. Paul Johnson		Eveleth	**State Champion**	
Wayzata	St. Paul Johnson			
St. Paul Harding	Eveleth			
Eveleth				

Third Place Winner:
St. Paul Johnson, 5 South St. Paul, 3

Consolation Champion:
St. Paul Harding, 1 Minneapolis South, 0

Johnson cut the deficit to 2-1 when Stu Anderson beat Eveleth goalie Tom Beste on a low wrister. But, Bob Kochevar tallied with less than 30 seconds left in the second to put the game away. Johnson's Jack Hoistrom added one late, but the Governors came up short losing 3-2.

On Saturday, February 27th, 1954, in front of 7,433 fans, Thief River Falls took the ice against Eveleth for the right to be called champion. The Prowlers were a disciplined team that were led by Lyle Guttu, Marv Jorde, Joe Poole, and the defensive tandem of Mike McMahon and Les Sabo, who loved to mix it up at the blue line. Eveleth, on the other hand featured Tom Beste, Jerry Judnick, Gene Klun, Bob Kochevar, Jerry Norman, Ed Oswald, and Dave Rodda. The game proved to be a defensive battle from the get-go, with both teams testing each other early. Finally, at 11:10 of the first, after peppering Eveleth keeper Tom Beste with a flurry of shots, Marv Jorde scored on a rebound to put the Prowlers up 1-0. The Falls just kept on coming after that, scoring three more goals in the second from both Lyle Guttu, who had a pair, and Jorde - who added one more only six seconds after Guttu's second wrister. Eveleth's Bob Kochevar did manage to score late, but Falls' goalie Jack Hoppe hung on down the stretch to lead his team to a 4-1 victory and their first state title.

(Incidentally, Harding went on to win the consolation title 1-0 over Minneapolis South. What is significant about that is the fact that Dick Jinks scored his eighth goal of the tournament in that game, which was also the exact number of goals that his team scored during the entire Tournament. That amazing individual performance is a record that still stands today.)

1955: Johnson vs. Southwest
Southwest, which lost to the Eveleth in both 1951 and 1953, was finally able to exact some sweet revenge against their old foes from the Range in the tourney opener, as the Indians went on to tomahawk the Golden Bears 4-1 thanks to three goals by Merv

Front Row: Neil Aase (Student Manager), Marvin Jorde, Jack Hoppe, Lyle Guttu, Denny Rolfe (Coach).
Back Row: Loren Vraa, James Zavoral, Robert Helgeland, Bradley Teal, Mike McMahon, Lester Sabo, Joe Poole, Darryl Durgin, Jack Quesnell.
Not on picture—Rodney Collins.

The 1954 State Champs from Thief River Falls

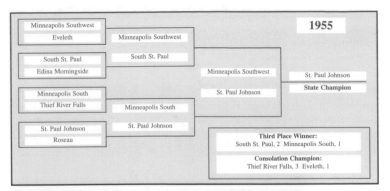

1955

Minneapolis Southwest			
Eveleth	Minneapolis Southwest		
South St. Paul	South St. Paul		
Edina Morningside		Minneapolis Southwest	
Minneapolis South		St. Paul Johnson	St. Paul Johnson
Thief River Falls	Minneapolis South		**State Champion**
St. Paul Johnson	St. Paul Johnson		
Roseau			

Third Place Winner:
South St. Paul, 2 Minneapolis South, 1
Consolation Champion:
Thief River Falls, 3 Eveleth, 1

Front Row: Karl Dahlberg, Herb Brooks, Roger Wigens, Tom Wahman, Jack Halstrom, John Patton.
Second Row: R. Gustafson (Coach), Rodney Anderson, Chuck Rodgers, Ken Fanger, Bill McKechnie, Ryan Ostebo, Stu Anderson, Tony Hudalla (Student Manager).

The 1955 State Champs from St. Paul Johnson

Meredith from Roger Rovick. In the afternoon matchup Edina showed just how "green" they really were, getting nailed by the South St. Paul Packers 4-0 on goals by Bob Sharrow, John Roth, Jack O'Brien and Bob Johnson.

The third game of the tourney would prove to be, arguably, the most famous of all-time. That's because the contest between Minneapolis South and Thief River Falls lasted an incredible 11 overtimes, the longest game ever to be played in Tournament history. South, the Minneapolis city champion, had seven players back from its tournament team of the year before, and felt good about their chances against the defending champs. The game started out innocently enough, with Dale Rasmussen putting South ahead 1-0 in the first, on a slapper from just inside the left circle. The Falls' came back to take a 2-1 lead on back-to-back goals by Loren Vraa and Glenn Carlson. Vraa's goal came off of Joe Poole's rebound in front of South goalie Roger Evenson, while Carlson's was a 30-foot blast from the left point. Then, at 6:03 of the third, Jerry Westby scored the tying goal for South on a deflected dribbler, to send the game into overtime.

As the teams began to play the five-minute overtimes, South's goalie Rog Evenson and Rod Collins of Thief River Falls both played tremendously. Time and again they stuffed everything that came their way. While Vraa and Poole both missed open goals in the first, South's Jim Westby missed a rebound from a Larry Alm shot in the second overtime that was a sure-goal. Finally, after nine overtimes, and no end in sight, Tournament officials decided to start the evening game between Johnson and Roseau at 11:33 pm. The two games then rotated in-between periods, giving the players a much needed rest between games. After Johnson's Ken Fanger scored at 6:32 of the first period to put the Govs ahead 1-0, South and the Falls then came back out to play a 10th overtime. Still scoreless, the game's switched back one more time. Perhaps inspired, Roseau goalie John Almquist and Johnson goalie Tom Wahman both earned shut outs for their second period games. Now, back to the 11th overtime. With both teams exhausted, South caught a break against the defending champs when Prowler's forward Duane Glass was called for a tripping penalty. Taking advantage of this rare power-play opportunity, South's Jim Westby struck again by slapping a rocket right through Collins' five-hole just as he was doing the splits, to end the unbelievable marathon at 1:50 of the 11th extra session. Both teams, fatigued, fell to the ice in disbelief. South's goaltender, Rog Evenson, who made a record 54 saves in the game, was wildly embraced by his teammates at the end of the four and a half hour grudge match.

The hero of the game was without question, Jim Westby. "I didn't aim," Westby later said. "If I had, I probably wouldn't have hit the goal. I just slapped it. I was all ready to tear in for the rebound because I didn't think it would go in."

Incidentally, and completely overshadowed, Ken Fanger's first period goal was all that Johnson needed to hang on for the 1-0 win over Roseau. Then, in the first-ever "All-Metro" semis, Southwest's Merv Meredith, Eric Sundquist and Ed Noble secured a 3-1 win over South St. Paul, who's lone goal was scored in the third by Bob Johnson. In the other semi, Herbie Brooks put his Johnson squad up 1-0 at 9:07 of the first, only to see Dick Koob tie it back up for South in the second. Finally, in the third, Stu Anderson and Roger Wigens tallied for Johnson to give the Governors a 3-1 win, and a ticket to the finals.

Johnson and Southwest faced off for the right to be called champion that next night, in front of a packed Auditorium crowd. The hero of the game would prove to be Herb Brooks, who got the Governors on the board at 2:32 of the first period. His teammate, Stu Anderson then tallied less than seven minutes later, only to see Brooks score his second of the game just a minute and a half after that. Merv Meredith added one in the third, but it was too little - too late for Southwest, as they lost the game 3-1 to Johnson. For the Governors, in seven Tournament appearances, it was their third state championship, and second in three years.

"Winning the state championship was great, but my most memorable moment is not from a game we played but a game we had to follow!" said Herb Brooks on the 11-overtime thriller. "We had to wait and wait in the dressing room; we'd take our skates off, put them on, shuffle our feet, this and that. It was hard to wait, and it was after one in the morning when our game was finally over, but we won and went on to win the championship."

Even today, Brooks still considers that high school tournament victory as his top career achievement, above the 1980 Olympics Miracle on Ice victory, winning three NCAA Championships with the Gophers, and even above being voted as the Sporting News' NHL (Rangers) Coach of the Year. "Winning the state championship for St. Paul Johnson, that represented your neighborhood," said Brooks, "and that was special."

1956: Thief River Falls vs. International Falls
Eveleth opened up the three-day affair by keeping its first-round win-

Front Row: Art Overbye, Glen Carlson, Jack Poole, Cliff Strand, Rod Collins and Duane Glass.
Second Row: Jim Hall, Darryl Smith, Ken Sauve, Ronald Reese, Art Cloutier, Fred Dablow, Wendy Johnson, Jim Reese, Dale Glass, Dennis Rolle (Coach).

The 1956 State Champs from Thief River Falls

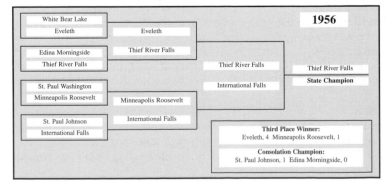

1956

White Bear Lake			
Eveleth	Eveleth		
Edina Morningside	Thief River Falls		
Thief River Falls		Thief River Falls	
St. Paul Washington		International Falls	Thief River Falls
Minneapolis Roosevelt	Minneapolis Roosevelt		**State Champion**
St. Paul Johnson	International Falls		
International Falls			

Third Place Winner:
Eveleth, 4 Minneapolis Roosevelt, 1
Consolation Champion:
St. Paul Johnson, 1 Edina Morningside, 0

ning streak in tact. Although Gary Fournelle's goal after the first minute of the game put White Bear up by one, Eveleth's Jim Drobnick, Gus Hendrickson and Jerry Judnick, each beat White Bear goalie Gordon Mackenhausen, to give Eveleth a 3-1 win. Game Two was an exciting contest that saw Edina's Larry Johnson score just 32 seconds after the opening face-off. While Thief River Falls tied it up in the second on a goal from Cliff Strand, Johnson scored again in the third, only to see Falls' winger Jack Poole tie it five minutes later. With the game tied at two apiece, the game went into overtime. There, after Edina controversially had a goal disallowed because of a man in the crease in the first extra session, Prowler's center Cliff Strand hooked up with Duane Glass to beat Edina goalie Murray Macpherson at 4:30 of the third sudden death for the 3-2 win. International Falls pulled off the tourney's the first upset in the first evening game, beating the defending champs from Johnson 3-1 thanks to a pair of Oscar Mahle goals. The late game featured the day's only shutout, as Roosevelt goalie Jerry Gangloff recorded 14 saves for a 4-0 Teddy victory over Washington. Four different Teddies scored in the game -- Bart Larson, Bob Carlson, Doug Larson and John Hrkal.

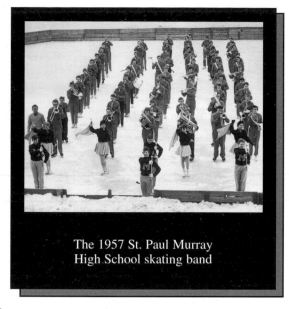

The 1957 St. Paul Murray
High School skating band

Thief River Falls then did something that had never been done before in the first semi. Thanks to goals from Duane Glass, Jack Poole and Cliff Strand, the Prowlers handed Eveleth the only shutout they had ever had in tournament play, winning the game 3-0. The second semifinal contest proved to be a classic, as International Falls hooked up with Roosevelt in a triple-overtime thriller. The Teddies jumped out to a quick lead, when Bob Carlson dug a puck out from behind the Bronco goal and stuffed it in past Falls' netminder Bob Laurion at 7:20 of the first. International Falls, coach Larry Ross' boys stormed back though, as Bill Cronkhite and Dave Frank each tallied to put the Broncos up 2-1. Roosevelt stormed right back in the third to tie it up, behind a text-book three-on-two breakaway where the Larsons, Bart and Doug, fed Gary Olin on a nice top-shelf wrister. The score held at 2-2 through the third, and forced the contest into overtime. It remained that way until midway through the third overtime, when defenseman Elmer Walls, who wound up playing every minute of every game in the tournament, ended it all on a 35-foot prayer that somehow found its way over Jerry Gangloff's shoulder and into the top corner of the net. When it was all over, an exhausted Ross called it "the best high school hockey game he'd ever seen."

With that dramatic win, the stage was now set for a championship game of Herculean proportions. In what was billed as the "battle of the Falls," Thief River Falls came out with something to prove. The Prowlers jumped all over the Broncos right out of the opening face-off, scoring just 10 seconds into the game when Glen Carlson and Duane Glass set up Cliff Strand on a nice one-timer. Thief River Falls made it 2-0 about six minutes later, when Jack Poole scored on another Glen Carlson assist. But the Broncos came right back when Oscar Mahle flipped one past Prowler goalie Rod Collins just 20 seconds later. Then, three minutes into the final period, Mahle scored his second of the game to tie it up at 2-2. The game went back and forth after that, with both northern squads mired in a physical and defensive battle. Finally at 9:55 of the second, Cliff Strand dished the biscuit to Jack Poole in front of the net, where he shoved it past goalie Bob Laurion, for what would turn out to be the game-winner.

So compelling of a tale was that Thief River Falls championship season, that it even inspired a local book by Mary Halverson Schofield, called "River of Champions." The book described how the boys persevered through so much adversity that year to win it all, including: nearly losing three of the boys who almost died in a blizzard the night before the St. Paul Johnson game, losing one of its star players to suspension just the day before playoffs began, and the fact that one of the boys had to scratch and claw his way through the tournament on novocaine, adrenaline and athletic tape because he was so hampered by injuries. The miraculous win was made possibly by Falls' goalie, Rod Collins, who Schofield remembered fondly. "The coach, Dennis Rolle, desperately needed a goalie," said Schofield. "So he took a bunch of kids, lined them up along a wall in the gym and hit tennis balls at them. Collins was the only one who didn't flinch."

Left to Right: Larry Ross (Coach), Ray Boyum, Robert Miggens, Tom Morse, John Kerry, Lester Etienne, David Frank, Oscar Mahle, James Wherley, Tom Neveaux (Capt.), Gene Steele, Lee Boyum, William Cronkhite, Richard Kalb, Tony Nagurski, Dennis Vance, Gary Thompson (Stu. Mgr.)

The 1957 State Champs from International Falls

1957: International Falls vs. Roseau

The 13th annual Tournament had a strange feeling to it in 1957. That was because for the first time since the event was held, Eveleth was not participating in it. While some were disappointed, there were eight teams in that year's field that were elated to not have to face them! Solid goaltending was the theme of this tournament, as there were a miraculous six shutouts recorded in the three day affair. Murray was the exception to the rule in that opening round, scoring one goal against Roseau - which got a pair each from Ed Bulauco and Neal Johnson in the 5-1 win. The other three opening round games were all shutouts, starting with South, which blanked Edina 6-0 on two-goal performances by both Rick Alm and Jim Ekberg. International Falls got four goals from Dave Frank, another three from Oscar Mahle, and five assists from Bob Miggins as they spanked the rookies from Hallock 10-0. And lastly, Johnson whipped South St. Paul 3-0 on goals from Harold Vinnes, Jim Cocchiarella and Dave Brooks.

International Falls got two goals from Gene Steele and Oscar Mahle in the first, and another two in the third from Tom Neveaux and Dave Frank as they beat South 4-0 in the first semifinal game. The other semifinal contest would prove to be much more dramatic, as Roseau battled the Johnson juggernaut for a ticket to the finals. Johnson's

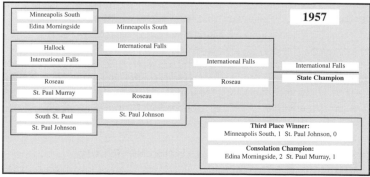

				1957	
Minneapolis South					
Edina Morningside	Minneapolis South				
Hallock	International Falls				
International Falls		International Falls			International Falls
Roseau		Roseau			State Champion
St. Paul Murray	Roseau				
South St. Paul	St. Paul Johnson				
St. Paul Johnson					

Third Place Winner:
Minneapolis South, 1 St. Paul Johnson, 0

Consolation Champion:
Edina Morningside, 2 St. Paul Murray, 1

Mark Skoog opened the scoring at 3:40 of the first period, only to see Roseau roar back for three quick goals in a span of three minutes -- two by Dave Wensloff and the third by Neal Johnson for a 3-1 lead. After Wensloff got his hat trick just 28 seconds into the second, Gary Ostedt, Harold Vinnes and Gary Schmalzbauer each scored for Johnson to tie it back up at 4-4. After a scoreless third, the game went into overtime. With back and forth play, Roseau's Arlyn Sjaaheim and Johnson's Tom Martinson played masterfully in net to force a second OT. Then, at 3:40 of the second overtime, Neal Johnson scored off of a perfect touch-pass from Dave Wensloff in front of the net to seal the deal for the Rams.

In the finals, Roseau took on International Falls in a battle of "northern exposure." After a scoreless first period, the Falls got on the board when Dave Frank tallied at 1:25 of the second. Then, only 16 seconds later, Mahle scored on a nice wrister from the slot. Mahle scored again 10 minutes later to give the Broncos a commanding 3-0 advantage. At 4:02 of the third, Jim Stordahl quieted the crowd when he scored on a Nystrom rebound to get to within two. But Bronco netminder Jim Wherley played big in the net from that point on, as Larry Ross' Bronco's went on to win their first championship 4-1.

The 1958 State Champs from Roseau

1958: Roseau vs. Harding

The festivities kicked off with Roosevelt taking on South St. Paul in the opener. The Teddies jumped out to a 1-0 lead on a Dick Wakefield score, only to see Ken Pedersen and Rich Brown score for the Packers in the second. Bud Bjerken then tied it back up for Roosevelt at 5:15 of the third to send the game into overtime. There, at 2:32 of the extra session Pedersen scored on a Grannis assist to give the Packers a 3-2 win. Game Two was a rematch of the 1957 title game, only this time it had a much different outcome. Roseau's Bill Bulauca scored at 7:31 of the second to open the scoring. The score remained that way until 7:07 of the third, when the Rams got three unanswered goals from Don Ross, Larry Anderson and Larry Stordahl. Roseau goalie Dick Roth stopped all 13 shots he faced to hang on for the 4-0 shutout.

Game Three would prove to be an upset, as St. Louis Park took on heavily favored Duluth East. After playing to a scoreless first, the Orioles' Bob Reith, Jim Boyce, Jack Burke and Don Brose all scored in a span of just seven minutes - pasting East goalie Paul Mehling. Tom Powell scored Duluth's only goal in the third, as Park's Lowell Nelson added one more for good measure in the 5-1 drubbing. A couple of St. Paulites got together in front of their home town fans for the final game of the day. Murray's Lindel Hess and Jerry Groebner each scored in the first, only to see Harding's Dougie McLellan tally in the second, followed by Ron DeMike's goal with less than a minute to go in the third to force an overtime. It didn't last long though, as Dougie McLellan notched his second of the game just 48 seconds into sudden death, to give Harding the 3-2 victory.

In the first semifinal contest, Roseau jumped out to a 4-1 first period lead over South St. Paul thanks to goals by Keith Brandt, Jim Stordahl, Dave Wensloff and Larry Anderson. Stordahl and Wensloff each added another one in the second, only to see the Packers answer with goals from Grannis and Pedersen to make it 6-2 after two. Pedersen added another in the third, but it was too little too late, as the Rams went on to beat the Packers 6-3. The second semi pitted Harding against St. Louis Park. Goalies Arnie Johnson and Mike Storm each pitched shutouts in the first, only to see Harding's Joe Schwartzbauer light the lamp at 4:56 of the second. Park's Bobby Reith answered with a goal of his own less than two minutes later to tie it, but Jim Olszewski got two quickies only 90 seconds apart for Harding, who went on to win 3-1.

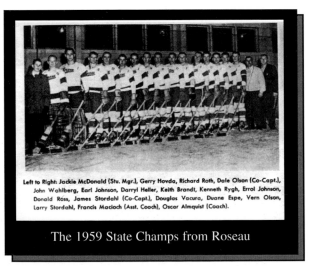

The 1959 State Champs from Roseau

The finals featured last year's runner-up's from Roseau, and first-time finalists Harding. At 4:37 of the first period, Dave Wensloff hit his off-side winger Larry Anderson, who was streaking down the side-boards. Anderson then deked Harding goalie Arnie Johnson and scored on a nice snap-shot. Amazingly, that would prove to be the game winner, as Roseau's Dick Roth stood his ground to give the Rams their second state championship. It was a tough loss for Harding, which outshot Roseau 38-12.

1959: Roseau vs. Washburn

Roseau came out of the gates with something to prove in 1959, beating Thief River Falls 7-2 in the Tournament opener. The Stordahl brothers were the heroes in the game, with Larry getting a hat trick, and his brother Jim grabbing two of his own. Dan Cullen's four goals led International Falls to a 6-2 win over Robbinsdale in Game Two. Then, in the first evening game, South St. Paul's Doug Woog scored on a nice pass from Rich Brown early in the third to seal a 1-0 victory over Henry, as Packer goalie Gary McAlpine stopped all 22 shots that came

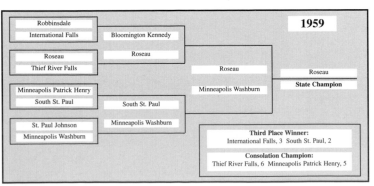

his way. In the late game, Washburn crushed Johnson 6-0 on pairs of goals from Jim Councilman and John Simus, while Jim Salmon made 23 saves for the shutout.

In the first semifinal game, Roseau's Stordahl brothers, Larry and Jim, were once again the difference, as they each scored to give the Rams a 2-0 win over International Falls. The second semi pitted Washburn against South St. Paul. The game got underway with Bill Egan and Doug Woog each scoring in the first to give the Packers a 2-0 lead. Then, Rich Brown made it 3-0 for South just 41 seconds into the third, only to see Washburn storm back. In an amazing span of less than four minutes, Russ Hardin, Tom Gould, Larry Hendrickson and Jim Nyholm each got goals to rally Washburn ahead 4-3 after two. The Packers didn't lie down though, as Doug Woog and Bill Egan each notched their second goals of the game in the third to once again put South St. Paul back on top. Washburn's Kenny Hanson tied it back up at 8:15 of the third, and sent the game into overtime. After one scoreless overtime, Hanson took a pass from Russ Hardin at 2:12 of the second OT and slid it past the outstretched Gary McAlpine to give Washburn the dramatic 6-5 victory.

In the title match, Don Ross and Earl Johnson each scored in the first period to give Roseau a 2-0 lead going into the second. Washburn's Kenny Hanson, narrowed the gap by one when he scored on a nice slapper from the slot. Ross answered back with his second and third goals of the game for Roseau though, and John Simus added one more for good measure, as the undefeated 30-0 Rams went on to win the game 4-2 for their second consecutive state championship.

1960: Duluth East vs. St. Paul Washington
Washburn opened the scoring of the opening match when Ken Hanson got an unassisted goal at 9:13 of the first. Duluth East forward Jim Ross tied it up on a nice pass from Bob Hoene early in the second, only to see Washburn jump ahead 3-1 on goals from Jim Nyholm and Jim Councilman. Ross tallied again for the Greyhounds at 6:49 of the second, which set off a Duluth scoring barrage. Within five minutes the Hounds had scored goals by Bill Sivertson, Bill Savolainen and another from Ross, this time on a sweet one-timer from winger Bill McGiffert at 10:53 of the third to give him the hat trick. Duluth held on to take the game by the score of 5-3, sending Washburn into the loser's bracket.

South St. Paul took on Thief River Falls in Game Two, as Arlan Hjelle kicked off the festivities for the Prowlers, when he scored at 6:08 of the first. After a scoreless second, Doug Woog got the Packers on the board early in the third to make it 1-1, only to see Jim Wegge score for the Falls less than a minute later. The Packers then tied it back up at two with only 33 seconds left in the game to force the contest into overtime. There, 19 seconds into the second extra session, South St. Paul center Rich Brown beat Prowler goalie Wayne Halvorson for the 3-2 game winner.

Don Laine and Jim Anderson each scored to make it 2-0 midway through the second in Henry's quarterfinal game against Eveleth, only to see Frank Judnick and Bill Stanisich tie it up in the third. Then, with just seconds to go in the final period, Henry's Jack Hanson beat Eveleth's netminder Ray Kloiber on a breakaway goal to seal the 3-2 victory for Henry.

The last quarterfinal contest of the day saw Washington's Jeff Sauer score an early pair of goals in the first and second periods against Edina. The Hornets came back to tie it up though, on Franz Jevne and Paul Rosendahl's goals midway through the second frame. Washington's Don Norqual and Edina's Chuck Plain each added another in the third to send the game into overtime. There, it was Norqual finding the net once again, this time at 3:51, on a nice touch-pass from Jack Bunde for a Washington victory.

In the semis, South St. Paul's Doug Woog hooked up with Rich Brown to take a quick 1-0 lead over Duluth East. This apparently upset a few people from the Port City, as the Hounds howled back by scoring an amazing six straight goals. Bill Sivertson notched three, while Tom Weyl, Dave Steones and Mike Hoene each added one of their own. The Wooger scored again late in the third for the Packers, but it was way too little - way too late, as East went on to win the game 6-2.

The other semifinal contest was a replay of the Twin Cities championship game between Washington and Henry. Henry's Terry McNabb scored at 6:20 of the first, only to see Washington's Bob Olson make it 1-1 late in that same period. After a scoreless second, Washington forward Bob Olson skated down on the Henry defensemen and set up his linemate Jeff Sauer, who beat Henry goalie Jack Toumie upstairs, for what would prove to be the game-winner at 4:24 of the third.

For the first time in a long time, the 1960 finals featured two teams that had never won it all -- Duluth East and St. Paul Washington. Bill Sivertson opened the scoring for the Hounds, after pouncing on a Jim Ross rebound to beat Washington goalie John Fiandaca. Up 1-0, East kept the heat on when Sivertson, this time, fed Bill McGiffert out front at 5:24 to make it two-zip. Don Norqual rallied Washington back midway through the second though, when he made a cross-ice pass to a wide open Bill Olson, who put it past Duluth goalie Don Hilsen. The game remained tight from that point on, with Duluth keeper Don Hilsen playing solid between the pipes. After thwarting several scoring chances to keep his Hounds in the game, Hilsen finally breathed a sigh of relief when Mike Hoene added an insurance goal at 9:52 of the third to ice the game for the Hounds at 3-1, thus giving them their first state title.

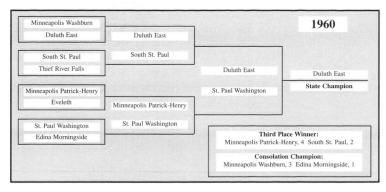

				1960
Minneapolis Washburn		Duluth East		
Duluth East				
South St. Paul		South St. Paul		
Thief River Falls			Duluth East	Duluth East
Minneapolis Patrick-Henry			St. Paul Washington	**State Champion**
Eveleth		Minneapolis Patrick-Henry		
St. Paul Washington		St. Paul Washington		
Edina Morningside				

Third Place Winner:
Minneapolis Patrick-Henry, 4 South St. Paul, 2

Consolation Champion:
Minneapolis Washburn, 3 Edina Morningside, 1

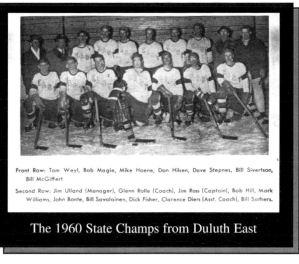

Front Row: Tom Weyl, Bob Magie, Mike Hoene, Don Hilsen, Dave Stepnes, Bill Sivertson, Bill McGiffert.

Second Row: Jim Ulland (Manager), Glenn Rolle (Coach), Jim Ross (Captain), Bob Hill, Mark Williams, John Bonte, Bill Savolainen, Dick Fisher, Clarence Diers (Asst. Coach), Bill Sathers.

The 1960 State Champs from Duluth East

A couple of Minnesota coaching legends: Bob Johnson, who coached Minneapolis Roosevelt, and Larry Ross, who coached International Falls

1961: Roseau vs. South St. Paul

North St. Paul opened up the tourney with a 4-1 win over Hallock thanks to a pair of goals by Dan Lindahl, as well as one each from both Bob Kohlman and Pat Goff. Roseau outlasted Roosevelt in the second game of the afternoon, as Rams winger Dave Backlund scored the 3-2 game-winner on a beautiful pass from Jeff Vacura at 4:08 of overtime. Defending champion Duluth East narrowly beat St. Paul Johnson 1-0 in the first evening game. With the game tied at 0-0 through regulation, Greyhound winger Bill Sivertson busted loose on a breakaway and beat Governor goalie Bob Johnson at the 3:37 mark of the extra session to get the dramatic game-winner. Meanwhile, Duluth goalie Jon Birch stopped all 21 shots he faced for the shutout. Then, in the night cap, South St. Paul, led by a pair of Doug Woog goals, pummelled Bloomington for 56 shots en route to an 8-1 victory.

Roseau then needed overtime to finish off North St. Paul in the first semifinal game. Roseau winger Dick Ulvin proved to be the hero in this one as he notched his third goal of the game at the 5:25 mark of the third overtime by beating Polar goalie Jim Durose, thus giving the Rams an exhausting 4-3 win. Meanwhile, in the other semi, South St. Paul's Doug Woog beat Duluth East goaltender Jon Birch midway through the first period on a pass from Brice Larson. East's Tom Weyl scored on an unassisted break-away to beat Packer keeper Gary McAlpine at 4:59 of the second, only to see South St. Paul's George Hocking tally at the 8:14 mark to give the Packers a 2-1 victory.

Roseau and South St. Paul got together in the finals, with Roseau's Dave Backlund striking first on a Paul Rygh centering pass midway through the first. The game went back and forth from there on out, with the Rams playing dump and chase in the last period to save their legs. Then, to really frustrate and tire out the Packers, Roseau iced the puck five times in a row during the final two minutes of the game. Oscar Almquist's Roseau Rams went on to shutout the Pack by the final score of 1-0, winning their third championship in four years. Roseau's Gary Johnson needed to make only 14 saves in goal that night, but he stopped them all, including several from future Gopher coach Doug Woog, who, incredibly, failed to score for only the first time in nine tournament games.

1962: International Falls vs. Roseau

South St. Paul got a pair of goals from Joe Frank as well as a goal and two assists from Doug Woog, as the Packers went on to beat Edina 4-2 in the opener. Game Two saw Roseau's Bob Lillo and Larry Skime each score a deuce as the Rams went on to beat St. Paul Monroe 5-1. Greenway-Coleraine came out and smoked Washburn in the first evening game on four quick goals from Jack Stebe, Ron Rollins, Jim Barle and Rian Tellor as the Raiders went on to clinch a 5-2 win, while Washburn's Bill Ronning scored a pair of goals in the loss. In the final quarterfinal game, the citizens of Minnesota got to witness the newest hockey phenome to come through the pipeline, International Falls' sensation, Keith "Huffer" Christensen, who opened the scoring early in the first for the Falls in its game against Richfield. While Glen Blumer added two more of his own in the second, goalie Mike Curran stopped all 20 shots that came his way as the Broncos cruised to a 4-0 win.

In a replay of the last year's title match, Roseau took on South St. Paul in the semifinal opener. Roseau's Larry Skime scored early in the first, only to see Joe Frank tie it right back up for the Pack. Dick Ulvin and Bob Lillo each scored for Roseau to put the Rams up 3-1, while Doug Woog assisted on a pretty Terry Abram goal for South St. Paul to narrow the gap. But when Lillo got his second goal of the game, it was all over. The Rams went on to beat the Packers 5-2.

The other semi saw Jack Stebe put Greenway up 1-0 at the 9:44 mark of the first, only to see International Falls' Jim Amidon get two goals and another from Matt Donahue, to take a 3-1 lead. Greenway's Jim Barle added one late in the third, but Falls' goalie Jim Lothrup stopped 12 third-period shots to preserve the 3-2 victory.

In the finals, International Falls met their northern neighbors from Roseau. Huffer Christensen came out and put his Broncos up 1-0 at the 3:49 mark of the first, only to see three more unanswered goals from Matt Donahue, Glen Blumer and Bob O'Leary get by Rams goalie Gary Johnson through the second. Falls' goalie Mike Curran, who had 29 saves in the game, held on and got the 4-0 shutout as Larry Ross' Broncos dethroned Roseau to win the title.

1963: St. Paul Johnson vs. International Falls

Roseau beat Richfield 2-1 in the opening game as Wendell Grand put Roseau in the black at 4:19 of the second. Richfield's Tim Olson answered three minutes later to tie it up, only to see Roseau freshman

Steve Wilson (Student Manager), Jackie McDonald (Student Manager), Gary Johnson, Richard Rygh, David Johnson, Gary Grugel, Jerome Swenson, Paul Rygh, David Backlund, Paul Dorwart, David Peterson, Richard Ulvin, Robert Lillo, David Mattson, Jeffrey Vacura, Gordon Hipsher, Charles Oseid, Francis Macioch, (Assist. Coach); Oscar Almquist (Coach).

The 1961 State Champs from Roseau

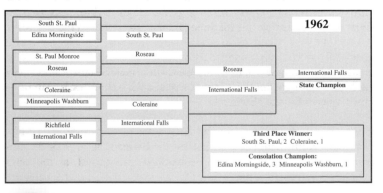

Left to Right: Larry Ross (Coach), Larry Roche, Don Milette,(Co-Capt), Jim Thompson (Co-Capt), Jim Amidon, Richard Haugland, Bob O'Leary, Charles Ketola, Matt Donahue, Glen Blumer, Bernard Woods, Les Eklund, Bob Hartje, Keith Christiansen, Mike Curran, Kevin Kennedy (Asst. Coach).

The 1962 State Champs from International Falls

Bryan Grand hit Dick Anderson in front of the net for what would prove to be the game-winner at 7:59 of the third. In the second game of the day, Johnson's Rob Shattuck put the Governor's on the board midway through the first, only to see Roosevelt's Chuck Gunderson and Jon Hall each tally to put the Teddy's up 2-1 after two. But, thanks to two third period goals from Bill Metzger, the Governors rallied to beat Roosevelt 3-2. Game Three saw St. Paul Murray's Jim Nylund score a natural hat trick in a time-frame of less than nine minutes. Bill Carrol added two goals of his own as well, as Murray cruised past Warroad 5-1 to reach the semis. In the evening game, International Falls took on the kids from Roseville's-Alexander Ramsey in what would prove to be a wild one. Down 4-1 midway through the second, Jim Amidon scored his second goal of the game to get the Bronco's rally started. Keith Bolin, Les Eklund, and Amidon scored in the third to give the Falls a 5-4 lead, only to see Ramsey's Jack Thoemke score with just 20 seconds left to send the contest into overtime. There, at 5:17 of the extra session, Falls' forward Pete Fichuk slipped a shot past Ramsey goalie Gary Martinson to give the Broncos a dramatic 6-5 victory. Bob Boysen had a hat trick and Jim Jaderston added a pair for Ramsey in the loss.

In the first semifinal game, Johnson narrowly got past a talented Roseau team by the final score of 2-1. After both teams went scoreless in the first, Governors wing Rob Shattuck scored two quick goals, both on beautiful feeds from Mike Crupi. Roseau's Larry Skime scored a goal to get the Rams back in it in the second period, but Johnson's goalkeeper Hank Remachel, who came up with 28 saves, held his ground to earn the win. The last semi was also a good game, as International Falls met St. Paul Murray. The Broncos got on the board first, when Gary Wood scored a pair of goals in the second. Murray's John Zellner got his squad to 2-1 late in the third, but Falls' forward Bob Hartje put the final nail in the coffin with just over a minute to go in the game to clinch the 3-1 win.

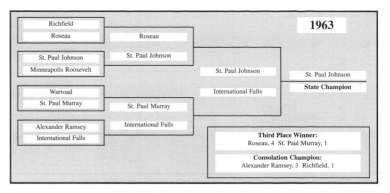

Front Row: Pat McKuskey, Frank Taylor, Rob Shattuck, Hank Remachel, Dick Peterson, Bill Weller, William Metzger, George Peltier.
Back Row: Rube Gustafson (Coach), Phil Kellor, Phil Parezino, Greg Hughes, Mike Crupi, Dick Nordlund, Ron Evenson, Jon Kulstad, Dean Stankey (Manager).

The 1963 State Champs from St. Paul Johnson

The 1963 championship game would go down in the annals of hockey history as one of the best ever, with the defending champs from International Falls taking on St. Paul Johnson. The Broncos, despite being shorthanded, struck first that night. Team captain Jim Amidon made it possible when he skated around four defenders to somehow find sophomore winger Gary Wood, from behind his own net, who caught the pass and scored on a 30-foot bullet at 7:32 of the first. Johnson came right back though, as Mike Crupi deflected a Shattuck shot only 45 seconds later. Then, just 17 seconds after that, Greg Hughes busted loose on a breakaway to score again at 8:35, for a 2-1 Governor's lead. The Falls, now rallying behind an injured Mike Crupi, scored just 89 seconds into the second on a long slapper by Bronco defenseman Dick Haugland to tie it up. (Incredibly, Haugland played the entire game with a ruptured appendix!) The play was fierce and physical by this point, as Bill Metzger scraped in front of the net for a rebound garbage goal at 5:08 to make the score 3-2. Then, with just 42 seconds left in the contest, who else but Jim Amidon grabbed a long rebound from just outside the blue line. As the crowd gasped, Amidon flew down the right side, floated to center ice and fired a bullet that found the back left side of the net, sending the game into overtime. With both teams going back and forth throughout the sudden death session, finally, at 4:31, Mike Crupi, back from his doctor's exam, took the puck in the corner and slid it over between a defender to Shattuck, who one-timed it past Falls goalie Larry Roche for the exhilerating 4-3 game-winner.

1964: International Falls vs. St. Paul Johnson

The opening game of the tourney proved to be a revenge match between Duluth East and International Falls, who the Hounds beat in the Region Seven finals, forcing the Broncos to come in through the back door as the Region Three champions. Duluth got on the board first that morning, when John McKay beat Larry Roche on a low slapper to make it 1-0. The Broncos came right back though, as Tim Sheehy tied it up at 1-1 at 9:20 of the first. The score remained tied until midway through the second, when Falls' winger Marshall Sether beat East goalie Ed Barbo for what would prove to be the game-winner.

Richfield powered past Roseau in the second game of the day, behind pairs of goals each from Ken Doerfler, Mike Burg and Dick Metz.

Then, in the first evening game, Henry tallied twice in all three periods with five different players scoring goals. Dick Subject got two for Henry as Scott Tarbox got the lone Bloomington goal in the 6-1 loss.

The last game of the day was a laugher, as the defending champs from Johnson blanked Alexander Ramsey 4-0. Bill Weller opened the scoring at 10:15 of the first, while Rob Shattuck added two and Mike Crupi got another. Johnson goalie Rich Peterson had to make only 12 saves for the shutout.

In the semifinal opener, International Falls played a dandy against Richfield. Keith Bolin struck first for the Broncos at 3:19 of the first period. Both keepers played well through the second, as the score remained 1-0 into the third. Tim Sheehy made it 2-0 for the Falls just

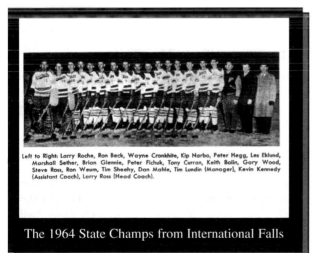

Left to Right: Larry Roche, Ron Beck, Wayne Cronkhite, Kip Narbo, Peter Hegg, Les Eklund, Marshall Sether, Brian Glennie, Peter Fichuk, Tony Curran, Keith Bolin, Gary Wood, Steve Ross, Ron Weum, Tim Sheehy, Dan Mahle, Tim Lundin (Manager), Kevin Kennedy (Assistant Coach), Larry Ross (Head Coach).

The 1964 State Champs from International Falls

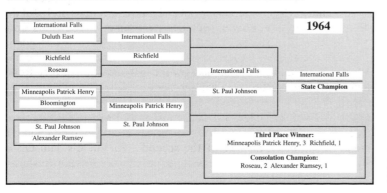

a minute into the last period, only to see Barry Bloomgren pull Richfield to within one at 5:58. Then, at 11:06, Tony Curran fed Sheehy in the slot for his second goal of the game. Richfield rallied late in the game, when Dick Metz scored with less than 30 seconds left, but it was too late as the Broncos held on for the 3-2 win.

The other semi was an onslaught, as Johnson mauled Henry 9-0. Mike Crupi, Bill Weller and Greg Hughes each had two goals in the win, while George Peltier, Gary LaMotte and Rob Shattuck each had one. Govs goalie Rich Peterson made just 18 saves for his second consecutive shutout.

In a rematch of the last year's finals, International Falls didn't waste much time in letting Johnson know just how they felt about losing the title to them the year before. Greg Hughes got Johnson on the board first on an assist from Rob Shattuck at 6:26 of the opening period. Broncos center Pete Fichuk came right back though, scoring on a nice wrister just a minute later. Shattuck again fed Hughes for another goal at 10:30 of the first, only to see Fichuk answer with his second goal of the period to tie it back up at 2-2. That's when the Falls said enough is enough, and brought out the heavy artillery. Led by goals from Keith Bolin, Les Eklund, Gary Wood and a pair from Tony Curran, the Broncos went on to blow out the Governors 7-3 to win their third title.

1965: International Falls vs. Bloomington
Johnson battled Alexander Ramsey in the opener, as Ramsey's Bob Olein scored first, only to see Johnson's Bert DeHate and Gary LaMotte give their team a 2-1 first-period lead. Ramsey tied it back up on a Jerry Christensen goal, only to see Skip Peltier and Bert DeHate each tally to give the Govs a 4-2 win.

Thief River Falls, on goals from Monte LeMoine and John Olson, jumped out to a quick two-goal lead over Bloomington in Game Two. Gordon Henry and Ron Wheeler tied it right back up for the Bears just three minutes later though. Then, after a scoreless second, Bloomington's Gene Carr scored at 2:44 of the third, as the Bears rolled to a 4-2 victory.

Game Three was all South St. Paul. The Packers went up 4-0 against Southwest, on goals by Jim LeMay, Roger Klegin, Larry Palodichuk and his brother Al Palodichuk. Southwest added one late, but Packer goalie Jim Quirk held on for the easy 4-1 win.

The last game of the day saw northern powers, International Falls and Roseau, got toe-to-toe. Roseau's Jerry Klema opened the scoring just 30 seconds into the game, while Gary Wood and Dan Mahle came right back to put the Broncos ahead 2-1. After playing a scoreless second, Austin Wallestad and Tom Billberg gave Roseau a 3-2 lead, only to see the Broncos roar back on goals from Keith Bolin, Dan Mahle and Pete Fichuk to win 5-4.

The first semifinal proved to be one of the biggest upsets in tourney history, as Bloomington, who got two goals from Jack Nichols and another from Gordy Henry, went on to beat St. Paul Johnson 3-2. While Roger Dupre and Bert DeHate each scored for Johnson in the loss, what made the game even more dramatic was the fact that while Governor goalie Jim Resch had only eight saves in the game, Johnson peppered Bloomington keeper Terry Smith with 38 shots.

In the second semifinal, International Falls' high-scoring center Tim Sheehy, got a hat trick to lead the Broncos over South St. Paul for a 5-1 win. Pete Fichuk and Tony Curran got the other two goals for the Falls, while Terry Abram managed the only Packer goal of the day.

Many thought that destiny would be on the side of the underdog Bloomington Bears in the title game, but oh were they wrong! The championship tilt proved to be a flop, as the boys from International Falls crushed the young cubs by the ugly final of 7-0. Dan Mahle got the hat trick and Pete Fichuk and Tony Curran each added a pair in the Bronco win. Amazingly, the game could've been even worse had it not been for the unbelievable netminding job from Bloomington's goalie, Terry Smith who set a championship game record by making 45 saves.

1966: International Falls vs. Roseau
South St. Paul met White Bear in the opener, and thanks to a pair of Chuck Mortel goals, the Packers went on to beat the Bears by the final of 3-1.

In the other afternoon game, the defending champs from International Falls took on Bloomington Kennedy. Tim Sheehy got the Broncos on the board first when he scored back-back goals late in the first and then early in the second. Jon Hammer got Bloomington on the board at 10:45 of the second to make it 2-1, but when John Mathews beat Bloomington goalie Bob Vroman late in the third to make it 3-1, it was all over.

Game Three had Roseau going against Greenway-Coleraine,

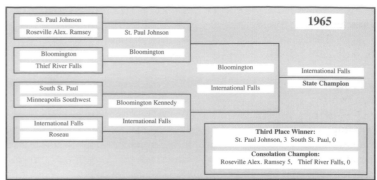

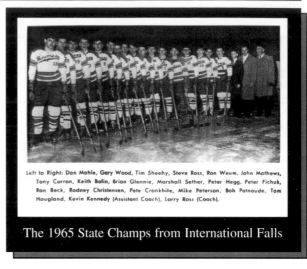

The 1965 State Champs from International Falls

Left to Right: Dan Mahle, Gary Wood, Tim Sheehy, Steve Ross, Ron Weum, John Mathews, Tony Curran, Keith Bolin, Brian Glennie, Marshall Sether, Peter Hegg, Peter Fichuk, Ron Beck, Rodney Christensen, Pete Cronkhite, Mike Peterson, Bob Patnaude, Tom Haugland, Kevin Kennedy (Assistant Coach), Larry Ross (Coach).

Front Row: Tim Sheehy, Mike Peterson, Rod Christensen, Steve Ross, Ron Beck, Peter Hegg, Ron Weum, Dan Mahle.

Back Row: Larry Ross (Coach), Tom Kuryla, Wayne Horgan, Bill Wiemer, Terry Shewchuk, Bob Patnaude, John Mathews, Duane Earnest, Tom Haugland (Student Manager), Kevin Kennedy (Asst. Coach).

The 1966 State Champs from International Falls

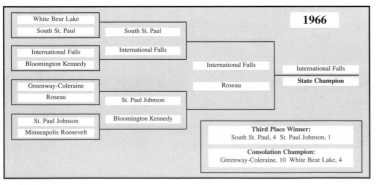

as Bryan Grand, who was making his fourth consecutive appearance in the tourney, scored all four of Roseau's goals to give the Rams a 4-2 win over Greenway. Kent Nyberg got both of Greenway's goals in the loss.

The last quarterfinal game of the day featured Johnson vs. Roosevelt. Glenn Goski scored for Johnson at 5:11 of the second and Gary Johnson added another in the third as the Governors cruised to a 2-0 victory behind 25 saves from Governor goalie John Anderson.

Both semifinals played out to be two of the best ever, with International Falls and South St. Paul going at it first. The two-time defending champs from International Falls who entered the 1966 tournament with a spotless 25-0 record and averaged better than seven goals per game while holding their opponents to just one, were led by Tim Sheehy, who had amassed 53 goals and 40 assists during that season. Coming out swinging, the Packers scored at 7:27 of the first when Terry Lawrence's long-range slapper was deflected in by Jon Bonk. Behind for only the second time all season, the Broncos lunged back into the game by scoring just seven minutes later in the first. The Falls caught the Pack during a line-change, and made them pay when Rod Christensen fed Peter Hegg out front for an easy backhander that beat South St. Paul goalie Jim Quirk. Then, striking while the irons were still hot, International Falls tallied just 10 seconds later when Sheehy stuffed in a Dan Mahle missed breakaway rebound in front of the net, as the Broncos hung on for a tough 2-1 win.

Johnson and Roseau hooked up in the other semifinal, as Governor winger Phil DeHate scored the first of his two first period goals at the 1:36 mark. Ryan Brandt and Mike Baumgartner each got one as well for Roseau that period to make it a 2-2 tie after one. Than, just 16 seconds into the second, Johnson's Ron Peltier scored on a couple of nice passes from Bert DeHate and Skip Peltier to regain the lead. Roseau's Rockford Ammerman tied it back up in the third, only to see Doug Peltier put Johnson back on top at 4:42. With the Govs up 4-3, Mike Lundbohm scored at 8:28 to send the game into overtime. Finally, at 7:06 of the third extra session, it finally came to an end when Rocky Ammerman beat Johnson goalie John Anderson on a nice wrist-shot from the top of the circle to get the 5-4 game-winner, despite being outshot 54-25.

So, after all that, it was Roseau and International Falls for all the beans. The fans expected another thriller, but what they got instead was a blow-out. The Broncos, who peppered goalie Jim Nelson with 44 shots, got goals from Rod Christensen, Ron Weum, Steve Ross, Dan Mahle and John Mathews, came out and squashed Roseau, 5-0, for their third straight state championship. It's amazing to think that the Bronco dynasty would have had an unprecedented five consecutive championships, had it not been for the overtime loss to St. Paul Johnson back in 1963.

1967: Greenway-Coleraine vs. St. Paul Johnson

The International Falls dynasty officially came to an end in 1967, when Greenway-Coleraine knocked them off in the Region Seven championships. The Raiders, riding high, took on Roosevelt in the opener, with the Teddies drawing first blood on a goal by Rich Bakke at 5:23. That would be all the scoring the Teddie's would be doing though, as the Raiders peppered Roosevelt goalie Steve Price with five unanswered goals from George Delich, Jeff Kosack, Mike Holland, Jim Stephens and Ken Lawson, en route to cruising to a 5-1 victory.

Game Two was highlighted by an amazing six-goal first period between Hibbing and White Bear. Nick Novak kicked off the period with a goal at 3:16, followed by a pair of Mike Barbato goals at 4:29 and 7:23 to give Hibbing a quick 3-0 lead. White Bear came back just a minute later when Steve Hall beat Blujacket goalie Andy Micheletti upstairs, only to see Dick Mlaker give Hibbing a 4-1 lead. Bears' forward Dennis Putney then made it 4-2 at 10:59, but that was all the scoring that would come from either team, as Hibbing went on to win by that same score.

The third game of the day between North St. Paul and Roseau proved to be the third highest scoring game in tournament history. The Polars started the scoring just 90 seconds into the game when Craig Sarner beat Roseau goalie Jim Nelson. Al Hansen and Keith Ebert then scored to give North a commanding 3-0 lead. From there Rams forward's Mike Lundbohm and Bruce Falk each scored a pair, only to see Dave Opsahl score two quick ones early in the third to give the Polars a 6-4 lead. Fifteen seconds later, Rams defenseman Lyle Olson made it 6-5, and five minutes after that Rocky Ammerman tied it up to send the game into OT. There, seven and a half minutes into the extra session, North's Keith Ebert took a pass from Sarner and slid it under the pads of Rams' goalie Jim Nelson to give his Polars the dramatic 7-6 upset.

In the last game of the day St. Paul Johnson's Peltier brothers, Ron and Doug, scored all three goals in a 3-1 victory over Edina. Tom Carlsen managed Edina's lone goal as Governor goalie Terry Del Monte posted just 11 saves in the quarterfinal win.

In the first semi, Greenway took on Hibbing in another wild one. Bill Baldrica scored late in the first to give the Bluejackets a 1-0 lead. His linemate Bob Collyard made it two-zip just after the four-minute mark of the second, only to see Mike Adams get one just 20 seconds later for Hibbing. That's when the people of St. Paul became formally introduced to a lightning quick 140-pound centerman by the name of Mike Antonovich, who tied it up at 7:48 of the second on a nice assist from Ken Lawson. Mike Metzer tallied early in the third to give Greenway its first lead of the day, but Bill Baldrica struck again to tie it back up with just a minute left. Sixteen seconds later, Ken Lawson put a dagger in the collective heart of Hibbingites everywhere, when he flipped the puck past Bluejacket goalie Andy Micheletti to give his Raiders a 4-3 win. (Incidentally, while these two teams were clearly two of the best in the state, they were both beaten soundly by Duluth Cathedral, who, because they were private, and won the Independant State Title, couldn't compete in the public school's state tournament.)

The other semifinal game had the Polars of North St. Paul going up against legendary coach Rube Gustafson's St. Paul Johnson Governors. Govs center Ron Peltier lit the lamp at 1:46 of the opening period, only to watch Terry Wasiluk tie it up just 21 seconds later on an assist from Al Hansen. Hansen then got a goal of his own at 3:19, while Johnson's

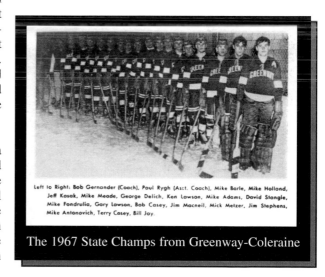

Left to Right: Bob Gernander (Coach), Paul Rygh (Asst. Coach), Mike Barle, Mike Holland, Jeff Kosak, Mike Meade, George Delich, Ken Lawson, Mike Adams, David Stangle, Mike Fondrulia, Gary Lawson, Bob Casey, Jim Macneil, Mick Metzer, Jim Stephens, Mike Antonovich, Terry Casey, Bill Joy.

The 1967 State Champs from Greenway-Coleraine

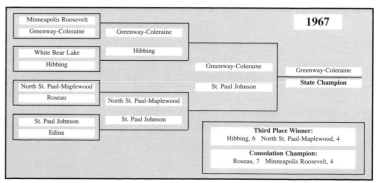

Doug Peltier tied it back up at 11:08 of the first. The Polars regained the lead just 17 seconds into the second on a goal by Dave Opsahl, only to see Johnson's George Fincel tie it up yet again. Then, early in the third, Craig Sarner beat Johnson goalie Terry Del Monte to regain the lead. But, as it had been all game, Johnson came right back on an Ed Giannini goal midway through the third. The score remained tied from there on in, and went into sudden death. That's where Ron Peltier took over, scoring his second goal of the game only 34 seconds into the extra session to give his Governors a 5-4 win.

So, the finals were set, it would be Greenway vs. Johnson, as Ronny Peltier set up Russ Zahradka at the 4:33 mark of the first period to get things started for the Govs. Greenway roared back though, as Ken Lawson, Jeff Kosak and Jim Macneil all got second period goals to give the Raiders a 3-1 lead. The game remained tight through the second and into the third, until, with just over a minute left in the game, Johnson's Glenn Goski beat Del Monte to get his team to within one. The Raiders pressed hard, but with just 10 seconds left in the game, the bespectacled wonder, Mike Antonovich, nailed an empty-netter to ice the game for Greenway, 4-2.

1968: Greenway-Coleraine vs. South St. Paul
As fate would have it, No. 1 ranked Mounds View, who was led by a pair of big, mobile twins named Bart and Brad Beutow, played the defending champs from Greenway in the opener. In a fabulous back and forth, wide open game which wound up going into overtime, Dave Stangl took a Mike Antonovich pass and beat Mounds View goalie Mike Schuett at 5:31 of the extra session to give his Raiders a 4-3 victory.

St. Paul Johnson then beat International Falls in the second game of the afternoon, as the Governors got a hat trick from Doug Peltier, a pair from Scott Frantzen, and goals from Steve Schwietz and Ed Giannini to cruise to a 7-4 win. Pat DeMarki scored twice for the Falls in the losing effort.

Southwest, which got a pair of goals from Jack Gravel, went on to beat Roseau 4-2 in the first evening game, as Ram's winger Earl Anderson put a pair of his own past Southwest goalie Brad Shelstad in the loss.

The last game of the day saw Edina roll over South St. Paul 6-2, thanks to Joe Bonk's hat trick and Dale Abram's pair of goals in the third. Hornet center Bob Krieger also added a deuce in the loss.

Greenway struck first in the semis on goals from Tom Peluso in the first and then Sandy Markovich in the second to give the Raiders a 2-0 lead over Johnson. Less than three minutes later, Governor winger John Horton made it 2-1, only to see Greenway's Ken Lawson and Jim Stephens score to make it a three-goal game. Then Ed Giannini and Horton both tallied for Johnson to cut the deficit to one, but Greenway goalie Terry Casey held off a late Johnson rally to preserve a 4-3 win for the Raiders.

South St. Paul played Southwest in the other semifinal contest, with the Packers blanking Southwest 2-0. Terry Madland scored first on a nice assist from Dick Todd, while Dale Abram found the back of the net with just under a minute to go in the second for the other. South St. Paul goaltender Mark Kronholm made 22 saves in earning the shutout.

The finals were hyped from every angle by the press, with the most obvious being Greenway's attempt to repeat as state champs. But another interesting sidebar was the fact that this was South St. Paul coach Lefty Smith's final game for the Packers, because he had recently been appointed as Notre Dame's head hockey coach. Greenway opened the scoring at the four minute mark, when Dave Stangl beat Packer goaltender Mark Kronholm. South St. Paul evened it up early in the second though, on George Tourville's wrister from Joe Bonk. That would unfortunately be as close as Lefty would ever get that day, as Greenway exploded for five unanswered goals in the third. Both Mike Antonovich and Tom Peluso each had a couple of tallies, while Jim Stephens added another in the 6-1 drubbing.

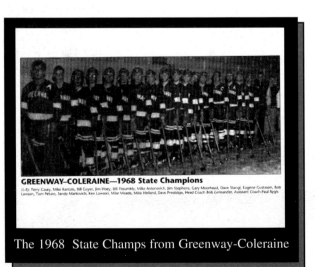

GREENWAY-COLERAINE—1968 State Champions
(l-R) Terry Casey, Mike Rantala, Bill Goyer, Jim Hoey, Bill Tromblit, Mike Antonovich, Jim Stephens, Gary Moorhead, Dave Stangl, Eugene Gustason, Bob Lawson, Tom Peluso, Sandy Markovich, Ken Lawson, Mike Meade, Mike Holland, Dave Prestidge, Head Coach Bob Gernander, Assistant Coach Paul Rygh.

The 1968 State Champs from Greenway-Coleraine

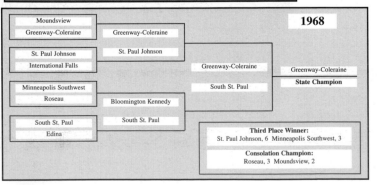

1969: Edina vs. Warroad
For its 25th anniversary, the Minnesota State High School Hockey Tournament changed venues. Because the new Civic Center was being constructed alongside of the old Auditorium, the tourney temporarily moved to Bloomington, where it resumed play in the newly constructed Met Center.

Harding took on Roseau in Game One, with Mike Broten opening the scoring for the Rams at 4:51 of the first period. The teams pounded each other back and forth until Dennis Trooien scored a power-play goal with just 16 seconds to go in the second. At 6:06 of the third, Roseau got what would prove to be the game-winner from young centerman by the name of John Harris. (Harris, in addition to winning a NCAA hockey championship with the Gophers in 1974, went on to become Minnesota's most prolific amateur golfer, winning several U.S. Amateur titles.) Anderson and Smedsmo each added goals later in the third as Roseau cruised to a 4-1 victory.

The second game of the afternoon pitted Southwest against a young Warroad team which was led by a kid named Henry Boucha. While Southwest jumped out to a quick 2-0 lead on a pair of goals from Dixon Shelstad, it was Boucha who led the rally back and ultimately beat Southwest goalie Brad Shelstad for what would prove to be the 4-3 game-winner.

Mounds View and Edina played the first evening game, with Edina blasting some 40 shots at Mustangs goalie Terry Moores. Five of them found the back of the net for the Hornets, with budding superstar Bobby Krieger getting the first one only a minute into the game. Mark Fretland added a pair of goals, as did his freshman brother Rick, as Bruce Carlson added another to make the final 5-0. Hornet's keeper Doug Hastings stopped only 14 shots in the shutout.

The best was saved for last though when it came to the final quarterfinal contest of the day. That's because South St. Paul and Greenway played a thrilling back and forth game that came right down to the wire. Junior center Paul Hanson put the Packers up first, when he beat Greenway goalie Mike Rantala at 2:15 of the first. Greenway answered back in the second by scoring three straight goals in a span of less than two minutes apart. Mike Antonovich got the first one, followed by Jim Hoey and Tom Peluso. Then, at 1:22 of the third, the Packers Gene Mortel got one, followed by Mike Neska's just five minutes later to tie it up. Both teams played a furious final few minutes, but with just 19 seconds left in the game, Packers winger Scott Sandison beat Rantala through the five-hole to give his team a dramatic 4-3 come-from-behind win.

Region Eight rivals Roseau and Warroad then got together for an all-northern semifinal shoot-out. Henry Boucha put Warroad up 3-1 at 7:01 in the third, only to see Mike Broten tally his second of the game just two minutes later. Roseau pressed hard to get the equalizer in the final minutes, but couldn't get the puck past Warroad tender Jeff Hallett, who's 14 saves were enough for the 3-2 win.

The last semi was a blow-out as Edina came out and scored the first six goals of the game against South St. Paul, en route to a 7-1 victory. Bruce Carlson and Bobby Krieger each had three points, while Tim Carlson, Mark Fretland, and Jim Knutson also tallied for Willard Ikola's Hornets. Edina's Doug Hastings registered 25 saves in the win.

The stage was now set for one of the most emotionally-charged championship games of all-time, Edina vs. Warroad. The sentimental favorite Warriors were led by Henry Boucha, who had been playing nearly every minute of his team's games up to that point. Edina, on the other hand, was the "cake-eating" team that everybody loved to hate. They were pompous, but they were good, having come into the game with an impressive 25-1 record. The Hornets had outscored their opponents that year by the insane margin of 142 to 19, while goalie Jim Hastings posted a whopping 13 shutouts.

The game got underway with Edina setting the tempo early. Just 22 seconds after the opening face-off, Rick Fretland buried a long-range wrist-shot over Jeff Hallett's outstretched glove. The Warriors came back to tie it up on a power-play goal at 7:32, when Hangsleben and Kvarnlov set up Leo Marshall out front for the equalizer. But, just two minutes later, Eddie Huerd whacked in a rebound that bounced past Hastings to give Warroad a 2-1 advantage. Threatening to blow the game wide open, John Taylor came down on a three-on-one and let a blast loose that nailed the pipe. Edina rallied thanks to a couple of pairs of brothers. First the Carlson brothers, Tim and Bruce, hooked up to tie the game only 47 seconds into the second. Then, Rick Fretland added his second of the game just a minute later, on a nice back-hander from his brother Mark from behind the net to give Edina a 3-2 lead.

Then something happened that will forever be remembered in the annals of tournament history. Henry Boucha came down the ice and fired the puck into the Edina net. He followed his own rebound towards the back-boards, and just as he got behind the goal, he got checked head first into the boards. Boucha went down in a heap and didn't get up. The record crowd stood in shock as Warroad coach Dick Roberts rushed onto the ice to check on his star player. Boucha was eventually helped off the ice from the controversial play and taken to the hospital where it was determined that he had ruptured his eardrum.

With their leader now out of the game, Warroad tried to get it together. But, when Edina's Tim McGlynn scored on a 20-footer only minutes later to go up 4-2, things started to look grim. Then, after an inspirational pep-talk from their coach, the courageous Warriors came back behind a pair of Frank Krahn goals to tie it back up in the second. The first came on a 20-foot blast from Bobby Storey, while the second came on a Al Hangsleben tip-in at 10:41.

The third period was fast and furious, but both keepers kept their teams in it to force a sudden-death overtime. The Warriors got the early break, but couldn't capitalize. Then Edina took over, as defenseman Skip Thomas fired a prayer of a slapshot through traffic that somehow found the back of the Warroad goal just over two minutes into the extra session. The Hornets had done it. The first suburban high school team ever to win a title, Edina had beaten Warroad 5-4, in one of the greatest title matches in tourney history.

1970: Southwest vs. Edina
Down 3-0 from North St. Paul winger Dan Leigh's pure hat trick, Southwest came back in the third period to put together one of the best rallies in tourney history. After Dan Casperson

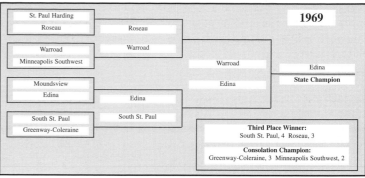

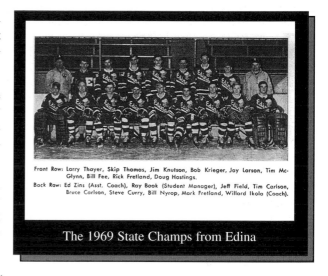

Front Row: Larry Thayer, Skip Thomas, Jim Knutson, Bob Krieger, Jay Larson, Tim Mc-Glynn, Bill Fee, Rick Fretland, Doug Hastings.
Back Row: Ed Zins (Asst. Coach), Ray Book (Student Manager), Jeff Field, Tim Carlson, Bruce Carlson, Steve Curry, Bill Nyrop, Mark Fretland, Willard Ikola (Coach).

The 1969 State Champs from Edina

Willard Ikola

Willard Ikola grew up in Eveleth, where he played goalie for three undefeated state championship teams from 1948-1950. From there he went on to become an All-American at the University of Michigan, where he led the Wolverines to a pair of national championships in 1952 and 1953. He later played for the silver medal-winning U.S. team in Cortina, Italy, before finally taking over as the coach for Edina High School in 1958. There, he became synonymous with high school hockey in our state. His Edina teams were among the most prolific in tourney history, winning 22 conference championships, 19 regional playoffs and 8 high school hockey championships (1969, '71, '74, '78, '79, '82, '84 and '88.) His 616-149-36 record over 33 years of coaching makes him not only the winningest coach in the history of Minnesota high school sports, but also the second all-time winningest coach in the history of high school hockey in America. Ike, with his trademark hounds-tooth hat, retired from coaching in 1991 to join the North Stars as a scout. A living legend, Ike truly is Minnesota hockey.

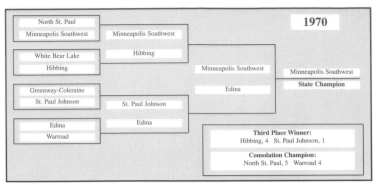

North St. Paul			
Minneapolis Southwest	Minneapolis Southwest		
White Bear Lake	Hibbing	Minneapolis Southwest	Minneapolis Southwest
Hibbing		Edina	**State Champion**
Greenway-Coleraine			
St. Paul Johnson	St. Paul Johnson		
Edina	Edina		
Warroad			

1970

Third Place Winner:
Hibbing, 4 St. Paul Johnson, 1

Consolation Champion:
North St. Paul, 5 Warroad 4

scored just 26 seconds into the third, Paul Miller got the next two goals to force the game into overtime. There, who else but Miller, scored on a low snap-shot just a minute into the extra session for not only the second pure hat trick of the afternoon, but also for the 4-3 game-winner.

Hibbing pummeled White Bear Lake 4-0 in Game Two, thanks to yet another pure hat trick from junior winger Ron Brager. Mike Polich got the other goal as sophomore goaltender George Milinovich came up with 20 saves to earn the shut out.

The third quarterfinal contest between Greenway and Johnson turned into a gut-wrenching thriller, that just seemed to go on and on. The game started on a bad note when Johnson captain Mark Kroll broke his collarbone on the game's first shift. Johnson forward Neal Barrette opened the game's scoring at 9:27 of the first when he tipped in future Gopher All-American Les Auge's slapper from the point. Greenway's Bob Lawson evened back up just a minute later when he knocked in a Tom Peluso shot in front of the net that beat Johnson goalie Doug Long. Johnson center Tom Holm put the Governors back up on top one more time at 7:50 of the second, only to see the Raiders answer with two quick ones from Bob Lynch and Joe Miskovich in the opening minutes of the third to regain the lead. But Johnson's third-line centerman Jim Metzger came to the rescue midway through the third when he deflected defenseman Bill Nyquist's shot past Greenway keeper Mike Rantala. The 3-3 score held up through regulation as the teams went into sudden death. Johnson missed two power play opportunities during the first and second overtime periods, but couldn't pull the trigger. Johnson defensemen Les Auge and Bob Peltier guarded their blue line like it was a baby. The game raged back and forth, finally going into a fifth extra session. Then, finally at the 3:24 mark of OT number five, Johnson center Fran McClellan flipped in a Bob Peltier missed shot to get the 4-3 game-winner. Johnson's goalie Doug Long, who made a tournament record 61 saves in the four-hour grudge match, was mobbed by his teammates when it was all through.

The 15,000 - plus fans figured that they had definitely gotten their money's worth that night, seeing such a fantastic overtime game. Little did they know, but there was another one starting right before their eyes. The last game of the day featured the defending champs from Edina against the Warriors from Warroad in a rematch of the 1969 finals. Bobby Krieger would prove to be the hero that night, as he opened the scoring not even a minute after the first face-off. Sophomore center Steve Eichorn then made it 2-0 Edina at 3:40 of the second, when he beat Warroad's Jeff Hallett on a couple of nice set-up passes from Marty Rogers and Bill Nyrop. Down but not out the Warriors came right back in the third, as Jerome Hodgson took an Ed Boucha pass and drilled it past Hornet netminder Larry Thayer. Lyle Kvarnlov added another goal just 15 seconds later to tie it up, and ultimately send the game into overtime. There, already a minute and a half into the second OT, Bobby Krieger scored his second goal of the game by beating Hallett for the 3-2 game-winner.

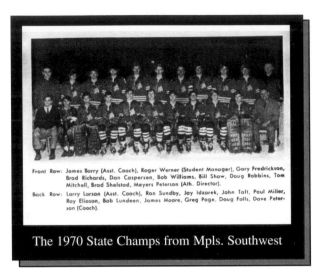

The 1970 State Champs from Mpls. Southwest

Front Row: James Barry (Asst. Coach), Roger Werner (Student Manager), Gary Fredrickson, Brad Richards, Dan Caspersen, Bob Williams, Bill Shaw, Doug Robbins, Tom Mitchell, Brad Shelstad, Meyers Peterson (Ath. Director).
Back Row: Larry Larson (Asst. Coach), Ron Sundby, Jay Idzorek, John Taft, Paul Miller, Ray Eliason, Bob Lundeen, James Moore, Greg Page, Doug Falls, Dave Peterson (Coach).

Southwest went on to beat Hibbing in a tough and physical semifinal contest which featured seven penalties. The Indians got two goals late in the first from Dan Casperson and Paul Miller, and another in the second from Brad Richards, as they rolled to the 3-1 win.

The other semi had Edina going against Johnson in yet another overtime match. Edina's Bruce Carlson put the Hornets on the board first at 4:20 of the opener, only to see Governors center Fran McClellan even it up just two minutes later. Fast-forward to the third overtime, still tied tied at one, when, finally at 4:34 of the third extra session, Edina's Bruce Carlson stuffed a Billy Nyrop pass by Johnson goalie Doug Long for the 2-1 game winner.

With that, an Edina repeat seemed eminent. The only thing standing in their way was coach Dave Peterson's Southwest Indians. The game was back and forth all night, as each team took its chances. Shelstad had his hands full all day, especially trying to keep tabs on the water-bug Bobby Krieger, who came at the keeper time and time again, only to be stuffed every time. His biggest chance came with just 10 seconds left in regulation, when Krieger stole the puck, flew in all alone, deked across the crease, and flipped a back-hander towards the top shelf. Shelstad, calm and collected, stoned him yet again. After both goalies posted shutouts through regulation, the championship match went into sudden death. Finally, at the six-minute mark of overtime, Jay Idzorek started a rush towards the Edina end and dished over to his defenseman, Bob Lundeen, who took an open shot from the right point. Bill Shaw, parked out in front of the net, saw the blast coming right toward him. Trying to deflect it with his stick, it instead flew right into his chest, and ricocheted into the top corner of the net for the dramatic, and bizarre 1-0 game-winner.

1971: Edina vs. Roseau

Hastings and Roseau hooked up in the opener, as Roseau's Mike Broten tallied two goals early in the first, followed by another from defenseman Gary Ross to give the Rams a 3-0 lead. After a scoreless second, Hastings roared back to tie it in the third behind three straight goals from Gary Wytaske (on an assist from future North Star Dean Talafous), Ron Regenscheid and Jerry Meier. Then, with just over a minute to go in the game, Roseau's Mitch Brandt beat Hasting's goalie Ron Savage for the 4-3 game winner.

International Falls hammered East Grand Forks in Game Two 6-2 as Brian Briggs, John Prettyman, Jeff Lindvall, Dave Brown, Jeff Boyum, Jim Knapp, and Mike Dalton all got goals in the win.

Southwest and Edina got together for a rematch of the previous year's overtime title match in Game Three, as Edina's Steve Eichorn got his club some sweet revenge when

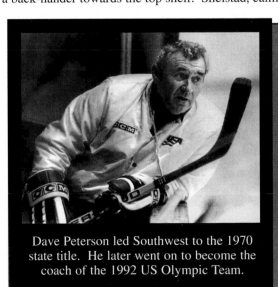

Dave Peterson led Southwest to the 1970 state title. He later went on to become the coach of the 1992 US Olympic Team.

he beat Southwest goalie Mike Dibble at the 5:22 mark of the first overtime to give the Hornets a dramatic 4-3 victory.

The last quarterfinal had St. Paul Johnson blanking Alexander Ramsey 3-0, as Bob Peltier and Scott Klinkerfues, who netted a pair, took care of the offense, while Governor goalie Doug Long made 14 saves in earning the shutout.

It was Roseau and International Falls going at it in the first semifinal, with Roseau coming out and scoring four quick ones from Jeff Tangan, Kent Lanlie and a pair from John Harris to beat Bronco goalie Peter Waselovich. Falls' forwards Dave Brown and Jeff Boyum halved the deficit in the second, but Merlin Nelson's late goal iced it for the Rams, who went on to win the game 5-2.

Edina now had to get by Johnson if they wanted to get back to the finals for the third time in three years. The Hornets jumped out to a quick 2-0 lead on goals from John Enquist and Tim Carlson. Then, Governor center Bob Peltier made it 2-1 at 2:43 of the second, only to watch the Hornet's Steve Eichorn tip in a Ron Sorem shot to make it 3-1. Johnson rallied behind Stan Blom's unassisted goal midway through the third, but Edina's Bill Brobak beat Doug Long on a nice wrist shot to make the final 4-2 in favor of the Hornets.

The championship game between Willard Ikola's Edina Hornets and Terry Abrams' Roseau Rams had a lot of hype going in. The record crowd of 15,319 at the Met Center was treated to a defensive gem that night, as Hornet's junior center Rick Wineberg got the game's only goal at 8:57 of the first, when he deked and beat Roseau goalie Tim Delmore on a low slapper. Dave Otness and Charlie Kelly got the assists, while junior goalie Dave Bremer posted just 19 saves to earn the shutout. The 1-0 victory gave the Hornets their second title in three years.

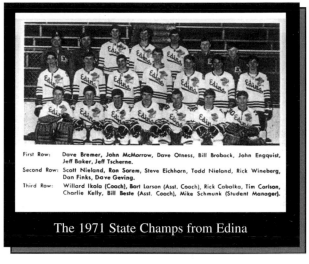

First Row: Dave Bremer, John McMorrow, Dave Otness, Bill Brobock, John Engquist, Jeff Baker, Jeff Tscherne.
Second Row: Scott Nieland, Ron Sorem, Steve Eichorn, Todd Nieland, Rick Wineberg, Dan Finks, Dave Geving.
Third Row: Willard Ikola (Coach), Bart Larson (Asst. Coach), Rick Cabalka, Tim Carlson, Charlie Kelly, Bill Beste (Asst. Coach), Mike Schmunk (Student Manager).

The 1971 State Champs from Edina

1972: International Falls vs. Grand Rapids

International Falls beat Bemidji 8-3 in the opener behind Craig Dahl's hat trick and Don Reuter's two goals. Bemidji's Gary Sargent, a future North Star, added a pair of goals in the loss.

Southwest beat Alexander Ramsey 3-1 in Game Two, as Mark Narum opened the scoring for the Rams at 9:06 of the first, only to see Murray Johnson tally twice in the second to beat Ramsey goalie Dave Miller for what would prove to be the game-winner.

South St. Paul played Harding in the third quarterfinal, as the Packers pounded Knight's goalie Gary Flash with 50 shots on goal, including a 23-shot barrage in the third alone, for the 4-2 victory. After falling behind 2-0, the Pack roared back for four straight on goals from Warren Miller, John Shewchuck, Rich Keogh and Tom Waldhauser to get the "W."

Grand Rapids then upset the defending champs from Edina in the last quarterfinal contest of the day by the final of 3-1. Led by Rapids defenseman Kelly Cahill's monster checks on several Hornet players, the Indians got goals from Jim Stacklie, Don Madson and Doug Christy, who hammered a Madson pass from behind the cage past Edina goalie Jeff Tscherne at 8:19 of the third. (For Gus Hendrickson, who starred for Eveleth High School in 1958, beating Eveleth folk-hero Willard Ikola was quite an accomplishment. "I remember going to church when I was a little kid and seeing Ike sit there," said Hendrickson. "I never took my eyes off of him - you'd have thought I was praying to the wrong guy all those years!")

International Falls and Southwest hooked up in the first semi, as the Broncos opened the scoring at 13:25 of the first when Allen Karsnia scored on a Craig Dahl rebound out front. Southwest came back to tie it when Tom Pontinen pounced on a rebound at 4:25 of the second. With the score remaining tied 1-1 through regulation, the game went into sudden death. The Broncos third line of Buzzy LaFond, Jim Jorgenson and Paul Brown, proved to be the heroes in this one. LaFond started out the rush by dumping the puck behind the Indian cage. Jorgenson then dug out the puck from behind the net and fed it out front to Paul Brown, who buried it past Indian keeper Peter Waselovich at 2:07 of the extra session to give the Broncos a dramatic 2-1 win.

Grand Rapids then beat South St. Paul 5-4 in the other semi. Greg Stanley opened the scoring for Grand Rapids early in the first, followed by Ken Yackel's shot from Roger Rothstein in the slot at 6:43. Jim Stacklie gave the Indians a 2-1 lead on a power-play goal midway through the second, followed by Mark Wenda's hard slap shot goal from the right circle. Doug Christy and Tom Clusiau made it 4-2 for the Indians, only to see Dan Bonk and John Shewchuck, who nailed a 40-footer, each score to tie it up late in the third. Then, with just minutes to go in the game, Indians forward Greg Stanley found the back of the net to give the Indians a 5-4 win.

International Falls and Grand Rapids then met for the championship in front of some 16,000-plus screaming fans. The Broncos erupted for three third period goals in this one, and then had to hang on for dear life as the Indians mounted a fierce rally. After both teams played to a scoreless first period, Rapids winger Dan Madson scored an unassisted

Front Row: Charles Holland, John Murray, Dave Hanson, Jim Jorgenson, Craig Dahl, Jim Knapp, Paul Green, Don Reuter, Allen Karsnia, Pete Waselovich. Back Row: Terry Burns (Asst. Coach), Cal Sandbeck, Buzzy LaFond, David Brown, Jim Lundquist, Steve Johnson, Mike Bolin, Paul Brown, Richard McBride (Student Manager), Larry Ross (Coach).

The 1972 State Champs from International Falls

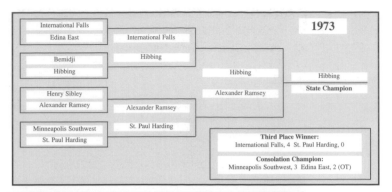

International Falls				
Edina East	International Falls			
Bemidji	Hibbing			
Hibbing		Hibbing	Hibbing	
Henry Sibley		Alexander Ramsey	State Champion	
Alexander Ramsey	Alexander Ramsey			
Minneapolis Southwest	St. Paul Harding			
St. Paul Harding				

Third Place Winner:
International Falls, 4 St. Paul Harding, 0

Consolation Champion:
Minneapolis Southwest, 3 Edina East, 2 (OT)

power-play goal with just less than a minute left in the second to give his club a 1-0 lead. The Broncos tied it at 2:40 of the third on David Brown's low wrister. It was Iron Range hockey at its best, as the game flip-flopped back and forth behind some great checking, as well as goaltending from both teams. At 3:40 of the third, Paul Brown caught the Indians on a line change and took off with the puck into the Rapids zone. There, he deked, and flipped a backhander into the back of the net to make it 2-1. Craig Dahl then made it 3-1 for the Broncos at the 10:45 mark, on a beautiful goal that followed his own rebound. Rapids winger Doug Christy added one with 28 seconds left, as the Indians attacked six-on-five, but the gritty Waselovich stood tall in the end and preserved the 3-2 victory for his school's sixth state hockey title.

1973: Hibbing vs. Alexander Ramsey

International Falls and Edina played to a scoreless first and second period in the opener before Bronco winger Buzzy LaFond finally scored at 8:35 of the third to put the Broncos up 1-0. Junior defenseman Craig Norwich then scored five minutes later to even it up, as the score stayed that way through the end of three. Then, at 2:19 of the game's second overtime, Falls' senior centerman David Brown took a Gary Beck pass and flipped it past Edina goalie Frank Zimmerman for a dramatic 2-1 Broncos win.

Game Two was also an exciting affair with Hibbing and Bemidji mixing it up. After Bemidji got two first period goals from Dick Howe and Andy Kannenberg, the Bluejackets stormed back behind Joe Micheletti's hat trick, and George Perpich, Jr.'s pair of assists to earn a 4-2 comeback victory.

Ramsey made quick work of Sibley in Game Three, as Bob Richards scored a pair of goals and Tim Fitzsimmons added another in the 3-0 blanking. Rams goalie Dave Tegenfeldt made 17 saves for the shutout.

In the last quarterfinal of the day, Harding and Southwest played a dandy. Harding center Paul Holmgren got his Knights on the board just 30 seconds into the game when he beat Southwest goalie Gene Tierney on an unassisted breakaway goal. The Indians came right back though, scoring two straight in the second on goals by Tom Pontinen and Mark Johnson. Harding's Tom Glancey answered at 12:54 of the second to tie it back up, only to see Indian center Tom Paulson score at 11:25 of the third. Then, with less than two minutes to go, Harding defenseman Nick Schwartz beat Tierney for what would prove to be the game-winner, as the Knights rolled into the semis with a 5-3 win.

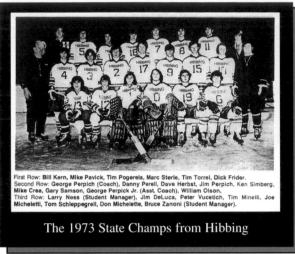

First Row: Bill Kern, Mike Pavick, Tim Pogerels, Marc Sterle, Tim Torrel, Dick Frider.
Second Row: George Perpich (Coach), Danny Perell, Dave Herbst, Jim Perpich, Ken Simberg, Mike Crea, Gary Samson, George Perpick Jr. (Asst. Coach), William Olson.
Third Row: Larry Ness (Student Manager), Jim DeLuca, Peter Vucetich, Tim Minelli, Joe Micheletti, Tom Schleppegrell, Don Michelette, Bruce Zanoni (Student Manager).

The 1973 State Champs from Hibbing

The Hibbing Bluejackets, coached by George Perpich, and the International Falls Broncos, coached by Larry Ross were both well disciplined Iron Range teams. Meeting for the third time that season, Hibbing was anxious to exact a little revenge for its 8-3 drubbing in the Region Seven finals, which forced the Jackets to come through the Region Three back door by beating Roseau. In a game that was very fast paced with a lot of hard hitting, the Falls jumped out to a quick 2-0 lead on Steve Johnson's 20-footer, followed by Kevin Nagurski's tip-in. Hibbing's Dave Herbst then added a pair of goals late in the first and early into the second to even the score at 2-2. The score remained that way until 1:31 of the third, when Joe Micheletti beat Bronco goalie Pete Waselovich. Up 3-2, Hibbing poured it on, as George Perpich Jr. got a pair of goals within a 30 second span to give the Jackets a commanding three-goal lead. The Broncos, visibly tired from their double-overtime win the night before, just wouldn't lie down though. They came right back on goals from Buzzy LaFond and Paul Brown with less than five minutes to go. The Broncos eventually pulled Waselovich for the game's final minute, but Hibbing keeper Tim Pogorels stood on his head, finishing the game with 22 hard fought saves to lead the Jackets to a thrilling 5-4 win.

The other semi had Harding and Ramsey playing to a scoreless first. Then, in the second, Ramsey took a quick two-goal lead on tallies from Ken Porten and Mike Green to go up 2-0. Harding came right back when Paul Holmgren fed Tom Glancey to bring the Knights to within one. Center Mike DiSanto then evened it up three minutes later, only to see Rams right wing Tom Williams beat Harding goalie Gary Flasch with less than two minutes to go in the game. Harding pulled their keeper in the waning minutes, but Ramsey hung on for a tough-fought 3-2 win.

The championship was finally set with Hibbing and underdog Ramsey. Hibbing's Tom Schleppegrell fed Mike Crea only 85 seconds into the game to get his squad on the board first. Ramsey center Pat Graizinger answered back with only five seconds to go in the first to make it 1-1. Ramsey then took the lead early in the second when Tom Fitzsimmons scored on a Mike Bailey pass. Then, Joe Micheletti tied it up on a short-handed goal to start a rally. First Micheletti fed George Perpich for a goal at 3:31 of the third, and then added one himself just nine seconds later. Perpich scored again just 14 seconds after that, only to see Micheletti notch his hat trick less than a minute later. The amazing barrage of artillery was unbelievable, as Hibbing went on to win the game by the final of 6-3.

1974: Edina East vs. Bemidji

Sibley jumped all over the defending champs from Hibbing in the first quarterfinal game, as John Albers, Doug Spoden, Tim Salscheider and Mark Prettyman all tallied in the 4-1 upset victory.

Edina East came out and absolutely destroyed Harding in the afternoon game, pummeling Knight goalie Ted Vanderbeek with 49 shots on goal. Both Tim Pavek and Steve Poltfuss had hat tricks, while Bill Thayer added a pair in the 9-0 onslaught.

Roosevelt and Grand Rapids got together in the first evening game, which would have to be settled in overtime. Mark DeCenzo's goal just 41 seconds into the game gave the Indians an early 1-0 lead,

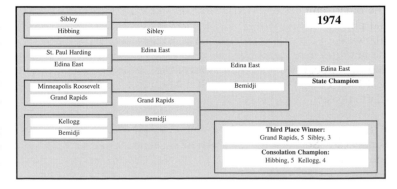

Sibley				
Hibbing	Sibley			
St. Paul Harding	Edina East			
Edina East		Edina East	Edina East	
Minneapolis Roosevelt		Bemidji	State Champion	
Grand Rapids	Grand Rapids			
Kellogg	Bemidji			
Bemidji				

1974

Third Place Winner:
Grand Rapids, 5 Sibley, 3

Consolation Champion:
Hibbing, 5 Kellogg, 4

but the Teddies went ahead 2-1 just four minutes later, thanks to goals by future NHL star Reed Larson and also by Brian Young. Rapids tied it back up just 20 seconds into the third when Tim McDonald tipped in a Mike Johnson shot to send the game into overtime. Then, Indians center Evin Roth took a Dan Lempe pass at the 1:40 mark of the extra session and fired it past Teddie goalie Richard Bain for the 3-2 game-winner.

Bemidji edged Kellogg in the final quarterfinal of the day, as the Lumberjacks got goals from Dick Howe, Jimmy Conway and Brian Nelson. Kellogg rallied in the third to get to within one, but Bemidji's goalie Jeff Wizner held on for the 3-2 win.

Sibley and Edina met in the first semifinal, as Sibley's left wing Bob Baumgartner got two first period goals to give the Warriors an early 2-0 lead. Edina, which hadn't been down by more than one goal that entire season, started to get worried. After a scoreless second, Doug Spoden made it three-nil, when he out-muscled two Edina defenders to slip a sweet backhander past Hornet keeper John Hughes just two minutes into the third. With the scent of upset now rancid, Edina geared up for what would prove to be one of the greatest third period comebacks of all time. Somehow pulling five straight unanswered goals out of their magic hat from Dick Pavek, Billy Thayer, Bob Frawley and a pair from Chas Peterson, the Hornets rolled to a fabulous come-from-behind 5-3 victory.

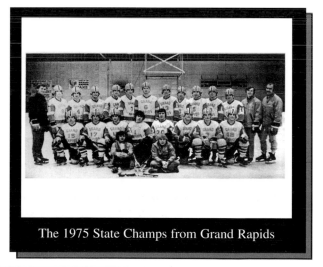

First Row: Jon Hughes, Bill Thayer, Charlie Petersen, Jerry Johnson, Steve Nichols, Tim Pavek, Steve Sherman.
Second Row: Coach Willard Ikola, Larry Johnson, Andy Overman, Mike Mastor, Matt Ikola, Dave Finks, Assistant Coach Ed Zins.
Third Row: Student Manager Adam White, Craig Norwich, Jim Anderson, Tom Brower, Bob Frawley, Steve Polsfuss, Student Manager John Senior.

The 1974 State Champs from Edina East

Bemidji knocked off Grand Rapids in the other semifinal, thanks to goals from Rod Beck, Jim Conway, Mike Fairchild and Bill Isrealson. The Indians got a couple of goals late from John Rothstein, but it was too little too late, as the Lumberjacks cruised to a 4-2 victory.

The next night Willard Ikola's Edina Hornets completed their perfect 24-0 championship season when they romped all over Bemidji by the final score of 6-0. Jerry Johnson opened the scoring just 30 seconds into the game and was followed by goals from Bob Frawley, Dave Finks, Jim Anderson, Andy Overman and Bill Thayer. Sophomore sensation Jon Hughes posted just 12 saves that night, as he earned a much coveted championship shut out.

1975: Grand Rapids vs. Southwest

A significant event took place in 1975 that had never happened before in Tournament history. Private schools, who in the past played in their own annual "Private or Independant School Tournament," were admitted to the Minnesota State High School League. Terry Skrypek's Hill-Murray Pioneers were the first team to make it into the tournament field that year, coming in with an undefeated record none-the-less.

Southwest and Roseau commenced Tournament play that year, with the Indians going on to beat the Rams 5-3, thanks to a late third period rally that was highlighted by Mark Gherity's game-tying and game-wining goals. Rams center Mike Burgraff added a pair in the loss.

Game Two had Bloomington Lincoln going against Hopkins-Lindbergh. The Bears opened the scoring when Bart Larson beat Hopkins-Lindbergh goalie Bill Perkl at 5:53 of the first on a low slapper. The Flyers came back in the second to take the lead on a pair of goals from Joe Lawless and Scott Whitney, only to see the Bears retort with three unanswered tallies in the second and third from Tim Harrer, Dave Gunderson and Bart Larson to win 4-2.

Hill-Murray beat Duluth East 3-1 in the first evening game, thanks to goals from Tom Conroy and Mike Hurt and Mike Regan. The Hounds mounted a rally in the second as Phil Verchota hit Steve Mars on a nice give-and-go, but it was too late as the Pioneers peppered East's sophomore goaltender Walt Aufderheide, and hung on for their first win.

Grand Rapids scored early and often in Game Four, as they were led by Pete DeCenzo's hat trick and John Rothstein's two goals and three assists to beat Sibley 8-3. The Rapids pelted Warrior's goalie Pat Farrington with an amazing 51 shots en route to the win.

Southwest and Bloomington met in the first semifinal, and after a scoreless first, Bloomington center Terry Houck put the puck past Indian goalie Dan Mott at 5:38 of the second to take a one goal lead. John Meredith answered for Southwest midway through the third to tie it up and ultimately send the game into overtime. There, at 7:49 of the extra session, Southwest winger Steve Lindmeier beat Bloomington keeper Mickey Pickens on assists from Bob Bonin and Jeff Blake, to score the 2-1 game-winner.

The 1975 State Champs from Grand Rapids

The other semi between Grand Rapids and Hill-Murray was a rough and physical contest that featured some eight penalty's ranging from elbowing, to slashing, to interference. Indians winger Erin Roth was the hero in this one, scoring the games only two goals, both coming midway through the second on assists from DeCenzo and Rothstein to beat Pioneer goalie Steve Janaszek. Meanwhile, Indians goalie Dan Clafton posted just 12 saves in the shut out victory.

With that, the finals were set between Grand Rapids and Minneapolis Southwest. Southwest's John Meredith scored the game's first goal late in the first, giving his Indians a 1-0 lead that would last until the seven-minute mark of the second. That's when Grand Rapids brought

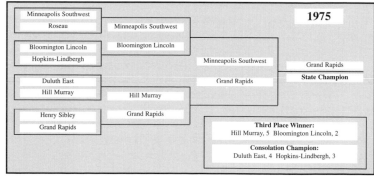

1975

Minneapolis Southwest			
Roseau	Minneapolis Southwest		
Bloomington Lincoln	Bloomington Lincoln		
Hopkins-Lindbergh		Minneapolis Southwest	Grand Rapids
		Grand Rapids	State Champion
Duluth East			
Hill Murray	Hill Murray		
	Grand Rapids		
Henry Sibley			
Grand Rapids			

Third Place Winner:
Hill Murray, 5 Bloomington Lincoln, 2

Consolation Champion:
Duluth East, 4 Hopkins-Lindbergh, 3

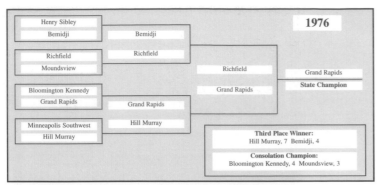

Henry Sibley			
Bemidji	Bemidji		
Richfield	Richfield		
Moundsview		Richfield	Grand Rapids
		Grand Rapids	State Champion
Bloomington Kennedy			
Grand Rapids	Grand Rapids		
Minneapolis Southwest	Hill Murray		
Hill Murray			

Third Place Winner:
Hill Murray, 7 Bemidji, 4

Consolation Champion:
Bloomington Kennedy, 4 Moundsview, 3

out the heavy artillery. At 7:54 John Rothstein blasted one by Southwest goalie Dan Mott to even it up at one apiece. Then, less than three minutes later Dan Lempe added a pair of goals, followed by Dennis Doyle's wrister at 13:33. Up 4-1, Rapids' coach Gus Hendrickson, himself a Tournament star as a member of the famous 1951 Eveleth team, showed no mercy in the third. Roth got one at 4:46 and DeCenzo got another five minutes later, as Grand Rapids went on to take the lopsided 6-1 championship finale.

1976: Grand Rapids vs. Richfield

After seven years, the bicentennial Tournament of 1976 said good-bye to Bloomington's Met Center, and said hello to its old stomping grounds in downtown St. Paul where she was originally groomed some 31 years prior. On March 4th, the tourney officially christened the new St. Paul Civic Center, a plush 16,188-seat arena, complete with see-thru plexiglas dasher-boards, that sat adjacent to the old St. Paul Auditorium, which was later renamed in honor of the late civil rights leader Roy Wilkins.

Bemidji edged out Sibley in Game One, as John Fairbanks got the first of his two goals just three minutes into the game. Sibley answered with three straight from Tom Cascalenda, Greg Cosgrove and Tim Fangel, only to see the Lumberjacks rally to score three unanswered goals of their own in the third from John Fairbanks, Eric Niskanen and Lee Hanson to rally for a 4-3 win.

A couple of future 1980 Olympic stars got together in Game Two, with Richfield's Steve Christoff and Mounds View's Robbie McClanahan squaring off for a trip to the semis. Richfield, who got a pair of goals each from Christoff and Tom Szepanski, held on to fend off a late Mustang charge that included goals from McClanahan, Brad Michaelson and Jeff Lundgren, to earn a 4-3 victory.

Bloomington Kennedy met Grand Rapids in the third game of the day, as Kennedy's Dave Dillon scored first with just five seconds to go in the opening period. Indians center Pete DeCenzo then added a pair of goals in the second and third to ice the game for Rapids 2-1. The first came on an Al Cleveland tip-in, while the second came off a nice set-up pass from Don Lucia (today the Gophers new head hockey coach).

Southwest and Hill-Murray met in the final quarterfinal, in what would turn out to be a wild one. With Southwest up 4-2 going into the final period, the Pioneers mounted a comeback which began just 26 seconds into the third when Jeff Lukas tallied to get to within one. With their goalie Len Eagon pulled, Hill-Murray was able to get the equalizer with just 53 seconds remaining on the clock to force overtime. There, at just 4:11 of the OT, Pioneer winger Mike Hurt came down and stuffed a Steve Pierce rebound past Indians goalie Mike Senescall to get the dramatic 5-4 game-winner.

The first semi pitted Bemidji and Richfield together, as the sticks were flying from the opening drop in this one. While Dan Dow opened the scoring for the Lumberjacks at 2:50 of the first, Richfield's Jan Lasserud and Bemidji's Lee Hanson each exchanged a pair of goals to make it 3-2 for Bemidji. Then, midway through the second and into the third, Spartans wingers Steve Christy, Tom Szepanksi and Tommy Scudder all tallied to give Richfield the 5-3 come-from-behind win.

The last semifinal of the day featured yet another wild one between Grand Rapids and Hill-Murray. Indians goalie Jim Jetland had to make only 13 saves compared to his counterpart from Hill, Len Eagon, who faced 42 shots that night. Rapids jumped out to a quick 3-0 lead on goals by Dan Lempe, Tom Madsen and Al Cleveland, only to see Hill-Murray answer with two goals from Pat Regan and Steve Pierce to get it close. Dave Akre and Mark Schroeder each scored in the second and Al Cleveland then got his hat trick on two back-to-back power-play goals late in the third to put it out of reach, as Grand Rapids went on to win 7-4.

Coach Jim Nelson's Grand Rapids Indians were now set to face Larry Hendrickson's Richfield Spartans for all the beans. Don Lucia set up Brad Nordberg to open the scoring at just 1:25 of the first when he beat Geof Haraway on a pretty goal. Rapids then made it 2-0 when Al Cleveland tallied at 7:42 of the second. But Richfield came back behind its star player, Steve Christoff, who beat Jetland with just over a minute to go in the second. Erin Roth scored for Rapids midway through the third, only to see Christoff get another one at 12:21 to make it 3-2. Dan Lempe and Dave Akre hooked up just a minute later to make it 4-2 for Grand Rapids on an empty netter, only to see Christoff hit Jan Lasserud on a pretty one-timer to get it to 4-3 with just nine seconds left. Richfield's six attackers tried in vain to tie it up, but Jetland stoned them for the 4-3 final.

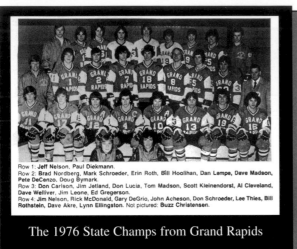

The 1976 State Champs from Grand Rapids

Row 1: Jeff Nelson, Paul Diekmann.
Row 2: Brad Nordberg, Mark Schroeder, Erin Roth, Bill Hoolihan, Dan Lempe, Dave Madson, Pete DeCenzo, Doug Bymark.
Row 3: Don Carlson, Jim Jetland, Don Lucia, Tom Madson, Scott Kleinendorst, Al Cleveland, Dave Welliver, Jim Leone, Ed Gregerson.
Row 4: Jim Nelson, Rick McDonald, Gary DeGrio, John Acheson, Don Schroeder, Lee Thies, Bill Rothstein, Dave Akre, Lynn Ellingston. Not pictured: Buzz Christensen.

1977: Rochester John Marshall vs. Edina

Hill-Murray and South St. Paul got together in Game One, as Packer winger Keith Peterson's hat trick proved to be the difference in the 5-2 victory.

Rochester John Marshall came right out of the shoots against Southwest, as Scott Lecy and Todd Bauernfeind each scored in the first six minutes to make it 2-0. The Indians came back on a Kurt Madgyra goal with only 29 seconds remaining in the second that beat JM goalie Paul Butters, but Lecy added his second of the game late in the third to ice it for the Rockets, 4-1.

Game Three was a blow-out, with the defending champs from Grand Rapids making quick work of Mounds View. Mark Roy, Scott

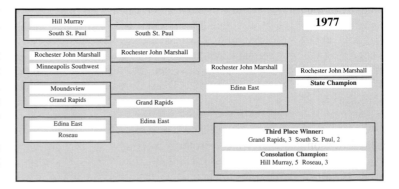

Hill Murray			
South St. Paul	South St. Paul		
Rochester John Marshall	Rochester John Marshall		
Minneapolis Southwest		Rochester John Marshall	Rochester John Marshall
		Edina East	State Champion
Moundsview			
Grand Rapids	Grand Rapids		
Edina East	Edina East		
Roseau			

1977

Third Place Winner:
Grand Rapids, 3 South St. Paul, 2

Consolation Champion:
Hill Murray, 5 Roseau, 3

Kleinendorst, Al Cleveland and Bill Rothstein (who netted a pair), all tallied for the Indians as they routed the Mustangs 5-1 to advance to the semis.

The last quarterfinal of the day saw the rather inauspicious debut of one of the greatest lines in Minnesota hockey history, Roseau's Neal Broten, Aaron Broten and Butsy Erickson. Edina East had other plans on that evening, as they got two goals from Bret Bjerken and John Donnelly in the third to blank the Rams 2-0. Hornet goalie Steve Carroll had 22 saves in the shutout.

The first semifinal contest had South St. Paul going up against Rochester. The game was very tight, with some six penalties being called through the first two periods alone. After both goalies put up zero's through two, Todd Lecy finally got one past Packer keeper Duane Bodle at the 7:24 mark to give his club a 1-0 lead. From there star goalie Paul Butters played phenomenally, making 37 straight saves in the 1-0 shutout.

The other semi had Edina playing Grand Rapids. The Indians, who came into the tournament averaging seven goals per game, were the odds-on favorites to three-peat, despite the fact that Edina had been ranked No. 1 for most of that season in the polls.

The two teams got started by trading a pair of goals each through the first as Mel Pearson tallied twice for Edina, and Gary DeGrio and Mark Roy scored for the Indians. Grand Rapids came out big in the second, scoring two straight within a minute's time on goals from Scott Kleinendorst and Steve Swentkofske. The Hornets remained calm though, and very quietly came back behind a pair of Steve Pepper goals to score four straight in a time span of just less than six minutes. Indians' center Kurt Kleinendorst closed the gap with just over a minute to play, but his team couldn't pull their goalie because the Hornets kept dumping the puck into their zone. Edina held on to get the upset victory by the final score of 6-5.

And so, in front of a record championship crowd of 17,083 at the new Civic Center, it was 24-1 Edina vs. 24-2 Rochester for all the works. Rochester came out the gates ready to go as Scott Lecy took the opening face-off draw, skated into the Edina zone, slipped a perfect pass over to his linemate Bruce Aikens, and watched him beat Hornet goalie Steve Carroll up high for the 1-0 lead. The Rockets took a 2-0 lead at 7:24 when Lecy took a long outlet pass from defenseman Paul Brandrup for a breakaway. He came in on Carroll, faked left, and went top-shelf on the other side. Edina came back just five minutes later on a Dave Terwilliger garbage goal out front, and then tied it up at 12:01 of the second when Tom Kelly's power-play blast from the blue-line rifled through traffic and into the back of the John Marshall net. Just a minute into the third, it was Lecy again for the Rockets, as he this time stuffed in a rebound in the crease. Up 3-2 with just a minute to go, Rochester got an insurance goal on a wild six-on-five play. Edina, who had pulled their goalie, was pressing hard to try and tie it up. Then, on a crucial face-off in the Rochester end, Lecy won the draw, passed it over to Brandrup for the give-and-go, and took the return pass the length of the ice for the open-net breakaway goal. Lecy, the hero, celebrated wildly with his teammates at center ice.

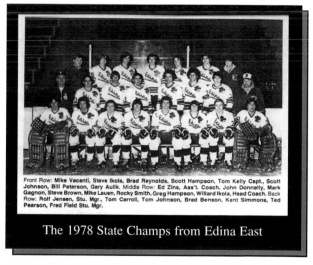
Front row, left to right: Scott Lecy, Bruce Aikens, Pat Taylor, Paul Butters, Todd Lecy, Jeff Nelson, Paul Brandrup.
Back row, left to right: Coach Gene Sack, Ken Roberts, Student Manager, Jeff Teal, Todd Bauernfeind, Dan Erickson, Jeff Meyer, Doug LeTourneau, Tom Taylor, Jon Erickson, Kevin Bakken, Tom Kothenbeutel, Scott Monarud, Bill Michaels, Ed Schroeder, Student Manager, Les Neeb, Asst. Coach.

The 1977 State Champs from Rochester J.M.

1978: Edina East vs. Grand Rapids

For the first time in tourney history, players were required to start wearing face-masks in 1978. It was a controversial decision that was met with much debate. While on one hand, it meant that the players would be further protected from eye and facial injuries, it also meant that smaller players could be every bit as aggressive as the bigger ones, without suffering the consequences. Kids who were 5-foot-5 and a buck forty soaking wet could now mouth off and deck just about any team's biggest goon with very little fear of getting punched in return, and this changed the game's chemistry.

Grand Rapids needed just a first period goal from Bill Rothstein to beat Hill-Murray 1-0 in the opener, as Jim Jetland recorded 24 saves in earning the shutout victory. Mounds View got goals from Steve Klein, Pat Conlin, Jeff Ness, Harry Geist and Pete Eastman, as they went on to beat South St. Paul 5-4 in Game Two, while Packer winger Tom Sadowski had a pair of goals in the loss. A pair of Aaron Broten goals late in the third clinched a 4-2 Roseau win over the defending champs from Rochester in Game Three, and Willard Ikola's protégé, Steve Ikola, beat Roosevelt goalie John Berke with just 54 seconds left to get the game-winner in Edina's 4-3 Game Four victory.

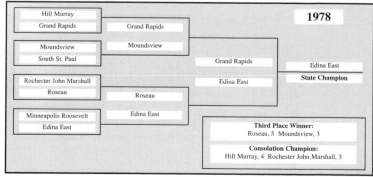
Front Row: Mike Vacanti, Steve Ikola, Brad Reynolds, Scott Hampson, Tom Kelly Capt., Scott Johnson, Bill Peterson, Gary Aulik. Middle Row: Ed Zins, Ass't. Coach, John Donnelly, Mark Gagnon, Steve Brown, Mike Lauen, Rocky Smith, Greg Hampson, Willard Ikola, Head Coach. Back Row: Rolf Jensen, Stu. Mgr., Tom Carroll, Tom Johnson, Brad Benson, Kent Simmons, Ted Pearson, Fred Field Stu. Mgr.

The 1978 State Champs from Edina East

Grand Rapids and Mounds View hooked up for the first semi, and thanks to goals from Tom Rothstein, Scott Kleinendorst, Irwin Frizzell and Don Schroeder, the Indians beat the Mustangs 4-2.

The other semifinal contest had Edina going up against the Roseau Rams. Roseau, led by the now infamous line of Aaron and Neal Broten and Butsy Erickson (a line that would later be reconnected at the U of M), came into the game with a perfect 23-0 record, having scored an amazing 10 or more goals in 11 games that season. Edina's Mark Gagnon opened the scoring on a short-handed goal midway through the first, only to see Neal Broten tie it up just two minutes later. Hornet winger Mike Lauen then beat Ram netminder Dean Grindahl at 10:59 of the first to regain the lead. After a Jeff Goos tying goal, Edina regained the lead at 7:13 of the second when Tom Kelly fired a prayer from center ice that bounced off of Grindahl's shoulder and into the back of the net. Butsy Erickson tied it off Aaron Broten's rebound three minutes later, only to see Lauen score again, this time grabbing a Broten rebound shot that had caromed off the pipe the length of the ice. Lauen added anoth-

				1978
Hill Murray				
Grand Rapids	Grand Rapids			
Moundsview				
South St. Paul	Moundsview			
		Grand Rapids		Edina East
Rochester John Marshall		Edina East		**State Champion**
Roseau	Roseau			
Minneapolis Roosevelt				
Edina East	Edina East			

Third Place Winner:
Roseau, 5 Moundsview, 3

Consolation Champion:
Hill Murray, 4 Rochester John Marshall, 3

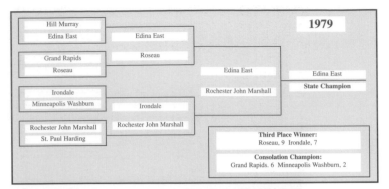

1979

Hill Murray
Edina East
Edina East

Grand Rapids
Roseau
Roseau

Edina East
Rochester John Marshall

Edina East
State Champion

Irondale
Minneapolis Washburn
Irondale

Rochester John Marshall
St. Paul Harding
Rochester John Marshall

Third Place Winner:
Roseau, 9 Irondale, 7

Consolation Champion:
Grand Rapids. 6 Minneapolis Washburn, 2

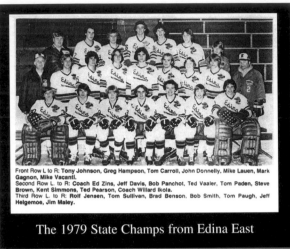

Front Row L to R: Tony Johnson, Greg Hampson, Tom Carroll, John Donnelly, Mike Lauen, Mark Gagnon, Mike Vacanti.
Second Row L. to R: Coach Ed Zins, Jeff Davis, Bob Panchot, Ted Vaaler, Tom Paden, Steve Brown, Kent Simmons, Ted Pearson, Coach Willard Ikola.
Third Row L. to R: Rolf Jensen, Tom Sullivan, Brad Benson, Bob Smith, Tom Paugh, Jeff Helgemoe, Jim Maley.

The 1979 State Champs from Edina East

er late in the third to complete his hat trick and ice the game for the Hornets by the final of 5-3.

Edina then faced another northern power in the finals, Grand Rapids, which had won it all in both 1975 and 1976, and finished third in 1977. Edina's Steve Ikola got the Hornets on the board first, when he took a couple of sweet passes from John Donnelly and Tom Kelly to beat Indians goalie Jim Jetland at the 10:00 mark. Bill Rothstein answered by scoring a power-play goal with just over a minute to go in the period to make it 1-1. Rapids then made it 2-1 just 29 seconds into the second on defenseman Irwin Frizzell's shot from the point, only to see the stubborn Hornets rally behind a Mark Gagnon shot out front just 25 seconds later. The Indians resumed the lead on a Gary DeGrio unassisted wrister from the high slot that beat Edina goalie Gary Aulik. Edina tied it up at 2:44 of the third on Greg Hampson's 30-foot slapper, and then took a 4-3 lead at 9:40 when Scott Johnson tipped a long shot from Donnelly past Jetland. Bill Rothstein then jammed in a loose puck in front of the cage just 14 seconds later to tie the game at four, and send it into overtime. After playing a scoreless first OT, Edina's Tommy Carroll, who came into the game as a substitute, got the game-winner by shooting his own rebound past Indians goalie Jeff Jetland at 1:06 of the second extra session. Edina, despite being outshot 52 to 23, held on for the 5-4 victory behind goalie Gary Aulik's championship game record 48 saves.

1979: Edina vs. Rochester John Marshall

The Hornets barely etched out a big and quick Hill-Murray team 4-3 in the opener, thanks to goals from Steve Brown, Mike Laven, John Donnelly and Mark Gagnon.

Game Two was a clash of the titans, with Roseau battling Grand Rapids, and their young goaltender by the name of Jon Casey, for the rights to northern supremacy. Glen DaMota's hat trick and Aaron Broten's two goals and two assists led the way for the Rams, as they hung on to win a very tough 6-4 nail-biter.

Game Three saw Washburn jump out to a 2-0 lead over Irondale, only to see the Knights rally back behind Scott Bjugstad's hat trick, and Mark Bader's two goals, to win the game by the final score of 6-4.

The last quarterfinal of the day pitted Rochester John Marshall against St. Paul Harding. Rochester jumped out to a 4-1 lead after the first, thanks to goals from Rick Ruesink, Pete Segar, Doug LeTourneau and Dirk Anderson. Harding then rallied back on a pair of second period goals from Jeff Thole and another from Bill Taleen, but Todd Lecy's goal at 5:30 of the third period iced it for the Rockets as goalie Paul Butters hung on for the 5-3 win.

Edina and Roseau got together yet again for the first semifinal contest. These two teams had created a great rivalry over the past several years, and the 16,000-plus fans in attendance were eager to see them beat the hell out of each other. Edina, wanting to send a clear message once and for all about how they felt, came out and annihilated the Rams 12-4. Five of the goals came on power-play situations, meaning that there were a lot of players sitting in the penalty box throughout this wild one. The Hornets got three goals from Mark Ganon, and a pair each from Tom Carroll and Mike Laven to lead the way.

The other semifinal game was also a high scoring affair, as Irondale met up with Rochester. The two teams methodically scored back-and-forth against each other, with Rochester finally winning the contest 7-4. While the Rockets got a hat trick from Todd Lecy and a pair from Doug LeTourneau, Mike Kelly scored two and added an assist for Irondale in the loss.

With that, the stage was now set for a rematch of the 1977 state championship game, Edina vs. Rochester. Lecy picked up where he left off, scoring first for Rochester just a minute into the game. Greg Hampson answered at the 4:56 mark of the first to make it 1-1. The score remained tied until the midway point of the second, when Brad Benson beat Rochester goalie Paul Butters on a nice breakaway goal. The Rockets responded with two power-play goals midway through the third from Scott Monsrud and Doug LeTourneau to make it 3-2. But, with just over a minute to go in the game, and their goalie sitting on the bench, Edina's Tom Carroll found the back of the net to send the game into overtime. It didn't take long to settle the score in sudden death. That's because at 3:27 of the extra session, Edina left winger Mike Laven deked and beat Rochester goalie Paul Butters on a nice pass from Mark Gagnon for the spine-tingling game-winner. The Civic Center's record crowd of 17,469 went berserk as the Edina players mobbed their goalie Mike Vacanti, who had 29 saves in the 4-3 victory. The win gave Willard Ikola's Hornets their third title in just six years.

1980: Grand Rapids vs. Hill-Murray

Southwest and South St. Paul hooked up in the opener, as the Indians got on the board first when Dan May scored a shorthanded goal at 4:08 of the first. The Packers evened it up three minutes later on a Gary Mausolf goal, only to see Southwest fire back with three straight goals from Charlie Lundeen, Doug Hackett and Dan Burns. After playing to a scoreless second, South St. Paul came out and got it to 4-3 on a pair of power-play goals from Steve Zweig. Then, with just 28 seconds to go in the game, and the Packers goalie pulled, South St. Paul defenseman Phil Housley beat Southwest goalie Greg Dick to tie it up at 4-4. The Packers just kept the pressure on after that, as May got his second of the game just 47 seconds into the extra session to give his squad a 5-4 win.

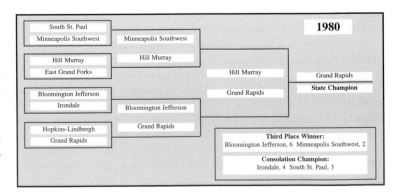

1980

South St. Paul
Minneapolis Southwest
Minneapolis Southwest

Hill Murray
East Grand Forks
Hill Murray

Hill Murray

Bloomington Jefferson
Irondale
Bloomington Jefferson

Grand Rapids

Grand Rapids
State Champion

Hopkins-Lindbergh
Grand Rapids
Grand Rapids

Third Place Winner:
Bloomington Jefferson, 6 Minneapolis Southwest, 2

Consolation Champion:
Irondale, 4 South St. Paul, 3

Game Two had the undefeated Hill-Murray Pioneers going against East Grand Forks. Thanks to a pair of goals from Pat Foley and another from Rob Schwietz, the Pioneers hung on to beat the Green Wave by the final of 3-1.

Bloomington Jefferson and Irondale met in the first evening game, and thanks to centerman Jay North's hat trick, Jefferson went on to beat the Knights 5-2.

The last quarterfinal featured Hopkins Lindbergh going against Grand Rapids, in a game that was all Indians. Rapids jumped out to a quick 2-0 lead within the game's first four minutes on goals from Jim Malwitz and Tom Rothstein that beat Hopkins' goalie Duffy Loney. The Flyers made it 2-1 at 11:38 on a Todd Bjorkstrand wrister that slipped past Rapids' netminder Jon Casey upstairs, followed up by a Pat Reichel power-play goal just over a minute later to tie it up. But, Grand Rapids took over from there, scoring six more goals in the second and third from Scott Billedeau, Jeff Hovanec, Todd Grina, Tom Rothstein and a pair from Todd Lempe to cruise to a 8-3 win.

The 1980 State Champs from Grand Rapids

Front Row, L. to R.: Jon Casey, Robert Madson, John DeCenzo, Scott Billeadeau, Thomas Rothstein, Michael Brill, Shawn Edwards, Jeffrey Hovanec, Todd Grina, Jeff Storlie. Second Row, L. to R.: Ted Brill, Asst. Coach, Todd Lempe, Bruce LaRoque, Pat Bowe, Steve LaRoque, Tony Kellin, Jim Malwitz, Brian Crippa, Glenn Palso, Will Sarkela, Athletic Director. Back Row, L. to R.: Lynn Ellingson, Ass't Coach, Rod (Buzzy) Christensen, Coach, Eric Lempe, David Casey, Don Carlson, Trainer, Bob Dunnell, Manager. Not Pictured: Chris LaVasseur.

Future North Star Jon Casey is mobbed after his Grand Rapids Indians win the 1980 state title

Hill-Murray and Southwest got together for the first semi and showed why there was no love loss between these two teams. In a game that included an incredible 14 penalties, Hill-Murray pounded the Indians by the final score of 7-2. Mark Kissner and Tom Xavier each netted a pair, while Pioneer goalie Jeff Poeschl registered 26 saves in the win

Grand Rapids and Bloomington met for the other semi, in a penalty-laden affair that kept the referees busy all night. Bloomington jumped out first on a low slapper by Tim Sullivan that beat Jon Casey at 10:48 of the first. But the Indians roared back for three unanswered goals from Tom Rothstein, Jim Malwitz and Shawn Edwards, who got an empty netter, to beat Jefferson by the final of 3-1. Jaguar goalie John Columbo had 23 saves in the game, while Jon Casey came up with 22 of his own for the win.

Grand Rapids drew first blood in the finals against Hill-Murray, when at 13:45 of the first John DeCenzo, the team's scoring leader, first dug the puck out of the corner, then skated around a Pioneer defender, and finally lifted a backhander past goalie Jeff Poeschl to make it 1-0. Hill-Murray tied it up at 6:35 of the second when Mark Kissner grabbed Sean Regan's blue line blast rebound and stuffed it into the back of the net. Six minutes later, Indian winger Todd Lempe got what would prove to be the game-winner when he deflected a Shawn Edwards shot past Poeschl to make it 2-1. Hill-Murray tried like hell to tie it up, but Casey played huge in earning the 2-1 victory. For the Pioneers, who outshot the Indians by a two to one margin (32 to 16), it was, incredibly, their fifth straight tournament defeat at the hands of Grand Rapids.

1981: Bloomington Jefferson vs. Irondale

The Jaguars jumped out to a 1-0 lead against Grand Rapids in the opener, thanks to defenseman Rob Ohno's power-play goal from Steve Bianchi at 10:04 of the second period. The Indians then tied it up with just 15 seconds to go in the period when Bruce LaRoque beat Jefferson netminder Chris Robideau. Rapids then added a pair of goals from Eric Lempe and Tony Kellin to go up 3-1, only to see Bloomington answer with a pair of their own from Dan Beaty and Steve Bianchi, who beat Indians goalie Paul Kaczor on a breakaway with just 11 seconds to go in the game. The game went into sudden death, where, just 49 seconds later, Bloomington's Steve Nornes assisted on Jim Gess' 4-3 game-winning goal.

North St. Paul and Apple Valley met for Game Two, in what would prove to be another overtime thriller. While Mike Anderson led the way for the Polars with a pair of tallies, it was Apple Valley's Bruce Heglund who finally got the overtime game-winner just 29 seconds into the extra session to give the Eagles a 4-3 win.

Edina West and South St. Paul met for the third quarterfinal of the day, as Wes Olson put the Cougars up 1-0 at 9:41 of the first on a power-play goal from Mike O'Connor and Tom Frisk. The Packers came back on a power-play goal of their own that was set up by Phil Housley, who dished to Dave Sobaski in front of the net to tie it up at 1-1 just 11 seconds into the second period. The very physical game raged back and forth, with a whopping 10 penalties between the two clubs occurring in the first two periods alone. Then, with just five seconds left in the contest, future NHL star Phil Housley skated in, deked, and beat Edina goalie Jim Lozinski up high for the game-winner.

The last quarterfinal game of the day had Irondale and Roseau going toe-to-toe. Roseau's Larry Goos opened the scoring at 2:27 of the first, only to see Irondale charge back for four straight goals from Marc Bader, Steve Hoppe, Mike Bjugstad and Steve Checco. Roseau answered with two more from Shawn Hallie and Keith Beito, but Irondale's Dana Hildreth and Steve Witucki responded with a pair of their own to give the Knights a 7-3 win.

Apple Valley and Bloomington met in the first semifinal match, as the Jaguars, who got goals from Joe Wech, Chris Gram and a pair from

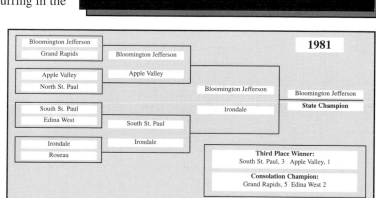

Front Row, L. to R.: Steve Nornes, Rob Ohno, Dan Beaty, Joe Wech, Chris Robideau, Scott Schoening, Kirk Nelson, Tom Kelly, Terry Sullivan, Steve Bianchi. Back Row, L. to R.: Asst. Coach John Bianchi, Craig Havlicek Mgr., Chris Gram, Scott Myklebust, Jim Becker, Jim Gess, Tony Mazzu, Paul Gess, Kyle Kranz, Lee Fjellman, Randy Thompson, Mgr., Coach Tom Saterdalen.

The 1981 State Champs from Bloomington Jefferson

Bloomington Jefferson				1981
Grand Rapids	Bloomington Jefferson			
Apple Valley	Apple Valley			
North St. Paul		Bloomington Jefferson	Bloomington Jefferson	
South St. Paul		Irondale	State Champion	
Edina West	South St. Paul			
Irondale	Irondale			
Roseau				

Third Place Winner:
South St. Paul, 3 Apple Valley, 1

Consolation Champion:
Grand Rapids, 5 Edina West 2

Dan Beatty, went on to beat the Eagles by a 4-1 margin. The other semi had Irondale and South St. Paul going at it in a wild one. The Packers came out and appeared to have this one in the bag after three goals by Tom Stiles, Phil Housley and Larry Housley. But, Irondale, who got second and third period goals from Loren Bayer, Lou Hedberg, Ken Brovold, Dave Kirwin and Steve Hoppe, rallied back to capture the 5-3 victory.

So, it would be the Jaguars and Knights for the title. Irondale opened the scoring at 9:44 of the first when defenseman Dave Kirwin beat Bloomington keeper Chris Robideau on an unassisted slapper to make it 1-0. The Jags answered back with two of their own, when Jim Becker and Paul Gess tallied late in the first period to take a 2-1 lead. The Jags added another goal less than a minute into the second on a Tony Mazzu goal from Steve Bianchi and Dan Beatty to give themselves a two goal lead. Irondale pressed hard in the last seconds of the game, finally getting one back with on the six-on-five advantage with just four seconds to go, but the Jags held on to win the game and the title by the final of 3-2.

1982: Edina vs. White Bear Mariner

Rochester Mayo and Edina (Edina-West was consolidated into Edina-East to form one combined school after eight years as two separate programs), played in a wild Game One, with the Hornets coming up victorious. Edina's John DeVoe started it out by scoring at 8:08 of the first, only to see Mayo come right back to score three quick ones for a 3-1 lead.

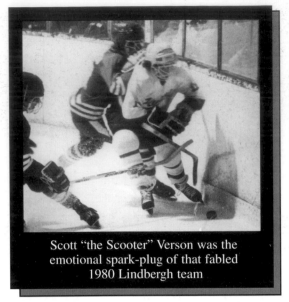

Scott "the Scooter" Verson was the emotional spark-plug of that fabled 1980 Lindbergh team

Edina, led by Dave Maley's two goals, then promptly responded by scoring six unanswered goals to win the game 7-3.

Game Two had Bloomington beating East Grand Forks 4-3 thanks to Steve Bianchi and Kyle Kranz' one goal and one assist, while Hibbing blanked Sibley 3-0 on a pair of Gary and Greg Hooper goals.

The last quarterfinal had Cloquet taking on White Bear Mariner in another blowout. White Bear's Brydges had a hat trick while his teammate McLeod added a pair in the 7-2 drubbing. For Cloquet, it was a tough loss. The Lumberjacks were making their first-ever appearance in the tourney, and to top it off, they were missing their star player, Cory Millen, who had broken his ankle in the sectional playoffs.

Edina then met Jefferson in the first semifinal contest, as the two teams skated to a scoreless first period. Hornets winger Paul Roff opened the scoring at 6:01 of the second period when he knocked in Jeff Vacanti's rebound to make it 1-0. The Jags answered at 8:17 when Kyle Kranz's 15-foot one-timer from Terry Sullivan found the roof of the net. The teams skated into the third when Roff got his second goal of the game at the 5:50 mark on a nice wrister from just outside the circle. With Jefferson's goalie pulled in favor of a sixth attacker, and less than a minute left in regulation, Scott Myklebust zipped a pass over to Kranz, who beat Galbraith on a beautiful slapper at the 14:39 mark to send the game into overtime. There, with just 57 seconds left in the eight-minute session, Edina's Dan Carroll passed the puck up to Mike DeVoe, who touch-passed it to Wally Chapman, who in turn tattoo'd a 30-foot slapper off the side of the crossbar and into the net for the dramatic 3-2 game-winner.

The other semi saw much less dramatics, as White Bear Mariner beat Hibbing 4-1, on goals from Baker, Schultz, and a pair from Anderson. Mariner goalie Bohrer made 28 saves in the semifinal win, to give his team its first ever trip to the finals.

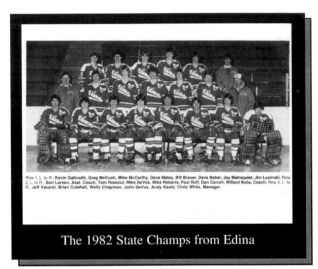

The 1982 State Champs from Edina

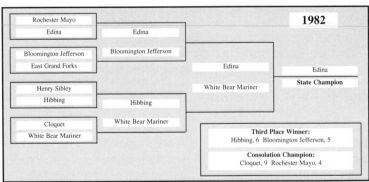

The Mariners and Hornets then met for the title, in what turned out to be a laugher. The 18,985 fans at the Civic Center could be seen leaving early in this one as Edina gave Willard Ikola his sixth state title by scoring six unanswered goals to blank White Bear 6-0. Edina goalie Kevin Galbraith posted just seven saves in the title game shutout, something that hadn't happened in Tournament history since 1974. Scoring for the Hornets were: Dan Carroll, Mike McCarthy, Jeff Vacanti, Dave Maley, Bill Brauer and Paul Roff.

1983: Hill-Murray vs. Burnsville

Two significant events happened in 1983 that gave the Minnesota State High School Tournament a lot of great local, as well as national exposure. First, WCCO-TV began televising the Tournament throughout the state, giving everyone at home the chance to follow the games. Secondly, Sports Illustrated's senior writer, E.M Swift, wrote a wonderful feature story about the Tournament, entitled: "The Thrill of a Lifetime." The 11-page article, complete with eight color illustrations, let the entire world know about our little secret up here in the great northwoods, and instantly put Minnesota high school hockey on the map.

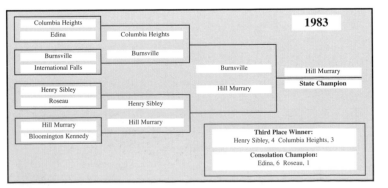

Edina, which joined most of the other schools at the tournament by

switching from the traditional hockey socks and breezers to those hideous "long-pant" incarnations called "Cooperalls," met Columbia Heights in the first quarterfinal game, as the Hylanders got two goals from Joe Mickelson and D.J. Haller to earn a 2-0 first round upset over the Hornets. Columbia Heights goalie Reggie Miracle recorded 29 saves in the shutout.

Game Two saw yet another shut out, as Burnsville blanked International Falls 4-0. Todd Okerlund (son of pro wrestling's "Mean-Gene" Okerlund), led the Braves with a pair of goals and an assist, while Braves goalie John Olson posted just 13 saves for the doughnut.

The third game of the day was also a blow-out, as Henry Sibley beat Roseau 4-1, on a pair of goals from Tom Genz. Brent Nagel and Steve Fleming also tallied for the Warriors, while defenseman Tom Pederson got Roseau's lone goal on a power-play at 6:38 of the third period.

The final quarter featured the undefeated Hill-Murray Pioneers against the Bloomington Kennedy Eagles in a contest that came down to the wire. Kennedy got on the board first when Larry Leeman scored just 26 seconds into the game, while Tim Cline evened it up just seven minutes later. Pioneer right wing Tony Curella made it 2-1 at 9:02, only to see Eagles winger Dallas Miller beat Pioneer goalie Tim Galash with only a minute to go in the first. Hill-Murray, down 3-1, came out swinging in the second and put up four straight goals from Nick Bede, Jeff Borndale, Curella and Mark Horvath to take the lead. Kennedy responded with a pair from Jim Hartman and Pat Swetela to tie it up yet again, but with only 43 seconds left in the game, Tony Curella notched his hat trick by beating Eagle keeper Jeff Miles for the 6-5 game winner.

Front Row, L. to R.: Tim Galash, Jeff Borndale, Mark Horvath, Tom Follmer, Mark Krois, Nick Belde, Scott Faust, Pat Heffernan, Mike Schwietz.
Back Row, L. to R.: Assistant Coach Bill Lechner, Diane Yarusso (stat), Trisha Driscoll (stat), Jim Jirele, Jeff Thomas, Jim Boryczka, Tom Graske, Paul Syfko, Mark Stonich, Mike Roth, Todd Norman, Mark Nowicki, Bob Leier, Tony Curella, Brian Zelenak, Head Coach Terry Skrypek. Missing: Managers John Rather and Joe Giannini.

The 1983 State Champs from Hill-Murray

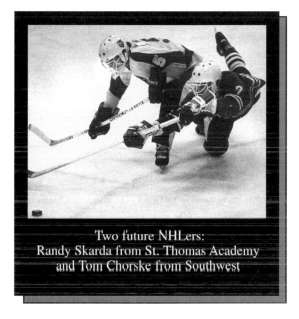

Two future NHLers:
Randy Skarda from St. Thomas Academy
and Tom Chorske from Southwest

Burnsville beat Columbia Heights in the first semifinal game when, Dave MacNulty, after being dragged down on a breakaway, broke a 2-2 tie on a an exciting penalty shot with less than five minutes to go in the game. (It was the first successful penalty shot in the state tournament since 1960.) The Braves then added two more empty netters in the final minute of the contest to grab the 5-2 win.

Henry Sibley and Hill-Murray met for the second semi, in a game that was all Hill-Murray. Center Mark Horvath had a pair of power-play goals in this one, while Jeff Borndale added another in the 3-1 win.

The finals then saw Hill-Murray and Burnsville go at it, as Braves center Louie Molnar opened the scoring at 4:32 of the first on a Dave Thon assist. Hill came back on Mark Krois' put-in eight minutes later, only to see Burnsville's Todd Skime tally on a power-pay goal at 4:11 of the second. Down 2-1, the Pioneers roared back to take the lead on goals from Tom Graske and Mark Krois at the end of the second period. Burnsville tied it up on Tom Campbell's goal from Todd Okerlund at 6:36, as the teams skated down the home-stretch locked at three-apiece. Then, after a flurry of activity from both teams, Hill-Murray center Jim Jirelle got the goal of a lifetime with just 3:12 remaining in the game, when he knocked in Scott Fausts' rebound past Braves goalie John Olson. The Braves tried to mount a rally, but Pioneer goalie Mike Schwietz stood on his head for the last three minutes to give his club a dramatic 4-3 win as well as its first title.

1984: Edina vs. Bloomington Kennedy

Edina pulverized Roseau in the opener, getting goals from sophomore sensation Pete Hankinson, Jerry Kaehler, Marty Nanne (as in the son of Lou), Tom Terwilliger, and also a pair from future NHL star Paul Ranheim. Edina keeper Chris Schwartzbauer posted 23 saves in the shutout.

Hill-Murray and Johnson met in Game Two, with the Governors winning a back-and forth slug-fest by the final of 3-2. Jim Hau led the way for Johnson with a pair of goals, while Tom Graske and Steve Rohlik each scored for the Pioneers in the losing effort.

The third game of the afternoon was another blowout, with Hibbing eliminating St. Cloud Apollo 6-2. Apollo jumped out to a quick 2-0 lead in the first thanks to goals by Mike Hiltner and Erik Halstrom, but the Bluejackets roared back for six unanswered goals in the second and third. Tallying for Hibbing that night were: Antonio Catani, Nick Andrich, Richie Bryant, Pat Iozzo, John Schwartz and Tom Hanson.

The last quarterfinal of the day saw Kennedy edge out Burnsville in a tight 4-2 contest. The two teams exchanged a pair of goals back and forth through the second period, but when Eagle's center Tracey Leeman beat Burnsville goalie Andy Luckraft at 7:03 of the third to give his team a 3-2 lead, it was all but over. Kennedy added an empty netter from John Reuder with 24 seconds to go to put the final nail in Burnsville's coffin.

Johnson and Kennedy played a wild semifinal opener, with Kennedy

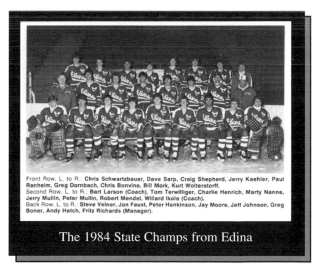

Front Row, L. to R.: Chris Schwartzbauer, Dave Sarp, Craig Shepherd, Jerry Kaehler, Paul Ranheim, Greg Dornbach, Chris Bonvino, Bill Mork, Kurt Wolterstorff.
Second Row, L. to R.: Bart Larson (Coach), Tom Terwilliger, Charlie Henrich, Marty Nanne, Jerry Mullin, Peter Mullin, Robert Mendel, Willard Ikola (Coach).
Back Row, L. to R.: Steve Velner, Jon Faust, Peter Hankinson, Jay Moore, Jeff Johnson, Greg Boner, Andy Hatch, Fritz Richards (Manager).

The 1984 State Champs from Edina

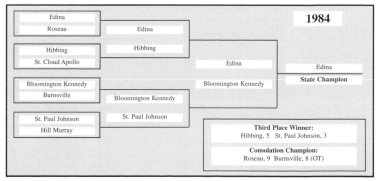

				1984
Edina				
Roseau	Edina			
Hibbing		Edina		
St. Cloud Apollo	Hibbing		Edina	
				State Champion
Bloomington Kennedy		Bloomington Kennedy		
Burnsville	Bloomington Kennedy			
St. Paul Johnson	St. Paul Johnson			
Hill Murray				

Third Place Winner:
Hibbing, 5 St. Paul Johnson, 3

Consolation Champion:
Roseau, 9 Burnsville, 8 (OT)

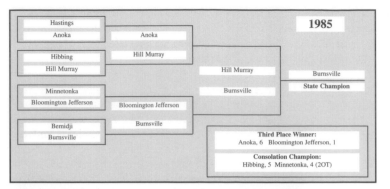

1985

Hastings
Anoka — Anoka
Hibbing — Hill Murray
Hill Murray — Hill Murray
Minnetonka — Bloomington Jefferson
Bloomington Jefferson — Burnsville
Bemidji
Burnsville

Burnsville
State Champion

Third Place Winner:
Anoka, 6   Bloomington Jefferson, 1

Consolation Champion:
Hibbing, 5   Minnetonka, 4 (2OT)

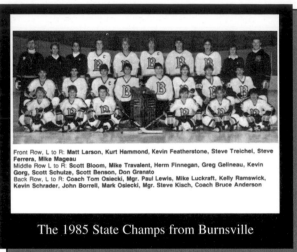

Front Row, L to R: Matt Larson, Kurt Hammond, Kevin Featherstone, Steve Treichel, Steve Ferrera, Mike Mageau
Middle Row L to R: Scott Bloom, Mike Travalent, Herm Finnegan, Greg Gelineau, Kevin Gorg, Scott Schulze, Scott Benson, Don Granato
Back Row, L to R: Coach Tom Osiecki, Mgr. Paul Lewis, Mike Luckraft, Kelly Ramswick, Kevin Schrader, John Borrell, Mark Osiecki, Mgr. Steve Kisch, Coach Bruce Anderson

The 1985 State Champs from Burnsville

jumping out to a quick 3-0 lead on goals from Dallas Miller, Jeff Kuester and Dan Tousignant. The Governors got two of their own in the second from Jim Hau and Mitch Converse, but when Miller and Kuester each tallied again for the Eagles late in the third, it was all but over for Johnson.

Edina and Hibbing met in the other semi, and, thanks to goals from Tom Terwilliger, Jay Moore, Paul Ranheim, Marty Nanne and Bill Mork, the Edina Hornets whipped Hibbing 5-1, to earn a return trip to the finals. Edina goalie Chris Schwartzbauer made 23 stops in the win.

In the championship game Edina picked up where they left off, going up 1-0 midway through the first on a goal from Jeff Johnson. They then made it 2-0 at 4:31 of the second when Greg Dornbach beat Bloomington goalie Bruce Wilson on a nice wrister from the circle. Kennedy marched back to tie it up late in the second on goals from Dallas Miller and Jeff Jungwirth, only to see the Hornets put it away in the third on a pair of goals from Marty Nanne and Paul Ranheim. For Willard Ikola's 21-4-1 Hornets, this was their unprecedented seventh state hockey championship.

1985: Burnsville vs. Hill-Murray

Anoka and Hastings hooked up for one of the wildest tourney openers of all-time. The Tornadoes came out and got two quick ones from Dave Boitz and Mike Bunker. Hastings then made it 2-1 at 4:43 when Brad Stepan beat Anoka goalie Tony Moore on a short-handed goal. The Tornadoes then stormed ahead with five straight goals in the second from Tod Hartje, Jeff Foss and a hat trick from Bill Carlson. Hastings then answered with four of its own from Jeff Pauletti, Gary Ruedy and a pair from Rob Williams. Anoka simply responded to that by scoring three more from Jeff Reiman, Pat Sullivan and another from Hartje, to seal the amazing 11-5 victory. All in all, the Tornadoes peppered Raiders' goalie Dave Fries with 46 shots on goal. So bizarre was this game, that four records were set in it by Anoka, including: Most Assists by One Team in One Period -- 10, Most Goals in a Period by Two Teams -- 8, Fastest Two Goals at the Start of a Game by One Team -- 1:16, and Fastest Four Goals by One Team -- 2:02 (Anoka, in the Second Period).

Hill-Murray and Hibbing met in Game Two, and after a back and forth first and second periods, Pioneer winger Tommy Quinlan beat Bluejackets goalie John Hyduke on a nice wrister to tie the game up at 3-3 with just a minute to go in the third. Then, just 34 seconds into overtime, Hill-Murray forward Nick Gerebi got the game-winner on an unassisted breakaway goal.

Jefferson and Minnetonka then played what would turn out to be the longest state tournament game since 1955 when Minneapolis South defeated Thief River Falls, 3-2, in 11 overtimes. The game got started innocently enough when Skipper defenseman Jim Wilharm scored on a power-play goal at the 3:25 mark of the first period. Jefferson answered only 28 seconds later when Brock Rendall beat Tonka goalie Dale Roehl to tie it up at 1-1. The scoring went back and forth through the second and early into the third with each team scoring a pair of goals to make it 3-3. Fred Holmner started it out at 1:01 for Minnetonka, followed by Jags center Kurt Svendsen at 3:06, and Tonka center Tom Walsh at 13:03. Pat Beaty got the equalizer at 1:44 of the third, only to see both goalies pucker up and force the game into overtime. The teams raged back and forth in the extra sessions, until finally, after the third overtime, Tournament officials decided to postpone the game until morning. So, after a good night's rest, the two teams picked up where they left off from the night before. Finally, at 2:21 of the fourth sudden death session, Brock Rendall took a pass from Mark Brandt and beat Roehl down low to get the dramatic game-winner.

Now, back to Friday night, for the fourth quarterfinal between Burnsville and Bemidji. Thanks to a pair of Herm Finnegan goals that beat Bemidji goalie Steve Peters, Burnsville won a close 5-3 victory. George Pelawa added two of his own in the Lumberjack loss.

Both semifinals ended in 4-1 spankings. Tray Tuomie had a hat trick for Hill-Murray in their 4-1 drubbing of Anoka in the first semi, while Burnsville got goals from Scott Bloom, Kevin Featherstone, Kelly Ramswick and Don Granato in their 4-1 win over Jefferson.

Burnsville then went on to win its first championship by virtue of a 4-3 triumph over Hill-Murray in the title game. Hill-Murray's Mark Johnson put his Pioneers on the board first when he beat Braves goalie Kevin Gorg just 26 seconds into the game. Burnsville answered with a goal from Herm Finnegan at 9:00, only to see Pioneer center Phil Zelenak make it 2-1 only three minutes later. Burnsville then answered with a pair of goals in the second and third from Mike Luckcraft and Scott Bloom to go up 3-2. Hill rallied early in the third on a goal from Tom Graske, but Bloom added his second of the night to seal the Braves' first championship. For Tom Osiecki's Burnsville squad, who finished the season with a 24-1-1 mark, it was a sweet victory that had been a long time in the making.

1986: Burnsville vs. Hill-Murray

Duluth Denfeld and Bloomington Jefferson played the opening quarterfinal game, as Minnesota got their first look at superstar goalie Rob Stauber of Denfeld. Another Stauber, Bill, opened the scoring for the Hunters, just 10 seconds after the opening draw, when he beat Jefferson keeper Bobby Hanson, arguably the school's best-ever to play between the pipes. Darren Matetich then tallied just 90 seconds later to give Denfeld a 2-0 lead, only to see Jefferson answer back at 2:57 of the second when Todd Olson beat Stauber from the top of the circle. Denfeld center Mike Vuconich made it 3-1 at the 6:36 mark, followed by Kevin Maas' goal six minutes later. Tommy Pederson added one late for the

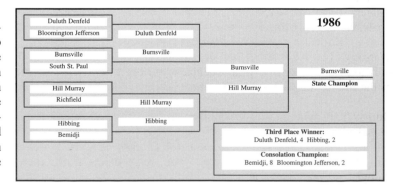

1986

Duluth Denfeld
Bloomington Jefferson — Duluth Denfeld
Burnsville — Burnsville
South St. Paul
Hill Murray — Hill Murray
Richfield
Hibbing — Hibbing
Bemidji

Burnsville — Burnsville
Hill Murray

Burnsville
State Champion

Third Place Winner:
Duluth Denfeld, 4   Hibbing, 2

Consolation Champion:
Bemidji, 8   Bloomington Jefferson, 2

The 1986 State Champs from Burnsville

Front Row L to R: Noel Manley, Marc Linsenman, Jon McDermott, Carl Anderson, Rob Granato, Brad Hendrickson. Middle Row L to R: Scott Bloom, Mike Gresser, Matt Larson, Matt Leegwater, Tom Dennis, Steve Ferrera, Mike Engfer, Steve Treichel. Back Row L to R: Coach Tom Osiecki, Manager Pete Heunisch, John Sundby, Dan Brettschneider, Mark Osiecki, Scott Schulze, Lance Werness, Manager Brian Ferrell, Coach Bruce Anderson.

Jaguars, but it wasn't nearly enough as Duluth went on to win the game 4-2.

Burnsville and South St. Paul met for Game Two, in what would prove to be a wild one. Led by Scott Bloom's hat trick and two assists, as well as Jon McDermit's pair of goals, the Braves went on to beat the Packers 7-4.

Richfield, led by star winger Danny Palmer, and Hill-Murray then hooked up in a rough Game Three, which saw some 10 penalties take place. Pioneer center Tray Tuomie got the first goal of the day when he beat Richfield goalie Damian Rhodes (who is presently starring in the NHL), at 2:55 of the first. The Spartans came right back on a pair of goals from Brian Provost and Trent Jutting to take the lead midway through the first. The score remained 2-1 until just 33 seconds into the second, when future Gopher Nicky Gerebi found the back of the net to tie it up. Steve Rohlik's goal at 11:46 of the period gave Hill-Murray the lead back at 3-2. Pioneers winger Tommy Quinlan went on to add a pair of goals in the third, as Hill rolled to a 5-3 win.

The last quarterfinal game of the day pitted Hibbing and Bemidji, as the Lumberjack's opened the scoring when George Pelawa, a specimen at 6-foot-3 and 240-plus pounds, beat Hibbing goalie Jim Monacelli at 6:14 of the first. The Bluejackets tied it up only three minutes later on a John Schwartz wrister, only to see Bemidji get the lead back just 23 seconds later when Pelawa set up Rob Sauer out front. Hibbing regained the lead midway through the second on goals from Pete Wohlers and John Schwartz, only to see Sauer get his second of the day on a shorthanded breakaway to deadlock it at 3-3. Wohlers iced the game at 7:29 of the third when he put his third goal of the game past Bemidji goalie Steve Peters, as Hibbing hung on for the 4-3 win. (Tragically, Pelawa, who was drafted by the Montreal Canadiens, was killed in an automobile accident just before he was set to attend UND on a hockey scholarship that next summer.)

Burnsville went on to beat Duluth Denfeld 3-1 in the first semifinal, as Jason Francisco got Duluth up 1-0 just one minute into the game, only to see Burnsville rally back on three unanswered third period goals from Mike Gresser, Dan Bretschnieder and Lance Werness.

Hill-Murray beat Hibbing 5-4 in the other semi, as the Pioneers got goals from Tom Quinlan, Sean Fabian, Todd Valento, Steve Rohlik and Tray Toumi, while Hibbing's Doug Torrell added a pair of goals in the loss.

So the stage was set for a rematch of epic proportions, Burnsville vs. Hill-Murray. The Braves had beaten the Pioneers 4-3 the year before in the finals, and Hill desperately wanted to get a little pay-back. The game got underway under a cloud of penalties, four alone in the first, that set the tone early. The Pioneers got on the board first when Tom Quinlan and Tray Tuomie set up Steve Rohlik on a nice one-timer at 11:43 of the first. Matt Larson then tied it up at 2:59 of the second, and then Scott Bloom took a Lance Werness pass at 9:55 and beat Horvath on a low wrister to give the Braves a 2-1 lead. Bloom then took over, first setting up Jon McDermott at 5:39 of the third, followed by an empty netter of his own with just 45 seconds to go. Braves goalie Tom Dennis hung on for the 4-1 victory, as head coach Tom Osiecki's Braves joined the elite fraternity of back-to-back state champions.

1987: Bloomington Kennedy vs. Burnsville

The Braves opened the tourney right where they left off -- in the winner's column. Burnsville and Roseville met in the opener, with Burnsville scoring the game's first four goals on shots by Jon Lindquist, Dan Brettschneider, Paul Kivi and Rob Granato. Raider's center Scott Marshall finally got his team on the board at 1:08, but the damage had been done as Burnsville cruised to a 4-1 final.

Warroad and Hill-Murray met for Game Two, in what proved to be another blow-out. Winger Greg Knox opened the scoring at the 9:45 mark of the first to give Warroad a 1-0 lead. Hill-Murray then answered back when Sean Fabian scored an unassisted power-play goal at 1:05 of the second. It was all Warriors from there though, as Warroad went on to tally four unanswered goals from Mike Flick, Jared Baines and a pair from Scott Peterson to win the game by the final of 5-1.

Greenway's Kenny Gernander tallied a hat trick en route to leading his team to an 8-3 spanking of Edina in Game Three. The Raiders also got goals from Corey Schoenrock, Chris Rauzi, Andrew Parker, Derek Vekich and Justin Tomberlin, as well as three assists from Craig Miskovich. Greenway goalie Jeff Stolp made just 13 saves in the win.

Kennedy pounded South St. Paul in the final quarterfinal contest of the day. Jason Miller netted the hat trick, while the Eagles also got goals from Pat McGowan, Chad Pittelkow, Joe Decker and Tom Hanson in the 7-3 win. Gary Lewandowski added a pair of goals for the Packers in the loss.

Bloomington Kennedy, who's only loss during the regular season was to Greenway-Coleraine, now had its chance to exact a little revenge against the Raiders in the first semifinal game, and thanks to Jason Miller's two goals, the Eagles went on to win 4-2.

Burnsville and Warroad met in the other semifinal as Warroad's Larry Olimb led the Warriors to a quick 3-1 lead in the first, only to see Burnsville rally back behind a pair of Lance Werness goals, as the Braves hung on to beat Warroad 5-3

Burnsville then hit the ice against its rivals from Kennedy in an attempt to make it three straight state titles. The Braves jumped out to a quick 1-0 lead when Lance Werness took a Rob Granato pass and buried it into the back of the Kennedy net. From there it was all Kennedy though, as the Eagles scored four unanswered goals from Pat

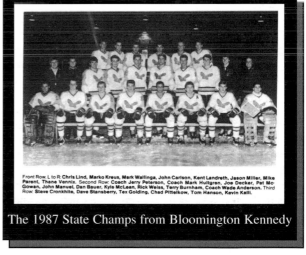

The 1987 State Champs from Bloomington Kennedy

Front Row, L to R: Chris Lind, Marko Kreus, Mark Wallinga, John Carlson, Kent Landreth, Jason Miller, Mike Parent, Thane Vennix. Second Row: Coach Jerry Peterson, Coach Mark Hultgren, Joe Decker, Pat McGowan, John Manuel, Dan Bauer, Kyle McLean, Rick Weiss, Terry Burnham, Coach Wade Anderson. Third Row: Steve Cronkhite, Dave Stansberry, Tex Golding, Chad Pittelkow, Tom Hanson, Kevin Kalli.

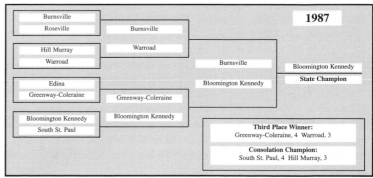

			1987
Burnsville			
Roseville	Burnsville		
Hill Murray	Warroad		
Warroad		Burnsville	Bloomington Kennedy
Edina		Bloomington Kennedy	**State Champion**
Greenway-Coleraine	Greenway-Coleraine		
Bloomington Kennedy	Bloomington Kennedy		
South St. Paul			

Third Place Winner:
Greenway-Coleraine, 4 Warroad, 3

Consolation Champion:
South St. Paul, 4 Hill Murray, 3

McGowan, Joe Decker, Chad Pittelkow and Jason Miller to upset the Braves 4-1, and win their first-ever state title. The emotional leader of that Kennedy team was a 5-foot-8, 140-pound junior center spark-plug by the name of Dave Stansberry, who's leadership and moxy made him the tournament's biggest fan-favorite.

1988: Edina vs. Hill-Murray

Bloomington's Tony Bianchi got the second fastest goal in tournament history when he beat Grand Rapids goalie Brett Nelson just 16 seconds into the opening game on a breakaway through the slot. Troy Cusey evened it up for the Indians just over a minute later on a nice slapper from the top of the circle, only to see Jags winger Todd Witcraft regain the lead for his club at 9:35 on a one-timer out front. Tommy Pederson then took a Chris Tucker pass and beat Nelson on a power-play goal from the left side at 5:43 of the second to make it 3-1 for Jefferson. The Indians then proceeded to mount a three goal rally, with Tom Murphy swatting a John Brill rebound past Jefferson keeper Derek Anderson just 49 seconds into the third, followed by a goal from John Murphy that was assisted by Chris Marinucci and Jeff Neilsen at 4:14, and finally Murphy's second of the game during a scrum out front at 11:40 to take the lead. But Jefferson didn't quit. With the Bloomington goalie on the bench, Jeff Saterdalen poked in a Tony Bianchi rebound to get the game-tying goal with just 17 seconds left on the clock to send it to OT. There, at the 5:05 mark, Jefferson's Chris Tucker would emerge as the hero as he took a Tommy Pederson pass and rifled it home from the point past Nelson for the dramatic 5-4 win.

Game Two was just as exciting, as Rochester John Marshall and Hill-Murray also found themselves in sudden death. Rochester opened the scoring on a Matt Brumm power-play goal at 5:13. The Pioneers came back on a pair of goals from Mike Hurley, who scored from the high slot, and Tim Carroll, who got alone for a breakaway. The next goal saw Doug Zmolek slide the puck over from the point to an awaiting Pat Ferschweiler, who beat Pioneer goalie Scott Cardinal on a nice one-timer. Hill took a 3-2 lead at 8:59 of the second when Greg Hagen caught Rochester goalie Jeff Kruesel way out of the net for an easy score. Then, with just 13 seconds to go in the game, and with their goalie pulled, Rochester pressed into the Pioneer zone. There, winger Gene Rebelatto came in across the crease and beat Cardinal on a beautiful backhander to send the game into overtime. The game raged back and forth until the 6:41 mark of the first extra session, when Hill-Murray defenseman Brian Krois unloaded a blast from just inside the blue line that found the top-shelf of the net for the amazing 4-3 win.

Edina and Cretin Derham Hall met in the third game of the day, as Greg Chapman, Kyle Humphrey and Scott Fronek all scored in the first period to give the Hornets a commanding 3-0 lead. Cretin came back on defenseman Tony Lancette's goal late in the first, and then late in the third, when Chris Weinke (who would go on to play pro baseball until 1998, when he became the starting quarterback at Florida State University), beat Edina goalie Matt Bertram to get to within one. But that was as far as they got that night, as Edina hung on for the 3-2 win.

Warroad then beat Duluth Denfeld in the final game of the day, as Larry Olimb, Jim Fish and Joey Biondi all tallied in the 3-1 victory over the Hunters.

Hill-Murray played Bloomington Jefferson in the first semifinal contest, and thanks to goals from Tim Carrol, Mike Hanson, Mark Tollefsbol, Jim Scott and a deuce from Todd Montpetit, the Pioneers hung on to beat the Jags 6-3 to advance to the title game. Edina and the undefeated Warroad Warriors played a defensive gem in the second semi, with John McCoy getting the Hornets on the board first when his wrister beat Warroad goalie Chad Erickson just 42 seconds into the game. After a scoreless second, Vince Huerd knocked in a Dan Marvin rebound at 4:21 to tie the game up at 1-1. The score remained that way until the 2:51 mark of overtime, when Mike Hiniker jammed in a loose puck out front into the side of the net for the 2-1 game-winner.

Edina then met Hill-Murray in a title game full of action and drama. John McCoy got Edina into the black at 4:41 of the first, only to see Pioneer forward Mark Tollefsbol tie it up three minutes later. Edina center Robbie Morris worked a nice give and go with Chris Justice to make it 2-1 less than two minutes after that, only to see Hill-Murray's Mike Hurley tie it back up at 2-2 off a pretty little backhander with just a second to go in the first. Edina then got a nice poke-in goal from Noel Rahn at 1:04 of the second, followed by Rob Morris' second of the day on a breakaway just six minutes later. The Pioneers got one back from Greg Hagen less than a minute into the third, but Hornet's centerman Chad Vandertop iced it at 5:46 when he beat Scott Cardinal down low. With the 5-3 victory, Willard Ikola's Hornets cruised to their eight state championship.

1989: Bloomington Jefferson vs. Rochester John Marshall

The state's top rated squad, Edina, lost to Rochester John Marshall in the opening quarterfinal game, 4-2. JM's Doug Zmolek and Edina's

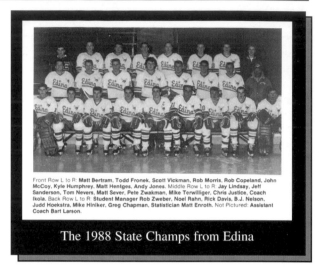

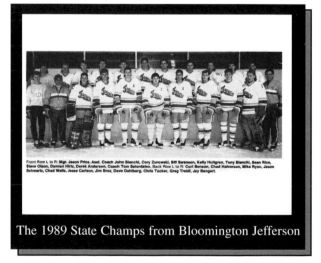

The 1988 State Champs from Edina

The 1989 State Champs from Bloomington Jefferson

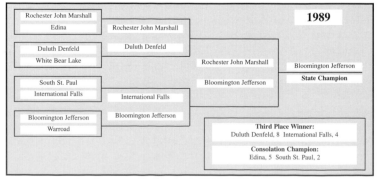

Dan Plante each had a pair of goals respectively.

In Game Three, International Falls upended South St. Paul 4-2 on a two-goal performance from Marty Olson.

In the last quarterfinal, Bloomington Jefferson pounced all over Warroad as Sean Rice and Dave Dahlberg each netted a pair of goals for the Jags, while Joey Biondi, who averaged three points per game that season for Warroad, added a goal and an assist in the loss.

In the first semifinal game, Denfeld, despite going up 1-0 on a break-away goal from Greg Christenson, fell to Rochester John Marshall 2-1, thanks to scores from both Eric Means and Jon Hilken. In the other semi, Jefferson got two goals from Sean Rice, and another five singles from Dave Dahlberg, Bill Swanson, Chad Halvorson, Chris Tucker and Jason Schwartz to pound International Falls 7-3.

So, the finals were set, it would be Bloomington Jefferson and Rochester John Marshall for all the marbles. Rochester's Jeff Fogarty opened the scoring at 6:10 of the first when he beat Jefferson goalie Derek Anderson on a shot from out front. Jefferson's Jason Schwartz got the equalizer with just 14 seconds to go in the first, while Chris Tucker got the go-ahead goal on a breakaway goal at 6:42 of the second. Rochester's Doug Zmolek answered back late in the second though, as the future NHL star netted a pair of goals to give his Rockets the lead once again. Tucker tied it up one more time at 7:41 of the third, only to see Jeff Fogarty tally for Rochester to go up 4-3. Then, at 11:01 of the third, Tony Bianchi took a Chris Tucker pass, deked, and found the back of the net to make it 4-4. The game roared back and forth for the final minutes, as neither team was able to get the go-ahead goal. Deadlocked, the two went in to sudden death. There, at 3:29 of the extra session, Chris Tucker took a Jesse Carlson pass and skated it all the way into the zone and beat Rochester goalie Sam Person on a beautiful wrister to win the Jags second state title in dramatic fashion. Ironically, it was the first overtime title game since in 1979, when Edina East beat Rochester John Marshall by the same 5-4 margin.

1990: Roseau vs. Grand Rapids

Down 1-0, Matt Bender and Steve Magnusson each scored in the third to rally Anoka past South St. Paul in the opening game of the Tourney by the final of 2-1.

Game Two was a wild one, as Bloomington Kennedy got beat by Grand Rapids 3-2 in overtime. While future UMD star and Hobey Baker winner, Chris Marinucci, had a goal and an assist, it was Jeff Wilson who played hero by beating Kennedy goalie Ben Schiebe just four minutes into the first overtime.

Minnetonka outlasted Burnsville in the third quarterfinal, as the Braves lost the lead on four different occasions in the 5-4 defeat. Justin McHugh, Mike Pankoff, Hoby Mork, Pat Ward, and Eric Haagenson all tallied for the Skippers in the win.

The last game of the day saw Roseau crush White Bear Lake, which was led by another future Hobey Baker winner, Brian Bonin, who would go on to star for the Gophers. The Rams proved to be too tough in this one though, as winger Chris Hites notched a pair, while Dale Genderson, Chris Gotziaman and Jason Hanson each tallied to lead the Rams to a 5-1 victory.

Grand Rapids secured its championship berth with a 3-2 victory over Anoka, as Troy Cusey, Jeff Wilson and Kelly Fairchild all tallied for the Indians. Roseau, led by goals from Chris Gotziaman, Dale Lund, Chris Hites and a deuce from Jamie Byfuglien, then advanced to the finals with a 5-2 win over Minnetonka.

The all-north finals got underway with the No. 2 ranked Roseau Rams vs. the No. 1 ranked Grand Rapids Indians. Interestingly, it was the first time since 1972, when International Falls edged Grand Rapids 3-2, that two northern Minnesota schools matched up against each other for the state title. The Indians drew blood first, as Troy Cusey fired home a Tony Retka pass at 9:23 in the first period. That lead held up for only 42 seconds into the second period, however, until Roseau's Chris Gotziaman beat Rapids goalie Chad Huson on a breakaway goal to tie it up. Todd Hedlund got the go-ahead goal for the Rams at 1:56 of the third, and Gotziaman scored his second goal of the game at 14:00 to secure the 3-1 final for Roseau. It was a big win for head coach Dean Blais' Rams, giving them their fifth state title, and first since 1961.

1991: Hill-Murray vs. Duluth East

Burnsville knocked off the defending champs from Roseau in the open-

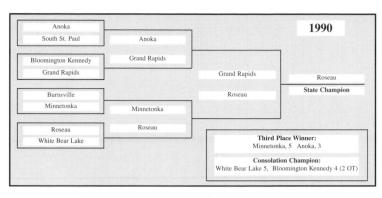

1990

Anoka / South St. Paul	Anoka		
Bloomington Kennedy / Grand Rapids	Grand Rapids	Grand Rapids	Roseau
Burnsville / Minnetonka	Minnetonka		**State Champion**
Roseau / White Bear Lake	Roseau	Roseau	

Third Place Winner:
Minnetonka, 5 Anoka, 3

Consolation Champion:
White Bear Lake 5, Bloomington Kennedy 4 (2 OT)

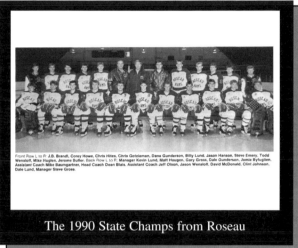

Front Row L to R: J.B. Brandl, Corey Howe, Chris Hites, Chris Gotziaman, Dana Gunderson, Billy Lund, Jason Hanson, Steve Emery, Todd Wensloff, Mike Huglen, Jerome Butler. Back Row L to R: Manager Kevin Lund, Matt Haugen, Gary Gross, Dale Gunderson, Jamie Byfuglien, Assistant Coach Mike Baumgartner, Head Coach Dean Blais, Assistant Coach Jeff Olson, Jason Wensloff, David McDonald, Clint Johnson, Dale Lund, Manager Steve Gross.

The 1990 State Champs from Roseau

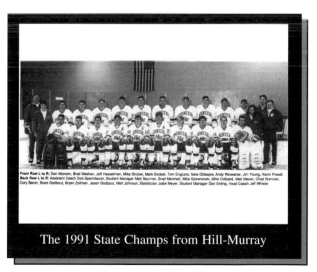

Front Row L to R: Don Monson, Brad Meehan, Jeff Hasselman, Mike Strobel, Mark Strobel, Tom Englund, Nate Gillaspie, Andy Woessner, Jim Young, Kevin Powell. Back Row L to R: Assistant Coach Dick Spannbauer, Student Manager Matt Bauman, Brad Marshall, Mike Govaronski, Mike Collyard, Matt Mauer, Chad Brennen, Cory Baron, Brent Godbout, Bryan Zollman, Jason Godbout, Matt Johnson, Statistician Jodie Meyer, Student Manager Dan Erding, Head Coach Jeff Whisler.

The 1991 State Champs from Hill-Murray

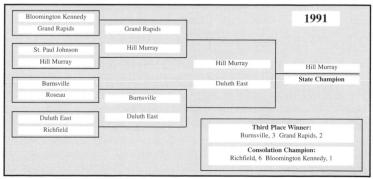

1991

Bloomington Kennedy / Grand Rapids	Grand Rapids		
St. Paul Johnson / Hill Murray	Hill Murray	Hill Murray	Hill Murray
Burnsville / Roseau	Burnsville	Duluth East	**State Champion**
Duluth East / Richfield	Duluth East		

Third Place Winner:
Burnsville, 3 Grand Rapids, 2

Consolation Champion:
Richfield, 6 Bloomington Kennedy, 1

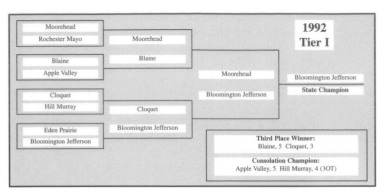

1992 Tier I

Moorehead		
Rochester Mayo	Moorehead	
Blaine	Blaine	
Apple Valley		Moorehead
		Bloomington Jefferson
Cloquet		**State Champion**
Hill Murray	Cloquet	
Eden Prairie	Bloomington Jefferson	
Bloomington Jefferson		

Third Place Winner:
Blaine, 5 Cloquet, 3

Consolation Champion:
Apple Valley, 5 Hill Murray, 4 (3OT)

er, as Chris Loken, Chad Hall and Rolf Simonson each tallied for the Braves in the 3-2 upset. Hill-Murray pounded on St. Paul Johnson in Game Two in a penalty-fest, as the Pioneers cruised to a 7-1 win behind winger Matt Mauer's hat trick. In the first evening game, Grand Rapids got goals from Matt Blade, Kirk Nielsen, Dave Holum and Troy Cusey to hold off Bloomington Kennedy 4-3. The last quarterfinal game of the day was all Duluth East, who, behind Kevin Rappana's two goals and two assists, defeated Richfield 5-1. Richfield's lone goal came from future NHLer Darby Hendrickson.

The first semifinal of Day Two was a goalie's nightmare. The Pioneers absolutely annihilated Grand Rapids in that opener by the unconscionable score of 11-3. Leading the charge for Hill-Murray was the identical twin tandem of Mike and Mark Strobel, who between them tallied seven points. In addition, Matt Mauer and Jeff Hasselman each added a pair for good measure. The other semi was a much different affair, as Duluth East needed overtime to defeat Burnsville 2-1. Derek Locker opened the scoring for the Hounds late in the second, only to see Chris Porter tie it up for the Braves midway through the third. It remained that way until 6:58 of the extra session, when Greyhound forward Rusty Fitzgerald played hero by beating Burnsville goalie Jeff Rathburn on a nice feed from Shawn Proudlock.

The championship tilt was another dandy, as Duluth East finally gave Hill-Murray a little bit of competition. After skating to a scoreless first, Duluth's Derek Locker opened the scoring that night at 2:35 of the second. Adam Vork made it 2-0 for the Hounds just a minute later, only to see Nate Gillespie cut the deficit to one at the 7:12 mark. Locker tallied again just 25 seconds later to give his club a commanding 3-1 lead midway through the game. That's when the Pioneers kicked it into overdrive, getting four unanswered goals down the stretch from Bryan Zollman, Jeff Hasselman and a pair from Mike Strobel. Hill-Murray goalie Kevin Powell came up with 27 saves down the stretch as the Pioneers hung on for a 5-3 victory and their second state title.

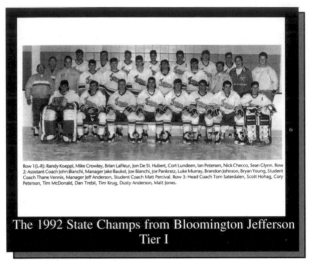

Row 1 (L-R): Randy Koeppl, Mike Crowley, Brian LaFleur, Jon De St. Hubert, Cort Lundeen, Ian Petersen, Nick Checco, Sean Glynn. Row 2: Assistant Coach John Bianchi, Manager Jake Baukol, Joe Bianchi, Joe Pankratz, Luke Murray, Brandon Johnson, Bryan Young, Student Coach Thane Vennix, Manager Jeff Anderson, Student Coach Matt Percival. Row 3: Head Coach Tom Saterdalen, Scott Hohag, Cory Peterson, Tim McDonald, Dan Trebil, Tim Krug, Dusty Anderson, Matt Jones.

The 1992 State Champs from Bloomington Jefferson
Tier I

1992: Bloomington Jefferson vs. Greenway-Coleraine

In 1992, following the recommendations of the state's High School Hockey Coaches Association, the Minnesota State High School League Board of Directors decided to try a two-year experiment of sorts, by changing the event's format to feature two "tiers" which included 16 teams. They figured that instead of dividing the schools based on enrollment, as was the case with all other activities, they suggested that the divisions should be based on performance and ability. With that, the coaches in each section then ranked all the teams based on their performances following the regular season. Based on their recommendations, the top-eight sectional teams were then placed in the Tier I, or upper division, and the remaining teams fell into Tier II division. Then, a post-section tournament, so to speak, was created, with the winners of each tier going on to represent the section at the state tournament.

Never in the Tournament's 48-year history, had anything ever been meet with so much controversy. The hockey purists went crazy, and started to scramble to try and save their tournament. Like "New Coke" in years past, people were concerned that another tournament would dilute the "Classic," which had long been the model for success in the eyes of the nation. While the die-hards stuck to the "If it ain't broken, then don't fix it," scenario. Many others, particularly from the small, non-traditional hockey hot-beds of the state, said "Hey, what about us? We'd like our kids to be able to have a shot at the post-season as well."

The new format, with all of its good intentions, was intended for those schools in the state that seemingly never had a prayer of making it to the big tournament. It wasn't supposed to "compete" with the original, rather, it was supposed to be another venue for some more kids to have a chance to play in the post-season. However, under the new format, two things came to the front burner that would prove to be controversial. First, the second tier lessened the chances of watching the classic big-school/small-school "David vs. Goliath" match-ups that, in part, made the tournament such a classic in so many people's eyes. I mean how great is it to see tiny Roseau come down to the tourney and kick the snot out of Edina or Burnsville? It's awesome! And secondly, it also allowed for team's with poor regular season records to get hot in the playoffs and make it to the tourney. And, in 1992, during the inaugural run of the new tiered format, that very scenario played out, when Greenway-Coleraine, a past state champ and perennial power, and Rosemount, a team that had won but two games all year, made it to the Tier II finals. Despite the fact that Greenway crushed Rosemount in the title game, the system showed some obvious flaws, that would need to be tweaked in the years to come.

In the first game of the Tier I quarterfinals, Moorhead pummeled

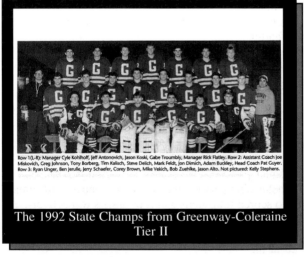

Row 1 (L-R): Manager Cyle Kohlhoff, Jeff Antonovich, Jason Koski, Gabe Troumbly, Manager Rick Flatley. Row 2: Assistant Coach Joe Miskovich, Greg Johnson, Tony Borberg, Tim Kalisch, Steve Delich, Mark Feldt, Jon Dimich, Adam Buckley, Head Coach Pat Guyer. Row 3: Ryan Unger, Ben Jerulle, Jerry Schaefer, Corey Brown, Mike Vekich, Bob Zuehlke, Jason Alto. Not pictured: Kelly Stephens.

The 1992 State Champs from Greenway-Coleraine
Tier II

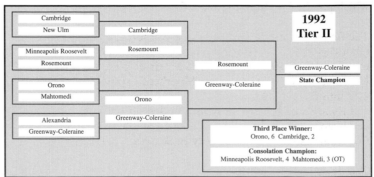

1992 Tier II

Cambridge		
New Ulm	Cambridge	
Minneapolis Roosevelt	Rosemount	
Rosemount		Rosemount
		Greenway-Coleraine
Orono		**State Champion**
Mahtomedi	Orono	
Alexandria	Greenway-Coleraine	
Greenway-Coleraine		

Third Place Winner:
Orono, 6 Cambridge, 2

Consolation Champion:
Minneapolis Roosevelt, 4 Mahtomedi, 3 (OT)

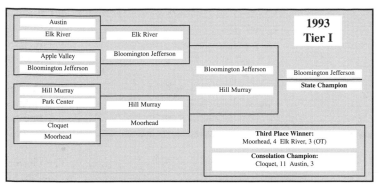

1993 Tier I

Austin				
Elk River	Elk River			
Apple Valley	Bloomington Jefferson	Bloomington Jefferson	Bloomington Jefferson	
Bloomington Jefferson		Hill Murray	**State Champion**	
Hill Murray				
Park Center	Hill Murray			
Cloquet	Moorhead			
Moorhead				

Third Place Winner:
Moorhead, 4 Elk River, 3 (OT)

Consolation Champion:
Cloquet, 11 Austin, 3

Rochester Mayo by the final of 7-1. Leading the charge for the Spuds were John Haberlach and Jim Jacobson, who each netted a pair of goals, while future Gopher Ryan Kraft added a goal and three assists as well. Game Two pitted Blaine against Apple Valley, in a much closer affair. Chad Marlow's two goals paced the Bengals in this one, as Blaine went on to a 4-2 win. The first evening game saw one of the state's biggest future stars in action, Cloquet's Jamie Langenbrunner, who starred as a member of the 1999 Stanley-Cup winning Dallas Stars. His power-play goal at 2:25 of the third gave his Lumberjacks a 3-2 lead, as they hung on to beat Hill-Murray by the final score of 5-3. The night game proved to be a laugher, as Joey Bianchi's hat trick and Tim McDonald's two goals led Bloomington Jefferson past Eden Prairie by the final of 7-1.

Moorhead and Blaine hooked up in the first semifinal contest, in what would prove to be a much closer game than the final 6-3 score indicated. With the score tied at 2-2 in the second, Moorhead got a goal from Ryan Kappes at 4:01, only to see Blaine tie it up just a minute later on Jim Garbe's one-timer from the inside the circle. Tied at three, the Spuds took over and went on to win it in the third, thanks to a pair of goals from a couple of future stars, Jason Blake and Ryan Kraft. The other semi came down to sudden death, as Jefferson's Nick Checco tied it at 4-4 with less than a minute to go in the game against a very tough Cloquet team. This set the heroics for Tim McDonald, who got the third of his three goals of the game at the 3:03 mark of overtime to give his Jaguars a dramatic 5-4 victory over the Lumberjacks.

In the finals, Moorhead opened the scoring at 3:31 when Greg Salvevold took a Jason Blake pass and beat Jefferson goalie Randy Koeppl downstairs. Cort Lundeen tied it up for the Jags six minutes later, and Matt Jones made it 2-1 for Bloomington less than two minutes after that. Moorhead star Jason Blake tied it up at two apiece on a power-play goal early in the second, only to see Jefferson's Joey Bianchi go nuts.

The 1993 State Champs from Bloomington Jefferson
Tier I

After Nick Checco gave Jefferson the lead at 7:22 of the second, Bianchi took a couple of sweet passes from future NHL star Mike Crowley to tally a pure hat trick in less than five minutes, giving his Jags a commanding 6-2 lead. (Incidentally, that feat surpassed the previous tournament record set by Eveleth's John Mayasich back in 1951.) Moorhead added one late, but couldn't get back into it as top-ranked Bloomington Jefferson rolled to a 6-3 victory and the state championship. (With the win, Joey Bianchi, son of Jaguars assistant coach John Bianchi, became the third Bianchi sibling to win a state title, as brother Steve won it in 1981, and Tory in 1989.)

Additionally, while the Tier I event remained at the Civic Center, much of the Tier II Tournament was held at the Target Center in Minneapolis, where Greenway-Coleraine beat Cinderella Rosemount 6-1 for the inaugural Tier II title.

1993: Bloomington Jefferson vs. Hill-Murray

Elk River welcomed the tourney first-timer's from Austin in the opening quarterfinal contest by giving them a 9-0 beating. Eight different Elk's scored in this one, including a pair from Clay Thompson. The defending champs from Bloomington Jefferson made quick work of Apple Valley in the second afternoon game, as John De St. Hubert notched two goals and two assists to lead the Jags to a 6-2 win over the Eagles. Hill-Murray went up 3-0 on Park Center in Game Three, only to see the Pirates roar back to score two goals in the final minute of the game. Jason and Brent Godbout figured into all of the scoring for the Pioneers, while Jason Bliven and Damian Ellis each had a goal and an assist in the 3-2 loss for Park. The night game was a scoring-fest, as Moorhead and Cloquet duked it out for the right to go to the semis. Cloquet jumped out to a 4-3 lead early into the third, thanks to the unbelievable performance of Sergei Petrov and Jamie Langenbrunner,

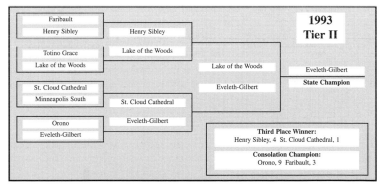

1993 Tier II

Faribault				
Henry Sibley	Henry Sibley			
Totino Grace	Lake of the Woods	Lake of the Woods	Eveleth-Gilbert	
Lake of the Woods		Eveleth-Gilbert	**State Champion**	
St. Cloud Cathedral	St. Cloud Cathedral			
Minneapolis South				
Orono	Eveleth-Gilbert			
Eveleth-Gilbert				

Third Place Winner:
Henry Sibley, 4 St. Cloud Cathedral, 1

Consolation Champion:
Orono, 9 Faribault, 3

who scored four goals and four assists respectively. At 1:32 of the third Matt Cullen got his third assist of the game when he fed Louis Paquin out front for a goal, only to see Cloquet answer back at the 10:05 mark. Then, with less than five minutes to go in the game, Ryan Kraft tied it at 5-5, followed by Josh Arnold's goal at 11:37 which put the Spuds up for good, 6-5.

The first semifinal contest had Elk River jumping out to a quick 1-0 lead on Woody Glines' goal at 3:58. But Bloomington Jefferson came right back though, and went on to win the game 4-1 thanks to a pair of goals each from Nick Checco and Tim McDonald. The other semi saw Moorhead explode out of the blocks just seven minutes into the game for a quick 3-1 lead on goals from Greg Salvevold, Josh Arnold and Ryan Kraft. Hill-Murray then pulled off one of the greatest comebacks in tourney history, getting goals from Mike Goveronski, Aaron Laszlo, Brent Godbout and two from Jason Godbout, to rally back for a 5-3 win.

The finals had all the hype in the world going in, but in the end it was Jefferson by a

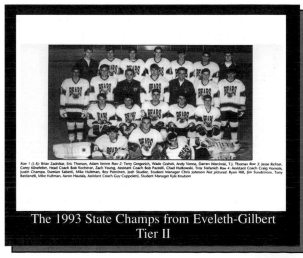

The 1993 State Champs from Eveleth-Gilbert
Tier II

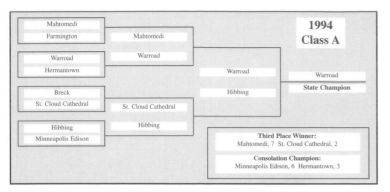

1994 Class A

Mahtomedi / Farmington	Mahtomedi		
Warroad / Hermantown	Warroad	Warroad	Warroad
Breck / St. Cloud Cathedral	St. Cloud Cathedral	Hibbing	**State Champion**
Hibbing / Minneapolis Edison	Hibbing		

Third Place Winner: Mahtomedi, 7 St. Cloud Cathedral, 2
Consolation Champion: Minneapolis Edison, 6 Hermantown, 3

landslide. Joey Bianchi opened the scoring at 3:55 of the first, and was followed by three second period goals from Ian Peterson, Nick Checco and Mike Crowley. Jaguar goalie Randy Koepple made just 13 saves in the championship shut out, to give the Jags their second straight title and a perfect 28-0 season.

In the Tier II finals, Eveleth-Gilbert, making just its first trip back to the tourney in 33 years, went on to beat the Lake of the Woods 3-2 in overtime. Eveleth's Zach Young got the game-winner at 2:05 of the extra session to finally bring the Golden Bears back to the promised land.

1994: Bloomington Jefferson vs. Moorhead

In 1994, the league's Board of Directors chose to reformat the tournament once again, opting this time to eliminate the Tier I & II system, and instead implementing a Class A and AA system. The new format would classify participating schools by enrollment, as it was for every other sport, instead of by performance. In addition, schools could now choose, at the beginning of the year, which level they wanted to participate in. That way, some of the smaller Class A programs that wanted to play against the bigger Class AA school's could move up if they so chose.

The 50th Tournament got underway with South St. Paul beating Rochester Mayo 4-1, thanks to a tremendous individual effort from Packers sophomore winger Ryan Huerta. Game Two saw Moorhead, behind Ryan Kraft, Josh Arnold,

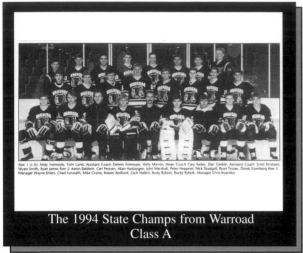

The 1994 State Champs from Warroad
Class A

Rob Gramer and Matt Cullen, pound on White Bear Lake 7-3, despite a solid performance from Bears winger Jesse Rooney. The first evening game saw the defending champs from Bloomington Jefferson win a hard-fought 1-0 win over Osseo, whose goalie Matt Jeffers, turned away a record-tying 20 shots in the first period alone. The last game of the day was a dandy, as Duluth East, which was led by Dave Spehar and Clint Johnson, beat a very talented Minnetonka team 3-1.

1994 Class AA

South St. Paul / Rochester Mayo	South St. Paul		
Moorhead / White Bear Lake	Moorhead	Moorhead	Bloomington Jefferson
Bloomington Jefferson / Osseo	Bloomington Jefferson	Bloomington Jefferson	**State Champion**
Duluth East / Minnetonka	Duluth East		

Third Place Winner: Duluth East, 5 South St. Paul, 3
Consolation Champion: White Bear Lake, 5 Osseo, 1

In the first semi, led by All-Stater's Mike Crowley and Joey Bianchi, Bloomington Jefferson edged out Duluth East 2-1, thanks to another outstanding performance from goalie Jeff Heil. Then, in the second semifinal, Moorhead barely hung on to beat South St. Paul by the final score of 4-3. Moorhead's lethal combo of Ryan Kraft, Josh Arnold and Matt Cullen all figured into the mix, which gave the Spud's a return trip to the finals. The Spuds, who finished second in 1992 and third in 1993, were eager to knock off the two-time defending champs from Bloomington.

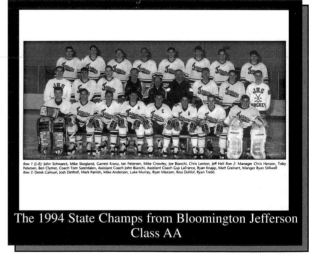

The 1994 State Champs from Bloomington Jefferson
Class AA

In the championship game, Moorhead standout right wing Ryan Kraft put the Spuds ahead late in the first period by stuffing in a rebound for his eighth goal of the tournament. Jaguars junior wing Mark Parrish, who would go on to NHL stardom, then tied the tilt with a 25-foot slapper at the 4:30 mark of the second period. Both goalies played outstanding hockey through the second, as the score remained deadlocked until just shy of six minutes into the third period. That's when 6-foot-1, 180-pound senior defenseman Derek Camuel barreled past both Moorhead defenders on a breakaway to score what would prove to be the game-winner. Mike Crowley, who would be named as the state's Mr. Hockey for the season, added an insurance goal late in the period as Jeff Heil hung on down the stretch for the 3-1 win. With the dramatic victory, the Jags had established themselves as one of the

The 1995 State Champs from Duluth East
Class AA

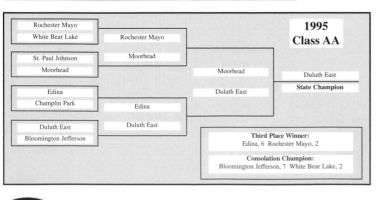

1995 Class AA

Rochester Mayo / White Bear Lake	Rochester Mayo		
St. Paul Johnson / Moorhead	Moorhead	Moorhead	Duluth East
Edina / Champlin Park	Edina	Duluth East	**State Champion**
Duluth East / Bloomington Jefferson	Duluth East		

Third Place Winner: Edina, 6 Rochester Mayo, 2
Consolation Champion: Bloomington Jefferson, 7 White Bear Lake, 2

state's all-time great dynasties, joining just Eveleth (1948-51) and International Falls (1964-1966) as the only other team to have won at least three titles in a row. Over those three years, the Jaguars, who finished the season at 26-1-1, put together 49 consecutive victories, sandwiched between a pair of ties and a 59-game unbeaten streak. (In fact, those 49 straight victories still rank sixth all-time in American high school hockey history.)

The Class A Tournament was played at both the Civic Center in St. Paul, and also at Mariucci Arena on the U of M campus. The event came to a close as Warroad beat rival Hibbing by the final score of 5-3 in the finals. The Warriors, which were led by Wyatt Smith's two goals, got the game-winner from Ryan James, who iced the victory on a break-away goal with just over three minutes left in the game. For Hockeytown USA, the victory had finally given the program something it was unable to do in nine previous tournament appearances, a championship. In the other tournament, Warroad had finished as the runner-up on three different occasions, including a heart-breaking over time loss to Edina in the 1969 title game. One of the other highlights of the Class A Tournament was the outstanding play of Farmington's third-line center Amber Hegland, who became the first girl to play in the boys' ice hockey tournament. (No stranger to competing with the boys, Amber also played cornerback on the Tigers football team which competed in the 1991 Prep Bowl.)

1995: Duluth East vs. Moorhead

Rochester Mayo and White Bear Lake hooked up in the opener, and thanks to Mayo junior winger Matt Leinbek's pure hat trick in the second, the Spartans came back from a 2-0 defect to beat the Bears by the final of 5-4. Tony Grosso got the game-winner for Rochester, while Bears winger Whitey Schwartzbauer scored a pair in the loss. After falling behind 2-1, Moorhead's Matt Cullen notched a goal and two assists in leading the Spud's past St. Paul Johnson in Game Two. The third game of the day saw John Farrell play hero for the Edina Hornets. Farrell got the go ahead goal at 11:13 of the first to make it 2-1, and then scored the game-winner at 5:54 of the third to give his Hornets a 3-2 win over a tough Champlin Park team. The last game of the day saw Duluth East exact a little revenge against Bloomington Jefferson, when, after losing 2-1 to the Jags in the 1994 tourney semifinals, they came out and spanked the three-time defending champs 5-0. While Greyhounds' phenom Dave Spehar opened the scoring by tallying a pure hat trick in the first nine minutes of the game, senior goalie Cade Ledingham made 18 saves for the shutout.

The first semifinal proved to be a classic as Moorhead and Mayo banged heads for all of regulation and then part of two overtimes, before Spuds' star winger Matt Cullen beat Spartan keeper Marc Ranfranz just 11 seconds into the second extra session. While Matt and Mark Cullen combined for five points in the win, Mayo forwards Tony Grosso and Jason Notermann each tallied a pair of goals in the loss. The other semi was all Duluth East, as Ryan Engle opened the scoring against Edina in the game's first 15 seconds. Spehar then made it 2-0 just six minutes later, and just kept on rolling after that, notching his second straight hat trick as the Greyhounds rolled over Edina by the final score of 6-2.

The championship tilt featured the state's three top-scoring players: Dave Spehar, who had 102 points for the season, teammate Chris Locker, who tallied 92, and Moorhead's Matt Cullen, who finished with 88 total points. In the title game, it was Dave Spehar once again getting the Hounds on the board first, when he beat Moorhead goalie Jason Gregoire at the 3:39 mark of the first. Matt Cullen answered for the Spuds late in the first period, and then made it 2-1 on a nice wrister just 14 seconds into the second. Duluth East came right back though, thanks to Chris Locker's goal late in the second to tie it up. Moorhead made it 3-2 at 5:21 of the third, when Cullen set up Joel Jamison on a nice one-timer, only to see Greyhound junior center Ted Suihkonen get the equalizer just 40 seconds later. From there, it was all Spehar, as he electrified the sell-out crowd by proceeding to get pulled down from behind on a breakaway to earn a penalty-shot. Moorhead's Rory Kortan had tripped the speedy centerman on to set up the dramatic scenario, which proved to be just the third successful penalty shot in tournament history. With the Hounds now up by one, Spehar made a little history. Just four minutes later, Dave Almquist went behind the net and floated a backhander to Spehar, who fired it home for his third straight hat trick of the tournament, tying the legendary John Mayasich of Eveleth who had also done the feat back in the 1951 tourney.

International Falls hung on to beat Totino-Grace in the Class A final, thanks to Jon Austin's 35-foot slapper from the top of the circle that beat Eagle goalie Aaron Ratfield with just eight seconds left in the game. (In addition, the Apple Valley girls team beat South St. Paul 2-0 to win the first-ever girls' state high school championship. For a complete history and recap, check out the women's hockey history chapter!)

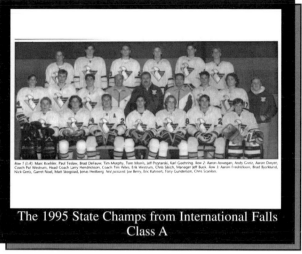

1995 Class A bracket

Third Place Winner:
Warroad, 7 Red Wing, 2

Consolation Champion:
Hutchinson, 5 Blake, 4

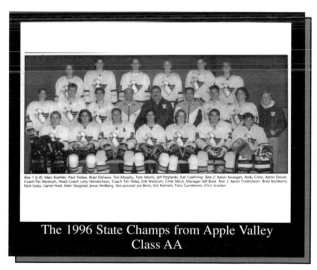

The 1995 State Champs from International Falls
Class A

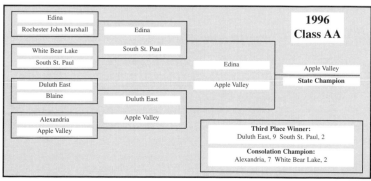

The 1996 State Champs from Apple Valley
Class AA

1996 Class AA bracket

Third Place Winner:
Duluth East, 9 South St. Paul, 2

Consolation Champion:
Alexandria, 7 White Bear Lake, 2

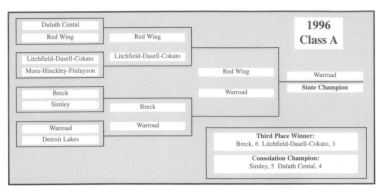

				1996 Class A
Duluth Cental / Red Wing	Red Wing			
Litchfield-Dasell-Cokato / Mora-Hinckley-Finlayson	Litchfield-Dasell-Cokato	Red Wing	Warroad	
Breck / Simley	Breck	Warroad	State Champion	
Warroad / Detroit Lakes	Warroad			

Third Place Winner:
Breck, 6 Litchfield-Dasell-Cokato, 3

Consolation Champion:
Simley, 5 Duluth Cental, 4

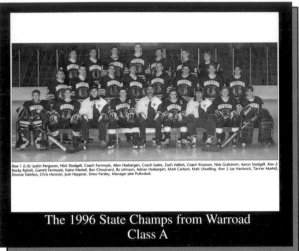

Row 1: (L-R): Justin Ferguson, Nick Stodgell, Coach Fermoyle, Allen Hasbargen, Coach Eades, Zach Hallett, Coach Knutson, Niels Grafstrom, Aaron Stodgell. Row 2: Rocky Rybolt, Garrett Fermoyle, Kaine Martell, Ben Chouinard, Bo Johnson, Adrian Hasbargen, Mark Carlson, Matt Ulwelling. Row 3: Jay Hardwick, Tanner Martell, Donnie DeMars, Chris Honsvet, Josh Heppner, Drew Parsley, Manager Jake Pulkrabek.

The 1996 State Champs from Warroad
Class A

1996: Apple Valley vs. Edina

Rochester John Marshall and Edina met in the first game of the 1996 state tournament, in what would prove to be a defensive gem. Rochester's Bryce Beckel opened the scoring at 2:40 of the first, only to see Edina's Dan Carlson tie it up at 13:14 of the first. The score remained that way until the final two minutes of the game, when Hornet forward Peter Armbrust beat Rocket goalie Derek Link for the game-winner. Game Two was also a good game, as South St. Paul rallied from a 2-1 deficit in the third to beat White Bear Lake 3-2. Packer center David Bonk got the tying goal midway through the final period, while Klint Nateau got the dramatic game-winner with just 56 seconds to go in the game. The defending champs from Duluth East steam-rollered over Blaine 7-1 in the first evening game. Dave Spehar's four goals and two assists led the charge for the Hounds, while Andy Wheeler also notched a pair and Chris Locker added one of his own for good measure. The night game was all Apple Valley, who, thanks to goals from Brad Defauw, Aaron Westrum and Chris Sikich, rallied from a 1-0 deficit early in the first to earn a 3-1 win over Alexandria.

Duluth East star Dave Spehar
now leads the Gophers

Edina kept it going into the next round, easily beating South St. Paul 3-1 in the first semifinal game. Edina's Brad and Dan Carlson led the way with a goal and an assist apiece. The next game would prove to be one of the tournament's all-time classics. Duluth East and Apple Valley squared off for the second semi without so much as a clue that they were about to make history. The game went back and forth all night, as the lead exchanged hands on numerous occasions. Down 3-2 midway through the third, Dave Spehar tied the game at 3-3, only to see Eagle's center Erik Westrum tally to give his team the lead yet again. Then, with Apple Valley leading 4-3 late in the third period, Duluth's Dave Spehar set up Chris Locker on a nice give-and-go to tie the game with just 38 seconds left in regulation. Five overtimes later, Eagles' defenseman Aaron Dwyer took a Chris Sikich pass from the top of the circle and slid it past Greyhound goalie Kyle Kolquist to give Apple Valley an incredible 5-4 victory, and put an end to the wild marathon. Apple Valley goalie Karl Goehring made 65 saves that night, including 17 in the fourth over time alone to break the old record of 61 saves held by St. Paul Johnson's Doug Long in 1970. (In addition, the 93 minute and 12 second game is recorded as the longest ever in state tournament history, surpassing the 1955 classic when South St. Paul needed 87:50 to defeat Thief River Falls 3-2 in 11 overtimes.)

Despite playing into the wee hours of the morning, the fatigued Eagles came back to defeat Edina in the title game that next night, giving the school its' first state title. Edina's Peter Fitzgerald got the Hornet's on the board first, when he lit the lamp at the 2:12 mark of the first. Chris Sikich tied it just four minutes later when he fired home a slapper from the right circle, followed by Aaron Fredrickson's goal at 3:22 of the second to make it 2-1 for the Eagles. Five minutes later Edina's Dan Carlson scored a short-handed goal to tie it back up at 2-2, setting the stage for Apple Valley's Matt Skogstad, who, on the power-play, found the back of the net at 14:21 of the second. Eagle goalie Karl Goehring stood tall for the final period, as Apple Valley hung on for the 3-2 victory.

Warroad annihilated the No. 3 ranked Red Wing Wingers by the final of 10-3 in the Class A final. The Warriors were leading 6-0 before Warroad goalie Aaron Stodgell gave up his first goal of the tournament to future Gopher Johnny Pohl, at the 13:31 mark. Matt Ulwelling and Zach Hallett each netted a pair in the lopsided win.

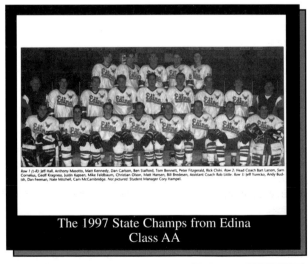

Row 1: (L-R): Jeff Hall, Anthony Masotto, Matt Kennedy, Dan Carlson, Ben Stafford, Tom Bennett, Peter Fitzgerald, Rick Chihi. Row 2: Head Coach Bart Larson, Sam Cornelius, Geoff Kragness, Justin Kapsen, Mike Feldbaum, Christian Olson, Matt Hansen, Bill Bredesen, Assistant Coach Rob Little. Row 3: Jeff Yurecko, Andy Budish, Dan Feeman, Nate Mitchell, Cam McCambridge. Not pictured: Student Manager Cory Hampel.

The 1997 State Champs from Edina
Class AA

1997: Edina vs. Duluth East

Moorhead pounced on Anoka in the opening game of the 1997 tourney, beating the Tornadoes 7-1. Brian Nelson led the charge by scoring an amazing four goals, while Mark Cullen added a goal and four assists in the win. The second game saw Duluth East hold off a late charge from Rochester Mayo to win by the final score of 3-2. Matt Mathias, Nick Anderson and Pat Finnegan all scored for the Hounds, while senior winger Brian Buskowiak tallied both goals for the Spartans. Game Three was all Edina as Tom Bennett, Sam Cornelius and Dan Carlson each scored for the Hornets, while junior goalie Jeff Hall stopped all

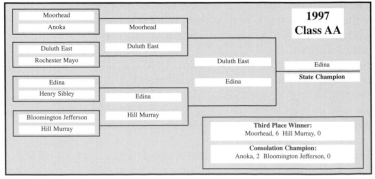

				1997 Class AA
Moorhead / Anoka	Moorhead			
Duluth East / Rochester Mayo	Duluth East	Duluth East	Edina	
Edina / Henry Sibley	Edina	Edina	State Champion	
Bloomington Jefferson / Hill Murray	Hill Murray			

Third Place Winner:
Moorhead, 6 Hill Murray, 0

Consolation Champion:
Anoka, 2 Bloomington Jefferson, 0

nine shots he faced to earn the 3-0 shut out. Hill-Murray and Bloomington Jefferson squared off in the nightcap, in what would prove to be no love-fest. Hill-Murray went up 3-0 early, only to see Bloomington's John Konrad score a couple of quick goals late in the third to get it to 3-2. The Jags pressed in the final minutes of the game but couldn't beat Pioneer goalie Jason Carey, as Hill added an empty netter and cruised to a 4-2 victory.

Duluth East rolled over Moorhead in the first semifinal game of the day, as Gabe Taggart opened the scoring with a power-play goal at 9:54 of the first. Senior centerman Matt Mathias then scored a pair of goals down the stretch and goalie Kyle Kolquist stopped all 12 shots that came his way to earn the 3-0 shut out.

Hill-Murray and Edina got together for a penalty-laden second semifinal game, with the Hornets holding on for an amazing 5-4 triple-overtime victory. This one went back and forth all night as the Pioneers went up 1-0 on Rick Brosseau's goal just a minute into the game. Edina's Tony Massotto then netted the first of his two first period goals to get the equalizer. Edina went up 4-2 into the third when Justin Kapsen tickled the twine, only to see the Pioneers come right back on a pair of goals from Tony Rockenbach and Steve Jones to tie it up at four apiece. The teams then battled it out for three overtimes until Edina's Sam Cornelius got the game-winning goal at the 5:26 mark of the third extra session.

This set up a final which featured a couple of team's who had been there before, the 1996 state runner-ups from Edina and the undefeated Duluth East Greyhounds. This one would prove to be a defensive battle from the start, with both goalies playing outstanding between the pipes. At the 13:20 mark of the first period, Hornets senior winger Dan Carlson took a pass from Ben Stafford and proceeded to score what turned out to be the game-winning goal. Edina goalie Jeff Hall stood on his head the rest of the game and stopped all 20 shots that came at him for the coveted championship shut out. The anti-climactic 1-0 win gave the Hornets their ninth boys' hockey championship trophy, two more than any other school in state history.

The 1997 State Champs from Red Wing
Class A

In a rematch of the 1996 Class A championship game, Red Wing and Warroad once again squared off for the title. This year, however, had a different outcome, as the undefeated Red Wing Wingers finally exorcised some demons by winning their first title in three consecutive tourney appearances. Red Wing got the championship game off to a quick start with three first-period goals, one each by the brother's Pohl -- Mark and John, and another by Tom Moore. Warroad answered with goals from Jackson Harren and Chris Heppner in the second, but at 1:22 of the third, Red Wing junior forward Mark Bang took a Mark Pohl pass and beat Warroad goalie Justin Ferguson for what would turn out to be the game-winner. The Wingers held on down the stretch behind goalie Joe Edstrom's 16 saves for the 4-3 victory.

1998: Duluth East vs. Anoka

Bloomington Jefferson and Owatonna got together in the opening quarterfinal game of the 1998 state tournament, in what would prove to be a laugher. Led by Dave Hergert's hat trick, the Jags pulled out the heavy artillery in this one, pounding the Huskies by the final of 8-0. Game Two saw Duluth East come from behind to earn a 5-4 victory over Hastings. Pat Finnegan, Gabe Taggart, Ross Carlson, Chad Roberg and Rheese Carlson all tallied for the Hounds in the win, while Jeff Taffe, Dan Welch and Ben Tharp combined for eight points for the Raiders in the loss. Anoka got two first period goals from Rick Talbot and never looked back in its 2-1 win over White Bear Lake in Game Three. The final game of the night between Roseau and Edina went back and forth three different times before finally going into overtime. With Edina up 3-2 after two, Roseau's David Lunbohm notched the equalizer at 2:33 of the third. The score remained that way until 4:14 of sudden death, when Phil Larson took a Lunbohm pass and sent it past Hornets' goalie Jeff Hall for the dramatic game-winner.

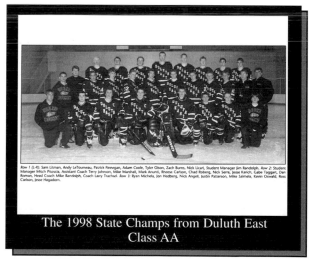

The 1998 State Champs from Duluth East
Class AA

The first semifinal featured Jefferson and Duluth East skating to a scoreless first period. Jake Heisler finally got the Jags on the board at 10:34 of the second, only to see Duluth East's Kevin Oswald and Nick Angel each tally in the third to go up 2-1. Todd Koehnen got the equalizer for Jefferson at 11:10 of the final session, which sent the game into overtime. There, just two minutes and 22 seconds later, Kevin Oswald put his second goal of the evening past Greyhound goalie Adam Coole to give the Jaguars a dramatic 3-2 victory. The other semi was a blowout as Anoka romped all over Roseau by the final of 6-1. While the Rams opened the scoring early in the first, the Tornadoes roared back for six unanswered goals, highlighted by Rick Talbot's hat trick.

The finals pitted the new kids on the block from Anoka, and the old stand-byes from Duluth East, in what would prove to be the last ever

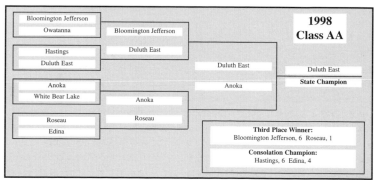

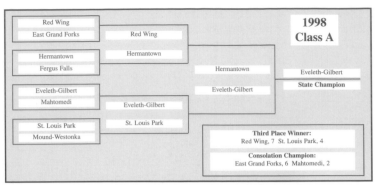

	1998 Class A	
Red Wing		
East Grand Forks	Red Wing	
Hermantown	Hermantown	
Fergus Falls		Hermantown
		Eveleth-Gilbert
Eveleth-Gilbert		Eveleth-Gilbert
Mahtomedi	Eveleth-Gilbert	**State Champion**
	Eveleth-Gilbert	
St. Louis Park	St. Louis Park	
Mound-Westonka		

Third Place Winner:
Red Wing, 7 St. Louis Park, 4

Consolation Champion:
East Grand Forks, 6 Mahtomedi, 2

game in the Civic Center. (The NHL's Minnesota Wild announced their plans to build a new arena on that site, and as a result, the tournament would move to the Target Center for a two-year hiatus before returning to St. Paul to play in the new arena.) The Hounds came in to the game riding a 22-game winning streak, and were eager to win their second title in four years. Gabe Taggart opened the scoring for Duluth East at the 7:31 mark when he came in on Danny Scott, deked and fired a nice wrist shot into the back of the net. Both teams had numerous opportunities in the second, but it was Ross Carlson's 19th goal of the season that put the Greyhounds ahead 2-0. Anoka's Jerrid Reinholz then answered back just 20 seconds later to make it 2-1. The third period was wide open, as Chad Roberg took a couple of passes from the Carlson brothers: Ross and Rheese, to go up 3-1 at 3:43 of the third. Greyhound goalie Adam Coole stopped the remaining 23 shots he faced that night as the Hounds went on to beat Anoka 3-1 for the state championship.

Eveleth-Gilbert then made it an all-northern Minnesota sweep when they beat Hermantown in the Class A finals. Hermantown took the early lead on Jon Francisco's quick slapper from the slot at 3:04 of the first period, only to see Eveleth come right back and spank Hawk goalie Chris Oppel in the second on a pair of goals from Steve Denny and Jeff Dolinsek. The score remained 2-1 until the third, when, after Pat Andrews tied it up at 8:18 of the final period, Kyle Hawley got what would prove to be the game-winner with just 4:38 left in regulation. Jeff Dolinsek added an empty-netter as the Golden Bears cruised to a 5-3 victory.

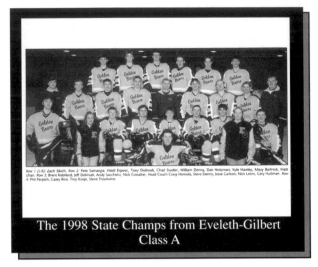

Row 1 (L-R): Zach Sikich. Row 2: Pete Samargia, Heidi Erjavec, Tony Dolinsek, Chad Studier, William Denny, Dan Heitzman, Kyle Hawley, Missy Bartnick, Matt Uhan. Row 3: Brent Robillard, Jeff Dolinsek, Andy Sacchetti, Nick Cossalter, Head Coach Craig Homola, Steve Denny, Jesse Carlson, Nick Leoni, Gary Hultman. Row 4: Phil Perpich, Casey Rice, Troy Korpi, Steve Troutwine

The 1998 State Champs from Eveleth-Gilbert
Class A

1999: Roseau vs. Hastings

Holy Angels and Eden Prairie got together in the first state tournament game ever played in the Target Center. The Eagles got on the board first when Brian Rasmussen scored a short-handed goal at 14:12 of the first period. That would be all the scoring Eden Prairie would do that day however, because Holy Angels fired back four unanswered goals from Casey Garven, Justin Hauge, Josh Singer and Adam Kaiser to roll to a 4-1 win. Game Two pitted Roseau and Rochester Mayo in a game that Mike Klema looked like a man among boys. Klema not only scored two goals in the game, he also was a physical presence on the ice, as the Rams beat up on the Spartans by the final of 4-2. The first evening game of the day was all Elk River, as the Elks, behind a pair of Joey Bailey goals, cruised to a 5-1 win over Hill-Murray. In the final semifinal of the day, Hastings and Blaine played one of the most wide-open games in tourney history. Jeff Taffe opened the scoring just 22 seconds into the first, while Adam Holmgren got the first of his three goals just 33 seconds later. Hastings got the next three to make it 4-1 going into the second, when the scoring frenzy reached epic proportions. At the start of the second period, the teams actually set a new state tournament record for the fastest three goals ever scored. (Blaine's Trevor Frischmon at 3:11, Hasting's Matt Van Der Bosch at 3:19 and Blaine's Erik Johnson at 3:27.) Blaine came out and scored three straight in the third to regain the lead, only to see Dan Welch score a pair down the stretch to seal the 7-6 victory for Hastings.

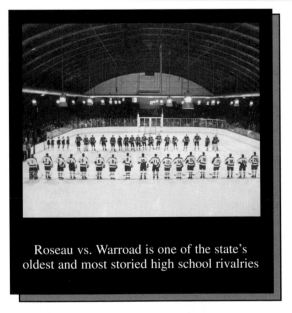

Roseau vs. Warroad is one of the state's oldest and most storied high school rivalries

Roseau scored early and often against Holy Angels in the first semifinal game, as the Mike Klema show continued to roll on. Klema scored an unbelievable four goals in this one as the Rams went on to beat the Stars by the final of 6-2. The other semi saw a much closer contest between Elk River and Hastings. Carson Ezati opened the scoring in this one at the 8:57 mark of the first when he beat Hasting's keeper Matt Klein out front. After playing to a scoreless second, Hastings' junior center Adam Gerlach found the back of the net at 1:56 of the third to tie it up.

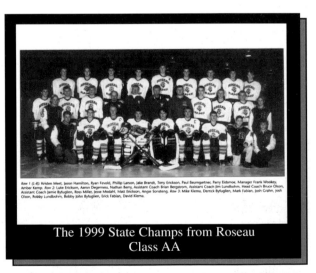

Row 1 (L-R): Kristen Meet, Jason Hamilton, Ryan Fevold, Phillip Larson, Jake Brandt, Tony Erickson, Paul Baumgartner, Parry Eidsmoe, Manager Frank Wookey, Amber Kemp. Row 2: Luke Erickson, Aaron Degermess, Nathan Berry, Assistant Coach Brian Bergstrom, Assistant Coach Jim Lundbohm, Head Coach Bruce Olson, Assistant Coach Jamie Byfuglien, Ross Miller, Jesse Modahl, Matt Erickson, Angie Sonsteng, Row 3: Mike Klema, Derrick Byfuglien, Mark Fabian, Josh Grahn, Josh Olson, Robby Lundbohm, Bobby John Byfuglien, Erick Fabian, David Klema

The 1999 State Champs from Roseau
Class AA

Both teams had plenty of opportunities down the stretch, but neither could capitalize, as the game went into overtime. Then, finally, at the 10:15 mark of the second extra session, Travis Kieffer took a couple of passes from Cody Swanson and Jeff Taffe, and buried the puck past Elk River goalie Mitch Glines for the 2-1 win. Hasting's goalie made 36 saves in the game, compared to just 19 by Glines, who got the loss.

The finals were now set with Roseau and Hastings ready to do battle. Both teams looked sharp in the first, and each missed a couple of solid

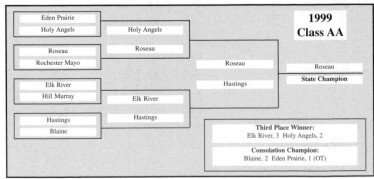

	1999 Class AA	
Eden Prairie		
Holy Angels	Holy Angels	
Roseau	Roseau	
Rochester Mayo		Roseau
		Roseau
Elk River		Hastings
Hill Murray	Elk River	**State Champion**
	Elk River	
Hastings	Hastings	
Blaine		

Third Place Winner:
Elk River, 3 Holy Angels, 2

Consolation Champion:
Blaine, 2 Eden Prairie, 1 (OT)

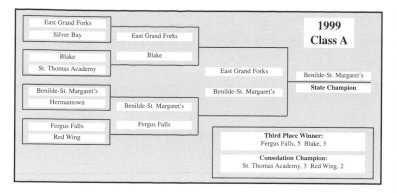

	1999 Class A

Bracket (Class A):
- East Grand Forks / Silver Bay → East Grand Forks
- Blake / St. Thomas Academy → Blake
- East Grand Forks vs Blake → East Grand Forks
- Benilde-St. Margaret's / Hermantown → Benilde-St. Margaret's
- Fergus Falls / Red Wing → Fergus Falls
- Benilde-St. Margaret's vs Fergus Falls → Benilde-St. Margaret's
- East Grand Forks vs Benilde-St. Margaret's → Benilde-St. Margaret's
- **State Champion:** Benilde-St. Margaret's

Third Place Winner:
Fergus Falls, 5 Blake, 3

Consolation Champion:
St. Thomas Academy, 3 Red Wing, 2

scoring chances to boot. At 6:40 of the second period Josh Olson finally put Roseau on the board, and from there on out the Rams didn't look back. Both Dan and Mike Klema, as well as Matt Erickson all scored goals after that as the Rams went on to cruise to a 4-0 victory. Ram's goalie Jake Brandt stopped all 19 shots that came his way that night en route to earning the oh so sweet shut out. And with that, Roseau, the smallest school in the AA Tournament, with just 339 students, won its sixth state championship, proving that those wonderful David vs. Goliath stories are still alive and well in Minnesota State High School Hockey.

In the Class A championship, Benilde St. Margaret's came back from an early 2-1 deficit to beat East Grand Forks by the final score of 4-2. Troy Riddle proved to be the hero in this one, scoring not only the game's opening goal, but then leading the rally back to also get the game-winner as well, as the Red Knights cruised to their first Class A title over the Green Wave.

The 1999 State Champs from Benilde St. Margaret's
Class A

Minnesota Hockey in the 21st Century

As we head into the new millenium, the state of the state of Minnesota hockey is better than ever. From what started as a mythical championship back around the turn of the century, to Gene Aldrich's dream in 1945 at the old St. Paul Auditorium, to today, where it is the largest, most action-packed tournament of its kind in the world, this is Minnesota's pride and joy— the tournament. For those who got to play in it, and especially for those lucky few who even got to skate off the ice with gold medals around their necks, it means a lifetime of memories. From the Eveleth dynasties of the 1940s, to Roseau, St. Paul Johnson and Thief River Falls in the 1950s, to International Falls and Greenway during the 1960s, to Grand Rapids and Edina during the 1970s, to Burnsville and Edina in the 1980s, and finally, to Bloomington Jefferson and Duluth East in the 1990s, Minnesota has seen it all.

Things have changed in the world of hockey since Eveleth's incredible high school run back in the 1940s. While the attendance for the first high school hockey tournament in 1945 was 8,434, today the tournament draws more than 120,000. More than 3 million people have seen the tourney live, and millions more have watched it on TV. Families even plan their vacations around it, as it has become a part of our way of life. Blizzard or not, people will show up just to scream "we've got spirit, yes we do, we've got spirit, how 'bout you?"

Today, the high school game continues to grow, all in an effort to showcase our best and brightest for their hopeful departure to the next level of competition. There are a handful of select teams and all-star squads to get kids noticed by college and junior coaches. One of the best is the Maroon and Gold Series, which started back in 1984 when the Minnesota High School Hockey Coach's Association and MAHA collaborated on a senior all-star series involving 42 of the state's top graduating seniors. From there it became the Great 68, and today it features 136 players at the "Super Rink" in Blaine, where the purpose has remained the same — to showcase the players for advanced level opportunities.

From seven-man hockey, to rovers, to no forward passing rules, the game has seen a lot of changes over the past century. Today people will attest to the fact that there is too much interference and too many defensive slowdown tactics. All the dumping-and-chasing and clutching-and-grabbing has taken away from the creativity of the game, and added a physical element that many don't care for. But, through it all, the game has evolved and changed with the times. From Cooperalls to spider web masks, the tourney has aspired. Now, with two classes, twice as many kids get to participate in the event. While that decision back in the early '90s was met with a great deal of controversy, today people like the fact that more Minnesota kids are getting the chance to play hockey. Period.

The support for the tourney continues to be amazing, with new communities embracing it every year. To watch tiny Roseau come down and kick the snot out of all of the bigger metro schools was a David and Goliath dream come true in '99. That is what the tourney is all about, and it is nothing for those northern schools to come down to the "Cities" by the bus-load to watch their teams play. And while many stay in hotels for the weekend, many others make the three to six hour round-trip back and forth each night - only to return in the morning to do it all over again. From the days at the old Auditorium on through to the Civic Center, for the fans, the tourney has become the premier gathering place. The sea of letter jackets, bands, cheerleaders, students, alumni, and face-painted psycho fanatics make for some classic sports theater that has made it all so special.

With apologies to the NCAA Basketball's Final-Four tournament, the real "March Madness" is right here, in Minnesota.

The 1985 Fairmont Cardinals High School juggernaut
(Yours truly - third from the right, bottom row!)

In Memory of Don Clark

This past summer a Minnesota hockey legend passed away. Don Clark did more for hockey in Minnesota than anyone. Period. While many of you may have never heard of Don, fittingly, that is probably the way he would have liked it. An incredibly humble, modest, and brilliant man, Don was the ultimate "behind the scene's" guy. He dedicated his entire life to the advancement of ice hockey in the United States, and did it all out of the goodness of his heart.

Don grew up in Faribault, where he was a three-sport athlete at Faribault High School. He went on to play both amateur baseball and hockey, but it was the latter that was his true passion. In 1934, at just 19, he organized the Southern Minnesota Hockey League , doing his part to advance the game south of the Twin Cities. While Don went on to become a successful agri-chemist, specializing in the dairy industry, his real job was developing hockey in the Gopher State.

In 1947, along with Bob Ridder and "Buck" Riley, Don founded the Minnesota Amateur Hockey Association (MAHA) and proceeded to build it into the most successful organization of its kind in the country. He would later serve as its president and secretary-treasurer, on and off for nearly a half-century. His many accomplishments there included organizing the nation's first state bantam hockey tournament in 1951.

In 1958 he became vice president of the Amateur Hockey Association of the United States (AHAUS, which later became USA Hockey), a position he would hold for more than 20 years. That same year Don managed the first U.S. National team to ever play in the Soviet Union. He would go on to serve as the Hall of Fame's first president in 1974, where he would later be inducted in 1978. In 1975 Don was awarded hockey's highest honor - the Lester Patrick Award - for all of his amazing contributions to the game. January 28, 1989 was even declared Don Clark Day in Minnesota, by Governor Rudy Perpich.

Don was a walking encyclopedia of American hockey history and all its lore, and truly represents everything that is good, and decent about sports. He was a tireless man who gave and gave and expected nothing in return. I initially met him back in 1991, when I wrote my first book, "Gopher Hockey by the Hockey Gopher." He helped me write the history for that book, and without his help I would have been truly lost. I was amazed at just how smart he was, and how incredible his memory was. He knew everything about everyone. I would mention a player from the 1920s and he could tell me his number, how he played, his stats, everything.

For the good of hockey, I am so glad that I was able to drive to his home in Cumberland, Wisc., this past summer and meet with him one last time before he passed. We sat with his two sons, and his wife of more than 50 years, Harriet, and ate some pie and talked hockey. It was marvelous, and something I will never forget. If you have ever read the book "Tuesday's with Morrie," by Mitch Albom, you will know exactly what I mean. He was a real mentor for me, and inspired me to be a better person. Selfishly, I am so sad that I won't be able to present him with my new book, and maybe even teach him something he didn't already know - although I doubt that would have been possible!

So many of the pictures in this book are from Don, and much of the history was compiled by him. I couldn't have done it without him, and want him to know that I miss him and want to thank him. He was truly a remarkable person, and without a doubt the biggest friend that Minnesota hockey will ever know. All kids, boys and girls, everywhere, should give thanks to Don Clark. He, more than anyone, blazed the trail for hockey in our great state. So, if Mr. Mariucci was the "Godfather" of Minnesota hockey, Don Clark would then have to be the "Grandfather."

The 1934 Faribault High School team led by Don Clark
(No. 35, second from the left in the front row)

Afterword by Brett Hull

Being the son of NHL Hall of Famer Bobby Hull and nephew of ex-NHLer Dennis Hull, Brett Hull was born into some pretty amazing "thoroughbred" lineage. Having first learned how to skate from his mother, who was a professional figure skater, Brett grew up learning the game of hockey from some of the game's greatest players. After playing in the Junior ranks, Brett hit the Minnesota scene in 1985, when he joined Mike Sertich's Minnesota-Duluth Bulldogs. In his first year with the Dogs, Hull won the WCHA Rookie of the Year Award, and led the team to the NCAA Final Four. Deciding to join the NHL's Calgary Flames in 1987, Brett finished his incredible career in Duluth with an amazing 84 goals and 60 assists for 144 points in just 90 games. But his fame in the Port City has lived on forever, as today he is without question the biggest celebrity in town.

Although there were some cynics early on who felt that Brett Hull might not have the right stuff to play in the NHL, somehow the nine-time All-Star, three-time NHL goal-scoring champion and 1991 league MVP managed to do all right for himself. An extremely intelligent and creative play-maker, Hull reigns as the NHL's top gun with one of the hardest shots in the game. Destined for the Hall of Fame, Brett has tallied 586 goals and 459 assists for 1,045 career points. Now that's a lot of goals, but on Saturday, June 19th, 1999, Brett got a goal he would've gladly traded all the others in for.

I can still remember watching it at my in-law's house on Lake Nichols, a little town just north of Duluth, with a bunch of die-hard UMD fans. It was late that Saturday night, and my Uncle Pete was dozing on and off as we were watching the most incredible Stanley Cup finals game that any of us had ever seen. Fast-forward now to the 14:51 mark of the third overtime of a 1-1 Game Six (with the Stars up three games to one), as Brett Hull took a rebound out front and proceeded to score the biggest goal of his life. In what has been referred to simply as the now infamous "toe in the crease goal," the crafty right winger beat Sabres' MVP goalie Dominik Hasek on a nice little wrister to win the Stanley Cup Championship. It was the middle of the night, but we all went nuts. While we all wished like hell that it could've been the Minnesota North Stars who were playing that night instead of the Dallas Stars, that bunch of Duluth die-hards felt vindicated that at least it was one of their own who was finally able to bring a Cup home to that storied franchise.

Brett made the Duluth fans happy yet again this summer, when he brought the Stanley Cup back to Duluth for a day. And, while he didn't take the Cup tubing behind his boat, like his teammate Jamie Langenbrunner, from Cloquet, did, he did manage to get it over to Grandma's Restaurant and Norman's Bar. Making the people of the Northland happy is nothing new to Brett Hull. Today the superstar lives on Pike Lake, just outside of Duluth, where he still hangs out with his old UMD buddies such as Bill Watson, Jim Toninato and Norm MacIver. He is a living legend in Northern Minnesota, and probably one of the nicest, and most down-to-earth guys you will ever meet. When I decided to write my new book about the history of Minnesota hockey, I couldn't think of anyone more deserving to represent it, than Brett Hull, hockey's premier sniper.

"When Ross first called me to tell me about his new book project, I was flattered that he considered me to be a part of it," said Brett. "I told him that there were probably a lot of other people much more worthy of doing the Afterword than myself though. I explained to him that I really only played in Duluth for two seasons, and that surely I couldn't have that much to say about the future of Minnesota hockey. But after he told me how much the fans and all the little kids back there had been following my career, it made me feel really proud to say that I am a Minnesotan.

"All in all, I think hockey in Minnesota is going great, and the future of the game is in good hands. The fans there truly know and understand the game. I have played in a lot of places over the years, including at the old Met Center against the North Stars, and I can tell you that those are some of the most loyal fans in the world. Some of the greatest hockey minds in the game are there as well, because the state wreaks of hockey tradition. The kids are born into it, much like they are in Canada, and it is really a special place to learn the game. I see kids up there roller-blading and playing constantly, and that's why Minnesota continues to be the top hockey state in the country. Even to see where it has gotten to since the mid-1980s, when I was at UMD, has been great. There a five D-I programs there now, the women's game is strong and the high school tournament is still the best in the country. The sport has continued to move onward and upward and Minnesota just continues to raise talent for the next levels."

"From Mr. Mariucci on down, Minnesota has produced a lot of great players over the years, and that is well known throughout the ranks of pro hockey. The people there know hockey and respect the game. I learned that right away from playing there, and as I spend more and more time there, I can see how important it is to all of the communities. It is obviously a great source of pride for the people there, and I am honored to be a part of the great tradition. I mean, just look at the little town of Cloquet. The fact that Derek Plante and Jamie Langenbrunner were both on the Stanley Cup team is amazing. That community must be so proud of those guys.

"I feel very lucky and very fortunate to have had the success that I have had in the game of hockey, and I am seriously dreading the day when I have to retire. But, when I do hang em' up, I know I can always become a bar-league star up in Duluth! I can play golf at Northland Country Club during the day, and then play hockey at night, it'll be great! But seriously, I am really honored and humbled that the people and fans of Minnesota have treated me so well through the years, and I can't thank them enough. I am also honored to be a part of Ross' book. If you liked his last one, "Fifty Years • Fifty Heroes," then you'll love this one. Reading about all my buddies from UMD brought back a lot of wonderful memories, and to learn so much about all of the old teams, like the North Stars and Fighting Saints was really fun. It was something that needed to be done, and he did a fabulous job of putting it all together for everyone to enjoy. And, after reading about all of the legends in there, it just makes me even more proud to be a part of Minnesota's wonderful hockey tradition."

Duluth's "Golden Brett"

List of Works Cited:

1. *Ross Bernstein: Interviews from over 100 Minnesota sports personalities and celebrities
2. "Gopher Hockey by the Hockey Gopher," by Ross Bernstein, Minneapolis, MN, 1992
3. "Fifty Years • Fifty Heroes" A Celebration of Minnesota Sports, by Ross Bernstein, Minneapolis, MN, 1997
4. "Hubert H. Humphrey Metrodome Souvenir Book": by Calvin Griffith, Jim Klobuchar, Halsey Hall, Muriel Humphrey Brown, Charles O. Johnson, Patrick Reusse, Joe Soucheray - compiled by Dave Mona. MSP Publications.
5. "An Investment of 26 Years Yields Nothing but Memories," Star Tribune Article by Curt Brown, March 11, 1993.
6. "The Official National Hockey League 75th Anniversary Commemorative Book": by Dan Diamond, NHL Pub., 1991.
7. "USA Hockey," by Kevin Allen, Triumph Books, Chicago, IL, 1997.
8. "A Thinking Man's Guide to Pro Hockey": by Eskenazi, Gerald, E. P. Dutton, 1972.
9. "The Hockey Encyclopedia": by Fischler, Stan, and Shirley Fischler, Macmillan, 1983.
10. "NHL The World of Professional Hockey": by Jay Greenberg, On Frarik, and Gary Ronberg, Rutledge Press, 1981.
11. "The Pictorial History of Hockey" by Joseph Romain, & Dan Diamond, Gallery Books, 1987.
12. "The Sporting News Hockey Guide & Register": Sporting News Publishing, 1984-90.
13. "Sid!" by Sid Hartman & Patrick Reusse - Voyager Press, 1997
14. "Broten Lived Out a Dream" by Dan Barriero, Star Tribune, Oct. 16, 1996
15. The U.S. Hockey Hall of Fame Handbook
16. "One Goal - A Chronicle of the 1980 US Olympic Hockey Team": by John Powers and Art Kaminsky: Harper Row, 1984
17. The US Olympic Hockey Guide -1996
18. North Stars article by Curt Brown, Star Tribune, March 11, 1993
19. "An Investment of 26 Years Yields Nothing But Memories" Star Tribune, 1981.
20. North Stars Media Guides (1970s -90s)
21. "Don Roberts Bids Farewell to Gustavus Adolphus," by Jim Rueda, Mankato Free Press
22. "The Christian Story": Christian Brothers, Inc. Press Release Information
23. "Minnesota Trivia," by Laurel Winter: Rutledge Hill Press, Nashville, TN, 1990
24. "NCAA Championships": The Official 1996 National Collegiate Championships & Records, by the NCAA
25. The Phoenix Coyotes Media Guide: 1997
26. The U.S. Olympic Comm. Olympian Report
27. The Star Tribune Minnesota Sports Hall of Fame insert publication
28. "Hockey": The Illustrated History, by Dan Diamond
29. "One Hundred Years of Hockey": by Brian McFarlane
30. "The Official NHL Stanley Cup Centennial," by Dan Diamond
31. "Can You Name That Team?" by David Biesel
32. Duluth News Tribune and Herald: UMD Hockey article, March 25, 1984
33. The Sporting News: UMD Hockey article - April 2, 1984
34. "Ivory Tower": John Mariucci article - "The Coach Behind the Comeback," by Peter Vanderpoel, 1953
35. "Hockey Chicago Style: The History of the Blackhawks," by Paul Greenland: Sagamore Publishing
36. "Dallas Stars" - Professional Team Histories
37. "Scoreboard," by Dunstan Tucker & Martin Schirber, St. John's University Press, Collegeville, MN, 1979.
38. "The Great American Hockey Dilemma," by Murray Williamson, Ralph Turtinen Publishing Co., Wayzata, MN, 1978.
39. "The Flakes of Winter," by Stan Fischler, Warwick Publishing Co, Toronto, Canada, 92.
40. "Icy Pleasures," by Paul Clifford Larson, Afton Historical Society Press, Afton, MN 98.
41. "Great Book of Hockey," by Stan & Shirley Fischler, Publications International, Ltd., Lincolnwood, IL, 1997.
42. "Awesome Almanac MN," by Jean Blashfield, B&B Pub. Inc., Fontana, WI, 93.
43. "Hockey America," by Kevin Hubbard & Stan Fischler, Masters Press, Indianapolis, 97.
44. "Minnesota State High School Hockey Tournament History," Art Solz Jr., Minneapolis, MN, 1968.
45. "The Goldy Shuffle: The Bill Goldsworthy Story," by Richard Rainbolt & Ralph Turtinen, Denison Pub., Minneapolis, 1971.
46. "Skate for Goal!," by Gary L. Phillips, Afton Press, Afton, MN 1982.
47. "The Blazing North Stars," by Stan Fischler, Prentice Hall Pub., Englewood Cliffs, NJ, 1972.
48. "Hockey Hall of Fame," by Dan Diamond and Joseph Romain, Doubleday Pub., NY, 1988.
49. "NHL Hockey: An Official Fans Guide, "by John Mackinnon, Triumph Books, Chicago, 97.
50. "Total Hockey," by Dan Diamond, Total Sports Publishing, NY, 1998
51. "The Encyclopedia of Sports," by Frank Menke, AC Barnes Pub., Cranbury, NJ, 1975.
52. "Sad and Mad," by Curt Brown, Star Tribune, March 11, 1993.
53. "Going for Gold," by Tim Wendel, Lawrence Hill Pub. Co. Westport, CT., 1980
54. "The Internet Hockey Database," by Ralph Slate
55. "My lifetime in sports," by George Barton, Stan Carlson Pub., Minneapolis, 1957.
56. "The Story of Hockey," by Frank Orr, Random House, NY, 1971.
57. "Hockey legends of all time," by Morgan Hughes, Pub. Intl., Lincolnwood, IL, 1996.
58. Sports Illustrated: Stars article, May 25, '81
59. Sports Illustrated: Stars article, June 1, 1981
60. "Ice Polo in Minnesota," 1883-1901, by DonClark
61. "Minn. Indoor Rinks," 1894-1982, by Don Clark
62. "Early Eveleth Hockey," First Fifty Years, 1903-1952, by Don Clark
63. "Early St. Paul Hockey," 1896-1942, by Don Clark
64. "Early Minneapolis Hockey," 1895-1942, by Don Clark
65. "Early Duluth Hockey," by Don Clark
66. "Hockey in the U.S.," by Don Clark
67. "USAHA - United States Amateur Hockey Association," 1920-1926, by Don Clark
68. "American Hockey Association," 1927-1942, by Don Clark
69. "Central Hockey League," 1931-1932, 1934-1935, by Don Clark
70. "Minnesota Amateur Hockey Association - The Early Years," by Don Clark
71. "The Great American Hockey Dilemma," by Murray Williamson (Ralph Turtinen Pub., 1978).
72. "Times have changed," by John Millea, Star Tribune, January 3, 1999.
73. "Something Wild is going on here," by John Millea, Star Tribune, December 6, 1998.
74. "Melting away," by Roman Augustoviz, Star Tribune, January 17, 1999.
75. "Heritage on ice," by Patrick Reusse, Star Tribune, February 28, 1999.
76. "Hockeytown Indeed," by Tim Klobuchar, Star Tribune, February 28, 1999.
77. "Tradition, meet reality," by Rachel Blount, Star Tribune, February 14, 1999.
78. "Too Many Men on the Ice," by Joanna Avery & Julie Stevens, Polestar Pub., Victoria, B.C., 1997.
79. "Girls Hockey in Minnesota, Where to from here?", by Dr. Robert H. May, T. S. Denison Publishing, Minneapolis, 1978
80. "NHL Hockey: An official Fans Guide," by Triumph Books, Chicago, IL, 1997.
81. "Hockey Hall of Fame," by Dan Diamond and Joseph Romain, Doubleday Pub., NY, 1988.
82. "Best of Hockey," by Morgan Hughes, Publications Int., Lincolnwood, IL, 1998.
83. "NHL Hockey - An official fans guide," Triumph Books, Chicago, IL, 1997.
84. "Hockey's young superstars," by Eric Dwyer, Polestar Press, Vancouver, BC, 1992.
85. "Great Moments in Hockey," by Brian Kendall, Penguin Pub., Toronto, 1994.
86. "The Official NHL Stanley Cup Centennial Book," by Dan Diamond, Firefly Books, Buffalo, NY, 1992.
87. "Legends of Hockey," by Opus Productions, Penguin Books, Toronto, Ont., 1996.
88. "Heritage on ice," by Patrick Reusse, Star Tribune, February 28, 1999.
89. "Hockeytown Indeed," by Tim Klobuchar, Star Tribune, February 28, 1999.
90. "The Official Notional Hockey League 75th Anniversary Commemorative Book," by Diamond, Dan, NHL Publications, 1991.
91. "A Thinking Man's Guide to Pro Hockey," by Eskenazi, Gerald, E. P. Dutton, 1972.
92. "The Hockey Encyclopedia," by Stan and Shirley Fischler, MacMillan, 1983.
93. "NHL: The World of Professional Hockey," by Greenberg, Jay, Frank Orr, and Gary Ronberg, Rutledge Press, 1981.
94. "The Pictorial History of Hockey," by Romain, Joseph, and Dan Diamond, Gallery Books, 1987.
95. "The Story of Hockey," by Frank Orr, Random House, NY, 1971.
96. "Professional Sports Teams Histories," by Michael LaBlanc, Gale Research Pub., Detroit, MI, 1994.
97. "The Great Book of Hockey," by Stan and Shirley Fischler, Publications International, Ltd., 1996.
98. "The Encyclopedia of Sports," by Frank Menke, AC Barnes Pub., Cranbury, NJ, 1975.
99. "The Encyclopedia of North American Sports History," by Ralph Hickock, 1992.
100. "Fischler's Illustrated History of Hockey Book," by Stan Fischler, Warwick Publishing, Toronto, Ontario, 1993.
101. "Skating by C.G. Tebbutt," Published by Longman, Green and Company, London , 1892.
102. "Municipal Hockey In Minneapolis," by W.W. Fox, Assistant Director of Recreation from article in "Parks and Recreation."
103. "Hockey in the US: The Canadian Influence," by Don Clark and Roger A. Godin
104. "My lifetime in sports," by George Barton, Stan Carlson Pub., Minneapolis, 1957.
105. "Organizations that Wield the Shinny Sticks on Ice," St. Paul Globe, January 25, 1888.
106. "Polo on Ice," Duluth News-Tribune, January 14, 1893.
107. "Ice Follies 20th Anniversary Brochure"
108. "Minnesota State Fair: The history and heritage of 100 years," Argus Publishing, 1964.
109. "The Origins Of American Hockey," By Kevin Allen
110. "The Eveleth Hockey Story," By G. P. Finnegan, Postmaster, Eveleth
111. "Eveleth: Where It All Began," By Bruce Brothers
112. "Eveleth Hockey," by Chuck Muhich, State Sports News, November 15, 1953.
113. "Wren Blair - in Living Color," By Paul Rimstead the Canadian magazine
114. "The Islanders sew it Up," by E.M. Swift, Sports Illustrated, 1980.
115. "Skates, Sticks, & Men," The Story of Amateur Hockey in the US by S. Kip Farrington, Jr., 1972.
116. "The Official NHL Stanley Cup Centennial Book," by Dan Diamond, Firefly Books, Buffalo, NY, 1992.
117. "Death Ended Masterton's Dream of Big Time Hockey," St. Paul Dispatch 1/15/68
118. "Masterton Dies of Head Injuries," St. Paul Dispatch 1/15/68
119. "NHL: The World of Professional Hockey," by Frank Orr.
120. "Glen Sonmor: The scrapper who led Gophers, the Fighting Saints and the Stars has mellowed," by Bruce Brothers, Minnesota Hockey Magazine, 1988.
121. "Glen Sonmor - full speed ahead!", by Charley Hallman, 1972 Saints program.
122. "More Bad Boys," by Stan Fischler, McGraw Hill Pub., Whitby, Ontario, 1995.
123. "Jon Casey: Always Proving Himself" - From Grand Rapids to Grand Forks to the pro's, it's been a constant battle, by Kent Youngblood.
124. "Hockey's young superstars," by Eric Dwyer, Polestar Press, Vancouver, BC, 1992.
125. "The Islanders sew it Up," by E.M. Swift, Sports Illustrated, 1980.
126. "The First 50 Years of Tournament Dominated by Dynasties," By Mike Cook.
127. "State Tournament: Premier Event Of Its Kind Nationwide," By Larry Larson.
128. "You think state tourney is great now? You shoulda been there..." By John Gilbert.
129. "From Humble Beginnings, Tournament Becomes Showcase," by J.G. Preston.
130. "Aldrich dream still growing" by Charley Hallman, St. Paul Pioneer Press/Dispatch, March 10, 1983.
131. "It's Becoming More Difficult to Attain Unbeaten Status," By Mike Fermoyle, St. Paul Pioneer Press Dispatch.
132. "The Thrill of a Lifetime," by E.M Swift, Sports Illustrated, March 7, 1983.
133. "The Warroad Lakers 1946-47 to 1996-97," by Roger A. Godin (Total Hockey)
134. "Marvin 'godfather' of Warroad hockey," by John Gilbert
135. "Lakers a Major Part of "Hockeytown USA," by Jess Myers
136. "Hockey Legends' Favorite State Tournament Memories," By J.G. Preston
137. "Fighting Saints - were they ever!" by John Gilbert
138. "Curling Club provided foundation for wealthy Duluth hockey tradition," by John Gilbert (MN Hockey Magazine, 11/89)
139. "Duluth's 1st college team had to wait for uniforms, competition," by Gary Bartness
140. "Rip Williams, now 80, Mr. Hockey in Duluth," By Jess Myers
141. "SCSU Hockey: Reestablishing the Tradition," by Kimberly Knutson.
142. "SCSU hockey: Old slapshots never die; they just fade away," by Kimberly Knutson and Greg Erickson.
143. "St. Cloud builds arena, tradition, respect," by Bruce Brothers.
144. "For Brose Hockey Is All About Goals," by Paul Allan, MSU Sports Information Director
145. "Saugestad 'cabin fever' to supplant hockey for a spell," by Dave Wright, MN Hockey, summer 1990.
146. "Beaulieu Brought Goals to St. Mary's," By Dave Wright
147. "Concordia Sports - The First One Hundred Years" by Vernon Finn Grinaker, Concordia Website.
148. "In-line skates: 'Not-so-new' product continues on a roll in Minnesota," by Judd Zulgad.
149. "Sports Leagues & Teams," by Mark Pollak, McFarland and Co. Publishing, Jefferson, NC, 1996.
150. "Too Many Men on the Ice," by Joanna Avery & Julie Stevens, Polestar Pub., Victoria, B.C., 1997.
151. "A Woman's Game," by Shirley Fischler Total Hockey, 1998.
152. "US women have golden moment in Nagano," by Rachel Blount, Star Tribune, Feb. 18, 1998.
153. "Precious Mettle," by Rachel Alexander, American Hockey, April/May 1998.
154. "Emotion pours out in victory, defeat," by Sharon Raboin, USA Today, 02/18/98.
155. "Curtin Call: Roseville senior is '99 Ms. Hockey," by Shane Frederick, Feb. 25, 1999.
156. "MIAC get's grant," Women's Hockey News, Vol. 2, 1999.
157. "Move from boys' ranks leads to record year for Krissy Wendell and her Pirates teammates," By Dave Pedersen.
158. "Rainy River Community College: A 30-Year History," by Dan Huntley, 1999.
159. " 'U' takes a step forward in second season," by Rachel Blount, Star Trib, Mar. 28, '99.
160. "Southern Minnesota's Pride on Ice: Rochester's Mustangs," by Mark Dayton.
161. "The Great American Hockey Dilemma," by Murray Williamson (Ralph Turtinen Publishing, 1978).
162. "Up from the Minor Leagues of Hockey," by Stan and Shirley Fischler, 1970.
163. "Hull says he's willing to make sacrifices for Stars," by Helene Elliott, Sporting News (Oct. 19, 1998)
164. "Shooting from the lip" Sports Illustrated article, 11/2/98 by Johnette Howard
165. "Hockey Showdown, The Canada-Russia Hockey Series," by Harry Sinden and Will McDon ough, Toronto: Doubleday, 1972.
166. "Golden Ice," by Stan Fischler, McGraw Hill Ryerson Ltd., Scarborough, Ontario, 1990.
167. "Going for Gold," Tim Wendel, Westport, CT: Lawrence Hill & Co., 1980.
168. "One Goal," by John Powers and Arthur Kaminsky, NY: Harper & Row Pub., 1984.
169. "USA Hockey," by Kevin Allen, Triumph Books, Chicago, IL, 1997.
170. "Minnesota NHLers: Remembering Their Roots," (www.nhlpa.com), March 2, 1999
171. University of Minnesota Men's Athletics Media Guides: Hockey
172. University of Minnesota Women's Athletics Media Guides: Hockey
173. Bemidji State Media Guides: Hockey
174. Moorhead State Media Guides: Hockey
175. UMD Media Guides: Hockey
177. Mankato State Media Guides: Hockey
178. St. Cloud State Media Guides: Hockey
179. Augsburg College Media Guides: Hockey
180. Bethel College Media Guides: Hockey
181. Carlton College Media Guides: Hockey
182. Concordia College Media Guides: Hockey
183. Hamline University Media Guides: Hockey
184. Macalaster College Media Guides: Hockey
185. St. John's Media Guides: Hockey
186. St. Mary's Media Guides: Hockey
187. St. Olaf College Media Guides: Hockey
188. St. Thomas College Media Guides: Hockey
189. Minnesota State High School League Hockey Tournament Programs: 1945-1999
190. "Eveleth Hockey - First Fifty Years (1903-1952)," By Don Clark
191. "Eveleth Hockey," By Don Clark
192. "Gopher Hockey," by Don M. Clark
193. "St. Paul Hockey 1896-1942," by Don Clark
194. "Ice Polo In Minnesota 1883-1901," by Don M. Clark
195. "Early Ice Games," By Don Clark
196. "Hockey - World Encyclopedia," 1967
197. WCHA Yearbook, 40th Anniversary Edition, 1991-92
198. NHL Guide and Record Book, 1991-1992
199. "Ice Hockey, U.S. Records, Olympics and World Championships 1920-86," By Don Clark
200. "Minn. Hockey History," By Don Clark
201. "Early Minneapolis Hockey - 1895-1942," by Don Clark
202. "Minneapolis Municipal Hockey," by W.W. Fox, Director Of Municipal Athletics
203. "The Origins of American Hockey," by Kevin Allen
204. "Early St. Paul Hockey 1896-1942," by Don Clark
205. Spalding Ice Hockey Guide, 1912
206. "A Chronological History of Minnesota Hockey," by Don Clark
207. "Ice Polo In Minnesota 1883-1901," By Don M. Clark
208. "United States Amateur Hockey Association," by Don Clark
209. MAHA Handbooks: 1952, 54, 58, 64
210. "Minnesota Amateur Hockey Association - The Early Years," By Don M. Clark
211. Spalding Ice Hockey Guide: 1921
213. "Eveleth Hockey-First Fifty Years" (1903-1952) By Don Clark
214. The United States Hockey Hall Of Fame: A Brief History